Structural Bioinformatics Handbook

Structural Bioinformatics Handbook

Edited by **Christina Marshall**

SYRAWOOD
PUBLISHING HOUSE

New York

Published by Syrawood Publishing House,
750 Third Avenue, 9th Floor,
New York, NY 10017, USA
www.syrawoodpublishinghouse.com

Structural Bioinformatics Handbook
Edited by Christina Marshall

International Standard Book Number: 978-1-68286-280-3 (Hardback)

Printed in the United States of America.

Contents

Preface   VII

Chapter 1   **Determination of minimal transcriptional signatures of compounds for target
             prediction**
             Florian Nigsch, Janna Hutz, Ben Cornett, Douglas W Selinger,
             Gregory McAllister, Somnath Bandyopadhyay, Joseph Loureiro and
             Jeremy L Jenkins   1

Chapter 2   **The role of feedback control mechanisms on the establishment of oscillatory
             regimes in the Ras/cAMP/PKA pathway in S. cerevisiae**
             Daniela Besozzi, Paolo Cazzaniga, Dario Pescini, Giancarlo Mauri,
             Sonia Colombo and Enzo Martegani   11

Chapter 3   **Relations between the set-complexity and the structure of graphs and their
             sub-graphs**
             Tomasz M Ignac, Nikita A Sakhanenko and David J Galas   28

Chapter 4   **Approximate maximum likelihood estimation for stochastic chemical kinetics**
             Aleksandr Andreychenko, Linar Mikeev, David Spieler and Verena Wolf   38

Chapter 5   **Feature ranking based on synergy networks to identify prognostic markers
             in DPT-1**
             Amin Ahmadi Adl, Xiaoning Qian, Ping Xu, Kendra Vehik and Jeffrey P Krischer   52

Chapter 6   **Subtyping glioblastoma by combining miRNA and mRNA expression data
             using compressed sensing-based approach**
             Wenlong Tang, Junbo Duan, Ji-Gang Zhang and Yu-Ping Wang   61

Chapter 7   **Optimal reference sequence selection for genome assembly using minimum
             description length principle**
             Bilal Wajid, Erchin Serpedin, Mohamed Nounou and Hazem Nounou   70

Chapter 8   **Map-invariant spectral analysis for the identification of DNA periodicities**
             Ahmad Rushdi, Jamal Tuqan and Thomas Strohmer   81

Chapter 9   **Identification of genomic functional hotspots with copy number alteration
             in liver cancer**
             Tzu-Hung Hsiao, Hung-I Harry Chen, Stephanie Roessler, Xin Wei Wang and
             Yidong Chen   102

Chapter 10   **Scientific knowledge is possible with small-sample classification**   112
Edward R Dougherty and Lori A Dalton

Chapter 11   **Relationships between kinetic constants and the amino acid composition of enzymes from the yeast *Saccharomyces cerevisiae* glycolysis pathway**   124
Peteris Zikmanis and Inara Kampenusa

Chapter 12   **Analysis of gene network robustness based on saturated fixed point attractors**   133
Genyuan Li and Herschel Rabitz

Chapter 13   **Effective gene prediction by high resolution frequency estimator based on least-norm solution technique**   160
Manidipa Roy and Soma Barman

Chapter 14   **On the impoverishment of scientific education**   173
Edward R Dougherty

Chapter 15   **Tracking of time-varying genomic regulatory networks with a LASSO-Kalman smoother**   184
Jehandad Khan, Nidhal Bouaynaya and Hassan M Fathallah-Shaykh

Chapter 16   **From microscopy data to *in silico* environments for *in vivo*-oriented simulations**   199
Noriko Hiroi, Michael Klann, Keisuke Iba, Pablo de Heras Ciechomski, Shuji Yamashita, Akito Tabira, Takahiro Okuhara, Takeshi Kubojima, Yasunori Okada, Kotaro Oka, Robin Mange, Michael Unger, Akira Funahashi and Heinz Koeppl

Chapter 17   **Simultaneous identification of robust synergistic subnetwork markers for effective cancer prognosis**   210
Navadon Khunlertgit and Byung-Jun Yoon

Chapter 18   **Application of discrete Fourier inter-coefficient difference for assessing genetic sequence Similarity**   220
Brian R King, Maurice Aburdene, Alex Thompson and Zach Warres

Chapter 19   **Discovering irregular pupil light responses to chromatic stimuli using waveform shapes of pupillograms**   232
Minoru Nakayama, Wioletta Nowak, Hitoshi Ishikawa, Ken Asakawa and Yoshiaki Ichibe

Chapter 20   **A comparison study of optimal and suboptimal intervention policies for gene regulatory networks in the presence of uncertainty**   246
Mohammadmahdi R Yousefi and Edward R Dougherty

Permissions

List of Contributors

Preface

Structural bioinformatics is a rapidly progressing field that deals with the determination and analysis of macromolecular biological structures. The chapters included herein discuss concepts of genome research and gene networks, stimulating biological networks, statistical and computational techniques for gene sequence analysis, etc. This book encompasses advanced techniques and instruments for data analysis and observations. It aims to present researches that have transformed this discipline and will serve as a valuable source of reference for graduate and post graduate students.

This book is a comprehensive compilation of works of different researchers from varied parts of the world. It includes valuable experiences of the researchers with the sole objective of providing the readers (learners) with a proper knowledge of the concerned field. This book will be beneficial in evoking inspiration and enhancing the knowledge of the interested readers.

In the end, I would like to extend my heartiest thanks to the authors who worked with great determination on their chapters. I also appreciate the publisher's support in the course of the book. I would also like to deeply acknowledge my family who stood by me as a source of inspiration during the project.

Editor

Determination of minimal transcriptional signatures of compounds for target prediction

Florian Nigsch[1*], Janna Hutz[2], Ben Cornett[2], Douglas W Selinger[2], Gregory McAllister[2], Somnath Bandyopadhyay[3], Joseph Loureiro[2] and Jeremy L Jenkins[2]

Abstract

The identification of molecular target and mechanism of action of compounds is a key hurdle in drug discovery. Multiplexed techniques for bead-based expression profiling allow the measurement of transcriptional signatures of compound-treated cells in high-throughput mode. Such profiles can be used to gain insight into compounds' mode of action and the protein targets they are modulating. Through the proxy of target prediction from such gene signatures we explored important aspects of the use of transcriptional profiles to capture biological variability of perturbed cellular assays. We found that signatures derived from expression data and signatures derived from biological interaction networks performed equally well, and we showed that gene signatures can be optimised using a genetic algorithm. Gene signatures of approximately 128 genes seemed to be most generic, capturing a maximum of the perturbation inflicted on cells through compound treatment. Moreover, we found evidence for oxidative phosphorylation to be one of the most general ways to capture compound perturbation.

Keywords: transcriptional profiling, target prediction, genetic algorithm, graphics processing unit (GPU) programming, compute unified device architecture (CUDA)

Introduction

Early drug discovery research involves target discovery and lead discovery. Target discovery is concerned with the identification and validation of the disease-relevance of a particular protein. Subsequent lead discovery is the task of finding a suitable molecule that can interact with the target in a specific, therapeutically relevant way. A typical strategy to identify potential lead compounds is the screening of large collections of molecules, up to several millions, in highly automated high-throughput assays. In biochemical assays, each molecule is tested against a purified target protein of interest; molecules that are found to significantly affect the assay readout are called hits and are selected for further follow-up experiments such as secondary- or counter-screens. Successful outcomes in those latter screens result in more confidence of having found a true modulator of the target protein, yielding a target-lead pair. An orthogonal approach where the target protein is unknown from the outset is a phenotypic screen: a collection of molecules is tested for their potential to induce (or abrogate) a complex phenotype, such as the ability of cells to divide successfully. Because the target protein of such screens is not known, they require the identification of the target that gives rise to the observed phenotype subsequent to the identification of active compounds.

Whereas biochemical assays have the advantage that the target protein is essentially a parameter of the experiment, they often lack biological relevance because compounds tested do not have to penetrate cell walls and are not subjected to other relevant biological processes such as active transport and metabolism. Phenotypic assays are a more realistic model for compound administration to living systems but entail the significant post-screen difficulty of target identification and mode of action (MoA) elucidation for any hits identified.

The identification of molecular target and MoA of compounds is a key hurdle in drug discovery. Significantly more hits are obtained from screening campaigns than are typically amenable to extensive experimental profiling such as proteomics. Computational methods that inform about the underlying, specific biological

* Correspondence: florian.nigsch@cantab.net
[1]Developmental and Molecular Pathways, Novartis Institutes for BioMedical Research, Forum 1, Novartis Campus Basel, CH-4056, Basel, Switzerland
Full list of author information is available at the end of the article

processes, for example targets and pathways, that are actually being perturbed by the compounds are much sought after, as they can help to uncover the molecular causes of the positive assay readout. Many such methods rely on the availability of compound annotations from previous experiments or specific profiling platforms. There is a considerable amount of literature on target prediction methods that work from chemical structure alone or composite data types using a variety of methods, and we refer the interested reader to [1-4] and the references therein. Profiling platforms are composed of a reference base of n-dimensional readouts, for example a panel of reporter gene assays [5], for a set of well-characterised compounds and a mechanism to position the readouts of novel samples in the context of the reference. This latter mechanism is often some kind of metric such as Euclidean distance or Pearson correlation, though more sophisticated methods can also be applied.

Transcriptional profiles, the mRNA levels of expressed genes as a result of treatment of cells with a compound, are routinely used to cluster or otherwise relate compounds that elicit a similar biological response [6-8]. For any such approach, it is important to choose which genes to include in the calculations. Typical human genome-wide chips cover approximately 22,000 genes, where the expression level of each gene is determined by a set of specific probes, a probeset [9]. Other experimental techniques, however, require the selection of a set of genes upfront, for example the Luminex technology of Panomics [10]. The selection of suitable genes, a gene signature, depends on the desired signature size, which is directly proportional to cost, as well as the biological questions that need to be addressed. The selection and evaluation of such gene signatures is the subject of the remainder of this article. Like many other companies, Novartis has several compound profiling platforms, including one based on expression profiles. The questions that we addressed in this article are directly related to some of our ongoing efforts to optimise such platforms.

We used a publicly available microarray dataset [7] in conjunction with extensive compound annotations to probe several important aspects of target and MoA prediction from gene signatures. We explored systematically to what extent transcriptional profiles of compounds can be used for target prediction. This study provided insight into questions such as the following: Is there and what is the minimal gene signature that can be used to reasonably predict molecular targets of compounds? Do designed signatures predict targets better than genes selected at random? How can such signatures be optimised in an automatic way, and what are the results of such an optimisation? We employed machine learning and biologically inspired algorithms implemented on state-of-the-art graphics processing units (GPUs) to answer these questions.

Results and discussion
Compound-target annotations
We retrieved all currently known targets for any compound in Connectivity Map 2 [7] where the compound had an activity (IC_{50}, K_i) of ≤ 5 μM. Each compound had an average number of 23 targets satisfying these criteria. The compound with the most targets was staurosporine with 386, whereas for 126 molecules only one target was known, for example hydroxysteroid (17-beta) dehydrogenase 1 (HSD17B1) for the horse steroid equilin. At least 5 targets were known for 502 compounds. These high numbers of high-affinity targets per compound illustrate the fact that many compounds, including many marketed drugs [4,11], are much less specific than is typically appreciated. A further compounding factor for this polypharmacology comes from the tissue expression of the drug targets. A compound with several high-affinity *in vitro* targets could not manifest its action at all of these proteins if most of them were not expressed. The tissue expression of many proteins, however, is relatively unspecific: recent RNA-sequencing experiments showed that approximately 6,000 genes were expressed in all of heart, liver, testis, skeletal muscle and cerebellum, all of which are important target tissues for therapeutics [12,13]. Targeted drug delivery and carefully designed pharmacokinetic compound properties can provide some relief; yet, it is obvious that the foundations for polypharmacology have been laid in evolutionary history [14], and that the man-made design of exquisitely specific drugs is a tremendous undertaking.

A common problem encountered by modellers of chemogenomics data (large repositories of compound-target associations) that is equally a common concern for reviewers of such modelling exercises is the extreme sparseness of the compound-target matrix. The nature of compound screening in drug discovery brings with it that often many structurally similar compounds are tested against the same target, or target family, to identify structural determinants of activity and selectivity. This results in disproportionately many data points for isolated proteins, whereas other proteins are relatively deprived of the honour of being probed to that extent [15]. Consequently, every single chemogenomics dataset, with few exceptions such as the BioPrint database from CEREP [16], is unbalanced and sparse. This is a severe drawback from a modelling perspective as most likely any number for false positives can be expected to be an overestimate. The dataset we used comprises 1,309 compounds and for 804 of these we had target annotations in our repository. These annotations covered a total of 4,428 distinct proteins (as identified by their UniProt primary accessions) in a total of 19,871 compound-target associations. Thus, merely 0.5% of the compound-target matrix that we base our studies on is populated. This extreme sparseness is sobering at best considering that we retrieved the annotations from one of the largest existing repositories of compound bioactivities. Conversely, it illustrates straightforwardly that there is ample space for novel discoveries.

Target prediction from gene signatures

We used a simple nearest neighbour technique to predict targets of compounds. To that end, we correlated the transcriptional profile of a query compound to all other profiles and retained the three nearest neighbours, that is the compounds corresponding to the three highest correlations. The targets of the neighbours are the predicted targets, and we consider a prediction successful if the intersection of predicted and real targets is non-zero. The overall accuracy for a given signature is the fraction of successful predictions; see section 'Materials and methods' for details. Unless otherwise stated,

accuracy refers to the accuracy obtained when only the first nearest neighbour is considered.

The term transcriptional signature is used for a subset of all probesets that is employed for the target predictions. Such signatures were derived using two data-driven methods: (1) based on all expression values; and (2) based on biological networks. For the latter part, we used all human interactions of the StringDB interaction database [17]. We retained the top-ranking 300 probesets for each of the selection methods described in section 'Methods and materials'. This cutoff was chosen as even for randomly selected signatures there was no increase in performance with more probesets (see next paragraph and Figure 1).

To establish a baseline for all further experiments, we determined the accuracy of guessing by using randomly shuffled compound-target associations. The accuracy obtained in this way ranges between 0.11 for one nearest neighbour and 0.26 for three nearest neighbours. It is interesting to note that even randomly selected probesets perform better than pure chance, for example with one nearest neighbour 0.11 versus 0.16 (Figure 1).

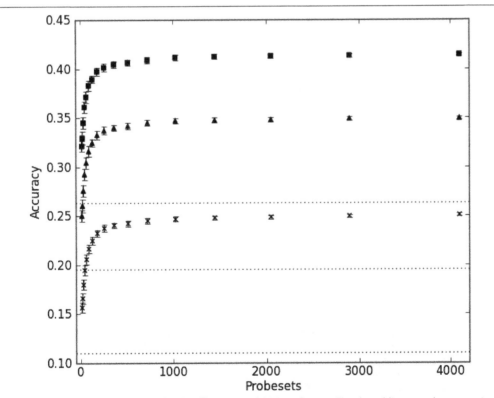

Figure 1 Performance of random signatures levels off at around 300 probesets. The dotted lines are the accuracies obtained (for increasing number of nearest neighbours from bottom to top) for randomly shuffled compound-target associations. This shows that although the signature probesets were selected randomly, they nonetheless yield a better target prediction accuracy than chance alone. One nearest neighbour: cross; two nearest neighbours: triangle; three nearest neighbours: square. Displayed data are the average accuracy values (n = 50) and the total length of the error bars is the corresponding standard deviation.

Designed signatures

We used two different groups of signatures for our experiments: one group was derived from the expression data itself, the other from biological interaction networks. Regardless of how the signatures were obtained, none produced an accuracy above 0.27. All signatures that were derived using expression data had accuracies in the range of 0.13 (for the minimum variance signature) to 0.26 (for the maximum variance signature, see Figure 2). Even with three nearest neighbours, the minimum variance signature was clearly the worst (Figure 2). The signature most different from all others consisted of the minimum variance probesets. This was consistent with what would be expected, as the genes corresponding to these probesets simply were not very responsive to perturbation. It is interesting to note that the genes that had the highest average expression were not very predictive; on the contrary, the signature comprised of the probesets that had the lowest average expression performed better. Consistent with the previous observations was that the probesets with the highest overall variance of expression were most useful for target prediction.

The signatures derived from biological networks all performed equally with accuracies around 0.23; all of them improved in a similar way with increasing numbers of nearest neighbours (Figure 3). The signature that performed best was based on the betweenness centrality of network nodes. This centrality is related to the number of shortest paths that go through a node. None of these signatures performed better than any signature derived from expression data.

Genetically optimised signatures

We used a genetic algorithm to evolve pools of 200 randomly initialised signatures for 150 generations. This resulted in an optimised set of genes for each signature size. Figure 4 shows the distribution of fitness scores over the range of the entire optimisation of 150 generations for a signature of 64 probesets. The decrease in the rate of improvement of the maximum fitness indicates that the genetic algorithm is close to converging to an optimal solution. Whereas there is no guarantee that it will ever be reached [18], Figure 4 shows that we are presumably very close to the maximally achievable accuracy for that signature size.

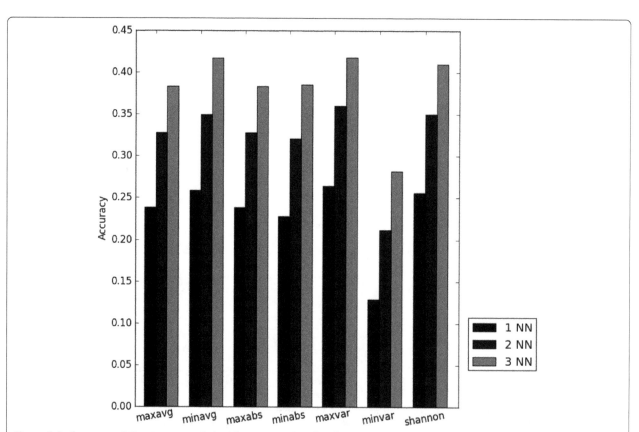

Figure 2 Performance of the signatures derived from expression data for one, two or three nearest neighbours (NN). maxavg: highest mean expression; minavg: lowest mean expression; maxvar: highest standard deviation; minvar: lowest standard deviation; maxabs: highest mean of absolute expression value; minabs: lowest mean of absolute expression value and shannon: Shannon entropy of binned expression values.

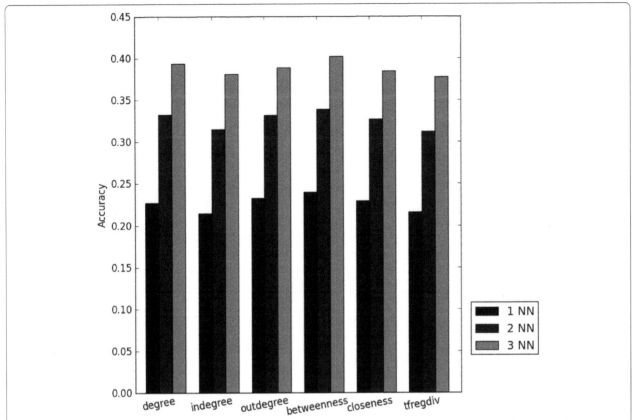

Figure 3 Performance of the signatures derived from biological networks for one, two or three nearest neighbours (NN). betweenness: betweenness centrality; closeness: closeness centrality; degree: degree centrality; in-degree: in-degree centrality; out-degree: out-degree centrality; tfregdiv: diverse set of genes that are downstream of regulators of gene expression.

Overall, all of the genetically optimised signatures achieved accuracies above 0.26. Therefore, the smallest optimised signature with 32 probesets outperformed many of the expression-based signatures and also all network-based signatures. The signature that performed best contained 128 probesets and achieved an accuracy just below 0.30.

An analysis of the overlap of selected probesets between all of the optimised signatures revealed that very few probesets are shared. The highest overlap is achieved between the two largest signatures with 136 shared probesets between the signatures with sizes 1,448 and 2,048. The maximum overlap between two signatures is equal to the size of the smaller signature. Therefore, overlaps are expressed here as the fraction of the smaller signature that is common to the larger signature. The largest fractional overlap is between the signatures of sizes 256 and 2,048: 37 probesets (14%) of the smaller signature are found in the larger signature.

Even the smallest genetically optimised signature (32 probesets) performed basically equally well as the best performing signature derived from expression values (the 300 most variable probesets). Each of the 32 probesets of the smaller signature therefore seems to capture at least 10% more information than the 300 probesets of the larger signature. It can also be noted that these two signatures only share one probeset. The smaller, optimised signature is therefore not merely a result of the genetic algorithm choosing the most variable probesets.

The good performance of very small, optimised signatures as well as the trend seen in Figure 5 indicates that larger signatures do not help in target prediction using our approach. Contrarily, they seem to add noise that is detrimental to performance. Obviously, such a trend might not be observed for other target prediction approaches such as reverse causal reasoning [19] where a larger signature might indeed provide more information to seed the reasoning algorithms.

Analysis of gene signatures

We analysed whether the signatures derived by data-driven processes or the genetic algorithm are representative of any major biological processes. To that end, we calculated pathway enrichments for the designed signatures and the best-performing optimised signature with 128 probesets.

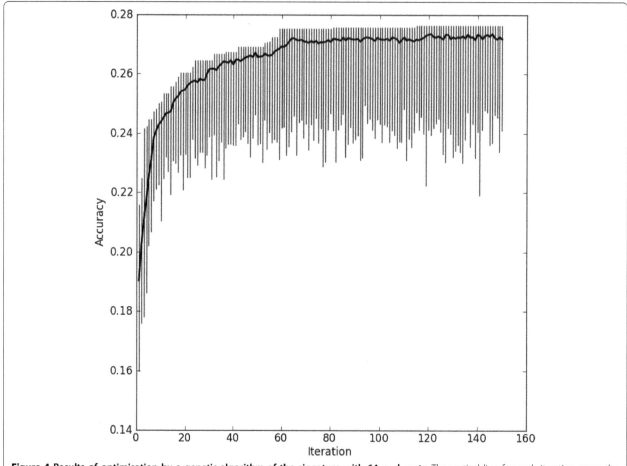

Figure 4 Results of optimisation by a genetic algorithm of the signature with 64 probesets. The vertical line for each iteration spans the range from worst to best fitness. The solid line indicates the mean fitness of all individuals in any iteration.

Overall, the signatures of the genes that have the highest absolute and highest mean expression yielded the most significant enrichments. The two most significantly enriched pathways were oxidative phosphorylation ($-\log p \sim 100$) and ubiquinone metabolism ($-\log p \sim 58$). The p-values increase rapidly to 10^{-5} within the top five ranked pathways. The best-performing expression-based signature is enriched for cytoskeleton remodelling, regulation of cell cycle checkpoint G_1/S and regulation of cellular metabolism ($-\log p$ values between 10 and 8).

The only other very significant enrichments were obtained with the network-derived signature based on the betweenness centrality of nodes. The enriched pathways were involved in protein folding ($p \sim 10^{-19}$) and regulation of G_1/S transition ($p \sim 10^{-18}$). Noteworthy enrichments were also found for the signatures based on the degree centrality of nodes in the interaction network. All three of these signatures (degree, in-degree and out-degree) yielded several highly enriched pathways for nucleotide metabolism ($10^{-20} < p < 10^{-17}$). The results of all the enrichment calculations are provided as an Excel spreadsheet, see additional file 1.

The best-performing optimised gene signature with 128 genes showed a similar result as the one obtained for the highest absolute and highest mean expression signatures: oxidative phosphorylation ($10^{-113} < p < 10^{-76}$) and ubiquinone metabolism ($p \sim 10^{-64}$) were consistently the most significant pathways across several of the optimised signatures from different runs of the genetic algorithm.

The low p-values for oxidative phosphorylation are due to the large size of this pathway compared to all other pathways. This pathway contains several large complexes of the respiratory chain (mammalian complexes 1 to 4 and ATP synthase) and is composed of a total of 105 proteins. The ubiquinone metabolism pathway counts 74 proteins, 46 of which pertain again to mammalian complex 1. The constituents of the oxidative phosphorylation pathway, especially so the parts of the electron transport chain composed of complexes 1 to 4, are highly expressed in the mitochondria of all cells. Furthermore, rapidly dividing cancerous cells in culture, such as the ones used to derive the expression values used in this study, also require a lot of energy;

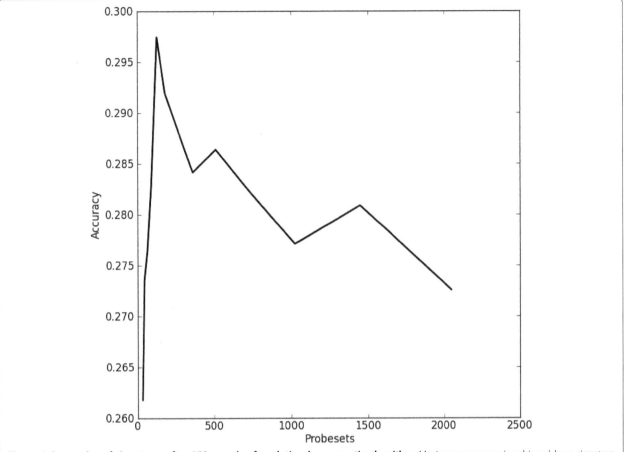

Figure 5 Accuracies of signatures after 150 rounds of evolution by a genetic algorithm. Maximum accuracy is achieved by a signature size of 128 probesets.

thus, high expression levels are to be expected for members of the respiratory chain. Naturally, such highly expressed genes were selected for inclusion into the signature of genes with highest expression, which in turn explains the observed enrichment.

A more intriguing fact is that the same enrichment is observed for the best-performing optimised signature. This suggests that there is at least some overlap in the functionality of the genes of the two signatures: given the large size of the mammalian complexes 1 to 4 there need not be an overlap of the same genes, but in genes that belong to the same complex. The optimised signature therefore contains a significant part of genes that have a high level of expression overall, whereas the other genes were selected by the algorithm for other reasons. These other reasons are likely to remain unfounded due to the inherent lack of interpretability of results obtained from genetic optimisations, and we do not intend to speculate about those reasons at this point and leave this for further study. We note, however, that the enrichments obtained for the optimised signature are fundamentally different from and much more

significant than those for an equal number of randomly selected probesets (data not included).

Conclusion
We established a baseline for achievable target prediction accuracy using a simple 'guilt-by-association' method based on correlation of transcriptional profiles. The main objective of this study, however, is not target prediction *per se* but an investigation about how this can be achieved with gene signatures of varying nature and length. Two distinct groups of transcriptional signatures—expression data driven and based on biological interaction networks—were analysed for their performance; no striking differences between these groups were found. The optimisation of transcriptional signatures by a genetic algorithm led to the best-performing signatures and indicated that a maximum size of approximately 128 probesets is optimal. A signature of this size therefore extracted a maximum of biological variation of the investigated cellular systems. The genes of this optimised signature were predominantly found in pathways relating to oxidative

phosphorylation and ubiquinone metabolism; this indicated that these biological processes might be the most generic way to capture compound perturbation of cells. We furthermore showed that it is possible to optimise very small signatures (32 probesets) for a particular purpose. Given that both groups of signatures—expression-based and network-based—perform similarly it is to be expected that a combination of both can lead to better signatures.

Methods and materials
Expression data and compound annotations

Our analyses are based on gene expression data from the Broad Institute's Connectivity Map 2 (CMAP2) [7]. Several cell lines were treated with a total of 1,309 different compounds and whole-genome expression levels were determined using Affymetrix gene chips. The cell lines with most measurements in CMAP2 were the human breast epithelial adenocarcinoma cell line MCF7, the prostate adenocarcinoma cell line PC3 and the human promyelocytic leukaemia cell line HL60. Expression levels were measured using the human Affymetrix chips (HT)HG-U133A [9]. The compounds were tested in batches with replicates, resulting in a total of 6,100 experiments. The combination of a compound, applied concentration, cell line and microarray platform used is referred to as a treatment instance.

We used a total of 22,267 probesets that were present in all treatment instances. CMAP2 data were downloaded from the Broad Institute's website and processed in R [20] using the *affy* [21] package. Robust multichip average [22] expression values were calculated for each treatment instance, and the expression values of each batch containing more than five treatment instances were then mean-centred on a probeset level using the average expression of each probeset in the corresponding batch [12]. In other words, the expression values we used correspond to expression after treatment relative to average expression in the batch; expression of vehicle (DMSO) treated cells does not enter the process. This procedure, originally proposed by Iskar et al. [12], has been found to be suitable for the elimination of batch effects for purposes very similar to ours.

The targets of any compound used in CMAP2 were obtained from an in-house bioactivity repository that comprises information both proprietary to Novartis and public such as ChEMBL and DrugBank [23,24]. We retained all targets of a compound at which it had an IC_{50} or K_i value of ≤ 5 µM.

Target prediction and accuracy measure

We determined nearest neighbours for each treatment instance by searching for treatments with highly correlated (Pearson product-moment correlation coefficient) gene signatures. Because the same molecule might have been tested several times under slightly different conditions (for example varying concentration, different cell line, different array platform), the nearest neighbour search was implemented in a way that prohibits it from finding a variation of a molecule as a neighbour for that molecule. The accuracies obtained would be higher without this restriction, but this would overestimate the true value that can be achieved in a real-world setting: in terms of target prediction the knowledge gained from a self-match is zero. We determined a maximum of three nearest neighbours for each treatment instance.

All of our analyses were assessed using the accuracy of target prediction, that is the fraction of all predictions that are considered successful. We considered a target prediction successful if the intersection of the target sets of query and nearest neighbour(s) is not empty. The main reason for this measure is the sparseness of compound-target annotations: any other measure would result in misleadingly low performance measures due to the large number of false positives/negatives; however, many of those predictions could actually be true if a complete compound-target matrix were available. An equally important factor for such a performance metric is the fact that in our setting all predicted targets have an equal rank. This is in contrast to other methods that provide a ranked list of targets. In separate experiments (not included here) we also used the F-measure, a weighted average of positive recall and positive precision that can be tuned to favour either recall or precision. The reliance on accuracy alone provides a realistic assessment of an achievable baseline for target prediction. Nevertheless, for certain applications it might indeed be worth to use other performance measures, for example to find a signature that minimises false negatives. For the precision of target prediction for the designed signatures, please refer to additional file 2.

The correlation calculations and nearest neighbour algorithms were implemented as a Python module using cython and CUDA on an NVIDIA GPU Tesla M2050 with 448 cores. This resulted in a speedup of more than two orders of magnitude compared to a single CPU implementation. The speed of this implementation was essential to get results from the genetic algorithm procedure in a reasonable amount of time. The source code used for any of the calculations is available from the authors upon request.

Signature selection

In addition to designed signatures, we used signatures that were made up of randomly selected probesets to estimate the improvement that can be achieved when designed signatures are employed. We used 17 signatures containing 16 to 4,096 probesets in half-logarithmic steps in base 2. The signature sizes used were thus 16, 22, 32, 45, 64, 90, 128, 181, 256, 362, 512, 724, 1024, 1448, 2048, 2896, 4096. We randomly sampled 50 different signatures for each signature size; the reported accuracies for these signatures are therefore sample averages.

For expression-based signatures, the probesets were ranked according to the following criteria determined across all expression arrays in CMAP2: (1) highest mean expression; (2) lowest mean expression; (3) highest standard deviation; (4) lowest standard deviation; (5) highest mean of absolute expression value; (6) lowest mean of absolute expression value and (7) Shannon entropy of binned expression values; expression values were binned into 200 bins in the range [-5, 8].

For network-based signatures, we used the following criteria to score network nodes: (1) betweenness centrality; (2) closeness centrality; (3) degree centrality; (4) indegree centrality; (5) out-degree centrality; (6) maximum average distance to reachable transcriptional modifiers.

The motivation for the last signature was to have a diverse set of genes that are downstream of regulators of gene expression. We first identified all regulators of gene expression (regulatory nodes) as any node in StringDB [17] that has at least one outgoing edge of mode 'expression'. For all nodes downstream of any regulatory node we then determined the average shortest path length to all reachable upstream regulators. Overall, this results in a total of 13 designed signatures.

Optimisation with genetic algorithm

We used a genetic algorithm to determine an optimal signature for a given number of probesets. A population of 200 randomly initialised signatures was evolved for 150 generations. The objective function maximised by the genetic algorithm is the accuracy of prediction as defined above. The top 20% of each iteration were included for any subsequent iteration (elitism), the remaining 80% were obtained through crossover and mutation operations (crossover rate 70%, mutation rate 30%). Genetically optimised signatures were derived for the following signature sizes: 32, 45, 64, 90, 128, 181, 256, 362, 512, 724, 1024, 1448, 2048. The genetic algorithm was based on an example in 'Programming collective intelligence' [25].

Pathway enrichments

We used GeneGO (now part of Thomson Reuters) Metacore to calculate pathway enrichments. This calculation is based on a hypergeometric null distribution for the intersection of the query set of genes and any given pathway [26]. The p-value corresponds to the probability of an intersection equal or greater to the observed one. This procedure is equal to a Fisher's exact test.

Additional material

> **Additional file 1: Pathway enrichment for the designed gene signatures**. Pathway enrichment for the designed gene signatures.
>
> **Additional file 2: Precision of prediction for designed signatures**. Excel spreadsheet with precision of prediction for designed signatures.

Abbreviations
CMAP: Broad Institute's Connectivity Map, build 02; GPU: graphics processing unit; MoA: mechanism of action.

Acknowledgements
FN and JH were supported by postdoctoral fellowships of the Education Office of the Novartis Institutes for BioMedical Research.

Author details
[1]Developmental and Molecular Pathways, Novartis Institutes for BioMedical Research, Forum 1, Novartis Campus Basel, CH-4056, Basel, Switzerland [2]Developmental and Molecular Pathways, Novartis Institutes for BioMedical Research, 220 Massachusetts Avenue, 02139 Cambridge, MA, USA [3]Immunology Clinical Biomarkers, Bristol Myers Squibb, Princeton, New Jersey

Competing interests
The authors declare that they have no competing interests.

References
1. D di Bernardo, MJ Thompson, TS Gardner, SE Chobot, EL Eastwood, AP Wojtovich, SJ Elliott, SE Schaus, JJ Collins, Chemogenomic profiling on a genome-wide scale using reverse-engineered gene networks. Nat Biotech. 23(3), 377–383 (2005). doi:10.1038/nbt1075
2. M Keiser, B Roth, B Armbruster, P Ernsberger, J Irwin, B Shoichet, Relating protein pharmacology by ligand chemistry. Nat Biotechnol. 25(2), 197–206 (2007). doi:10.1038/nbt1284
3. F Nigsch, A Bender, JL Jenkins, JBO Mitchell, Ligand-target prediction using winnow and naive bayesian algorithms and the implications of overall performance statistics. J Chem Inf Model. 48(12), 2313–2325 (2008). doi:10.1021/ci800079x
4. M Campillos, M Kuhn, A Gavin, L Jensen, P Bork, Drug target identification using side-effect similarity. Science. 321(5886), 263–266 (2008). doi:10.1126/science.1158140
5. FJ King, DW Selinger, FA Mapa, J Janes, H Wu, TR Smith, Q-Y Wang, P Niyomrattanakitand, DG Sipes, A Brinker, JA Porter, VE Myer, Pathway reporter assays reveal small molecule mechanisms of action. J Assoc Lab Autom. 14(6), 374–382 (2009). doi:10.1016/j.jala.2009.08.001
6. PE Blower, C Yang, MA Fligner, JS Verducci, L Yu, S Richman, JN Weinstein, Pharmacogenomic analysis: correlating molecular substructure classes with microarray gene expression data. Pharmacogen J. 2(4), 259–271 (2002). doi:10.1038/sj.tpj.6500116
7. J Lamb, ED Crawford, D Peck, JW Modell, IC Blat, MJ Wrobel, J Lerner, J-P Brunet, A Subramanian, KN Ross, M Reich, H Hieronymus, G Wei, SA Armstrong, SJ Haggarty, PA Clemons, R Wei, SA Carr, ES Lander, TR Golub, The connectivity map: using gene-expression signatures to connect small molecules, genes, and disease. Science. 313(5795), 1929–1935 (2006). doi:10.1126/science.1132939
8. F Iorio, R Bosotti, E Scacheri, V Belcastro, P Mithbaokar, R Ferriero, L Murino, R Tagliaferri, N Brunetti-Pierri, A Isacchi, D di Bernardo, Discovery of drug mode of action and drug repositioning from transcriptional responses. Proc Natl Acad Sci USA. 107(33), 14621–14626 (2010). doi:10.1073/pnas.1000138107
9. Affymetrix Human Genome U133 Set http://www.affymetrix.com/support/help/faqs/hgu133/index.jsp. Accessed 06 Jan 2012
10. Panomics Luminex Assays http://www.panomics.com/index.php?id=products_luminexAssays. Accessed 06 Jan 2012

11. R Morphy, C Kay, Z Rankovic, From magic bullets to designed multiple ligands. Drug Discov Today. **9**(15), 641–651 (2004). doi:10.1016/S1359-6446 (04)03163-0

12. M Iskar, M Campillos, M Kuhn, LJ Jensen, V van Noort, P Bork, Drug-induced regulation of target expression. PLoS Comput Biol. **6**(9), e1000925 (2010). doi:10.1371/journal.pcbi.1000925

13. D Emig, T Kacprowski, M Albrecht, Measuring and analyzing tissue specificity of human genes and protein complexes. EURASIP J Bioinf Syst Biol. **2011**(1), 5 (2011). doi:10.1186/1687-4153-2011-5

14. I Nobeli, AD Favia, JM Thornton, Protein promiscuity and its implications for biotechnology. Nat Biotech. **27**(2), 157–167 (2009). doi:10.1038/nbt1519

15. AM Edwards, R Isserlin, GD Bader, SV Frye, TM Willson, FH Yu, Too many roads not taken. Nature. **470**(7333), 163–165 (2011). doi:10.1038/470163a

16. CM Krejsa, D Horvath, SL Rogalski, JE Penzotti, B Mao, F Barbosa, JC Migeon, Predicting ADME properties and side effects: the BioPrint approach. Curr Opin Drug Discov Dev. **6**(4), 470–480 (2003)

17. D Szklarczyk, A Franceschini, M Kuhn, M Simonovic, A Roth, P Minguez, T Doerks, M Stark, J Muller, P Bork, LJ Jensen, C von Mering, The STRING database in 2011: functional interaction networks of proteins, globally integrated and scored. Nucleic Acids Res. **39**(suppl 1), D561–D568 (2011)

18. D Whitley, A genetic algorithm tutorial. Stat Comput. **4**(2), 65–85 (1994)

19. R Kumar, S Blakemore, C Ellis, E Petricoin, D Pratt, M Macoritto, A Matthews, J Loureiro, K Elliston, Causal reasoning identifies mechanisms of sensitivity for a novel AKT kinase inhibitor, GSK690693. BMC Genomics. **11**(1), 419 (2010). doi:10.1186/1471-2164-11-419

20. R Development Core Team, *R: A Language and Environment for Statistical Computing*, (R Foundation for Statistical Computing, Vienna, 2011)

21. L Gautier, L Cope, BM Bolstad, RA Irizarry, Affy–analysis of Affymetrix GeneChip data at the probe level. Bioinformatics. **20**(3), 307–315 (2004). doi:10.1093/bioinformatics/btg405

22. RA Irizarry, BM Bolstad, F Collin, LM Cope, B Hobbs, TP Speed, Summaries of Affymetrix GeneChip probe level data. Nucleic Acids Res. **31**(4), e15 (2003). doi:10.1093/nar/gng015

23. A Gaulton, LJ Bellis, AP Bento, J Chambers, M Davies, A Hersey, Y Light, S McGlinchey, D Michalovich, B Al-Lazikani, JP Overington, ChEMBL: a large-scale bioactivity database for drug discovery. Nucleic Acids Res. **40**, D1100–D1107 (2012). doi:10.1093/nar/gkr777

24. C Knox, V Law, T Jewison, P Liu, S Ly, A Frolkis, A Pon, K Banco, C Mak, V Neveu, Y Djoumbou, R Eisner, AC Guo, DS Wishart, DrugBank 3.0: a comprehensive resource for 'omics' research on drugs. Nucleic Acids Res , 39 Database: D1035–D1041 (2011)

25. T Segaran, *Programming Collective Intelligence: Building Smart Web 2.0 Applications*, 1st edn. (O'Reilly Media, USA, 2007)

26. RK Curtis, M Orešič, A Vidal-Puig, Pathways to the analysis of microarray data. Trends Biotechnol. **23**(8), 429–435 (2005). doi:10.1016/j. tibtech.2005.05.011

The role of feedback control mechanisms on the establishment of oscillatory regimes in the Ras/cAMP/PKA pathway in *S. cerevisiae*

Daniela Besozzi[1][*], Paolo Cazzaniga[2], Dario Pescini[3], Giancarlo Mauri[4], Sonia Colombo[5] and Enzo Martegani[5]

Abstract

In the yeast *Saccharomyces cerevisiae*, the Ras/cAMP/PKA pathway is involved in the regulation of cell growth and proliferation in response to nutritional sensing and stress conditions. The pathway is tightly regulated by multiple feedback loops, exerted by the protein kinase A (PKA) on a few pivotal components of the pathway. In this article, we investigate the dynamics of the second messenger cAMP by performing stochastic simulations and parameter sweep analysis of a mechanistic model of the Ras/cAMP/PKA pathway, to determine the effects that the modulation of these feedback mechanisms has on the establishment of stable oscillatory regimes. In particular, we start by studying the role of phosphodiesterases, the enzymes that catalyze the degradation of cAMP, which represent the major negative feedback in this pathway. Then, we show the results on cAMP oscillations when perturbing the amount of protein Cdc25 coupled with the alteration of the intracellular ratio of the guanine nucleotides (GTP/GDP), which are known to regulate the switch of the GTPase Ras protein. This multi-level regulation of the amplitude and frequency of oscillations in the Ras/cAMP/PKA pathway might act as a fine tuning mechanism for the downstream targets of PKA, as also recently evidenced by some experimental investigations on the nucleocytoplasmic shuttling of the transcription factor Msn2 in yeast cells.

Introduction

In living cells many processes are regulated by negative and positive feedback mechanisms, which are usually interlaced in complex regulatory networks and can function to either attenuate, amplify or even exploit molecular noise and stochasticity (see, e.g., [1-3] and references therein). As a matter of fact, molecular fluctuations do not always represent a negative feature for the proper functioning of a cellular system, on the contrary they can be advantageous to widen the range of stimulus-response to different perturbations, therefore promoting the adaptability to changeable environments. In this context, computational models represent an indispensable tool to investigate the complexity of the systems where multiple feedback and feedforward loops occur, multiple feedback and feedforward loops, as well as to reveal their emergent behaviors, as the use of experimental analysis

alone is typically not able to unravel the whole picture of these (inhibitory or activatory) molecular interactions cascade [4-6].

A signal transduction pathway that is characterized by such complexity is the Ras/cAMP/PKA pathway in the yeast *Saccharomyces cerevisiae*, which regulates metabolism and cell cycle progression in response to nutritional sensing and stress conditions [7-10]. In budding yeast, five interlocked systems are known to participate in glucose signaling, which altogether result in a massive restructuring of the transcriptional state of the genome, as well as in a rapid change in the pattern of protein phosphorylation when glucose is added to cells growing on a non-fermentable carbon source [11]. Among these five pathways, the Ras/cAMP/PKA system plays a central role in responding to changes in glucose concentration and in turning on the processes that lead to cellular growth and division.

In particular, the Ras/cAMP/PKA pathway controls more than 90% of all genes that are regulated by glucose through the activation of the protein kinase A (PKA), that is able to phosphorylate a plethora of downstream

*Correspondence: besozzi@di.unimi.it
[1] Università degli Studi di Milano, Dipartimento di Informatica, Via Comelico 39, 20135 Milano, Italy
Full list of author information is available at the end of the article

proteins [11]. PKA is activated by the binding of the second messenger cyclic-AMP (cAMP), which is synthesized by the adenylate cyclase Cyr1. The activity of Cyr1 is controlled by the monomeric GTPases Ras1 and Ras2, which cycle between a GTP-bound active state and a GDP-bound inactive state. In turn, Ras proteins are positively regulated by protein Cdc25, a Ras-GEF (Guanine Nucleotide Exchange Factor) that stimulates the GDP to GTP exchange, and negatively regulated by proteins Ira1 and Ira2, two Ras-GAP (GTPase Activating Proteins) that stimulate the GTPase activity of Ras proteins. The degradation of cAMP is governed by two phosphodiesterases, Pde1 and Pde2. These two enzymes constitute a major negative feedback in this pathway: the low-affinity phosphodiesterase Pde1 is active under the positive regulation of PKA, while the high-affinity phosphodiesterase Pde2 is active in the basal level regulation of cAMP [7,12]. Experimental evidences suggest that the negative feedback loop exerted by PKA operates also at the level of Ras2-GTP [13-15]: PKA can phosphorylate Cdc25, reducing its exchange activity, as well as Ira proteins, increasing the Ras-GAP activity (in both cases, this regulation results in a decrease of the activity of the adenylate cyclase).

Because of such complex interplay, it is not easy to predict the behavior of the Ras/cAMP/PKA pathway in different growth conditions or in response to various stress signals. To understand the role of the negative feedback controls, in [16,17] we defined and analyzed a stochastic model of the Ras/cAMP/PKA pathway. In particular, we focused our attention on the mechanisms that allow the emergence of oscillatory regimes, since recent experiments evidenced *in vivo* the presence of continuous oscillations related to this pathway under specific stress conditions [18,19]. Furthermore, the effects of some regulatory mechanisms related to the stress response in the Ras/cAMP/PKA pathway were also highlighted through the analysis of the nucleocytoplasmic shuttling of Msn2, a transcription factor whose localization is controlled in yeast by the periodic activation of PKA [20,21]. This periodicity can be ascribed to an oscillatory behavior of the intracellular cAMP concentration and of PKA activity, though no direct measurements of the dynamics of these components have been executed *in vivo* so far. In this context, our previous computational investigations indicated that stable oscillatory regimes of cAMP amount can be established when the feedback operating on Ira proteins is activated, and that this dynamics seems to be regulated by the balance between the activities of the Ras protein modulators, i.e., Cdc25 and Ira proteins. In addition, we previously showed that also the intracellular ratio of guanine nucleotides pools (GTP/GDP) could represent an important metabolic signal for the regulation of the pathway, as also suggested in [22,23].

In this article, we extend the study presented in [24] and continue the analysis on the establishment of oscillatory regimes of cAMP by investigating the modulation of other feedback mechanisms. In particular, we study the influence that a change in the activity of phosphodiesterases - coupled with the perturbation of Cdc25 amount - have on the existence of stable oscillations of cAMP, and we highlight that the deletion of Pde1 can induce marked variations in the cAMP dynamics, while the deletion of Pde2 fosters the establishment of oscillations. Moreover, a preliminary analysis carried out on the oscillations frequency of cAMP in both the conditions of deletion of Pde1 and Pde2, considering different values for the ratio Cdc25/Ira2, shows that the deletion of Pde2 is able to diminish the oscillations frequency of cAMP with respect to the wild type condition, while the deletion of Pde1 has a minor effect on the frequency modulation.

Then, we continue the investigation initiated in [17] and study the role played by the guanine nucleotide concentrations, which control the exchange activity of Cdc25. Through the investigation of the simultaneous modulation of the amount of Cdc25 and of the intracellular ratio of guanine nucleotides, we show here that a decrease in the ratio GTP/GDP—which mimics a reduced nutritional condition in yeast cells—is able to control the transition between stable steady states and oscillations, independently from the amount of Cdc25.

Methods
Mechanistic model of the Ras/cAMP/PKA pathway
The mechanistic model of the Ras/cAMP/PKA pathway that we previously presented in [16,17] was developed according to the stochastic formulation of chemical kinetics [25], defined by specifying the set of molecular species occurring in the pathway and the set of biochemical reactions, together with their related stochastic constants (see Table 1). In particular, the model describes the major interactions between the pivotal components of the Ras/cAMP/PKA pathway, as well as the negative feedback mechanisms which are able to regulate the intracellular levels of cAMP. The model consists of six functional modules, which correspond to the following processes:

1. The switch cycle of Ras2 protein between its inactive state (Ras2-GDP) and active state (Ras2-GTP), regulated by the activity of the GEF Cdc25 and of the GAP Ira2 (reactions $r_1, \ldots, r_{10}$ in Table 1).
2. The synthesis of cAMP through the activation of the adenylate cyclase Cyr1, mediated by Ras2-GTP (reactions r_{11}, r_{12}, r_{13} in Table 1).
3. The activation of PKA, mediated by the reversible binding of cAMP to its two regulatory subunits, and the subsequent dissociation of the PKA tetramer,

Table 1 Mechanistic model of the Ras/cAMP/PKA pathway in *S. cerevisiae*

No.	Reagents	Products	Constant c_i
r_1	Ras2-GDP + Cdc25	Ras2-GDP-Cdc25	1.0
r_2	Ras2-GDP-Cdc25	Ras2-GDP + Cdc25	1.0
r_3	Ras2-GDP-Cdc25	Ras2-Cdc25 + GDP	1.5
r_4	Ras2-Cdc25 + GDP	Ras2-GDP-Cdc25	1.0
r_5	Ras2-Cdc25 + GTP	Ras2-GTP-Cdc25	1.0
r_6	Ras2-GTP-Cdc25	Ras2-Cdc25 + GTP	1.0
r_7	Ras2-GTP-Cdc25	Ras2-GTP + Cdc25	1.0
r_8	Ras2-GTP + Cdc25	Ras2-GTP-Cdc25	1.0
r_9	Ras2-GTP + Ira2	Ras2-GTP-Ira2	$*1.0 \times 10^{-2}$
r_{10}	Ras2-GTP-Ira2	Ras2-GDP + Ira2	$*2.5 \times 10^{-1}$
r_{11}	Ras2-GTP + Cyr1	Ras2-GTP-Cyr1	1.0×10^{-3}
r_{12}	Ras2-GTP-Cyr1 + ATP	Ras2-GTP-Cyr1 + cAMP	2.1×10^{-6}
r_{13}	Ras2-GTP-Cyr1 + Ira2	Ras2-GDP + Cyr1 + Ira2	1.0×10^{-3}
r_{14}	cAMP + PKA	cAMP-PKA	1.0×10^{-5}
r_{15}	cAMP + cAMP-PKA	(2cAMP)-PKA	1.0×10^{-5}
r_{16}	cAMP + (2cAMP)-PKA	(3cAMP)-PKA	1.0×10^{-5}
r_{17}	cAMP + (3cAMP)-PKA	(4cAMP)-PKA	1.0×10^{-5}
r_{18}	(4cAMP)-PKA	cAMP + (3cAMP)-PKA	1.0×10^{-1}
r_{19}	(3cAMP)-PKA	cAMP + (2cAMP)-PKA	1.0×10^{-1}
r_{20}	(2cAMP)-PKA	cAMP + cAMP-PKA	1.0×10^{-1}
r_{21}	cAMP-PKA	cAMP + PKA	1.0×10^{-1}
r_{22}	(4cAMP)-PKA	C + C + R-2cAMP + R-2cAMP	1.0
r_{23}	R-2cAMP	R + cAMP + cAMP	1.0
r_{24}	R + C	R-C	7.5×10^{-1}
r_{25}	R-C + R-C	PKA	1.0
r_{26}	C + Pde1	C + Pde1p	1.0×10^{-6}
r_{27}	cAMP + Pde1p	cAMP-Pde1p	1.0×10^{-1}
r_{28}	cAMP-Pde1p	cAMP + Pde1p	1.0×10^{-1}
r_{29}	cAMP-Pde1p	AMP + Pde1p	7.5
r_{30}	Pde1p + PPA2	Pde1 + PPA2	1.0×10^{-4}
r_{31}	cAMP + Pde2	cAMP-Pde2	1.0×10^{-4}
r_{32}	cAMP-Pde2	cAMP + Pde2	1.0
r_{33}	cAMP-Pde2	AMP + Pde2	1.7
r_{34}	C + Cdc25	C + Cdc25p	1.0
r_{35}	Cdc25p + PPA2	Cdc25 + PPA2	1.0×10^{-2}
r_{36}	Ira2 + C	Ira2p + C	1.0×10^{-3}
r_{37}	Ras2-GTP + Ira2p	Ras2-GTP-Ira2p	1.25
r_{38}	Ras2-GTP-Ira2p	Ras2-GDP + Ira2p	2.5
r_{39}	Ira2p	Ira2	10.0

The mechanistic model of the Ras/cAMP/PKA pathway in *S. cerevisiae*, developed according to the stochastic formulation of chemical kinetics, consists of 39 reactions among 33 molecular species. Each reaction is described by a set of reagents and a set of products, and is characterized by a stochastic constant ($c_i, i = 1, \ldots, 39$, here expressed in arbitrary time units (time^{-1})). The following notation has been used in writing the reactions: (*i*) X + Y represents an interaction between the molecular species X and Y; (*ii*) X-Y describes a molecular complex between species X and Y; (*iii*) Xp denotes the phosphorylated form of species X; (*iv*) the regulatory and catalytic subunits of PKA are indicated by symbols R and C, respectively. Note that the values of the stochastic constants of reactions r_9 and r_{10}—highlighted with an asterisk in the table—are changed to 3.0×10^{-2} and 7.0×10^{-1}, respectively, when reactions $r_{36}, \ldots, r_{39}$ are not active, that is, when the negative feedback exerted by PKA on Ira2 is switched off.

which releases the two catalytic subunits (reactions $r_{14}, \ldots, r_{25}$ in Table 1).

4. The activity of the two phosphodiesterases Pde1 and Pde2, that carry out the degradation of cAMP. The activation of Pde1 is regulated by the catalytic subunits of PKA, and it represents one of the main negative feedback control exerted by PKA within this pathway [12] (reactions $r_{26}, \ldots, r_{33}$ in Table 1).

5. The negative feedback exerted by PKA on Cdc25, whose effect is modeled as a partial inactivation of the GEF activity, as stated in [15,26], and a reduction of the active state level of Ras2-GTP (reactions r_{34}, r_{35} in Table 1).

6. The negative feedback exerted by PKA on Ira2 which, according to [13,14], is assumed to increase the GAP activity and to induce a faster decrease of the Ras2-GTP level (reactions $r_{36}, \ldots, r_{39}$ in Table 1).

In Figure 1, we give a schematic picture of the main inhibitory and activatory regulations existing among the components of the pathway. The complete network of the interactions between all molecular species, as well as the SBML version of the model, are available for free download at the BioSimWare website (http://biosimware.disco.unimib.it). A "generalized mass-action based" [27] version of this mechanistic model was derived, in order to compare the outcome of stochastic and deterministic approaches, as also discussed in [17].

Unless otherwise specified, all the simulations of our mechanistic model were performed starting from an initial state in which the Ras/cAMP/PKA pathway is switched off, that is, in a condition where no cAMP molecules are present in the system and the main components of the pathway (Ras2, adenylate cyclase, PKA) are inactive. The switch on of the pathway is triggered by the presence of an initial amount of the inactive form of Ras2 protein (Ras2-GDP complex), that can be transformed into the active form Ras2-GTP thanks to the presence of guanine nucleotide pools and of the Ras regulator proteins (the values of molecular species initially occurring in the system are given in Table 2). In cascade, the downstream components of the pathway are activated one after the other, giving rise to the emergent dynamics of the whole system and the resulting steady states. This situation is close to that observed *in vivo* when *S. cerevisiae* cells bearing a deletion in the GPR1 gene were starved for nutrients and then stimulated by glucose addition [28].

The rationale behind this choice is that this initial condition allows us to investigate the transient accumulation as well as the oscillatory dynamics of cAMP according to a sequential activation of the different regulatory mechanisms within the pathway. To this aim, as also described in [16], the validation of the model was carried out by simulating the first functional module (the switch cycle

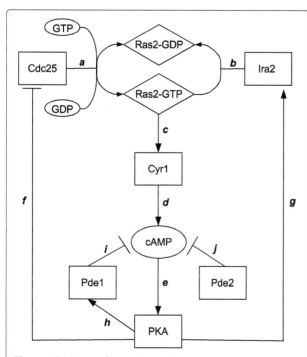

Figure 1 Positive and negative regulations in the Ras/cAMP/PKA pathway. The diagram shows the logical relationships among the principal components of the Ras/cAMP/PKA pathway. The switch cycle of Ras2 protein between its inactive state (Ras2-GDP) and active state (Ras2-GTP) is regulated by the activity of Cdc25 (**a**) and Ira2 (**b**). The intracellular ratio of GTP and GDP also contributes to the regulation of the activity of Ras proteins (**a**), since Cdc25 stimulates the exchange of these nucleotides on Ras according to their relative concentration. Ras2-GTP controls the activity of the adenylate cyclase Cyr1 (**c**), which mediates the synthesis of the second messenger cAMP (**d**). cAMP activates PKA (**e**) by binding to its regulatory subunits and releasing its catalytic subunits. The degradation of cAMP is governed by Pde1 (**i**) and Pde2 (**j**), which constitute a major negative feedback in this pathway, as they both contribute to decrease the intracellular level of the second messenger. The active form of PKA exerts three main regulations in this pathway through the phosphorylation of different components: a positive regulation of Pde1 (**h**) and of Ira2 (**g**), and a negative regulation of Cdc25 (**f**). Since the increased activity of the phosphorylated forms of both Pde1 and Ira2 result in switching off the signal—that is, they both contribute to reducing the intracellular level of cAMP—due either to a faster degradation of cAMP by Pde1 (**i**) or to a diminished fraction of active Ras2 by Ira2 proteins (**b**), these two positive regulations actually have the effect of a negative feedback control on the whole pathway. The negative regulation of Cdc25 by PKA results in a partial inactivation of the GEF activity (**a**), and thus a reduced activation of the Ras2 protein, which results in a decreased activity of the adenylate cyclase and therefore contributes to lowering the cAMP level.

Table 2 Molecular amounts of initial species in the Ras/cAMP/PKA model

Molecular species	Copy number (molecules/cell)	Reference
Cyr1	200	[16]
Cdc25	300	[29]
Ira2	200	[16]
Pde1	1,400	[29]
PKA	2,500	[29]
PPA2	4,000	[29]
Pde2	6,500	[29]
Ras2-GDP	20,000	[29]
GDP	$*1.5 \times 10^6$	[23]
GTP	$*5.0 \times 10^6$	[23]
ATP	$*2.4 \times 10^7$	[23]

The molecular amounts of the species initially occurring in the system are expressed as number of molecules per cell. The number of molecules for Ras2, Cdc25, PKA, Pde1, Pde2 and PPA2 were evaluated using the data presented in [29] (available online at http://yeastgfp.ucsf.edu/). The number of molecules for Ira2 and Cyr1 were estimated in [16] by comparing the fluorescence of yeast cells expressing fusion with eGFP (obtained by http://yeastgfp.ucsf.edu/) using Cdc25-eGFP as a standard (300 molecules/cell). The number of molecules for ATP, GTP and GDP were calculated by considering experimental data presented in [23] and assuming an internal free water volume of about 30 fL [16], obtained by considering an average cell volume of 45 fL [30,31] and taking into account that part of this volume is occupied by the cell wall and internal structures. Therefore, assuming a concentration of 1 mM, for ATP we obtained about 2.4×10^7 molecules/cell, while for GTP and GDP we estimated 5.0×10^6 and 1.5×10^6 molecules/cell, respectively, for yeast cells growing in minimal glucose medium [16]. Unless otherwise specified, the amounts of GDP, GTP and ATP—highlighted with an asterisk in the table—are kept constant during the execution of simulations.

of Ras2 protein) and then adding, in a sequential and iterative way, all the other modules of the model. So doing, we can easily identify the role played by every functional module of reactions on the emergent behaviors of the Ras/cAMP/PKA pathway, avoiding possible interferences with the molecular mechanisms that are already turned on in the system when starting the simulations from a

different initial condition such as, e.g., a steady state corresponding to the basal level of cAMP. Nevertheless, we will show later on that the system response (e.g., the establishment of oscillatory regimes when the sixth functional module is activated) is actually independent of the chosen initial state of the system. For this reason, knowing that we obtain qualitatively and quantitatively comparable system responses starting from either a steady state condition or when the pathway is totally switched off, we prefer the latter initial state in order to analyze the pathway behaviors—in relation to both the initial transient and the subsequent dynamics in response to given stimuli—and to better compare the simulation outcomes under different perturbations.

Simulation and analysis tools
The model was simulated and analyzed with the software BioSimWare [32], using a personal computer with an Intel Core2 CPU (2.66 GHz) running Linux. All stochastic simulations were performed by exploiting the tau-leaping algorithm [33], which represents one of the most efficient methods for simulating the temporal evolution of biochemical systems. This method is an approximated but accurate version of the stochastic simulation algorithm

(SSA) defined in [25], which allows to select and execute in parallel several reactions per step—instead of executing the reactions in a sequential manner, as it is done with SSA—thus speeding up the computation. The mean duration time to execute one run of the tau-leaping algorithm to simulate the dynamics of the Ras/cAMP/PKA pathway over 1500 arbitrary time units is about 30 s, using the initial values of molecular amounts given in Table 2 and the stochastic constants reported in Table 1. Deterministic simulations were executed using the LSODA algorithm [34].

In this study, the efficiency of tau-leaping and LSODA algorithms was exploited to carry out a parameter sweep analysis (PSA), to the aim of investigating the effect of the variation of the values of molecular amounts and of reaction constants on the dynamics of cAMP and of other pivotal components of the Ras/cAMP/PKA pathway. PSA was performed using a computational tool that generates a set of different initial conditions for the model and then automatically executes the corresponding stochastic or deterministic simulations. With this tool, the value of each analyzed parameter varies within a specified range (with respect to a reference value), according to the following procedures:

- The sweep analysis for single parameters (PSA-1D) is performed considering a linear (logarithmic, respectively) sampling of values within the specified range in the case of molecular amounts (reaction constants, respectively). The logarithmic sampling allows to uniformly span different orders of magnitude of the value of the chosen parameter using a reduced but fine-grained set of samples, therefore efficiently analyzing the dynamics of the system in a broad range of environmental conditions.
- The sweep analysis over pairs of parameters (PSA-2D) is performed by exploiting the quasi-random series method [35]. Quasi-random series, also called low discrepancy sequences, allow to efficiently sample a multidimensional space of numerical values. The discrepancy of a sequence represents a measure of its uniformity, and is computed by comparing the actual number of sampled points in a given multidimensional space with the number of points that would be sampled by assuming a uniform distribution. Therefore, the aim of quasi-random series is to uniformly cover the chosen parameter sweep space with "few" samples (i.e., with a lower number of points with respect to classic uniform distributions).

Since we are interested in the analysis of the oscillatory regimes related to the Ras/cAMP/PKA pathway, we also developed a numerical procedure, implemented with the LabVIEW 2009 (National Instruments) environment, in

order to evaluate the amplitude and frequency of stochastic oscillations. In particular, we considered the dynamics of cAMP as the target of this analysis. To this aim, for any simulation outcome we choose a portion of the dynamics where oscillations of cAMP occur (e.g., the time interval $[200, 1, 400]$ after the initial transient accumulation of cAMP in Figure 2, bottom left), we evaluate the mean amount of cAMP within this interval, and use this value as a threshold to identify the disjoint sets of consecutive points that are all above (or all below) the threshold. Then, within each of these sets, we identify the global maximum (or minimum, respectively) amount of cAMP, and finally we evaluate the mean and standard deviation of all the maxima (or minima) points previously identified. So doing, we can evaluate the maximum, minimum and average amplitude of the amount of cAMP during stochastic oscillations. The frequency of oscillations of cAMP can then be easily calculated by dividing the number of maxima (minima) by the length of the chosen time interval. We refer to [17] for additional details on this method.

Results and discussion

The computational methods previously described were exploited in this study to test different hypotheses on the mechanisms that activate and regulate the components of the Ras/cAMP/PKA pathway in single yeast cells. In this context, our previous analysis on the Ras/cAMP/PKA model suggested that stable oscillatory regimes in the amount of cAMP can be regulated by the ratio between Cdc25 and Ira2 proteins, which both control the activation of the adenylate cyclase by means of the active fraction of Ras proteins (that is, Ras2-GTP) [17]. Hence, we start here by briefly presenting the effects of modulating the feedback mechanisms on Cdc25 and Ira2 proteins. Then, we study the role of the feedback mechanism exerted by PKA at the level of Pde1, as well as the influence of the deletion and of the overexpression of both phosphodiesterases on the establishment of oscillatory regimes. Finally, we investigate the presence of oscillations in the pathway through the variation of the intracellular amounts of GTP and Cdc25. Indeed, as we previously suggested [16], one of the signals that can modulate the activity of the Ras/cAMP/PKA pathway is the ratio between GTP and GDP, since the exchange activity of Cdc25 depends on the relative concentration of these guanine nucleotides [23].

The role of feedback mechanisms on Ras activation

Starting from the initial condition of the system previously described, the simulation of the switch cycle of Ras2 protein—together with the activation of the adenylate cyclase and of the downstream components—shows a transient accumulation of cAMP in response to the

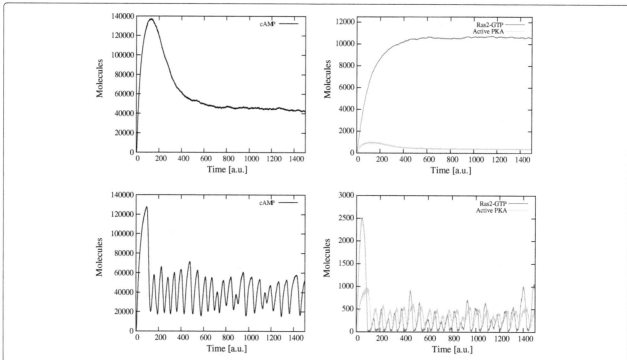

Figure 2 Dynamics of cAMP, Ras2-GTP and active PKA with and without the feedback on Ira2. When the feedback control on Ira2 proteins is not activated, the dynamics of cAMP shows an initial transient increase and the successive establishment of a stable steady state (*top left*). In this condition, neither Ras2-GTP nor active PKA show oscillatory behavior (*top right*). On the contrary, when the feedback on Ira2 proteins is activated, the initial peak on cAMP amount is followed by the establishment of a stable oscillatory state (*bottom left*), as also reflected in the dynamics of both Ras2-GTP and of the active fraction of PKA (*bottom right*). In *S. cerevisiae*, cAMP was experimentally determined to be around 2×10^5 molecules after stimulation, while basal levels vary from 2×10^4 to 5×10^4 molecules/cell; as a consequence of stimulation, a cAMP peak was observed after 45–60 s, and then a new steady-state was reached in 3–5 min (see, e.g., Figure 2 in [28]). The expected number of cAMP molecules derived from stochastic simulations was calculated here by considering our own measurements [16] and data presented in [28].

formation of the complex Ras2-GTP. More precisely, when we only activate the feedback mechanisms based on the phosphorylation of Cdc25 and of the phosphodiesterase Pde1 (functional modules 1–5), we obtain a stable steady state in the levels of cAMP, Ras2-GTP and active PKA, as shown in Figure 2 (top plots). On the contrary, if the feedback control on Ira2 proteins is activated (functional module 6), then the system is able to generate stable oscillatory states of cAMP amount, as well as of Ras2-GTP and active PKA (Figure 2, bottom plots). We previously analyzed this oscillatory regime in [17], showing that the range of cAMP oscillations depends on the ratio between the Ras regulator proteins Cdc25 and Ira2, and that the oscillations frequency increases as the ratio Cdc25/Ira2 decreases, meaning that an unbalance between the GEF and GAP activity with respect to the wild type condition is able to induce a frequency modulation.

In Figure 3, we show that the occurrence of the oscillatory regime in cAMP dynamics is affected only by the activation of these negative feedback mechanisms, and is actually independent of the chosen initial condition of the system. The plots show the establishment of stable oscillations in cAMP amount (left plot), as well as in

Ras2-GTP and active PKA amounts (right plot), when the simulation is executed starting from an initial condition where the level of cAMP is already at the stable steady state.

Then, we investigated how an increased or a reduced phosphorylation activity of PKA over Cdc25 and Ira2 can influence the establishment of oscillatory regimes. Figures 4 and 5 represent the simulation results on the dynamics of cAMP (left plots) and of Ras2-GTP (right plots), carried out through a PSA-1D over the reaction constants corresponding to the negative feedback over Cdc25 and Ira2, respectively. Figure 4 shows that oscillations occur for any value of the stochastic constant of reaction r_{34}, that is, regardless of the magnitude of the feedback exerted by PKA on Cdc25. On the contrary, the feedback on Ira2 is effectively able to control the establishment of oscillatory regimes (Figure 5): for values of the constant of reaction r_{36} lower than the reference value, only stable steady states can be reached. Conversely, if the value of this reaction constant is higher than the reference value, that is, if the GTPase activity of Ras2 proteins is strongly enhanced by the phosphorylation of Ira2, then the oscillatory regime is lost.

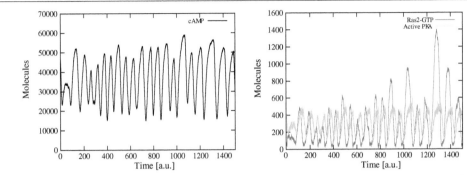

Figure 3 Activation of the feedback on Ira2: cAMP oscillations starting from a steady state condition. The occurrence of oscillatory regimes in the cAMP dynamics is only affected by the activation of negative feedback mechanisms and is independent of the initial condition of the system. The plots show the establishment of stable oscillations in cAMP amount (*left*), as well as in Ras2-GTP and active PKA amounts (*right*), starting the simulation from an initial condition where the system is at a stable steady state. In this simulation, the initial amounts of cAMP, Ras2-GTP and active PKA are around 47,000, 50, and 400 molecules, respectively.

In addition, the stochastic simulations of the oscillatory regimes in the Ras/cAMP/PKA pathway were compared to the outcome of deterministic simulations of the "generalized mass-action model" [17]. In Figure 6, we show the dynamics of cAMP with different initial amounts of Cdc25, obtained by means of stochastic (left plot) and deterministic (right plot) simulations. It is worth noting that the deterministic and stochastic behaviors are comparable for Cdc25 equal to 200 and 300 molecules (sustained oscillations occur in both cases) and for Cdc25 equal to 400 (damped oscillations). On the other hand, by setting the initial amount of Cdc25 to smaller values, e.g., 150 molecules, the two approaches show qualitatively different outcomes: the stochastic approach provides stable oscillations of cAMP, while in the deterministic case, under the same initial conditions, the dynamics show damped oscillations. This result highlights the usefulness of stochastic modeling and the role played by noise in the Ras/cAMP/PKA pathway, which seems to support the robustness of the system with respect to the variation of the amount of pivotal components of the pathway (in

this case, protein Cdc25), ensuring the presence of stable oscillatory regimes.

The negative regulation by phosphodiesterases
To determine the influence of phosphodiesterases on the existence of stable oscillations of cAMP, we conducted three different parameter sweep analyses:

1. A PSA-1D over the reaction constant corresponding to the negative feedback exerted by PKA on Pde1, whereby higher values of this parameter represent a stronger activation of the phosphodiesterase activity, and hence a higher net effect of the negative feedback. In Figure 7, we plot the dynamics of cAMP (top left plot), Ras2-GTP (top right plot), phosphorylated Ira2 (bottom left plot) and phosphorylated Pde1 (bottom right plot) with respect to the variation of this reaction constant in the interval $[1.0 \times 10^{-9}, 1.0 \times 10^{-3}]$. This interval corresponds to 3 orders of magnitude below and 3 above the reference value given in Table 1, whose

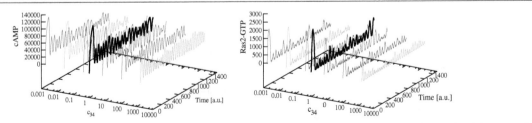

Figure 4 Effects of the modulation of the negative feedback on Cdc25 (reaction constant c_{34}). The figure shows the simulated dynamics of cAMP (*left*) and Ras2-GTP (*right*) resulting from a PSA-1D on the value of the reaction constant that modulates the phosphorylation of Cdc25 by means of active PKA. The varied parameter is constant c_{34} (see Table 1), within the interval $[1.0 \times 10^{-3}, 1.0 \times 10^{3}]$, being 1.0 the reference value (represented with the black thick line). Stable oscillations occur in both cAMP and Ras2-GTP dynamics, for any value of the reaction constant, regardless of the magnitude of the feedback exerted by PKA on Cdc25. For larger values of the constant, namely c_{34} greater than 1.0, the only effect is a reduction in the amount of cAMP and Ras2-GTP (whose average values are reduced from around 40,000 to 35,000 molecules, and from around 270 to 130 molecules, respectively) and an increase of about fifty per cent in the frequency of oscillations with respect to the reference value.

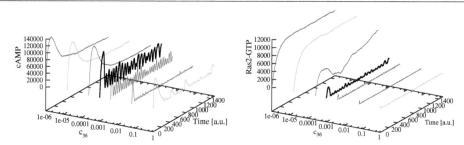

Figure 5 Effects of the modulation of the negative feedback on Ira2 (reaction constant c_{36}). The figure shows the simulated dynamics of cAMP (*left*) and Ras2-GTP (*right*) resulting from a PSA-1D on the value of the reaction constant that modulates the phosphorylation of Ira2 by means of active PKA. The varied parameter is constant c_{36} (see Table 1), within the interval [1.0×10^{-6}, 1.0], being 1.0×10^{-3} the reference value (represented with the black thick line). The reaction that describes the feedback on Ira2 is able to control the establishment of oscillatory regimes: for values of the reaction constant lower than the reference value, only stable steady states can be reached. In particular, cAMP and Ras2-GTP reach a noisy steady state around 60,000 and 10,000 molecules, respectively. Conversely, by increasing the value of the constant, that is, enhancing the GTPase activity of Ras2 proteins by means of the phosphorylation of Ira2, the amplitude of oscillations of cAMP and Ras2-GTP is reduced from around 40,000 to 25,000 molecules and from 600 to 140 molecules, respectively, as well as their average amounts, that decrease from around 40,000 to 20,000 and from around 270 to 50 molecules, respectively. For values of constant c_{36} greater than 1.0×10^{-2} the oscillatory regime is lost and the average values of cAMP and Ras2-GTP drop to around 5,000 and 20 molecules, respectively.

related dynamics is represented in the plots with the black thick line.

2. A PSA-2D over the amounts of Pde1 and of Pde2 in the intervals [0, 2,800] and [0, 13,000] molecules, respectively, which mimic the biological conditions ranging from the deletion to a two-fold overexpression of each phosphodiesterase. In Figure 8 we plot the amplitude of cAMP oscillations generated with these parameters, where the values on the x- and y-axis were normalized to [0, 1]. In this figure, an amplitude value equal to zero corresponds to a non oscillating dynamics. Figure 9 shows the dynamics of cAMP in the four extreme conditions of the phosphodiesterases amounts, as highlighted in Figure 8, where **A** corresponds to Pde1 = 0, Pde2 = 0 molecules; **B** corresponds to Pde1 = 0, Pde2 = 13,000 molecules; **C** corresponds to Pde1 = 2,800,

Pde2 = 0 molecules; **D** corresponds to Pde1 = 2,800, Pde2 = 13,000 molecules.

3. A PSA-1D over the amount of Cdc25 in the interval [0, 900] molecules, ranging from the deletion to a three-fold overexpression of the GEF proteins, in both conditions of deletion of Pde1 or Pde2. In Figures 10 and 11, we plot the diagrams of the amplitude of cAMP oscillations with respect to the number of Cdc25 molecules, under the deletion of Pde1 and Pde2, respectively. In these figures, square points represent the mean value of cAMP amount, circle (triangular) points the maximum (minimum) value of oscillations with the respective standard deviation, the left and right shady areas correspond to noisy stochastic fluctuations and stable steady states, respectively, while the white area corresponds to oscillatory regimes.

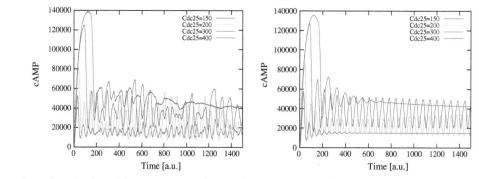

Figure 6 Comparison of stochastic and deterministic simulations of cAMP dynamics with different initial amounts of Cdc25. The figure shows the dynamics of cAMP with different initial amounts of Cdc25 (150, 200, 300, and 400 molecules) obtained by means of stochastic (*left*) and deterministic (*right*) simulations. The deterministic and stochastic behaviors are comparable for Cdc25 equal to 200 and 300 molecules (sustained oscillations occur in both cases) and for Cdc25 equal to 400 (damped oscillations). On the contrary, when the initial amount of Cdc25 is low (i.e., 150 molecules), with the stochastic approach we obtain stable oscillations of cAMP, while in the deterministic case the dynamics shows damped oscillations.

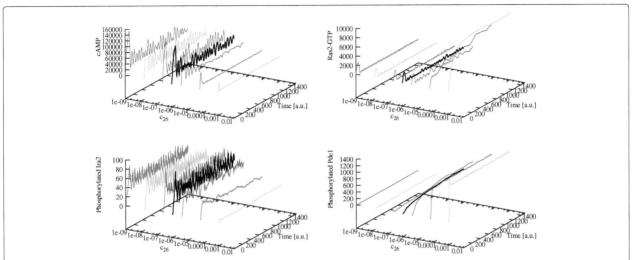

Figure 7 Effects of the modulation of the negative feedback on Pde1 (reaction constant c_{26}). The figure shows the simulated dynamics of cAMP (*top left*), Ras2-GTP (*top right*), phosphorylated Ira2 (*bottom left*) and phosphorylated Pde1 (*bottom right*) resulting from a PSA-1D on the value of the reaction constant that modulates the phosphorylation of Pde1 by means of active PKA. The varied parameter is constant c_{26} (see Table 1), within the interval $[1.0 \times 10^{-9}, 1.0 \times 10^{-3}]$, being 1.0×10^{-6} the reference value (represented with the black thick line). For values of the constant lower than the reference value, stable oscillations still occur. On the contrary, by increasing the value of the reaction constant, that is, if we simulate a marked promotion of the activity of Pde1, after an initial transient increase the amount of cAMP gets almost completely degraded and no oscillations occur anymore (cAMP reaches a noisy steady state around 5,000 molecules, *top left*). Under the same condition, the amount of Ras2-GTP tends to a high steady state level (around 10,000 molecules, *top right*), which would intuitively induce a promotion of the cyclase activity and thus an expectable increase in the cAMP amount, which is instead counterbalanced by two concurrent processes: (*i*) the reduced activity of Ira2 proteins, whereby only a few copies of phosphorylated Ira2 are present inside the system (around 5 molecules, *bottom left*), and (*ii*) the strong phosphodiesterase activity taking place in this condition, that is also confirmed by the high level of phosphorylated Pde1 (around 1,200 molecules, *bottom right*).

Taken altogether, the results of these simulations show that the deletion of the high-affinity phosphodiesterase Pde2 fosters the establishment of oscillations of cAMP, whose amplitude increases with the increase of Pde1 amount. On the contrary, the deletion of the low-affinity cAMP phosphodiesterase Pde1 has the effect of

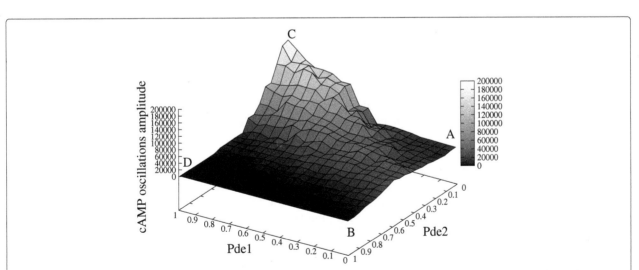

Figure 8 Influence of the amount of Pde1 and Pde2 on the establishment of cAMP oscillatory regimes. The figure shows the oscillations amplitude of cAMP dynamics resulting from a PSA-2D on the values of the initial amounts of Pde1 and Pde2, varied in the intervals $[0, 2,800]$ and $[0, 13,000]$, respectively (being Pde1 $= 1,400$ and Pde2 $= 6,500$ molecules the reference values—see Table 2). In the plot, the values on the x- and y-axis were normalized in the interval $[0, 1]$; a total of 200 initial conditions were sampled from the specified bidimensional parameters space. This analysis shows that the deletion of the high-affinity phosphodiesterase Pde2 fosters the establishment of oscillations of cAMP, whose amplitude increases with the increase of Pde1 amount (from point **A** to point **C**); on the contrary, the deletion of the low-affinity cAMP phosphodiesterase Pde1 has the effect of diminishing or even abolishing the oscillations irrespective of the amount of Pde2 (from point **A** to **B**). The overexpression of both phosphodiesterases (point **D**) does not allow the establishment of oscillatory regimes.

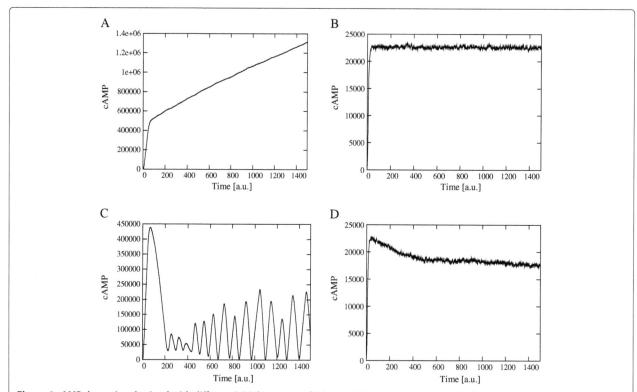

Figure 9 cAMP dynamics obtained with different initial amounts of Pde1 and Pde2. Dynamics of cAMP with different initial amounts of the phosphodiesterases, as given in Figure 8, where **A**: Pde1 = 0, Pde2 = 0; **B**: Pde1 = 0, Pde2 = 13,000; **C**: Pde1 = 2,800, Pde2 = 0; **D**: Pde1 = 2,800, Pde2 = 13,000 molecules. The plots show that in the absence of both phosphodiesterases (**A**) we achieve, as expected, an unlimited accumulation of cAMP, since our model does not include any other mechanism to reduce the intracellular level of cAMP; with a very high initial amount of Pde2 (**B** and **D**), cAMP reaches a noisy steady state but no oscillations are observed; in the absence of Pde2, when only Pde1 is active (**C**), oscillations of cAMP can then be established, showing a very large amplitude and a mean cAMP amount that is slightly higher than standard conditions. The molecular amounts of cAMP reached in conditions **A** and **C** are higher than the physiological levels measured in corresponding experimental settings [12,14] though, from a computational point of view, they are indicative of the role played by the two phosphodiesterases, since they highlight the different dynamical behaviors of the pathway in extreme conditions.

diminishing or even abolishing the oscillations irrespective of the amount of Pde2 (see Figure 8). This might indicate that the negative feedback on Pde1 is effectively able to regulate the oscillatory regime of cAMP, independently from the presence of Pde2.

Indeed, if we simulate a stronger activity of PKA over Pde1, that is, a marked promotion of the activity of Pde1, we see that after an initial transient increase the intracellular cAMP gets almost completely degraded and no oscillations occur anymore (Figure 7, top left plot). Interestingly, in the same condition the amount of Ras2-GTP tends to a high steady state level (Figure 7, top right plot), which would intuitively induce a promotion of the cyclase activity and thus an increase in the cAMP amount. This counterintuitive behavior is an overall effect due to two concurrent factors: (*i*) the strong negative feedback exerted by Pde1 (Figure 7, bottom right plot), that causes the immediate degradation of cAMP and does not allow its intracellular accumulation, and (*ii*) the lack of the effect of the feedback on Ira2, that causes the increase in the

amount of Ras2-GTP, a consequence of the fact that Ira2 proteins are basically not phosphorylated by PKA in this condition (Figure 7, bottom left plot).

In addition, Figure 10 shows that in the absence of Pde1 the oscillatory regimes are established even when the amount of Cdc25 is at a two-fold overexpression with respect to its physiological amount, which corresponds to about 300 molecules/cell [29]. These data can be compared to the analysis shown in [17], which highlights that in normal conditions and in presence of Pde1, the oscillatory regimes can only be established when Cdc25 is approximately between 150 and 400 molecules, that is, when the ratio Cdc25/Ira2 is not higher than 2 (being the amount of Ira2 around 200 molecules in normal conditions). Therefore, the deletion of Pde1 with respect to the ratio Cdc25/Ira2 has the effect of widening the conditions under which sustained oscillations of cAMP occur. Similar considerations can be done for the deletion of Pde2, whereby oscillatory regimes occur with Cdc25 in between 200 and 600 molecules (Figure 11).

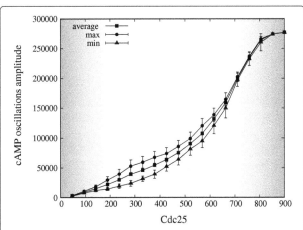

Figure 10 Diagram of cAMP oscillations amplitude with respect to Cdc25 amount when deleting Pde1. The figure shows the oscillations amplitude of cAMP dynamics resulting from a PSA-1D where the amount of Cdc25 varies in the interval [0, 900], in the condition of deletion of Pde1. The mean and standard deviation of the average (squares), maximum (circles) and minimum (triangles) amount of cAMP during oscillations are plotted. The left and right shady areas correspond to noisy stochastic fluctuations and stable steady states, respectively, while the white area corresponds to oscillatory regimes. This analysis highlights that, when deleting Pde1, oscillatory regimes in cAMP can be established even when the amount of Cdc25 is at a two-fold overexpression with respect to the physiological amount of 300 molecules/cell (Table 2). Therefore, the deletion of Pde1 has the effect of widening the range of Cdc25 molecules under which sustained oscillations of cAMP occur, being approximately [150, 400] the interval whereby oscillatory regimes in cAMP are found when Pde1 is present in the system (see [17] for more details).

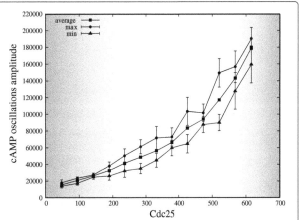

Figure 11 Diagram of cAMP oscillations amplitude with respect to Cdc25 amount when deleting Pde2. The figure shows the oscillations amplitude of cAMP dynamics resulting from a PSA-1D where the amount of Cdc25 varies in the interval [0, 900], in the condition of deletion of Pde2. The mean and standard deviation of the average (squares), maximum (circles) and minimum (triangles) amount of cAMP during oscillations are plotted. The left and right shady areas correspond to noisy stochastic fluctuations and stable steady states, respectively, while the white area corresponds to oscillatory regimes. Similarly to Figure 10, the analysis highlights that, under the deletion of Pde2, oscillatory regimes in cAMP can be established even when the amount of Cdc25 is at a two-fold overexpression with respect to its physiological amount. Therefore, also the deletion of Pde2 has the effect of changing the range of Cdc25 molecules under which sustained oscillations of cAMP occur.

The computational results corresponding to the conditions of deletion of the phosphodiesterases are in line with recent experimental measurements of the nucleocytoplasmic localization of the transcription factor Msn2, carried out in *S. cerevisiae pde1Δ* and *pde2Δ* mutant cells, under continuous light-induced stress conditions [21]. In yeast cells, the nuclear localization of Msn2 is under the negative control of PKA: it is mainly localized in the cytoplasm under non-stressed conditions, but in response to environmental stresses Msn2 is dephosphorylated and translocates to the nucleus. The observations presented in [21] highlight that both deletion mutants—that are characterized by a higher PKA activity with respect to the control strain—show a decrease in Msn2 nuclear localization, with *pde2Δ* exhibiting the strongest effect, that is, a marked reduction of nuclear Msn2 with respect to both *pde1Δ* and the control strain. Moreover, both phosphodiesterases seem to be involved in the regulation of cAMP intracellular amount under light-induced stress. Indeed, in cells lacking the phosphodiesterases, the PKA activity was shown to increase, in agreement to our simulation outcomes, therefore inducing a decrease in the nuclear fraction of Msn2 [21].

Finally, an analysis similar to that presented in Figures 10 and 11 was performed for the deterministic case, though achieving different results with respect to the stochastic approach. As shown in Figure 12, which represents the dynamics of cAMP under different initial amounts of Cdc25, in both cases of deletion of Pde1 (left plot) and Pde2 (right plot) no sustained oscillations of cAMP are obtained (for this reason, the diagram of oscillations amplitude corresponding to the deterministic simulations—as given in Figures 10 and 11 in relation to the stochastic approach—is not shown, as it would be non informative). Instead, in Figure 13 we show the comparison between the dynamics of cAMP obtained with stochastic and deterministic simulations, under the deletion of Pde1 (left plot) and Pde2 (right plot), and with an initial amount of Cdc25 equal to 300 molecules, which represents, the physiological level in yeast cells (Table 2). The plots clearly show that in both conditions, while with the deterministic approach oscillations are damped or even not occurring, stochastic simulations show sustained oscillations of cAMP. Therefore, we can hypothesize that the introduction of noise in the Ras/cAMP/PKA pathway is able to stabilize the oscillatory regimes.

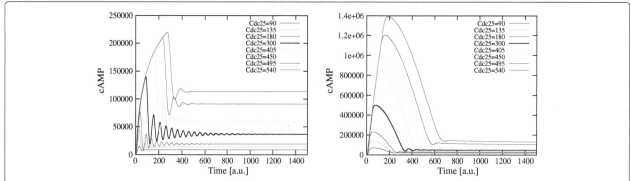

Figure 12 Deterministic simulations of cAMP dynamics under deletion of Pde1 or Pde2 with different initial amounts of Cdc25. The figure shows the dynamics of cAMP with different initial amounts of Cdc25, obtained by means of deterministic simulations when deleting Pde1 (*left*) and Pde2 (*right*). In both conditions, no sustained oscillations are present in the system for any value of the initial amount of Cdc25.

In this context, we also carried out a preliminary analysis on the oscillations frequency of cAMP in both the conditions of deletion of Pde1 and Pde2, considering different values for the ratio Cdc25/Ira2, as already mentioned in the previous section for the wild type condition. In Figure 14, we compare the oscillations frequency of cAMP in these three conditions showing that, while the deletion of Pde1 has a minor effect with respect to the wild type on the frequency modulation, the deletion of Pde2 is able to diminish the oscillations frequency of cAMP, as can also be gained by comparing the stochastic simulations of cAMP dynamics presented in Figure 13 and in Figure 2, bottom left.

The role of guanine nucleotide pools

We previously suggested that one of the signals able to modulate the activity of the Ras/cAMP/PKA pathway is the ratio between GTP and GDP, since the exchange activity of Cdc25 depends on the relative concentration of GTP and GDP [16,23]. In normal growth conditions, the concentration of GTP is 3 to 5 times higher than GDP,

allowing the activation of Ras protein; anyway, under limited nutrient availability (when the relative amount of GTP decreases), the activity of Cdc25 does not result in Ras proteins activation, since in this case the unproductive binding/unbinding with GDP is mostly favored.

To investigate the role played by guanine nucleotides concentrations on the establishment of oscillations, we carried out a PSA-2D to simulate the behavior of the system in perturbed conditions, where the concentration of GTP varies in the interval $[1.9 \times 10^4, 5.0 \times 10^6]$ molecules (ranging from a reduced nutrient availability to a normal growth condition) and, at the same time, also the amount of Cdc25 varies in the interval $[0, 600]$ molecules (ranging from the deletion to a two-fold overexpression of the GEF proteins). In Figure 15, we plot the amplitude of cAMP oscillations obtained in these conditions. In this figure, the values on the *x*- and *y*-axis were normalized to $[0, 1]$, and an amplitude value equal to zero corresponds to a non oscillating dynamics. Figure 16 shows the dynamics of cAMP in the four extreme conditions of GTP and Cdc25 amounts, as highlighted in Figure 15,

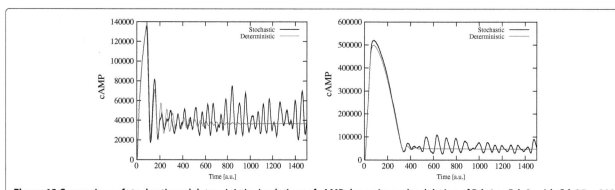

Figure 13 Comparison of stochastic and deterministic simulations of cAMP dynamics under deletion of Pde1 or Pde2, with Cdc25 = 300 molecules. The figure shows the comparison of the dynamics of cAMP obtained by means of stochastic and deterministic simulations when deleting Pde1 (*left*) or Pde2 (*right*), with an initial amount of Cdc25 equal to 300 molecules. We note that, while in the deterministic case oscillations are damped or even not occurring, the stochastic case shows sustained oscillations of cAMP in both cases.

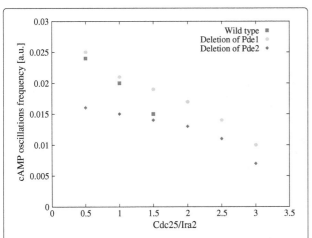

Figure 14 Frequency modulation of cAMP oscillations in the wild type condition and under the deletion of Pde1 and Pde2.
The figure shows the comparison of the oscillations frequency of cAMP in the wild type condition (red square dots) and under the deletion of Pde1 (green circle dots) or Pde2 (blue diamond dots), with respect to the ratio Cdc25/Ira2 (with the initial amount of Cdc25 ranging from 100 to 600 molecules, and Ira2 = 200 molecules). The plot shows that the deletion of Pde1 has a minor effect with respect to the wild type condition on the modulation of frequency, while the deletion of Pde2 is able to diminish the oscillations frequency of cAMP. For values of the ratio Cdc25/Ira2 greater than 1.5, the points related to the wild type condition are not plotted, since no stable oscillations are established in these cases [17].

where **A** corresponds to Cdc25 = 10, GTP = 1.9×10^4 molecules; **B** corresponds to Cdc25 = 10, GTP = 5.0×10^6 molecules; **C** corresponds to Cdc25 = 600, GTP = 1.9×10^4 molecules; **D** corresponds to Cdc25 = 600, GTP = 5.0×10^6 molecules.

The simulations show that when the amount of Cdc25 is approximately at normal condition or slightly lower, the oscillatory regimes are established for basically any value of GTP, being the amplitude of oscillations smaller in lower nutrient availability conditions. On the contrary, when the amount of Cdc25 increases, no oscillations of cAMP occur when GTP is high, but oscillatory regimes are still present if GTP is low. This result can be motivated considering that when the ratio GTP/GDP decreases, Ras proteins are more frequently loaded with GDP instead that with GTP, and their activity is therefore decreased, inducing the establishment of an oscillatory regime.

Conclusion

With this study we determined, in a quantitative way, that the coupling between feedback mechanisms and the molecular levels of the Ras modulators can influence the oscillatory regimes of cAMP and PKA. In this context, our study highlights the role played by the feedback exerted by PKA on phosphodiesterases and on Ira2 proteins, that was never directly investigated so far. To this aim, stochastic

and deterministic simulations were carried out to analyze the behavior of the Ras/cAMP/PKA pathway under different conditions. As also presented in [17], the comparison between the two approaches indicates that with deterministic simulations the interval of Cdc25 amount for obtaining stable oscillations of cAMP is reduced with respect to stochastic simulations. In particular, in [17] it was shown that stable oscillations occur when Cdc25 amount is approximately between 200 and 350 molecules in the first case, while in the second case noisy oscillations are still evident for lower and higher Cdc25 amounts (being the oscillatory regime interval around [150, 400] molecules). Within this oscillatory interval, the frequency and the amplitude of oscillations are well comparable in the stochastic and the deterministic simulations in standard conditions.

On the contrary, the comparison between stochastic and deterministic analysis performed in the perturbed conditions (that is, under the deletion of phosphodiesterases) shows qualitatively and quantitatively different results. Indeed, the dynamics of cAMP with different initial amounts of Cdc25, in both cases of deletion of Pde1 and Pde2, does not present sustained oscillations in the deterministic case, while stochastic simulations show stable oscillations.

Therefore, we can argue that molecular noise within the Ras/cAMP/PKA pathway can enhance the robustness of the system at least in response to the different perturbations we considered here, ensuring the presence of stable oscillatory regimes as also previously discussed for other biological systems (see [2] and references therein). Indeed, stochastic simulations show that the cell might be able to respond appropriately to an alteration of its pivotal components—such as the amount of protein Cdc25, which is related to the stress level [19,36]—fostering the maintenance of stable oscillations during the signal propagation (i.e., the synthesis of the second messenger cAMP) and the activation of PKA. As such, this might suggest a stronger adaptation capability of yeast cells to various environmental stimuli or endogenous variations.

In [37] it was shown that in MIN6 beta cells PKA, cAMP and calcium are highly integrated in an oscillatory circuit that allows a fine spatiotemporal regulation of the kinase activity. Similarly, we think that the multi-level regulation carried out with different feedback mechanisms in the Ras/cAMP/PKA pathway in yeast might represent a way to extend the regulatory span of the system, therefore acting as a tuning mechanism for the numerous downstream targets of PKA. This assumption might be in line with the hypothesis of the "frequency-modulated" regulation that was recently proposed in yeast in relation to calcium oscillations [38], though further computational and experimental investigations should be carried out to ascertain the validity of this hypothesis also in relation to cAMP and

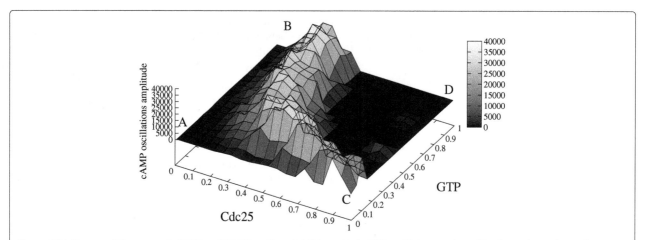

Figure 15 Influence of the amount of GTP and Cdc25 on the establishment of cAMP oscillatory regimes. The figure shows the oscillations amplitude of cAMP dynamics resulting from a PSA-2D on the values of the initial amounts of GTP and Cdc25, varied in the intervals $[1.9 \times 10^4, 5.0 \times 10^6]$ and $[0, 600]$, respectively (being GTP $= 5.0 \times 10^6$ and Cdc25 $= 300$ molecules the reference values—see Table 2). In the plot, the values on the x- and y-axis have been normalized in the interval $[0, 1]$; a total of 200 initial conditions were sampled from the specified bidimensional parameters space. This analysis shows that when the amount of Cdc25 is approximately at normal condition or slightly lower, oscillatory regimes are established for basically any value of GTP (from point **A** to point **B**), being the amplitude of oscillations smaller in lower nutrient availability conditions. On the contrary, when the amount of Cdc25 increases, no oscillations of cAMP occur when GTP is high (point **D**), but oscillatory regimes are still present if GTP is low (point **C**).

PKA oscillations induced by the molecular interactions within the Ras/cAMP/PKA pathway.

Indeed, oscillations related to the Ras/cAMP/PKA pathway were experimentally observed, but only in indirect ways, e.g., through the analysis of the periodic nucleocytoplasmic shuttling of Msn2 [18,19]. In this context, the observations presented in [21] show that, in single yeast cells subject to continuous light exposure, the oscillations frequency of Msn2 between the nucleus and the cytoplasm can be influenced by PKA as well as by Pde1 and Pde2, whereby phosphodiesterases indirectly affect the activity of PKA through the degradation of cAMP. In particular, in [21] it was shown that the oscillation frequency of Msn2 increases alongside the increase in the induced-stress condition, which can be also ascribed to a reduced activity of Cdc25 protein [19,36], as tested in our study. Anyway, it is not clear whether the nucleocytoplasmic oscillations frequency of Msn2 can be interpreted solely in terms of the above mentioned frequency modulation control, since the response of the cell to cumulative light-induced stress might suggest a more complex scenario that is still to be unraveled [21].

The computational results presented in this study and in [17], in relation to the amplitude and the frequency of oscillations within the Ras/cAMP/PKA pathway, suggest that a frequency modulation can be achieved when perturbing the ratio between the amounts of Cdc25 and Ira2 proteins, that is, the Ras regulator proteins. In particular we showed here that, with respect to the wild type condition, the deletion of Pde2 is able to diminish

the oscillations frequency of cAMP, while the deletion of Pde1 has a minor effect on its variation. These results represent a first step towards an in depth analysis of oscillatory regimes in the Ras/cAMP/PKA pathway, that we plan to carry out in different ways. On the one hand, we will investigate the correlation between the oscillations of cAMP, PKA and its downstream targets (such as Msn2) to analyze how this behavior propagates through the signal transduction pathway. On the other hand, we are currently developing a computational tool to quantitatively characterize the oscillations (whether stochastic, deterministic or noise-induced) by means of Fourier analysis, as already proposed for the study of the oscillatory shuttling of NF-κB [39], whereby the power spectrum of simulated dynamics was analyzed to verify the occurrence of peaks at non-zero frequencies, as well as to calculate the signal-to-noise ratio, in order to inspect the presence of oscillations. In addition, qualitative analysis of the nature of bifurcation points, based on dynamical systems theory (see, e.g., [40] for an application to the study of noise-induced stabilization in a genetic circuit, and [41] for a broad overview of the subject), could be exploited to better investigate how stochastic fluctuations are able to originate the stable oscillatory regimes in the Ras/cAMP/PKA model, which do not occur in the absence of noise.

Furthermore, as a future development of our study, we will investigate the response of the Ras/cAMP/PKA pathway to nutrients and to intracellular acidification (that likely causes an inhibition of GAP activity of the Ira proteins [42]), its crosstalk and integration with

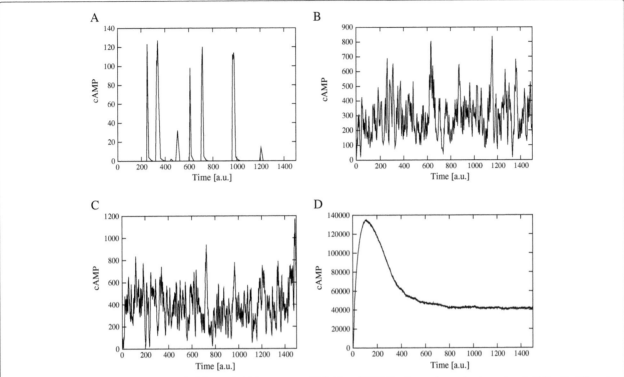

Figure 16 cAMP dynamics obtained with different initial amounts of Cdc25 and GTP. The figure shows the dynamics of cAMP with different initial amounts of Cdc25 and GTP, as given in Figure 15, where **A**: Cdc25 = 10, GTP = 1.9×10^4; **B**: Cdc25 = 10, GTP = 5.0×10^6; **C**: Cdc25 = 600, GTP = 1.9×10^4; **D**: Cdc25 = 600, GTP = 5.0×10^6 molecules. The plots show that low amounts of Cdc25 (**A** and **B**), or high amounts of Cdc25 coupled with low amounts of GTP (**C**), lead to the production of very low amounts of cAMP, showing a noisy dynamics. On the other hand, when the amounts of both Cdc25 and GTP are high (**D**), we observe a dynamics of cAMP similar to that obtained without the feedback on Ira2 proteins (see Figure 2, top left), and no oscillations are established.

other pathways co-involved in glucose signaling and yeast metabolism, as well as the regulated expression of downstream target genes. In particular, we will define additional functional modules of reactions to describe the Gpr1/Gpa2 pathway, a signaling mechanism that responds only to high glucose concentration and operates in an addictive redundant way with Ras2-GTP to activate the adenylate cyclase [28,42]. We also plan to define a multi-volume version of our mechanistic model, in order to characterize the intracellular localization of the central components of this pathway, since there exist experimental evidences that most of the Cdc25, Cyr1, Ira2 and Ras2 proteins localize at internal membranes, suggesting the presence of large signaling complexes inside yeast cells [43,44]. Investigations about the topological distribution of the molecular species in distinct cellular regions will be performed by means of the tau-DPP framework [45]. This will enable us, for instance, to study the dynamical movement of Cdc25 proteins to plasma membrane in response to nutrient starvation, and the hyper-activity of PKA to counteract the localization of Cdc25 and Ira2 proteins.

In conclusion, the computational model we developed allows to investigate in details the mechanisms that regulate the transition between stable and oscillatory regimes in the Ras/cAMP/PKA pathway, to make predictions on the conditions that lead to the insurgence of oscillations, and to eventually plan focused validation experiments. In particular, by directly operating on the modulation of specific components of the pathway, such as molecular amounts and reaction constants, we are able to study in details the influence of every molecular interaction on the pathway behavior. Nonetheless, although the Ras/cAMP/PKA pathway has gone through extensive investigations in *S. cerevisiae*, accurate wet data on the spatiotemporal dynamics of cAMP in single yeast cells are still lacking. To this aim, we are carrying out extensive laboratory work to develop a FRET-sensor based on Epac able to respond to cAMP levels in *S. cerevisiae*, in order to measure the changes in the level of cAMP in single cells and to directly test the presence of long term cAMP oscillations *in vivo* [46]. This setup will allow us to conduct an in depth analysis of the response of the pathway to different nutritional and stress conditions, as well as to perform an accurate parameter estimation analysis [47], therefore working thoroughly on the experimental and computational validation of our model.

Competing interests
The authors declare that they have no competing interests.

Acknowledgements
The study of Enzo Martegani was partially supported by the University of Milano-Bicocca (FAR funds) and by EC-Project UNICELLSYS. Dario Pescini and Giancarlo Mauri acknowledge the partial funding by Regione Lombardia, research project "Network Enabled Drug Design (NEDD)". The authors would like to thank the anonymous reviewers for their valuable comments and suggestions to improve the quality of the article.

Author details
[1] Università degli Studi di Milano, Dipartimento di Informatica, Via Comelico 39, 20135 Milano, Italy. [2] Università degli Studi di Bergamo, Dipartimento di Scienze della Persona, Piazzale S. Agostino 2, 24129 Bergamo, Italy. [3] Università degli Studi di Milano-Bicocca, Dipartimento di Statistica, Via Bicocca degli Arcimboldi 8, 20126 Milano, Italy. [4] Università degli Studi di Milano-Bicocca, Dipartimento di Informatica, Sistemistica e Comunicazione,Viale Sarca 336, 20126 Milano, Italy. [5] Università degli Studi di Milano-Bicocca, Dipartimento di Biotecnologie e Bioscienze, Piazza della Scienza 2, 20126 Milano, Italy.

References
1. A Eldar, M Elowitz, Functional roles for noise in genetic circuits. Nature. **467**, 167–173 (2010)
2. R Steuer, C Zhou, J Kurths, Constructive effects of fluctuations in genetic and biochemical regulatory systems. BioSystems. **72**, 241–251 (2003)
3. V Shahrezaei, P Swain, The stochastic nature of biochemical networks. Curr. Opin. Biotech. **19**, 369–374 (2008)
4. SH Strogatz, Exploring complex networks. Nature. **410**, 268–276 (2001)
5. CV Rao, DM Wolf, AP Arkin, Control, exploitation and tolerance of intracellular noise. Nature. **420**, 231–237 (2002)
6. J Intosalmi, T Manninen, K Ruohonen, M Linne, Computational study of noise in a large signal transduction network. BMC Bioinf. **12**(252), 1–12 (2011)
7. GM Santangelo, Glucose signaling in *Saccharomyces cerevisiae*. Microbiol. Mol. Biol. R. **70**, 253–282 (2006)
8. JM Thevelein, Signal transduction in yeast. Yeast. **10**, 1753–1790 (1994)
9. JM Thevelein, JH de Winde, Novel sensing mechanisms and targets for the cAMP-protein kinase A pathway in the yeast *Saccharomyces cerevisiae*. Mol. Microbiol. **33**, 904–918 (1999)
10. JM Thevelein, L Cauwenberg, S Colombo, JH de Winde, M Donaton, F Dumortier, L Kraakman, K Lemaire, P Ma, D Nauwelaers, F Rolland, A Teunissen, PV Dijck, M Versele, S Wera, J Winderickx, Nutrient-induced signal transduction through the protein kinase A pathway and its role in the control of metabolism, stress resistance, and growth in yeast. Enzyme Microb. Tech. **26**, 819–825 (2000)
11. S Zaman, SI Lippman, L Schneper, N Slonim, JR Broach, Glucose regulates transcription in yeast through a network of signaling pathways. Mol. Syst. Biol. **5**, 1–14 (2009)
12. P Ma, S Wera, PV Dijck, JM Thevelein, The PDE1-encoded low-affinity phosphodiesterase in the yeast *Saccharomyces cerevisiae* has a specific function in controlling agonist-induced cAMP signaling. Mol. Biol. Cell. **10**, 91–104 (1999)
13. S Colombo, D Ronchetti, JM Thevelein, J Winderickx, E Martegani, Activation state of the Ras2 protein and glucose-induced signaling in *Saccharomyces cerevisiae*. J. Biol. Chem. **279**, 46715–46722 (2004)
14. J Nikawa, S Cameron, T Toda, KM Ferguson, M Wigler, Rigorous feedback control of cAMP levels in *Saccharomyces cerevisiae*. Gene Dev. **1**, 931–937 (1987)
15. D Jian, Z Aili, B Xiaojia, Z Huansheng, H Yun, Feedback regulation of Ras2 guanine nucleotide exchange factor (Ras2-GEF) activity of Cdc25p by Cdc25p phosphorylation in the yeast *Saccharomyces cerevisiae*. FEBS Lett. **584**(23), 4745–4750 (2010)
16. P Cazzaniga, D Pescini, D Besozzi, G Mauri, S Colombo, E Martegani, Modeling and stochastic simulation of the Ras/cAMP/PKA pathway in the yeast *Saccharomyces cerevisiae* evidences a key regulatory function for intracellular guanine nucleotides pools. J. Biotechnol. **133**(3), 377–385 (2008)
17. D Pescini, P Cazzaniga, D Besozzi, G Mauri, L Amigoni, S Colombo, E Martegani, Simulation of the Ras/cAMP/PKA pathway in budding yeast highlights the establishment of stable oscillatory states. Biotechnol. Adv. **30**, 99–107 (2012)
18. C Garmendia-Torres, A Goldbeter, M Jacquet, Nucleocytoplasmic oscillations of the yeast transcription factor Msn2: Evidence for periodic PKA activation. Curr. Biol. **17**, 1044–1049 (2007)
19. O Medvedik, D Lamming, K Kim, D Sinclair, MSN2 and MSN4 link calorie restriction and TOR to Sirtuin-mediated lifespan extension in *Saccharomyces cerevisiae*. PLoS Biol. **5**, 2330–2341 (2007)
20. D Gonze, M Jacquet, A Goldbeter, Stochastic modelling of nucleocytoplasmic oscillations of the transcription factor Msn2 in yeast. J. Roy. Soc. Interface. **5**(Suppl 1), S95–S109 (2008)
21. K Bodvard, D Wrangborg, S Tapani, K Logg, P Sliwa, A Blomberg, M Kvarnström, M Käll, Continuous light exposure causes cumulative stress that affects the localization oscillation dynamics of the transcription factor Msn2p. Biochim. Biophys. Acta. **1813**, 358–366 (2011)
22. SA Haney, JR Broach, Cdc25p, the guanine nucleotide exchange factor for the Ras proteins of *Saccharomyces cerevisiae*, promotes exchange by stabilizing Ras in a nucleotide-free state. J. Biol. Chem. **269**, 16541–16548 (1994)
23. S Rudoni, S Colombo, P Coccetti, E Martegani, Role of guanine nucleotides in the regulation of the Ras/cAMP pathway in *Saccharomyces cerevisiae*. Biochim. Biophys. Acta. **1538**, 181–189 (2001)
24. D Besozzi, P Cazzaniga, D Pescini, G Mauri, S Colombo, E Martegani, Investigating oscillatory regimes in the Ras/cAMP/PKA pathway in *S. cerevisiae*: the role of feedback control mechanisms. in ed. by H Koeppl, J Acimovic, J Kesseli, T Mäki-Marttunen, A Larjo, O Yli-Harja, *Eigth International Workshop on Computational Systems Biology, WCSB 2011* (vol. 57 of TICSP Series, Zürich, Switzerland, 2011), pp. 33–36
25. DT Gillespie, Exact stochastic simulation of coupled chemical reactions. J. Phys. Chem. **81**(25), 2340–2361 (1977)
26. E Gross, D Goldberg, A Levitzki, Phosphorylation of the *S. cerevisiae* Cdc25 in response to glucose results in its dissociation from Ras. Nature. **360**, 762–765 (1992)
27. O Wolkenhauer, M Ullah, W Kolch, C Kwang-Hyun, Modeling and simulation of intracellular dynamics: choosing an appropriate framework. IEEE T. Nanobiosci. **3**(3), 200–207 (2004)
28. F Rolland, J de Winde, K Lemaire, E Boles, J Thevelein, J Winderickx, Glucose-induced cAMP signalling in yeast requires both a G-protein coupled receptor system for extracellular glucose detection and a separable hexose kinase-dependent sensing process. Mol. Microbiol. **38**, 348–358 (2000)
29. S Ghaemmaghami, W Huh, K Bower, R Howson, A Belle, N Dephoure, E O'Shea, J Weissman, Global analysis of protein expression in yeast. Nature. **425**, 737–741 (2003)
30. B Carter, P Sudbery, Small-sized mutants of *Saccharomyces cerevisiae*. Genetics. **96**, 561–566 (1980)
31. P Jorgensen, J Nishikawa, B Breitkreutz, M Tyers, Systematic identification of pathways that couple cell growth and division in yeast. Science. **297**, 395–400 (2002)
32. D Besozzi, P Cazzaniga, G Mauri, D Pescini, BioSimWare: a software for the modeling, simulation and analysis of biological systems. in ed. by M Gheorghe, T Hinze, G Păun, G Rozenberg, A Salomaa, *Membrane Computing, 11th International Conference, CMC 2010*. Revised Selected Papers 2010 (vol. 6501 of LNCS, Springer-Verlag, Jena, 2010), pp. 119–143
33. Y Cao, DT Gillespie, LR Petzold, Efficient step size selection for the tau-leaping simulation method. J. Chem. Phys. **124**, 044109 (2006)
34. L Petzold, Automatic selection of methods for solving stiff and nonstiff systems of ordinary differential equations. SIAM J. Sci. Stat. Comput. **4**, 136–148 (1983)
35. H Niederreiter, *Random Number Generation and Quasi-Monte Carlo Methods* (Society for Industrial and Applied Mathematics, Philadelphia, 1992)
36. L Wang, G Renault, H Garreau, M Jacquet, Stress induces depletion of Cdc25p and decreases the cAMP producing capability in *Saccharomyces cerevisiae*. Microbiology. **150**, 3383–3391 (2004)
37. Q Ni, A Ganesan, NN Aye-Han, X Gao, MD Allen, A Levchenko, J Zhang, Signaling diversity of PKA achieved via a Ca^{2+}-cAMP-PKA oscillatory circuit. Nat. Chem. Biol. **7**, 34–40 (2011)

38. L Cai, C Dalal, M Elowitz, Frequency-modulated nuclear localization bursts coordinate gene regulation. Nature. **455**(7212), 485–490 (2008)
39. J Joo, SJ Plimpton, JL Faulon, Noise-induced oscillatory shuttling of NF-κB in a two compartment IKK-NF-κB-IκB-A20 signaling model. arXiv:1010.0888v1 [q-bio.MN] (2010)
40. M Turcotte, J Garcia-Ojalvo, GM Süel, A genetic timer through noise-induced stabilization of an unstable state. PNAS. **105**(41), 15732–15737 (2008)
41. S Strogatz, *Nonlinear Dynamics and Chaos: With Applications to Physics, Biology, Chemistry, and Engineering* (Westview Press, Boulder, 2001)
42. S Colombo, P Ma, L Cauwenberg, J Winderickx, M Crauwels, A Teunissen, D Nauwelaers, JH de Winde, MF Gorwa, D Colavizza, JM Thevelein, Involvement of distinct G-proteins, Gpa2 and Ras, in glucose- and intracellular acidification-induced cAMP signalling in the yeast *Saccharomyces cerevisiae*. EMBO J. **17**, 3326–3341 (1998)
43. R Tisi, F Belotti, C Paiardi, F Brunetti, E Martegani, The budding yeast RasGEF Cdc25 reveals an unexpected nuclear localization. BBA-Mol. Cell Res. **1783**(12), 2363–2374 (2008)
44. F Belotti, R Tisi, S Paiardi, E Groppi, Martegani, PKA-dependent regulation of Cdc25 RasGEF localization in budding yeast. FEBS Lett. **585**(24), 3914–3920 (2011)
45. P Cazzaniga, D Pescini, D Besozzi, G Mauri, Tau leaping stochastic simulation method in P systems. in ed. by HJ Hoogeboom, G Păun, G Rozenberg, A Salomaa, *7th International Workshop, WMC 2006, Leiden, Netherlands, July 17–21 2006, Revised, Selected, and Invited Papers* (vol. 4361 of LNCS, Springer-Verlag, 2006), pp. 298–313
46. S Colombo, S Broggi, L D'Alfonso, G Collini, E Chirico, E Martegani, Monitoring cyclic-AMP changes in a single yeast cell. in *Special Issue: 36th FEBS Congress, Biochemistry for Tomorrow's Medicine, Lingotto Conference Center, Torino, Italy, June 25–30, 2011*, FEBS J. 278(Suppl. 1 – Poster Presentations), P21.37, p.362 (2011)
47. MS Nobile, D Besozzi, P Cazzaniga, G Mauri, D Pescini, A GPU-based multi-swarm PSO method for parameter estimation in stochastic biological systems exploiting discrete-time target series. in ed. by M Giacobini, L Vanneschi, W Bush, *Evolutionary Computation, Machine Learning and Data Mining in Bioinformatics* (vol. 7246 of LNCS, Springer-Verlag, 2012), pp. 74–85

3

Relations between the set-complexity and the structure of graphs and their sub-graphs

Tomasz M Ignac[1,2]*, Nikita A Sakhanenko[1] and David J Galas[1,2]

Abstract

We describe some new conceptual tools for the rigorous, mathematical description of the "set-complexity" of graphs. This set-complexity has been shown previously to be a useful measure for analyzing some biological networks, and in discussing biological information in a quantitative fashion. The advances described here allow us to define some significant relationships between the set-complexity measure and the structure of graphs, and of their component sub-graphs. We show here that modular graph structures tend to maximize the set-complexity of graphs. We point out the relationship between modularity and redundancy, and discuss the significance of set-complexity in this regard. We specifically discuss the relationship between complexity and entropy in the case of complete-bipartite graphs, and present a new method for constructing highly complex, binary graphs. These results can be extended to the case of ternary graphs, and to other multi-edge graphs, which are fundamentally more relevant to biological structures and systems. Finally, our results lead us to an approach for extracting high complexity modular graphs from large, noisy graphs with low information content. We illustrate this approach with two examples.

Keywords: Set-complexity, Biological networks, Modularity, Modular graphs, Bipartite graphs, Multi-partite graphs

Introduction

Most physical, communications, social, and biological networks are usefully represented as graphs, with varying levels of complexity. The topology and the statistical structures of these graphs are central to understanding the functional properties of these systems. Our primary concern here is the representation and properties of biological networks, as reflected in the graphs used to represent these complex systems. The application of our results, however, is significantly broader. Previous attempts to elucidate the fundamental concept of biological information have led to a proposed, general measure of complexity, or information content, based on Kolmogorov complexity [1,2], that resolves some of the perplexing paradoxes of biologically relevant meaning that arise in definitions of information and complexity [1]. We used this approach successfully in analyzing the information in gene interaction networks of yeast [3,4]. It was shown that the

most informative networks are those with the highest set-complexity (a detailed discussion about applications of the set-complexity to biology and related problems can be found in the cited articles). The properties of our measure, which we call "set-complexity", are expected to be fruitful in describing a large class of problems in biology. It is clear, however, that we need more mathematical understanding of the properties of this complexity measure, and we have therefore focused initially on the set-complexity of graphs, and begun by analyzing the mathematical properties of relatively simple structures.

The results here extend our previous results and increase understanding of the structure of graphs and sub-graphs with the highest set-complexity. We have previously suggested, for example, that highly complex graphs have a more modular architecture than others [4]. The aim of this article is twofold. First, we aim to provide a mathematical foundation for this suggestion, the relation between the set-complexity and the graph structure. Second, we show that this research has practical uses. To accomplish the first goal we develop a formalism that allows us to analyze the set-complexity in a rigorous fashion and capture some of its essential properties. Our approach uses stochastic methods to analyze graphs by

*Correspondence: tomasz.ignac@uni.lu
[1] Institute for Systems Biology, 401 N. Terry Avenue, Seattle, WA 98109, USA
[2] Luxembourg Centre for Systems Biomedicine, University of Luxembourg, Campus Belval, 7, Avenue des Hauts-Fourneaux, L-4362 Esch-sur-Alzette, Luxembourg

defining specific random variables describing interactions between nodes in a graph. Information-theoretical features of the variables defined are then used to investigate the set-complexity, Ψ, measure. To accomplish the second goal, we present two examples illustrating how the set-complexity theory can be used to identify specific sub-graphs with modular properties. Note that the theoretical formalism of this article extends the ideas from our previous article [5] that presented a technical background of set-complexity and its computation as well as initial analysis of complexity of some graphs. Article [5] does not touch the application of this formalism in finding modular structure from real-world networks, which is a major goal of this article.

The article is structured as follows. First, we describe basic definitions and notation, and present the relation between the complexity and the entropy for complete bipartite graphs (CBG), an important class of binary graph for this analysis. We then describe a method for constructing highly complex binary graphs and provide two examples which show how to use the set-complexity to analyze information content of a graph and its sub-graphs. We conclude the article by discussing results, open questions and plans for future work.

Preliminaries

Let $G = (V, E)$ denote a graph, where V stands for the set of vertices and E the set of edges. The number of nodes in a graph is denoted by N, i.e., $V = \{1, \ldots, N\}$. Existence of an edge between nodes i and j is denoted by $(i, j) \in E$, and M labels for the graph edges are assumed. The labels are enumerated from 0 to $M - 1$. Let us take $a \in \{0, \ldots, M - 1\}$. The notation $(i, j) = a$ states that the label of the edge connecting nodes i and j is equal to a. We also assume that the graphs are fully connected in the following sense. A graph can always be formally extended to a multi-labeled, fully connected graph by defining an edge label 0, the usual designation for no connection. For example, in binary graphs, which are the main subject of this article, $(i, j) = 1$ means that nodes i and j are connected and $(i, j) = 0$ stands for a pair of disconnected nodes.

For each node $i \in V$ we define the probability distribution $P_i(a)$, which is the fraction of nodes connected to node i by edges labeled a. In other words, if we choose a particular i and then randomly select another node, j, from the remaining $N - 1$ nodes, the value of $P_i(a)$ is the probability of $(i, j) = a$. In a binary graph, $P_i(1)$ is the number of nodes connected to node i divided by $N - 1$.

If we select two nodes, i and j, and randomly choose a third node k, $P_{ij}(a, b)$ is the probability that $(i, k) = a$ and $(j, k) = b$. For example, to calculate $P_{ij}(1, 0)$ in a binary graph, we count the number of nodes connected to i and not connected to j and divide it by $N - 2$. The notation

$P_{ij}(a, \cdot)$ and $P_{ij}(\cdot, b)$ stands for marginalization of $P_{ij}(a, b)$ over j and i respectively, i.e.,

$$P_{ij}(a, \cdot) = \sum_{b=0}^{M-1} P_{ij}(a, b) \text{ and } P_{ij}(\cdot, b) = \sum_{a=0}^{M-1} P_{ij}(a, b).$$

$$(1)$$

Finally, conditional probabilities are defined as:

$$P_{ij}(a \mid b) = \frac{P_{ij}(a, b)}{P_{ij}(\cdot, b)}. \tag{2}$$

Remark 1. $P_i(a)$ and $P_{ij}(a, \cdot)$ are two probability distributions of random variables defined on the same alphabet $\{0, \ldots, M - 1\}$. The difference between these two quantities is small: both tend to zero as N goes to infinity. $P_i(a)$ describes a situation when only one node is selected, and we randomly choose another node. $P_{ij}(a, \cdot)$ describes a situation when we are given a pair of nodes and a third node is chosen at random. The value of the random variable is the label of the edge between i and the selected node.

Shannon's entropy will be denoted by $H[\,\cdot\,]$, e.g.,

$$H[P_i(a)] = -\frac{1}{\log M} \sum_{a=0}^{M-1} P_i(a) \log P_i(a). \tag{3}$$

All logarithms in this article are to the base two. To normalize, the entropies are multiplied by $1/\log M$. Note that although the values of $H[P_i(a)]$ and $H[P_{ij}(a, \cdot)]$ are normalized to the interval $[0, 1]$, the value of $H[P_{ij}(a, b)]$ is normalized to $[0, 2]$, since the maximal value of the entropy of a joint distribution is equal to the sum of entropies of the single variables. We want to preserve this property of entropies after normalization. The notation of $H[P_i(a)]$ and $H[P_{ij}(a, b)]$ will be abbreviated as H_i and H_{ij}, respectively. The set-complexity of a graph G is defined as

$$\Psi(G) = C \sum_{i=2}^{N} \sum_{j=1}^{i-1} \max(H_i, H_j) m_{ij}(1 - m_{ij}), \tag{4}$$

where C is a normalization factor of the form $8/(N(N-1))$ and m_{ij} is the normalized mutual information between nodes i and j,

$$m_{ij} = \frac{1}{\log M} \sum_{a,b=0}^{M-1} P_{ij}(a, b) \log \frac{P_{ij}(a, b)}{P_{ij}(a, \cdot) P_{ij}(\cdot, b)}. \tag{5}$$

We previously introduced the definition of mutual information for graphs [1]. Intuitively, it measures the reduction of the uncertainty about the connectivity of one node given the connectivity pattern of a second node. It is therefore natural to define this quantity as mutual information between random variables described by distributions $P_{ij}(a, \cdot)$ and $P_{ij}(\cdot, b)$, c.f., Remark 1.

In the remainder of the article we will be exploiting a useful fact [6] that m_{ij} can be rewritten as

$$m_{ij} = H[P_{ij}(a, \cdot)] + C_1 \sum_{a,b=0}^{M-1} P_{ij}(a, b) \log P_{ij}(a \mid b), \quad (6)$$

where $C_1 = 1/\log M$. Consequently,

$$m_{ij} = H[P_{ij}(a, \cdot)] + H[P_{ij}(\cdot, b)] - H_{ij}. \quad (7)$$

Complexity of CBGs

A set of nodes in a CBG can be represented as a sum of two disjoint sets O_1 and O_2 such that if nodes i and j belong to different sets, then $(i, j) = 1$, and if they belong to the same set, then $(i, j) = 0$. Sets O_1 and O_2 are referred to as *orbits*. This is consistent with the graph theory definition of an orbit, which holds that an orbit is an equivalence class of nodes under the action of an automorphism [7]. This means that all nodes in an orbit are connected in the same way to other nodes. The symbol $K_{m,N-m}$ is used to denote a CBG of size N, where m is the size of O_1.

Consider nodes i and j from the same orbit. By the definition of CBGs, $(i, k) = (k, j)$ for any third node k. Thus, $P_{ij}(0, 1) = P_{ij}(1, 0) = 0$. Consequently, $P_{ij}(0, 0) = P_{ij}(0, \cdot) = P_{ij}(\cdot, 0)$ and $P_{ij}(1, 1) = P_{ij}(1, \cdot) = P_{ij}(\cdot, 1)$. This leads us to $P_{ij}(0 \mid 0) = P_{ij}(1 \mid 1) = 1$ and $P_{ij}(0 \mid 1) = P_{ij}(1 \mid 0) = 0$. Similar reasoning holds for nodes from different orbits such that $P_{ij}(a \mid a) = 0$ and $P_{ij}(a \mid b) = 1$ for $a \neq b$. If we apply this result to Equation (6), we can see that the second component of the sum on the right hand side of the equation is zero. Therefore, we have proved the following lemma.

Lemma 1. *If G is a CBG, then for any pair of nodes i and j*

$$m_{ij} = H[P_{ij}(a, \cdot)].$$

Next we elucidate the relationship between entropy and the set-complexity of CBGs. However, we first have to deal with the difference between H_i and $H[P_i(a, \cdot)]$. This problem can be resolved by introducing a common approximation for these two entropies. This is doable, because the difference between $P_{ij}(a, \cdot)$ and $P_i(a)$ converges to zero with the increasing size of the graph, c.f., Remark 1. Let us show a common approximation of these entropies in the case of binary graphs. Suppose nodes i and j are in O_1, then $P_i(0) = (m-1)/(N-1)$, $P_i(0, \cdot) = P_{ij}(0, 0) = (m-2)/(N-2)$. Both values can be reasonably approximated by m/N for large N. A similar analysis reveals that $P_{ij}(1, \cdot)$ and $P_i(1)$ can be approximated by $(N-m)/N$.

Thus, the common approximation for H_i and $H[P_{ij}(a, \cdot)]$ should have the following form:

$$H(q) = -q \log q - (1 - q) \log(1 - q), \quad (8)$$

where $q = m/N$. A similar analysis shows that Equation (8) can also be used to approximate entropies when $i, j \in O_2$ or $i \in O_1, j \in O_2$. The notation $H(q)$ emphasizes that this quantity depends only on the proportion of nodes in orbits O_1 and O_2 and does not depend on the size of the graph.

Theorem 1. *Let G_N be a sequence of complete bipartite graphs, such that the ratio $q = m/N$ is constant for all N. Then,* $\lim_{N \to \infty} \Psi(G_N) = 4(H^2(q) - H^3(q))$.

Proof. Lemma 1 allows us to rewrite each component of the sum on the right hand side of Equation (4) as

$$\max(H_i, H_j) H[P_{ij}(a, \cdot)] (1 - H[P_{ij}(a, \cdot)]). \quad (9)$$

$\square$

Since the values of all entropies presented above converge to $H(q)$, it holds that

$$\lim_{N \to \infty} \Psi(G_N) = C \sum_{i=2}^{N} \sum_{j=1}^{i-1} (H^2(q) - H^3(q)). \quad (10)$$

Note that the sum on the right hand side of Equation (10) consists of $N(N-1)/2$ identical elements. Thus, Equation (10) can be rewritten to the equation of the theorem. QED.

We see that the complexity of CBGs depends only on the entropy (mutual information is fully expressible in terms of the entropy for CBGs); thus, the complexity depends only on the sizes of O_1 and O_2. The equation in Theorem 1 is maximized for $H(q) = 2/3$ leading to $\Psi_{\max} \approx 0.59$, the highest obtainable value of Ψ for CBGs. The complexity of CBGs is maximized when $q \approx 0.174$, i.e., when one of two orbits contains about 17.4% of nodes, see Figure 1. On the other hand, if both orbits are equal, entropies are close to one (more formally, they tend to one, when N goes to infinity), and the value of the set-complexity is close to zero.

We can easily see that the complexity can be bounded:

$$\Psi(G) \leq \frac{2}{N(N-1)} \sum_{i=2}^{N} \sum_{j=1}^{i-1} \max(H_i, H_j). \quad (11)$$

Figure 1 shows that CBGs with low values of q have complexity that is very close to the upper bound. Complexity of CBGs with high node entropies tends to zero (as

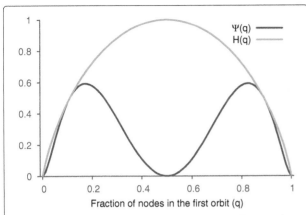

Figure 1 Set-complexity and entropy versus sizes of orbits. The set-complexity of CBGs (red) and their entropy (green) as functions of the proportion of nodes in one orbit to the other.

the upper bound raises at the same time). This suggests a method for construction of complex graphs from CBGs.

Complex binary graphs

At the end of the last section we show that the graphs with high values of Ψ (close to one) should exhibit high values of node entropies similar to $K_{N/2,N/2}$ graphs. This section shows that, even though $K_{N/2,N/2}$ graphs have zero complexity, they are a good starting point for constructing highly complex graphs, in that a relatively small number of modifications is needed to increase Ψ substantially. We propose a stochastic transformation F_p of a graph such that for any pair of nodes i and j the label of (i,j) is flipped to the opposite value with a probability p. We use G^* to denote the graph produced by this transformation applied to G.

Let us consider a sequence of graphs G_N. We have seen already that in this case the non-zero joint probabilities converge to 0.5 when N tends to infinity. Therefore, the entropies H_i and mutual information m_{ij} converge to one, which implies

$$\lim_{N \to \infty} \Psi(G_N) = 0. \qquad (12)$$

Let us apply the transformation F_p to G_N. We want to describe the complexity of the sequence of transformed graphs G_N^*. To illustrate the impact of the transformation on the joint probabilities $P_{ij}(a,b)$, take nodes i, j, and k from the same orbit, so that $(i,k) = (j,k) = 0$. The probability that labels of both edges will be flipped to one is equal to p^2, the probability that only one label will be flipped is $2p(1-p)$, and the probability that both labels will not be flipped is $(1-p)^2$. Thus, if for the original graph $P_{ij}(a,a) \approx 0.5$ (i.e., nodes i and j are from the same orbit as in the example above), then after the transformation we expect that the probabilities $P_{ij}(a,b)$ (for $a \neq b$)

will be equal to $p(1-p)$, and the probabilities $P_{ij}(a,a)$ will become $1/2 - p(1-p)$, or more formally

$$
\begin{aligned}
E[P_{ij}(0,0)] &= E[P_{ij}(1,1)] = \tfrac{1}{2} - p(1-p), \\
E[P_{ij}(1,0)] &= E[P_{ij}(0,1)] = p(1-p),
\end{aligned}
\qquad (13)
$$

where $E[\,\cdot\,]$ stands for the expected value. A similar analysis conducted for nodes from different orbits reveals that $E[P_{ij}(a,a)] = p(1-p)$ and $E[P_{ij}(a,b)] = 1/2 - p(1-p)$, where $a \neq b$.

We see that the expected value of the node entropies remains one, i.e., the transformation preserves the entropy of nodes in $K_{N/2,N/2}$ graphs, but it alters the mutual information m_{ij}. The complexity is maximized when $m_{ij} = 1/2$. Since the node entropies are close to one, it follows from Equation (7) that $m_{ij} = 1/2$ when $H_{ij} = 3/2$. We can calculate that for the transformation F_p, $E[H_{ij}] = 3/2$ iff $p \approx 0.058428$. This discussion can be summarized in the following theorem.

Theorem 2. *Let G_N be a sequence of graphs, and let G_N^* be a sequence of corresponding outputs of the transformation F_p with $p \approx 0.058428$. Then,* $\lim_{N \to \infty} E[\Psi(G_N^*)] = 1$.

This argument demonstrates that if we apply the transformation F_p to large graphs, the outcome will be a graph with the complexity close to one. Since the relative number of transformed edges is low, the bipartite structure of the graph is largely preserved. The relation between the probability of transforming an edge and the expected value of the set-complexity of a CBG is plotted in Figure 2. In this figure, we can see that the complexity grows rapidly for small values of the probability. The decrease after the maximum can be inferred from the fact increased randomness beyond this point decreases the

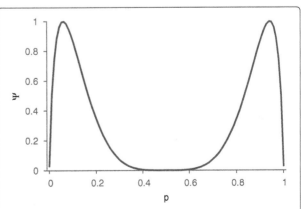

Figure 2 Dependency of the set-complexity on the flip probability. The relation between the probability, p, that an edge of a CBG will be flipped and the set-complexity, Ψ, of the CBG.

mutual information between nodes severely, degrading the set-complexity.

To illustrate this theorem experimentally, we applied the transformation to $K_{N/2,N/2}$ graphs with $N = 50, 100, 200, 300, 500$ nodes. The average values of $\Psi(G^*)$ ranged from 0.9154 (with standard deviation 0.0185 on 500 experiments) for $N = 50$ to 0.9926 (with standard deviation 0.0004 on 50 experiments) for $N = 500$.

Applications

We have shown how to construct high Ψ graphs. The method used for this construction enforces modular structure of these graphs. One may ask whether modularity is a property of all complex graphs. The answer, for these binary graphs, is yes. In [8], we proved that any complex graph must exhibit a modular structure; however, there can be some "noise" in the structure. The nature of that noise is similar to that described above. In other words, a binary graph with the set-complexity score close to one exhibits a structure similar to an outcome of the transformation F_p applied to $K_{N/2,N/2}$ with $p \approx 0.058$. This result was generalized to graphs with $M > 2$, so-called multi-colored graphs. For this generalization we extended the definition of a CBG, and defined complete multi-partite graphs (see [8] for more details). In the same article we analyzed some examples of complex graphs (Ψ of these graphs was close to one). To describe the information content of these graphs we used a histogram of

$$\phi_{ij} = \max(H_i, H_j)m_{ij}(1 - m_{ij}). \tag{14}$$

It is obvious that Ψ can be expressed as the average of ϕ_{ij}.

One way of extending the analysis of a graph may be described as a problem similar to retrieving a signal from a noisy transmission of information. Here, the signal is a sub-graph showing some type of regular structure, e.g., a set of nodes with similar connectivity pattern, and the noise comes from all the nodes that do not exhibit any regular connectivity patterns, such as the nodes of a random graph. Structures like this arise in biology whenever we locate members of a large set of objects based on some common properties, for example, when we select genes based on their correlated expression levels. In contrast to [8], we focus our attention on graphs with very low values of the complexity score. Low complexity graphs can have different characters: some of them may be simple random graphs, while others can have a very regular structure, like CBGs. Both of these types of graphs are uncommon in biological applications. On one hand, biological systems are not random; thus, characteristics of their network representations cannot exhibit values similar to those of randomly generated graphs. On the other hand, such graphs are not completely regular. In biological

sciences we almost always deal with an interesting mixture of randomness and regularity. We will focus our attention here on graphs whose structure is a mix of random and regular connectivity patterns.

Generally speaking the proposed approach focuses on finding a specific subset of nodes, a sub-graph, with a high contribution to Ψ. In order to do this we construct a histogram of ϕ_{ij}, the complexity score for a specific pair of nodes, and for every node i define the following quantity:

$$\Phi_i(T) = \sum_{j=1}^{N} \langle \phi_{ij} > T \rangle, \tag{15}$$

where T is a threshold for values of ϕ_{ij} and $\langle \cdot \rangle$ stands for the Iverson's bracket, i.e., a logic function that takes value 1, if the statement inside the bracket is true, and 0 otherwise. In summary, for a specific i, $\Phi_i(T)$ is the number of pairs (i, j) in the graph such that $\phi_{ij} > T$. By looking at the rightmost tail of the histogram of $\Phi_i(T)$ we can identify nodes with the highest contribution to Ψ.

We now present two examples. The first one is an artificially generated graph and the second is based on a biological data set. The two examples are followed by the discussion of the proposed approach: relation to community detection, modularity of networks/data sets, possible applications and plans for future work. We want to stress that the purpose of this discussion is to show that the set-complexity, and its components ϕ_{ij}, of a graph gives us an insight into the graph's structural properties. Nevertheless, this approach may also be interesting for analyzing real biological data.

Example 1: artificially generated graph

In the first example we use a 300 node graph consisting of two sub-graphs. The first sub-graph is a $K_{25,25}$ graph and the second is a random graph (also randomly connected to the CBG) in which the probability that two nodes are connected is $1/2$. The probability of an edge between a pair of nodes from different sub-graphs is $1/2$. Another example, based on real biological data, is given in the second example.

The graph overall exhibits a very low value of Ψ, relative to most CBGs, about 0.011. Low complexity indicates, in this case, a graph with a high number of randomly connected nodes. On the other hand, a low Ψ graph can be characteristic of a very regular graph structure. Looking at mutual information simply allows us to distinguish between a very regular and a very random graph. In the present example mutual information is low: its mean value is about 0.02. At the same time all node entropies are close to one. This indicates that the structure of the graph is more random than regular. Nevertheless, there is a modular sub-graph in this graph.

There are 299 ϕ_{ij} values for every node i in the graph (number of undirected pairs that include i). The values of ϕ_{ij} for nodes within the CBG sub-graph should be, on average, higher than for nodes from a random sub-graph. Figure 3a,b show values of ϕ_{1j} and ϕ_{51j} respectively. We can see that for $i = 51$ most of ϕ_{ij} values are lower than 0.05, while for $i = 1$, a considerable fraction of pairs (i, j) have $\phi_{ij} > 0.05$ (most of these belong to the complete bipartite sub-graph).

Figure 3c shows the histogram of ϕ_{ij}. As expected, most of these values are concentrated close to zero, and the right tail is almost invisible. Nevertheless, the right tail is present, and the comparison of ϕ_{ij} for $i = 1$ and $i = 51$ indicates that nodes from the complete bipartite sub-graph make stronger contributions to the tail than nodes from the random sub-graph. To illustrate this we fixed the threshold, $T = 0.05$, and calculated the number of pairs with $\phi_{ij} > 0.05$, defined as $\Phi_i(0.05)$. Figure 3d shows the histogram of $\Phi_i(0.05)$.

Two groups of nodes are clearly distinguishable. The nodes in the right component of the histogram ($\Phi_i(0.05) > 25$) are the 50 nodes of the complete bipartite

sub-graph, whereas the nodes in the left component are from the random sub-graph. Figure 4 illustrates the entire graph and highlights the detected component.

Let us take a closer look at what happens when we change T. Figure 3e,f show histograms of $\Phi_i(0.025)$ and $\Phi_i(0.1)$, respectively. The complete bipartite sub-graph can be identified in both cases; however, in the first case ($T = 0.025$) both groups of nodes are close to one another. Decreasing T below 0.025 will result in misclassification of a significant number of nodes (mixing the two classes clearly separable in the present case). On the other hand, increasing T makes the group on the right more flat, therefore it becomes more difficult to distinguish between these groups. For example, in Figure 3f we show the histogram of $\Phi_i(0.1)$ where the right group looks almost like a long tail of the group on the left.

As we can see the choice of the threshold T can be somewhat arbitrary at the outset. Our approach yields a tool for analyzing graphs. Thus, it could be used in a supervised mode, where T is specified by the user, or the threshold could be systematically scanned in an unsupervised mode.

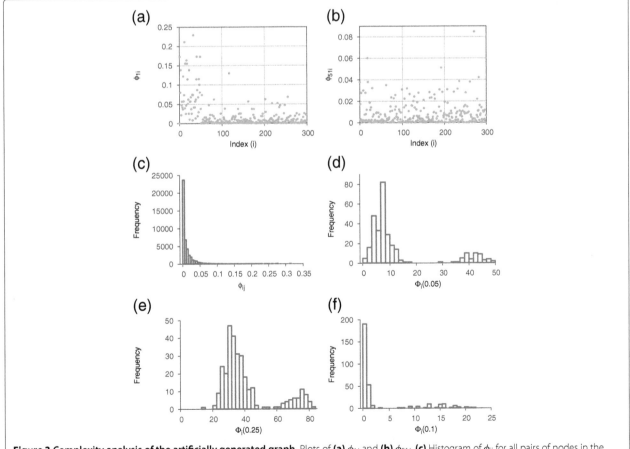

Figure 3 Complexity analysis of the artificially generated graph. Plots of **(a)** ϕ_{1j} and **(b)** ϕ_{51j}. **(c)** Histogram of ϕ_{ij} for all pairs of nodes in the graph. Histograms of $\Phi_i(T)$ for **(d)** $T = 0.05$, **(e)** $T = 0.025$, and **(f)** $T = 0.1$.

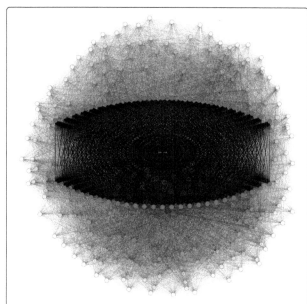

Figure 4 Capturing the regular structure in the artificially generated graph. This graph (disregarding the color) represents the binary graph from the first example of the article. The graph, which is mainly random, contains a complete bipartite sub-graph $K_{25,25}$. This highly structured sub-graph, highlighted in the figure, was successfully detected by the set-complexity-based approach. The two modules of the $K_{25,25}$ graph are shown in red and blue.

Example 2: biological data set

The second example is based on a real biological data set, and is both more realistic and more difficult. The data is a set of cross-correlations between time series of expression levels of 547 genes showing periodic variations during the cell cycle of the HeLa cells. These correlations were computed from data presented in [9]. Figure 5 shows a histogram of this data set. We represented this data as a network with three types of edges (I, II, III) corresponding to high positive correlation (>0.8) between two genes,

high negative correlation (< -0.8), and intermediate-to-no correlation (between -0.8 and 0.8). Up to now we have considered only binary graphs. This example, however, requires a ternary graph, $M = 3$.

We want to solve the problem of finding a set, or sets, of nodes with a similar connectivity pattern, which might represent a modular sub-graph. This case is more difficult, because we do not know *a priori* that there is any modular structure. Consequently, we initially choose low values for T, to avoid omitting potentially relevant nodes.

We start by analyzing the set-complexity and its components, ϕ_{ij}. The value of Ψ is small: about 0.06. Figure 6a shows the histogram of ϕ_{ij} for the correlation graph. The histogram is similar to the one discussed in the previous example (see Figure 3c). We set the threshold, T, to 0.05 and compute $\Phi_i(0.05)$ for all i, resulting in the histogram in Figure 6b. Note that this histogram is different from that presented in Figure 3d, where a subgroup of nodes is clearly separated from the others. We define a sub-graph of the original correlation graph by identifying only nodes for which $\Phi_i(0.05) > 200$. We then redefine the graph as the sub-graph containing only these nodes, and then repeat the analysis. Since only nodes within the sub-graph are used in this calculation, the ϕ_{ij} will, in general, all be different, and a new threshold will need to be set.

The new graph consists of 251 nodes. Recomputing Ψ and ϕ_{ij} shows that the set-complexity of this graph is significantly higher—about 0.32. The histogram of the recalculated ϕ_{ij}, presented in Figure 6c, is very different from the histogram in Figure 6a. We set a new threshold T equal to 0.5 and calculate the values of $\Phi_i(0.5)$ for all i. The histogram of this is presented in Figure 6d. Selecting 97 nodes for which $\Phi_i(0.5) > 60$ results in a graph whose complexity is about 0.7. It exhibits a bi-modular structure containing 33 and 64 nodes in each of the two modules. The nodes within each module are strongly connected via edges of type I (strong positive correlation), and nodes from different modules are usually connected via edges of type II (strong negative correlation). Some nodes are also connected via the type III edges. Table 1 shows the exact number of edges of different types within and between the modules. The genes present in the modules indicated in Table 1 are significantly enriched for genes known to be directly involved in the cell cycle. The detailed analysis of this network, however, its structure and biology, will be discussed in a future publication.

Conclusion

We have shown that, in general, a modular structure maximizes the set-complexity of a graph. It has been formally proved, however, that this is not always the case. If a binary graph is composed of two modules of identically connected nodes (orbits) and the modules have the same sizes, then the complexity of such a graph is

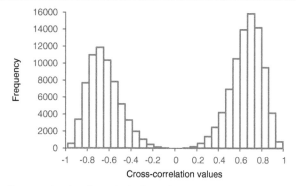

Figure 5 The data from the biological example. Histogram of cross-correlations between time series of expression levels of 547 genes during the cell cycle of the HeLa cells.

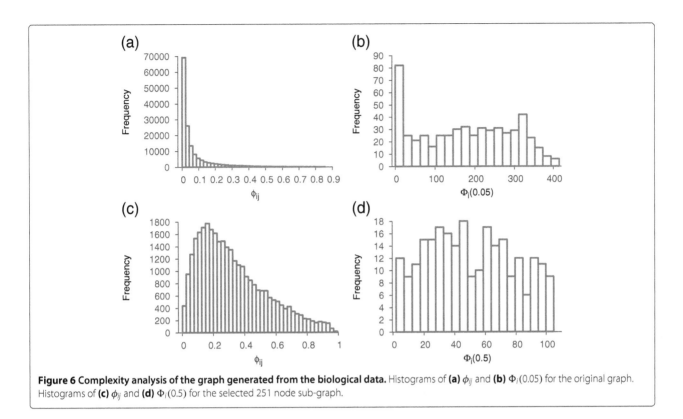

Figure 6 Complexity analysis of the graph generated from the biological data. Histograms of **(a)** ϕ_{ij} and **(b)** $\Phi_i(0.05)$ for the original graph. Histograms of **(c)** ϕ_{ij} and **(d)** $\Phi_i(0.5)$ for the selected 251 node sub-graph.

almost zero. The complexity grows rapidly, however, when we perturb the graph structure by breaking this symmetry. The symmetry can be broken in two ways: either the number of nodes in the components of the CBG can be made unequal, or the complete bipartite character can be broken by adding or deleting edges [8]. Actually, the number of altered edges that can significantly increase Ψ is a relatively small number; and the bi-modular structure of the graph is essentially preserved in a graph with significant Ψ. Similar results can be obtained for multi-colored edge graphs, with $M > 2$ [8]. We presented a method and two examples here that suggest useful applications of the described theory to analyzing real biological data—finding highly informative modular sub-graphs in a large graph.

There are several technical aspects of the analysis presented above that need to be considered. First, in the second example, the procedure was applied iteratively, twice. We chose a sub-graph of interest and repeated the procedure on this sub-graph. It is important to note that in the iterations the values of ϕ_{ij} were recomputed for the sub-graph only: the nodes and edges that are not in the sub-graph are omitted from computation. Since the set-complexity is defined as a context dependent measure, we treat one subset of nodes as a context for the other subset. Therefore, by omitting a group of nodes we change the context for the remaining nodes and change the complexity. It is clear that the subset of nodes considered is an important part of the definition of the set-complexity.

Our examples illustrate how to use set-complexity to capture the information content of a graph. For instance, histograms on Figure 6a,c show the increase of information when we narrow the original graph from 541 to 251 nodes. This information gain is also quantified by the set-complexity, which increases from 0.06 to 0.32. This can be useful for an evaluation of a network. Even if a

Table 1 Distribution of different types of edges in the 97 node sub-graph of the original correlation graph

	Type I edges	Type II edges	Type III edges
	(strong positive correlation)	(strong negative correlation)	
Module 1 (33 nodes)	**373 (70.6%)**	25 (4.7%)	130 (24.6%)
Module 2 (64 nodes)	**1644 (81.6%)**	46 (2.3%)	326 (16.2%)
Connections between modules	109 (5.2%)	**1405 (66.5%)**	598 (28.3%)

In parentheses we show the percentage of edges of each type in the set of all edges for each module as well as between the modules. In bold we indicate the largest edge type for each graph component.

network seems to be uninformative, we can attempt to extract an informative set of hidden regular patterns by narrowing down the set of nodes. This can be especially useful for networks with multiple types of edges (multicolor graphs), for which existing community detection and clustering methods are not suitable.

We wish to point out a significant potential relationship between two ideas presented here. The notion of modularity, based on the common connectedness of sets of nodes, as reflected in the measure of mutual information in the graph, is closely related to the idea of redundancy. This is because the modularity often stems from sets of nodes that are connected in similar ways to other nodes. Redundancy, in turn, has a strong functional significance in all functional systems, which is that it provides a robustness against damage or loss. If there are two or more nodes that are connected in almost the same fashion, loss of one of these nodes or its connection(s) can be mitigated to some extent by having a stand in, or partial stand in, in another node. Clearly this is a quantitative issue that needs more attention to fully characterize. What is also clear is that with too much redundancy, or regularity, the range of responses and the sensitivity to a variety of inputs is limited. This qualitative notion parallels the very idea of maximizing Ψ in that regularity (similar to redundancy) is balanced against variety (similar to randomness). The idea is appealing in thinking about biology, in that the robustness to perturbation or damage and the sensitivity to perturbation of damage are two general properties that biological evolution seeks to balance in many ways. It may be that Ψ can provide some quantitative insight into this biological balancing act.

Though the concept of set-complexity, defining a balance between regularity and randomness, is promising for future applications in biology, the two examples in this article are illustrations of a possible approach based on set-complexity and should be viewed as complementary to traditional community detection algorithms. At the current stage of development, the proposed approach requires supervision, but it is clear that scanning through threshold parameter space will be a key to automating the method. Since this article (as well as [8]) provides a rigorous theoretical background for the set-complexity of graphs, it should be possible to derive an automated approach for performing an analysis as illustrated in the examples. One possible direction for future research is to combine the search for a maximally complex sub-graph with optimization techniques, such as hill-climbing, using stochastic sampling methods.

Another interesting extension to our work is to look at how to use set-complexity as a specific measure of the modularity of graphs and of data sets. This extension would allow us to analyze modularity of multi-labeled graphs, which is currently impossible using traditional measures of modularity, since there is no defined interpretation of modularity for graphs with various types of labels. This will be a direction for future work.

The set-complexity was originally defined as a measure of complexity of sets of binary strings [1]. This definition can easily be used for characterizing the complexity of dynamics of various types of Boolean networks (for example, random, probabilistic), in which a binary string represents a state of a network and, thus, a dynamic trajectory of a network is a set of strings [1,10]. We have defined the set-complexity in terms of Kolmogorov complexity [1]. Unfortunately, since Kolmogorov complexity is incomputable, it needs to be approximated by algorithmic compression of binary strings, which represent states of the network. This approach has two drawbacks: (1) the approximated set-complexity is not normalized, so it is difficult to compare complexities of networks with different size, and (2) we can say nothing about the structure of the sequences: we can only hypothesize that these strings should be somewhat similar to one another but, in contrast to the graph case, we cannot quantify these relations. It may be interesting to calculate the complexity of a set of strings in a manner similar to that presented in the current article. We have begun this type of analysis, and the preliminary results look promising. We believe that such an approach may give us interesting insights into the dynamics and information structures of various types of Boolean networks.

We have demonstrated that the probabilistic description of the set-complexity sets up a formal framework for reasoning about some properties of our measure of complexity. We are able to prove some important properties of the set-complexity of graphs. Such an approach can be fruitful in the further investigations of this subject. This may result in better understanding of the nature of complexity in system biology, which may play a key role from the perspective of practical applications of that theory.

Abbreviations
CBG: complete bipartite graph.

Competing interests
The authors declare that they have no competing interests.

Acknowledgements
This work was supported by the ISB-Luxembourg Program, and by the FIBR program of NSF (0527023). TI is a fellow of the Luxembourg, LCSB-ISB fellowship program. We gratefully acknowledge stimulating conversations with Greg Carter and Ilya Shmulevich at various stages of this work. We thank Marek Ostaszewski from LCSB for providing the data and Paul Shannon for generating Figure 4.

References
1. DJ Galas, M Nykter, GW Carter, ND Price, I Shmulevich, Biological information as set-based complexity. IEEE Trans. Inf. Theory. **56**, 667–677 (2010)

2. AN Kolmogorov, Three approaches to the definition of the concept quantity of information (Russian). Probl. Peredachi Inf. **1**, 3–11 (1965)

3. GW Carter, DJ Galas, T Galitski, Maximal extraction of biological information from genetic interaction data. PLOS Comput. Biol. **54**, e1000347 (2009)

4. GW Carter, CG Rush, F Uygun, NA Sakhanenko, DJ Galas, T Galitski, A systems-biology approach to modular genetic complexity. Chaos. **20**, 026102 (2010)

5. TM Ignac, NA Sakhanenko, DJ Galas, in *Proceedings of the Eighth International Workshop on Computational Systems Biology: 6–8 June 2011*, vol. 57, ed. by H Koeppl, J Acimovic, J Kesseli, T Maki-Marttunen, A Larjo, and O Yli-Harja. Relation between the set-complexity of a graph and its structure (Tampere University of Technology, TICSP Series, Zurich, Switzerland, 2011), pp. 81–84

6. TM Cover, JA Thomas, *Elements of Information Theory*. (Wiley-Interscience, New York, 1991)

7. J Gross, J Yellen, *Graph Theory and its Applications*. (CRC Press Inc, Boca Raton, 1999)

8. TM Ignac, NA Sakhanenko, DJ Galas, Complexity of networks II: the set complexity of edge-colored graphs. Complexity. **17**, 23–36 (2012)

9. ML Whitfield, G Sherlock, AJ Saldanha, JI Murray, CA Ball, KE Alexander, JC Matese, CM Perou, MM Hurt, PO Brown, D Botstein, Identification of genes periodically expressed in the human cell cycle and their expression in tumors. Mol. Biol. Cell. **13**, 1977–2000 (2002)

10. T Maki-Marttunen, J Kesseli, S Kauffman, O Yli-Harja, M Nykter, in *Proceedings of the Eighth International Workshop on Computational Systems Biology:*, vol. 57, ed. by H Koeppl, J Acimovic, J Kesseli, T Maki-Marttunen, A Larjo, and O Yli-Harja. On the complexity of Boolean network state trajectories (Tampere University of Technology, TICSP Series, Zurich, Switzerland, 6–8 June 2011, 2011), pp. 137–140

4

Approximate maximum likelihood estimation for stochastic chemical kinetics

Aleksandr Andreychenko, Linar Mikeev, David Spieler and Verena Wolf*

Abstract

Recent experimental imaging techniques are able to tag and count molecular populations in a living cell. From these data mathematical models are inferred and calibrated. If small populations are present, discrete-state stochastic models are widely-used to describe the discreteness and randomness of molecular interactions. Based on time-series data of the molecular populations, the corresponding stochastic reaction rate constants can be estimated. This procedure is computationally very challenging, since the underlying stochastic process has to be solved for different parameters in order to obtain optimal estimates. Here, we focus on the maximum likelihood method and estimate rate constants, initial populations and parameters representing measurement errors.

Introduction

During the last decade stochastic models of networks of chemical reactions have become very popular. The reason is that the assumption that chemical concentrations change deterministically and continuously in time is not always appropriate for cellular processes. In particular, if certain substances in the cell are present in small concentrations the resulting stochastic effects cannot be adequately described by deterministic models. In that case, discrete-state stochastic models are advantageous because they take into account the discrete random nature of chemical reactions. The theory of stochastic chemical kinetics provides a rigorously justified framework for the description of chemical reactions where the effects of molecular noise are taken into account [1]. It is based on discrete-state Markov processes that explicitly represent the reactions as state-transitions between population vectors. When the molecule numbers are large, the solution of the deterministic description of a reaction network and the mean of the corresponding stochastic model agree up to a small approximation error. If, however, species with small populations are involved, then only a stochastic description can provide probabilities of events of interest such as probabilities of switching between different expression states in gene regulatory networks or the distribution of gene expression products. Moreover, even the mean behavior of the stochastic model can largely deviate from the behavior of the deterministic model [2]. In such cases the parameters of the stochastic model rather then the parameters of the deterministic model have to be estimated [3-5].

Here, we consider noisy time series measurements of the system state as they are available from wet-lab experiments. Recent experimental imaging techniques such as high-resolution fluorescence microscopy can measure small molecule counts with measurement errors of less than one molecule [6]. We assume that the structure of the underlying reaction network is known but the stochastic reaction rate constants of the network are unknown parameters. Then we identify rate constants that maximize the likelihood of the time series data. Maximum likelihood estimators are the most popular estimators since they have desirable mathematical properties. Specifically, they become minimum variance unbiased estimators and are asymptotically normal as the sample size increases.

Our main contribution consists in devising an efficient algorithm for the numerical approximation of the likelihood and its derivatives w.r.t. the stochastic reaction rate constants. Furthermore, we show how similar techniques can be used to estimate the initial molecule numbers of a network as well as parameters related to the measurement error. We also present extensive experimental results that give insights about the identifiability of certain parameters. In particular, we consider a simple gene expression model and the identifiability of reaction rate constants w.r.t. varying observation interval lengths and

*Correspondence: wolf@cs.uni-saarland.de
Computer Science Department, Saarland University, 66123 Saarbrücken, Germany

varying numbers of time series. Moreover, for this system we investigate the identifiability of reaction rate constants if the state of the gene cannot be observed but only the number of mRNA molecules. For a more complex gene regulatory network, we present parameter estimation results where different combinations of proteins are observed. In this way we reason about the sensitivity of the estimation of certain parameters w.r.t. the protein types that are observed.

Previous parameter estimation techniques for stochastic models are based on Monte-Carlo sampling [3,5] because the discrete state space of the underlying model is typically infinite in several dimensions and a priori a reasonable truncation of the state space is not available. Other approaches are based on Bayesian inference which can be applied both to deterministic and stochastic models [7-9]. In particular, approximate Bayesian inference can serve as a way to distinguish among a set of competing models [10]. Moreover, in the context of Bayesian inference linear noise approximations have been used to overcome the problem of large discrete state spaces [11].

Our method is not based on sampling but directly calculates the likelihood using a dynamic truncation of the state space. More precisely, we first show that the computation of the likelihood is equivalent to the evaluation of a product of vectors and matrices. This product includes the transition probability matrix of the associated continuous-time Markov process, i.e., the solution of the Kolmogorov differential equations (KDEs), which can be seen as a matrix-version of the chemical master equation (CME). Solving the KDEs is infeasible because of the state space of the underlying Markov model is very large or even infinite. Therefore we propose an iterative approximation algorithm during which the state space is truncated in an on-the-fly fashion, that is, during a certain time interval we consider only those states that significantly contribute to the likelihood. This technique is based on ideas presented in [12], but here we additionally explain how the initial molecule numbers can be estimated and how an approximation of the standard deviation of the estimated parameters can be derived. Moreover, we provide more complex case studies and run extensive numerical experiments to assess the identifiability of certain parameters. In these experiments we assume that not all molecular populations can be observed and estimate parameters for different observation scenarios, i.e., we assume different numbers of observed cells and different observation interval lengths. We remark that this article is an extension of a previously published extended abstract [13].

The article is further organized as follows: After introducing the stochastic model in Section "Discrete-state stochastic model", we discuss the maximum likelihood method in Section "Parameter inference" and present our approximation method in Section "Numerical approximation algorithm". Finally, we report on experimental results for two reaction networks in Section "Numerical results".

Discrete-state stochastic model

According to Gillespie's theory of stochastic chemical kinetics, a well-stirred mixture of n molecular species in a volume with fixed size and fixed temperature can be represented as a continuous-time Markov chain $\{\mathbf{X}(t), t \geq 0\}$ [1]. The random vector $\mathbf{X}(t) = (X_1(t), \ldots, X_n(t))$ describes the chemical populations at time t, i.e., $X_i(t)$ is the number of molecules of type $i \in \{1, \ldots, n\}$ at time t. Thus, the state space of $\mathbf{X}$ is $\mathbb{Z}_+^n = \{0, 1, \ldots\}^n$. The state changes of $\mathbf{X}$ are triggered by the occurrences of chemical reactions, which are of m different types. For $j \in \{1, \ldots, m\}$ let $\mathbf{v}_j \in \mathbb{Z}^n$ be the nonzero $change\ vector$ of the j-th reaction type. Thus, if $\mathbf{X}(t) = \mathbf{x}$ and the j-th reaction is possible in $\mathbf{x}$, then $\mathbf{X}(t + dt) = \mathbf{x} + \mathbf{v}_j$ is the state of the system after the occurrence of the j-th reaction within the infinitesimal time interval $[t, t + dt)$.

Each reaction type has an associated $propensity\ function$, denoted by $\alpha_1, \ldots, \alpha_m$, which is such that $\alpha_j(\mathbf{x}) \cdot dt$ is the probability that, given $\mathbf{X}(t) = \mathbf{x}$, one instance of the j-th reaction occurs within $[t, t + dt)$. The value $\alpha_j(\mathbf{x})$ is proportional to the number of distinct reactant combinations in state $\mathbf{x}$ and to the reaction rate constant c_j. The probability that a randomly selected pair of reactants collides and undergoes the j-th chemical reaction within $[t, t + dt)$ is then given by $c_j dt$. The value c_j depends on the volume and the temperature of the system as well as on the microphysical properties of the reactant species.

Example 1. *We consider the simple gene expression model described in [4] that involves three chemical species, namely DNA$_{ON}$, DNA$_{OFF}$, and mRNA, which are represented by the random variables $X_1(t)$, $X_2(t)$, and $X_3(t)$, respectively. The three possible reactions are DNA$_{ON}$ $\rightarrow$ DNA$_{OFF}$, DNA$_{OFF}$ $\rightarrow$ DNA$_{ON}$, and DNA$_{ON}$ $\rightarrow$ DNA$_{ON}$ + mRNA. Thus, $\mathbf{v}_1 = (-1, 1, 0)$, $\mathbf{v}_2 = (1, -1, 0)$, $\mathbf{v}_3 = (0, 0, 1)$. For a state $\mathbf{x} = (x_1, x_2, x_3)$, the propensity functions are $\alpha_1(\mathbf{x}) = c_1 \cdot x_1$, $\alpha_2(\mathbf{x}) = c_2 \cdot x_2$, and $\alpha_3(\mathbf{x}) = c_3 \cdot x_1$. Note that given the initial state $\mathbf{x} = (1, 0, 0)$, at any time, either the DNA is active or not, i.e. $x_1 = 0$ and $x_2 = 1$, or $x_1 = 1$ and $x_2 = 0$. Moreover, the state space of the model is infinite in the third dimension. For a fixed time instant $t > 0$, no upper bound on the number of mRNA is known a priori. All states $\mathbf{x}$ with $x_3 \in \mathbb{Z}_+$ have positive probability if $t > 0$ but these probabilities will tend to zero as $x_3 \rightarrow \infty$.*

The CME

For a state $\mathbf{x} \in \mathbb{Z}_+^n$ and $t \geq 0$, let $p(\mathbf{x}, t)$ denote the probability $\Pr(\mathbf{X}(t) = \mathbf{x})$, i.e., the probability that the process is in state $\mathbf{x}$ at time t. Furthermore, let $\mathbf{p}(t)$ be the row vector with entries $p(\mathbf{x}, t)$ where we assume a fixed enumeration of all possible states.

Given $\mathbf{v}_1, \ldots, \mathbf{v}_m, \alpha_1, \ldots, \alpha_m$, and some initial populations $\mathbf{x}(0) = (x_1(0), \ldots, x_n(0))$ with $P(\mathbf{X}(0) = \mathbf{x}(0)) = 1$, the Markov chain $\mathbf{X}$ is uniquely specified and its evolution is given by the CME

$$\frac{d}{dt}\mathbf{p}(t) = \mathbf{p}(t)Q, \tag{1}$$

where Q is the infinitesimal generator matrix of $\mathbf{X}$ with $Q(\mathbf{x}, \mathbf{y}) = \alpha_j(\mathbf{x})$ if $\mathbf{y} = \mathbf{x} + \mathbf{v}_j$ and reaction type j is possible in state $\mathbf{x}$. Note that, in order to simplify our presentation, we assume here that all vectors $\mathbf{v}_j$ are distinct. All remaining entries of Q are zero except for the diagonal entries which are equal to the negative row sum. The ordinary first-order differential equation in (1) is a direct consequence of the Kolmogorov forward equation but standard numerical solution techniques for systems of first-order linear equations cannot be applied to solve (1) because the number of nonzero entries in Q typically exceeds the available memory capacity for systems of realistic size. If the expected populations of all species remain small (at most a few hundreds) then the CME can be efficiently approximated using projection methods [14-16] or fast uniformization methods [17,18]. The idea of these methods is to avoid an exhaustive state space exploration and, depending on a certain time interval, restrict the analysis of the system to a subset of states.

We are interested in the partial derivatives of $\mathbf{p}(t)$ w.r.t. a certain parameter λ such as reaction rate constants $c_j, j \in \{1, \ldots, m\}$ or initial populations $x_i(0), i \in \{1, \ldots, n\}$. Later, they will be used to maximize the likelihood of observations and to find optimal parameters. In order to explicitly indicate the dependence of $\mathbf{p}(t)$ on λ we may write $\mathbf{p}_\lambda(t)$ instead of $\mathbf{p}(t)$ and $p_\lambda(\mathbf{x}, t)$ instead of $p(\mathbf{x}, t)$. We define the row vector $\mathbf{s}_\lambda(t)$ as the derivative of $\mathbf{p}_\lambda(t)$ w.r.t. λ, i.e.,

$$\mathbf{s}_\lambda(t) = \frac{\partial \mathbf{p}_\lambda(t)}{\partial \lambda} = \lim_{\Delta \to 0} \frac{\mathbf{p}_{\lambda+\Delta}(t) - \mathbf{p}_\lambda(t)}{\Delta}.$$

We denote the entry in $\mathbf{s}_\lambda(t)$ that corresponds to state $\mathbf{x}$ by $s_\lambda(\mathbf{x}, t)$. Note that we use bold face for vectors. By (1), we find that $\mathbf{s}_\lambda(t)$ is the solution of the system of ODEs

$$\frac{d}{dt}\mathbf{s}_\lambda(t) = \mathbf{s}_\lambda(t)Q + \mathbf{p}_\lambda(t)\frac{\partial}{\partial \lambda}Q, \tag{2}$$

when choosing $\lambda = c_j$ for $j \in \{1, \ldots, m\}$. In this case, the initial condition is $s_\lambda(\mathbf{x}, 0) = 0$ for all $\mathbf{x}$ since $p(\mathbf{x}, 0)$ is independent of c_j. If the unknown parameter is the i-th initial population, i.e., $\lambda = x_i(0)$, then we get

$$\frac{d}{dt}\mathbf{s}_\lambda(t) = \mathbf{s}_\lambda(t)Q, \tag{3}$$

with initial condition $\mathbf{s}_\lambda(0) = \frac{\partial}{\partial \lambda}\mathbf{p}_\lambda(0)$ since Q is independent of $x_i(0)$. Similar ODEs can be derived for higher order derivatives of the CME.

Parameter inference

Following the notation in [4], we assume that observations of the reaction network are made at time instances $t_1, \ldots, t_R \in \mathbb{R}_{\geq 0}$ where $t_1 < \cdots < t_R$. Since it is unrealistic to assume that all species can be observed, we assume w.l.o.g. that the species are ordered such that we have observations of $X_1, \ldots, X_d$ for some fixed d with $1 \leq d \leq n$, i.e. $O_i(t_\ell)$ is the observed number of species i at time t_ℓ for $i \in \{1, \ldots, d\}$ and $\ell \in \{1, \ldots, R\}$. Let $\mathbf{O}(t_\ell) = (O_1(t_\ell), \ldots, O_d(t_\ell))$ be the corresponding vector of observations. Since these observations are typically subject to measurement errors, we assume that $O_i(t_\ell) = X_i(t_\ell) + \epsilon_i(t_\ell)$ where the error terms $\epsilon_i(t_\ell)$ are independent and identically normally distributed with mean zero and standard deviation σ. Note that $X_i(t_\ell)$ is the true population of the i-th species at time t_ℓ. Clearly, this implies that, conditional on $X_i(t_\ell)$, the random variable $O_i(t_\ell)$ is independent of all other observations as well as independent of the history of $\mathbf{X}$ before time t_ℓ.

We assume further that we do not know the values of the rate constants $\mathbf{c} = (c_1, \ldots, c_m)$ and our aim is to estimate these constants. Similarly, the initial populations $\mathbf{x}(0)$ and the exact standard deviation σ of the error terms are unknown and must be estimated. We remark that it is straightforward to extend the estimation framework such that a covariance matrix for a multivariate normal distribution of the error terms is estimated. In this way, different measurement errors of the species can be taken into account as well as dependencies between error terms.

Let f denote the joint density of $\mathbf{O}(t_1), \ldots, \mathbf{O}(t_R)$ and, by convenient abuse of notation, for a vector $\mathbf{x}_\ell = (x_1, \ldots, x_d)$ let $\mathbf{X}(t_\ell) = \mathbf{x}_\ell$ represent the event that $X_i(t_\ell) = x_i$ for $1 \leq i \leq d$. In other words, $\mathbf{X}(t_\ell) = \mathbf{x}_\ell$ means that the populations of the observed species at time t_ℓ equal the populations of vector $\mathbf{x}_\ell$. Note that this event corresponds to a set of states of the Markov process since d may be smaller than n. More precisely, $\Pr(\mathbf{X}(t_\ell) = \mathbf{x}_\ell) = \sum_{\mathbf{y}: y_i = x_i, i \leq d} p(\mathbf{y}, t_\ell)$. Now the likelihood of the observation sequence $\mathbf{O}(t_1), \ldots, \mathbf{O}(t_R)$ is given by

$$\begin{aligned}
\mathcal{L} &= f(\mathbf{O}(t_1), \ldots, \mathbf{O}(t_R)) \\
&= \sum_{\mathbf{x}_1} \cdots \sum_{\mathbf{x}_R} f(\mathbf{O}(t_1), \ldots, \mathbf{O}(t_R) \mid \\
&\qquad \mathbf{X}(t_1) = \mathbf{x}_1, \ldots, \mathbf{X}(t_R) = \mathbf{x}_R) \\
&\qquad \Pr(\mathbf{X}(t_1) = \mathbf{x}_1, \ldots, \mathbf{X}(t_R) = \mathbf{x}_R).
\end{aligned} \tag{4}$$

Note that $\mathcal{L}$ depends on the chosen rate parameters $\mathbf{c}$ and the initial populations $\mathbf{x}(0)$ since the probability measure $\Pr(\cdot)$ does. Furthermore, $\mathcal{L}$ depends on σ since the density f does. When necessary, we will make this dependence explicit by writing $\mathcal{L}(\mathbf{x}(0), \mathbf{c}, \sigma)$ instead of $\mathcal{L}$. We now seek constants $\mathbf{c}^*$, initial populations $\mathbf{x}(0)$ and a standard deviation σ^* such that

$$\mathcal{L}(\mathbf{x}(0)^*, \mathbf{c}^*, \sigma^*) = \max_{\mathbf{x}(0), \sigma, \mathbf{c}} \mathcal{L}(\mathbf{x}(0), \mathbf{c}, \sigma) \qquad (5)$$

where the maximum is taken over all $\sigma > 0$ and vectors $\mathbf{x}(0)$, $\mathbf{c}$ with all components strictly positive. This optimization problem is known as the maximum likelihood problem [19]. Note that $\mathbf{x}(0)^*$, $\mathbf{c}^*$ and σ^* are random variables because they depend on the (random) observations $\mathbf{O}(t_1), \ldots, \mathbf{O}(t_R)$.

If more than one sequence of observations is made, then the corresponding likelihood is the product of the likelihoods of all individual sequences. More precisely, if $\mathbf{O}^k(t_l)$ is the k-th observation that has been observed at time instant t_l where $k \in \{1, \ldots, K\}$, then we define $\mathcal{L}_k(\mathbf{x}(0), \mathbf{c}, \sigma)$ as the probability to observe $\mathbf{O}^k(t_1), \ldots, \mathbf{O}^k(t_R)$ and maximize

$$\prod_{k=1}^{K} \mathcal{L}_k(\mathbf{x}(0), \mathbf{c}, \sigma). \qquad (6)$$

In what follows, we concentrate on expressions for $\mathcal{L}_k(\mathbf{x}(0), \mathbf{c}, \sigma)$ and $\frac{\partial}{\partial c_j} \mathcal{L}_k(\mathbf{x}(0), \mathbf{c}, \sigma)$. We first assume $K = 1$ and drop index k. We consider the case $K > 1$ later. In (4) we sum over all population vectors $\mathbf{x}_1, \ldots, \mathbf{x}_R$ of dimension d such that $\Pr(\mathbf{X}(t_\ell) = \mathbf{x}_\ell, 1 \leq \ell \leq R) > 0$. Since $\mathbf{X}$ has a large or even infinite state space, it is computationally infeasible to explore all possible sequences. In Section "Numerical approximation algorithm" we propose an algorithm to approximate the likelihoods and their derivatives by dynamically truncating the state space and using the fact that (4) can be written as a product of vectors and matrices. Let ϕ_σ be the density of the normal distribution with mean zero and standard deviation σ. Then

$$f\left(\mathbf{O}(t_1), \ldots, \mathbf{O}(t_R) \mid \mathbf{X}(t_1) = \mathbf{x}_1, \ldots, \mathbf{X}(t_R) = \mathbf{x}_R\right)$$
$$= \prod_{\ell=1}^{R} \prod_{i=1}^{d} f\left(O_i(t_\ell) \mid X_i(t_\ell) = x_{i\ell}\right)$$
$$= \prod_{\ell=1}^{R} \prod_{i=1}^{d} \phi_\sigma\left(O_i(t_\ell) - x_{i\ell}\right),$$

where $\mathbf{x}_\ell = (x_{1\ell}, \ldots, x_{d\ell})$. If we write $w(\mathbf{x}_\ell)$ for $\prod_{i=1}^{d} \phi_\sigma(O_i(t_\ell) - x_{i\ell})$, then the sequence $\mathbf{x}_1, \ldots, \mathbf{x}_R$ has "weight" $\prod_{\ell=1}^{R} w(\mathbf{x}_\ell)$ and, thus,

$$\mathcal{L} = \sum_{\mathbf{x}_1} \cdots \sum_{\mathbf{x}_R} \Pr(\mathbf{X}(t_1) = \mathbf{x}_1, \ldots, \mathbf{X}(t_R) = \mathbf{x}_R) \prod_{\ell=1}^{R} w(\mathbf{x}_\ell). \qquad (7)$$

Moreover, for the probability of the sequence $\mathbf{x}_1, \ldots, \mathbf{x}_R$ we have

$$\Pr(\mathbf{X}(t_1) = \mathbf{x}_1, \ldots, \mathbf{X}(t_R) = \mathbf{x}_R) = p(\mathbf{x}_1, t_1) P_2(\mathbf{x}_1, \mathbf{x}_2) \ldots$$
$$P_R(\mathbf{x}_{R-1}, \mathbf{x}_R)$$

where $P_\ell(\mathbf{x}, \mathbf{y}) = \Pr(\mathbf{X}(t_\ell) = \mathbf{y} \mid \mathbf{X}(t_{\ell-1}) = \mathbf{x})$ for d-dimensional population vectors $\mathbf{x}$ and $\mathbf{y}$. Hence, (7) can be written as

$$\mathcal{L} = \sum_{\mathbf{x}_1} p(\mathbf{x}_1, t_1) w(\mathbf{x}_1) \sum_{\mathbf{x}_2} P_2(\mathbf{x}_1, \mathbf{x}_2) w(\mathbf{x}_2) \ldots$$
$$\sum_{\mathbf{x}_R} P_R(\mathbf{x}_{R-1}, \mathbf{x}_R) w(\mathbf{x}_R). \qquad (8)$$

Assume that $d = n$ and let P_ℓ be the matrix with entries $P_\ell(\mathbf{x}, \mathbf{y})$ for all possible states $\mathbf{x}, \mathbf{y}$. Note that P_ℓ is the transition probability matrix of $\mathbf{X}$ for time step $t_\ell - t_{\ell-1}$ and thus the general solution $e^{Q(t_\ell - t_{\ell-1})}$ of the Kolmogorov forward and backward differential equations

$$\frac{d}{dt} P_\ell = Q P_\ell, \qquad \frac{d}{dt} P_\ell = P_\ell Q.$$

In this case, using $\mathbf{p}(t_1) = \mathbf{p}(t_0) P_1$ with $t_0 = 0$, we can write (8) in matrix-vector form as

$$\mathcal{L} = \mathbf{p}(t_0) P_1 W_1 P_2 W_2 \ldots P_R W_R \mathbf{e}. \qquad (9)$$

Here, $\mathbf{e}$ is the vector with all entries equal to one and W_ℓ is a diagonal matrix whose diagonal entries are all equal to $w(\mathbf{x}_\ell)$ with $\ell \in \{1, \ldots, R\}$, where W_ℓ is of the same size as P_ℓ.

If $d < n$, then we still have the same matrix-vector product as in (9), but define the weight $w(\mathbf{x})$ of an n-dimensional population vector as

$$w(x_1, \ldots, x_n) = \prod_{i=1}^{d} \phi_\sigma(O_i(t_\ell) - x_i),$$

i.e. the populations of the unobserved species have no influence on the weight.

Since it is in general not possible to analytically obtain parameters that maximize $\mathcal{L}$, we use numerical optimization techniques to find $\mathbf{c}^*$, $\mathbf{x}(0)^*$ and σ^*. Typically, such techniques iterate over values of $\mathbf{c}, \mathbf{x}(0)$ and σ and increase the likelihood $\mathcal{L}(\mathbf{c}, \sigma)$ by following the gradient. Therefore, we need to calculate the derivatives $\frac{\partial}{\partial c_j} \mathcal{L}$, $\frac{\partial}{\partial x_i(0)} \mathcal{L}$ and $\frac{\partial}{\partial \sigma} \mathcal{L}$. For $\frac{\partial}{\partial c_j} \mathcal{L}$ we obtain

$$\frac{\partial}{\partial c_j} \mathcal{L} = \frac{\partial}{\partial c_j} \left(\mathbf{p}(t_0) P_1 W_1 P_2 W_2 \ldots P_R W_R \mathbf{e}\right)$$
$$= \mathbf{p}(t_0) \left(\sum_{\ell=1}^{R} \left(\frac{\partial}{\partial c_j} P_\ell\right) W_\ell \prod_{\ell' \neq \ell} P_{\ell'} W_{\ell'}\right) \mathbf{e}. \qquad (10)$$

The derivative of $\mathcal{L}$ w.r.t. $x_i(0)$ and σ is derived analogously. The only difference is that $\mathbf{p}(t_0)$ is dependent on $x_i(0)$ and $P_1, \ldots, P_R$ are independent of σ but $W_1, \ldots, W_R$

depend on σ. It is also important to note that expressions for partial derivatives of second order can be derived in a similar way. These derivatives can then be used for an efficient gradient-based local optimization.

For $K > 1$ observation sequences we can maximize the log-likelihood

$$\log \prod_{k=1}^{K} \mathcal{L}_k = \sum_{k=1}^{K} \log \mathcal{L}_k, \tag{11}$$

instead of the likelihood in (6). Note that the derivatives are then given by

$$\frac{\partial}{\partial \lambda} \sum_{k=1}^{K} \log \mathcal{L}_k = \sum_{k=1}^{K} \frac{\frac{\partial}{\partial \lambda} \mathcal{L}_k}{\mathcal{L}_k}, \tag{12}$$

where λ is c_j, $x_i(0)$ or σ. It is also important to note that only the weights $w(\mathbf{x}_\ell)$ depend on k, that is, on the observed sequence $\mathbf{O}^k(t_1), \ldots, \mathbf{O}^k(t_R)$. Thus, when we compute $\mathcal{L}_k$ based on (9) we use for all k the same transition matrices $P_1, \ldots, P_R$ and the same initial conditions $\mathbf{p}(t_0)$, but possibly different matrices $W_1, \ldots, W_R$.

Numerical approximation algorithm

In this section, we focus on the numerical approximation of the likelihood and the corresponding derivatives. Our algorithm calculates an approximation of the likelihood based on (9) by traversing the matrix-vector product from the left to the right. The main idea behind the algorithm is that instead of explicitly computing the matrices P_ℓ, we express the vector-matrix product $\mathbf{u}(t_{\ell-1}) P_\ell$ as a system of ODEs similar to the CME (cf. Equation (1)). Note that even though P_ℓ is sparse the number of states may be very large or infinite, in which case we cannot compute P_ℓ explicitly. Let $\mathbf{u}(t_0), \ldots, \mathbf{u}(t_R)$ be row vectors that are obtained during the iteration over time points $t_0, \ldots, t_R$, that is, we define $\mathcal{L}$ recursively as $\mathcal{L} = \mathbf{u}(t_R)\mathbf{e}$ with $\mathbf{u}(t_0) = \mathbf{p}(t_0)$ and

$$\mathbf{u}(t_\ell) = \mathbf{u}(t_{\ell-1}) P_\ell W_\ell \quad \text{for all } 1 \le \ell \le R,$$

where $t_0 = 0$. We solve R systems of ODEs

$$\frac{d}{dt} \tilde{\mathbf{u}}(t) = \tilde{\mathbf{u}}(t) Q \tag{13}$$

with initial condition $\tilde{\mathbf{u}}(t_{\ell-1}) = \mathbf{u}(t_{\ell-1})$ for the time interval $[t_{\ell-1}, t_\ell)$ where $\ell \in \{1, \ldots, R\}$. After solving the ℓ-th system of ODEs we set $\mathbf{u}(t_\ell) = \tilde{\mathbf{u}}(t_\ell) W_\ell$ and finally compute $\mathcal{L} = \mathbf{u}(t_R)\mathbf{e}$. We remark that this is the same as solving the CME for different initial conditions and due to the largeness problem of the state space we use the dynamic truncation of the state space that we proposed in previous work [17]. The idea is to consider only the most relevant equations of the system (13), i.e., the equations that correspond to those states $\mathbf{x}$ where the relative contribution $\tilde{u}(\mathbf{x}, t)/(\tilde{\mathbf{u}}(t_\ell)\mathbf{e})$ is greater than a threshold δ. Since

during the integration the contribution of a state might increase or decrease we add/remove equations on-the-fly depending on the current contribution of the corresponding state. Note that the structure of the CME allows us to determine in a simple way which states will become relevant in the next integration step. For a small time step of length h we know that the probability being moved from state $\mathbf{x} - \mathbf{v}_j$ to $\mathbf{x}$ is approximately $\alpha_j(\mathbf{x} - \mathbf{v}_j)h$. Thus, we can simply check whether a state that receives a certain probability inflow receives more than the threshold. In this case we consider the corresponding equation in (13). Otherwise, if a state does not receive enough probability inflow, we do not consider it in (13). For more details on this technique we refer to [17].

Since the vectors $\tilde{\mathbf{u}}(t_\ell)$ do not sum up to one, we scale all entries by multiplication with $1/(\tilde{\mathbf{u}}(t_\ell)\mathbf{e})$. This simplifies the truncation of the state space using the significance threshold δ since after scaling it can be interpreted as a probability. In order to obtain the correct (unscaled) likelihood, we compute $\mathcal{L}$ as $\mathcal{L} = \prod_{\ell=1}^{R} \tilde{\mathbf{u}}(t_\ell)\mathbf{e}$. For our numerical implementation we used a threshold of $\delta = 10^{-15}$ and handle the derivatives of $\mathcal{L}$ in a similar way. To shorten our presentation, we only consider the derivative $\frac{\partial}{\partial c_j} \mathcal{L}$ in the sequel of the article. Iterative schemes for $\frac{\partial}{\partial \sigma} \mathcal{L}$ and $\frac{\partial}{\partial x_i(0)} \mathcal{L}$ are derived analogously. From (10) we obtain $\frac{\partial}{\partial c_j} \mathcal{L} = \mathbf{u}_j(t_R)\mathbf{e}$ with $\mathbf{u}_j(t_0) = \mathbf{0}$ and

$$\mathbf{u}_j(t_\ell) = (\mathbf{u}_j(t_{\ell-1}) P_\ell + \mathbf{u}(t_{\ell-1}) \frac{\partial}{\partial c_j} P_\ell) W_\ell \quad \text{for all } 1 \le \ell \le R,$$

where $\mathbf{0}$ is the vector with all entries zero. Thus, during the solution of the ℓ-th ODE in (13) we simultaneously solve

$$\frac{d}{dt} \tilde{\mathbf{u}}_j(t) = \tilde{\mathbf{u}}_j(t) Q + \tilde{\mathbf{u}}(t) \frac{\partial}{\partial c_j} Q \tag{14}$$

with initial condition $\tilde{\mathbf{u}}_j(t_{\ell-1}) = \mathbf{u}_j(t_{\ell-1})$ for the time interval $[t_{\ell-1}, t_\ell)$. As above, we set $\mathbf{u}_j(t_\ell) = \tilde{\mathbf{u}}_j(t_\ell) W_\ell$ and obtain $\frac{\partial}{\partial c_j} \mathcal{L}$ as $\mathbf{u}_j(t_R)\mathbf{e}$.

Solving (13) and (14) simultaneously is equivalent to the computation of the partial derivatives in (2) with different initial conditions. Numerical experiments show that the approximation errors of the likelihood and its derivatives are of the same order of magnitude as those of the transient probabilities and their derivatives. For instance, for a finite-state enzymatic reaction system that is small enough to be solved without truncation we found that the maximum absolute error in the approximations of the vectors $\mathbf{p}(t)$ and $\mathbf{s}_\lambda(t)$ is 10^{-8} if the truncation threshold is $\delta = 10^{-15}$ (details not shown).

In the case of K observation sequences we repeat the above algorithm in order to sequentially compute $\mathcal{L}_k$ for $k \in \{1, \ldots, K\}$. We exploit (11) and (12) to compute the total log-likelihood and its derivatives as a sum of individual terms. In a similar way, second derivatives can be approximated. Obviously, it is possible to parallelize the algorithm by computing $\mathcal{L}_k$ in parallel for all k.

In order to find values for which the likelihood becomes maximal, global optimization techniques can be applied. Those techniques usually use a heuristic for different initial values of the parameters and then follow the gradient to find local optima of the likelihood. In this step the algorithm proposed above is used since it approximates the gradient of the likelihood. The approximated global optimum is then chosen as the minimum/maximum of the local optima, i.e, we determine those values of the parameters that give the largest likelihood. Clearly, this is an approximation and we cannot guarantee that the global optimum was found. Note that this would also be the case if we could compute the exact likelihood. If, however, a good heuristic for the starting points is chosen and the number of starting points is large, then it is likely that the approximation is accurate. Moreover, since we have approximated the second derivative of the log-likelihood, we can compute the entries of the Fisher information matrix and use this to approximate the standard deviation of the estimated parameters, i.e., we consider the square root of the diagonal entries of the inverse of a matrix H which is the Hessian matrix of the negative log-likelihood. Assuming that the second derivative of the log-likelihood is computed exactly, these entries asymptotically tend to the standard deviations of the estimated parameters.

We remark that the approximation proposed above becomes unfeasible if the reaction network contains species with high molecule numbers since in this case the number of states that have to be considered is very large. A numerical approximation of the likelihood is, as the solution of the CME, only possible if the expected populations of all species remain small (at most a few hundreds) and if the dimension of the process is not too large. Moreover, if many parameters have to be estimated, the search space of the optimization problem may become unfeasibly large. It is however straightforward to parallelize local optimizations starting from different initial point.

Numerical results
In this section we present numerical results of our parameter estimation algorithm applied to two models, the simple gene expression in Example 1 and a multi-attractor model. The corresponding SBML files are provided as Additional files 1 and 2. For both models, we generated time series data using Monte-Carlo simulation where we added white noise to represent measurement errors, i.e. we added random terms to the populations that follow a normal distribution with mean zero and a standard deviation of σ. Our algorithm for the approximation of the likelihood is implemented in C++ and linked to MATLAB's optimization toolbox [20] which we use to minimize the negative log-likelihood. The global optimization method

(Matlab's GlobalSearch [21]) uses a scatter-search algorithm to generate a set of trial points (potential starting points) and heuristically decides when to perform a local optimization. We ran our experiments on an Intel Core i7 at 2.8 GHz with 8 GB main memory.

Simple gene expression
For our first model, the simple gene expression as introduced in Example 1, we chose the same parameters as Reinker et al.[4] multiplied by a factor of 10, i.e., $c = (0.270, 1.667, 4.0)$ and as the initial condition we have ten mRNA molecules and the DNA is inactive. We generated K observation sequences of length $T = 100.0$ and observed all species at R equidistant observation time points. We added white noise with standard deviation $\sigma = 1.0$ to the observed mRNA molecule numbers at each observation time point. For the case $K = 5, R = 100$ we plot the generated observation sequences in Figure 1. We estimated the reaction rate constants, the initial molecule numbers, and the parameter σ of the measurement errors for the case $K = 5, R = 100$ where we chose the interval $[10^{-5}, 10^3]$ as a constraint for the rate constants, the interval $[0, 100]$ for the initial number of mRNA molecules and $[0, 5]$ for σ. Since we use a global optimization method, the running time of our method depends on the number of trial points generated by GlobalSearch. In Figure 2 we plot the trial points (red points) and local optimization runs (differently colored lines) for the case of 10 (a), 100 (b) and 1000 (c) trial points. The intersection of the dashed blue lines represents the location of the original parameters. In the case of ten trial points, the running time was about one minute and the local optimization was performed only once. In the case of 100 and 1000 trial points, the running times were about 22 min and 1.9 h, respectively and several local optimization runs converged in nearly the same point. However, we remark that in general the landscape of the target function might have multiple local minima and require more trial points resulting in longer running times.

We ran experiments for varying values of K and R ($K, R \in \{1, 2, 5, 10, 20, 50, 100\}$) to get insights whether for this network it is more advantageous to have many observation sequences with long observation intervals or few observation sequences with a short time between two successive observations. In addition, we ran the same experiments with the restriction that only the number of mRNA molecules was observable but not the state of the gene. In both cases we approximated the standard deviations of our estimators as a measure of quality by repeating our estimation procedure 100 times and by the Fisher information matrix as explained at the end of the previous section. We used 100 trial points for the global optimization procedure and chose tighter constraints than above

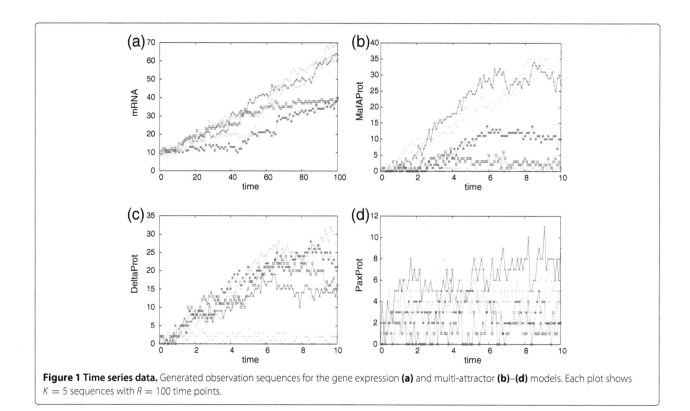

Figure 1 Time series data. Generated observation sequences for the gene expression **(a)** and multi-attractor **(b)**–**(d)** models. Each plot shows $K = 5$ sequences with $R = 100$ time points.

for the rate constants ($[0.01, 1]$ for c_1 and $[0.1, 10]$ for c_2, c_3) to have a convenient total running time.

The results are depicted in Figure 3 for the fully observable system and in Figure 4 for the restricted system, where the state of the gene was not visible. In these figures we present the estimations of the parameters c_1, c_2, c_3, σ, and an estimation of the initial condition, i.e. the number of mRNA molecules at time point $t = 0$. Moreover, we give the total running time of the procedure (Figures 3f and 4f). Our results are plotted as a gray landscape for all combinations of K and R. The estimates are bounded by a red grid enclosing an environment of one standard deviation around the respective average over all 100 estimates that we approximated. The real value of the parameter is indicated by a dotted blue rectangle.

At first, we remark that neither the quality of the estimation nor the running time of our algorithm is significantly dependent on whether we observe the state of the gene in addition to the mRNA level or not. Moreover, concerning the estimation of all of the parameters, one can witness that the estimates converge more quickly against the real values along the K axis than the R axis and also the standard deviations decrease faster. Consequently, at least for the gene expression model, it is more advantageous to increase the number of observation sequences, than the number of measurements per sequence. For example, $K = 100$ sequences with only one observation each already provide enough information to estimate c_1 up to

a relative error of around 2.1%. Unfortunately, in this case the computation time is the highest since we have to compute K individual likelihoods (one for each observation sequence). Moreover, if R is small then the truncation of the state space is less efficient. The reason is that we have to integrate for a long time until we multiply with the weight matrix W_ℓ. After this multiplication we decide which states contribute significantly to the likelihood and which states are neglected. We can, however, trade off accuracy against running time by varying K.

For the measurement noise parameter σ we see that it is more advantageous to increase R. Even five observation sequences with a high number of observations per sequence ($R = 100$) suffice to estimate the noise up to a relative error of around 10.2%. For the estimation of the initial conditions, both K and R seem to play an equally important role.

The standard deviations of the estimators give information about the accuracy of the estimation. In order to approximate the standard deviation we used statistics over 100 repeated experiments. In a realistic setting one would rather use the Fisher information matrix to approximate the standard deviation of the estimators since it is in most cases difficult to observe $100 \cdot K$ observation sequences of a real system. Therefore we compare the results of one experiment with K observation sequences and standard deviations approximated using the Fisher information matrix to the case where the experiment is

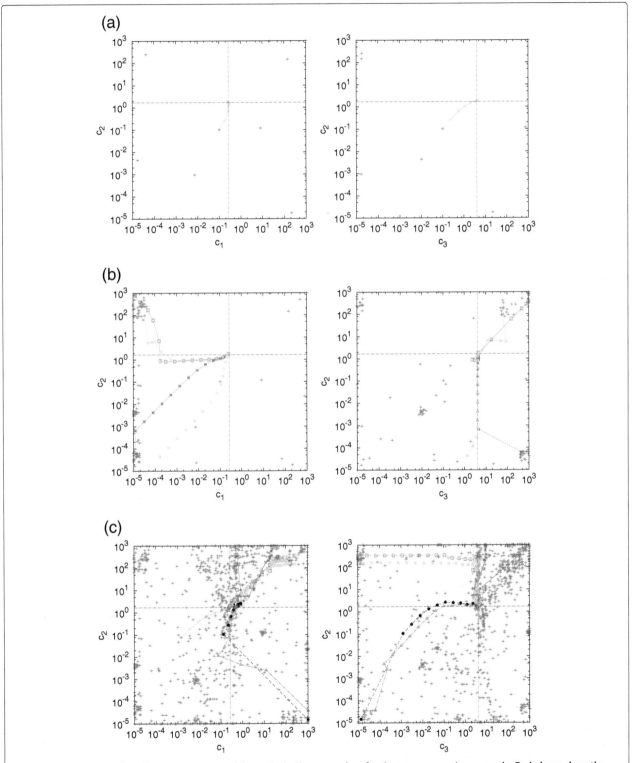

Figure 2 Start points and gradient convergence of the optimization procedure for the gene expression example: Red pluses show the potential start points. We use 10, 100, and 1000 start points in case **(a)**, **(b)**, and **(c)**, respectively. The markers that are connected by lines show the iterative steps of the gradient convergence while the dashed blue line shows the true values of the parameters. We chose $K = 5, R = 100$ and assume that the parameters are in the range $[10^{-5}, 10^{3}]$.

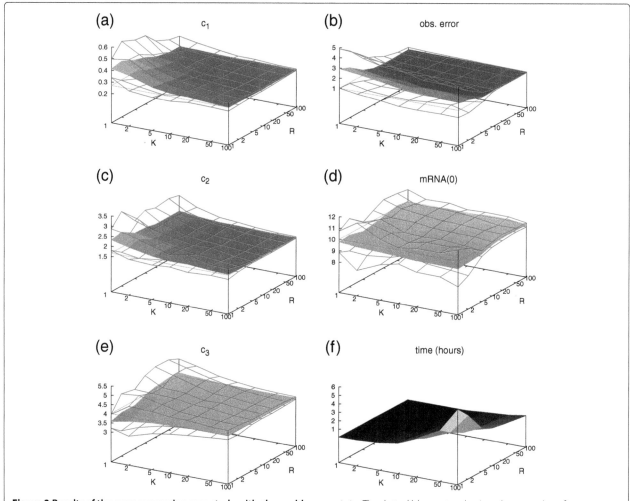

Figure 3 Results of the gene expression case study with observable gene state. The dotted blue rectangle gives the true value of c_1, c_2, c_3, σ (obs. error), and mRNA(0). The red grid corresponds to the approximated standard deviation of the estimators.

repeated 100 times. The results for varying values of K and R are given in Table 1 We observe that the approximation using the Fisher information matrix is in most cases close to the approximation based on 100 repetitions as long as K and R are not too small. This comes from the fact that the Fisher information matrix converges to the true standard deviation as the sample size increases.

Multi-attractor model

Our final example is a part of the multi-attractor model considered by Zhou et al. [22]. It consists of the three genes *MafA*, *Pax4*, and δ-gene, which interact with each other as illustrated in Figure 5. The corresponding proteins bind to specific promoter regions on the DNA and (de-)activate the genes. The reaction network has 2^3 different gene states, also called modes, since each gene can be on or off. It is infinite in three dimensions since for the proteins there is no fixed upper bound. The edges

between the nodes in Figure 5 show whether the protein of a specific gene can bind to the promoter region of another gene. Moreover, edges with normal arrow heads correspond to binding without inhibition while the edges with line heads show inhibition.

We list all 24 reactions in Table 2 For simplicity we first assume that there is a common rate constant for all protein production reactions (p), for all protein degradations (d), binding (b), and unbinding (u) reactions. We further assume that initially all genes are active and no proteins are present. For the rate constants we chose $\mathbf{c} = (p, d, b, u) = (5.0, 0.1, 1.0, 1.0)$ and generated $K \in \{1, 5\}$ sample paths of length $T = 10.0$. We added normally distributed noise with zero mean and standard deviation $\sigma = 1.0$ to the protein levels at each of the $R = 100$ observation time points. Plots of the generated observation sequences are presented in Figure 1 b–d for the case $K = 5$. For the global optimization we used ten trial points. We chose the interval $[0.1, 10]$ as a constraint for

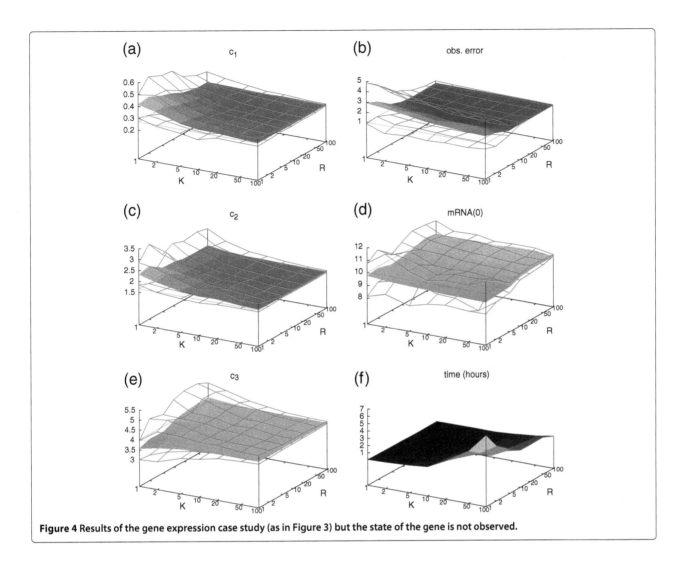

Figure 4 Results of the gene expression case study (as in Figure 3) but the state of the gene is not observed.

the rate constants p, b, u and the interval $[0.01, 1]$ for d. We estimated the parameters for all $2^3 - 1 = 7$ possibilities of observing or not observing the three protein numbers where at least one of them had to be observable. In addition we repeated the parameter estimation for the fully observable system where in addition to the three proteins also the state of the genes was observed.

The results are depicted in Figure 6 where the x-axis of the plots refers to the observed proteins. For instance, the third entry on the x-axis of the plot in Figure 6 a shows the result of the estimation of parameter $c_1 = 5$ based on observation sequences where only the molecule numbers of the proteins MafAProt and DeltaProt were observed. For this case study, we used the Fisher information matrix

Table 1 Different approximations of the standard deviations of the estimators

Method	K	R	c_1	c_2	c_3	σ	mRNA(0)
Fisher inf. matrix	10	10	0.0545104	0.561963	0.935324	0.364339	0.639471
100 experiments			0.0358142	0.198700	0.262223	0.392884	0.490305
Fisher inf. matrix	20	20	0.0324508	0.299487	0.451476	0.174095	0.594820
100 experiments			0.0304157	0.167431	0.287471	0.134506	0.436059
Fisher inf. matrix	50	50	0.0139185	0.110709	0.152229	0.0440282	0.238033
100 experiments			0.0140331	0.078516	0.146232	0.0353837	0.183888
Fisher inf. matrix	100	100	0.00866066	0.0548249	0.0728129	0.0182564	0.208469
100 experiments			0.00691956	0.0430123	0.0641821	0.0217544	0.187968

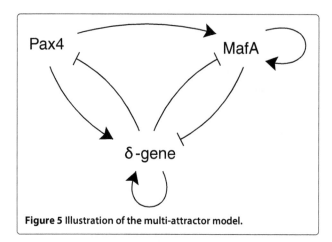

Figure 5 Illustration of the multi-attractor model.

to approximate the standard deviations of our estimators, plotted as bars in Figure 6 with the estimated parameter as midpoint. The fully observable case is labelled by "full".

We observe in Figure 6 that as expected the accuracy of the estimation and the running time of our algorithm is best when we have full observability of the system and gets worse with an increasing number of unobservable

Table 2 Chemical reactions of the multi-attractor model

PaxDna	$\xrightarrow{p}$	PaxDna + PaxProt
PaxProt	$\xrightarrow{d}$	$\emptyset$
PaxDna + DeltaProt	$\xrightarrow{b}$	PaxDnaDeltaProt
PaxDnaDeltaProt	$\xrightarrow{u}$	PaxDna + DeltaProt
MafADna	$\xrightarrow{p}$	MafADna + MafAProt
MafAProt	$\xrightarrow{d}$	$\emptyset$
MafADna + PaxProt	$\xrightarrow{b}$	MafADnaPaxProt
MafADnaPaxProt	$\xrightarrow{u}$	MafADna + PaxProt
MafADnaPaxProt	$\xrightarrow{p}$	MafADnaPaxProt + MafAProt
MafADna + MafAProt	$\xrightarrow{b}$	MafADnaMafAProt
MafADnaMafAProt	$\xrightarrow{u}$	MafADna + MafAProt
MafADnaMafAProt	$\xrightarrow{p}$	MafADnaMafAProt + MafAProt
MafADna + DeltaProt	$\xrightarrow{b}$	MafADnaDeltaProt
MafADnaDeltaProt	$\xrightarrow{u}$	MafADna + DeltaProt
DeltaDna	$\xrightarrow{p}$	DeltaDna + DeltaProt
DeltaProt	$\xrightarrow{d}$	$\emptyset$
DeltaDna + PaxProt	$\xrightarrow{b}$	DeltaDnaPaxProt
DeltaDnaPaxProt	$\xrightarrow{u}$	DeltaDna + PaxProt
DeltaDnaPaxProt	$\xrightarrow{p}$	DeltaDnaPaxProt + DeltaProt
DeltaDna + MafAProt	$\xrightarrow{b}$	DeltaDnaMafAProt
DeltaDnaMafAProt	$\xrightarrow{u}$	DeltaDna + MafAProt
DeltaDna + DeltaProt	$\xrightarrow{b}$	DeltaDnaDeltaProt
DeltaDnaDeltaProt	$\xrightarrow{u}$	DeltaDna + DeltaProt
DeltaDnaDeltaProt	$\xrightarrow{p}$	DeltaDnaDeltaProt + DeltaProt

species. Still the estimation quality is very high when five observation sequences are provided for almost all combinations and parameters. When only one observation sequence is given ($K = 1$), the parameter estimation becomes unreliable and time consuming. This comes from the fact that the quality of the approximation highly depends on the generated observation sequence. It is possible to get much better and faster approximations with a single observation sequence. However, we did not optimize our results but generated one random observation sequence and ran our estimation procedure once based on this.

Recall that we chose common parameters p, d, b, u for production, degradation, and (un-)binding for all three protein species. Next we "decouple" the binding rates and estimate the binding rate of each protein independently. We illustrate our results in Figure 7. Again, in case of a single observation sequence ($K = 1$) the estimation is unreliable in most cases. If the true value of the parameter is unknown, then the high standard deviation shows that more information (more observation sequences) is necessary to estimate the parameter. In order to estimate the binding rate of PaxProt, we see that observing MafAProt yields the best result while for the binding rate of MafAProt observing PaxProt is best. Only for the binding rate of DeltaProt, the best results are obtained when the corresponding protein (DeltaProt) is observed. The running times of the estimation procedure are between 10 and 80 h, usually increase with K and depend on the observation sequences.

In Table 3 we list the results of estimating the production rate 5.0 in the multi-attractor model where we chose $R = 100$. More precisely, we estimated the production rate of each protein independently when the other two proteins were observed. Since the population of the PaxProt is significantly smaller than the populations of the other two proteins, its production rate is more difficult to estimate. The production rate of MafAProt is accurately estimated even if only a single observation sequence is considered. For estimating the production rate of DeltaProt, $K = 5$ observation sequences are necessary to get an accurate result.

Finally, we remark that for the multi-attractor model it seems difficult to predict whether for a given parameter the observation of a certain set of proteins yields a good accuracy or not. It can, however, be hypothesized that, if we want to accurately estimate the rate constant of a certain chemical reaction, then we should observe as many of the involved species as possible. Moreover, it is reasonable that constants of reactions that occur less often are more difficult to estimate (such as the production of PaxProt). In such a case more observation sequences are necessary to provide reliable information about the speed of the reaction.

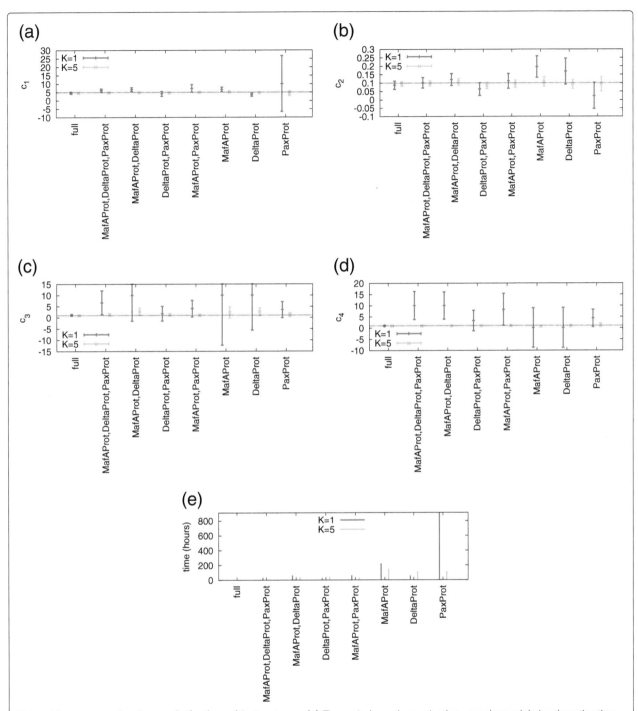

Figure 6 Parameter estimation results for the multi-attractor model. The x-axis shows the species that were observed during the estimation procedure. The dotted blue line corresponds to the true value of c_1, c_2, c_3, and c_4, respectively. The error bars in **(a)**–**(d)** show the mean (plus/minus the standard deviation) of the estimators. In **(e)** we plot the running time of the estimation procedure.

Conclusion

Parameter inference for stochastic models of cellular processes demands huge computational resources. We proposed an efficient numerical method to approximate maximum likelihood estimators for a given set of observations. We consider the case where the observations are subject to measurement errors and where only the molecule numbers of some of the chemical species are observed at certain points in time. In our experiments we show that if the observations provide sufficient information then parameters can be accurately identified. If only little information is available then the approximations of

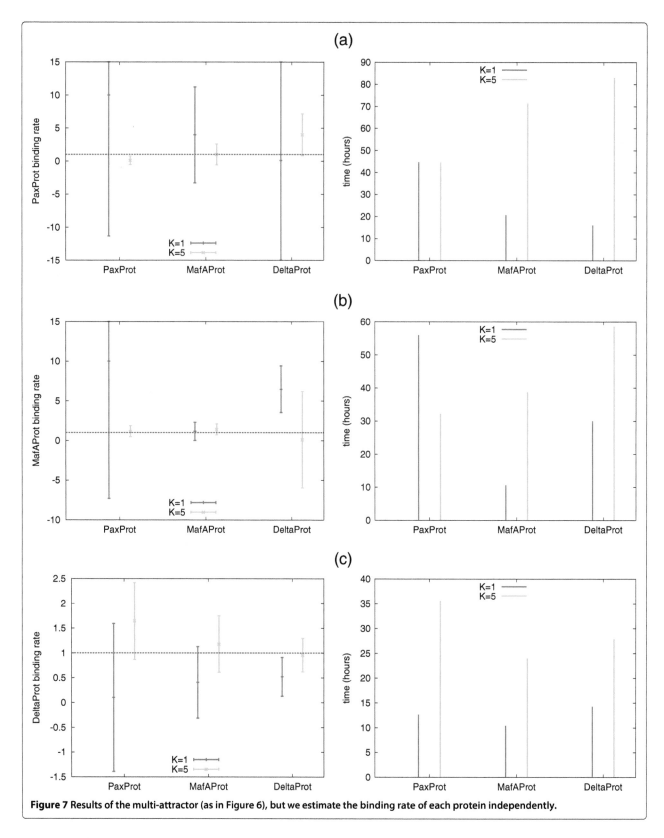

Figure 7 Results of the multi-attractor (as in Figure 6), but we estimate the binding rate of each protein independently.

the standard deviations of the estimators indicate whether more observations are necessary to accurately calibrate certain parameters.

As future work we plan a comparison of our technique to parameter estimation based on Bayesian inference. In addition, we will examine whether a combination of

Table 3 Production rate estimation in the multi-attractor model

Protein	K	Estimated rate constant	Standard deviation	Time (hours)	Observed proteins
PaxProt	1	10.0	13.6159	7.45	MafAProt, DeltaProt
	5	0.5693	2.1842	6.34	
MafAProt	1	4.9998	4.9884	11.62	PaxProt, DeltaProt
	5	5.4853	2.3873	13.86	
DeltaProt	1	2.5453	1.8075	4.35	PaxProt, MafAProt
	5	5.3646	1.4682	12.39	

methods based on prior knowledge and the maximum likelihood method is useful. Future plans further include parameter estimation methods for systems where some chemical species have small molecule numbers while others are high rendering a purely discrete representation infeasible. In such cases, hybrid models are advantageous where large populations are represented by continuous deterministic variables while small populations are still described by discrete random variables [23].

Additional files

Additional file 1: SBML file of the gene expression example.

- File name: genexpression.xml
- File format: SBML (see http://www.sbml.org/sbml/level2/version4)
- File extension: xml

Additional file 2: SBML file of the multiattractor model.

- File name: multiattractor.xml
- File format: SBML (see http://www.sbml.org/sbml/level2/version4)
- File extension: xml

Competing interests
The authors declare that they have no competing interests.

Acknowledgements
This research was been partially funded by the German Research Council (DFG) as part of the Cluster of Excellence on Multimodal Computing and Interaction at Saarland University and the Transregional Collaborative Research Center "Automatic Verification and Analysis of Complex Systems" (SFB/TR 14 AVACS).

References
1. DT Gillespie, Exact stochastic simulation of coupled chemical reactions, J. Phys. Chem. **81**(25), 2340–2361 (1977)
2. A Loinger, A Lipshtat, NQ Balaban, O Biham, Stochastic simulations of genetic switch systems, Phys. Rev. E. **75**, 021904 (2007)
3. T Tian, S Xu, J Gao, K Burrage, Simulated maximum likelihood method for estimating kinetic rates in gene expression, Bioinformatics. **23**, 84–91 (2007)
4. S Reinker, R Altman, J Timmer, Parameter estimation in stochastic biochemical reactions, IEEE Proc. Syst. Biol. **153**, 168–178 (2006)
5. B Uz, E Arslan, I Laurenzi, Maximum likelihood estimation of the kinetics of receptor-mediated adhesion, J. Theor. Biol. **262**(3), 478–487 (2010)
6. I Golding, J Paulsson, S Zawilski, E Cox, Real-time kinetics of gene activity in individual bacteria, Cell. **123**(6), 1025–1036 (2005)
7. R Boys, D Wilkinson, T Kirkwood, Bayesian inference for a discretely observed stochastic kinetic model, Stat. Comput. **18**, 125–135 (2008)
8. JJ Higgins, Bayesian inference and the optimality of maximum likelihood estimation, Int. Stat. Rev. **45**, 9–11 (1977)
9. CS Gillespie, A Golightly, Bayesian inference for generalized stochastic population growth models with application to aphids, J. R. Stat. Soc. Ser. C. **59**(2), 341–357 (2010)
10. T Toni, D Welch, N Strelkowa, A Ipsen, M Stumpf, Approximate Bayesian computation scheme for parameter inference and model selection in dynamical systems, J. R. Soc. Interface. **6**(31), 187–202 (2009)
11. M Komorowski, B Finkenstädt, C Harper, D Rand, Bayesian inference of biochemical kinetic parameters using the linear noise approximation, J. R. Stat. Soc. Ser. **C 10**(343) (2009)
12. A Andreychenko, L Mikeev, D Spieler, V Wolf, in *Computer Aided Verification - 23rd International Conference, CAV 2011, Snowbird, UT, USA, July 14-20, 2011. Proceedings, Volume 6806 of Lecture Notes in Computer Science.* Parameter Identification for Markov Models of Biochemical Reactions, (Springer, Heidelberg, 2011), pp. 83–98
13. A Andreychenko, L Mikeev, D Spieler, V Wolf, in *Computational Systems Biology - 8th International Workshop, WCSB 2011, Zürich, Switzerland, June 6-8, 2011. Proceedings.* Approximate maximum likelihood estimation for stochastic chemical kinetics ((Tampere International Center for Signal Processing. TICSP series # 57, Tampere, Finland, 2011)
14. TA Henzinger, M Mateescu, V Wolf, in *Computer Aided Verification, 21st International Conference, CAV 2009, Grenoble, France, June 26 - July 2, 2009. Proceedings, Volume 5643 of Lecture Notes in Computer Science.* Sliding Window Abstraction for Infinite Markov Chains, (Springer, Heidelberg, 2009), pp. 337–352
15. B Munsky, M Khammash, The finite state projection algorithm for the solution of the chemical master equation, J. Chem. Phys. **124**, 044144 (2006)
16. K Burrage, M Hegland, F Macnamara, B Sidje, in *Proceedings of the Markov 150th Anniversary Conference.* A Krylov-based finite state projection algorithm for solving the chemical master equation arising in the discrete modelling of biological systems, (Boson Books, Bitingduck Press, Altadena, CA, USA, 2006), pp. 21–38
17. M Mateescu, V Wolf, F Didier, T Henzinger, Fast adaptive uniformisation of the chemical master equation, IET Syst. Biol. **4**(6), 441–452 (2010)
18. R Sidje, K Burrage, S MacNamara, Inexact uniformization method for computing transient distributions of Markov chains, SIAM J. Sci. Comput. **29**(6), 2562–2580 (2007)
19. L Ljung, *System Identification: Theory for the, User*, 2nd edn, (Prentice Hall, PTR, New Jersey, USA, 1998)
20. Global Optimization Toolbox: User's Guide (r2011b). Mathworks 2011. [www.mathworks.com/help/pdf_doc/gads/gads_tb.pdf]
21. Z Ugray, L Lasdon, JC Plummer, F Glover, J Kelly, R Marti, Scatter search and local NLP solvers: a multistart framework for global optimization, INFORMS J. Comput. **19**(3), 328–340 (2007)
22. JX Zhou, L Brusch, S Huang, Predicting pancreas cell fate decisions and reprogramming with a hierarchical multi-attractor model, PLoS ONE. **6**(3), e14752 (2011)
23. TA Henzinger, L Mikeev, M Mateescu, V Wolf, in *Computational Methods in Systems Biology, 8th International Conference, CMSB 2010, Trento, Italy, September 29 - October 1, 2010. Proceedings.* Hybrid numerical solution of the chemical master equation, (ACM, New York, USA, 2010), pp. 55–65

5

Feature ranking based on synergy networks to identify prognostic markers in DPT-1

Amin Ahmadi Adl[1], Xiaoning Qian[1,2]*, Ping Xu[3], Kendra Vehik[3] and Jeffrey P Krischer[3]

Abstract

Interaction among different risk factors plays an important role in the development and progress of complex disease, such as diabetes. However, traditional epidemiological methods often focus on analyzing individual or a few 'essential' risk factors, hopefully to obtain some insights into the etiology of complex disease. In this paper, we propose a systematic framework for risk factor analysis based on a synergy network, which enables better identification of potential risk factors that may serve as prognostic markers for complex disease. A spectral approximate algorithm is derived to solve this network optimization problem, which leads to a new network-based feature ranking method that improves the traditional feature ranking by taking into account the pairwise synergistic interactions among risk factors in addition to their individual predictive power. We first evaluate the performance of our method based on simulated datasets, and then, we use our method to study immunologic and metabolic indices based on the Diabetes Prevention Trial-Type 1 (DPT-1) study that may provide prognostic and diagnostic information regarding the development of type 1 diabetes. The performance comparison based on both simulated and DPT-1 datasets demonstrates that our network-based ranking method provides prognostic markers with higher predictive power than traditional analysis based on individual factors.

Keywords: DPT-1; Type 1 diabetes; Biomarker identification; Interaction; Synergy network; Feature ranking

Introduction

Type 1 diabetes (T1D) is an autoimmune disorder and one of the common pediatric diseases with a diverse pathogenesis, clinical phenotype, and outcome [1]. Despite the emergence of T1D as a global issue with a steady increase in incidence worldwide over the past decade [2], the etiology of T1D is still not fully understood. Recent studies, including the Diabetes Prevention Trial-Type 1 (DPT-1) [3], have suggested that this complex disease has multiple risk factors, including genetic predisposition, diet, viruses, and geography in addition to autoimmunity [1,4-7]. The previous epidemiology studies mostly focus on studying hypotheses regarding individual risk factors, which have obtained important initial understanding, including the predisposing roles from genetic markers such as human leukocyte antigens [5]. However, traditional hypothesis-driven approaches focusing on 'essential' factors may not be sufficient for fully understanding T1D [6]. With large-scale perspective studies such as DPT-1, we believe that data-driven investigation considering all candidate factors with their interactions can serve as a critical complement for previous hypothesis-driven research.

Data-driven methods have been proven to be useful in both identifying probable mechanisms involved in disease and providing accurate biomarkers for early prediction [8,9]. However, as shown in genome-wide association studies (GWAS), single marker analysis is not sufficient for genetic studies of complex diseases [10,11]. In order to better explain the missing heritability of complex disease through analyzing high-dimensional genotype data, several methods have been proposed to take into account the interactive effect among single-nucleotide polymorphisms as well as multiple genes in GWAS and other -omic data analysis [12-14]. In this work, we propose a network-based mathematical model for systematically analyzing candidate risk factors for disease. We consider that the individual effect and interactions

---

*Correspondence: xqian@ece.tamu.edu
[1] Department of Computer Science and Engineering, University of South Florida, Tampa, FL, 33620, USA
[2] Department of Electrical & Computer Engineering, Texas A&M University, College Station, TX, 77843, USA
Full list of author information is available at the end of the article

from potential risk factors are all manifested as statistical associations with the disease outcome. Based on this, we construct a synergy network which integrates both the individual and synergistic interactive effects of factors in one single graph structure. We then propose a novel algorithm based on this synergy network to identify biomarkers for early prediction of disease. Specifically, we verify the effectiveness of our method using simulated case-control datasets. With such validated results, we apply our method to identify biomarkers for prognosis of T1D from measured immunologic and metabolic indices in DPT-1. The performance of the identified markers is then compared to the performance of traditional forward feature selection which only considers the individual statistical association with outcome. Our comprehensive results show that our network-based method identifies better biomarkers with better predictive performance.

Methods

Feature selection approaches are commonly used to identify biomarkers by finding a subset of biomedical measurements with high predictive power with respect to disease outcome [15-17]. As it is computationally very expensive to exhaustively search for the best subset of variables, these methods mostly rely on heuristic approaches. Filtering variables based on their individual effect on disease outcome has been a common practice in biomedical research. Heuristic approaches based on filtering have been successful in identifying biomarkers with strong individual effects. However, they may miss variables with weak individual effects but having synergistic interactive effects that produce high predictive accuracy [15,17]. To avoid missing these critical variables with high synergistic effects on outcome, we propose a new approach which takes into account both individual and synergistic interactive effects. In our approach, we first construct a synergy network based on the individual and synergistic effects of all the observed variables. Then, we solve the problem of finding the best subnetwork by an efficient graph spectral algorithm which leads to a novel feature ranking that improves the traditional ranking by taking into account the interaction among variables. Finally, we use this feature ranking together with traditional forward feature selection to achieve the final set of biomarkers.

Synergy network

To construct the synergy network, we need to measure the individual predictive power of all variables together with their pairwise synergistic power. One natural way to measure both individual and synergistic powers is to use a logistic regression model. In order to measure the individual power of variable v_i, we can learn the following logistic model $\log(g/(1-g)) = \alpha_0 + \alpha_1 v_i$ in which g is the probability $p(y = 1|v_i)$, where y denotes the disease outcome of interest. After fitting this model to the given data, the magnitude of the coefficient α_1 measures the individual power of v_i. To make sure that the measurements for different variables are with the same unit and comparable to each other, we use $-\log(p_i)$ as the individual power of variable v_i, in which p_i is the coefficient p-value for α_1 and measures the statistical significance of the individual power of v_i. Similarly, in order to measure the synergistic predictive power between two variables v_i and v_j, we fit the following logistic model $\log(g/(1-g)) = \alpha_0 + \alpha_1 v_i + \alpha_2 v_j + \beta v_i v_j$ (where $g = p(y = 1|v_i, v_j)$) to data and consider $-\log(p_{ij})$ as the synergistic power of variables v_i and v_j, in which p_{ij} is the coefficient p-value of β. With that, we construct the synergy network which can be represented by a graph $G(V, E)$. In this synergy network, V is the set of nodes corresponding to all the variables, and each $v_i \in V$ has the node weight $f(v_i)$ equal to $-\log(p_i)$; E is the set of edges (v_i, v_j) with the edge weight $s(v_i, v_j)$ equal to $-\log(p_{ij})$.

Finding subnetworks for biomarker identification

As explained, the synergy network integrates both individual and synergistic powers of candidate risk factors in a single graph structure. Similar to the traditional problem of feature selection, here we are looking for subsets of risk factors or subnetworks in the synergy network, with the highest possible discriminative power regarding disease outcome y. To simplify the problem, we approximate the discriminative power of subnetworks by the summation of the node weights and edge weights induced in them. We note that this approximation is expected to perform better than traditional feature selection approaches based on only individual effects [16] due to the integration of synergistic effects in our synergy network. The biomarker identification problem is then reduced to solve the following optimization problem:

$$\max_{C \subseteq G} \sum_{v_i \in C} f(v_i) + \lambda \sum_{v_i, v_j \in C} s(v_i, v_j), \qquad (1)$$

where C denotes potential subnetworks and $0 \leq \lambda \leq 1$ is a weighting coefficient between individual and synergistic effects. As both $f(v_i)$ and $s(v_i, v_j)$ are nonnegative, the previous optimization problem has the degenerated solution to include all the risk factors in C. To overcome this problem, we further impose another constraint to restrict the size of selected subnetworks to have $|C| \leq K$. This formulation is in fact the problem of finding a maximum weighted clique (MWCP) [18] which is a generalization of the classical maximum clique problem (MCP). As MCP is nondeterministically polynomial (NP)-hard [19], it can be easily shown that MWCP is NP-hard as well. Thus, our biomarker identification problem formulated in Equation 1 is also an NP-hard problem. Several approaches have been previously proposed to find the exact optimal solution of the problem by employing branch-and-bound techniques, but it is probable that exhaustive search over all possible subnetworks is needed [18]. In this paper, we propose a fast approximate algorithm for MWCP which also provides a ranked list of features based on both their individual and synergistic effects.

Feature ranking by a graph spectral algorithm

We first rewrite the optimization problem given in Equation 1 as a quadratic integer programming problem as follows: For each node v_i in G, we consider an integer variable x_i which is equal to 1 if the node v_i is selected in the subnetwork C and is 0 otherwise. Using this variable, we can rewrite Equation 1 as $\max_{\mathbf{x}} = [x_1, x_2, \ldots x_n]^T \sum_{i=1}^{n} f(v_i)x_i^2 + \lambda \sum_{i,j=1}^{n} s(v_i, v_j)x_i x_j$, where n is the number of feature nodes in G. We further define the matrix $M_{(n \times n)}$ with diagonal entries $M_{i,i}$ equal to the individual power $f(v_i)$, and off-diagonal entries $M_{i,j}$ equal to the synergistic power $\lambda \times s(v_i, v_j)$. We can rewrite the optimization problem for biomarker identification in the following matrix format:

$$\max_{\mathbf{x}} \ \mathbf{x}^T M \mathbf{x} \qquad (2)$$
$$\text{s.t.} \quad \mathbf{x}^T \mathbf{x} \leq K;$$
$$x_i \in \{0, 1\},$$

in which $\mathbf{x} = [x_1, \cdots, x_n]^T$ is a binary integer vector. In fact, the size constraint is equivalent to putting in a sparse penalty on $\mathbf{x}$ to select the smallest number of risk factors that have high predictive power. In order to solve this constrained quadratic integer programming problem, we develop a spectral approximate algorithm. We first relax the integer variable $x_i \in \{0, 1\}$ to $x_i \in \mathbb{R}$. Then, using Lagrangian relaxation, we can transform the original optimization problem given in Equation 2 to the following quadratic programming optimization problem:

$$\max_{\mathbf{x}} \ \mathbf{x}^T M \mathbf{x} + \alpha(K - \mathbf{x}^T \mathbf{x}), \qquad (3)$$

where α is the Lagrangian multiplier. Based on the Karush-Kuhn-Tucker condition [20], the optimal solution of this relaxed quadratic programming problem has to (necessarily) satisfy the condition that the derivative of the relaxed objective function equals to 0:

$$\frac{\partial}{\partial \mathbf{x}} \left[\mathbf{x}^T M \mathbf{x} + \alpha(K - \mathbf{x}^T \mathbf{x}) \right] = 0. \qquad (4)$$

By straightforward algebraic manipulations, we can show that the potential solution $\mathbf{x}^*$ has to satisfy $M\mathbf{x}^* = \alpha \mathbf{x}^*$. Therefore, the relaxed solution $\mathbf{x}^*$ to the MWCP is

an eigenvector of the matrix M. Furthermore, we want the objective function $\mathbf{x}^{*T} M \mathbf{x}^* = \alpha \mathbf{x}^{*T} \mathbf{x}^* = \alpha K$ to have the maximum value with $\mathbf{x}^*$, which means that we want α to be as large as possible. Hence, the solution $\mathbf{x}^*$ will be the eigenvector of M with the largest corresponding eigenvalue. Also given the relaxed solution $\mathbf{x}^*$, for any K, the approximate solution to the original integer programming optimization problem is to take top K nodes with the largest corresponding magnitudes in $\mathbf{x}^*$. This also shows that the candidate risk factors with larger magnitudes in $\mathbf{x}^*$ are more desirable to be selected in the final subset of risk factors as potential prognostic biomarkers. Thus, we can use the absolute values in $\mathbf{x}^*$ as a score to rank the risk factors. We note that K can be an arbitrary number without loss of generality, which will not affect our final ranking as the $\mathbf{x}^*$ only depends on the matrix M. As one can see, the proposed method combines both individual power and synergistic power among all candidate risk factors into one single score that can be used to rank them.

Biomarker identification using network-based spectral ranking

In order to select a subset of risk factors based on any ranking, a common approach is to use forward feature selection [16]. We replace the ranking step of the forward feature selection, which is only based on individual power, by our network-based spectral ranking which takes into account the interaction among factors as well. In forward feature selection, we sequentially add potential risk factors from the top of the ranked list to the current set of selected factors only if it improves the classification performance; otherwise, we move to the next factor in the ranked list. This procedure is repeated until we reach the end of the ranked list.

Experiments and discussions

We evaluate the performance of our network-based biomarker identification based on both simulated datasets and datasets obtained from the DPT-1 study and compare it with the individual-based biomarker identification, which only considers individual effects. In order to properly estimate and compare the performance of biomarker identification methods, we perform an 'embedded' cross-validation procedure.

Performance evaluation procedure

As explained earlier, our feature selection approach includes two steps: First, we construct a synergy network based on the given dataset and rank the candidate risk factors using our spectral algorithm. Second, we use the ranked list of factors obtained in the first step to perform a forward feature selection [16]. To make sure that we do not overestimate the performance of our biomarker identification approach, we perform the following embedded cross-validation procedure: Similar to the regular ten-fold cross validation, we first randomly divide the dataset into ten folds, within which one fold is used as the *testing set* to test the performance and the remaining nine folds are used as the *training set* to select biomarkers and learn the classifier. In order to select biomarkers based on the training set, we first use all the data points in the training set to construct a synergy network and perform our spectral algorithm to obtain the ranked list. Then, using the ranked list, we perform a forward feature selection method to select the best performing set of biomarkers. In the forward feature selection method, we sequentially add candidate factors to the current feature set (starting with an empty set), if it improves the classification performance; otherwise, we move to the next factor in the ranked list. To evaluate the performance of a set of potential risk factors during forward feature selection, we use another standard ten-fold cross validation in which we further divide the training set into ten folds, nine of which are used to train the classifier and the remaining is used to test the performance. After performing the forward feature selection and identifying the biomarkers, we learn a classifier based on the *training dataset* using those selected features and compute the performance based on the testing set. During our performance evaluation procedure, we adopt the MATLAB implementation of quadratic discriminant analysis as the classifier [21] to make sure that the pairwise interaction among risk factors is taken into account by the classifier. To measure the performance of any classifier in our performance evaluation procedure, in addition to the accuracy, we also compute the area under the ROC curve (AUC) which is a more reliable measure of prediction performance [22] in our experiments. When we use accuracy as the performance measure during forward feature selection, the identified biomarkers are optimized to provide better accuracy. We also take AUC as the performance measure for forward feature selection so that the biomarkers are optimized to provide better AUC. This two sets of biomarkers are not necessarily the same, especially with unbalanced datasets, as they are supposed to optimize for different criteria. Thus, for each dataset, we have two sets of results: one based on accuracy and one based on AUC.

Performance comparison based on the simulated datasets

We simulate a case-control disease model, in which the outcome y (disease) follows a Bernoulli distribution with the success parameter equal to $p(y = 1|\mathbf{v})$ given the input variables $\mathbf{v}$. We first simulate 30 random variables as input variables $\mathbf{v} = [v_1, v_2, \ldots, v_{30}]^T$. From all 435 potential pairs of these randomly simulated variables, ten of them are randomly selected to have synergistic effects with respect to the outcome. Based on this, we follow the following logistic model to simulate the disease outcome y:

$$\log \left(\frac{p(y = 1|\mathbf{v})}{1 - p(y = 1|\mathbf{v})} \right) = \alpha_0 + \sum_{i=1}^{30} \alpha_i v_i + \sum_{i \neq j} \beta_{ij} v_i v_j.$$

(5)

In this logistic model, the magnitude of each individual coefficient α_i determines the individual effect of the corresponding variable v_i on outcome y, and the magnitude of the interaction coefficient β_{ij} determines the amount of synergistic effect of two variables v_i and v_j on the outcome. To obtain the previously described case-control data, we simulate 30 random features with each variable v_i following a mixture-of-Gaussian distribution with equally weighted (mixture parameters equal to 0.5) Gaussian distributions with the same variance of 1.0 and the means equal to -1.0 and 1.0, respectively. For 435 interaction coefficients β_{ij}, we randomly set 425 of them to zero, and the values of the other ten are drawn from the standard normal distribution (mean 0.0 and variance 1.0). We also set all the individual coefficients α_i to zero which means that there is no feature with significant individual effect. To simulate the outcome y, we first compute the probability $p(y = 1|\mathbf{v})$ based on the previous logistic model (Equation 5). Then, we generate the value for y from a Bernoulli distribution with the success parameter equal to $p(y = 1|\mathbf{v})$. We have generated 20 of such case-control datasets with 200 data samples in each set for the performance evaluation of our method. In order to make sure that our performance comparison results are independent of how we set the values of these coefficients, each of these 20 datasets is simulated with different random values for coefficients β_{ij}.

To demonstrate the advantage of our network-based feature ranking, we compare the performance of our ranking with the traditional individual-based feature ranking. We use our embedded cross-validation procedure to evaluate the performance of both network-based ranking and individual-based ranking. We repeat the embedded cross validation 100 times for both individual- and network-based rankings and calculate the average accuracy and AUC for both methods. The performance comparison for our 20 simulated datasets is shown in Figure 1. The average accuracy and average AUC of our network-based method among 20 datasets are 65.17% and 0.6518, respectively, compared to 55.74% and 0.5577 obtained by individual-based ranking. As expected, the performance of our network-based ranking is significantly better than individual-based ranking. This clearly shows that filtering methods based on individual ranking are unable to capture those risk factors with synergistic effects but weak individual effects, which are critical biomarkers for better prediction.

In order to further show that our network-based method does not only bias toward risk factors with

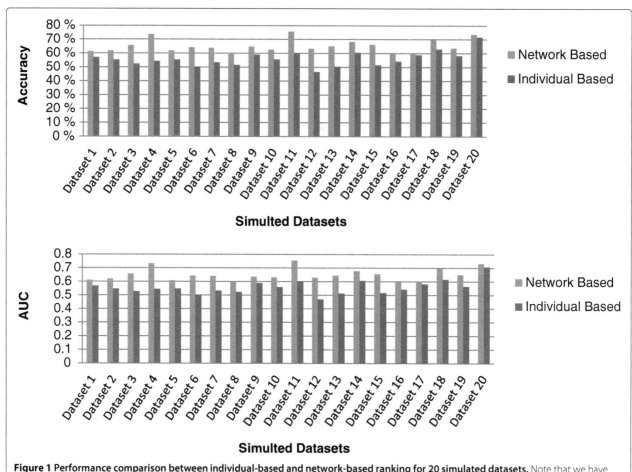

Figure 1 Performance comparison between individual-based and network-based ranking for 20 simulated datasets. Note that we have weak individual effects and significant synergistic effects in this ensemble of datasets.

only synergistic effects, we further check the performance of our network-based ranking when there are risk factors with significant individual effects in the case-control disease model. We use the same logistic regression model in Equation 5 where in addition to 10 nonzero interaction coefficients β_{ij}, we also have five random nonzero individual coefficients α_i (α_0 is set to zero as well). The values for those nonzero α_i are also drawn from a standard normal distribution. We have also generated 20 datasets of this new model, each with 200 samples. Similar to the previous 20 datasets, each of these 20 datasets is simulated with different random values for coefficients α_i and β_{ij}. The performance evaluation results based on these 20 new simulated datasets are shown in Figure 2. The average accuracy and average AUC obtained by our network-based method among these 20 new datasets are 65.47% and 0.6536, respectively, both of which are significantly higher than 60.38% and 0.6040 obtained by individual-based ranking. This shows that our network-based ranking consistently performs better than individual ranking

even when there are features with significant individual effects.

Finally, in our simulation model, we always have $p(y = 1) = p(y = 0)$, which is due to the symmetry of the logistic function, symmetry of distribution of all features, and symmetry of distribution of coefficients around zero. As a result, the datasets simulated from the model are balanced, i.e., they have almost the same number of case and control samples. Because of this, the accuracy and AUC performance measures are very similar for all of our simulated datasets which might not be the case for unbalanced datasets.

Biomarker identification in DPT-1

DPT-1 was a study designed to determine if T1D can be prevented or delayed by preclinical intervention of insulin supplement. It focuses on first- and second-degree nondiabetic relatives of patients with T1D before the age of 45, since they have more than tenfold risk of developing T1D compared to the general population [3]. DPT-1 screened 103,391 subjects altogether and categorized

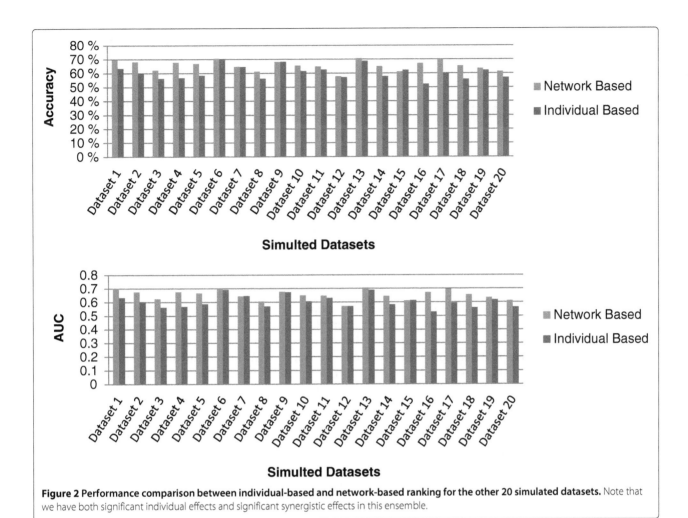

Figure 2 Performance comparison between individual-based and network-based ranking for the other 20 simulated datasets. Note that we have both significant individual effects and significant synergistic effects in this ensemble.

them into four risk groups based on genetic susceptibility, age, the presence of autoantibodies (including islet cell autoantibodies (ICA), insulin autoantibodies (IAA), glutamic acid decarboxylase (GAD), insulinoma-associated protein 2 (ICA512)), and the change of metabolic markers during oral glucose tolerance test (OGTT) and IV glucose tolerance test (IVGTT). The 3,483 subjects positive for ICA were staged to quantify the projected 5-year risk of diabetes [7]. Our analysis focuses on the study for the 'high risk' and 'intermediate risk' groups [7-9], which contain 339 and 372 subjects, respectively. The subjects of each group were randomly divided into two roughly equal subgroups: one received parenteral or oral insulin supplement, while the other was assigned to the placebo arm of the study. In this paper, we focus on the subjects of the placebo group. We consider the placebo subgroups of both high-risk and intermediate-risk groups as a dataset for our data-driven analysis (analysis based on the treated group is provided in Additional file 1). The dataset contains the following 19 features from baseline characteristics in

DPT-1, focusing on immunologic and metabolic markers. We have taken the available titer values for different autoantibodies, including ICA, IAA, GAD, ICA512, and micro-insulin autoantibodies. For metabolic indices, we have fasting glucose, glycated hemoglobin (HbA1c), fasting insulin, and first-phase insulin response (FPIR) from IVGTTs. Homeostasis model assessment of insulin resistance (HOMA-IR) and FPIR-to-HOMA-IR ratio are also computed as in [9]. From OGTTs, in addition to 2-h glucose and fasting glucose, we have collected blood samples for C-peptide measurements in the fasting state and then 30, 60, 90, and 120 min after oral glucose, from which we have computed peak C-peptide as the maximum point of all measurements and AUC C-peptide using the trapezoid rule. Furthermore, as age and body mass index (BMI) have been conjectured to be important confounding factors, we also include them in our set of features. We are interested in identifying the most predictive group of features as biomarkers from the above described candidates to predict the outcome

Table 1 Accuracy and AUC performance of network-based ranking and individual-based ranking based on the DPT-1 dataset

Performance measure	Individual ranking	Network-based ranking	p-value
Accuracy	68.31%	69.14%	6.8e−04
AUC	0.6524	0.6724	7.17e−11

which is the development of T1D at the end of the DPT-1 study. The dataset contains 356 subjects within which 133 subjects developed T1D at the end of the study.

To check the performance of our network-based biomarker identification for DPT-1, similar to simulated datasets, we repeat the embedded cross validation 100 times and use the average performance. In order to show the advantage of our network-based method, we also compute the performance of individual-based feature ranking. The results based on both accuracy and AUC measurements are given in Table 1. As one can see, both accuracy and AUC obtained by our network-based ranking are significantly higher than individual-based ranking with p-values of 6.8e−04 and 7.17e−11, respectively. The results obtained based on both simulated and DPT-1 dataset clearly show that our spectral network-based feature ranking provides biomarkers with significantly better predictive power than individual-based feature ranking. This also verifies our expectation that the integration of synergistic interaction among features provides biomarkers with higher prediction accuracies.

In each run of the embedded ten-fold cross validation procedure, we in fact have ten possibly different sets of selected features as we perform feature selection for each fold based on a different subset of training samples at each run of the cross-validation procedure. By repeating this procedure 100 times, we obtain 1,000 (100×10) different subsets of biomarkers. In order to report a single reliable set of biomarkers, we first compute the frequency of the appearance of each feature and then select the features that at least appeared in 40% of the 1,000 (i.e., 400) selected subsets. The single set of biomarkers based on both individual and network-based rankings is provided in Table 2. We have also evaluated the performance of those final biomarkers by 100 repeated ten-fold cross validations. Their corresponding accuracies and AUCs are also given in Table 2.

Note that, as mentioned previously, the features selected during the forward feature selection step of our biomarker identification method might vary when we optimize different performance measures. As a result, the final set of biomarkers when we use accuracy in our performance evaluation is different from the final set of biomarkers when we use AUC. The final set of biomarkers using both accuracy and AUC is reported; however, based on the fact that AUC measurement is more reliable than accuracy for unbalanced datasets, we believe that the final set of biomarkers obtained by AUC is more reliable.

Due to the relatively small number of features in this study, it is feasible to perform an exhaustive search over all possible subsets of features to find the biomarker set with the best performance. We computed the AUC and accuracy of all $2^{19} - 1$ possible subsets based on 100 repeated ten-fold cross validations. The best performing subsets together with their corresponding measured performances are also given in Table 2. The results in Table 2 clearly show that the network-based feature ranking method provides more predictive biomarkers than the individual-based feature ranking which are

Table 2 Final sets of biomarkers and their corresponding accuracy and AUC performances for the DPT-1 dataset

Performance Measure	Individual ranking		Network-based ranking		Exhaustive search	
Accuracy	2-h glucose, IAA, ICA512, peak C-peptide, AUC C-peptide	70.59%	2-h glucose, IAA, fasting glucose (IVGTT), ICA512, peak C-peptide, AUC C-peptide, FPIR-to-HOMA-IR ratio	73.40%	2-h glucose, AUC C-peptide, BMI, FPIR-to-HOMA-IR ratio, fasting insulin (IVGTT), HOMAIR, HbA1c, IAA, ICA512, peak C-peptide	73.48%
AUC	age, 2-h glucose, IAA, ICA512, peak C-peptide, AUC C-peptide	0.6779	2-h glucose, IAA, FPIR, fasting glucose (IVGTT), ICA512, peak C-peptide, AUC C-peptide, FPIR-to-HOMA-IR ratio	0.7154	2-h glucose, age, FPIR-to-HOMA-IR ratio, fasting glucose (IVGTT), IAA, peak C-peptide, weight	0.7227

Individual ranking, network-based ranking, and exhaustive search methods were used.

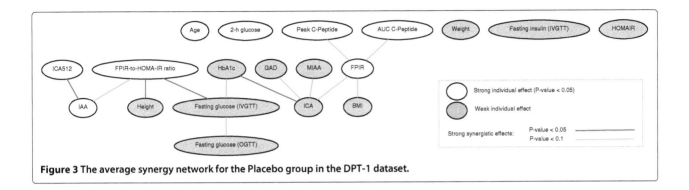

Figure 3 The average synergy network for the Placebo group in the DPT-1 dataset.

closer to the best performing biomarkers by exhaustive search. Furthermore, the average of 1,000 synergy networks obtained from 100×10 generation of synergy network in our embedded cross-validation procedure is provided in Figure 3. This synergy network shows that the nodes 'FPIR-to-HOMA-IR ratio', 'fasting glucose (IVGTT)', and 'ICA' are important nodes with high centrality in the average synergy network. From those three risk factors, FPIR-to-HOMA-IR ratio and fasting glucose (IVGTT) are also among the best biomarkers. This again verifies the effectiveness of our systematic network-based analysis in identifying important factors. Furthermore, as shown in Table 2, our network-based biomarker identification has successfully identified both of those important biomarkers, while the individual-based feature ranking has ignored them. We further provide in Figure 4 the Venn diagrams of selected biomarkers which show the intersection of biomarkers selected by different methods. As one can see, the intersection between biomarkers selected by our network-based ranking and best possible performing biomarkers is larger

than the intersection between biomarkers selected by individual-based ranking and the best possible performing biomarkers.

Conclusions

We have proposed a new feature ranking method that significantly improves the traditional feature ranking by considering the synergistic interaction among potential risk factors. The comprehensive results based on simulated datasets and the dataset from DPT-1 have shown that our network-based feature ranking can help identify more predictive biomarkers than traditional individual-based feature ranking. The set of final biomarkers identified for T1D may help find more predictive models for T1D which may provide early prediction of disease for timely treatment. Furthermore, the improvement obtained by our network-based data-driven method suggests that a more comprehensive systematic data-driven analysis of biomedical variables will be helpful for the better understanding of T1D etiology.

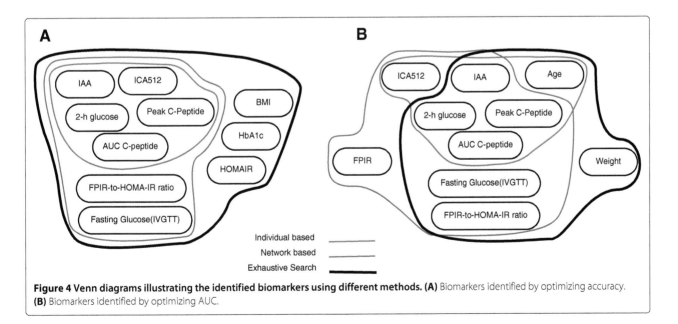

Figure 4 Venn diagrams illustrating the identified biomarkers using different methods. **(A)** Biomarkers identified by optimizing accuracy. **(B)** Biomarkers identified by optimizing AUC.

Additional file

> **Additional file 1: Supplementary material.** The results for network-based analysis based on the treated subjects from DPT-1 as well as a stability analysis for λ are provided in this file.

Abbreviations

AUC: Area under ROC curve; BMI: Body mass index; DPT-1: Diabetes Prevention Trial-Type 1 (DPT-1) study; FPIR: First-phase insulin response; GAD: Glutamic acid decarboxylase; GWAS: Genome-wide association studies; HOMA-IR: Homeostasis model assessment of insulin resistance; IAA: Insulin autoantibodies; ICA: Islet cell autoantibodies; ICA512: Insulinoma-associated protein 2; IVGTTI: IV glucose tolerance test; MCP: Maximum clique problem; MWCP: Maximum weighted clique problem; NP: Nondeterministically polynomial; OGTT: Oral glucose tolerance test; ROC: Receiver operating characteristic; T1D: Type 1 diabetes.

Competing interests

The authors declare that they have no competing interests.

Authors' contributions

AAA designed and implemented the algorithms, designed and carried out the experiments, analyzed the results, and drafted the manuscript. XQ conceived the study, designed the algorithms and the experiments, analyzed the results, and drafted the manuscript. PX, KV, and JPK helped analyze the results and drafted the manuscript. All authors read and approved the final manuscript.

Acknowledgements

The project was supported in part by Award R21DK092845 from the National Institute Of Diabetes and Digestive and Kidney Diseases, National Institutes of Health. The data from the DPT-1 reported here were supplied by the NIDDK Central Repositories. This manuscript was not prepared in collaboration with Investigators of the DPT-1 study and does not necessarily reflect the opinions or views of the DPT-1 study, the NIDDK Central Repositories, or the NIDDK.

Author details

[1]Department of Computer Science and Engineering, University of South Florida, Tampa, FL, 33620, USA. [2]Department of Electrical & Computer Engineering, Texas A&M University, College Station, TX, 77843, USA. [3]Department of Pediatrics, College of Medicine, University of South Florida, Tampa, FL, 33613, USA.

References

1. A Lernmark, J Ott, Sometimes it's hot, sometimes it's not. Nat. Genet. **19**(3), 213–214 (1998)
2. Group, D.S, Secular trends in incidence of childhood IDDM in 10 countries. Diab. Epidemiol. Res. Int. Group. Diab. **39**, 858–864 (1990)
3. Group D.P.T.-T.D.S, Effects of insulin in relatives of patients with type 1 diabetes mellitus. N. Engl. J. Med. **346**, 1685–1691 (2002)
4. G Bottazzo, A Florin-Christensen, D Doniach, Islet-cell antibodies in diabetes mellitus with autoimmune polyendocrine deficiencies. Lancet **2**(7892), 1280–1283 (1974)
5. J Nerup, P Platz, O Andersen, M Christy, J Lyngsoe, J Poulsen, L Ryder, L Nielsen, M Thomsen, A Svejgaard, HL-A antigens and diabetes mellitus. Lancet **2**(7885), 864–866 (1974)
6. P Bougnères, A Valleron, Causes of early-onset type 1 diabetes: toward data-driven environmental approaches. J. Exp. Med. **205**, 2953–2957 (2009)
7. J Krischer, D Cuthbertson, L Yu, T Orban, N Maclaren, R Jackson, W Winter, DA Schatz, J Palmer, GS Eisenbarth, Screening strategies for identification of multiple antibody-positive relatives of individuals with type 1 diabetes. J. Clin. Endocrinol. Metab. **88**, 103–108 (2003)
8. J Sosenko, J Palmer, C Greenbaum, J Mahon, C Cowie, J Krischer, H Chase, N White, B Buckingham, K Herold, D Cuthbertson, J Skyler, The Diabetes Prevention Trial-Type 1 Study Group, Increasing the accuracy of oral glucose tolerance testing and extending its application to individuals with normal glucose tolerance for the prediction of type 1 diabetes. Diab. Care **30**, 38–42 (2007)
9. P Xu, Y Wu, Y Zhu, G Dagne, G Johnson, D Cuthbertson, J Krischer, J Sosenko, J Skyler, The DPT-1 Study Group, Prognostic performance of metabolic indexes in predicting onset of Type 1 Diabetes. Diabetes Care **33**(12), 2508–2513 (2010). doi:10.2337/dc10-0802
10. R Culverhouse, BK Suarez, J Lin, T Reich, A perspective on epistasis: limits of models displaying no main effect. Am. J. Hum. Genet. **70**(2), 461–471 (2002)
11. JH Moore, The ubiquitous nature of epistasis in determining susceptibility to common human diseases. Human. Hered. **56**(1-3), 73–82 (2003)
12. LW Hahn, MD Ritchie, JH Moore, Multifactor dimensionality reduction software for detecting gene–gene and gene–environment interactions. Bioinformatics **19**(3), 376–382 (2003)
13. Y Chung, SY Lee, RC Elston, T Park, Odds ratio based multifactor-dimensionality reduction method for detecting gene–gene interactions. Bioinformatics **23**(1), 71–76 (2007)
14. J Gayan, A Gonzalez-Perez, F Bermudo, M Saez, J Royo, A Quintas, J Galan, F Moron, R Ramirez-Lorca, L Real, A Ruiz, A method for detecting epistasis in genome-wide studies using case-control multi-locus association analysis. BMC Genomics **9**(1), 360 (2008)
15. H Peng, F Long, C Ding, Feature selection based on mutual information: criteria of max-dependency, max-relevance, and min-redundancy. IEEE Trans. Pattern Anal. Mach. Intell. **27**(8), 1226–1238 (2005)
16. Y Saeys, I Inza, P Larra naga, A review of feature selection techniques in bioinformatics. Bioinformatics **23**(19), 2507–2517 (2007)
17. J Watkinson, X Wang, T Zheng, D Anastassiou, Identification of gene interactions associated with disease from gene expression data using synergy networks. BMC Syst. Biol. **2**, 10 (2008)
18. S Sajjadi, A Adl, B Zeng, X Qian, in *Abstracts of the 6th INFORMS Workshop on Data Mining and Health Informatics*. Finding the most discriminating sets of biomarkers by maximum weighted clique (Charlotte, North Carolina, November 12, 2011)
19. P Pardalos, J Xue, The maximum clique problem. J. Glob. Optimization **4**(3), 301–328 (1994)
20. D Bertsekas, *Nonlinear Programming*. (Athena Scientific, Belmont, 1995)
21. W Krzanowski, *Principles of Multivariate Analysis: A User's Perspective*. (Oxford University Press, New York, 1988)
22. CX Ling, J Huang, H Zhang, in *Proceedings of International Joint Conference on Artificial Intelligence*. AUC: a statistically consistent and more discriminating measure than accuracy (Acapulco, Mexico, August 9–15, 2003). vol. 3(Morgan Kaufmann, 2003), pp. 519–524

Subtyping glioblastoma by combining miRNA and mRNA expression data using compressed sensing-based approach

Wenlong Tang[1], Junbo Duan[1], Ji-Gang Zhang[2] and Yu-Ping Wang[1,2,3*]

Abstract

In the clinical practice, many diseases such as glioblastoma, leukemia, diabetes, and prostates have multiple subtypes. Classifying subtypes accurately using genomic data will provide individualized treatments to target-specific disease subtypes. However, it is often difficult to obtain satisfactory classification accuracy using only one type of data, because the subtypes of a disease can exhibit similar patterns in one data type. Fortunately, multiple types of genomic data are often available due to the rapid development of genomic techniques. This raises the question on whether the classification performance can significantly be improved by combining multiple types of genomic data. In this article, we classified four subtypes of glioblastoma multiforme (GBM) with multiple types of genome-wide data (e.g., mRNA and miRNA expression) from The Cancer Genome Atlas (TCGA) project. We proposed a multi-class compressed sensing-based detector (MCSD) for this study. The MCSD was trained with data from TCGA and then applied to subtype GBM patients using an independent testing data. We performed the classification on the same patient subjects with three data types, i.e., miRNA expression data, mRNA (or gene expression) data, and their combinations. The classification accuracy is 69.1% with the miRNA expression data, 52.7% with mRNA expression data, and 90.9% with the combination of both mRNA and miRNA expression data. In addition, some biomarkers identified by the integrated approaches have been confirmed with results from the published literatures. These results indicate that the combined analysis can significantly improve the accuracy of classifying GBM subtypes and identify potential biomarkers for disease diagnosis.

Keywords: Glioblastoma, Data integration, Compressed sensing, Classification, mRNA, miRNA

Introduction

Many diseases including cancers have multiple subtypes. For example, leukemia has four main categories: acute lymphoblastic leukemia (ALL), acute myelogenous leukemia, chronic lymphocytic leukemia, and chronic myelogenous leukemia. Each of these categories can be further divided into different subtypes [1]; for example, ALL can be further subtyped into six types [2]. Glioma has four subtypes, including oligodendroglioma, anaplastic oligodendroglioma, anaplastic astrocytoma, and glioblastoma multiforme (GBM) [3]. Prostate cancer has three major subtypes [4]. An accurate and effective classification of those subtypes based on genomic data will result in personalized treatments of the cancer in terms of a particular subtype. In this article, we are interested in the subtyping of GBM, which is a kind of glioma and is the most common form of malignant brain cancer in adults [5]. There is an increasing interest in classifying multiple subtypes of GBM based on its genomic measurements. Most of the existing works are based on gene expression data only. Benjamin et al. [6] classified two types of GBM in adults and found that the genes EGFR and TP53 were important in discriminating the two subtypes. Nutt et al. [7] built a k-nearest neighbor model with 20 features to classify 28 glioblastomas and 22 anaplastic oligodendrogliomas and found that the class distinctions were significantly associated with survival outcome ($p = 0.05$). Noushmehr et al. [8] separated a subset of samples in GBM from The Cancer Genome Atlas (TCGA) project, which displayed concerted

* Correspondence: wyp@tulane.edu
[1]Department of Biomedical Engineering, Tulane University, New Orleans, LA, USA
[2]Department of Biostatistics and Bioinformatics, Tulane University, New Orleans, LA, USA
Full list of author information is available at the end of the article

hypermethylation at a large number of loci. The datasets we used to subtype GBM are also from TCGA. The subtypes of GBM samples in TCGA includes: pro-neural, neural, classical, and mesenchymal [9]. The GBM data we have tested include both miRNA expression and mRNA expression data. The miRNAs, also called microRNAs, are short non-coding RNA molecules that were recently found in all eukaryotic cells except fungi, algae, and marine plants. The human genome may contain over 1,000 miRNAs [10]. Aberrant expressions of miRNAs have been found to be related to many diseases, including cancers [11,12]. They play an essential role in tissue differentiation during normal development and tumorigenesis [13].

In the last decade, the development of genomic techniques enables the availability of multiple data types on the same patient, such as mRNA or gene expression, SNP, miRNA expression, and copy number variation data. It is well recognized that a more comprehensive analysis result could be obtained based on integrating multiple types of genomic data than using an individual dataset. Soneson et al. [14] investigated the correlation between gene expression and copy number alterations using canonical correlation analysis for leukemia data. A web-based platform, called Magellan, was developed for the integrated analysis of DNA copy number and expression data in ovarian cancer [15], which found significant correlation between gene expression and patient survival. Troyanskaya et al. [16] developed a Bayesian framework to combine heterogeneous data sources to predict gene function with improved accuracy. A kernel-based statistical learning algorithm was also proposed in the combined analysis of multiple genome-wide datasets [17]. In this article, we propose a novel classifier based on the compressed sensing (CS) theory that we have been working with.

The CS technique enables compact storage and rapid transmission of large amounts of information. The technique can be used to extract significant statistical information from high-dimensional datasets [18]. The CS technology has been proven to be a powerful tool in the signal processing and statistics fields. It demonstrates that a compressible signal can be recovered from far fewer samples than that needed by the Nyquist sampling theorem [19]. Our recent work used a CS-based detector (CSD) for subtyping leukemia with gene expression data [20]. The CSD achieved high classification accuracies, with 97.4% evaluated with cross-validation and 94.3% evaluated with an independent dataset. The CSD showed better performance in subtyping two types of leukemia compared to some traditional classifiers such as the support vector machine (SVM), indicating the advantage of the CSD in analyzing high-dimensional genomic data. In this article, we extended the CSD to multiple data types and proposed a detector called MCSD. In particular, we applied the MCSD to the subtyping of four types of

GBM by combining miRNA expression and mRNA expression data. We present a novel combined analysis method based on the CS and demonstrate that the classification performance can significantly be improved in subtyping four types of GBM, with both miRNA expression and mRNA expression data.

Methods and materials
Data collection
The GBM data used in this study are publicly available from the website of TCGA [21]. The patients in the dataset can be classified into four subtypes, i.e., pro-neural, neural, classical, and mesenchymal [9]. The genomic data include miRNA expression (1,510 probes) and mRNA expression data (22,277 probes). We randomly divided the data (including 115 patients with both miRNA and mRNA expression data) into two sets: training and testing datasets. The total number of patients in the training dataset was 60 with 15 patients in each group. The testing dataset had 55 patients, with 17 pro-neural, 3 neural, 17 classical, and 18 mesenchymal subtypes (as listed in Table 1). The same number of patients in each subtype for training data was used for reducing the bias in the model building. Meanwhile, the numbers of patients in training and testing were approximately the same.

For multiple types of genomic data (e.g., miRNA expression data, mRNA expression data, etc.), we used x_{1i} to denote the data vector for the ith sample in data 1 (e.g., miRNA expression), x_{2i} to denote the data vector for the ith sample in data 2 (e.g., mRNA expression), and x_{ni} to denote the data vector for the ith sample in data n. The combined data for the ith sample is $x_i = \left(x_{1i}^T, x_{2i}^T, \ldots, x_{ni}^T \right)^T$, which is arranged in a cascaded manner.

MCSD
Bayesian classifier
To classify a given observation y to one of n classes, we define the actual class ("ground truth") to which it belongs as g; the class to which it is assigned ("decision") as d. The n classes are defined as: $\pi_1, \pi_2, \ldots, \pi_n$. Let $U_{\pi i}(y, g)$ be the

Table 1 GBM subtypes and their corresponding samples used for the training and the testing

Glioblastoma subtypes	Training (total 60)	Testing (total 55)
Pro-neural	15	17
Neural	15	3
Classical	15	17
Mesenchymal	15	18

These datasets are publicly available from the TCGA project.

utility of assigning y, actually from π_g, to π_i. The "utility" is negative relevant to the Bayes Risk (BR) [22], which is the minimum classification error. Thus, we make: $U = 1-BR$. The two-class one-dimensional BR (shaded area in Figure 1) can be calculated by

$$BR = P_2 \int_{-\infty}^{y_0} p_2(y)dy + P_1 \int_{y_0}^{\infty} p_1(y)dy, \qquad (1)$$

where y_0 is the decision boundary, P_1, P_2 are the prior probabilities and $P_1(y), P_2(y)$ are the conditional probability density functions of the two classes, respectively (shown in Figure 1).

Let us extend the BR to n classes and N dimensions. Then Equation (1) can be rewritten as

$$BR_N = \sum_{i=1}^{n} \sum_{\substack{j=1 \\ j \neq i}}^{n} P_j \int_{\Omega i} p_j(y)dy, \qquad (2)$$

where P_j is the prior probability of a given subject belonging to the class π_j, $j = 1,\ldots,n$; $P_j(y)$ is the conditional probability density function of the class π_j, and Ω_i is the Bayesian decision region for class π_i [23].

For multi-class classification, an ideal detector should yield

$$P\big(d = \pi_i | g = \pi_j\big) = \delta_{ij},$$

where

$$\delta_{ij} = \begin{cases} 0, & i \neq j \\ 1, & i = j \end{cases}, \qquad (3)$$

where $P(d = \pi_i | g = \pi_j)$ denotes the probability of

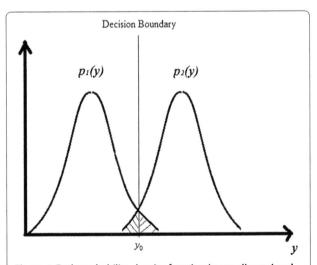

Decision Boundary

$p_1(y)$ $p_2(y)$

y_0

y

Figure 1 Each probability density function is one-dimensional normal distribution (area under each curve sums to 1).

assigning a given observation y, actually belonging to π_j, to π_i. δ_{ij} is the Kronecker's delta.

According to the ideal observer decision theory [22], a decision is selected only if its expected utility is greater than the expected utility of any others. Thus, for any given observation y, we decide $d = \pi_i$ iff

$$E\{U_{\pi_i}(y,g)|y\} > E\{U_{\pi_j}(y,g)|y\}, i \neq j \quad j = 1, 2, \ldots, i-1, i+1, \ldots, n. \qquad (4)$$

From Equation (2) and the relationship of utility and BR, we know "utility" is a number that can be calculated. We denote that number as $U_{i|j}$ to express the utility of assigning a given observation y, actually belonging to π_j, to π_i. The inequality (4) can be written as

$$\sum_{k=1}^{n} U_{i|k} P(g = \pi_k|y) > \sum_{k=1}^{n} U_{j|k} P(g = \pi_k|y), \qquad (5)$$

$$i \neq j, j = 1, 2, \ldots, i-1, i+1, \ldots, n, .$$

We apply Bayes' rule

$$P(g = \pi_k | y) = \frac{P_y(y|g = \pi_k) P(g = \pi_k)}{P_y(y)}, \qquad (6)$$

where $P_y(y|g = \pi_k)$, $k = 1,\ldots,n$, is the probability density function for the signal observations. According to Inequality (5), we decide $d = \pi_i$ iff

$$\sum_{k=1}^{n} U_{i|k} P(g = \pi_k) p_y(y|g = \pi_k) > \sum_{k=1}^{n} U_{j|k} P(g = \pi_k)$$

$$p_y(y|g = \pi_k) \ i \neq j \ j = 1, 2, \ldots, i-1, i+1, \ldots, n. \qquad (7)$$

That is known as maximum likelihood estimation. Specifically, the class label of the testing sample y is given by

$$ID = \underset{l}{\operatorname{argmax}} \left[\sum_{k=1}^{n} U_{l|k} P(g = \pi_k) p_y(y|g = \pi_k) \right]. \qquad (8)$$

If we assume $\pi_1, \pi_2, \ldots, \pi_n$ have the same prior probability, i.e., $P(g = \pi_k) = \frac{1}{n}$. The detector (8) can be rewritten as

$$ID = \underset{l}{\operatorname{argmax}} \left[\sum_{k=1}^{n} U_{l|k} p_y(y|g = \pi_k) \right]. \qquad (9)$$

The calculation of the utility is shown in the Additional file 1.

Dimension reduction using CS
To reduce the dimension of original sample, we design a projection (sparse) matrix Φ, called compress matrix.

The generation of the compress matrix can be formulated as a sparse representation problem as in Equation (10)

$$Y = \Phi S, \tag{10}$$

where $Y = \{y_i\} \in \mathbb{R}^{M \times c}$ is the projected sample, M is the dimension of the sample after the projection, y_i is the ith column in the compressed signal, c is the total number of columns in the compressed signal, $S = \{s_i\} \in \mathbb{R}^{N \times c}$ is the original signal, and N is the dimension of the original signal and $N \gg M$. The matrix $\Phi \in \mathbb{R}^{M \times N}$ is a sparse matrix, with most of the entries '0's. The compress matrix Φ projects the original sample S to a much smaller dimensional signal Y. The original sample may contain redundancy; through this projection, the original sample can significantly be compressed and compactly represented, which usually lead to better classification performance. Suppose we have n groups, with c_1 training samples in group 1, c_2 training samples in group 2, and so forth, c_n training samples in group n, and $c = c_1 + c_2 + \cdots + c_n$ for $S = [s_1, s_2, \ldots, s_c] \in \mathbb{R}^{N \times c}$ and $Y = [y_1, y_2, \ldots, y_c] \in \mathbb{R}^{M \times c}$. The transpose of Equation (10) is

$$S^T \Phi^T = Y^T. \tag{11}$$

Let $(\Phi^T)_j \in \mathbb{R}^{N \times 1}$ denote the jth column of Φ^T, and $(Y^T)_j \in \mathbb{R}^{c \times 1}$ denote the jth column of Y^T, where $j = 1, 2, \ldots, M$. Then Equation (11) can be rewritten as

$$S^T (\Phi^T)_j = (Y^T)_j. \tag{12}$$

The linear system given by (12) is an underdetermined system, which can be solved by using l-1 norm minimization algorithm such as Homotopy method, or the least angle regression method [24]. The l-1 norm optimization problem reads

$$(\Phi^T)_j = \underset{(\Phi^T)_j}{\text{argmin}} \left\| (\Phi^T)_j \right\|_1, \tag{13}$$

subject to

$$S^T (\Phi^T)_j = (Y^T)_j,$$

where $\|(\Phi^T)_j\|_1$ is the l-1 norm of the vector $(\Phi^T)_j$, i.e., the sum of the absolute values of entries in vector $(\Phi^T)_j$. Obviously, the compress matrix Φ projects the original signal $s_i \in \mathbb{R}^{N \times 1}$ to a much smaller dimensional signal $\Phi s_i \in \mathbb{R}^{M \times 1}$. Instead of dealing with the original signal, we only use $\Phi s_i \in \mathbb{R}^{M \times 1}$ and $\Phi \Phi^T \in \mathbb{R}^{M \times M}$ in the subtyping procedure, leading to a fast classification.

Determination of feature vector

We need to select significant features to represent the original data before we classify the data. For each sample, we extracted five feature characteristics [20]: the mean and the standard deviation of each group's standard deviation (*MeanStd, StdStd*), the standard deviation of the means of all the groups (*StdMean*), and the mean and standard deviation of Pearson's linear correlation coefficient (*Mean-Corr, StdCorr*) between the samples and their class label vector. Therefore, for the ith sample, we have a five-dimensional feature vector as follows:

$$V_i = \{MeanStd_i, StdStd_i, StdMean_i, MeanCorr_i StdCorr_i\}$$

where $i = 1, 2, \ldots, N$, and N is the number of samples. Each element in the vector V_i has been normalized by its overall maximum value so that its value is between 0 and 1, i.e., $V_i \in [0, 1]$. A number of M informative features were selected by setting the threshold values of V_i. If a feature is informative or significant, we expect that the values from different patients within the same subtype are similar while the differences among different subtypes are relatively large. In addition, it is easy to understand that, if the correlation between the feature vector and the class label is high, the feature vector can serve as a significant biomarker to distinguish the subtypes. According to the above analysis, matrix Y in Equation (10) is built by those features with low *MeanStd, StdStd, StdCorr* while high *StdMean, MeanCorr*, which are significant for the classification.

Classifier based on CS

In this particular study of subtyping four types of GBM with miRNA expression and mRNA expression data, we make a hypothesis that the data follow a normal distribution. In other words, the probability density function for the data is

$$p_y(\hat{y}|g = \pi_k) = (2\pi\sigma^2)^{-\frac{N}{2}} \exp\left(-\frac{\|\hat{y} - s\|_2^2}{2\sigma^2}\right), \tag{14}$$

where $\hat{y} \in \mathbb{R}^N$ is a given observation; $s \in \mathbb{R}^N$ is the mean of a sample; and σ is the standard deviation of the data.

After compressing the original sample, the probability density function (Equation 14) is still Gaussian but with different mean and standard deviation given by [18]

$$p_y(y|g = \pi_k) = \frac{\exp\left(-\frac{1}{2}(y - \Phi s)^T (\sigma^2 \Phi \Phi^T)^{-1} (y - \Phi s)\right)}{|\sigma^2 \Phi \Phi^T|^{\frac{1}{2}} (2\pi)^{\frac{N}{2}}} \tag{15}$$

where $\hat{y} \in \mathbb{R}^M$ is a compressed observation; $s \in \mathbb{R}^N$ is a known signal and Φ is the compress matrix. The MCSD used in this study is constructed by substituting Equation (15) into Equation (9) for maximum likelihood estimation.

The classification algorithm is described as below.

1. Inputs: training dataset and testing dataset
2. Normalize the rows of the training and the testing datasets to the range of [0,1]
3. Select informative features according to the feature selection criteria
4. Calculate compress matrix $\boldsymbol{\Phi} \in \mathbb{R}^{M \times N}$ by the training dataset by Equation (14)
5. Identify the class of the compressed testing data by Equation (9), where the probability density function is given by Equation (15).

There are many other classifiers such as SVM that can be used. But our purpose here is to show that dimension reduction with the CS can improve subsequent classification and the often used Bayesian classifier is chosen.

Results

We subtyped four types of GBM with multiple genomic data types (e.g., miRNA expression, mRNA expression, and their combinations) from TCGA. The MCSD was first trained by the training data with known class labels, and was then employed to detect subtypes in another independent testing dataset. The classification accuracy by the MCSD was compared with that without using MCSD. The classification performance between using the combined data types and using a single type of data was also compared.

Table 2 shows the comparison of the GBM classification accuracy for the testing dataset, with and without the compress matrix used in our algorithm (see Section "Methods and materials"). The results were obtained on three types of data, i.e., miRNA expression data, mRNA expression data, and their combinations. The classification accuracy is defined as the ratio between the number of correctly labeled samples and the number of total samples. The result calculated by the non-compressed detector had a classification accuracy of 41.8% with miRNA expression data. However, when we used the MCSD to classify the four subtypes, the accuracy of classifying the testing dataset was 69.1%, with 54 selected informative features out of 1,510 features. When we tested the classifiers on the mRNA expression data, the result calculated by the non-compressed detector was 32.7%.

However, the classification result with the MCSD was 52.7%, which employed a subset of the features, 432 out of 22,277 features.

We also tested if the classification performance of the MCSD was better than non-compressed detector in the combined analysis of both miRNA expression and mRNA expression data as shown in Table 2. The subtyping accuracy by the non-compressed detector was 32.7%. The classification accuracy by the MCSD showed a significant improvement over the non-compressed detector. The accuracy was 90.9% (121 informative features selected or 145 informative features selected). The 121 features selected are shown in Additional file 2 with the probes and the corresponding symbols.

Figure 2 demonstrates the classification accuracy when different numbers of informative features were employed. The combined analysis of the two types of genome-wide data was always able to achieve a significant higher subtyping accuracy than any single data type analysis when the same number of informative features were used (with a subset of features less than 450), indicating the advantages of the combined analysis. Figure 2 also shows that the classification accuracy was low when only a few features were used, indicating that the subset was too small to represent the characteristics of the entire dataset. When we increased the number of features used in the MCSD, the classification accuracy went up. The accuracy of classifying the testing dataset reached the highest value, 69.1, 52.7, and 90.9% on the miRNA expression, mRNA expression, and their combinations, respectively. However, more features may also add redundancy and thus cause the decrease of the classification accuracy. Therefore, we conclude that the use of

Table 2 Comparison of classification accuracy between MCSD and non-compressed detector using combined and single data type

	MCSD		Non-compressed accuracy (%)
	Accuracy (%)	Number of features	
Combined analysis	90.9	121	32.7
miRNA	69.1	54	41.8
Gene expression	52.7	432	32.7

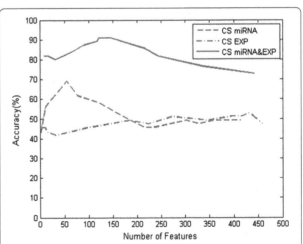

Figure 2 The comparison of the classification accuracies between the combined analysis and the single data type analysis. All of them employed MCSD method to subtype four types of GBM. Note that a significant improvement of the classification accuracy has been achieved by using the combined analysis.

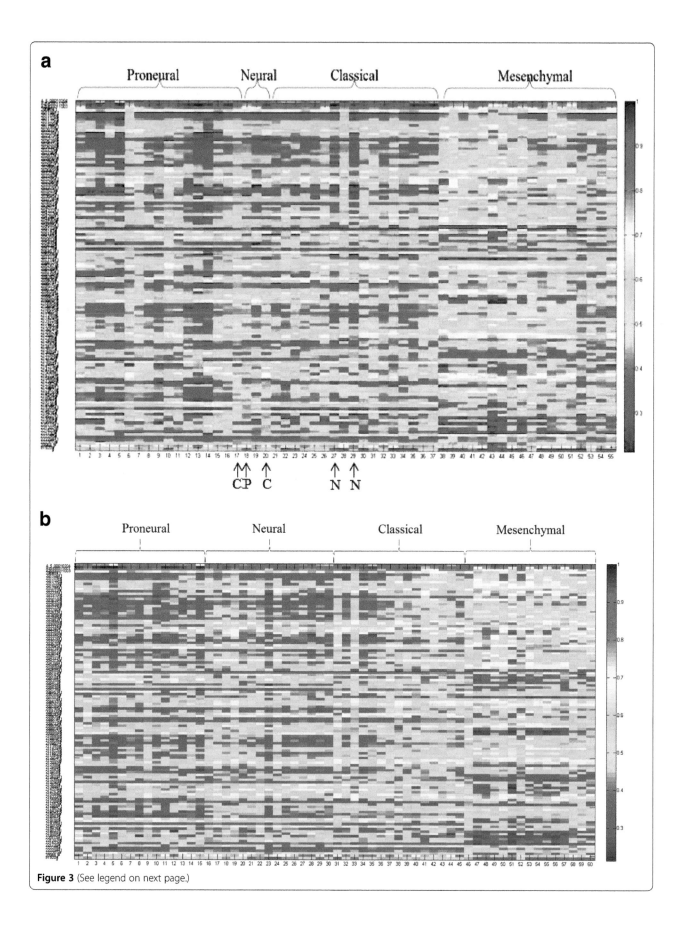

Figure 3 (See legend on next page.)

fewer but significant features will achieve better classification accuracy.

Figure 3a displays the normalized levels of the 121 selected features (118 mRNAs and 3 miRNAs) from both miRNA expression and mRNA expression data for the combined analysis, with the highest classification accuracy of 90.9%. If using the mRNA and miRNA data separately, they only give the accuracy as 49.1 and 47.3%, respectively. The samples with arrows were misclassified to the subtypes pointed by the arrows (e.g., the 17th sample that belongs to pro-neural was misclassified to classical). Each column represents a patient/sample and each row represents a feature (a probe from miRNA expression or mRNA expression data). The four subtypes of GBM are pro-neural, neural, classical, and mesenchymal. Each feature was normalized by the largest value in each row. It can be found that the misclassification only happens among the subtypes of pro-neural, neural, and classical. The number of misclassified samples in each subtype is one sample in pro-neural, two samples in neural, two samples in classical, and zero samples in mesenchymal. The expression levels in the subtype mesenchymal exhibit a significant difference from other three subtypes as shown in Figure 3a. Figure 3b displays the same selected features in the training dataset.

Conclusion and discussion

In this study, we applied the proposed MCSD to subtype four types of GBM: pro-neural, neural, classical, and mesenchymal with multiple genetic data from TCGA. High classification accuracy was achieved by using CS-based technique (i.e., MCSD) along with the combination of multiple datasets. The results from combining two types of genomic data were compared with those from single type of data. Moreover, the performance of the classification with and without MCSD technique had also been compared. The comparisons showed that the CS-based combined analysis of multiple types of genetic data could significantly improve the accuracy of detecting GBM subtypes.

Combining different types of genomic data allows us to interpret the information in the datasets comprehensively. The information from miRNA and mRNA are complementary to each other; so a combined analysis can give a better result than single data type analysis. miRNAs are a recently discovered class of small non-coding RNAs that regulate gene expression [25], which can be combined

with mRNA data for better disease subtyping. However, if no dimension reduction with CS was applied, we found from Table 2 that the classification accuracy from combined analysis was comparable to that from the single mRNA expression because of the redundancy added. The classification performance was significantly improved after we used CS method, indicating that CS may reduce redundancy [26] in the combined datasets and thus improve the classification accuracy.

Informative features/biomarkers selected in this study have also been validated to be associated with GBM and have been reported in the literatures. In the combined data analysis, the 121 features/probes selected (shown in Additional file 2), the 3 miRNA expression probes and 118 mRNA expression probes are listed. Two of the selected miRNAs probes that represent the same miRNA, "hsa-miR-9" (sequence "TCATACAGCTAGATAACCAA"), have been validated to have stemness potential and chemoresistance to GBM cells [27-29], and known to be specifically expressed during brain neurogenesis. In the listed mRNA expression probes, the four probes of "CD44" and the three probes of "ASCL1" are selected. Both of the genes have been validated as biomarkers in subtyping GBM in multiple genomic studies [9,30-32]. It demonstrates the significance of "CD44" and "ASCL1" in discriminating different subtypes of GBM. The three probes from "THBS1" are also selected in the 121 probes list. "THBS1" is a subunit of a disulfide-linked homotrimeric protein. This protein has been shown to play roles in platelet aggregation, angiogenesis, and tumorigenesis [33]. "THBS1" is also a major activator of "TGFB1" and the "TGFB1" expression is associated with GBM [34]. Moreover, it has been found that "TbRII", a receptor of "TGFB1", has a strong relationship with human malignant glioblastoma cells [35]. There are biomarkers listed in Additional file 2 that have not been reported yet. However, they may be potential biomarkers for GBM, deserving further study.

We also performed Gene Ontology (GO) analyses to determine that these genes were enriched in specific GO terms (biological processes). The GO term "antigen processing" and presentation "lymphocyte mediated immunity" ($p = 1.78 \times 10^{-6}$), and several GO terms related to wounding healing [e.g. "response to wounding" ($p = 1.26 \times 10^{-8}$); "wound healing" ($p = 2.44 \times 10^{-6}$)], and cell adhesion [e.g. "biological adhesion" ($p = 6.53 \times 10^{-7}$); "cell adhesion" ($p = 6.41 \times 10^{-7}$)] showed highly significant enrichment for our selected genes. These results were expected. Taking "lymphocyte mediated immunity"-related GO categories as an example, lymphocyte-mediated cellular responses play a critical role in the body's ability to generate an antitumor immune response, and activation status of lymphocytes is an important determinant of sensitivity to tumor-mediated apoptosis [36]. In addition, according to previous studies, the miRNAs we identified are related to glioblastoma. For example, it was found that "has-miR-9" inhibit differentiation of glioblastoma stem cells, and the cal-modulin-binding transcription activator 1 (CAMTA1) as "has-miR-9" target is a tumor suppressor in glio-blastoma [37].

To test the stability of the classification results, the samples in training and testing were randomly rear-ranged ten more times. The number of samples from each subtype in training and testing was maintained the same as in the description in the section "Data collec-tion". The overall classification rate has an average value of 87.1% with a standard deviation of 4.5%, indicating that the results are rather robust.

In summary, we have developed a CS-based technique for combining multiple genomic data to subtype glio-blastoma more accurately. The biomarkers identified with our approaches have also been validated or re-ported in some existing literatures, indicating that the integrated approach can provide comprehensive infor-mation for better disease diagnosis.

Additional files

Additional file 1: Calculation of U for the MCSD.
Additional file 2: List of 121 selected features.

Competing interests
The authors declare that they have no competing interests.

Acknowledgments
This study was supported by the NIH grant R21 LM010042, NSF Advances in Biological informatics (ABI) grant and The Program for Professor of Special Appointment (Eastern Scholar) at Shanghai Institutions of Higher Learning. The authors deeply appreciate the anonymous referees for their valuable suggestions.

Author details
[1]Department of Biomedical Engineering, Tulane University, New Orleans, LA, USA. [2]Department of Biostatistics and Bioinformatics, Tulane University, New Orleans, LA, USA. [3]Center for Systems Biomedicine, Shanghai University for Science and Technology, Shanghai, China.

References
1. *Leukemia-Topic Overview*, http://www.webmd.com/cancer/tc/leukemia-topic-overview
2. KY Yeung, RE Bumgarner, AE Raftery, Bayesian model averaging: development of an improved multi-class, gene selection and classification tool for microarray data. Bioinformatics 21, 2394–2402 (2005)
3. K Seungchan, ER Dougherty, I Shmulevich, KR Hess, SR Hamilton, JM Trent, GN Fuller, W Zhang, Identification of combination gene sets for glioma classification. Mol. Cancer Ther. 1, 1229–1236 (2002)
4. J Lapointe, C Li, JP Higgins, M Rijn, E Bair, K Montgomery, M Ferrari, L Egevad, W Rayford, U Bergerheim, P Ekman, AM DeMarzo, R Tibshirani, D Botstein, PO Brown, JD Brooks, JR Pollack, Gene expression profiling identifies clinically relevant subtypes of prostate cancer. PNAS 101, 811–816 (2003)
5. H Ohgaki, P Kleihues, Epidemiology and etiology of gliomas. Acta Neuropathol. 109, 93–108 (2005)
6. R Benjamin, J Capparella, A Brown, Classification of glioblastoma multiforme in adults by molecular genetics. Cancer J. 9, 82–90 (2003)
7. CL Nutt, DR Mani, RA Betensky, P Tamayo, JG Cairncross, C Ladd, U Pohl, C Hartmann, ME McLaughlin, TT Batchelor, PM Black, AV Deimling, SL Pomeroy, TR Golub, DN Louis, Gene expression-based classification of malignant gliomas correlates better with survival than histological classification. Cancer Res. 63, 1602–1607 (2003)
8. H Noushmehr, DJ Weisenberger, K Diefes, HS Phillips, K Pujara, BP Berman, F Pan, CE Pelloski, EP Sulman, KP Bhat, RGW Verhaak, KA Hoadley, DN Hayes, CM Perou, HK Schmidt, L Ding, RK Wilson, DV Den Berg, H Shen, H Bengtsson, P Neuvial, LM Cope, J Buckley, JG Herman, SB Baylin, PW Laird, K Aldape, The cancer genome atlas research network. Identification of a CpG island methylator phenotype that defines a distinct subgroup of glioma. Cancer Cell 17, 510–522 (2010)
9. RGW Verhaak, KA Hoadley, E Purdom, V Wang, Y Qi, MD Wilkerson, CR Miller, L Ding, T Golub, JP Mesirov, G Alexe, M Lawrence, MO Kelly, P Tamayo, BA Weir, S Gabriel, W Winckler, S Gupta, L Jakkula, HS Feiler, JG Hodgson, CD James, JN Sarkaria, C Brennan, A Kahn, PT Spellman, RK Wilson, TP Speed, JW Gray, M Meyerson et al., Integrated genomic analysis identifies clinically relevant subtypes of Glioblastoma characterized by abnormalities in PDGFRA, IDH1, EGFR, and NF1. Cancer Cell 17, 98–110 (2010)
10. I Bentwich, A Avniel, Y Karov, R Aharonov, S Gilad, O Barad, A Barzilai, P Einat, U Einav, E Meiri, E Sharon, Y Spector, Z Bentwich, Identification of hundreds of conserved and nonconserved human microRNAs. Nat. Genet. 37, 766–770 (2005). doi:10.1038/ng1590
11. P Fasanaro, S Greco, M Ivan, M Capogrossi, F Martelli, MicroRNA: emerging therapeutic targets in acute ischemic diseases. Pharmacol. Ther. 125, 92–104 (2010). doi:10.1016/j.pharmthera.2009.10.003
12. MV Iorio, M Ferracin, C-G Liu, A Veronese, R Spizzo, S Sabbioni, E Magri, M Pedriali, M Fabbri, M Campiglio, S Ménard, JP Palazzo, A Rosenberg, P Musiani, S Volinia, I Nenci, GA Calin, P Querzoli, M Negrini, CM Croce, MicroRNA gene expression deregulation in human breast cancer. Cancer Res. 65, 7065–7070 (2005). doi:10.1158/0008-5472.CAN-05-1783
13. JA Bishop, H Benjamin, H Cholakh, A Chajut, DP Clark, WH Westra, Accurate classification of non-small cell lung carcinoma using a novel MicroRNA-based approach. Clin. Cancer Res. 16, 610–619 (2010)
14. C Soneson, H Lilljebjörn, T Fioretos, M Fontes, Integrative analysis of gene expression and copy number alterations using canonical correlation analysis. BMC Bioinforma 11, 191 (2010)
15. CB Kingsley, W-L Kuo, D Polikoff, A Berchuck, JW Gray, AN Jain, Magellan: a web based system for the integrated analysis of heterogeneous biological data and annotations; application to DNA copy number and expression data in ovarian cancer. Cancer Inf. 2, 10–21 (2006)
16. OG Troyanskaya, K Dolinski, AB Owen, RB Altman, D Botstein, A Bayesian framework for combining heterogeneous data sources for gene function prediction (in *Saccharomyces cerevisiae*). PNAS 100, 8348–8353 (2003)
17. GRG Lanckriet, TD Bie, N Cristianini, MI Jordan, WS Noble, A statistical framework for genomic data fusion. Bioinformatics 20, 2626–2635 (2004)
18. MA Davenport, MB Wakin, RG Baraniuk, *Detection and estimation with compressive measurements. Technical Report*, 2007
19. EJ Cand`es, MB Wakin, An introduction to compressive sampling. IEEE Signal Process. Mag. 25(2), 21–30 (2008)
20. W Tang, H Cao, J Duan, Y-P Wang, A compressed sensing based approach for subtyping of leukemia from gene expression data. J. Bioinfo. Comput. Biol. 9, 631–645 (2011). doi:10.1142/S0219720011005689
21. *TCGA Data*, http://tcga-data.nci.nih.gov/tcga/tcgaHome2.jsp
22. DC Edwards, CE Metz, MA Kupinski, Ideal observers and optimal ROC hypersurfaces in N-class classification. IEEE Trans. Med. Imag. 23, 891–895 (2004)
23. SA Starks, V Kreinovich, Environmentally-oriented processing of multi-spectral satellite images: new challenges for Bayesian methods, in *Proceedings of the 17th International Workshop on Maximum Entropy and Bayesian Methods of Statistical Analysis, Boise, Idaho*, 1998, p. 271

24. B Efron, T Hastie, I Johnstone, R Tibshirani, Least angle regression. Ann. Stat. **32**, 407–451 (2004)

25. S Volinia, GA Calin, C-G Liu, S Ambs, A Cimmino, F Petrocca, R Visone, M Iorio, C Roldo, M Ferracin, RL Prueitt, N Yanaihara, G Lanza, A Scarpa, A Vecchione, M Negrini, CC Harris, CM Croce, A microRNA expression signature of human solid tumors defines cancer gene targets. PNAS **103**, 2257–2261 (2006)

26. Y Tsaig, DL Donoho, Extensions of compressed sensing. Signal Process. **86**, 549–571 (2006)

27. H-M Jeon, Y-W Sohn, S-Y Oh, S-H Kim, S Beck, S Kim, H Kim, ID4 imparts chemoresistance and cancer stemness to glioma cells by derepressing miR-9*-mediated suppression of SOX2. Cancer Res. **71**, 3410–3421 (2011)

28. MH Ko, S Kim, W Hwang, HY Ko, YH Kim, DS Lee, Bioimaging of the unbalanced expression of microRNA9 and microRNA9* during the neuronal differentiation of P19 cells. FEBS J. **275**, 2605–2616 (2008)

29. AS Yoo, BT Staahl, L Chen, GR Crabtree, MicroRNA-mediated switching of chromatin-remodelling complexes in neural development. Nature **460**, 642–646 (2009)

30. Y Liang, M Diehn, N Watson, AW Bollen, KD Aldape, MK Nicholas, KR Lamborn, MS Berger, D Botstein, PO Brown, MA Israel, Gene expression profiling reveals molecularly and clinically distinct subtypes of glioblastoma multiforme. PNAS **102**, 5814–5819 (2005)

31. A Ariza, D López, JL Mate, M Isamat, E Musulen, J Pujol, A Ley, J Navas-palacios, Role of CD44 in the invasiveness of glioblastoma multiforme and the noninvasiveness of meningioma: an immunohistochemistry study. Hum. Pathol. **26**, 1144–1147 (1995)

32. HS Phillips, S Kharbanda, R Chen, WF Forrest, RH Soriano, TD Wu, A Misra, JM Nigro, H Colman, L Soroceanu, PM Williams, Z Modrusan, BG Feuerstein, K Aldape, Molecular subclasses of high-grade glioma predict prognosis, delineate a pattern of disease progression, and resemble stages in neurogenesis. Cancer Cell **9**, 157–173 (2006)

33. AF Galvez, L Huang, MMJ Magbanua, K Dawson, RL Rodriguez, Differential expression of thrombospondin (THBS1) in tumorigenic and nontumorigenic prostate epithelial cells in response to a chromatin-binding soy peptide. Nutr. Cancer **63**, 623–636 (2011). doi:10.1080/01635581.2011.539312

34. B Lin, A Madan, J-G Yoon, X Fang, X Yan, T-K Kim, D Hwang, L Hood, G Foltz, Massively parallel signature sequencing and bioinformatics analysis identifies up-regulation of TGFBI and SOX4 in human glioblastoma. PLoS One **5**, e10210 (2010)

35. A Wesolowska, M Sliwa, B Kaminska, Development of siRNA against TbRII blocking efficiently TGFb1 signaling pathways in glioma cells. Eur. J. Biochem. **271**, 35–58 (2004). Supplement 1 July: abstract number P2.5-05

36. A Chahlavi, P Rayman, A-L Richmond, K Biswas, R Zhang, M Vogelbaum, C Tannenbaum, G Barnett, J-H Finke, Glioblastomas induce T-lymphocyte death by two distinct pathways involving gangliosides and CD70. Cancer Res. **65**, 5428–5438 (2005)

37. J Gil-Ranedo, M Mendiburu-Elicabe, M Garcia-Villanueva, D Medina, M del Alamo, M Izquierdo, An off-target nucleostemin RNAi inhibits growth in human glioblastoma-derived cancer stem cells. PLoS One **6**, e28753 (2011)

Optimal reference sequence selection for genome assembly using minimum description length principle

Bilal Wajid[1,2]*, Erchin Serpedin[1], Mohamed Nounou[3] and Hazem Nounou[4]

Abstract

Reference assisted assembly requires the use of a reference sequence, as a model, to assist in the assembly of the novel genome. The standard method for identifying the best reference sequence for the assembly of a novel genome aims at counting the number of reads that align to the reference sequence, and then choosing the reference sequence which has the highest number of reads aligning to it. This article explores the use of minimum description length (MDL) principle and its two variants, the two-part MDL and Sophisticated MDL, in identifying the optimal reference sequence for genome assembly. The article compares the MDL based proposed scheme with the standard method coming to the conclusion that "counting the number of reads of the novel genome present in the reference sequence" is not a sufficient condition. Therefore, the proposed MDL scheme includes within itself the standard method of "counting the number of reads that align to the reference sequence" and also moves forward towards looking at the model, the reference sequence, as well, in identifying the optimal reference sequence. The proposed MDL based scheme not only becomes the sufficient criterion for identifying the optimal reference sequence for genome assembly but also improves the reference sequence so that it becomes more suitable for the assembly of the novel genome.

1 Introduction

Rissanen's minimum description length (MDL) is an inference tool that learns regular features in the data by data compression. MDL uses "code-length" as a measure to identify the best model amongst a set of models. The model which compresses the data the most and presents the smallest code-length is considered the best model. MDL principle stems from Occam's razor principle which states that "entities should not be multiplied beyond necessity", http://www.cs.helsinki.fi/group/cosco/Teaching/Information/2009/lectures/lecture5a.pdf, stated otherwise, the simplest explanation is the best one, [1-5]. Therefore, MDL principle tries to find the simplest explanation (model) to the phenomenon (data).

The MDL principle has been used successfully in inferring the structure of gene regulatory networks [6-13], compression of DNA sequences [14-18], gene clustering [19-21], analysis of genes related to breast cancer [22-25] and transcription factor binding sites [26].

The article is organized as follows. Section 2 discusses briefly, the variants of MDL and their application to the comparative assembly. Section 3 explains the algorithm used for the purpose. Section 4 elaborates on the simulations carried out to test the proposed scheme. Section 5 explains the results and finally Section 6 points out the main features of this article.

2 Methods

The relevance of MDL to Genome assembly can be realized by understanding that Genome assembly is an inference problem where the task at hand is to infer the novel genome from read data obtained from sequencing. Genome assembly is broadly divided into comparative assembly and de-novo assembly. In comparative assembly, all reads are aligned with a closely related reference sequence. The alignment process may allow one or more mismatches between each individual read and the reference sequence depending on the user. The alignment

*Correspondence: bilalwajidabbas@hotmail.com
[1] Department of Electrical and Computer Engineering, Texas A&M University, College Station,TX 77843-3128, USA
[2] Department of Electrical Engineering, University of Engineering & Technology, Lahore, Punjab 54890, Pakistan
Full list of author information is available at the end of the article

of all the reads creates a "Layout", beyond which the reference sequence is not used any more. The layout helps in producing a consensus sequence, where each base in the sequence is identified by simple majority amongst the bases at that position or via some probabilistic approach. Therefore, this "Alignment-Layout-Consensus" paradigm is used by genome assemblers to infer the novel genome, [27-35].

Comparative assembly, therefore, is an inference problem which requires to identify a model that best describes the data. It begins the process by identifying a model, the "reference sequences", most closely related to the set of reads. It then uses the set of reads to build on this model producing a model which overfits the data, the "novel genome", [27,28,34,36-41]. The task of MDL is to identify the model that best describes the data and within comparative assembly framework the same meaning applies to finding the reference sequences that best describes the set of reads.

MDL presents three variants Two-Part MDL, Sophisticated MDL and MiniMax Regret [1]. The application of these will be briefly discussed in what follows.

2.1 Two-part MDL
Also called old-style MDL, the two-part MDL chooses the hypothesis which minimizes the sum of two components:

A) The code-length of the hypothesis.
B) Code-length of the data given the hypothesis.

The two-part MDL selects the hypothesis which minimizes the sum of the code-length of the hypothesis and code-length of the data given the hypothesis, [1,42-47]. The two-part MDL fits perfectly to the comparative assembly problem. The potential hypothesis which is closely related to the data, in comparative assembly, happens to be the reference sequence whereas the data itself happens to be the read data obtained from the sequencing schemes.

2.2 Sophisticated MDL
The two components of the two-part MDL can be further divided into three components:

A) Encoding the model class: $l(M_i)$, where M_i belongs in model class, and $l(M_i)$ denotes the length of the model class in bits.
B) Encoding the parameters (θ) for any model M_i : $l_i(\theta)$.
C) Code-length of the data given the hypothesis is $log_2 \frac{1}{p_{\bar{\theta}}(\mathcal{X})}$.

where $p_{\bar{\theta}}(\mathcal{X})$ denotes the distribution of the Data $\mathcal{X}$ according to the model $\bar{\theta}$. The three part code-length assessment process again can be converted into a two-part

code-length assessment by combining steps B and C into a single step B.

A) Encoding the model class: $l(M_i)$, where M_i belongs to any Model class.
B) Code-length of the Data given the hypothesis class $(M_i) = l_{(M_i(\mathcal{X}))}$, where $\mathcal{X}$ stands for any data set.

Item (B) above, i.e., the 'length of the encoded data given the hypothesis' is also called the "stochastic complexity" of the model. Furthermore, if the data is fixed, or if item (B) is constant, then the job reduces to minimizing $l(M_i)$, otherwise, reducing part (A), [1,48-53].

2.3 MiniMax regret
MiniMax Regret relies on the minimization of the worst case regret, [49,50,53-59]:

$$\min_{M} \max_{\mathcal{X}} \left[loss(M, \mathcal{X}) - \min_{\widehat{M}} loss(\widehat{M}, \mathcal{X}) \right], \quad (1)$$

where M can be any model, $\widehat{M}$ represents the best model in the class of all models and $\mathcal{X}$ denotes the data. The Regret, $R_{M_i, \mathcal{X}}$, is defined as

$$R_{M_i, \mathcal{X}} = \left[loss(M_i, \mathcal{X}) - \min_{\widehat{M}} loss(\widehat{M}, \mathcal{X}) \right] \quad (2)$$

Here the loss function, $loss(M_i, \mathcal{X})$, could be defined as the code-length of the data $\mathcal{X}$, given the model class M_i. The application of Sophisticated MDL in the framework of comparative assembly will be discussed in what follows.

2.4 Sophisticated MDL and genome assembly
In reference assisted assembly, also known as comparative assembly, a reference sequence is used to assemble a novel genome from a set of reads. Therefore, the best model is the reference sequence most closely related to the novel genome and the data at hand are the set of reads.

However, it should be pointed out that the aim is not to find a general model, rather, the aim is to find a "model that best overfits the data" since there is just one or maybe two instances of the data, based on how many runs of the experiment took place. One "run" is a technical term specifying that the genome was sequenced once and the data was obtained. The term "model that best overfits the data" can be explained using the following example.

Assume one has three Reads {X, Y, and Z} each having n number of bases. Say reference sequences (L) and (M), where (L) = XXYYZZ and (M) = XYZ contains all three reads placed side by side. Since both models contain all the three reads, the stochastic complexity of both (L) and (M) is the same and both overfit the data perfectly. However, since (M) is shorter than (L), therefore (M) is the model of choice on account of being the model that "best" overfits the data.

Table 1 Counting number of reads not enough

S.No.	Reference sequence	Number of bases in genomes	Number of reads found
1	Fibrobacter succinogenes subsp. succinogenes S85 (NC_013410.1)	3842635	157
2	Human Chromosome 21 (AC_000044.1)	32992206	158

The table shows that choosing the reference sequence which has the highest number of reads present is not a sufficient condition. Just by looking at the "Data given the model" ≡ "Number of reads found" one ends up choosing Human Chromosome 21. However, looking at the fact that Chromosome 21 is about 9× larger than S85 one realizes that actually S85 is the model of choice. Furthermore, S85 is a bacterial genome whereas Chromosome 21 comes from a eukaryote genome. PAb1 is also a bacteria, therefore, S85 is most definitely the model of choice.

To formalize the MDL process, the first step would be to identify the following considerations:

A) Encoding the model class: $l(M_i)$, M_i belongs to Model classes.
B) Encoding the parameters (θ) of the Model M_i : $l_i(\theta)$.
C) Code-length of the data given the hypothesis is $log_2 \frac{1}{p_{\hat{\theta}}(\mathcal{D})}$.

The model class in comparative assembly would be the reference (Ref.) sequence itself. The parameters of the model θ, are such that, $\theta \in \{-1, 0, 1\}$. In the process of encoding the model class regions of the genome that are covered by the reads of the unassembled genome are flagged with "1"(s). Areas of the Ref. genome not covered by the reads are flagged as "0"(s), whereas areas of the Ref. genome that are inverted in the novel genome are marked with "−1"(s). In the end, every base of the Ref. sequence is flagged with {−1, 0, 1}. Therefore, the code-length of the parameters of the model is proportional to length of the sequence.

Data given the hypothesis is typically defined as "Number of reads that align to the Ref. sequence". In the case presented below "data given the hypothesis" is defined in an inverted fashion as the "Number of reads that do not align to the reference sequence". These two are interchangeable as the "Total number of reads" is the sum total of the "number of reads that aligned to the Ref." and the "number of reads that do not align to the Ref.".

Table 1 shows that choosing the reference sequence having the highest number of reads present is not a sufficient condition for selecting the optimal reference sequence. The simulation carried out compared two reference sequences Fibrobacter succinogenes S85 (NC_013410.1), [60,61], and Human Chromosome 21 (AC_000044.1), [62-64], with the reads of Pseudomonas aeruginosa PAb1 (SRX000424), [48,65,66]. It shows that in order to choose the optimal reference sequence one has to take into account both the "Code-length of the model" and "Number of reads found" to be the sufficient conditions for choosing the optimal reference sequence.

Therefore, a simple yet novel scheme is proposed for the solution to the problem, see Figure 1 and Table 2. The proposed scheme follows the three assessment process of Sophisticated MDL. The MDL based proposed scheme stores the model class (Ref. sequence), the parameters of the model (where each base of the sequence is flagged with {−1, 0, 1}) and the data given the hypothesis (reads of the novel genome that do not align to the Ref. sequence) is one file. The file is than encoded using either Huffman Coding [67-70] or Shannon-Fano coding [68-71] to determine the code-length. For a simplistic three bits per character coding the code-length is measured according to Equation (3).

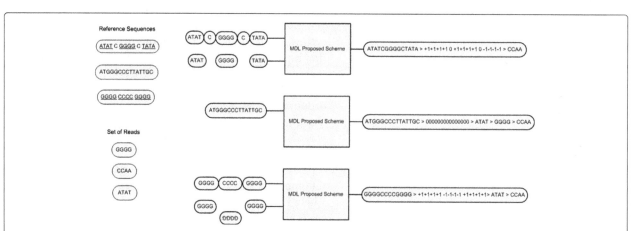

Figure 1 MDL proposed scheme: The output of the system shows that the three components of the encoding scheme are separated from one another by ">". The scheme follows the format "Model > Model given the Data > Data given the hypothesis". In the genome assembly framework the scheme mentioned above translates into "Reference Sequence > Reference Sequence according to the set of reads > Set of reads according to the Reference sequence". "Model given the Data" is identified using {−1, 0, 1}. "1"(s) represent the base locations where the reads are found. "0"(s) represents the locations which are not covered by any read. "−1"(s) represents the locations of the genome that are inverted.

Table 2 Summary of the experiment using three reads {ATAT, GGGG, CCAA} and three reference sequences {1, 2, 3}

| S.No. | Ref. Seq. | Model given by the Data | Reads that do not align to the reference sequence | Data given the hypothesis (Bits) | Regret | Proposed scheme | Code-length (Bits) |
							Code-length (Bits)
1	ATATCGGGGCTATA	1111011110-1-1-1-1	CCAA	12	0	ATATCGGGGCATAT>1111 0 1111 0 -1-1-1-1>CCAA	102
2	ATGGGCCCTTATTGC	000000000000000	ATAT>GGGG>CCAA	42	30	ATGGGCCCTTATTGC> 000000000000000 >ATAT>GGGG >CCAA	138
3	GGGGCCCCGGGG	1111-1-1-1-11111	ATAT>CCAA	27	15	GGGGCCCGGGGG>1111-1-1-1-11111>ATAT>CCAA	105

Regret is defined as $R_{M_i, \mathcal{X}} = \left[loss(M_i, \mathcal{X}) - min_{\widehat{M}} loss(\widehat{M}, \mathcal{X}) \right]$. Here the loss function, $loss(M_i, \mathcal{X})$, happens to be code-length of the data $\mathcal{X}$, given the model class M_j. Whereas, "Data given the hypothesis", is the code-length of the "Reads that do not align to the reference sequence". The code-length in the last column is measured according to Equation (3). The experiment shows that given the MDL proposed scheme Ref. 1 is the optimal choice for a reference sequence.

The proposed scheme not only allows to determine the best model, amongst the pool of models to choose from, but also improves the model to be better suited according to the novel genome to be assembled. This is done by identifying all insertions and inversions, larger than one read length. It then removes those insertions and rectifies those inversions to get a better model, better suited to assemble the novel genome compared to what was started from, see Figures 2 and 3.

$$\text{Code length} = (\text{Length}_{\text{Ref. Seq.}} \times 3)$$
$$+ (\text{Length}_{\text{Parameters of the Model}} \times 3)$$
$$+ (\text{Length}_{\text{Read}} \times 3 \times \text{No. of Unique}$$
$$\text{Unaligned Reads}). \qquad (3)$$

3 MDL algorithm

The pseudo code for analysis using sophisticated MDL and the scheme proposed in Section 2.4 is shown in Algorithm 1.

Given the reference sequence S_R and K set of reads, $\{r_1, r_2, \ldots, r_K\} \in R$, obtained from the FASTQ [72,73] file, the first step in the inference process is to filter all low quality reads. Lines 3–10 filters all the reads that contain the base N in them and also the reads which are of low quality leaving behind a set of O reads to be used for further analysis. This pre-processing step is common to all assemblers. Once all the low quality reads are filtered out, the remaining set of O reads are sorted and then collapsed so that only unique reads remain.

Lines 13–27 describe the implementation of the proposed scheme as defined in Section 2.4. Assume that S_R is l bases long, and the length of each read is p. Therefore, ϕ_{S_R} picks up p bases at a time from S_R and checks whether or not ϕ_{S_R} is present in the set of collapsed reads R'. In the event $\phi_{S_R} \in R'$ then the corresponding location on S_R, i.e., $j \to j + p$ are flagged with "1(s)". If $\phi_{S_R} \notin R'$, then invert

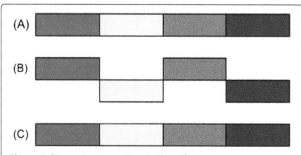

Figure 2 Correcting inversions in the reference sequence.
(a) Reads are derived from the novel sequence. **(b)** The reference sequence, S_R, contains two inversions, shown as yellow and blue regions. **(c)** The sequence generated Θ has both yellow and blue regions rectified. Notice that using a simple ad-hoc scheme of counting the number of reads in the reference sequence one would have made use of **(b)** for assembly of novel genome. However, using MDL one can now use **(c)** for the assembly of the novel genome.

Algorithm 1 MDL Analysis of a Ref. sequence given a set of reads of the unassembled genome.

1: Input reference sequence S_R;
2: Input read data set $\{r_1, r_2, \ldots, r_K\} \in R$;
3: **for** $i : 1 \to K$ **do**
4:      **if** r_i contains base N **then**
5:          remove r_i from the set of reads;
6:      **end if**
7:      **if** r_i has low quality bases **then**
8:          remove r_i from the set of reads;
9:      **end if**
10: **end for**
11: Sort remaining set of reads $\{r_1, r_2, \ldots, r_O\} \in R'$
12: Collapse duplicated reads.
13: **for** $j : 1 \to l$ **do**
14:     read $\phi_{S_R} = \{S_R^j, S_R^{j+1}, \ldots, S_R^{j+p}\}$;
15:     **if** $\phi_{S_R} = r_k \in R'$ **then**
16:         flag 1(s) in locations $j \to j + p$
17:         flag read r_k to be present.
18:     **else**
19:         invert read $\phi_{S_R} \to \psi_{S_R}$
20:         **if** $\psi_{S_R} = r_q \in R'$ **then**
21:             flag -1(s) in locations $j \to j + p$
22:             flag read r_q to be present
23:         **else**
24:             flag 0(s) in locations $j \to j + p$
25:         **end if**
26:     **end if**
27: **end for**
28: **for** $j : 1 \to l$ **do**
29:     modified sequence $\Theta \leftarrow S_R$
30:     identify all inversions by looking at -1 flags
31:     start = start of an inversion
32:     end = end of an inversion
33:     invert genome $\Theta^{\text{start}} \to \Theta^{\text{end}}$
34: **end for**
35: **for** $j : 1 \to l$ **do**
36:     identify all insertions by looking at 0 flags
37:     start = start of an insertion
38:     end = end of an insertion
39:     **if** $\tau_1 < \text{end} - \text{start} < \tau_2$ **then**
40:         remove segment of genome $\Theta^{\text{start}} \to \Theta^{\text{end}}$
41:     **else**
42:         segment of genome is either too large or too small.
43:     **end if**
44: **end for**
45: **for** $i : 1 \to O$ **do**
46:     if read r_i is flagged, remove from R;
47: **end for**
48: ζ = Code-length of encoded modified sequence Θ
49: γ = Code-length of reads R' not present in S_R
50: Total code-length $\xi = \zeta + \gamma$.

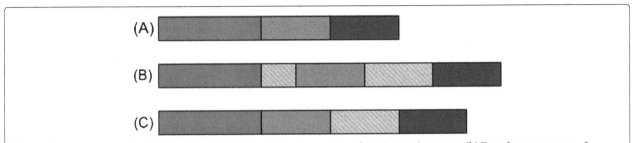

Figure 3 Removing insertions in the reference sequence. (a) Reads are derived from the novel sequence. **(b)** The reference sequence, S_R, contains two insertions, shown as shaded grey boxes. **(c)** The proposed MDL process generates Θ. The process removes only those insertions which are larger than τ_1 but smaller than τ_2; where τ_1 and τ_2 are user-defined. To remove the other insertion the value of τ_2 could be increased.

$\phi_{S_R} \rightarrow \psi_{S_R}$ and check whether or not $\psi_{S_R} \in R'$. If yes, then mark the corresponding location on S_R, i.e., $j \rightarrow j+p$ with "$-1(s)$" and flag ϕ_{S_R} to be present in R'. Otherwise, mark the corresponding locations on S_R as "$0(s)$".

Lines 28–34 generates a modified sequence Θ which has all the inversions rectified in the original sequence S_R. Lines 35–44 identifies all insertions larger than τ_1 and smaller than τ_2 and removes them, see Figure 3. Here τ_1 and τ_2 are user-defined. Care should be taken to avoid removing very large insertions as this may affect the overall performance in deciding the best sequence for genome assembly. Lines 45–47 removes all the reads that are present in the original S_R and the modified sequence Θ identified by flags 1 and -1. In the end the code-lengths are identified by any popular encoding scheme like Huffman [67-70] or Shannon-Fano coding [68-71]. If ξ is the smallest code-length amongst all models then use Θ as a reference for the assembly of the unassembled genome rather than using S_R.

4   Results

Simulations were carried out on both synthetic data as well as real data. At first, the MDL process was analyzed on synthetic data on four different sets of mutations by varying the number and length of {Single nucleotide polymorphisms (SNPs), Inversions, Insertions, and Deletions}. The experiments using synthetic data were carried out by generating a sequence S_N. The set of reads were derived from S_N and sorted using quick sort algorithm [74,75]. Each experiment modified S_N to produce two reference sequences S_{R1} and S_{R2} by randomly putting in the four set of mutations. The choice of the best reference sequence was determined by the code-length generated by the MDL process. See Tables 3, 4, 5, and 6 for results.

Once the robustness of MDL scheme on each of the four types of mutations was confirmed two-set of experiments were carried out on real data using Influenza viruses A, B, and C which belong to the Orthomyxoviridae group. Influenza virus A has five different strains, i.e., {H1N1, H5N1, H2N2, H3N2, H9N2}, while Influenza viruses B and C each have just one. The genomes of Influenza viruses is divided into a number of segments. Influenza virus A and B each have eight segments while virus C has seven segments, [76-78]. Amongst the first segments of each of the viruses only one was randomly selected and then modified to be our novel genome, S_N. Reads were then derived from S_N and compared

Table 3 Variable number of SNPs: the experiment shows the effect of increasing the number of SNPs on choice of the reference sequence

Ref. Seq.	SNPs	No. of inversions	No. of insertions	No. of deletions	Code-length using proposed scheme (Kb)
1	183	52 / 52	62 / 59	62	1815.14
2	224	50 / 51	66 / 58	63	1843.35

S_{R2} has higher number of SNPs as opposed to S_{R1}. The code-length suggests that S_{R1} is the model of choice as it has a smaller code-length. The results show that the MDL scheme works successfully on variable number of SNPs by choosing the model with a lower number of SNPs in them.

Table 4 Variable number of insertions: the experiment shows the effect of increasing the number of insertions on choice of the reference sequence

Ref. Seq.	SNPs	No. of inversions	No. of insertions	No. of deletions	Code-length using proposed scheme (Kb)
1	0	0	136 / 196	0	1200.3
2	0	0	132 / 203	0	1228.25

The location and length of these insertions was chosen randomly. $\frac{136}{196}$ shows that out of 196 insertions in S_{R1} only 136 were removed. The remaining insertions were not recovered due to the choice of τ_1 and τ_2. S_{R2} has higher number of insertions as opposed to S_{R1}. The code-length suggests that S_{R1} is the model of choice as it has a smaller code-length.

Table 5 Variable number of deletions: the experiment shows the effect of increasing the number of deletions on choice of the reference sequence

Ref. Seq.	SNPs	No. of inversions	No. of insertions	No. of deletions	Code-length using proposed scheme (Kb)
1	0	0	2 / 0	182	1997.28
2	0	0	3 / 0	189	2015.35

The location and length of these deletions was chosen randomly. S_{R2} has higher number of deletions as opposed to S_{R1}. The code-length suggests that S_{R1} is the model of choice as it has a smaller code-length. The experiment show that although no insertions were put in the actual sequence yet still two and three insertions were found for S_{R1} and S_{R2}, respectively. This may be due to a large section of reads that could not align to the reference sequence on the edges of these deletions.

with all the seven reference sequences. See Table 7 for results.

The second-set of experiments analyzed the performance of the MDL proposed scheme on reference sequences of various lengths. The test was designed to check whether the proposed scheme chooses smaller reference sequence with more number of unaligned reads or does it choose the optimal reference sequence for assembly. The reads were derived from Influenza A virus (A Puerto Rico 834 (H1N1)) segment 1. All the reference sequences used in this test were also derived from the same H1N1 virus, however, with different lengths, see Tables 8 and 9.

5 Discussion

The MDL proposed scheme was tested using two-set of experiments. In the first set the robustness of the proposed scheme was tested using reference sequences, both real and simulated, having four types of mutations {Inversions, Insertions, Deletions, SNPs} compared to the novel genome. This was done with the help of a program called change_sequence. The program 'change_sequence' requires the user to input Υ_m, the probability of mutation, in addition to the original sequence from which the reference sequences are being derived. It start by traversing along the length of the genome, and each time it arrives at a new base, a uniformly distributed random generator generates a number between 0 and 100. If the number generated is less than or equal to Υ_m a mutation is introduced. Once the decision to introduce a mutation is made, the choice of which mutation still needs to be made. This is done by rolling a biased four sided dice. Where each face of the dice represents a particular mutation, i.e., {inversion, deletion, insertion, and SNPs}. The percentage bias for each face of the dice is provided by the user as four additional inputs, Υ_{inv}, for the percentage bias for inversions, Υ_{indel}, representing percentage bias for insertions and deletions and Υ_{SNP} for SNPs. If

Table 6 Variable number of inversions: the experiment shows the proposed scheme is robust to the number of inversions in the reference sequence

Ref. Seq.	SNPs	No. of inversions	No. of insertions	No. of deletions	Code-length using proposed scheme (Kb)
1	0	0	0	0	586.04
2	0	176 / 176	0	0	586.04

Both S_{R1} and S_{R2} have the same code-length. This is because the MDL scheme not only detected all the inversions for S_{R2} but also recovered all of them. So effectively $S_{R2} \equiv S_{R1}$ after the MDL process as explained in Figure 2.

Table 7 Simulations with Influenza virus A, B, and C

S.No.	Ref. Seq. (Influenza virus)	No. of inversions	No. of deletions	Code-length using proposed scheme (Kb)
1	A, H1N1 (NC_002023.1)	0 / 4	1	254.109
2	A, H5N1 (NC_007357.1)	0 / 4	1	254.109
3	A, H2N2 (NC_007378.1)	0 / 4	1	254.109
4	A, H3N2 (NC_007373.1)	0 / 4	1	254.109
5	A, H9N2 (NC_004910.1)	0 / 4	1	254.109
6	B (NC_002204.1)	4 / 4	1	68.62
7	C (NC_006307.1)	0 / 4	1	254.027

One of the sequences from Influenza virus {A, B, C} was randomly selected and modified to include {SNPs = 7, inversions = 4, deletions = 1, insertions = 3}. As Influenza virus A has five different strains while both Influenza viruses B and C each have one the MDL process was used to compare the seven sequences to determine which is the best reference sequence. Ref. Seq. 6, Influenza virus B was found to have the smallest code-length (68.62 Kb), and is therefore, the model of choice. The experiment also shows that given the optimal reference sequence, in this case Influenza virus B, the MDL process rectifies all inversions (4/4). However, given non-optimal reference sequences, the proposed MDL process is not able to rectify the inversions (0/4). So the proposed algorithm chooses the optimal reference sequence, and given the optimal reference sequence if not all, at least most of the inversions are also corrected.

Table 8 The experiment uses the proposed MDL scheme on the same set of reads but different set of reference sequences

S.No.	Ref. Seq. (%)	No. of unaligned reads	Code-length (KB)	Execution time (s)	Length of new Seq.
1	1	696	128.60	0.046	14
2	2	696	128.73	0.031	47
3	5	693	128.575	0.046	113
4	10	684	127.576	0.046	229
5	25	668	126.615	0.093	565
6	50	650	126.615	0.109	650
7	100	3	14.276	0.078	2342
8	150	2	21.164	0.062	2341
9	200	2	27.808	0.124	2341
10	300	2	41.525	0.140	2341

The set of reads contained 3817 reads all of which were derived from 'Influenza A virus (A Puerto Rico 834 (H1N1)) segment 1, complete sequence'. Out of 3817 reads the method extracted 696 unique reads which were then used in the MDL proposed scheme. All the reference sequences were derived from the same Influenza A (H1N1) virus. Ref. Seq. 1% used in S.No. 1, has a length which is 1% of the actual genome. Similarly Ref. Seq. 25% has a length which is a quarter of the length of the actual genome. All other genomes were derived in a similar way. For, e.g., Ref. Seq. 200% has two H1N1 viruses concatenated together making the length twice that of the original H1N1 sequence. The code-length is calculated using Equation (3). The results show that the MDL proposed scheme chooses the best reference sequence, one which has the smallest code-length as determined by Equation (3). The MDL scheme does not choose smaller reference sequences with more unaligned reads rather than choosing larger reference sequence with smaller unaligned reads. The experiment also proves the correctness of the optimal reference sequence as it chooses Ref. Seq. 7, (shown underlined), since it has the smallest code-length, as the optimal reference sequence. It was Ref. Seq. 7 from which all the reads were derived from. Since the MDL scheme chooses Ref. Seq. 7 as the optimal sequence, the experiment also proves the correctness of the reference sequence chosen.

the dice chooses inversion, insertion or deletion as a possible mutation it still needs to choose the length of the mutation. This requires one last input from the user, Υ_{len}, identifying the upper threshold limit of the length of the mutation. A uniformly distributed random generator generates a number between 1 and Υ_{len}, and the number generated corresponds to the length of the mutation.

The proposed MDL scheme is shown to work successfully, as it chooses the optimal reference sequence to be the one which has smaller number of SNPs, see Table 3, smaller number of insertions, see Table 4, and smaller number of deletions compared to the novel genome, see Table 5. The proposed MDL scheme is also seen to detect and rectify most, if not all, of the inversions present in the reference sequence, see Table 6. Since the code-length of

S_{R1} is the same as S_{R2}, and all the inversions of S_{R2} are rectified, the corrected S_{R2} sequence and S_{R1} sequence are equally good for reference assisted assembly.

The experiment carried out using Influenza viruses is shown in Table 7. One sequence was randomly chosen amongst the seven sequences and modified at random locations, using the same 'change_sequence' program, to form the novel sequence S_N. The novel sequence contained {SNPs = 7, inversions = 4, deletions = 1, insertions = 3} as compared to the original sequence. The MDL process used the reads derived from S_N to compare seven sequences and determined Influenza virus B to be optimal reference sequence as it had the smallest code-length. The MDL process rectified all inversions while only one insertion was found. This meant that the remaining two

Table 9 The exeriment tests the proposed MDL scheme on a single set of reads yet on a number of reference sequences

S.No.	Ref. Seq. (%)	No. of unaligned reads	Code-length (KB)	Length of new Seq.
1	75	172	25.91	1755
2	85	148	25.10	1989
3	95	123	24.20	2223
4	100	109	23.62	2341
5	105	108	24.22	2458
6	115	107	25.50	2692
7	125	106	26.78	2926

The set of reads, 390 in total, were derived from 'Influenza A virus (A Puerto Rico 834 (H1N1)) segment 1, complete sequence' using the ART read simulator for NGS with read length 30, standard deviation 10, and mean fragment length of 100, [79]. Similarly the reference sequences were also derived from the same H1N1 virus. Ref. Seq. 75% used in S.No. 1, has a length which is 75% of the actual genome. Similarly Ref. Seq. 125% has a quarter of the actual genome concatenated with the complete H1N1 genome making the total length 125% of H1N1. All other genomes were derived in a similar way. The code-length is calculated using Equation (3). The results show that the MDL proposed scheme chooses the correct reference sequence, Ref. Seq. 100%, (shown underlined) even when all the contending sequences are closely related to one another in terms of their genome and length.

insertions were smaller than τ_1. The set of reads and Influenza virus B was then fed into MiB (**M**DL-**I**DITAP-**B**ayesian estimation comparative assembly pipeline) [80]. The MiB pipeline removes insertions and rectifies inversions using the MDL proposed scheme. IDITAP is a de-bruijn graph based denovo assembler that **I**dentifies the **D**eletions and **I**nserts them a**T** **A**ppropriate **P**laces. BECA (**B**ayesian **E**stimator **C**omparative **A**ssembler) helps in rectifying all the SNPs. The novel genome reconstructed by the MiB pipeline was one contiguous sequence with a length of 2368 bases and a completeness of 96.62%.

The second-set of experiment tests the correctness of the MDL proposed scheme, by testing the MDL scheme on a single set of reads but on a number of different reference sequences having a wide range of lengths. In the first test 3817 reads were derived from 'Influenza A virus (H1N1) segment 1' without any mutations, of which only 696 reads remained after collapsing duplicate reads. The reference sequences were also derived from the same H1N1 virus, with reference sequence (Ref. Seq.) 1% having a length which is 1% of the actual genome. Similarly Ref. Seq. 25% has a length which is a quarter of the length of the actual genome. Similarly Ref. Seq. 125% has a quarter of the actual genome concatenated with the complete H1N1 genome making the total length 125% of H1N1. All other reference sequences were derived in a similar way, see Table 8. The unique set of reads and the reference sequences were tested using the MDL proposed scheme, where the code-length was calculated using Equation (3). The results show that the MDL scheme does not choose smaller reference sequences with more unaligned reads rather it chooses the correct reference sequence, Ref. Seq. 7. It was Ref. Seq. 7 from which all the reads were derived from. Since the MDL scheme chooses Ref. Seq. 7 as the optimal sequence, this experiment further proves the correctness of the reference sequence chosen.

Lastly, the above experiment was repeated using a single set of reads derived from the same H1N1 virus segment 1, but this time containing mutations. The set of reads, 390 in total, were derived using the ART read simulator for NGS with read length 30, standard deviation 10, and mean fragment length of 100, [PUT ART Reference], see Table 9. The results show that the MDL proposed scheme chooses the correct reference sequence, Ref. Seq. 100%, even when all the contending reference sequences are closely related to one another in terms of their genome and length.

All simulations were carried out on Intel Core i5 CPU M430 @ 2.27 GHz, 4 GB RAM. Execution time of MDL proposed scheme have been provided in Table 8.

6 Conclusions

The article explored the application of Two-Part MDL qualitatively and the application of Sophisticated MDL both qualitatively and quantitatively for selection of the optimal reference sequence for comparatively assembly. The article compared the MDL scheme with the standard method of "counting the number of reads that align to the reference sequence" and found that the standard method is not sufficient for finding the optimal sequence. Therefore, the proposed MDL scheme encompassed within itself the standard method of 'counting the number of reads' by defining it in an inverted fashion as 'counting the number of reads that did not align to the reference sequence' and identified it as the 'data given the hypothesis'. Furthermore, the proposed scheme included the model, i.e., the reference sequence, and identified the parameters (θ_{M_i}) for the model (M_i) by flagging each base of the reference sequence with $\{-1, 0, 1\}$. The parameters of the model helped in identifying inversions and thereafter rectifying them. It also identified locations of insertions. Insertions larger than a user defined threshold τ_1 and smaller than τ_2 were removed. Therefore, the proposed MDL scheme not only chooses the optimal reference sequence but also fine-tunes the chosen sequence for a better assembly of the novel genome.

Experiments conducted to test the robustness and correctness of the MDL proposed scheme, both on real and simulated data proved to be successful.

Competing Interests
The authors declare that they have no competing interests.

Acknowledgements
This article has been partly funded by the University of Engineering and Technology, Lahore, Pakistan (No. Estab/DBS/411, Dated Feb 16, 2008), National Science Foundation grant 0915444 and Qatar National Research Fund—National Priorities Research Program grant 09-874-3-235. The first author would like to extend special thanks to his family. The authors acknowledge the Texas A&M Supercomputing Facility (http://sc.tamu.edu/) for providing computing resources useful in conducting the research reported in this article.

Author details
[1]Department of Electrical and Computer Engineering, Texas A&M University, College Station,TX 77843-3128, USA. [2]Department of Electrical Engineering, University of Engineering & Technology, Lahore, Punjab 54890, Pakistan. [3]Department of Chemical Engineering, Texas A&M University, Doha, Qatar. [4]Department of Electrical and Computer Engineering, Texas A&M University, Doha, Qatar.

References
1. T Roos. (Helsinki University Printing House, Helsinki, 2007), pp. 1–82
2. P Domingos, The role of Occam's razor in knowledge discovery. Data Min Knowledge Discovery. **3**(4), 409–425 (1999)
3. M Li, P Vitányi, *An Introduction to Kolmogorov Complexity and its Applications*. (Springer-Verlag Inc., New York, 2008)
4. C Rasmussen, Z Ghahramani, Occam's razor. Adv. Neural Inf. Process Systs. **13**, 294–300 (2001)
5. V Vapnik, *The Nature of Statistical Learning Theory*. (Springer-Verlag Inc., New York, 2000)
6. J Dougherty, I Tabus, J Astola, Inference of gene regulatory networks based on a universal minimum description length. EURASIP J. Bioinf. Systs. Biol. **2008**, 1–11 (2008)

7. W Zhao, E Serpedin, E Dougherty, Inferring gene regulatory networks from time series data using the minimum description length principle. Bioinformatics. **22**(17), 2129 (2006)

8. V Chaitankar, P Ghosh, E Perkins, P Gong, Y Deng, C Zhang, A novel gene network inference algorithm using predictive minimum description length approach. BMC Systs. Biol. **4**(Suppl 1), S7 (2010)

9. I Androulakis, E Yang, R Almon, Analysis of time-series gene expression data: Methods, challenges, and opportunities. Annual Rev. Biomed. Eng. **9**, 205–228 (2007)

10. H Lähdesmäki, I Shmulevich, O Yli-Harja, On learning gene regulatory networks under the Boolean network model. Mach. Learn. **52**, 147–167 (2003)

11. V Chaitankar, C Zhang, P Ghosh, E Perkins, P Gong, Y Deng, in *IEEE International Joint Conference on Bioinformatics, Systems Biology and Intelligent Computing, 2009. IJCBS09.* Gene regulatory network inference using predictive minimum description length principle and conditional mutual information, (Shanghai, China, 2009), pp. 487–490

12. E Dougherty, Validation of inference procedures for gene regulatory networks. Curr.Genom. **8**(6), 351 (2007)

13. X Zhou, X Wang, R Pal, I Ivanov, M Bittner, E Dougherty, A Bayesian connectivity-based approach to constructing probabilistic gene regulatory networks. Bioinformatics. **20**(17), 2918–2927 (2004)

14. G Korodi, I Tabus, An efficient normalized maximum likelihood algorithm for DNA sequence compression. ACM Trans. Inf Systs. (TOIS). **23**, 3–34 (2005)

15. G Korodi, I Tabus, J Rissanen, J Astola, DNA sequence compression-Based on the normalized maximum likelihood model. IEEE Signal Process. Mag. **24**, 47–53 (2006)

16. I Tabus, G Korodi, J Rissanen, in *IEEE Proceedings on Data Compression Conference, Snowbird.* DNA sequence compression using the normalized maximum likelihood model for discrete regression, (Utah, USA, 2003), pp. 253–262

17. S Evans, S Markham, A Torres, A Kourtidis, D Conklin, in *IEEE Fortieth Asilomar Conference on Signals, Systems and Computers, 2006. ACSSC'06.* An improved minimum description length learning algorithm for nucleotide sequence analysis, (Pacific Grove, CA, 2006), pp. 1843–1850

18. A Milosavljević, J Jurka, Discovery by minimal length encoding: a case study in molecular evolution. Mach. Learn. **12**, 69–87 (1993)

19. R Jornsten, B Yu, Simultaneous gene clustering and subset selection for sample classification via MDL. Bioinformatics. **19**(9), 1100 (2003)

20. I Tabus, J Astola, in *Proceedings of the Seventh International Symposium on Signal Processing and its Applications, ISSPA 2003, vol. 2.* Clustering the non-uniformly sampled time series of gene expression data, (Paris, France, 2003), pp. 61–64

21. A Jain, Data clustering: 50 years beyond K-means. Pattern Recogn. Lett. **31**(8), 651–666 (2010)

22. S Evans, A Kourtidis, T Markham, J Miller, D Conklin, A Torres, MicroRNA target detection and analysis for genes related to breast cancer using MDLcompress. EURASIP J. Bioinf. Syst. Biol. **2007**, 1–16 (2007)

23. E El-Sebakhy, K Faisal, T Helmy, F Azzedin, A Al-Suhaim, in *the 4th ACS/IEEE International Conf. on Computer Systems and Applications.* Evaluation of breast cancer tumor classification with unconstrained functional networks classifier, (Los Alamitos, CA, USA (0), 2006), pp. 281–287

24. A Bulyshev, S Semenov, A Souvorov, R Svenson, A Nazarov, Y Sizov, G Tatsis, Computational modeling of three-dimensional microwave tomography of breast cancer. IEEE Trans. Biomed. Eng. **48**(9), 1053–1056 (2001)

25. D Bickel, *Minimum description length methods of medium-scale simultaneous inference.* (Ottawa Institute of Systems Biology, Tech Rep, Ottawa, 2010)

26. J Schug, G Overton, in *Proc Int Conf Intell Syst Mol Biol, vol. 5.* Modeling transcription factor binding sites with Gibbs sampling and minimum description length encoding, (Halkidiki, Greece, 1997), pp. 268–271

27. B Wajid, E Serpedin, Review of general algorithmic features for genome assemblers for next generation sequencers. Genomics, Proteomics & Bioinformatics. **10**(2), 58–73 (2012)

28. B Wajid, E Serpedin, Supplementary information section: review of general algorithmic features for genome assemblers for next generation sequencers. Genomics, Proteomics & Bioinformatics. **10**(2), 58–73 (2012). [https://sites.google.com/site/bilalwajid786/research]

29. J Miller, S Koren, G Sutton, Assembly algorithms for next-generation sequencing data. Genomics. **95**(6), 315–327 (2010)

30. M Pop, Genome assembly reborn: recent computational challenges. Brief. Bioinf. **10**(4), 354–366 (2009)

31. C Alkan, S Sajjadian, E Eichler, Limitations of next-generation genome sequence assembly. Nat. Methods. **8**, 61–65 (2010)

32. P Flicek, E Birney, Sense from sequence reads: methods for alignment and assembly. Nat. Methods. **6**, S6–S12 (2009)

33. E Mardis, Next-generation DNA sequencing methods. Annu. Rev. Genom. Hum. Genet. **9**, 387–402 (2008)

34. M Schatz, A Delcher, S Salzberg, Assembly of large genomes using second-generation sequencing. Genome Res. **20**(9), 1165 (2010)

35. M Pop, S Salzberg, Bioinformatics challenges of new sequencing technology. Trends Genet. **24**(3), 142–149 (2008)

36. M Pop, A Phillippy, A Delcher, S Salzberg, Comparative genome assembly. Brief. Bioinf. **5**(3), 237 (2004)

37. S Kurtz, A Phillippy, A Delcher, M Smoot, M Shumway, C Antonescu, S Salzberg, Versatile and open software for comparing large genomes. Genome Biol. **5**(2), R12 (2004)

38. M Pop, D Kosack, S Salzberg, Hierarchical scaffolding with Bambus. Genome Res. **14**, 149 (2004)

39. S Salzberg, D Sommer, D Puiu, V Lee, Gene-boosted assembly of a novel bacterial genome from very short reads. PLoS Comput. Biol. **4**(9), e1000186 (2008)

40. M Schatz, B Langmead, S Salzberg, Cloud computing and the DNA data race. Nat. Biotechnol. **28**(7), 691 (2010)

41. S Gnerre, E Lander, K Lindblad-Toh, D Jaffe, Assisted assembly: how to improve a de novo genome assembly by using related species. Genome Biol. **10**(8), R88 (2009)

42. J Rissanen, MDL denoising. IEEE Trans. Inf. Theory. **46**(7), 2537–2543 (2000)

43. J Rissanen, Hypothesis selection and testing by the MDL principle. Comput. J. **42**(4), 260–269 (1999)

44. R Baxter, J Oliver, *MDL and MML: Similarities and Differences, vol. 207.* (Dept. Comput. Sci. Monash Univ, Clayton, Victoria, Australia, Tech. Rep, 1994)

45. P Adriaans, P Vitányi, in *IEEE International Symposium on Information Theory, ISIT.* The power and perils of MDL, Nice, France, 2007), pp. 2216–2220

46. J Rissanen, I Tabus, Kolmogorov's Structure function in MDL theory and lossy data compression Chap. 10 *Adv. Min. Descrip. Length Theory Appl.* (MIT Press, 5 Cambridge Center, Cambridge, MA 02412, 2005), pp. 245–262

47. P Grünwald, P Kontkanen, P Myllymäki, T Silander, H Tirri, in *Proceedings of the Fourteenth conference on Uncertainty in artificial intelligence.* Minimum encoding approaches for predictive modeling (Morgan Kaufmann Publishers Inc, San Francisco, CA, USA, 1998), pp. 183–192

48. B Wajid, E Serpedin, in *2011 IEEE International Workshop on Genomic Signal Processing and Statistics (GENSIPS).* Minimum description length based selection of reference sequences for comparative assemblers, (San Antonio, TX, USA, 2011), pp. 230–233

49. T Silander, T Roos, P Kontkanen, P Myllymäki, in *4th European Workshop on Probabilistic Graphical Models, Hirtshals.* Factorized normalized maximum likelihood criterion for learning Bayesian network structures, (Denmark, 2008), pp. 257–264

50. P Grunwald, A tutorial introduction to the minimum description length principle. Arxiv preprint math/0406077 (2004)

51. J Oliver, D Hand, *Introduction to Minimum Encoding Inference,* (Dept. of Comp. Sc., Monash University, Clayton, Vic. 3168, Australia, Tech. Rep, 1994)

52. C Wallace, D Dowe, Minimum message length and Kolmogorov complexity. Comput. J. **42**(4), 270–283 (1999)

53. P Grünwald, in *Advances in Minimum Description Length: Theory and Applications.* Minimum description length tutorial (MIT Press, 5 Cambridge Center, Cambridge, MA 02412, 2005), pp. 1–80

54. A Barron, J Rissanen, B Yu, The minimum description length principle in coding and modeling. IEEE Trans. Inf. Theory. **44**(6), 2743–2760 (1998)

55. Q Xie, A Barron, Asymptotic minimax regret for data compression, gambling, and prediction. IEEE Trans. Inf. Theory. **46**(2), 431–445 (2000)

56. S De Rooij, P Grünwald, An empirical study of minimum description length model selection with infinite parametric complexity. J. Math. Psychol. **50**(2), 180–192 (2006)

57. T Roos, in *IEEE Information Theory Workshop, 2008. ITW'08.* Monte Carlo estimation of minimax regret with an application to MDL model selection, (Porto, Portugal, 2008), pp. 284–288

58. Y Yang, Minimax nonparametric classification. II. Model selection for adaptation. IEEE Trans. Inf. Theory. **45**(7), 2285–2292 (1999)

59. F Rezaei, C Charalambous, in *IEEE Proceedings International Symposium on Information Theory, 2005. ISIT*. Robust coding for uncertain sources: a minimax approach, (Adelaide, SA, 2005), pp. 1539–1543

60. G Suen, P Weimer, D Stevenson, F Aylward, J Boyum, J Deneke, C Drinkwater, N Ivanova, N Mikhailova, O Chertkov, L Goodwin, C Currie1, D Mead, P Brumm, The complete genome sequence of Fibrobacter succinogenes S85 reveals a cellulolytic and metabolic specialist. PloS one. **6**(4), e18814 (2011)

61. C Luo, D Tsementzi, N Kyrpides, T Read, K Konstantinidis, Direct comparisons of Illumina vs. Roche 454 sequencing technologies on the same microbial community DNA sample. PloS one. **7**(2), e30087 (2012)

62. M Hattori, A Fujiyama, T Taylor, H Watanabe, T Yada, H Park, A Toyoda, K Ishii, Y Totoki, D Choi, *et al*, The DNA sequence of human chromosome 21. Nature. **405**(6784), 311–319 (2000)

63. R Waterston, E Lander, J Sulston, On the sequencing of the human genome. Proc. Natl. Acad. Sci. **99**(6), 3712 (2002)

64. S Istrail, G Sutton, L Florea, A Halpern, C Mobarry, R Lippert, B Walenz, H Shatkay, I Dew, J Miller, *et al*, Whole-genome shotgun assembly and comparison of human genome assemblies. Proc. Natl. Acad. Sci. US Am. **101**(7), 1916 (2004)

65. S Salzberg, D Sommer, D Puiu, V Lee, Gene-boosted assembly of a novel bacterial genome from very short reads. PLoS Comput. Biol. **4**(9), e1000186 (2008)

66. N Croucher, From small reads do mighty genomes grow. Nature Rev. Microbiol. **7**(9), 621–621 (2009)

67. D Huffman, A method for the construction of minimum-redundancy codes. Proc. IRE. **40**(9), 1098–1101 (1952)

68. T Cover, J Thomas, J Wiley, *et al*, *Elements of information theory*, vol. 6. (Wiley InterScience, New York, 1991)

69. M Rabbani, P Jones, *Digital image compression techniques*. (SPIE Publications, Bellingham, Washington, vol. TT7, 1991)

70. J Kieffer, *Data Compression*. (Wiley InterScience, New York, 1971)

71. R Fano, D Hawkins, Transmission of information: a statistical theory of communications. Am. J. Phys. **29**, 793 (1961)

72. P Cock, C Fields, N Goto, M Heuer, P Rice, The Sanger FASTQ file format for sequences with quality scores, and the Solexa/Illumina FASTQ variants. Nucleic Acids Res. **38**(6), 1767–1771 (2010)

73. N Rodriguez-Ezpeleta, M Hackenberg, A Aransay, *Bioinformatics for High Throughput Sequencing*. (Springer Verlag, New York, 2011)

74. C Hoare, Quicksort. Comput. J. **5**, 10 (1962)

75. J Kingston, *Algorithms and Data Structures: Design, Correctness, Analysis*. (Addison-Wesley, Sydney, 1990)

76. K Renegar, Influenza virus infections and immunity: a review of human and animal models. Lab. Animal Sci. **42**(3), 222 (1992)

77. K Myers, C Olsen, G Gray, Cases of swine influenza in humans: a review of the literature. Clin. Infect. Diseases. **44**(8), 1084 (2007)

78. D Suarez, S Schultz-Cherry, Immunology of avian influenza virus: a review. Develop. Comparat. Immunol. **24**(2–3), 269–283 (2000)

79. W Huang, L Li, JR Myers, GT Marth, ART: a next-generation sequencing read simulator. Bioinf. **28**(4), 593–594 (2012)

80. B Wajid, E Serpedin, M Nounou, H Nounou, in *2012 IEEE International Workshop on Genomic Signal Processing and Statistics (GENSIPS'12)*. MiB: a comparative assembly processing pipeline, (Washington DC., USA, 2012)

8

Map-invariant spectral analysis for the identification of DNA periodicities

Ahmad Rushdi[1][*], Jamal Tuqan[2] and Thomas Strohmer[3]

Abstract

Many signal processing based methods for finding hidden periodicities in DNA sequences have primarily focused on assigning numerical values to the symbolic DNA sequence and then applying spectral analysis tools such as the short-time discrete Fourier transform (ST-DFT) to locate these repeats. The key results pertaining to this approach are however obtained using a very specific symbolic to numerical map, namely the so-called Voss representation. An important research problem is to therefore quantify the sensitivity of these results to the choice of the symbolic to numerical map. In this article, a novel algebraic approach to the periodicity detection problem is presented and provides a natural framework for studying the role of the symbolic to numerical map in finding these repeats. More specifically, we derive a new matrix-based expression of the DNA spectrum that comprises most of the widely used mappings in the literature as special cases, shows that the DNA spectrum is in fact invariable under all these mappings, and generates a necessary and sufficient condition for the invariance of the DNA spectrum to the symbolic to numerical map. Furthermore, the new algebraic framework decomposes the periodicity detection problem into several fundamental building blocks that are totally independent of each other. Sophisticated digital filters and/or alternate fast data transforms such as the discrete cosine and sine transforms can therefore be always incorporated in the periodicity detection scheme regardless of the choice of the symbolic to numerical map. Although the newly proposed framework is matrix based, identification of these periodicities can be achieved at a low computational cost.

1 Introduction

Many researchers have noted that the occurrence of repetitive structures in a DNA sequence is symptomatic of a biological phenomena. Specific applications of this observation include identification of diseases [1], DNA forensics [2], and detection of pathogen exposure [3]. Some of these structures are simple repetition of short DNA segments such as exons [4], tandem repeats [5], dispersed repeats [6], and unstable triplet repeats in the noncoding regions [7] while other forms more elaborate patterns such as palindromes [8] and the period-3 component [9-13], a strong periodic characteristic found primarily in genes and pseudogenes [14]. Methods that detect these DNA periodicities are either probabilistic or deterministic. Most of the deterministic techniques rely on spectral analysis of the DNA sequence using the short-time discrete Fourier transform (ST-DFT) [15-17]. The main idea is as follows: given a DNA sequence of length N, numerical values are first assigned to every element in $\mathbb{F} = \{A, C, G, T\}$, where these letters denote the four nucleotides in the DNA, namely the two purines: adenine (A) and guanine (G) and the two pyrimidines: thymine (T) and cytosine (C). A typical DNA double helix is shown in Figure 1.

The symbolic to numerical map is clearly not unique, typically has a biological interpretation, and needs to preserve the specific structure of the DNA sequence under study. One such popular map is the Voss representation $\mathbb{F} \longmapsto \mathbb{D} = \{0, 1\}$, where four binary indicator sequences $x_l(n)$, $l \in \mathbb{F}$, are generated with 1 indicating the presence of a nucleotide and 0 its absence [18]. An example of the mapping of a single DNA strand to $x_l(n), \forall\, l \in \mathbb{F}$ is shown in Figure 2.

Once the DNA symbolic sequence is mapped into numerical version(s), a set of discrete time sequences are generated and are the numerical equivalent of the DNA

*Correspondence: aarushdi@ieee.org
[1] Department of Electrical and Computer Engineering at the University of California, Davis, CA 95616, USA, and is now with Cisco Systems, Inc., San Jose CA 95134, USA
Full list of author information is available at the end of the article

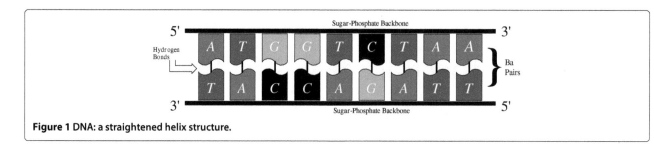

Figure 1 DNA: a straightened helix structure.

sequence. These numerical sequences can then by processed using standard signal processing techniques. In particular, the ST-DFT for each elementary sequences can be computed as

$$X_l(Rn, k) \triangleq \sum_{m=-M+1}^{0} x_l(Rn + m)h(m)e^{-j\frac{2\pi mk}{M}}, \quad (1)$$

$\forall\ l\ \in\ \mathbb{F}$, where n is the window starting point, R is the amount of window shift, and $h(m) = 1$ for $-M + 1 \leq m \leq 0$ and zero otherwise. If $R = 1$, then, the window slides one nucleotide at a time whereas if $R = 3$, the displacement of the window is on a 3-nucleotide basis. Note that the all-ones function $h(m)$ does not affect the value of $X_l(Rn, k)$. However, it serves as a place holder for other filters that can be used to replace it, as will be shown in the following section. One popular application of the ST-DFT based technique that has received considerable attention in the past is the identification of the period-3 component using the DNA spectrum, defined for $R = 3$ as follows

$$S(n) = \sum_{l\in\mathbb{F}} |X_l\left(3n, \frac{M}{3}\right)|^2$$

$$= \sum_{l\in\mathbb{F}} \left| \sum_{m=-M+1}^{0} x_l(3n + m)e^{-j\frac{2\pi m}{3}} \right|^2. \quad (2)$$

A number of researchers have advocated the use of the period-3 component to discriminate between coding and non coding regions (see for example [11,13,16,19-23] to name a few) but the subject remains highly controversial as it is successful for certain genes but does not work for others. To better comprehend the underlying reasons behind this disparity in performance, a new multirate DSP model that provides a full understanding of the inner workings of the DNA periodicity has been first proposed in [24], and studied in details in [25]. This model is shown in Figure 3.

This model provides closed form expressions for the DNA spectrum that generalize and unify some of the already existing results in the literature were obtained. One of these expressions in particular clearly shows that the identification of the period-3 component in the DNA spectrum, a signal processing problem, is equivalent to the detection of the nucleotide distribution disparity in the codon structure of a DNA sequence, a genomic problem. The disparity in the nucleotide distribution within the codon structure of a DNA sequence is termed the codon bias. Using this model, the DNA spectrum is completely characterized by a set of digital sequences, termed the *filtered polyphase sequences*. By processing these sequences, signal processing techniques can potentially have an impact on understanding and detecting biological structures of this nature. From a computational cost perspective, the computation of the DNA spectrum

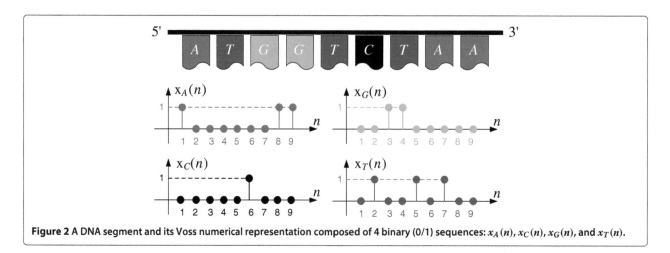

Figure 2 A DNA segment and its Voss numerical representation composed of 4 binary (0/1) sequences: $x_A(n)$, $x_C(n)$, $x_G(n)$, and $x_T(n)$.

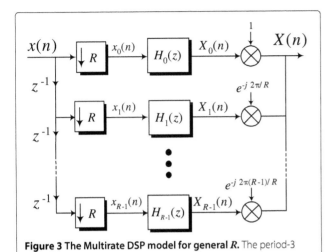

Figure 3 The Multirate DSP model for general R. The period-3 case is easily obtained by setting $R = 3$.

using this model does not require any complex valued operations [26]. This finding is rather surprising given the existence of complex multipliers in the proposed DSP model as clearly illustrated in Figure 3. It is shown that the direct computation of the DNA spectrum using (2) requires essentially double the amount of arithmetic operations compared to the DSP model approach.

It is important, however, to keep in mind that the above conclusions and results were obtained using the Voss symbolic to numerical transformation. A fundamental research issue is to therefore determine the sensitivity of the signal processing based method to the choice of the *symbolic to numerical map*. In particular, the core question here is: how dependent are the above results on the Voss representation? Are these results invariant with respect to the other popular maps in the literature? Can we derive necessary and/or sufficient conditions for the invariance of the DNA spectrum to the symbolic to numerical transformation? Is there a general mathematical framework that can help us generate new symbolic to numerical maps for which the DNA spectrum remains essentially the same? These are the type of questions we address in this article and provide answers to. One approach to answer this question was presented in [27], where a novel framework for the analysis of the equivalence of the mappings used for numerical representation of symbolic data based on signal correlation was presented, along with strong and weak equivalence properties. In [28], we attempted to answer the same question starting at the aforementioned DSP model for a limited set of mappings. Our main goal in this study is to de-embed the symbolic to numerical mapping process from the DNA spectrum computation process. We answer a set of other relevant questions along the way.

A key remark is in order at this point: while the DSP model approach proposed in Figure 3 has many

advantages, it is not well suited for investigating the role of the symbolic to numerical map in the identification of DNA harmonics. It follows that *a completely new paradigm for detecting DNA harmonics is required*. The main contribution of this article is therefore the derivation of a novel matrix-based framework for the computation of the DNA spectrum that is extremely well fitted to the study of the symbolic to numerical transformation. Specifically, we first derive a new matrix-based expression of the DNA spectrum that:

1. comprises most of the existing mappings in the literature as special cases,
2. shows that the DNA spectrum is in fact invariable under all these mappings,
3. generates a necessary condition for the invariance of the DNA spectrum to the symbolic to numerical mapping used to compute it.

Furthermore, the new algebraic framework presented here decomposes the frequency identification problem into several fundamental components that are *totally independent of each other*. It follows that sophisticated digital filters and/or alternative transformations to the DFT such as the discrete cosine, sine, and Hartley transforms can *always* be easily incorporated in the harmonics detection scheme irrespective of the choice of the symbolic to numerical map. Finally, although the newly proposed framework is matrix based, we show that similar to the DSP model approach, the computation of the DNA spectrum using this new framework is very efficient.

The article is organized as follows. In Section 2, we derive a new matrix based framework to efficiently compute the ST-DFT-based spectrum. New expressions for the ST-DFT $X_l(Rn, \frac{M}{R})$ and its magnitude squared $|X_l(Rn, \frac{M}{R})|^2$ are obtained and indicate that these quantities are completely parameterized by some pre-defined matrices. The numerical values of these matrices simply depend on our choice of filtering (e.g., rectangular window versus non-rectangular one versus general FIR filters) as well as our choice of data transform (e.g., the DFT versus the DCT versus the DST).

Using these results, in Section 3, a new expression of the DNA power spectrum is derived and is also completely defined by these matrices. The elegance of this matrix based approach is that it allows the incorporation of general symbolic to numerical maps into the newly derived DNA spectrum expression *provided these generic maps can be expressed as affine transformations of the Voss representation*. This last assumption is motivated by the fact that all the popular maps that are available in the literature satisfy the affine condition. Furthermore, the maps are now completely characterized by the affine transformation (two matrices **A** and **b**) and can be therefore changed *without affecting the remaining matrices* in the DNA spectrum expression. In conclusion, the newly derived DNA spectrum expression is stated as a function of a number of matrices. Each of these matrices captures an essential component of the process (filtering, data transform, symbolic to numerical map) and the elements of each matrix can be changed without affecting the other matrices.

In Section 4 and using the above results, we show that the Voss-based DNA spectrum is essentially invariant under some of the most popular maps in the literature. A **necessary and sufficient** condition for the invariance of the DNA spectrum under any map is also derived.

In Section 5, we show how the special structure of the filtering matrix allows the efficient use of sophisticated digital filters to improve the detection performance of DNA harmonics through the computation of the DNA spectrum. We also show how to replace the DFT by other fast transforms such as the discrete cosine transform (DCT), the discrete sine transform (DST), and the discrete Hartley transform (DHT). Finally, some concluding remarks are mentioned in Section 6. A list of the different notation used in the article is summarized in Table 1.

2 A new algebraic framework for computing the ST-DFT

Given a sequence $x(n)$ of length N, the ST-DFT is typically implemented using a sliding window approach as shown in Figure 4. Windows of length M that overlap with a factor R are first generated to form $\mathbf{x}_r(n), r = 1, 2, \ldots, N_w$, where $N_w = \lceil (N - M + 1)/R \rceil$ is the number of resulting windows. Once we map the DNA sequence into an integer number of numeric sequences γ, given by $x_l(n)$, $l = 1, \ldots, \gamma$ ($\mathbb{F} \longmapsto \mathbb{D}$), the ST-DFT's $X_l(n)$, $l = 1, \ldots, \gamma$ can be found and their squared magnitudes are added to result in the DNA Spectrum $S(n)$ as summarized in Figure 5.

It was shown in [26] that the ST-DFT of $x(n)$ can be written as

$$X(Rn, \frac{M}{R}) = X_0(n) + X_1(n)e^{-j\frac{2\pi}{R}} + \cdots + X_{R-1}(n)e^{-j2\pi\frac{R-1}{R}},$$

(3)

where the quantities $X_r(n), \forall\, r \in \{0, 1, \ldots, R-1\}$ are the so-called filtered polyphase sequences given by

$$X_r(n) \doteq X_r\left(Rn, \frac{M}{R}\right)$$

$$= \sum_{m=r,r+R,\ldots}^{\lfloor\frac{M}{R}-1\rfloor} x(Rn + Rm + r)h_r(m),$$

(4)

$\forall\, r \in \{0, 1, \ldots, R-1\}$. The impulse response $h_r(m)$ is the inverse $\mathcal{Z}$-transform of $H_r(z)$ in Figure 3. Equations (3) and (4) can be used to compute the ST-DFT of a

Table 1 Summary of the article notations

$\mathbb{F}$	$\{A, C, G, T\}$, the field of DNA nucleotides
$\mathbb{V}$	$\{0, 1\}$, the field of Voss binary elements
$\mathbb{D}$	A general field of complex valued elements
$\mathbb{F} \longmapsto \mathbb{D}$	Field mapping operation from set $\mathbb{F}$ to set $\mathbb{D}$, resulting in γ sequences $x_l(n)$, where $l = 1, \ldots, \gamma$. For example, when $\mathbb{D} = \mathbb{V}$, $\mathbb{F} \longmapsto \mathbb{D}$ results in $\gamma = 4$ binary sequences, namely: $x_A(n), x_C(n), x_G(n)$, and $x_T(n)$
$x_l(n)$	A discrete time sequence of length N whose elements belong to the mapped field $\mathbb{D}$
$\mathbf{x}_l(n)$	The nth window of length M, extracted from $x_l(n)$, $l = 1, \ldots, \gamma$
$\hat{\mathbf{x}}_l(n)$	The interleaved version of $\mathbf{x}(n)$ with an interleaving factor $R, l = 1, \ldots, \gamma$
$X_l(Rn, \frac{M}{R})$	The ST-DFT of $x_l(n)$, generated using a sliding window of length M and a window shift of length R
$\Upsilon_v(n)$	$[X_A(n)\, X_C(n)\, X_G(n)\, X_T(n)]^T$, the array of the four $\mathbb{V}$-based ST-DFTs
$\Upsilon_d(n)$	$[X_1(n)\, X_2(n) \ldots X_\gamma(n)]^T$, the array of the γ $\mathbb{D}$-based ST-DFTs
$X_{lr}(n)$	The rth filtered polyphase component of $X_l(n)$, where $r = 0, 1, \ldots, R-1$ and $l = 1, \ldots, \gamma$
$S_v(n)$	The DNA spectrum computed by adding the magnitude squared of the ST-DFT of the four $\mathbb{V}$-based sequences
$S_d(n)$	The DNA spectrum computed by adding the magnitude squared of the ST-DFT of the γ $\mathbb{D}$-based sequences
$\Gamma_l(n)$	$[X_{l0}(n)\, X_{l1}(n) \ldots X_{l,R-1}(n)]^T$, the array of the R filtered polyphase components $X_{lr}(n)$, $r = 0, 1, \ldots, R-1$ and $l = 1, \ldots, \gamma$
$\mathbf{I}_\gamma$	An identity matrix of size $\gamma \times \gamma$
$\mathbf{c}$	An array of length R whose elements are equally spaced on the unit circle
$\mathbf{h}$	An array of length M/R whose elements are all equal to one
$\mathbf{D}$	$\mathbf{c}^*\mathbf{c}^T$, an $R \times R$ matrix
$\mathbf{H}$	$\mathbf{I}_R \otimes \mathbf{h}^T$, an $R \times R$ block matrix of $\frac{M}{R} \times 1$ blocks
$\mathbf{W}$	$\mathbf{H}^H\mathbf{DH}$, an $R \times R$ block matrix of $\frac{M}{R} \times \frac{M}{R}$ blocks
$\mathbf{A}, \mathbf{b}$	The affine transformation matrices of size $\gamma \times 4$ and $\gamma \times 1$, respectively, that map the four $\mathbb{V}$-based sequences into the γ $\mathbb{D}$-based sequences.
$\mathbf{B}$	$\mathbf{A}^H\mathbf{A}$, a 4×4 matrix
$\tilde{\mathbf{C}}$	A complex valued array of R elements
$\tilde{\mathbf{h}}$	A complex valued array of M/R elements
$\tilde{\mathbf{D}}$	$\tilde{\mathbf{C}}^*\tilde{\mathbf{C}}^T$, an $R \times R$ matrix
$\tilde{\mathbf{H}}$	$\mathbf{I}_R \otimes \tilde{\mathbf{h}}^T$, an $R \times R$ block matrix of $\frac{M}{R} \times 1$ blocks
$\tilde{\mathbf{W}}$	$\tilde{\mathbf{H}}^H\tilde{\mathbf{D}}\tilde{\mathbf{H}}$, an $R \times R$ block matrix of $\frac{M}{R} \times \frac{M}{R}$ blocks

discrete time sequence, and subsequently its magnitude squared. In this section, we re-express these equations in matrix form, and then use the new formula to derive an expression for $|X(Rn, \frac{M}{R})|^2$. Throughout the article, vectors and matrices (arrays) are always expressed in bold

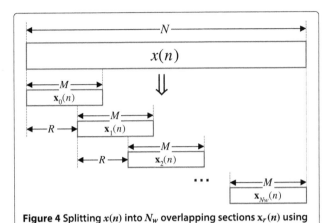

Figure 4 Splitting $x(n)$ into N_w overlapping sections $x_r(n)$ using a sliding window approach.

letters. The notation for the various matrix operations is given in Table 2.

2.1 Matrix formulation of the ST-DFT
Using the defined matrix notation, we can restate Equation (3) as

$$X\left(Rn, \frac{M}{R}\right) = \left[\begin{array}{cccc} 1 & e^{-j\frac{2\pi}{R}} & \cdots & e^{-j2\pi\frac{R-1}{R}} \end{array}\right] \left[\begin{array}{c} X_0(n) \\ X_1(n) \\ \vdots \\ X_{R-1}(n) \end{array}\right]$$

$$\doteq \mathbf{C}^T \Gamma(n). \tag{5}$$

The real valued array

$$\Gamma(n) = [X_0(n) \; X_1(n) \; \ldots \; X_{R-1}(n)]^T \tag{6}$$

Table 2 Notation of matrix operations

$\{\cdot\}^*$	Matrix complex conjugate
$\{\cdot\}^T$	Matrix transpose
$\{\cdot\}^H$	Matrix hermitian
$\{\otimes\}$	Kronecker product of two matrices
$vec\{.\}$	Vector of columns of a matrix

is the vector whose elements are the R filtered polyphase components. Similarly, the complex valued R-element array

$$\mathbf{C} = \left[\begin{array}{cccc} 1 & e^{-j\frac{2\pi}{R}} & \cdots & e^{-j2\pi\frac{R-1}{R}} \end{array}\right]^T \tag{7}$$

is the vector whose elements are the R equispaced phasors located on the unit circle with $\frac{2\pi}{R}$ phase deviations as shown in Figure 6 for $R = 3$ and $R = 8$. Note that

$$\sum_{r=0}^{R-1} e^{-j2\pi r/R} = \frac{1 - (e^{-j2\pi/R})^R}{1 - e^{-j2\pi/R}} = 0, \tag{8}$$

$\forall R \neq 1$, which implies that the sum of elements in $\mathbf{C}$ is equal to 0. This is a key feature of the complex array $\mathbf{C}$ that will be used in later sections to simplify important expressions.

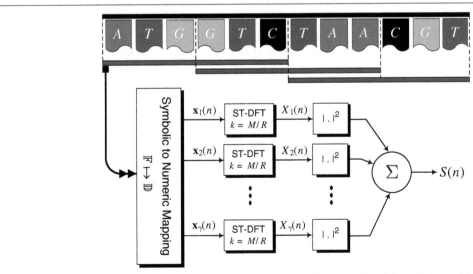

Figure 5 System structure to find the DNA power spectrum $S(n)$ by extracting successive sliding windows of the symbolic DNA sequence, mapping each to γ numeric sequences, finding their DFT's at $k = \frac{M}{R}$, and finally adding the corresponding squared magnitudes. In this example, $N_w = \lceil (N - M + 1)/R \rceil = \lceil (12 - 6 + 1)/3 \rceil = 3$ windows are generated.

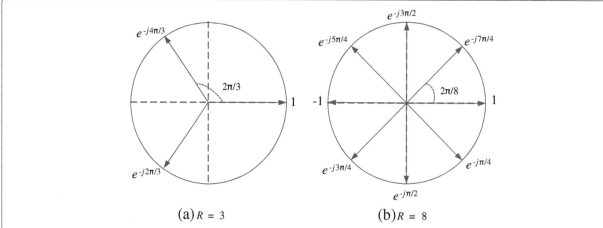

Figure 6 Elements of array **C** of Equation (7), represented as phasors on the unit circle for (a) $R = 3$, and (b) $R = 8$.

On the other hand, we observe that (4) can be written in the following matrix format

$$X_r(n) = \begin{bmatrix} 1 & 1 & \cdots & 1 \end{bmatrix} \begin{bmatrix} x(Rn + r) \\ x(Rn + r + R) \\ \vdots \\ x(Rn + r + M - R) \end{bmatrix} \doteq \mathbf{h}^T \hat{\mathbf{x}}_r(n),$$

(9)

$\forall\ r \in \{0, 1, \ldots, R - 1\}$, where $\mathbf{h}$ is an all-one vector of length M/R, and $\hat{\mathbf{x}}_r(n)$ of length M/R is the rth polyphase component of the window $\mathbf{x}(n)$ of length M. Using (9), the R filtered polyphase components $X_r(n)$ can be arranged in the following array format

$$[X_0(n)\ X_1(n)\ \ldots\ X_{R-1}(n)] = \mathbf{h}^T [\hat{\mathbf{x}}_0(n)\ \hat{\mathbf{x}}_1(n)\ \ldots$$
$$\hat{\mathbf{x}}_{R-1}(n)].$$ (10)

Using the identity

$$vec(\mathbf{A}_1 \mathbf{A}_2) = (\mathbf{I} \otimes \mathbf{A}_1) vec(\mathbf{A}_2),$$ (11)

it follows that

$$\begin{bmatrix} X_0(n) \\ X_1(n) \\ \vdots \\ X_{R-1}(n) \end{bmatrix} = \left(\mathbf{I}_R \otimes \mathbf{h}^T\right) \begin{bmatrix} \hat{\mathbf{x}}_0(n) \\ \hat{\mathbf{x}}_1(n) \\ \vdots \\ \hat{\mathbf{x}}_{R-1}(n) \end{bmatrix},$$

which can be restated in matrix format as

$$\Gamma(n) = \left(\mathbf{I}_R \otimes \mathbf{h}^T\right) \hat{\mathbf{x}}(n) = \mathbf{H}\, \hat{\mathbf{x}}(n),$$ (12)

where $\mathbf{H} \doteq \mathbf{I}_R \otimes \mathbf{h}^T$ is an $R \times R$ matrix of $1 \times \frac{M}{R}$ blocks, given by

$$\mathbf{H} = \begin{bmatrix} \mathbf{h}^T & 0 & \cdots & 0 \\ 0 & \mathbf{h}^T & \ddots & \vdots \\ \vdots & \ddots & \ddots & 0 \\ 0 & \cdots & 0 & \mathbf{h}^T \end{bmatrix} = \begin{bmatrix} 1\,1..1 & \cdots & 0\,0..0 \\ \vdots & \ddots & \vdots \\ 0\,0..0 & \cdots & \underbrace{1\,1..1}_{M/R} \end{bmatrix}.$$

The window $\hat{\mathbf{x}}(n)$ of length M is a block interleaved version of the sliding window $\mathbf{x}(n)$ of length M starting at index n. Generating $\hat{\mathbf{x}}(n)$ can be accomplished by blocking the window $\mathbf{x}(n)$ into an array of R elements per row (hence M/R rows), and then reading the array out column by column. The ST-DFT $X(Rn, \frac{M}{R})$ can therefore be completely identified as a function of $\mathbf{C}$, $\mathbf{h}$, and $\hat{\mathbf{x}}(n)$ as follows

$$X(Rn, \frac{M}{R}) = \mathbf{C}^T \left(\mathbf{I}_R \otimes \mathbf{h}^T\right) \hat{\mathbf{x}}(n) = \mathbf{C}^T \mathbf{H}\, \hat{\mathbf{x}}(n).$$ (13)

The complex row vector $\mathbf{C}^T \mathbf{H}$ is an array of R blocks, each of length $\frac{M}{R}$ as given by

$$\mathbf{C}^T \mathbf{H} = \left[\underbrace{1..1}_{M/R}\ \underbrace{e^{-j\frac{2\pi}{R}}..e^{-j\frac{2\pi}{R}}}_{M/R}\ \cdots\ \underbrace{e^{-j2\pi\frac{R-1}{R}}..e^{-j2\pi\frac{R-1}{R}}}_{M/R} \right],$$

which represents M/R repetitions of the elements in $\mathbf{C}$. Similar to $\mathbf{C}$, the sum of elements in $\mathbf{C}^T \mathbf{H}$ is equal to 0.

2.2 A matrix based expression for the magnitude squared of the ST-DFT

Using (5), the magnitude squared of the ST-DFT can be expressed as

$$\left| X\left(Rn, \frac{M}{R}\right) \right|^2 = X^H(n)X(n) \doteq \Gamma^H(n)\mathbf{D}\Gamma(n),$$ (14)

where matrix $\mathbf{D} \doteq \mathbf{C}^\star \mathbf{C}^T$ is an $R \times R$ matrix given by

$$\mathbf{D} = \begin{bmatrix} 1 & e^{-j\frac{2\pi}{R}} & \cdots & e^{-j2\pi\frac{R-1}{R}} \\ e^{j\frac{2\pi}{R}} & 1 & \ddots & \vdots \\ \vdots & \ddots & \ddots & e^{-j\frac{2\pi}{R}} \\ e^{j2\pi\frac{R-1}{R}} & \cdots & e^{j\frac{2\pi}{R}} & 1 \end{bmatrix}.$$

$\mathbf{D}$ is obviously a right circulant (hence Toeplitz) matrix whose rows and columns are rotated versions of $\mathbf{C}$. Obviously, the sum of any row or column elements in $\mathbf{D}$ is equal to 0. Substituting (12) in (14), or equivalently using (13), implies that the spectrum $S(n)$ can be stated as

$$
\begin{aligned}
\left| X\left(Rn, \frac{M}{R}\right) \right|^2 &= \hat{\mathbf{x}}^H(n) \left[\left(\mathbf{I}_R \otimes \mathbf{h}^T \right)^H \mathbf{C}^\star \right] \\
&\quad \times \left[\mathbf{C}^T \left(\mathbf{I}_R \otimes \mathbf{h}^T \right) \right] \hat{\mathbf{x}}(n) \\
&= \hat{\mathbf{x}}^H(n)\, \mathbf{H}^H \mathbf{D}\, \mathbf{H}\, \hat{\mathbf{x}}(n) \\
&= \hat{\mathbf{x}}^H(n)\, \mathbf{W}\, \hat{\mathbf{x}}(n),
\end{aligned}
\tag{15}
$$

where

$$
\mathbf{W} \doteq \mathbf{H}^H \mathbf{D} \mathbf{H} = (\mathbf{C}^T \mathbf{H})^H (\mathbf{C}^T \mathbf{H}),
$$

is an $R \times R$ matrix of $\frac{M}{R} \times \frac{M}{R}$ blocks, given by

$$
\mathbf{W} = \begin{bmatrix}
1 & e^{-j\frac{2\pi}{R}} & \cdots & e^{-j2\pi \frac{R-1}{R}} \\
e^{j\frac{2\pi}{R}} & 1 & \ddots & \vdots \\
\vdots & \ddots & \ddots & e^{-j\frac{2\pi}{R}} \\
e^{j2\pi \frac{R-1}{R}} & \cdots & e^{j\frac{2\pi}{R}} & 1
\end{bmatrix}
\begin{matrix} \\ \\ \\ \underbrace{}_{\frac{M}{R} \times \frac{M}{R}} \quad \underbrace{}_{\frac{M}{R} \times \frac{M}{R}} \end{matrix}.
$$

Matrix $\mathbf{W}$ can be represented as a Kronecker product of $\mathbf{D}$ and an $\frac{M}{R} \times \frac{M}{R}$ all-one matrix. Note that any row or column in $\mathbf{W}$ is a rotated version of $\mathbf{C}^T \mathbf{H}$, therefore, the sum of the elements of any row or column in $\mathbf{W}$ is equal to 0.

3 The new DNA spectrum expression

A first step towards finding the DNA spectrum $S(n)$ is the symbolic to numeric mapping $\mathbb{F} \longmapsto \mathbb{D}$ as was shown in Figure 5. Once the symbolic DNA sequence is mapped into γ numeric sequence(s), the short-time discrete Fourier transform is applied to each of them and the sum of the squared magnitudes of the ST-DFTs will result in the DNA spectrum at the frequency point $k = \frac{M}{R}$ as given by

$$
S(Rn, k)|_{k=\frac{M}{R}} = \sum_{l=1}^{\gamma} \left| X_l\left(Rn, \frac{M}{R}\right) \right|^2.
\tag{16}
$$

For simplicity, we denote $S(Rn, k)|_{k=\frac{M}{R}}$ as $S(n)$ in the following sections. Several mappings were introduced in the literature using both real and complex numerical values with typical number of sequences $\gamma = 1$ up to 4 to maintain reasonable computation complexity. In this section, we use the results of Section 2 to derive general expressions for the M/R ST-DFT and spectrum for any symbolic to numeric mapping.

3.1 The Voss-based DNA spectrum

The simplest and most commonly used map of a DNA sequence is the Voss representation $\mathbb{F} \longmapsto \mathbb{V}$: that is to form $\gamma = 4$ binary indicator sequences $x_A(n), x_C(n), x_G(n)$, and $x_T(n)$ where a 1 would indicate the presence

of a base and 0 indicates its absence [18]. This approach has been extensively used in relevant genomic research. Note that the four sequences are not linearly independent since for any index n, the four sequences will add up to one. That is

$$
x_A(n) + x_C(n) + x_G(n) + x_T(n) = 1.
$$

This redundancy plays an important role in the derivations of this section. Moreover, it follows that for any length-M window starting at n, the four mapped Voss windows will add up to an all-one length-M sequence and the same fact holds for the interleaved windows

$$
\begin{aligned}
\mathbf{x}_A(n) + \mathbf{x}_C(n) + \mathbf{x}_G(n) + \mathbf{x}_T(n) &= \hat{\mathbf{x}}_A(n) + \hat{\mathbf{x}}_C(n) \\
&\quad + \hat{\mathbf{x}}_G(n) + \hat{\mathbf{x}}_T(n) \\
&= [1\ 1\ \cdots\ 1]^T.
\end{aligned}
\tag{17}
$$

For illustration, Figure 7a shows a sample DNA window that is mapped into the corresponding numeric windows $\mathbf{x}_l(n), \forall l \in \mathbb{F}$ in Figure 7b,d,f,h. With an example interleaving factor $R = 3$, the interleaved windows $\hat{\mathbf{x}}_l(n), \forall l \in \mathbb{F}$ are shown in Figure 7c,e,g,i. Each of the four sequences is a discrete time sequence that can be processed using the analysis of Section 2.

Therefore, the ST-DFT of each sequence can be found using (13) to be

$$
X_l(n) = \mathbf{C}^T \mathbf{H}\, \hat{\mathbf{x}}_l(n),
\tag{18}
$$

$\forall l \in \mathbb{F}$, and the power spectrum of each sequence can hence be derived as in (15) to be

$$
S_l(n) = |X_l(n)|^2 = \hat{\mathbf{x}}_l^H(n)\, \mathbf{W}\, \hat{\mathbf{x}}_l(n),
$$

$\forall l \in \mathbb{F}$. It follows that the Voss-based DNA spectrum $S_v(n)$ is

$$
\begin{aligned}
S_v(n) &\doteq |X_A(n)|^2 + |X_C(n)|^2 + |X_G(n)|^2 + |X_T(n)|^2 \\
&= \sum_{l \in \mathbb{F}} \hat{\mathbf{x}}_l^H(n)\, \mathbf{W}\, \hat{\mathbf{x}}_l(n).
\end{aligned}
\tag{19}
$$

An obvious step at this point is to simplify (19) to avoid the summation over different bases. To do this, we use Equation (18) to arrange the ST-DFT's of $x_l(n), \forall l \in \mathbb{F}$ in the following format

$$
[X_A(n)\ X_C(n)\ X_G(n)\ X_T(n)] = \mathbf{C}^T \mathbf{H}\, [\hat{\mathbf{x}}_A(n)\ \hat{\mathbf{x}}_C(n)
$$
$$
\hat{\mathbf{x}}_G(n)\ \hat{\mathbf{x}}_T(n)].
\tag{20}
$$

Using (11), it follows that

$$
\begin{bmatrix}
X_A(n) \\
X_C(n) \\
X_G(n) \\
X_T(n)
\end{bmatrix}
=
\left(
\begin{bmatrix}
1 & 0 & 0 & 0 \\
0 & 1 & 0 & 0 \\
0 & 0 & 1 & 0 \\
0 & 0 & 0 & 1
\end{bmatrix}
\otimes \mathbf{C}^T \mathbf{H}
\right)
\cdot
\begin{bmatrix}
\hat{\mathbf{x}}_A(n) \\
\hat{\mathbf{x}}_C(n) \\
\hat{\mathbf{x}}_G(n) \\
\hat{\mathbf{x}}_T(n)
\end{bmatrix}.
$$

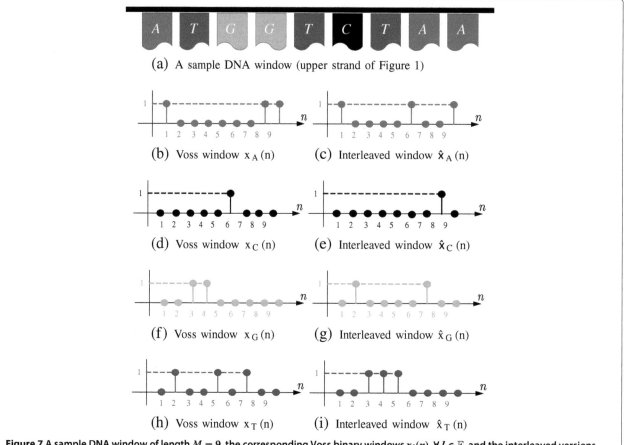

(a) A sample DNA window (upper strand of Figure 1)

(b) Voss window $x_A(n)$

(c) Interleaved window $\hat{x}_A(n)$

(d) Voss window $x_C(n)$

(e) Interleaved window $\hat{x}_C(n)$

(f) Voss window $x_G(n)$

(g) Interleaved window $\hat{x}_G(n)$

(h) Voss window $x_T(n)$

(i) Interleaved window $\hat{x}_T(n)$

Figure 7 A sample DNA window of length $M = 9$, the corresponding Voss binary windows $x_l(n), \forall l \in \mathbb{F}$, and the interleaved versions $\hat{x}_l(n), \forall l \in \mathbb{F}$ with an interleaving factor $R = 3$. The interleaved windows are generated by rearranging the original windows in an $R = 3$-interleaved format. In this example, data points of $\hat{x}_l(n)$ at (1,2,3),(4,5,6),(7,8,9) are mapped from those in $x_l(n)$ at (1,4,7),(2,5,8),(3,6,9).

We define $\Upsilon_v(n)$: the array of the four Voss-based ST-DFTs. It can now be written as

$$\Upsilon_v(n) = \begin{bmatrix} X_A(n) & X_C(n) & X_G(n) & X_T(n) \end{bmatrix}^T$$
$$= \left(\mathbf{I}_4 \otimes \mathbf{C}^T \mathbf{H} \right) \hat{\mathbf{x}}_v(n), \qquad (21)$$

where $\mathbf{I}_4$ is the 4×4 identity matrix, and the vector $\hat{\mathbf{x}}_v(n)$ of length $4M$ is an array of the four Voss interleaved windows starting at index n: $\hat{\mathbf{x}}_l(n), \forall l \in \mathbb{F}$. Using the identity

$$(\mathbf{A}_1 \otimes \mathbf{A}_2)(\mathbf{A}_3 \otimes \mathbf{A}_4) = (\mathbf{A}_1 \mathbf{A}_3 \otimes \mathbf{A}_2 \mathbf{A}_4), \qquad (22)$$

the Voss-based DNA power spectrum can be manipulated into

$$S_v(n) \doteq \Upsilon_v^H(n) \Upsilon_v(n)$$
$$= \hat{\mathbf{x}}_v^H(n) \left(\mathbf{I}_4^H \otimes (\mathbf{C}^T \mathbf{H})^H \right) \left(\mathbf{I}_4 \otimes \mathbf{C}^T \mathbf{H} \right) \hat{\mathbf{x}}_v(n)$$
$$= \hat{\mathbf{x}}_v^H(n) \left(\mathbf{I}_4 \otimes \mathbf{W} \right) \hat{\mathbf{x}}_v(n). \qquad (23)$$

In (23), $\mathbf{I}_4$ and $\mathbf{W}$ are constant matrices $\forall n$. Hence the computation of the spectrum $S_v(n)$ for different windows of a DNA sequence needs only the evaluation of the Voss interleaved array $\hat{\mathbf{x}}_v(n)$.

3.2 Computing the DNA spectrum under general symbolic to numerical maps

Similar to the Voss representation case, any map $\mathbb{F} \longmapsto \mathbb{D}$ of γ sequences can be processed using the analysis of Section 2. It directly follows that the ST-DFT and spectrum of a single sequence are given by

$$X_l(n) = \mathbf{C}^T \mathbf{H} \, \hat{\mathbf{x}}_l(n),$$
$$S_l(n) = \hat{\mathbf{x}}_l^H(n) \, \mathbf{W} \, \hat{\mathbf{x}}_l(n),$$

where $l = 1, 2, \ldots, \gamma$. The array of $\gamma \mathbb{D}$-mapped ST-DFTs $\Upsilon_d(n)$ is therefore given by

$$\Upsilon_d(n) = \begin{bmatrix} X_1(n) & X_2(n) & \ldots & X_\gamma(n) \end{bmatrix}^T$$
$$= \left(\mathbf{I}_\gamma \otimes \mathbf{C}^T \mathbf{H} \right) \hat{\mathbf{x}}_d(n). \qquad (24)$$

The $\mathbb{D}$-based DNA spectrum can easily be shown to be

$$S_d(n) = \hat{\mathbf{x}}_d^H(n) \left(\mathbf{I}_\gamma \otimes \mathbf{W} \right) \hat{\mathbf{x}}_d(n), \qquad (25)$$

where the vector $\hat{\mathbf{x}}_d(n)$ of length γM is an array of the $\gamma \mathbb{D}$-mapped and interleaved windows starting at index n: $\hat{\mathbf{x}}_l(n), \forall l = 1, 2, \ldots, \gamma$. It is clear that for every different map $\mathbb{F} \longmapsto \mathbb{D}$, a new interleaved windows array

$\hat{\mathbf{x}}_d(n)$ has to be evaluated in order to compute a spectrum point $S_d(n)$. In this following, we introduce a different new approach to recompute (25) without updating $\hat{\mathbf{x}}_d(n)$ for every map. Basically, we derive a new expression for $S_d(n)$ in terms of $\hat{\mathbf{x}}_v(n)$ and a new constant matrix so that we incorporate the map dependance in the matrix part rather than the interleaved array part. In other words, since the map $\mathbb{F} \longmapsto \mathbb{V}$ is already well-defined, we use the map $\mathbb{V} \longmapsto \mathbb{D}$ to complete the chain $\mathbb{F} \longmapsto \mathbb{V} \longmapsto \mathbb{D}$ and hence find the spectrum $S_d(n)$. Consider the following affine transformation from Voss sequences to a general array of $\mathbb{D}$-mapped sequences

$$\begin{bmatrix} x_1(n) \\ x_2(n) \\ \vdots \\ x_\gamma(n) \end{bmatrix}_{\gamma \times 1} = \mathbf{A}_{\gamma \times 4} \begin{bmatrix} x_A(n) \\ x_C(n) \\ x_G(n) \\ x_T(n) \end{bmatrix}_{4 \times 1} + \mathbf{b}_{\gamma \times 1},$$

where $\mathbf{A}_{\gamma \times 4}$ and $\mathbf{b}_{\gamma \times 1} = \begin{bmatrix} b_1 & b_2 & \ldots & b_\gamma \end{bmatrix}^T$ are constant possibly complex valued arrays. It follows that the array of the $\mathbb{D}$-mapped interleaved windows $\hat{\mathbf{x}}_d(n)$ can be written in terms of the array the Voss-mapped interleaved windows $\hat{\mathbf{x}}_v(n)$ in the following form

$$\hat{\mathbf{x}}_d(n)_{\gamma M \times 1} = \left(\mathbf{A}_{\gamma \times 4} \otimes \mathbf{I}_M \right) \hat{\mathbf{x}}_v(n)_{4M \times 1} + \hat{\mathbf{b}}_{\gamma M \times 1}, \quad (26)$$

where $\hat{\mathbf{b}}$ defined as

$$\hat{\mathbf{b}} = \left[\underbrace{b_1 .. b_1}_{M} \; \underbrace{b_2 .. b_2} \; \ldots \; \underbrace{b_\gamma .. b_\gamma}_{M} \right]$$

is an array of γ M-element blocks, each block is M repetitions of one element of $\mathbf{b}$. Substituting for $\hat{\mathbf{x}}_d(n)$ in (24) results in a new formula for the array of $\mathbb{D}$-mapped ST-DFTs $\Upsilon_d(n)$ into

$$\Upsilon_d(n) = \left(\mathbf{I}_\gamma \otimes \mathbf{C}^T \mathbf{H} \right) \left[(\mathbf{A} \otimes \mathbf{I}_M) \hat{\mathbf{x}}_v(n) + \hat{\mathbf{b}} \right]. \quad (27)$$

An important result at this point is that the second term in $\Upsilon_d(n)$ is actually equal to 0. This can be verified by reducing it into the following form

$$\left(\mathbf{I}_\gamma \otimes \mathbf{C}^T \mathbf{H} \right) \hat{\mathbf{b}} = \begin{bmatrix} \mathbf{C}^T \mathbf{H} & 0 & \cdots & 0 \\ 0 & \mathbf{C}^T \mathbf{H} & \ddots & \vdots \\ \vdots & \ddots & \ddots & 0 \\ 0 & \cdots & 0 & \mathbf{C}^T \mathbf{H} \end{bmatrix} \begin{bmatrix} \hat{\mathbf{b}}_1 \\ \hat{\mathbf{b}}_2 \\ \vdots \\ \hat{\mathbf{b}}_\gamma \end{bmatrix}.$$

Recall that the sum of elements in $\mathbf{C}^T \mathbf{H}$ is equal to 0. Therefore, since $\hat{\mathbf{b}}_l$ is a constant vector, the product $(\mathbf{C}^T \mathbf{H}) . \hat{\mathbf{b}}_l$ is equal to 0, $\forall l = 1, 2, \ldots, \gamma$ and hence

$$\left(\mathbf{I}_\gamma \otimes \mathbf{C}^T \mathbf{H} \right) \hat{\mathbf{b}} = \sum_{l=1}^{\gamma} \left(\mathbf{C}^T \mathbf{H} \right) . \hat{\mathbf{b}}_l = 0. \quad (28)$$

The ST-DFTs array $\Upsilon_d(n)$ can therefore be simplified using the Kronecker product identity (22) into

$$\Upsilon_d(n) = \left(\mathbf{I}_\gamma \otimes \mathbf{C}^T \mathbf{H} \right) (\mathbf{A} \otimes \mathbf{I}_M) \hat{\mathbf{x}}_v(n)$$
$$= \left(\mathbf{A} \otimes \mathbf{C}^T \mathbf{H} \right) \hat{\mathbf{x}}_v(n). \quad (29)$$

It follows that the $\mathbb{D}$-based DNA spectrum $S_d(n)$ is

$$S_d(n) = \Upsilon_d^H(n) \Upsilon_d(n)$$
$$= \hat{\mathbf{x}}_v^H(n) \left(\mathbf{A} \otimes \mathbf{C}^T \mathbf{H} \right)^H \left(\mathbf{A} \otimes \mathbf{C}^T \mathbf{H} \right) \hat{\mathbf{x}}_v(n)$$
$$= \hat{\mathbf{x}}_v^H(n) \left(\mathbf{B} \otimes \mathbf{W} \right) \hat{\mathbf{x}}_v(n), \quad (30)$$

where $\mathbf{B} \doteq \mathbf{A}^H \mathbf{A}$. Equation (30) indicates that when a certain symbolic to numeric mapping $\mathbb{F} \longmapsto \mathbb{D}$ is used, the DNA power spectrum $S_d(n)$ is completely defined in terms of the Voss-based interleaved array $\hat{\mathbf{x}}_v(n)$ along with constant matrices $\mathbf{W}$ and $\mathbf{B}$ which is a function of the transformation matrix $\mathbf{A}$ ($\mathbb{V} \longmapsto \mathbb{D}$). Note that if $\mathbf{A} = \mathbf{I}_4$ then $\mathbf{B} = \mathbf{I}_4$ at which (30) reduces to (23) which is the Voss-based spectrum case.

4 Invariance of the DNA spectrum under popular mappings

The results found in Section 3 can be applied to some mappings that are widely used in the literature. In specific, by defining the corresponding transformation matrices $\mathbf{A}$ and $\mathbf{B}$ ($\mathbb{V} \longmapsto \mathbb{D}$), closed form expressions for $S_d(n)$ are obtained. Furthermore, for a number of mappings, we show that the $\mathbb{D}$-mapped spectrum $S_d(n)$ is in fact a scaled version of the Voss-based spectrum $S_v(n)$.

4.1 Four-to-four ($\gamma = 4$) representations

In this scheme, each Voss sequence is scaled by a possibly complex coefficient according to the following transformations matrices

$$\mathbf{A} = \begin{bmatrix} a & 0 & 0 & 0 \\ 0 & c & 0 & 0 \\ 0 & 0 & g & 0 \\ 0 & 0 & 0 & t \end{bmatrix}, \quad \mathbf{B} = \begin{bmatrix} |a|^2 & 0 & 0 & 0 \\ 0 & |c|^2 & 0 & 0 \\ 0 & 0 & |g|^2 & 0 \\ 0 & 0 & 0 & |t|^2 \end{bmatrix},$$

where a, a, g, and t are real or complex coefficients used to scale $x_A(n), x_C(n), x_G(n)$, and $x_T(n)$, respectively. The corresponding array of ST-DFT's $\Upsilon_d(n)$ is subsequently given by

$$\Upsilon_d(n) = \left(\begin{bmatrix} a & 0 & 0 & 0 \\ 0 & c & 0 & 0 \\ 0 & 0 & g & 0 \\ 0 & 0 & 0 & t \end{bmatrix} \otimes \mathbf{C}^T \mathbf{H} \right) \hat{\mathbf{x}}_v(n),$$

and the DNA spectrum $S_d(n)$ is

$$S_d(n) = \hat{\mathbf{x}}_v^H(n) \left(\begin{bmatrix} |a|^2 & 0 & 0 & 0 \\ 0 & |c|^2 & 0 & 0 \\ 0 & 0 & |g|^2 & 0 \\ 0 & 0 & 0 & |t|^2 \end{bmatrix} \otimes \mathbf{W} \right) \hat{\mathbf{x}}_v(n).$$

Now, we extend this result to certain transformations where numeric values of the scale factors a, a, g, and t are specified.

§ *Tetrahedral mapping.*

The so-called tetrahedral representation has been proposed in [13,29]. In this mapping scheme, the four nucleotides are represented by four equal length vectors oriented towards the corners of a tetrahedron. Projecting the basic tetrahedron on a plane will reduce the dimensionality of the representation to two. This mapping can be defined by the mapping matrix

$$\mathbf{A} = \begin{bmatrix} 1+j & 0 & 0 & 0 \\ 0 & -1+j & 0 & 0 \\ 0 & 0 & -1-j & 0 \\ 0 & 0 & 0 & 1-j \end{bmatrix}.$$

It can be easily seen that in this case: $|a| = |c| = |g| = |t| = \sqrt{2}$ which implies that $\mathbf{B} = 2\mathbf{I}_4$. The corresponding DNA spectrum is

$$S_d(n) = 2\hat{\mathbf{x}}_v^H(n)(\mathbf{I}_4 \otimes \mathbf{W})\hat{\mathbf{x}}_v(n) = 2S_v(n). \quad (31)$$

Since $\mathbf{B} = \alpha\mathbf{I}_4 (\alpha = 2)$, the tetrahedral-based DNA spectrum is a scaled version of the Voss-based spectrum.

§ *Quaternion mapping.*

A more involved step is to replace the complex number set of the tetrahedral mapping with its algebraic generalization, the set of quaternions. Quaternions have been used to map DNA sequences $\mathbb{F} \longmapsto \mathbb{H}$ [30] and are simply defined as hypercomplex numbers given by $p \in \mathbb{H} = \{a + bi + cj + dk | a,b,c,d \in \mathbb{R}\}$, where i,j,k are complex coefficients such that $i^2 = j^2 = k^2 = ijk = -1$ and $|p| = \sqrt{pp^*} = \sqrt{a^2 + b^2 + c^2 + d^2}$. The transformation matrix is given by

$$\mathbf{A} = \begin{bmatrix} i+j+k & 0 & 0 & 0 \\ 0 & i-j-k & 0 & 0 \\ 0 & 0 & -i-j+k & 0 \\ 0 & 0 & 0 & -i+j-k \end{bmatrix}.$$

In this case, $|a| = |c| = |g| = |t| = \sqrt{3}, \mathbf{B} = 3\mathbf{I}_4$. The corresponding DNA spectrum is

$$S_d(n) = 3\hat{\mathbf{x}}_v^H(n)(\mathbf{I}_4 \otimes \mathbf{W})\hat{\mathbf{x}}_v(n) = 3S_v(n) \quad (32)$$

§ *Higher order mappings.*

An alternative Quaternion transformation is given by $\mathbf{A} = \mathrm{diag}(1+i+j+k, 1+i-j-k, 1-i-j+k, 1-i+j-k)$, which results in $\mathbf{B} = 4\mathbf{I}_4$ and consequently $S_d(n) =$

$4S_v(n)$. In general, for a complex representation system with η dimensions and equal amplitude coefficients: $\mathbf{B} = \eta\mathbf{I}_4$ and hence the spectrum $S_d(n) = \eta S_v(n)$.

4.2 Four-to-three ($\gamma = 3$) mappings

In order to reduce the DNA spectrum computational cost, several mappings have been proposed with smaller numbers of sequences.

§ *Z-curve mapping.*

One such important symbolic-to-numeric map is the Z-curve mapping [24], which is a unique 3-dimensional curve representation whose sequences have values 1 and -1. One advantage of the Z-curve mapping is that each of its three sequences has a biological interpretation. This scheme is given by

$$\begin{bmatrix} x(n) \\ y(n) \\ z(n) \end{bmatrix} = 2 \begin{bmatrix} 1 & 0 & 1 & 0 \\ 1 & 1 & 0 & 0 \\ 1 & 0 & 0 & 1 \end{bmatrix} \begin{bmatrix} x_A(n) \\ x_C(n) \\ x_G(n) \\ x_T(n) \end{bmatrix} - \begin{bmatrix} 1 \\ 1 \\ 1 \end{bmatrix}.$$

Therefore, the transformation matrices are

$$\mathbf{A} = \begin{bmatrix} 2 & 0 & 2 & 0 \\ 2 & 2 & 0 & 0 \\ 2 & 0 & 0 & 2 \end{bmatrix}, \quad \mathbf{B} = \begin{bmatrix} 12 & 4 & 4 & 4 \\ 4 & 4 & 0 & 0 \\ 4 & 0 & 4 & 0 \\ 4 & 0 & 0 & 4 \end{bmatrix}.$$

Matrix $\mathbf{B}$ in this case can be written as

$$\mathbf{B} = 4 \left(\mathbf{I}_4 + \begin{bmatrix} 1 & 1 & 1 & 1 \\ 0 & 0 & 0 & 0 \\ 0 & 0 & 0 & 0 \\ 0 & 0 & 0 & 0 \end{bmatrix} + \begin{bmatrix} 1 & 0 & 0 & 0 \\ 1 & 0 & 0 & 0 \\ 1 & 0 & 0 & 0 \\ 1 & 0 & 0 & 0 \end{bmatrix} \right)$$

$$= 4(\mathbf{I}_4 + \mathbf{B}_1 + \mathbf{B}_2).$$

Note that the term involving $\mathbf{B}_1$ in $S_d(n)$ can be manipulated into

$$S_d(n)|_{\mathbf{B}_1} = \hat{\mathbf{x}}_v^H(n)(\mathbf{B}_1 \otimes \mathbf{W})\hat{\mathbf{x}}_v(n)$$

$$= 4\hat{\mathbf{x}}_v^H(n) \begin{bmatrix} \mathbf{W} & \mathbf{W} & \mathbf{W} & \mathbf{W} \\ 0 & 0 & 0 & 0 \\ 0 & 0 & 0 & 0 \\ 0 & 0 & 0 & 0 \end{bmatrix} \begin{bmatrix} \hat{\mathbf{x}}_A(n) \\ \hat{\mathbf{x}}_C(n) \\ \hat{\mathbf{x}}_G(n) \\ \hat{\mathbf{x}}_T(n) \end{bmatrix}$$

$$= 4\hat{\mathbf{x}}_v^H(n) \begin{bmatrix} \mathbf{W}\left(\sum_{l\in\mathbb{F}}\hat{\mathbf{x}}_l(n)\right) \\ 0 \\ 0 \\ 0 \end{bmatrix}.$$

Recall from (17) that $\sum_{l\in\mathbb{F}}\hat{\mathbf{x}}_l(n) = [1\ 1\cdots 1]^T$. Take also into consideration that the sum of elements of any row or column in $\mathbf{W}$ is equal to 0. This implies that $\mathbf{W}\left(\sum_{l\in\mathbb{F}}\hat{\mathbf{x}}_l(n)\right) = \mathbf{0}$, at which it is easy to see that $S_d(n)|_{\mathbf{B}_1} = 0$. Similarly, $S_d(n)|_{\mathbf{B}_2} = 0$. Therefore, only the first term in $\mathbf{B}$ contributed to $S_d(n)$ at which the Z-curve mapped DNA spectrum is a scaled version of the

Voss-based DNA spectrum

$$S_d(n) = \hat{\mathbf{x}}_v^H(n)\,(4\mathbf{I_4} \otimes \mathbf{W})\,\hat{\mathbf{x}}_v(n) = 4S_v(n). \qquad (33)$$

This ratio is consistent with the result we first derived in [24] for $R = 3$, but is now shown to be general for any value of R. We are now ready to state an important result.

Theorem. *Necessary and Sufficient condition for the invariance of the DNA spectrum.* Consider the following affine transformation from Voss sequences to a general array of $\mathbb{D}$-mapped sequences

$$\begin{bmatrix} x_1(n) \\ x_2(n) \\ \vdots \\ x_\gamma(n) \end{bmatrix}_{\gamma \times 1} = \mathbf{A}_{\gamma \times 4} \begin{bmatrix} x_A(n) \\ x_C(n) \\ x_G(n) \\ x_T(n) \end{bmatrix}_{4 \times 1} + \mathbf{b}_{\gamma \times 1},$$

where $\mathbf{A}_{\gamma \times 4}$ and $\mathbf{b}_{\gamma \times 1} = \begin{bmatrix} b_1 & b_2 & \dots & b_\gamma \end{bmatrix}^T$ are constant possibly complex valued arrays. Define the 4×4 matrix $\mathbf{B} = \mathbf{A}^H \mathbf{A}$. The DNA spectrum is invariant under this map, i.e., $S_d(n) = \alpha S_v(n)$ if the transformation matrix $\mathbf{B}$ can be written as $\mathbf{B} = \alpha \mathbf{I_4} + \sum_i \mathbf{B}_i$, where $\mathbf{B}_i$ holds constant rows and/or constant columns $\forall\, i$.

The proof follows by simply observing that if $\mathbf{B}_i$ has constant rows and/or constant columns, then $S_d(n)|_{\mathbf{B}_i} = 0$. We remind the reader at this point that the vector $\mathbf{b}_{\gamma \times 1}$ has no bearing on the invariance of the DNA spectrum.

§ *Simplex mapping.*

The simplex mapping is essentially another tetrahedron structured mapping that aims to eliminate the computational redundancy. Its transformations matrices are

$$\mathbf{A} = \frac{1}{3} \begin{bmatrix} 0 & -\sqrt{2} & -\sqrt{2} & 2\sqrt{2} \\ 0 & \sqrt{6} & -\sqrt{6} & 0 \\ 3 & -1 & -1 & -1 \end{bmatrix}, \quad \mathbf{B} = \frac{1}{3} \begin{bmatrix} 1 & -1 & -1 & -1 \\ -1 & 1 & -1 & -1 \\ -1 & -1 & 1 & -1 \\ -1 & -1 & -1 & 1 \end{bmatrix}.$$

Matrix $\mathbf{B}$ in this case can be written as

$$\mathbf{B} = \left(\frac{4}{3}\right)\left(\mathbf{I_4} - \frac{1}{4}\begin{bmatrix} 1 & 1 & 1 & 1 \\ 1 & 1 & 1 & 1 \\ 1 & 1 & 1 & 1 \\ 1 & 1 & 1 & 1 \end{bmatrix}\right) = \left(\frac{4}{3}\right)(\mathbf{I_4} + \mathbf{B_1}).$$

Similar to the $\mathcal{Z}$-curve case, $S_d(n)|_{\mathbf{B_1}} = 0$. It follows that the simplex-based DNA spectrum is also a scaled version of the Voss-based spectrum, and is given by

$$S_d(n) = \hat{\mathbf{x}}_v^H(n)\left(\frac{4}{3}\mathbf{I_4} \otimes \mathbf{W}\right)\hat{\mathbf{x}}_v(n) = \left(\frac{4}{3}\right)S_v(n). \qquad (34)$$

This ratio is consistent with the result in [31] which was limited to direct DFT and is now shown to be extended to M/R ST-DFT with any value of R.

4.3 Four-to-two ($\gamma = 2$) mappings

Pairing couples of nucleotides together was proposed in the literature in order to exploit certain biological features in addition to complexity reduction. For example, it was suggested that exons are rich in nucleotides C and G, while introns have more A and T [29]. This claim inspired the transformation

$$\mathbf{A} = \begin{bmatrix} 0 & 1 & 1 & 0 \\ -1 & 0 & 0 & -1 \end{bmatrix}, \quad \mathbf{B} = \begin{bmatrix} 1 & 0 & 0 & 1 \\ 0 & 1 & 1 & 0 \\ 0 & 1 & 1 & 0 \\ 1 & 0 & 0 & 1 \end{bmatrix}.$$

It is obvious that the DNA spectrum in this case can be simplified to

$$S_d(n) = \hat{\mathbf{x}}_v^H(n) \begin{bmatrix} \mathbf{W} & 0 & 0 & \mathbf{W} \\ 0 & \mathbf{W} & \mathbf{W} & 0 \\ 0 & \mathbf{W} & \mathbf{W} & 0 \\ \mathbf{W} & 0 & 0 & \mathbf{W} \end{bmatrix} \hat{\mathbf{x}}_v(n), \qquad (35)$$

which obviously is not a scaled version of $S_v(n)$ since $\mathbf{B}$ in this case can not be written as $\alpha \mathbf{I_4} + \sum_i \mathbf{B}_i$, where $\mathbf{B}_i$ holds constant rows and/or constant columns $\forall\, i$.

4.4 Four-to-one ($\gamma = 1$) mappings

Single sequence representations can be generated by assigning each nucleotide a certain coefficient [4,13] in order to keep the single sequence structure using the transformation array and matrix

$$\mathbf{A} = \begin{bmatrix} a & c & g & t \end{bmatrix}, \quad \mathbf{B} = \begin{bmatrix} |a|^2 & a^*c & a^*g & a^*t \\ c^*a & |c|^2 & c^*g & c^*t \\ g^*a & g^*c & |g|^2 & g^*t \\ t^*a & t^*c & t^*g & |t|^2 \end{bmatrix}.$$

Note that the coefficients chosen for the tetrahedral, quaternion, and paired coupled mappings can be reused along with the single sequence formulation. For example, the paired couples case can be reformulated in a single sequence of 1's and -1's using $\mathbf{A} = \begin{bmatrix} -1 & 1 & 1 & -1 \end{bmatrix}$ and

$$\mathbf{B} = \begin{bmatrix} 1 & -1 & -1 & 1 \\ -1 & 1 & 1 & -1 \\ -1 & 1 & 1 & -1 \\ 1 & -1 & -1 & 1 \end{bmatrix},$$

at which the DNA spectrum is

$$S_d(n) = \hat{\mathbf{x}}_v^H(n) \begin{bmatrix} \mathbf{W} & -\mathbf{W} & -\mathbf{W} & \mathbf{W} \\ -\mathbf{W} & \mathbf{W} & \mathbf{W} & -\mathbf{W} \\ -\mathbf{W} & \mathbf{W} & \mathbf{W} & -\mathbf{W} \\ \mathbf{W} & -\mathbf{W} & -\mathbf{W} & \mathbf{W} \end{bmatrix} \hat{\mathbf{x}}_v(n).$$

Similar to the previous case, $S_d(n)$ is not a scaled version of $S_v(n)$.

Experimental verification. To briefly verify the results of this section experimentally, we apply Equation (30) to real DNA sequences, when the Voss, tetrahedral, quaternion, Z-curve, and simplex maps are employed. For comparison with previous study, we consider first the DNA sequence F56F11.4 in the *C. elegans* chromosome III. This sequence is 8060 nucleotides and has been used as a benchmark by many researchers [13] to extract the periodicity component at $R = 3$. The DNA spectra at $R = 3$ are shown in Figure 8 for the five former mappings, and are obviously related by the constant scale factors derived earlier in the section which clearly verifies our results. Although we lack the space for more general simulations, it is important to state that all the spectra relations are maintained experimentally at other values of R associated with higher order periodicities.

For generality purposes, we test two more sequences extracted from the well known Burset-Guigo database [32].

In specific, DNA spectra at $R = 3$ of the zeta globin gene (ECZGL2) of length 1563, and the Alouatta seniculus epsilon-globin gene (ALOEGLOBIM) of length 1691 are shown in Figures 9 and 10, respectively, for the five former mappings. It can be seen that the relations are still preserved.

5 Alternative measures of DNA periodicities

Alternative DNA periodicity measures using fast data transforms [33-35], wavelets, and finite impulse response (FIR) digital filters [25,36] were recently proposed to improve the detection performance of these periodicities. However, each method was obtained separately from the other using seemingly a different approach. In this section, we show that our proposed framework can systematically generate all these results by simply changing a number of matrices. It therefore provides a *generic unified framework* for generating alternative measures of DNA periodicities.

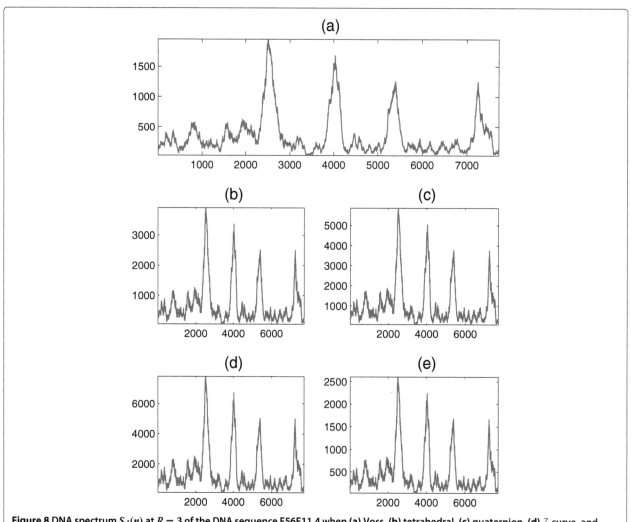

Figure 8 DNA spectrum $S_d(n)$ at $R = 3$ of the DNA sequence F56F11.4 when (a) Voss, (b) tetrahedral, (c) quaternion, (d) Z-curve, and (e) simplex mappings are used.

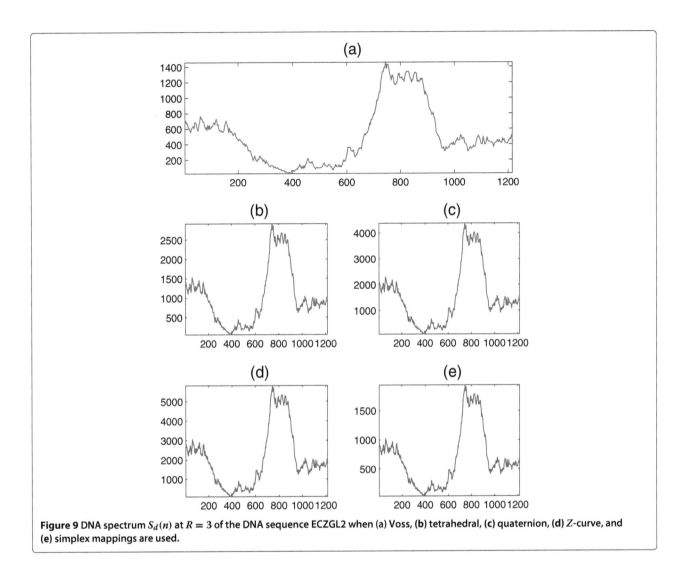

Figure 9 DNA spectrum $S_d(n)$ at $R = 3$ of the DNA sequence ECZGL2 when (a) Voss, (b) tetrahedral, (c) quaternion, (d) Z-curve, and (e) simplex mappings are used.

For example, we can re-express the matrices $\mathbf{D}$ and $\mathbf{W}$ in terms of general digital filters and use these filters to modify (30) in order to generate new spectrum formulas. Furthermore, using symmetry based decompositions of $\mathbf{D}$ and $\mathbf{W}$, we simplify (30) into a formula with low computational complexity.

5.1 Modified periodicity measures

Recall from Section '2' that matrix $\mathbf{W}$ is given by

$$\mathbf{W} = \mathbf{H}^H \mathbf{D} \mathbf{H} = (\mathbf{I}_R \otimes \mathbf{h}^T)^H \mathbf{C}^\star \mathbf{C}^T (\mathbf{I}_R \otimes \mathbf{h}^T).$$

Obviously, $\mathbf{W}$ is completely defined by the real array $\mathbf{h}$ and the generally complex array $\mathbf{C}$. Note that $\mathbf{h}$ and $\mathbf{C}$ can be viewed as the impulse responses of two FIR filters defined by the z-transforms $H(z)$ and $C(z)$.

5.1.1 Updating the real filter h

The FIR filter $H(z)$ is the standard rectangular window filter and has a low pass frequency response with a -13 dB attenuation. To improve its filtering performance, we can use a more general FIR filter, denoted by $\tilde{H}(z)$ and expressed as

$$\tilde{H}(z) = h_0 + h_1 z^{-1} + \cdots + h_{\frac{M}{R}} z^{-\frac{M}{R}},$$

which is the $\mathcal{Z}$-transform of the general array $\tilde{\mathbf{h}}$ given by

$$\tilde{\mathbf{h}} = \begin{bmatrix} h_0 & h_1 & \cdots & h_{\frac{M}{R}} \end{bmatrix}.$$

From a signal processing perspective, achieving better performance can be obtained by replacing the rectangular window with another one, $\tilde{H}(z)$, that has slightly wider main lobes but much more attenuated side lobes, as shown in Table 3. The impulse responses of such windows are depicted in Figure 11a for $R = 8$ and $M = 96$. Better harmonics characterization can be achieved by giving each nucleotide position within the window a relative weight in contrast to the rectangular where equal

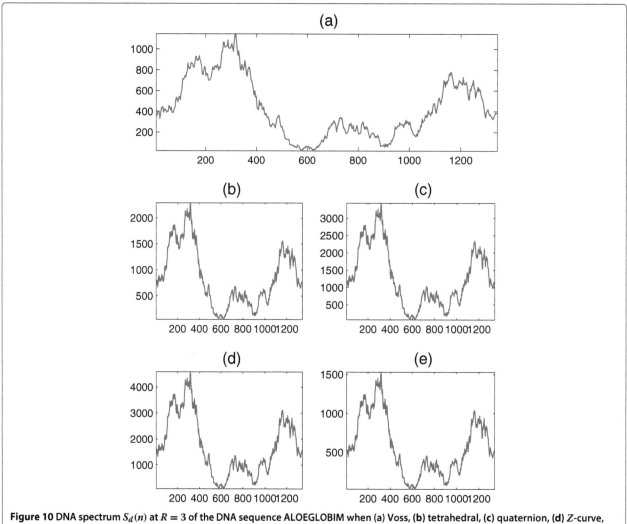

Figure 10 DNA spectrum $S_d(n)$ at $R = 3$ of the DNA sequence ALOEGLOBIM when (a) Voss, (b) tetrahedral, (c) quaternion, (d) Z-curve, and (e) simplex mappings are used.

weighting is given to all nucleotides. It turns out that the Blackman window has the best main-to-first side lobe attenuation behavior as shown in Figure 11b compared to the rectangular window case and therefore provides the best smoothing of the DNA spectrum.

By replacing $\mathbf{h}$ with $\tilde{\mathbf{h}}$, the matrix $\mathbf{H}$ can be in turn expressed as

$$
\tilde{\mathbf{H}} = \begin{bmatrix} h_0\, h_1 \,..\, h_{M/R-1} & \cdots & 0\,0\,..\,0 \\ \vdots & \ddots & \vdots \\ 0\,0\,..\,0 & \cdots & \underbrace{h_0\, h_1 \,..\, h_{M/R-1}}_{M/R} \end{bmatrix},
$$

and the complex row vector $\mathbf{C}^T\tilde{\mathbf{H}}$ is now given by

$$
\mathbf{C}^T\tilde{\mathbf{H}} = \begin{bmatrix} \underbrace{h_0\,..\,h_{\frac{M}{R}-1}}_{M/R} & \cdots & \underbrace{h_0 e^{-j2\pi\frac{R-1}{R}} \,..\, h_{\frac{M}{R}-1} e^{-j2\pi\frac{R-1}{R}}}_{M/R} \end{bmatrix}.
$$

It can be easily seen that the sum of elements in $\mathbf{C}^T\tilde{\mathbf{H}}$ is still equal to zero as was the case for $\mathbf{C}^T\mathbf{H}$. Consequently, it follows that the sum of any row or column in

Table 3 FIR window Specifications: relative peak side lobe A_1/A_0 in dB, approximate width of main lobe $\Delta\omega$, equivalent Kaiser window coefficient β, and transition width $\Delta\omega_\beta$

FIR Window	A_1/A_0	$\Delta\omega$	β	$\Delta\omega_\beta$
Rectangular	−13	$4\pi/(M/R+1)$	0	$1.81\pi R/M$
Bartlett	−25	$8\pi R/M$	1.33	$2.37\pi R/M$
Hanning	−31	$8\pi R/M$	3.86	$5.01\pi R/M$
Hamming	−41	$8\pi R/M$	4.86	$6.27\pi R/M$
Blackman	−57	$12\pi R/M$	7.04	$9.19\pi R/M$

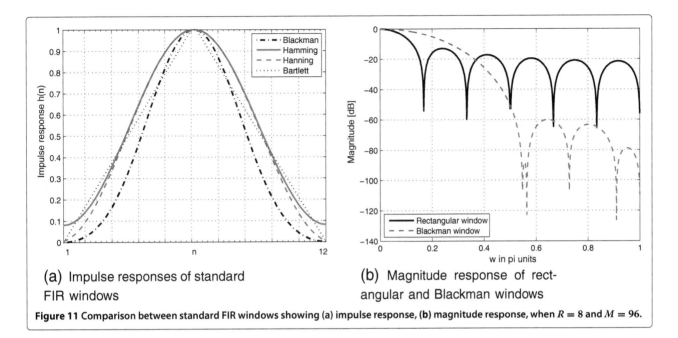

(a) Impulse responses of standard FIR windows

(b) Magnitude response of rectangular and Blackman windows

Figure 11 Comparison between standard FIR windows showing (a) impulse response, (b) magnitude response, when $R = 8$ and $M = 96$.

$\tilde{\mathbf{W}} = \tilde{\mathbf{H}}^H \mathbf{D} \tilde{\mathbf{H}}$ is still equal to zero. This is a fundamental result which, in turn, implies that all the derivations of Section 3 are still the same even when $\tilde{\mathbf{h}}$ replaces $\mathbf{h}$. In particular, the $\mathbb{V}$-based DNA spectrum $\tilde{S}_v(n)$ and the $\mathbb{D}$-based one $\tilde{S}_d(n)$ can be stated as

$$\tilde{S}_v(n) = \hat{\mathbf{x}}_v^H(n)(\mathbf{I}_4 \otimes \tilde{\mathbf{W}})\hat{\mathbf{x}}_v(n),\ \tilde{S}_d(n)$$
$$= \hat{\mathbf{x}}_v^H(n)(\mathbf{B} \otimes \tilde{\mathbf{W}})\hat{\mathbf{x}}_v(n). \qquad (36)$$

Moreover, all the mathematical relations derived in Section 3 between the $\mathbb{D}$-based spectrum and the Voss-based one are all still valid even when $\mathbf{h}$ is replaced by $\tilde{\mathbf{h}}$.

Experimental verification. To experimentally verify this result, we consider finding the DNA spectrum $\tilde{S}_d(n)$ of the three DNA sequences used in the previous section when $\tilde{\mathbf{h}}$ is set to a Blackman window. The relations between the spectra when using the Voss, tetrahedral, quaternion, Z-curve, and simplex mappings are still the same as shown in Figures 12, 13, and 14.

5.1.2 Updating the complex filter C
Similar to $H(z)$, the FIR filter $C(z)$ can be replaced by a more sophisticated filter $\tilde{C}(z)$ expressed as

$$\tilde{C}(z) = C_0 + C_1 z^{-1} + \cdots + C_{R-1} z^{-(R-1)},$$

which is the $\mathcal{Z}$-transform of the general array $\tilde{\mathbf{C}}$ given by

$$\tilde{\mathbf{C}} = [C_0\ \ C_1\ \ \ldots\ \ C_{R-1}].$$

Note that, in this case, the elements in array $\tilde{\mathbf{C}}$ do not necessarily add to zero anymore. Consequently, the sum of elements in any row or any column in $\tilde{\mathbf{D}} = \tilde{\mathbf{C}}^\star \tilde{\mathbf{C}}^T$ or $\tilde{\mathbf{W}} = \mathbf{H}^H \tilde{\mathbf{D}} \mathbf{H}$ is not necessarily zero. We also note that

unlike the case of $\tilde{\mathbf{h}}$, using $\tilde{\mathbf{C}}$ instead of $\mathbf{C}$ keeps the spectrum formulas in (36) correct but does not preserve the mathematical relations between the different $\mathbb{D}$-mapped spectra and the Voss-based spectrum.

5.1.3 Joint optimization of $\tilde{\mathbf{h}}$ and $\tilde{\mathbf{C}}$
It should be clear at this point that better DNA harmonics detection performance can be potentially achieved through a joint "optimization" of $\tilde{\mathbf{h}}$ and $\tilde{\mathbf{C}}$. For example, a learning paradigm can be used with a least-mean-square (LMS) criterion to find the optimal set, $\tilde{\mathbf{h}}$ and $\tilde{\mathbf{C}}$. Alternatively, a biologically induced criterion can yield a substantial boost in performance but it is not clear which criterion to use. This interesting but challenging research topic is however outside the scope of this article and will not be further pursued here.

Example. Standard discrete time transforms have been proposed to replace the ST-DFT in the periodicity detection problem. In particular, the short time discrete cosine transform (ST-DCT), sine transform (ST-DST), and Hartley transform (ST-DHT) were introduced and analyzed for this purpose [33]. In this example, we show that these three transforms fit naturally within our proposed analysis when the two arrays $\tilde{\mathbf{h}}$ and $\tilde{\mathbf{C}}$ are adjusted correctly for each case. Although these standard transforms are not optimized for certain data sets, they can serve as preliminary tests for better periodicity detection. In [33], the short time DFT, DCT, DST, and DHT at $k = M/R$ were shown to be given by

$$X^{(t)}(n) = \sum_{r=0}^{R-1} C_r^{(t)} \sum_{m=r,r+R,\ldots}^{\frac{M}{R}-1} x(n + mR + r) h^{(t)}(m), \qquad (37)$$

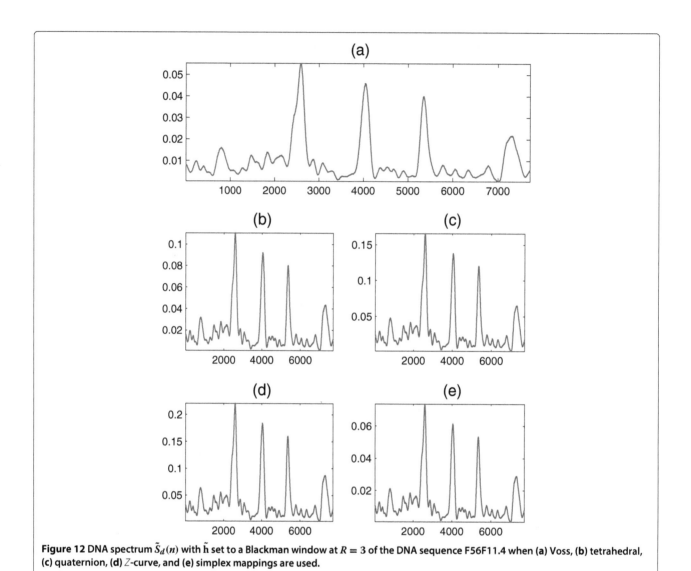

Figure 12 DNA spectrum $\tilde{S}_d(n)$ with $\tilde{\mathbf{h}}$ set to a Blackman window at $R = 3$ of the DNA sequence F56F11.4 when (a) Voss, (b) tetrahedral, (c) quaternion, (d) Z-curve, and (e) simplex mappings are used.

where $t \in \{f, c, s, h\}$ indicates Fourier, cosine, sine, and Hartley transforms, respectively, $C_r^{(t)} = a^{(t)} e^{j\theta_r^{(t)}} + b^{(t)} e^{-j\theta_r^{(t)}}$ are possibly complex coefficients, and $h^{(t)}(m) = (\alpha^t)^m$. Values of the parameters α, a, b, and θ_r for every transform are adjusted according to Table 4. For illustration, setting $\alpha = 1$, $a = 1$, $b = 0$, and $\theta_r = -2\pi r/R$ in (37) results in the ST-DFT case. An efficient implementation to calculate Equation (37) is shown in Figure 15 which generalizes Figure 3.

This model provides a general framework that encapsulates the computation of the short-time Fourier, cosine, sine, and Hartley transforms at frequency point $k = M/R$. Therefore, the same matrix-based analysis of Sections 2 and 3 can be used. Matrix $\mathbf{W}$ will be updated into

$$\tilde{\mathbf{W}} = \tilde{\mathbf{H}}^H \tilde{\mathbf{D}} \tilde{\mathbf{H}} = \left(\mathbf{I}_R \otimes \tilde{\mathbf{h}}^T\right)^H \tilde{\mathbf{C}}^\star \tilde{\mathbf{C}}^T \left(\mathbf{I}_R \otimes \tilde{\mathbf{h}}^T\right),$$

and therefore the $\mathbb{D}$-based DNA spectrum $\tilde{S}_d(n)$ when one of the ST-DFT, DCT, DST, or DHT is employed can be stated as

$$\tilde{S}_d(n) = \hat{\mathbf{x}}_v^H(n)(\mathbf{B} \otimes \tilde{\mathbf{W}})\hat{\mathbf{x}}_v(n), \qquad (38)$$

where the values of $\tilde{\mathbf{h}}$ and $\tilde{\mathbf{C}}$ are adjusted according to Table 5.

Note that similar to the Fourier case, the sum of elements in $\tilde{\mathbf{C}}$ for the cosine and Hartley transforms cases is equal to zero. Therefore, under these two cases, the relations between different $\mathbb{D}$-based DNA spectra and the $\mathbb{V}$-based DNA spectrum are still the same as given in Section 3.

At this point, it can be concluded that the $\mathbb{D}$-based DNA spectrum $\tilde{S}_d(n)$ is completely defined in terms of the Voss-based array of interleaved windows $\hat{\mathbf{x}}_v(n)$, the

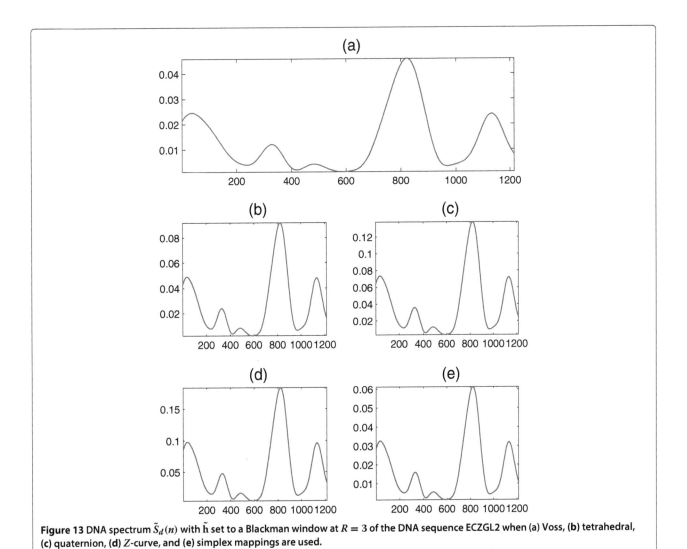

Figure 13 DNA spectrum $\tilde{S}_d(n)$ with $\tilde{\mathbf{h}}$ set to a Blackman window at $R = 3$ of the DNA sequence ECZGL2 when (a) Voss, (b) tetrahedral, (c) quaternion, (d) Z-curve, and (e) simplex mappings are used.

$\mathbb{V} \longmapsto \mathbb{D}$ mapping matrix $\mathbf{A}$, the real array $\tilde{\mathbf{h}}$, and the generally complex array $\tilde{\mathbf{C}}$. This conclusion is summarized in Figure 16.

5.2 A real approach for the spectrum computation

A real computationally-efficient alternative for the evaluation of $S_d(n)$ can be found by observing the special properties of the circulant/toeplitz matrix $\mathbf{D}$ or equivalently the block matrix $\mathbf{W}$. We use the fact that for a generally-complex matrix $\mathbf{Q}$: $y^H \mathbf{Q} y = 0$, $\forall y \in \mathbb{R}$, if $\mathbf{Q}$ is an antisymmetric matrix. We start by splitting $\mathbf{D}$ into its symmetric and antisymmetric parts

$$\mathbf{D} = \underbrace{\frac{1}{2}\left(\mathbf{D} + \mathbf{D}^T\right)}_{\text{symmetric}} + \underbrace{\frac{1}{2}\left(\mathbf{D} - \mathbf{D}^T\right)}_{\text{antisymmetric}} = \mathbf{D}_s + \mathbf{D}_{as},$$

where $\mathbf{D}_s$ is a circulant and Toeplitz real $R \times R$ matrix given by

$$\mathbf{D}_s = \begin{bmatrix} 1 & 2\cos\frac{2\pi}{R} & \cdots & 2\cos\frac{2\pi(R-1)}{R} \\ 2\cos\frac{2\pi}{R} & 1 & \ddots & \vdots \\ \vdots & \ddots & \ddots & 2\cos\frac{2\pi}{R} \\ 2\cos\frac{2\pi(R-1)}{R} & \cdots & 2\cos\frac{2\pi}{R} & 1 \end{bmatrix},$$

and $\mathbf{D}_{as}$ is a circulant and Toeplitz complex $R \times R$ matrix given by

$$\mathbf{D}_{as} = 2j \begin{bmatrix} 0 & -\sin\frac{2\pi}{R} & \cdots & -\sin\frac{2\pi(R-1)}{R} \\ \sin\frac{2\pi}{R} & 0 & \ddots & \vdots \\ \vdots & \ddots & \ddots & -\sin\frac{2\pi}{R} \\ \sin\frac{2\pi(R-1)}{R} & \cdots & \sin\frac{2\pi}{R} & 0 \end{bmatrix}.$$

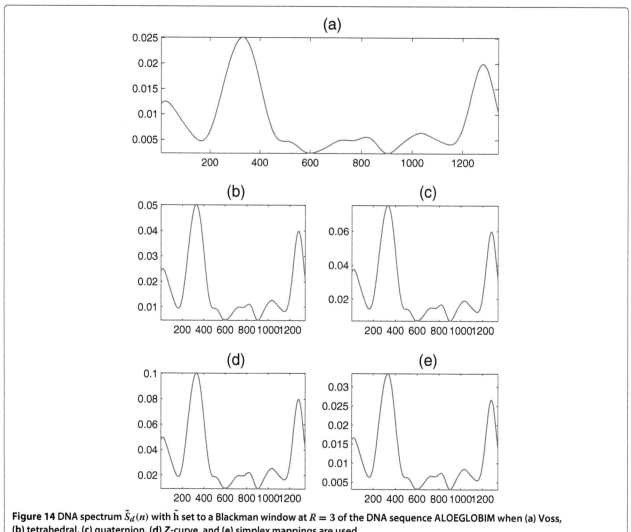

Figure 14 DNA spectrum $\tilde{S}_d(n)$ with $\tilde{h}$ set to a Blackman window at $R = 3$ of the DNA sequence ALOEGLOBIM when (a) Voss, (b) tetrahedral, (c) quaternion, (d) Z-curve, and (e) simplex mappings are used.

Substituting for $\mathbf{D}$ in (15), we get a simple form of the spectrum $S(n)$

$$
\begin{aligned}
S(n) &= \hat{\mathbf{x}}^H(n)\,\mathbf{H}^H\mathbf{D}\mathbf{H}\,\hat{\mathbf{x}}(n) \\
&= \hat{\mathbf{x}}^H(n)\,\mathbf{H}^H\,(\mathbf{D}_s + \mathbf{D}_{as})\,\mathbf{H}\,\hat{\mathbf{x}}(n) \\
&= \hat{\mathbf{x}}^H(n)\,\mathbf{W}_s\,\hat{\mathbf{x}}(n),
\end{aligned} \tag{39}
$$

where $y^H\mathbf{D}_{as}y = 0, \forall l \in \mathbb{F}, y = \mathbf{H}\,\hat{\mathbf{x}}(n)$. The block matrix

$$
\mathbf{W}_s \doteq \mathbf{H}^H\mathbf{D}_s\mathbf{H} = \frac{1}{2}\mathbf{H}^H\left(\mathbf{D} + \mathbf{D}^T\right)\mathbf{H}
$$

is an $R \times R$ matrix of $\frac{M}{R} \times \frac{M}{R}$ blocks. Using (39) to update the DNA spectrum (19), $S_v(n)$ simplifies into

$$
S_v(n) = \sum_{l \in \mathbb{F}} \hat{\mathbf{x}}_l^H(n)\,\mathbf{W}_s\,\hat{\mathbf{x}}_l(n). \tag{40}
$$

Following the same analysis of Section 3, (40) can be easily manipulated into a more elegant completely real form given by

$$
S_v(n) = \hat{\mathbf{x}}_v^H(n)\,(\mathbf{I}_4 \otimes \mathbf{W}_s)\,\hat{\mathbf{x}}_v(n),
$$

or more generally, (30) can be updated into

$$
S_d(n) = \hat{\mathbf{x}}_v^H(n)\,(\mathbf{B} \otimes \mathbf{W}_s)\,\hat{\mathbf{x}}_v(n), \tag{41}
$$

which provides a completely real approach for the computation of the $\mathbb{D}$-mapped spectrum $S_d(n)$. Note that all

Table 4 Parameter settings in Figure 15 to compute the short time Fourier, cosine, sine, and Hartley transforms

Transform	α	a	b	θ_r
ST-DFT	1	1	0	$-2\pi r/R$
ST-DCT	-1	1/2	$-1/2$	$(2r+1)\pi/2R$
ST-DST	-1	$1/2j$	$-1/2j$	$(2r+1)\pi/2R$
ST-DHT	1	$\frac{1}{2}(1-j)$	$-\frac{1}{2}(1-j)$	$2\pi r/R$

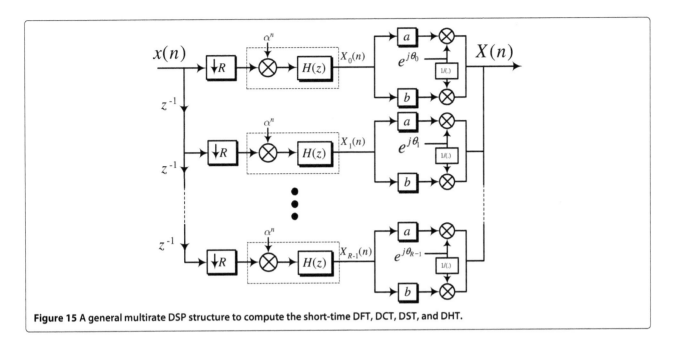

Figure 15 A general multirate DSP structure to compute the short-time DFT, DCT, DST, and DHT.

results and different spectra relations in Section 3 still hold when $\mathbf{W}_s$ replaces $\mathbf{W}$ as in (41).

Computational complexity comparison. To quantify the computational credit of this real approach, we compare the complexity of (39) to that of (15) of a single discrete time sequence. Since $\hat{\mathbf{x}}(n)$ can be complex as well according to the mapping used, we find the number of real multiplications and additions needed to evaluate (39) when each of $\hat{\mathbf{x}}(n)$ and $\mathbf{W}$ is either real or complex, as given in Table 6. Recall that the multiplication of the complex numbers x and y, where $x = a + jb$ and $y = c + jd$ requires the computation of $ac - bd$ and $ad + bc$, which requires four real multiplications and two real additions.

Example. For illustration, we evaluate the spectrum $S_v(n)$ using $\mathbf{W}_s$ when $R = 3$, and compare the result to the

Table 5 Modified arrays $\tilde{\mathbf{h}}$ and $\tilde{\mathbf{C}}$ to compute the short time Fourier-, cosine-, sine-, and Hartley-based DNA spectrum of (38)

ST-DFT	$\tilde{\mathbf{h}} = \mathbf{h} = \{(1)^i, i = 1, 2, \ldots M/R\}$
	$\tilde{\mathbf{C}} = \mathbf{C} = \{e^{-j2\pi r/R}, r = 1, 2, \ldots R\}$
ST-DCT	$\tilde{\mathbf{h}} = \{(-1)^i, i = 1, 2, \ldots M/R\}$
	$\tilde{\mathbf{C}} = \{\cos((2r + 1)\pi/2R), r = 1, 2, \ldots R\}$
ST-DST	$\tilde{\mathbf{h}} = \{(-1)^i, i = 1, 2, \ldots M/R\}$
	$\tilde{\mathbf{C}} = \{\sin((2r + 1)\pi/2R), r = 1, 2, \ldots R\}$
ST-DHT	$\tilde{\mathbf{h}} = \mathbf{h} = \{(1)^i, i = 1, 2, \ldots M/R\}$
	$\tilde{\mathbf{C}} = \{\cos(2\pi r/R) + \sin(2\pi r/R), r = 1, 2, \ldots R\}$

formula derived in [37]. In specific, we use (40) to find the spectrum $S(n)$ as follows

$$S_v(n) = \sum_{l \in \mathbb{F}} \hat{\mathbf{x}}_l^H(n) \mathbf{H}^H \mathbf{D}_s \mathbf{H} \hat{\mathbf{x}}_l(n) = \sum_{l \in \mathbb{F}} \Gamma_l^H(n) \mathbf{D}_s \Gamma_l(n)$$

$$= \sum_{l \in \mathbb{F}} [X_{l0} \ X_{l1} \ X_{l2}] \begin{bmatrix} 1 & -1 & -1 \\ -1 & 1 & -1 \\ -1 & -1 & 1 \end{bmatrix} \begin{bmatrix} X_{l0} \\ X_{l1} \\ X_{l2} \end{bmatrix}.$$

Expanding and completing the square, it follows that

$$\begin{aligned} S_v(n) &= \sum_{l \in \mathbb{F}} [X_{l0}^2(n) + X_{l1}(n)(X_{l1}(n) - X_{l0}(n)) \\ &\quad + X_{l2}(n)(X_{l2}(n) - X_{l0}(n) - X_{l1}(n))] \\ &= \frac{1}{2} \sum_{l \in \mathbb{F}} \sum_{r=0}^{2} (X_{lr}(n) - X_{lq}(n))^2, \end{aligned} \qquad (42)$$

where $q = (r + 1) \bmod 3$. The matrix-based DNA spectrum formula in (42) is consistent with the result derived using a different approach in [37].

6 Concluding remarks

In this article, we have introduced a matrix based framework for locating hidden DNA periodicities using spectral analysis techniques that are invariant to the choice of the symbolic to numerical map. The primary advantage of the presented approach over some of the previous study is the decomposition of the spectrum expression into key matrices whose values can be set *independently from each other*. Each matrix represents one of the essential components involved in the computation of the spectrum such as the

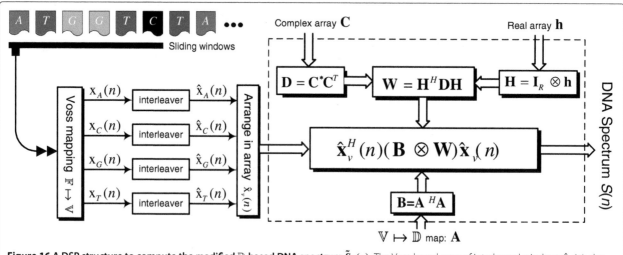

Figure 16 A DSP structure to compute the modified $\mathbb{D}$-based DNA spectrum $\tilde{S}_d(n)$. The Voss-based array of interleaved windows $\hat{\mathbf{x}}_v(n)$, the $\mathbb{V} \longmapsto \mathbb{D}$ mapping matrix $\mathbf{A}$, the real array $\tilde{\mathbf{h}}$, and the generally complex array $\tilde{\mathbf{C}}$ are the system design parameters.

symbolic to numerical map, the data transform, and the filtering scheme. The above framework is derived under the assumption that the symbolic to numerical map can be obtained from the Voss representation using an affine transformation. This assumption is however quite loose given that most (if not all) of the proposed maps in the literature satisfy this requisite. Using the new framework, we have then shown that the DNA spectrum expression is invariant under these maps. We have also derived a necessary and sufficient condition for the invariance of the DNA spectrum in terms of the affine transformation matrix $\mathbf{A}$ (the $\mathbf{b}$ vector in the affine transformation does not affect the DNA spectrum).

This condition can serve as the basis for generating novel symbolic to numerical map that preserve the DNA spectrum expression. Finally, in the latter sections of the article, we have shown the potential of using different filtering schemes, e.g., windows other than the rectangular one as well as alternate fast data transforms, e.g., the DCT, DST, and the Hartley transform. A number of simulation results that verify the findings of this article and a brief quantitative analysis of the computational complexity of the new approach were given in the same sections. Future research study would consider the optimization of the

different building blocks, namely the symbolic to numerical map, the data transform, and the filtering scheme. This, in turn, requires a deep understanding of the biological significance of different DNA periodicities in order to set up a meaningful objective function and appropriate constraints. Ultimately, the framework proposed here can be incorporated in a more sophisticated system to study the complex structure of genomic sequences and understand the functionality of its various components. Finally, this efficient framework can be extended to the analysis of other types of symbolic sequences of various limited alphabets, either biological sequences (such as protein sequences) or even non-biological ones.

Competing interests
The authors declare that they have no competing interests.

Acknowledgements
TS acknowledges partial support from the NSF via grants DMS 0811169 and DMS-1042939.

Author details
[1] Department of Electrical and Computer Engineering at the University of California, Davis, CA 95616, USA, and is now with Cisco Systems, Inc., San Jose CA 95134, USA. [2] Department of Electrical and Computer Engineering at the University of California, Davis, CA 95616, USA. [3] Department of Mathematics, University of California, Davis, CA 95616, USA.

Table 6 Real multiplications and additions needed for the evaluation of (39) and (15)

$\hat{x}(n), W$	Real multiplications	Real additions
real,real	$M(M+1)$	$M^2 - 1$
real,complex	$2M(M+1)$	$2(M^2 - 1)$
complex,real	$2M(M+1)$	$2(M^2 - 1)$
complex,complex	$4M(M+1)$	$2(2M^2 + M - 1)$

References
1. G Benson, Tandem repeat finder: a program to analyze DNA sequences. Nucleic Acids Res. **27**(2), 573–580 (1999)
2. J Butler, *Forensic DNA Typing: Biology and Technology behind STR Markers* (Academic Press, MA, Burlington, 2003)
3. CA Cummings, DA Relman, Microbial forensics: cross-examining pathogens. Science. **296**, 1976–1979 (2002)
4. P Ramachandran, W Lu, A Antoniou, Filter-based methodology for the location of hot spots in proteins and exons in DNA. IEEE Trans. Biomed. Eng. **59**(6), 1598–1609 (2012)

5. T Strachan, AP Read, *Human Molecular Genetics*. (John Wiley and Sons, New York, 1999)
6. AF Smit, The origin of interspersed repeats in the human genome. Curr. Opin. Genet. Dev. **6**, 743–748 (1996)
7. DC Rubinsztein, MR Hayden, *Analysis of triplet repeat Disorders* (Bios Scientific Pub, Oxford, England, 1999)
8. R Gupta, A Mittal, S Gupta, An efficient algorithm to detect palindromes in DNA sequences using periodicity transform. Signal Process. **18**(4), 8–20 (2001)
9. VR Chechetkin, AY Turygin, Size-dependence of three-periodicity and long-range correlations in DNA sequences. Phys. Lett A. **199**, 75–80 (1995)
10. VR Chechetkin, AY Turygin, Search of hidden periodicities in DNA sequences. J. Theor. Biol. **175**, 477–494 (1995)
11. BD Silverman, R Linsker, A measure of DNA periodicity. J. Theor. Biol. **118**(3), 295–300 (1986)
12. D Holste, I Grosse, S Beirer, P Schieg, H Herzel, Repeats and correlations in human DNA sequences. Physic. Rev. E. **67**(06913) (2003)
13. D Anastassiou, Genomic signal processing. IEEE Signal Process. Mag. **18**(4), 8–20 (2001)
14. VR Chechetkin, VV Lobzin, Anticodons, frameshifts, and hidden periodicities in tRNA sequences. J. Biomol. Struct. Dyn. **24**(2), 189–202 (2006)
15. D Anastassiou, Frequency domain analysis of biomolecular sequences. Bioinformatics. **16**(12), 1073–1082 (2000)
16. S Tiwari, S Ramachandran, A Bhattacharya, S Bhattacharya, R Ramaswamy, Prediction of probable genes by Fourier analysis of genomic sequences. Comput. Appl. Biosci. **13**(3), 263–270 (1997)
17. M Akhtar, E Ambikairajah, in *Proceedings of ICASSP*, vol. 2. Time and frequency domain methods for gene and exon prediction in Eukaryotes (Honolulu, Hawaii, USA, 2007), pp. 573–576
18. RF Voss, Evolution of long-range fractal correlations and 1/f noise in DNA base sequences. Phys. Rev. Lett. **68**(25), 3805–3808 (1992)
19. JW Fickett, The gene identification problem: an overview for developers. Comput. Chem. **20**, 103–118 (1996)
20. N Bouaynaya, D Schonfeld, Non-stationary analysis of coding and non-coding regions in nucleotide sequences. IEEE J. Sel. Top. Signal Process. **2**(3), 357–364 (2008)
21. PP Vaidyanathan, BJ Yoon, in *Gensips Proc*. Gene and exon prediction using all pass-based filters, (Raleigh, North Carolina, USA, 2003), pp. 1–4
22. PP Vaidyanathan, B Yoon, in *Proc. Asilomar conference*, vol. 1. Digital filter for gene prediction applications, (Pacific Grove, CA, USA, 2003), pp. 306–310
23. M Akhtar, J Epps, E Ambikairajah, in *Proceedings of the workshop on Genomic Signal Processing and Statistics*. On DNA numerical representations for period-3 based exon prediction, (Tuusula, Finland, 2007), pp. 1 - 4
24. A Rushdi, J Tuqan, in *Proceedings of the 31st IEEE ICASSP conference*, vol. II. Gene identification using the Z-curve representation (Toulouse, France, 2006), pp. 1024–1027
25. J Tuqan, A Rushdi, A DSP approach for finding the codon bias in DNA sequences. IEEE J. Sel. Top. Signal Process. **2**(3), 343–356 (2008)
26. A Rushdi, J Tuqan, in *Proceedings of the 3rd IEEE Cairo International Biomedical Engineering Conference (CIBEC)*, vol. BI. An efficient algorithm for DNA discrete Fourier analysis (Cairo, Egypt, 2006), pp. 1–4
27. L Wang, D Schonfeld, Mapping equivalence for symbolic sequences: Theory and applications. IEEE Trans. Signal Process. **57**(12), 4895–4905 (2009)
28. A Rushdi, J Tuqan, in *Proceedings of the workshop on Genomic Signal Processing and Statistics*. The role of the Symbolic-to-Numerical Mapping in the detection of DNA Periodicities, (Phoenix, AZ, USA, 2008), pp. 1–4
29. PD Cristea, Conversion of nucleotides sequences into genomic signals. J. Cellul. Mol. Med. **6**(2), 279–303 (2002)
30. AK Brodzik, in *Proceedings of the IEEE Int. Conf. on Acoustics, Speech, and Signal Processing*, vol. 5. O Peters, Symbol-balanced quaternionic periodicity transform for latent pattern detection in DNA sequences (Philadelphia, PA, USA, 2005), pp. 373–376
31. E Coward, Equivalence of two Fourier methods for biological sequences. J. Math. Biol. **36**, 64–70 (1997)
32. M Burset, R Guigo, Evaluation of gene structure prediction programs. Genomics. **34**, 353–357 (1996)
33. A Rushdi, J Tuqan, in *Proceedings of the workshop on Genomic Signal Processing and Statistics*. Trigonometric Transforms for Finding Repeats in DNA sequences, (Phoenix, AZ , USA, 2008), pp. 1–4
34. JA Berger, SK Mitra, J Astola, in *Proceedings of the International Symposium on Signal Processing and its Applications*, vol. 2. Power spectrum analysis for DNA sequences, (Paris, France, 2003), pp. 29–32
35. D Kotlar, Y Lavner, Gene prediction by spectral rotation measure: a new method for identifying protein-coding regions. Genome Res. **13**(8), 1930–1937 (2003)
36. A Rushdi, J Tuqan, in *Proceedings of the 40th IEEE Asilomar Conference on Signals, Systems, and Computers*. The filtered spectral rotation measure, (CA, USA, 2006), pp. 1875–1879
37. S Datta, A Asif, in *Proc. of the ICASSP*, vol. 5. A fast DFT based gene prediction algorithm for identification of protein coding regions, (Philadelphia, PA, USA, 2005), pp. 113–116

9

Identification of genomic functional hotspots with copy number alteration in liver cancer

Tzu-Hung Hsiao[1], Hung-I Harry Chen[1], Stephanie Roessler[2], Xin Wei Wang[3] and Yidong Chen[1,4*]

Abstract

Copy number alterations (CNAs) can be observed in most of cancer patients. Several oncogenes and tumor suppressor genes with CNAs have been identified in different kinds of tumor. However, the systematic survey of CNA-affected functions is still lack. By employing systems biology approaches, instead of examining individual genes, we directly identified the functional hotspots on human genome. A total of 838 hotspots on human genome with 540 enriched Gene Ontology functions were identified. Seventy-six aCGH array data of hepatocellular carcinoma (HCC) tumors were employed in this study. A total of 150 regions which putatively affected by CNAs and the encoded functions were identified. Our results indicate that two immune related hotspots had copy number alterations in most of patients. In addition, our data implied that these immune-related regions might be involved in HCC oncogenesis. Also, we identified 39 hotspots of which copy number status were associated with patient survival. Our data implied that copy number alterations of the regions may contribute in the dysregulation of the encoded functions. These results further demonstrated that our method enables researchers to survey biological functions of CNAs and to construct regulation hypothesis at pathway and functional levels.

Keywords: Copy number alteration; Gene set enrichment; Pathway analysis; Liver cancer

Introduction

Chromosomal instability is one of the characteristics in cancer [1] and results in the numerical and structural alterations of DNA copy number variations (CNAs). Recently, some literatures have reported the association of CNAs and patient survival in different tumors [2-4]. Several important oncogenes or tumor suppressors were also showed with high frequency of gain or loss status in different cancers. For example, the copy number amplification of gene Her2, which is the addicted oncogene in the HER2+ subtype of breast cancer, was highly correlated with the gene overexpression [5]. However, in addition to focal amplification, most tumors display multiple and broad ranges of copy number change, where large number of genes are involved in and potentially to be induced or suppressed due to copy number amplifications or deletions. Some *in vitro* studies were performed to survey the affected functions of CNAs [6-8]. For example,

Nicole et al. utilized the shRNA library to identify the GO and STOP genes which positively and negatively regulate proliferation to evaluate the effect of gene deletions [7], respectively. They also proposed a model called 'Cancer Gene Island', which encompasses high density of genes with the same function within a genomic region [7]. However, the *in vitro* studies were labor intensive if not cost prohibitive. Moreover, it is hard to perform a systematic analysis based on these approaches, thus, leaving the gene island model and their functions unexplored.

In conventional gene expression data analysis, several bioinformatics methods based on the concept of 'gene set enrichment analysis' (GSEA) have been successfully utilized to explore the underlying molecular pathways and Gene Ontology functions [9-12]. The GSEA method assesses the number of overlap genes between two gene sets: the differentially expressed genes of a certain functional annotation and genes from the entire genome with the same annotation, to estimate the probability of the overlapping through the statistical test. The procedure provides a high throughput and systematic analysis to explore the putative activated pathways or functions.

* Correspondence: cheny8@uthscsa.edu
[1]Greehey Children's Cancer Research Institute, University of Texas Health Science Center at San Antonio, San Antonio, TX 78229, USA
[4]Department of Epidemiology and Biostatistics, University of Texas Health Science Center at San Antonio, San Antonio, TX 78229, USA
Full list of author information is available at the end of the article

Hepatocellular carcinoma (HCC) is one of the malignant cancers and the third leading cause of cancer death worldwide [13]. Major etiologies associated with HCC are hepatitis B virus (HBV) and hepatitis C virus (HCV) infection [14]. Previous studies have been reported in which comparative genomic hybridization by microarray (aCGH) was utilized to examine CNAs in HCC. Several regions with frequent copy number gain and loss were identified. The CNA-associated oncogenes and tumor suppressors, such as *MYC*, *JAG1*, *TP53*, and *RB1*, were also found [15-18]. The association between survival and CNAs has been investigated, and ten associated genes were reported [19]. However, the biological functions altered by CNAs remain unknown and thus need to be dissected.

According to the concept of Cancer Gene Island, here, we propose an algorithm to identify the spatial functional hotspots (SFHs) in human genome based on the enrichment analysis. The human genome is divided firstly into segments along the genomic sequence coordinate. Then, the tests of enrichment between the segments and whole genome functional categories are performed. Finally, a method which identifies the optimal regions of enriched functions between the segments was applied to examine putative SFHs. To demonstrate the ability of our method, we applied the method to an aCGH data set of HCC. The result showed several immune-related SFHs which showed gain and loss in HCC samples. Also, survival-associated SFHs were identified. The result also indicated that our system could serve as a useful method to understand the CNAs-affected functions.

Methods

To identify the SFHs in human genome, we proposed a novel enrichment analysis that compares the genes contained within a genomic segment with all genes belonging to the same function categories associated to the genes within the segment under consideration based on the concept of gene set enrichment. As shown in Figure 1A, two matrixes, **B** and **P**, were constructed first. The indicator matrix **B** contains information whether or not a gene belongs to a genomic region (spatial segment) determined by a sliding window along the genomic position of all chromosomes or $\mathbf{B} = (b_{k,i})_{K \times M}$, where M is the number of genes and K is the number of genome segments pre-determined and where $b_{k,i} = 1$ when ith gene is in the kth segment, otherwise 0. The matrix $\mathbf{P} = \{p_{i,l}\}_{M \times L}$ is also an indicator matrix of functional gene sets, where L is the number of functional gene sets and $p_{i,l} = 1$ when ith gene is in the lth GO (Gene Ontology) function, otherwise 0. The enrichment is defined as scoring function C of the two matrixes **B** and **P**.

$$ES = C(\mathbf{B}, \mathbf{P}) \tag{1}$$

Here, we use Fisher's exact test as the score function C (**B**, **P**) (Figure 1B). Let $x_k = \sum_{i=1}^{M} b_{k,i}$ is the number of genes in the kth segment, $y_l = \sum_{i=1}^{M} p_{i,l}$ is the number of total genes in gene set l, and $z_{k,l} = \sum_{i=1}^{M} b_{k,i} p_{i,l}$ is the number of overlapped genes between the kth segment and gene set l. The p value of Fisher's exact test between the genome segment and the gene set can be calculated by

$$P(x > z_{k,l}) = \sum_{h=z_{k,l}}^{\infty} \frac{\binom{x_k}{h}\binom{M-x_k}{y_l-h}}{\binom{M}{y_l}} \tag{2}$$

Based on the p values, we can determine if the function l was enriched at the genome segment k. Then, we merge and extend the enriched segments to a merged window to include all genes involved in the function l if the segments were located nearby and have position overlapping. As shown in Figure 1C, assuming qth to $(q + R)$th segments have enrichment for the function l, the genes involved in the merged windows can be expressed as vector $\boldsymbol{d}$:

$$d_i = \begin{cases} 1, & \text{if } s_i > 1 \\ 0, & \text{else} \end{cases}, \tag{3}$$

where $s_i = \sum_{t=q}^{(q+R)} b_{t,i}$. Assuming there are G genes (from eth to $(e + G)$th) located in the qth to $(q + R)$th enriched window, we defined the subsets of the G genes which exclude out genes gradually from left or right side according to the genome coordinate. Two parameters, pL and pR, which perform enrichment analysis (Fisher's exact test) between the subsets with the gene set of function l were introduced (Figure 1C). pL and pR are defined as:

$$pR_g = C(\{d_{e+g}, ..., d_{(e+G)}\}, \mathbf{p}_l) \tag{4}$$

$$pL_g = C(\{d_e, ..., d_{e+g}\}, \mathbf{p}_l), \tag{5}$$

where $g = 1, ..., G$ and $C(.)$ is the enriched score function. Then, the optimal enriched region o of function l can be defined as:

$$o = \{\text{argmin}(pR), ..., \text{argmin}(pL)\}. \tag{6}$$

If the p value of the region o passed the selection threshold, o was defined as the SFHs of function l.

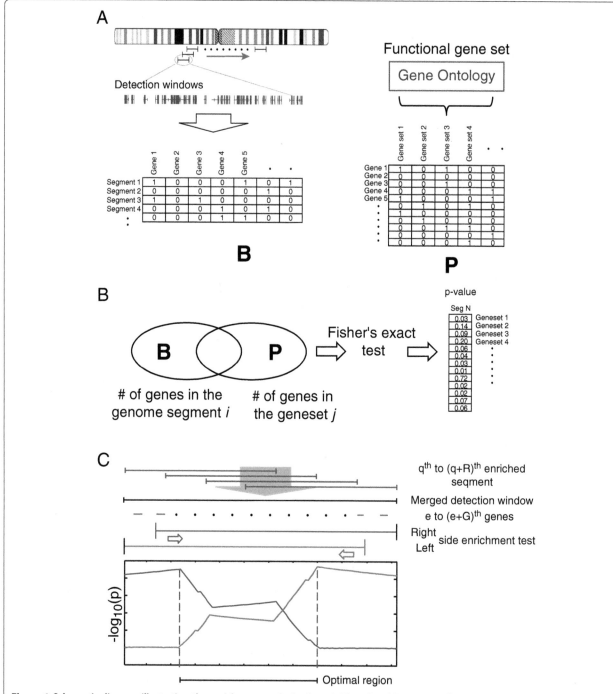

Figure 1 Schematic diagram illustrating the enrichment analysis of spatial functional hotspots in human genome. (A) The indicator matrix **B** was generated by sliding the detection window along the genome. It contains the information of genes located in each segment. The matrix **P** records the gene sets of Gene Ontology. **(B)** By comparing the two matrices assessed with Fisher's exact test, the *p* values of gene sets in each segment were generated. The enriched functions of each segment were then identified if passed the selection criteria. **(C)** The nearby segments with the same enriched function were merged to a detection window. The enrichment analysis between the function and the subset of genes in the windows were performed. The subset was constructed by excluding gene by gene along the left side or right side of the genome coordinate. The position with the smallest *p* value of left side and right side excluding subset was defined as the boundaries of the optimal region of the functional hotspot.

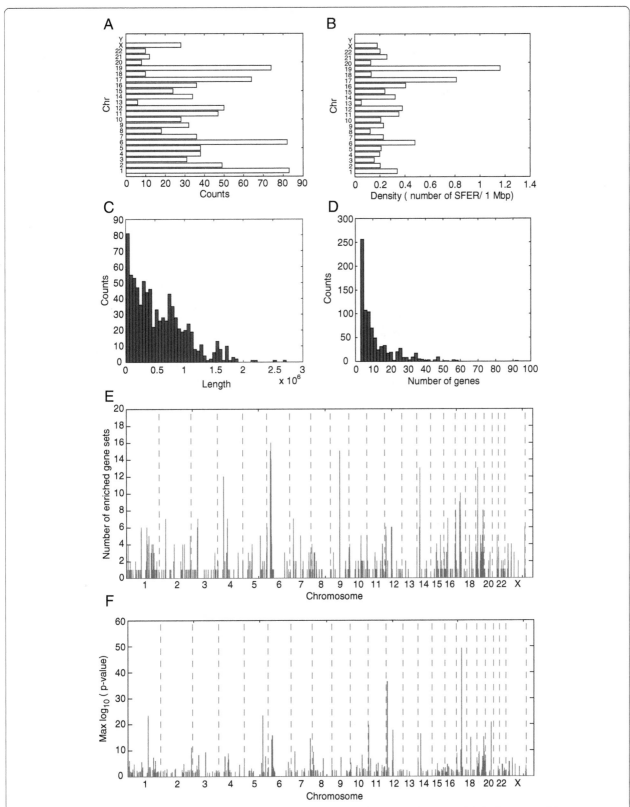

Figure 2 The summary of the spatial functional hotspots. (A) The histogram of the length of the SFHs. **(B)** The histogram of the gene numbers in the SFHs. **(C)** The SFH number in each chromosome. **(D)** The SFH density (numbers of SFHs per million base pair) in each chromosome. **(E)** The most significant *p* value and **(F)** the number of SFHs in the position of human genome. In **(E)** and **(F)**, the chromosomes were separated by red broken lines.

Gene sets of genome segments and biological functions

To define the genome segments, the detection window size was set as one million base pairs (Mbp) after the testing of three different conditions (Additional file 1: Figure S1). The sliding distance was set at 0.25 Mbp. The genomic position of each gene was obtained from Ensembl (version Homo Sapiens 65) [20], or equivalent to NCBI human genome GRCh37. Therefore, a total of 12,098 segments were defined. To construct the functional gene sets, we downloaded all records of Gene Ontology from the BioMart website of Ensembl 65 (http://useast.ensembl.org/info/data/biomart.html) [20]. A total of 7,654 GO terms were downloaded. After excluding the gene sets containing fewer than 15 genes, 1,091, 404, and 275 gene sets associated to biological process (BP), molecular function (MF), and cellular component (CC) terms were utilized in this study, respectively.

aCGH arrays of hepatocellular carcinoma

To identify the functional effect of CNAs in HCC, the aCGH array data set, GSE14322, was downloaded from GEO/NCBI website. The data set contains 76 HCC samples. The determination of CNAs was through the NEXUS software (BioDiscovery, San Diego, CA, USA). The CBS segmentation algorithm was performed to identify the segments of CNAs [21] using the thresholds of log2 values of fold change larger or smaller than ±0.2.

Results

Identification of spatial functional hotspots

By using adjusted p values of Fisher's exact test < 0.05 after Bonferroni adjustment as the criteria, a total of 540 GO gene sets showed the functional enrichment in 838 SFHs. There are 443, 269, and 126 of SFHs belonging to BP, MF, and CC terms, respectively. On average, each chromosome contains 57 SFHs. Chromosome 1 has the largest number (147) of SFHs, and chromosome Y has no SFH (Figure 2A). The averaged SFH density is 0.43 SFHs per million base pairs (Mbp). Chromosome 6 has the highest SFH density (0.48 SFHs/Mbp) (Figure 2B). For the 838 SFHs, the average length of SFHs was 0.56 Mbp (Figure 2C) and the averaged 11.5 genes are in a SFH (Figure 2D). The SFH of 'sugar binding' enrichment, which is located in the 7.88 to 10.6 Mbp region at chromosome 12, has the longest region length. The SFH of 'immune response' enrichment (31.2 to 33 Mbp at chromosome 6), which contains 93 genes, has the largest number of genes. The region located in 29.7 to 31.5 Mbp at chromosome 6 contained the most number of enriched gene sets (16) (Figure 2E and Additional file 1: Table S1). The region includes lots of SFHs which have enrichment of immune-related gene sets, such like MHC class I protein complex, type I interferon-mediated signaling pathway, and immune response. Our finding indicated that the two regions are important for cell immunity.

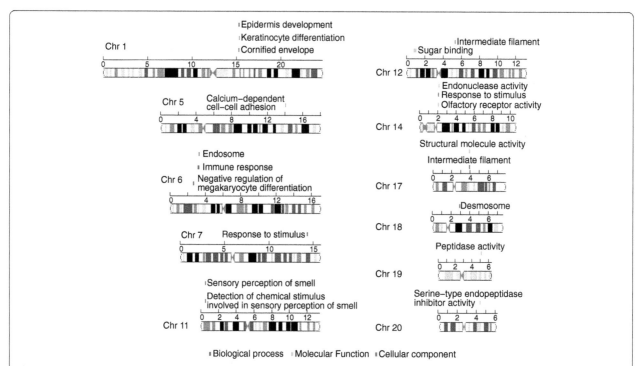

Figure 3 The top 20 enriched function in human genome. The top 20 significant SFHs, which contain 18 functions, were showed in the figure. The function of 'intermediate filament' was enriched at both chromosomes 12 and 17. The 'response to stimulus' function was enriched at chromosomes 7 and 14.

Table 1 Top ten gain/loss spatial functional hotspots (SFHs) of HCC with enriched functions

Chr	Start pos	End pos	Number of CNVs		Presented gene set	Number gene sets
Gain						
1	153.33	153.59	59	bp	Response to lipopolysaccharide	4
1	153.27	153.43	59	bp	*Innate immune response*	4
1	153.33	153.36	59	bp	Response to zinc ion	2
1	152.27	153.43	59	bp	Epidermis development	13
1	152.27	153.23	59	mf	Structural molecule activity	8
1	152.88	153.43	58	bp	Keratinocyte differentiation	12
1	152.88	153.23	58	bp	Peptide cross-linking	6
1	152.88	153.23	58	mf	Protein binding, bridging	4
1	153.50	153.60	57	mf	Protein homodimerization activity	5
1	153.50	153.60	57	cc	Perinuclear region of cytoplasm	5
Loss						
8	6.84	6.88	42	bp	*Response to virus*	3
4	190.39	191.01	40	mf	Sequence-specific DNA binding	6
4	190.39	191.01	40	mf	Sequence-specific DNA binding transcription Factor activity	6
8	6.35	6.91	40	cc	Extracellular space	7
4	90.80	91.76	40	cc	Platelet alpha granule lumen	2
4	90.80	91.76	40	bp	Platelet degranulation	2
8	26.61	27.47	39	bp	Response to stress	3
17	10.35	10.56	38	bp	Actin filament-based movement	2
8	26.37	27.31	37	bp	Response to cocaine	2
8	22.88	23.08	37	mf	Caspase activator activity	2

Immune-related functions are in italics.

The smallest p values of the enriched gene sets in the genomic positions were showed in Figure 2F. There are nine SFHs which have adjusted p value smaller than 1×10^{-20}. The 'intermediate filament' gene set has the most significant adjusted p value (7.4×10^{-50}) of the enrichment in the SFH of 38.8 to 39.4 Mbp region at chromosome 17. Twenty-nine out of 57 genes in the 'intermediate filament' gene set are located at the hotspots. All of them belong to the keratin family genes, which are components of the cytoskeleton of epithelial cells. The top 20 SFHs were showed in Figure 3. Another SFH which is located at 52.6 to 53.3 Mbp region at chromosome 12 also showed the enrichment of intermediate filament. Other 12 keratin genes were contained. The SFH located at 31.2 to 33 Mbp regions of chromosome 6, which code 16 human leukocyte antigen (HLA) genes, enriched the immune response gene set. In summary, our result indicates that there are several functional hotspots within human genome related to the immune function.

The affected function of copy number variation in liver cancer

To evaluate the effect function of CNAs in liver cancer, the dataset GSE14322, which contains 76 aCGH arrays

of HCC samples, was downloaded and analyzed. The percentage of CNA status of each SFH was calculated. There are 61 and 89 SFHs that contained copy number gain and loss in more than 30% patients (25). The result was showed in Table S2 in Additional file 1, and the top ten SFHs were listed in Table 1. One immune-related gene set had the gain status in most of the samples (innate immune response), and one had loss status (response to virus), since the major etiologies of HCC are the infection of HBV and HCV. We hypothesize that those immune-related SFHs that harbor CNAs may play a role in the HCC carcinogenesis.

We also analyzed the association between disease-free survival and the CNAs of the SFHs through log rank test. Using $p < 0.01$ as the threshold, a total of 20 and 19 SFHs of which gain and loss status were identified with survival association, respectively (see Table 2). The copy number gain status in the SFH which located at 41.1 to 41.9 Mbp at chromosome 19 had the smallest p value of the survival testing. The SFH had the enrichment of 'oxygen binding'. As shown in Figure 4A, the patients with copy number gain in the SFH had reduced survival comparing with neutral status. Interestingly, all the SFHs with survival-associated gain status were all located at

Table 2 The SFHs of which copy number status were associated with patient survival

Chr	Start pos	End pos	p value		Presented gene set	Number of overlapped genes
Gain						
19	41.38	41.63	2.6E-04	mf	Oxygen binding	2
19	43.23	44.29	0.001	bp	Defense response	4
19	54.72	55.11	0.002	bp	Defense response	6
19	54.72	55.11	0.002	bp	Cell surface receptor linked Signaling pathway	6
19	40.09	40.23	0.003	mf	Lysophospholipase activity	2
19	40.09	40.23	0.003	mf	Carboxylesterase activity	2
19	39.41	39.52	0.004	cc	SCF ubiquitin ligase complex	2
19	39.41	39.52	0.004	mf	Glycoprotein binding	2
19	51.63	52.15	0.007	mf	Sugar binding	9
19	54.78	55.38	0.007	bp	Regulation of immune response	8
19	51.63	52.27	0.007	bp	Cell adhesion	11
19	42.18	44.32	0.007	cc	Anchored to membrane	9
19	54.72	55.55	0.007	mf	Transmembrane receptor activity	8
19	54.80	55.30	0.007	mf	Antigen binding	5
19	54.78	55.42	0.007	bp	Cellular defense response	5
19	54.72	55.55	0.007	cc	Integral to plasma membrane	12
19	58.55	59.08	0.007	bp	Viral reproduction	7
19	54.78	55.40	0.007	bp	Immune response	6
19	50.86	51.59	0.008	mf	Peptidase activity	17
19	45.41	45.45	0.008	mf	Lipid transporter activity	2
Loss						
8	11.83	12.18	2.4E-04	bp	Defense response to bacterium	4
4	55.10	55.99	0.001	bp	Vascular endothelial growth Factor receptor signaling pathway	2
4	55.10	55.99	0.001	mf	Growth factor binding	2
8	22.88	23.08	0.001	mf	Caspase activator activity	2
8	22.30	23.02	0.002	bp	Apoptosis	5
4	74.61	74.97	0.003	bp	Inflammatory response	5
8	26.37	27.47	0.004	cc	Growth cone	3
8	26.37	27.32	0.004	bp	Response to cocaine	2
8	22.01	23.08	0.005	bp	Cellular response to mechanical stimulus	3
4	68.69	69.36	0.006	mf	Serine-type endopeptidase activity	5
4	68.69	69.36	0.006	bp	Proteolysis	5
4	68.69	69.36	0.006	mf	Peptidase activity	5
4	70.86	71.40	0.007	bp	Biomineral tissue development	5
4	71.06	71.47	0.007	bp	Odontogenesis of dentine-containing tooth	3
4	74.26	74.85	0.007	cc	Platelet alpha granule lumen	3
4	74.26	74.85	0.007	bp	Platelet degranulation	3
4	76.92	76.94	0.008	bp	Defense response to virus	2
4	74.70	75.32	0.008	bp	Cell-cell signaling	4
8	38.13	38.33	0.008	bp	Cell growth	2

chromosome 19 and ranged from 33.7 M to 59 Mbp. Four immune-related functions, defense response, regulation of immune response, antigen binding, and immune response, were enriched in the region. The finding indicated that the immune functional island located at the region is sensitive to patient survival. The SFH located at 11.8 to 12.2

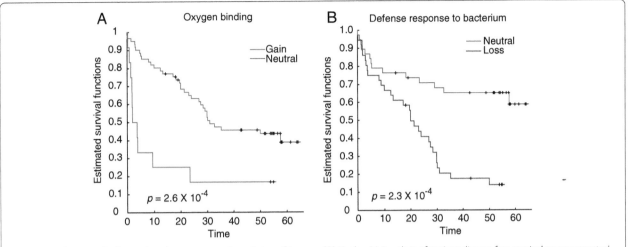

Figure 4 Patient survival correlated to copy number status of tumor. (A) Kaplan-Meier plots of patient disease-free survival were separated by the status of copy number in the SFH located at 41.1 to 41.9 Mbp at chromosome 19. The SFH has enrichment of 'oxygen binding'. Samples were assigned to two groups, copy number gain (red line) and neutral (blue line). The p values was statistically significant (<0.01). **(B)** Kaplan-Meier plots of the copy number status in SFH at 11.8 to 12.2 Mbp at chromosome 8. Samples were assigned to two groups, copy number loss (green line) and neutral (blue line). The SFH had enrichment of 'defense response to bacterium'. The p value of test was also significant.

Mbp at chromosome 8, which has enrichment of 'defense response to bacterium', has the smallest p value of copy number loss status (Figure 4B). For SFHs with survival-associated loss status, 12 of them were located at 55 to 76.9 Mbp region at chromosome 4, and 7 of them were located at 11.1 to 38.3 Mbp at chromosome 8.

Discussion

We introduced a system biology method, motivated by Cancer Gene Island, to identify the spatial functional hotspots in human genome. A statistical assay was presented to estimate the enrichment within genome regions to functional gene sets. By applying the terms of Gene Ontology into our method, the result provided the details of the function encoded in human genome. We set the two parameters of the algorithm, the length of window size and shift distance, as 1 and 0.25 Mbp, respectively. Although the setting of the parameters will affect the p value of enrichment testing for each segment, our algorithm performed an optimal procedure which merge the continual enriched segments and find the region with maximum p values by removing the gene one by one from both sides. Different settings of window size will not affect the results of final optimal regions. However, the detection of continual functional enriched segments could be missed under the condition of small window size because the windows contained no and less genes. To find out the workable parameters, we tested three conditions of window sizes, 0.5, 1, and 1.5 Mbp and found out that the condition of 0.5 Mbp contains large numbers of segments of which the gene number is less than three. The parameters of 1 and 1.5 Mbp

contain fewer segments with low numbers of genes. Through the testing, we set the window size as 1 Mbp to analyze the human genome.

We applied the method in HCC data set to estimate the effect of hotspots in the genome. Using the data set GSE14322 as an example, a total of 150 SFHs have been identified with copy number alterations in most of the HCC patients, and the novelty of our analysis is to identify the functional hotspots in human genome. The region we identified is located with high density of genes that share the same biological function, and as we demonstrated in the HCC dataset, these functions may also be sensitive to CNAs. Two immune-related functional regions were identified with gain or loss in most of patients in the HCC dataset. The major carcinogenesis of HCC is the chronic and acute inflammation under HBV or HCV infection; thus, we hypothesize that these two regions we identified may also play a role in HCC oncogenesis.

We also identified 39 SFHs of which the copy number status was associated with patient survival. The result indicates that the copy number alterations in these regions may affect the function of tumor progression and then reflect on patient survival. For example, the patients who have copy number loss in the SFH which was enriched in inflammatory response have shorter survival. The chronic and acute inflammations induced by HBV and HCV infection have been proved to play an important role in HCC tumorgenesis [22,23]. Our data implied that copy number alterations may contribute in the inflammatory response. Also, other enriched functions in survival-related SFHs have been reported, such as regulation of immune response, cell growth, apoptosis, and caspase activator activity. The SFHs and enriched function we identified provided the clues of the association between CNAs and the regulations of the enriched functions. We expected that the SFHs we identified will provide further insight of affected functions of CNAs to uncover the mechanism of cancer.

Conclusions

In this paper, we systematically surveyed human genome and identified 838 functional hotspots based on Gene Ontology classification. To substantiate our findings, 76 HCC tumors and their DNA copy number gain/loss statuses were examined closely. Among the 838 hotspots, a total of 150 regions affected by CNAs, and the encoded enriched functions were identified. Our results indicate that two immune-related hotspots had copy number alterations in most of the patients and might be involved in HCC oncogenesis. In addition, 39 survival-related hotspots were identified. Taken together, our results demonstrated that the method presented in the paper is a powerful tool to survey biological functions of CNAs and to construct regulation hypothesis at pathway and functional levels.

Additional file

Additional file 1: Supplemental materials. This file contains tables and a figure showing the enriched functions, spatial functional hotspots, and histogram of the gene numbers.

Competing interests
All authors declare that they have no competing interests.

Acknowledgements
This work was supported by the NIH/NCI Cancer Center grant (P30 CA054174-17), NSF grant (NSF CCF-1246072), and Qatar National Research Foundation (NPRP09 -874-3-235). TH is supported by NIH/NCI grant (U54 CA113001) and the Greehey Children Cancer Research Institute (GCCRI) Intramural Research fund. SR and XWW were supported by grants (Z01-BC 010313) from the Intramural Research Program of the Center for Cancer Research, the National Cancer Institute. The funders had no role in the study design, data collection and analysis, decision to publish, or preparation of the manuscript.

Author details
[1]Greehey Children's Cancer Research Institute, University of Texas Health Science Center at San Antonio, San Antonio, TX 78229, USA. [2]Institute of Pathology, University Hospital, Im Neuenheimer Feld 224, Room 2.034, Heidelberg 69120, Germany. [3]Laboratory of Human Carcinogenesis, National Cancer Institute, NIH, Bethesda, MD 20892, USA. [4]Department of Epidemiology and Biostatistics, University of Texas Health Science Center at San Antonio, San Antonio, TX 78229, USA.

References
1.   SL Carter, AC Eklund, IS Kohane, LN Harris, Z Szallasi, A signature of chromosomal instability inferred from gene expression profiles predicts clinical outcome in multiple human cancers. Nat. Genet. 38, 1043–1048 (2006)

2.   HG Russnes, HK Vollan, OC Lingjaerde, A Krasnitz, P Lundin, B Naume, T Sørlie, E Borgen, IH Rye, A Langerød, SF Chin, AE Teschendorff, PJ Stephens, S Månér, E Schlichting, LO Baumbusch, R Kåresen, MP Stratton, M Wigler, C Caldas, A Zetterberg, J Hicks, AL Børresen-Dale, Genomic architecture characterizes tumor progression paths and fate in breast cancer patients. Sci. Transl. Med 2, 38ra47 (2010)

3.   P Micke, K Edlund, L Holmberg, HG Kultima, L Mansouri, S Ekman, M Bergqvist, L Scheibenflug, K Lamberg, G Myrdal, A Berglund, A Andersson, M Lambe, F Nyberg, A Thomas, A Isaksson, J Botling, Gene copy number aberrations are associated with survival in histologic subgroups of non-small cell lung cancer. J. Thorac. Oncol. 6, 1833–1840 (2011)

4.   K Kurashina, Y Yamashita, T Ueno, K Koinuma, J Ohashi, H Horie, Y Miyakura, T Hamada, H Haruta, H Hatanaka, M Soda, YL Choi, S Takada, Y Yasuda, H Nagai, H Mano, Chromosome copy number analysis in screening for prognosis-related genomic regions in colorectal carcinoma. Cancer Sci. 99, 1835–1840 (2008)

5.   M Tan, D Yu, Molecular mechanisms of erbB2-mediated breast cancer chemoresistance. Adv. Exp. Med. Biol. 608, 119–129 (2007)

6.   JE Lucas, HN Kung, JT Chi, Latent factor analysis to discover pathway-associated putative segmental aneuploidies in human cancers. PLoS Comput. Biol. 6, e1000920 (2010)

7.   NL Solimini, Q Xu, CH Mermel, AC Liang, MR Schlabach, J Luo, AE Burrows, AN Anselmo, AL Bredemeyer, MZ Li, R Beroukhim, M Meyerson, SJ Elledge, Recurrent hemizygous deletions in cancers may optimize proliferative potential. Science 337, 104–109 (2012)

8.   X Tang, JE Lucas, JL Chen, G LaMonte, J Wu, MC Wang, C Koumenis, JT Chi, Functional interaction between responses to lactic acidosis and hypoxia regulates genomic transcriptional outputs. Cancer Res. 72, 491–502 (2012)

9.   W da Huang, BT Sherman, RA Lempicki, Bioinformatics enrichment tools: paths toward the comprehensive functional analysis of large gene lists. Nucleic Acids Res 37, 1–13 (2009)

10. SA Tomlins, R Mehra, DR Rhodes, X Cao, L Wang, SM Dhanasekaran, S Kalyana-Sundaram, JT Wei, MA Rubin, KJ Pienta, RB Shah, AM Chinnaiyan, Integrative molecular concept modeling of prostate cancer progression. Nat. Genet. 39, 41–51 (2007)

11. Q Zheng, XJ Wang, GOEAST: a web-based software toolkit for Gene Ontology enrichment analysis. Nucleic Acids Res 36, W358–W363 (2008)

12. W da Huang, BT Sherman, RA Lempicki, Systematic and integrative analysis of large gene lists using DAVID bioinformatics resources. Nat. Protoc. 4, 44–57 (2009)

13. DM Parkin, F Bray, J Ferlay, P Pisani, Global cancer statistics, 2002. CA. Cancer. J. Clin. 55, 74–108 (2005)

14. PA Farazi, RA DePinho, Hepatocellular carcinoma pathogenesis: from genes to environment. Nat. Rev. Cancer 6, 674–687 (2006)

15. C Schlaeger, T Longerich, C Schiller, P Bewerunge, A Mehrabi, G Toedt, J Kleeff, V Ehemann, R Eils, P Lichter, P Schirmacher, B Radlwimmer, Etiology-dependent molecular mechanisms in human hepatocarcinogenesis. Hepatology 47, 511–520 (Feb 2008)

16. MA Patil, I Gutgemann, J Zhang, C Ho, ST Cheung, D Ginzinger, R Li, KJ Dykema, S So, ST Fan, S Kakar, KA Furge, R Buttner, X Chen, Array-based comparative genomic hybridization reveals recurrent chromosomal aberrations and Jab1 as a potential target for 8q gain in hepatocellular carcinoma. Carcinogenesis 26, 2050–2057 (2005)

17. L Zender, MS Spector, W Xue, P Flemming, C Cordon-Cardo, J Silke, ST Fan, JM Luk, M Wigler, GJ Hannon, D Mu, R Lucito, S Powers, SW Lowe, Identification and validation of oncogenes in liver cancer using an integrative oncogenomic approach. Cell 125, 1253–1267 (2006)

18. L Zender, W Xue, J Zuber, CP Semighini, A Krasnitz, B Ma, P Zender, S Kubicka, JM Luk, P Schirmacher, WR McCombie, M Wigler, J Hicks, GJ Hannon, S Powers, SW Lowe, An oncogenomics-based in vivo RNAi screen identifies tumor suppressors in liver cancer. Cell 135, 852–864 (2008)

19. S Roessler, EL Long, A Budhu, Y Chen, X Zhao, J Ji, R Walker, HL Jia, QH Ye, LX Qin, ZY Tang, P He, KW Hunter, SS Thorgeirsson, PS Meltzer, XW Wang, Integrative genomic identification of genes on 8p associated with hepatocellular carcinoma progression and patient survival. Gastroenterology 142, 957–966 (2012)

20. P Flicek, MR Amode, D Barrell, K Beal, S Brent, D Carvalho-Silva, P Clapham, G Coates, S Fairley, S Fitzgerald, L Gil, L Gordon, M Hendrix, T Hourlier, N Johnson, AK Kähäri, D Keefe, S Keenan, R Kinsella, M Komorowska, G Koscielny, E Kulesha, P Larsson, I Longden, W McLaren, M Muffato, B Overduin, M Pignatelli, B Pritchard, HS Riat, Ensembl 2012. Nucleic Acid Res 40, D84–D90 (2012)

21. AB Olshen, ES Venkatraman, R Lucito, M Wigler, Circular binary
     segmentation for the analysis of array-based DNA copy number data.
     Biostatistics **5**, 557–572 (2004)
22. M Levrero, Viral hepatitis and liver cancer: the case of hepatitis C. Oncogene
     25, 3834–3847 (2006)
23. D Kremsdorf, P Soussan, P Paterlini-Brechot, C Brechot, Hepatitis B virus-
     related hepatocellular carcinoma: paradigms for viral-related human
     carcinogenesis. Oncogene **25**, 3823–3833 (2006)

Scientific knowledge is possible with small-sample classification

Edward R Dougherty[1,2]* and Lori A Dalton[3]

Abstract

A typical small-sample biomarker classification paper discriminates between types of pathology based on, say, 30,000 genes and a small labeled sample of less than 100 points. Some classification rule is used to design the classifier from this data, but we are given no good reason or conditions under which this algorithm should perform well. An error estimation rule is used to estimate the classification error on the population using the same data, but once again we are given no good reason or conditions under which this error estimator should produce a good estimate, and thus we do not know how well the classifier should be expected to perform. In fact, virtually, in all such papers the error estimate is expected to be highly inaccurate. In short, we are given no justification for any claims.

Given the ubiquity of vacuous small-sample classification papers in the literature, one could easily conclude that scientific knowledge is impossible in small-sample settings. It is not that thousands of papers overtly claim that scientific knowledge is impossible in regard to their content; rather, it is that they utilize methods that preclude scientific knowledge. In this paper, we argue to the contrary that scientific knowledge in small-sample classification is possible provided there is sufficient prior knowledge. A natural way to proceed, discussed herein, is via a paradigm for pattern recognition in which we incorporate prior knowledge in the whole classification procedure (classifier design and error estimation), optimize each step of the procedure given available information, and obtain theoretical measures of performance for both classifiers and error estimators, the latter being the critical epistemological issue. In sum, we can achieve scientific validation for a proposed small-sample classifier and its error estimate.

Review

Introduction

It is implicit in the title of this paper that one can entertain the possibility that scientific knowledge is impossible with small-sample classification. In fact, not only might one entertain this impossibility, but perusal of the related literature would most likely lead one to seriously consider that impossibility. It is not that thousands of papers overtly claim that scientific knowledge is impossible with regards to their content; rather, it is that they utilize methods that, *ipso facto*, cannot lead to knowledge. Even though it appears to be almost universally, if tacitly, assumed that scientific knowledge is impossible with small-sample classification - otherwise, why do so many not aspire to such knowledge - we argue to the contrary in this paper that

scientific knowledge is possible. But before we make our case, let us examine in more detail why the literature may lead one to believe otherwise.

Consider the following common motif for a small-sample-classification paper, for instance, one proposing a classifier based on gene expression to discriminate types of pathology, stages of a disease, duration of survival, or some other phenotypic difference. Beginning with 30,000 features (genes) and less than 100 labeled sample points (microarrays), some classification rule (algorithm) is selected, perhaps an old one or a new one proposed in the paper. We are given no good reason why this algorithm should perform well. The classification rule is applied to the data and, using the same data, an error estimation rule is used to estimate the classification error on the population, meaning in practice the error rate on future observations. Once again, we are given no good reason why this error estimator should produce a good estimate; in fact, virtually, in all such papers, from what we know about the error estimation rule we would expect

*Correspondence: edward@ece.tamu.edu
[1] Department of Electrical and Computer Engineering, Texas A&M University, College Station, TX 77843, USA
[2] Computational Biology Division, Translational Genomics Research Institute, Phoenix, AZ 85004, USA
Full list of author information is available at the end of the article

the estimate to be inaccurate. At this point, one of two claims is made. If the classification rule is a well-known rule and the purpose of the paper is to produce a classifier for application (say, a biomarker panel), we are told that the authors have achieved their goal of finding such a classifier and its accuracy is validated by the error estimate. If, on the other hand, the purpose is to devise a new classification rule, we are told that the efficacy of the new rule has been validated by its performance, as measured by the error estimate or, by several such error estimates on several different data sets. In either case, we are given no justification for the validation claim. Moreover, in the second case, we are not told the conditions under which the classification rule should be expected to perform well or how well it should be expected to perform.

Amid all of this vacuity, perhaps the reporting of error estimates whose accuracy is a complete mystery is the most puzzling from a scientific perspective. To borrow a metaphor [1], one can imagine Harold Cramér leisurely sailing on the Baltic off the coast of Stockholm, taking in the sights and sounds of the sea, when suddenly a gene-expression classifier to detect prostate cancer pops into his head. No classification rule has been applied, nor is that necessary. All that matters is that Cramér's imagination has produced a classifier that operates on the feature-label distribution of interest with a sufficiently small error rate. Since scientific validity depends on the predictive capacity of a model, while an appropriate classification rule is certainly beneficial to classifier design, epistemologically, the error rate is paramount. Were we to know the feature-label distribution of interest, we could exactly determine the error rate of the proposed classifier. Absent knowledge of the feature-label distribution, the actual error must be estimated from data and the accuracy of the estimate judged from the performance of the error estimation rule employed. Consequently, any paper that applies an error estimation rule without providing a performance characterization relevant to the data at hand is scientifically vacuous. Given the near universality of vacuous small-sample classification papers in the literature, one could easily reach the conclusion that scientific knowledge is impossible in small-sample settings. Of course, this would beg the question of why people are writing vacuous papers and why journals are publishing them. Since the latter are sociological questions, they are outside the domain of the current paper. We will focus on the scientific issues.

Epistemological digression

Before proceeding, we digress momentarily for some very brief comments regarding scientific epistemology (referring to [2] for a comprehensive treatise and to [3] for a discussion aimed at biology and including classifier validity). Our aim is narrow, simply to emphasize the role of prediction in scientific knowledge, not to indulge in broad philosophical issues.

A scientific theory consists of two parts: (1) a *mathematical model* composed of symbols (variables and relations between the variables), and (2) a set of *operational definitions* that relate the symbols to data. A mathematical model alone does not constitute a scientific theory. The formal mathematical structure must yield experimental predictions in accord with experimental observations. As put succinctly by Richard Feynman, "It is whether or not the theory gives predictions that agree with experiment. It is not a question of whether a theory is philosophically delightful, or easy to understand, or perfectly reasonable from the point of view of common sense" [4]. Model validity is characterized by predictive relations, without which the model lacks empirical content. Validation requires that the symbols be tied to observations by some semantic rules that relate not necessarily to the general principles of the mathematical model themselves but to conclusions drawn from the principles. There must be a clearly defined tie between the mathematical model and experimental methodology. Philipp Frank writes, "Reichenbach had explicitly pointed out that what is needed is a bridge between the symbolic system of axioms and the protocols of the laboratory. But the nature of this bridge had been only vaguely described. Bridgman was the first who said precisely that these *relations of coordination* consist in the description of physical operations. He called them, therefore, *operational definitions*" [5]. Elsewhere, we have written, "Operational definitions are required, but their exact formulation in a given circumstance is left open. Their specification constitutes an epistemological issue that must be addressed in mathematical (including logical) statements. Absent such a specification, a purported scientific theory is meaningless" [6].

The validity of a scientific theory depends on the choice of validity criteria and the mathematical properties of those criteria. The observational measurements and the manner in which they are to be compared to the mathematical model must be formally specified. The validity of a theory is relative to this specification, but what is not at issue is the necessity of a set of relations tying the model to operational measurements. Formal specification is mandatory and this necessarily takes the form of mathematical (including logical) statements. Formal specification is especially important in stochastic settings where experimental outcomes reflect the randomness of the stochastic system so that one must carefully define how the outcomes are to be interpreted.

Story telling and intuitive arguments cannot suffice. Not only is complex-system behavior often unintuitive, but stochastic processes and statistics often contradict naïve probabilistic notions gathered from simple experiments like rolling dice. Perhaps even worse is an appeal to pretty pictures drawn with computer software. The literature abounds with data partitioned according to some clustering algorithm whose partitioning performance is unknown or, even more strangely, justified by some "validation index" that is poorly, if at all, correlated with the error rate of the clustering algorithm [7]. The pretty pictures are usually multi-colored and augmented with all kinds of attractive-looking symbols. They are inevitably followed by some anecdotal commentary. Although all of this may be delightful, it is scientifically meaningless. Putting the artistic touches and enormous calculations aside, all we are presented with is a radical empiricism. Is there any knowledge here? Hans Reichenbach answers, "A mere report of relations observed in the past cannot be called knowledge. If knowledge is to reveal objective relations of physical objects, it must include reliable predictions. A radical empiricism, therefore, denies the possibility of knowledge" [2]. A collection of measurements together with a commentary on the measurements is not scientific knowledge. Indeed, the entire approach "denies the possibility of knowledge," so that its adoption constitutes a declaration of meaninglessness.

Classification error

For two-class classification, the population is characterized by a feature-label distribution F for a random pair $(\mathbf{X}, Y)$, where $\mathbf{X}$ is a vector of D features and Y is the binary label, 0 or 1, of the class containing $\mathbf{X}$. A classifier is a function, ψ, which assigns a binary label, $\psi(\mathbf{X})$, to each feature vector. The error, $\varepsilon[\psi]$, of ψ is the probability, $P(\psi(\mathbf{X}) \neq Y)$, that ψ yields an erroneous label. A classifier with minimum error among all classifiers is known as a *Bayes classifier* for the feature-label distribution. The minimum error is called the *Bayes error*. Epistemologically, the error is the key issue since it quantifies the predictive capacity of the classifier.

Abstractly, any pair $\mathcal{M} = (\psi, \varepsilon_\psi)$ composed of a function $\psi : \mathbb{R}^D \rightarrow \{0, 1\}$ and a real number $\varepsilon_\psi \in [0, 1]$ constitutes a *classifier model*, with ε_ψ being simply a number, not necessarily specifying an actual error probability corresponding to ψ. $\mathcal{M}$ becomes a scientific model when it is applied to a feature-label distribution. In practice, the feature-label distribution is unknown and a *classification rule* Ψ_n is used to design a classifier ψ_n from a random sample $S_n = \{(\mathbf{X}_1, Y_1), (\mathbf{X}_2, Y_2), \ldots, (\mathbf{X}_n, Y_n)\}$ of pairs drawn from the feature-label distribution. Note that a classification rule is a sequence of rules depending on the sample size n. If feature selection is involved, then it is part of the classification rule. A designed classifier produces a classifier model, namely, $(\psi_n, \varepsilon[\psi_n])$. Since the true classifier error $\varepsilon[\psi_n]$ depends on the feature-label distribution, which is unknown, $\varepsilon[\psi_n]$ is unknown. The true error must be estimated by an *estimation rule*, Ξ_n. Thus, the random sample S_n yields a classifier $\psi_n = \Psi_n(S_n)$ and

an error estimate $\hat{\varepsilon}[\psi_n] = \Xi_n(S_n)$, which together constitute a classifier model $(\psi_n, \hat{\varepsilon}[\psi_n])$. Overall, classifier design involves a *rule model* (Ψ_n, Ξ_n) used to determine a sample-dependent classifier model $(\psi_n, \hat{\varepsilon}[\psi_n])$. Both $(\psi_n, \varepsilon[\psi_n])$ and $(\psi_n, \hat{\varepsilon}[\psi_n])$ are random pairs relative to the sampling distribution.

Given a feature-label distribution, error estimation accuracy is commonly measured by the *mean-square error* (*MSE*), defined by $\mathrm{MSE}(\hat{\varepsilon}) = \mathrm{E}[(\hat{\varepsilon} - \varepsilon)^2]$, where for notational ease we denote $\varepsilon[\psi_n]$ and $\hat{\varepsilon}[\psi_n]$ by ε and $\hat{\varepsilon}$, respectively, or, equivalently, by the square root of the MSE, known as the *root-mean-square* (*RMS*). The expectation used here is relative to the sampling distribution induced by the feature-label distribution. The MSE is decomposed into the bias, $\mathrm{Bias}(\hat{\varepsilon}) = \mathrm{E}[\hat{\varepsilon} - \varepsilon]$, of the error estimator relative to the true error, and the deviation variance, $\mathrm{Var}_{\mathrm{dev}}(\hat{\varepsilon}) = \mathrm{Var}(\hat{\varepsilon} - \varepsilon)$, by

$$\mathrm{MSE}(\hat{\varepsilon}) = \mathrm{Var}_{\mathrm{dev}}(\hat{\varepsilon}) + \mathrm{Bias}(\hat{\varepsilon})^2. \tag{1}$$

When a large amount of data is available, the sample can be split into independent training and test sets, the classifier being designed on the training data and its error being estimated by the proportion of errors on the test data, which is known as the holdout estimator. For holdout, we have the distribution-free bound $\mathrm{RMS}(\hat{\varepsilon}_{\mathrm{holdout}}|S_{n-m}, F) \leq 1/\sqrt{4m}$, where m is the size of the test sample, S_{n-m} is the training sample and F is any feature-label distribution [8]. $\mathrm{RMS}(\hat{\varepsilon}|Z)$ indicates that the expectation in the RMS is conditioned on the random vector Z. But when data are limited, the sample cannot be split without leaving too little data to design a good classifier. Hence, training and error estimation must take place on the same data set.

The consequences of training-set error estimation are readily explained by the following formula for the deviation variance:

$$\mathrm{Var}_{\mathrm{dev}}(\hat{\varepsilon}) = \sigma_{\hat{\varepsilon}}^2 + \sigma_\varepsilon^2 - 2\rho\sigma_{\hat{\varepsilon}}\sigma_\varepsilon, \tag{2}$$

where $\sigma_{\hat{\varepsilon}}^2, \sigma_\varepsilon^2$, and ρ are the variance of the error estimate, the variance of the error, and the correlation between the estimated and true errors, respectively. The deviation variance is driven down by small variances or a correlation coefficient near 1.

Consider the popular cross-validation error estimator. For it, the error is estimated on the training data by randomly splitting the training data into k folds (subsets), S_n^i, for $i = 1, 2, ..., k$, training k classifiers on $S_n - S_n^i$, for $i = 1, 2, ..., k$, calculating the proportion of errors of each designed classifier on the appropriate left-out fold, and then averaging these proportions to obtain the cross-validation estimate of the originally designed classifier. Various enhancements are made, such as by repeating the process some number of times and averaging. Letting $k = n$ yields the leave-one-out estimator. The problem with cross-validation is evident from (2): for small samples, it has large variance and little correlation with the true error. Hence, although with small folds, cross-validation does not suffer too much from bias, it typically has large deviation variance.

To illustrate the matter, we reproduce an example from [9] based on real patient data from a study involving microarrays prepared with RNA from breast tumor specimens from 295 patients, 115 and 180 belonging to the good-prognosis and poor-prognosis classes, respectively. The dataset is reduced to the 2,000 genes with highest variance, these are reduced to 10 via t test feature selection, and a classifier is designed using linear discriminant analysis (LDA). In the simulations, the data are split into two sets. The first set, consisting of 50 examples drawn without replacement from the full dataset, is used for both training and error estimation via leave-one-out cross-validation. The remaining examples are used as a hold-out test set to get an accurate estimate of the true error, which is taken as the true error. There is an assumption that such a hold-out size will give an accurate estimate of the true error. This procedure is repeated 10,000 times. Figure 1 shows the scatter plot for the pairs of true and estimated errors, along with the linear regression of the true error on the estimated error. The means are shown on the axes. What we observe is typical for small samples: large variance and negligible regression between the true and estimated errors [10]. Indeed, one even sees negatively sloping regression lines for cross-validation and bootstrap (another resampling error estimator), and negative

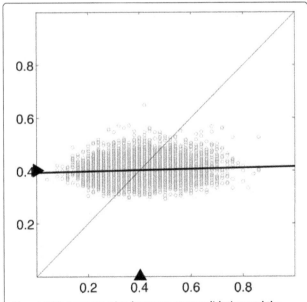

Figure 1 Linear regression between cross-validation and the true error. Scatter plot and linear regression for cross-validation (horizontal axis) and the true error (vertical axis) with sample size 50 for linear discrimination between two classes of breast cancer patients.

correlation between the true and cross-validation estimated errors has been mathematically demonstrated in some basic models [11]. Such error estimates are worthless and can lead to a huge waste of resources in trying to reproduce them [9].

RMS bounds

Suppose a sample is collected, a classification rule Ψ_n applied, and the classifier error estimated by an error-estimation rule Ξ_n to arrive at the classifier model $(\psi_n, \hat{\varepsilon}[\psi_n])$. If no assumptions are posited regarding the feature-label distribution, then the entire procedure is completely distribution-free. There are three possibilities. First, if no validity criterion is specified, then the classifier model is *ipso facto* epistemologically meaningless. Second, if a validity criterion is specified, say RMS, and no distribution-free results are known about the RMS for Ψ_n and Ξ_n, then again the model is meaningless. Third, if there exist distribution-free RMS bounds concerning Ψ_n and Ξ_n, then these bounds can, in principle, be used to quantify the performance of the error estimator and thereby quantify model validity.

Regarding the third possibility, the following is an example of a distribution-free RMS bound for the leave-one-out error estimator with the discrete histogram rule and tie-breaking in the direction of class 0 [8]:

$$\text{RMS}(\hat{\varepsilon}_{\text{loo}}|F) \leq \sqrt{\frac{1 + 6/e}{n} + \frac{6}{\sqrt{\pi(n-1)}}}, \tag{3}$$

where F is any feature-label distribution. Although this bound holds for all distributions, it is useless for small samples: for $n = 200$ this bound is 0.506. In general, there are very few cases in which distribution-free bounds are known and, when they are known, they are useless for small samples.

Distribution-based bounds are needed. These require knowledge of the RMS, which means knowledge concerning the second-order moments of the joint distribution between the true and estimated errors. More generally, to fully understand an error estimator we need to know its joint distribution with the true error. Oddly, this problem has historically been ignored in pattern recognition, notwithstanding the fact that error estimation is the epistemological ground for classification. Going back to the 1970s there were some results on the mean and variance of some error estimators for the Gaussian model using LDA. In 1966, Hills obtained the expected value of the resubstitution and plug-in estimators in the univariate model with known common variance [12]. The resubstitution estimate is simply a count of the classification errors on the training data and the plug-in estimate is found by using the data to estimate the feature-label distribution and then finding the error of the designed classifier on the estimated distribution. In 1972, Foley obtained the expected value of resubstitution in the multivariate model with known common covariance matrix [13]. In 1973, Sorum derived results for the expected value and variance for both resubstitution and leave-one-out in the univariate model with known common variance [14]. In 1973, McLachlan derived an asymptotic representation for the expected value of resubstitution in the multivariate model with unknown common covariance matrix [15]. In 1975, Moran obtained new results for the expected value of resubstitution and plug-in for the multivariate model with known covariance matrix [16]. In 1977, Goldstein and Wolf obtained the expected value of resubstitution for multinomial discrimination [17]. Following the latter, there was a gap of 15 years before Davison and Hall derived asymptotic representations for the expected value and variance of bootstrap and leave-one-out in the univariate Gaussian model with unknown and possibly different covariances [18]. This is the only paper we know of providing analytic results for moments of common error estimators between 1977 and 2005. None of these papers provided representation of the joint distribution or representation of second-order mixed moments, which are needed for the RMS.

This problem has only recently been addressed beginning in 2005, in particular, for the resubstitution and leave-one-out estimators. For the multinomial model, complete enumeration was used to obtain the marginal distributions for the error estimators [11] and then the joint distributions [19]. Exact closed-form representations for second-order moments, including the mixed moments, were obtained, thereby obtaining exact RMS representations for both estimators [11]. For the Gaussian model using LDA in 2009, we obtained the exact marginal distributions for both estimators in the univariate model (known but not necessarily equal class variances) and approximations in the multivariate model (known and equal class covariance matrices) [20]. Subsequently, these were extended to the joint distributions for the true and estimated errors in a Gaussian model [21]. Recently exact closed-form representations for the second-order moments in the univariate model without assuming equal covariances were discovered, thereby providing exact expression of the RMS for both estimators [22]. Moreover, double asymptotic representations for the second-order moments in the multivariate model, sample size and dimension approaching infinity at a fixed rate between the two, were found, thereby providing double asymptotic expressions for the RMS [23]. Finite sample approximations from the double asymptotic method have been shown to possess better accuracy than various simple asymptotic representations (although much more work is needed on this issue) [24,25].

Validity

Let us now consider validity. An obvious way to proceed would be to say that a classifier model (ψ, ε_ψ) is valid for the feature-label distribution F to the extent that ε_ψ approximates the classifier error, $\varepsilon[\psi]$, on F, where the degree of approximation is measured by some distance between ε_ψ and $\varepsilon[\psi]$. For a classifier ψ_n designed from a specific sample, this would mean that we want to measure some distance between $\varepsilon = \varepsilon[\psi_n]$ and $\hat{\varepsilon} = \hat{\varepsilon}[\psi_n]$, say $|\varepsilon - \hat{\varepsilon}|$. To do this, we would have to know the true error and to know that we would need to know F. But if we knew F, we would use the Bayes classifier and would not need to design a classifier from sample data. Since it is the precision of the error estimate that is of consequence, a natural way to proceed would be to characterize validity in terms of the precision of the error estimator $\hat{\varepsilon}[\psi_n] = \Xi_n(S_n)$ as an estimator of $\varepsilon[\psi_n]$, say by RMS($\hat{\varepsilon}$). This makes sense because both the true and estimated errors are random functions of the sample and the RMS measures their closeness across the sampling distribution. But again there is a catch: the RMS depends on F, which we do not know. Thus, given the sample without knowledge of F, we cannot compute the RMS.

To proceed, prior knowledge is required, in the sense that we need to assume that the actual (unknown) feature-label distribution belongs to some *uncertainty class*, $\mathcal{U}$, of feature-label distributions. Once RMS representations have been obtained for feature-label distributions in $\mathcal{U}$, distribution-based RMS bounds follow: RMS($\hat{\varepsilon}$) $\leq$ $\max_{G \in \mathcal{U}}$ RMS($\hat{\varepsilon}|G$) , where RMS($\hat{\varepsilon}|G$) is the RMS of the error estimator under the assumption that the feature-label distribution is G. We do not know the actual feature-label distribution precisely, but prior knowledge allows us to bound the RMS. For instance, consider using LDA with a feature-label distribution having two equally probable Gaussian class-conditional densities sharing a known covariance matrix. For this model the Bayes error is a one-to-one decreasing function of the distance, m, between the means. Figure 2a shows the RMS to be a one-to-one increasing function of the Bayes error for leave-one-out for dimension $D = 10$ and sample sizes $n = 20, 40, 60$, the RMS and Bayes errors being on the y and x axes, respectively.

Assuming a parameterized model in which the RMS is an increasing function of the Bayes error, ε_{bay}, we can pose the following question: Given sample size n and $\lambda > 0$, what is the maximum value, maxBayes(λ), of the Bayes error such that RMS($\hat{\varepsilon}$) $\leq \lambda$? If RMS is the measure of validity and λ represents the largest acceptable RMS for the classifier model to be considered meaningful, then the epistemological requirement is characterized by maxBayes(λ). Given the relationship between model parameters and the Bayes error, the inequality $\varepsilon_{\text{bay}} \leq$ maxBayes(λ) can be solved in terms of the parameters to

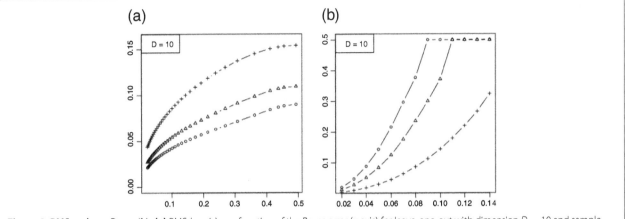

Figure 2 RMS and maxBayes(λ). **(a)** RMS (y-axis) as a function of the Bayes error (x-axis) for leave-one-out with dimension $D = 10$ and sample sizes $n = 20$ (plus sign), 40 (triangle), 60 (circle); **(b)** maxBayes(λ) curves corresponding to the RMS curves in part **(a)**.

arrive at a necessary modeling assumption. In the preceding Gaussian example, since ε_{bay} is a decreasing function of m, we obtain an inequality $m \geq m(\lambda)$. Figure 2b shows the maxBayes(λ) curves corresponding to the RMS curves in Figure 2a [26]. These curves show that, assuming Gaussian class-conditional densities and a known common covariance matrix, further assumptions must be made to insure that the RMS is sufficiently small to make the classifier model meaningful.

To have scientific content, small-sample classification requires prior knowledge. Regarding the feature-label distribution, there are two extremes: (1) the feature-label distribution is known, in which case the entire classification problem collapses to finding the Bayes classifier and Bayes error, so there is no classifier design or error estimation issue; and (2) the uncertainty class consists of all feature-label distributions, the distribution-free case, and we typically have no bound, or one that is too loose for practice. In the middle ground, there is a trade-off between the size of the uncertainty class and the size of the sample. The uncertainty class must be sufficiently constrained (equivalently, the prior knowledge must be sufficiently great) that an acceptable bound can be achieved with an acceptable sample size.

MMSE error estimation

Given that one needs a distributional model to achieve useful performance bounds for classifier error estimation, an obvious course of action is to find or define a prior over the uncertainty class of feature-label distributions, and then find an optimal minimum-mean-square-error (MMSE) error estimator relative to that class [27]. This results in a Bayesian approach with the uncertainty class being given a prior distribution and the data being used to construct a posterior distribution, which quantifies everything we know about the feature-label distribution.

Benefits of the Bayesian approach are (1) we can incorporate prior knowledge in the whole classification procedure (classifier design and error estimation), which, as we have argued above, is desperately needed in a small-sample setting where the data provide only a meager amount of information; (2) given the mathematical framework, we can optimize each step of the procedure, further addressing the poor performance suffered in small samples; and (3) we can obtain theoretical measures of the performance for both arbitrary classifiers (via the MMSE error estimator) and arbitrary error estimators (via the sample conditioned MSE), perhaps the most important advantage epistemologically. We begin with an overview of optimal MMSE error estimation.

Assume that a sample point has a prior probability c of coming from class 0, and that the class-0 conditional distribution is parameterized by θ_0 and class 1 is parameterized by θ_1. Considering both classes, our model is completely parameterized by $\theta = \{c, \theta_0, \theta_1\}$. Given a random sample, S_n, we design a classifier ψ_n and wish to minimize the MSE between its true error, ε (a function of θ and ψ_n), and an error estimate, $\widehat{\varepsilon}$ (a function of S_n and ψ_n). A key realization is that the expectation in the MSE may now be taken over the uncertainty class conditioned on the observed sample, rather than over the sampling distribution for a fixed (unknown) feature-label distribution. The MMSE error estimator is thus the expected true error, $\widehat{\varepsilon}(\psi_n, S_n) = \mathrm{E}_\theta[\varepsilon(\psi_n, \theta)|S_n]$. The expectation given the sample is over the posterior density of θ, denoted by $\pi^*(\theta)$. Thus, we write the Bayesian MMSE error estimator with the shorthand $\widehat{\varepsilon} = \mathrm{E}_{\pi^*}[\varepsilon]$.

The Bayesian error estimate is not guaranteed to be the optimal error estimate for any particular feature-label distribution but optimal for a given sample, and assuming the parameterized model and prior probabilities, it is both optimal on average with respect to MSE and unbiased when averaged over all parameters and samples. These implications apply for any classification rule as long as the classifier is fixed given the sample. To facilitate analytic representations, we assume c, θ_0 and θ_1 are all mutually independent prior to observing the data. Denote the marginal priors of c, θ_0 and θ_1 by $\pi(c)$, $\pi(\theta_0)$ and $\pi(\theta_1)$, respectively, and suppose data are used to find each posterior, $\pi^*(c)$, $\pi^*(\theta_0)$ and $\pi^*(\theta_1)$, respectively. Independence is preserved, i.e., $\pi^*(c, \theta_0, \theta_1) = \pi^*(c)\pi^*(\theta_0)\pi^*(\theta_1)$ [27].

If ψ_n is a trained classifier given by $\psi_n(\mathbf{x}) = 0$ if $\mathbf{x} \in R_0$ and $\psi_n(\mathbf{x}) = 1$ if $\mathbf{x} \in R_1$, where R_0 and R_1 are measurable sets partitioning the sample space, then the true error of ψ_n under the distribution parameterized by θ may be decomposed as

$$\varepsilon(\psi_n, \theta) = c \int_{R_1} f_{\theta_0}(\mathbf{x}|0) \, d\mathbf{x} + (1-c) \int_{R_0} f_{\theta_1}(\mathbf{x}|1) \, d\mathbf{x} \quad (4)$$

$$= c\varepsilon^0(\psi_n, \theta_0) + (1-c)\varepsilon^1(\psi_n, \theta_1),$$

where $f_{\theta_y}(\mathbf{x}|y)$ is the class-y conditional density assuming parameter θ_y is true and ε^y is the error contributed by class y. Owing to the posterior independence between c and θ_0 and between c and θ_1, the Bayesian MMSE error estimator can be expressed as [28]

$$\hat{\varepsilon}(\psi_n, S_n) = \mathrm{E}_{\pi^*}[c] \, \mathrm{E}_{\pi^*}[\varepsilon^0] + (1 - \mathrm{E}_{\pi^*}[c]) \mathrm{E}_{\pi^*}[\varepsilon^1]. \quad (5)$$

With a fixed sample and classifier, and given θ_y, the true error, $\varepsilon^y(\psi_n, \theta_y)$, is deterministic. Thus, letting Θ_y be the parameter space of θ_y,

$$\mathrm{E}_{\pi^*}[\varepsilon^y] = \int_{\Theta_y} \varepsilon^y(\psi_n, \theta_y)\pi^*(\theta_y)d\theta_y. \quad (6)$$

Just as the true error for a fixed feature-label distribution is found from the class-conditional densities, $f_{\theta_y}(\mathbf{x}|y)$, the Bayesian MMSE error estimator for an uncertainty class can be found from *effective class-conditional densities*, which are derived by taking the expectations of the individual class-conditional densities with respect to the posterior distribution,

$$f(\mathbf{x}|y) = \int_{\Theta_y} f_{\theta_y}(\mathbf{x}|y) \, \pi^*(\theta_y) \, d\theta_y. \quad (7)$$

Specifically, we obtain an equation for the expected true error that parallels that of the true error in (4) [29]:

$$\hat{\varepsilon}(\psi_n, S_n) = \mathrm{E}_{\pi^*}[c] \int_{R_1} f(\mathbf{x}|0) \, d\mathbf{x} + (1 - \mathrm{E}_{\pi^*}[c]) \int_{R_0} f(\mathbf{x}|1) \, d\mathbf{x}. \quad (8)$$

Application of Bayesian error estimation to real data, in particular gene-expression microarray data, has been addressed in [30]. This work provides C code implementing the Bayesian error estimator for Gaussian distributions and normal-inverse-Wishart priors for both linear classifiers, with exact closed-form representations, and non-linear classifiers, where closed form-solutions are not available and we instead implement a Monte-Carlo approximation. The code and a toolbox of related utilities are publicly available. In [30] we discuss the suitability of a Gaussian model with normal-inverse-Wishart priors for microarray data and propose a feature selection scheme employing a Shapiro-Wilk Gaussianity test to validate Gaussian modeling assumptions. Furthermore, we propose a methodology for calibrating normal-inverse-Wishart priors for microarray data based on a method-of-moments approach using features discarded by the feature-selection scheme.

Sample-conditioned MSE

The RMS of an error estimator is used to characterize the validity of a classifier model. As we have discussed, if we are in possession of RMS expressions for the feature-label distributions in an uncertainty class, we can bound the RMS, so as to insure a given level of performance. In the case of MMSE error estimation, the priors provide a mathematical framework that can be used for both the analysis of any error estimator and the design of estimators with desirable properties or optimal performance. The posteriors of the distribution parameters imply a (sample-conditioned) distribution on the true classifier error. This randomness in the true error comes from our uncertainty in the underlying feature-label distribution (given the sample). Within the assumed model, this sample-conditioned distribution of the true error contains the full information about error estimator accuracy and we may speak of moments of the true error (for a fixed sample and classifier), in particular the expectation, variance, and sample-conditioned MSE, as opposed to simply the MSE relative to the sampling distribution as in classical error estimation.

Finding the sample-conditioned MSE of MMSE Bayesian error estimators amounts to evaluating the variance of the true error conditioned on the observed sample [28]. The sample-conditioned MSE converges to zero almost surely in both discrete and Gaussian models provided in [31], where closed form expressions for the MSE are available. Further, the exact MSE for arbitrary error estimators falls out naturally in the Bayesian model. That is, if $\hat{\varepsilon}_\bullet$ is a constant representing an arbitrary error estimate computed from the sample, then the MSE of $\hat{\varepsilon}_\bullet$ can be evaluated directly from that of the Bayesian error estimator:

$$\mathrm{MSE}(\hat{\varepsilon}_\bullet|S_n) = \mathrm{MSE}(\hat{\varepsilon}|S_n) + (\hat{\varepsilon} - \hat{\varepsilon}_\bullet)^2.$$

$\mathrm{MSE}(\widehat{\varepsilon}_\bullet|S_n)$, as well as its square root $\mathrm{RMS}(\widehat{\varepsilon}_\bullet|S_n)$, are minimized when $\widehat{\varepsilon} = \widehat{\varepsilon}_\bullet$.

In a classical approach, nothing is known given a sample, whereas in a Bayesian approach, the sample conditions uncertainty in the RMS and different samples may condition it to different extents. Figure 3 shows probability densities of the sample-conditioned RMS for both the leave-one-out estimator and Bayesian error estimator in a discrete model with $b = 16$ bins. The simulation generates 10,000 distributions drawn from a prior given in [31] and 1,000 samples from each distribution. The unconditional RMS (averaged over both distributions and samples) for both error estimators is also shown, as well as the distribution-free RMS bound on leave-one-out given in (3). In Figure 3, the RMS of the Bayesian error estimator tends to be very close to 0.05 whereas the leave-one-out error estimator has a long tail with substantial mass between 0.05 and 0.2, demonstrating that different samples can condition the RMS to a very significant extent. In addition, the unconditional RMS of the Bayesian error estimator is less than half that of leave-one-out, while Devroye's distribution-free bound on the unconditional RMS is too loose to be useful. Hence, not only does a Bayesian framework permit us to obtain an optimal error estimator and its RMS conditioned on the sample, but performance improvement can be significant.

In [31], a bound on the sample-conditioned RMS of the Bayesian error estimator is provided for the discrete model. With any classifier, beta priors on c and Dirichlet priors on the bin probabilities satisfying mild conditions, and given a sample S_n, $\mathrm{RMS}(\widehat{\varepsilon}_{\mathrm{BEE}}|S_n) \le 1/\sqrt{4n}$. For comparison, consider the holdout bound $\mathrm{RMS}(\widehat{\varepsilon}_{\mathrm{holdout}}|S_{n-m}, F) \le 1/\sqrt{4m}$, where m is the size of the test sample. Both bounds still hold if we remove the conditioning, and in this way they become comparable. Since $1/\sqrt{4n} \le 1/\sqrt{4m}$, under a Bayesian model not only does using the full sample to train the classifier result in a lower true error, but we expect to achieve better RMS performance using training-data error estimation than we would by holding out the entire sample for error estimation. This is a testament to the power of modeling.

Optimal classification

Since prior knowledge is required to obtain a good error estimate in small-sample settings, an obvious course of action would be to utilize that knowledge for classifier design [29,32]. Whereas ordinary *Bayes classifiers* minimize the misclassification probability when the underlying distributions are known, *optimal Bayesian classification* trains a classifier from data assuming the feature-label distribution is contained in a family parameterized by $\theta \in \Theta$ with some assumed prior density over the states. Formally, we define an optimal Bayesian classifier, ψ_{OBC}, as any classifier satisfying

$$\mathrm{E}_{\pi^*}[\varepsilon(\psi_{\mathrm{OBC}}, \theta)] \le \mathrm{E}_{\pi^*}[\varepsilon(\psi, \theta)] \qquad (9)$$

for all $\psi \in \mathcal{C}$, where $\mathcal{C}$ is an arbitrary family of classifiers. Under the Bayesian framework, this is equivalent to minimizing the probability of error as follows:

$$\begin{aligned}
\mathrm{P}(\psi_n(\mathbf{X}) \ne Y|S_n) &= \mathrm{E}_{\pi^*}[\mathrm{P}(\psi_n(\mathbf{X}) \ne Y|\theta, S_n)] \\
&= \mathrm{E}_{\pi^*}[\varepsilon(\psi_n, \theta)] \\
&= \widehat{\varepsilon}(\psi_n, S_n). \qquad (10)
\end{aligned}$$

An optimal Bayesian classifier can be found by brute force using the closed form solutions for the expected true error (the Bayesian error estimator), when available. However, if $\mathcal{C}$ is the set of all classifiers (with measurable decision regions), then an optimal Bayesian classifier can be found analogously to Bayes classification for a fixed distribution using the effective class-conditional densities. To wit, we can realize an optimal solution without explicitly finding the error for every classifier because the solution can be found pointwise. Specifically, an optimal Bayesian classifier, ψ_{OBC}, satisfying (9) for all $\psi \in \mathcal{C}$, the set of all classifiers with measurable decision regions, exists and is given pointwise by [29]

$$\psi_{\mathrm{OBC}}(\mathbf{x}) = \begin{cases} 0 & \text{if } \mathrm{E}_{\pi^*}[c]f(\mathbf{x}|0) \ge (1 - \mathrm{E}_{\pi^*}[c])f(\mathbf{x}|1), \\ 1 & \text{otherwise.} \end{cases}$$

$$(11)$$

If $\mathrm{E}_{\pi^*}[c] = 0$, then this optimal Bayesian classifier is a constant and always assigns class 1, and if $\mathrm{E}_{\pi^*}[c] = 1$ it always assigns class 0. Hence, we will typically assume that $0 < \mathrm{E}_{\pi^*}[c] < 1$.

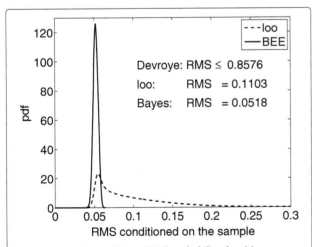

Devroye: RMS ≤ 0.8576

loo: RMS = 0.1103

Bayes: RMS = 0.0518

Figure 3 Sample-conditioned RMS probability densities.
Probability densities for the sample-conditioned RMS of leave-one-out (dashed line) and the Bayesian error estimator (solid line) in a discrete model with $b = 16$ bins, prior probability $c = 0.5$, $n = 30$ training points, and an average true error of 0.25.

Essentially, the optimal thing to do is to find the Bayes classifier using $f(\mathbf{x}|y)$ as the true class-conditional distributions. This is like a plug-in rule, only $f(\mathbf{x}|y)$ is not necessarily in the family of distributions $\{f_{\theta_y}(\mathbf{x}|y)\}$, but some other kind of density that happens to result in the optimal classifier. We find the optimal Bayesian classifier without explicitly evaluating the expected true error, $E_{\pi^*}[\varepsilon(\psi,\theta)]$, for every possible classifier ψ. With regards to both optimal Bayesian classification and Bayesian MMSE error estimation, $f(\mathbf{x}|y)$ contains all of the necessary information in the model about the class-conditional distributions and we do not have to deal with the uncertainty class or priors directly. Upon defining a model, we find $f(\mathbf{x}|y)$ (which depends on the sample because it depends on π^*) and then the whole problem is solved by treating $f(\mathbf{x}|y)$ as the true distribution: optimal classification, the error estimate of the optimal classifier, and the optimal error estimate for arbitrary classifiers. That being said, there is no short-cut to finding the sample-conditioned MSE via the effective density; indeed, there is no notion of variance in the true error of a fixed classifier under the effective class-conditional densities. Moreover, the approach of using the effective class-conditional densities finds an optimal Bayesian classifier over all possible classifiers. On the other hand, there may be advantages to restricting the space of classifiers, for example, in a Gaussian model one may prefer linear classifiers where closed-form Bayesian error estimators have been found [33].

We will present a Bayesian MMSE classifier for the discrete model, which has already been solved. More generally, what we are proposing is not just a few new classifiers, but a new paradigm in classifier design focused on optimization over a concrete mathematical framework. Furthermore, this work ties Bayesian modeling and the Bayesian error estimator together with the old problem of optimal robust filtering; indeed, in the absence of observations, the optimal Bayesian classifier reduces to the Bayesian robust optimal classifier [32,34].

Optimal discrete classification

To illustrate concepts in optimal Bayesian classification, we consider discrete classification, in which the sample space is discrete with b bins. We let p_i and q_i be the class-conditional probabilities in bin $i \in \{1,\ldots,b\}$ for class 0 and 1, respectively, and we define U_j and V_j to be the number of sample points observed in bin $j \in \{1,\ldots,b\}$ from class 0 and 1, respectively. The class sizes are given by $n_0 = \sum_{i=1}^{b} U_i$ and $n_1 = \sum_{i=1}^{b} V_i$. A general discrete classifier assigns each bin to a class, so $\psi_n : \{1,\ldots,b\} \rightarrow \{0,1\}$.

The discrete Bayesian model defines $\theta_0 = [p_1,\ldots,p_{b-1}]$ and $\theta_1 = [q_1,\ldots,q_{b-1}]$. The last bin probabilities are not needed since $p_b = 1 - \sum_{i=1}^{b-1} p_i$ and $q_b = 1 - \sum_{i=1}^{b-1} q_i$.

The parameter space of θ_0 is defined to be the set of a valid bin probabilities, e.g., $[p_1,\ldots,p_{b-1}] \in \Theta_0$ if and only if $0 \le p_i \le 1$ for $i \in \{1,\ldots,b-1\}$ and $\sum_{i=1}^{b-1} p_i \le 1$. The parameter space Θ_1 is defined similarly. With the parametric model established, we define conjugate Dirichlet priors

$$\pi(\theta_0) \propto \prod_{i=1}^{b} p_i^{\alpha_i^0 - 1} \text{ and } \pi(\theta_1) \propto \prod_{i=1}^{b} q_i^{\alpha_i^1 - 1}. \quad (12)$$

For proper priors, the hyperparameters, α_i^y for $i \in \{1,\ldots,b\}$ and $y \in \{0,1\}$, must be positive, and for uniform priors $\alpha_i^y = 1$ for all i and y. In this setting, the posteriors are again Dirichlet, and when normalized they are given by

$$\pi^*(\theta_0) = \frac{\Gamma\left(n_0 + \sum_{i=1}^{b} \alpha_i^0\right)}{\prod_{k=1}^{b} \Gamma\left(U_k + \alpha_k^0\right)} \prod_{i=1}^{b} p_i^{U_i + \alpha_i^0 - 1}, \quad (13)$$

$$\pi^*(\theta_1) = \frac{\Gamma\left(n_1 + \sum_{i=1}^{b} \alpha_i^1\right)}{\prod_{k=1}^{b} \Gamma\left(V_k + \alpha_k^1\right)} \prod_{i=1}^{b} q_i^{V_i + \alpha_i^1 - 1}, \quad (14)$$

where Γ is the Gamma function.

In the discrete model, for $j \in \{1,\ldots,b\}$ the effective class-conditional densities can be shown to be equal to

$$f(j|0) = \frac{U_j + \alpha_j^0}{n_0 + \sum_{i=1}^{b} \alpha_i^0} \text{ and } f(j|1) = \frac{V_j + \alpha_j^1}{n_1 + \sum_{i=1}^{b} \alpha_i^1}. \quad (15)$$

$f(j|0)$ and $f(j|1)$ may be viewed as effective bin probabilities for each class after combining prior knowledge and observed data. Hence, from (8), the Bayesian MMSE error estimator for an arbitrary classifier ψ_n is

$$\widehat{\varepsilon} = \sum_{j=1}^{b} E_{\pi^*}[c] \frac{U_j + \alpha_j^0}{n_0 + \sum_{i=1}^{b} \alpha_i^0} \mathbf{I}_{\psi_n(j)=1}$$
$$+ (1 - E_{\pi^*}[c]) \frac{V_j + \alpha_j^1}{n_1 + \sum_{i=1}^{b} \alpha_i^1} \mathbf{I}_{\psi_n(j)=0}, \quad (16)$$

where $\mathbf{I}_E$ is an indicator function equal to one if E is true and zero otherwise. Exactly the same expression was derived using a brute-force approach in [27]. The optimal Bayesian classifier may now be found directly using (11):

$$\psi_{\text{OBC}}(j) = \begin{cases} 1 \text{ if } E_{\pi^*}[c] \frac{U_j + \alpha_j^0}{n_0 + \sum_{i=1}^{b} \alpha_i^0} < (1 - E_{\pi^*}[c]) \frac{V_j + \alpha_j^1}{n_1 + \sum_{i=1}^{b} \alpha_i^1}, \\ 0 \text{ otherwise.} \end{cases} \quad (17)$$

The optimal Bayesian classifier minimizes the Bayesian error estimator by minimizing each term in the sum (16). This is achieved by assigning $\psi_{\text{OBC}}(j)$ the class with the smaller constant scaling the indicator function. The expected error of the optimal classifier is

$$\widehat{\varepsilon}_{\text{OBC}} = \sum_{j=1}^{b} \min \left\{ \text{E}_{\pi^*}[c] \frac{U_j + \alpha_j^0}{n_0 + \sum_{i=1}^{b} \alpha_i^0}, \right.$$
$$\left. (1 - \text{E}_{\pi^*}[c]) \frac{V_j + \alpha_j^1}{n_1 + \sum_{i=1}^{b} \alpha_i^1} \right\}. \tag{18}$$

In the special case where we have uniform c and uniform priors for the bin probabilities ($\alpha_i^y = 1$ for all i and y), the Bayesian MMSE error estimate is

$$\widehat{\varepsilon} = \sum_{j=1}^{b} \frac{n_0 + 1}{n + 2} \frac{U_j + 1}{n_0 + b} \mathbf{I}_{\psi_n(j)=1} + \frac{n_1 + 1}{n + 2} \frac{V_j + 1}{n_1 + b} \mathbf{I}_{\psi_n(j)=0}, \tag{19}$$

the optimal Bayesian classifier is

$$\psi_{\text{OBC}}(j) = \begin{cases} 1 & \text{if } \frac{n_0+1}{n_0+b}(U_j + 1) < \frac{n_1+1}{n_1+b}(V_j + 1), \\ 0 & \text{otherwise,} \end{cases} \tag{20}$$

and the expected error of the optimal classifier is

$$\widehat{\varepsilon}_{\text{OBC}} = \sum_{j=1}^{b} \min \left\{ \frac{n_0 + 1}{n + 2} \frac{U_j + 1}{n_0 + b}, \frac{n_1 + 1}{n + 2} \frac{V_j + 1}{n_1 + b} \right\}. \tag{21}$$

Hence, under uniform priors, when the total number of samples observed in each class is the same ($n_0 = n_1$), the optimal Bayesian classifier is equivalent to the classical discrete histogram rule, which assigns a class to each bin by a majority vote: $\psi_{\text{DHR}}(j) = 1$ if $U_j < V_j$ and $\psi_{\text{DHR}}(j) = 0$ if $U_j \geq V_j$; otherwise, the discrete histogram rule is not necessarily optimal within an arbitrary Bayesian framework.

We take a moment to compare optimal Bayesian classification over an uncertainty class of distributions with Bayes classification for a fixed feature-label distribution. With fixed class-0 probability c and bin probabilities p_i and q_i, the true error of an arbitrary classifier, ψ, is given by

$$\varepsilon = \sum_{j=1}^{b} c p_j \mathbf{I}_{\psi(j)=1} + (1 - c) q_j \mathbf{I}_{\psi(j)=0}. \tag{22}$$

Note a similarity to (16) and (19). The Bayes classifier is given by $\psi_{\text{Bayes}}(j) = 1$ if $c p_j < (1-c)q_j$ and zero otherwise,

corresponding to (17) and (20). Finally, the Bayes error is given by

$$\varepsilon_{\text{Bayes}} = \sum_{j=1}^{b} \min\{c p_j, (1 - c)q_j\}, \tag{23}$$

corresponding to (18) and (21). Throughout, c corresponds to $\text{E}_{\pi^*}[c]$, p_j corresponds to the effective bin probability $f(j|0) = (U_j + \alpha_j^0)/(n_0 + \sum_{i=1}^{b} \alpha_i^0)$ and similarly q_j corresponds to the effective bin probability $f(j|1)$. In this case, the effective density is a member of our uncertainty class (which contains all possible discrete feature-label distributions), so that the optimal thing to do is simply plug the effective parameters in the fixed-distribution problem.

That being said, the effective density is not always a member of our uncertainty class. Consider an example with $D = 2$ features, an uncertainty class of Gaussian class-conditional distributions with independent arbitrary covariances, and a proper posterior with fixed class-0 probability $c = 0.5$ (hyperparameters are provided in [32]). We consider three classifiers. First is a plug-in classifier, which is the Bayes classifier corresponding to the posterior expected parameters, $c = 0.5$, $\mu_0 = [0, 0, \ldots, 0]$, $\mu_1 = [1, 1, \ldots, 1]$, and $\Sigma_0 = \Sigma_1 = I_D$. Since the expected covariances are homoscedastic, this classifier is linear. The second is a state-constrained optimal Bayesian classifier, ψ_{SCOBC}, in which we search for a state with corresponding Bayes classifier having smallest expected error over the uncertainty class [34]. Since the Bayes classifier for any particular state in the uncertainty class is quadratic, this classifier is quadratic. Finally, we have the optimal Bayesian classifier, which has been solved analytically in [29], although details are omitted here. In this case, the effective densities are not Gaussian but multivariate student's t distributions, resulting in an optimal Bayesian classifier having a polynomial decision boundary that is higher than quadratic order. Figure 4 shows $\psi_{\text{plug-in}}$ (red), ψ_{SCOBC} (black) and ψ_{OBC} (green). Level curves for the class-conditional distributions corresponding to the expected parameters used in $\psi_{\text{plug-in}}$ are shown in red dashed lines, and level curves for the distributions in the state corresponding to ψ_{SCOBC} are shown in black dashed lines. These were found by setting the Mahalanobis distance to 1. Each classifier is quite distinct, and in particular, the optimal Bayesian classifier is non-quadratic even though all class-conditional distributions in the uncertainty class are Gaussian.

To demonstrate the performance advantage of optimal Bayesian classification via a simulated experiment, we return to the discrete classification problem. Let c and the bin probabilities be generated randomly according to uniform prior distributions. For each fixed feature-label

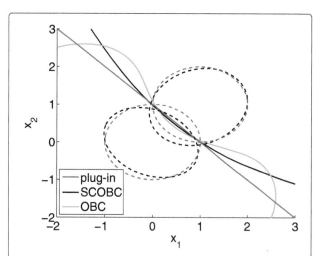

Figure 4 Classifiers for an independent arbitrary covariance Gaussian model. Classifiers for an independent arbitrary covariance Gaussian model with $D = 2$ features and proper posteriors. Whereas the optimal Bayesian classifier (in green) is polynomial with expected true error 0.2007, the state-constrained optimal Bayesian classifier (in black) is quadratic with expected true error 0.2061 and the plug-in classifier (in red) is linear with expected true error 0.2078. These expected true errors are averaged over the posterior on the uncertainty class of states.

distribution, a binomial(n, c) experiment is used to determine the number of sample points in class 0 and the bin for each point is drawn according to the bin probabilities corresponding to its class, thus generating a non-stratified random sample of size n. Both the histogram rule and the new optimal Bayesian classifier from (20), assuming correct priors, are trained from the sample. The true error for each classifier is also calculated exactly via (22) . This is repeated 100,000 times to obtain the average true error for each classification rule, presented in Figure 5 for $b = 2$, 4 and 8 bins. Observe that the average performance of optimal Bayesian classification is indeed superior to that of the discrete histogram rule, especially for larger bin

sizes. However, note that optimal Bayesian classifiers are not guaranteed to be optimal for a specific distribution (the optimal classifier is the Bayes classifier), but only optimal when averaged over all distributions in the assumed Bayesian framework.

Conclusions

Scientific knowledge is possible for small-sample classification.

Given the importance of classification throughout science and the crucial epistemological role played by error estimation, it is remarkable that only one paper providing analytic results for moments of common error estimators was published between 1977 and 2005, and that up until 2005, there were no papers providing representation of the joint distribution or of the second-order mixed moments. Today, we are paying the price for this dearth of activity as we are now presented with very large feature sets and small samples across different disciplines, in particular, in high-throughput biology, where the advance of medical science is being hamstrung by a lack of basic knowledge regarding pattern recognition. Moreover, in spite of this obvious crippling lack of knowledge, there is only a minuscule effort to rectify the situation, whereas billions of dollars are wasted on gathering an untold quantity of data that is useless absent the requisite statistical knowledge to make it useful.

No doubt this unfortunate situation would make for a good sociological study. But that is not our field of expertise. Nonetheless, we will put forth a comment made by Thomas Kailath in 1974, about the time that fundamental research in error estimation for small-sample classification came to a halt. He writes, "It was the peculiar atmosphere of the sixties, with its catchwords of 'building research competence,' 'training more scientists,' etc., that supported the uncritical growth of a literature in which quantity and formal novelty were often prized over significance and attention to scholarship. There was little

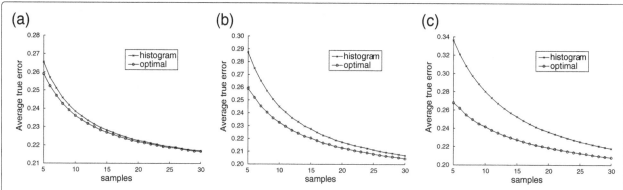

Figure 5 Average true errors for discrete classification. Average true errors on discrete distributions from known priors with uniform c and bin probabilities versus sample size. **(a)** $b = 2$; **(b)** $b = 4$; **(c)** $b = 8$.

concern for fitting new results into the body of old ones; it was important to have 'new' results!" [35]. Although Kailath's observation was aimed at signal processing, the "peculiar atmosphere" of which he speaks is not limited to any particular discipline; rather, he had perceived an "uncritical growth of a literature" lacking "attention to scholarship." One can only wonder what Prof. Kailath's thoughts are today when he surveys a research landscape that produces orders of magnitude more papers but produces less knowledge than that produced by the relative handful of scientists, statisticians, and engineers a half century ago. For those who would question this latter observation in pattern recognition, we suggest a study of the early papers by such pioneers as Theodore Anderson, Albert Bowker, and Rosedith Sitgreaves.

Competing interests
Both authors declare that they have no competing interests.

Author details
[1] Department of Electrical and Computer Engineering, Texas A&M University, College Station, TX 77843, USA. [2] Computational Biology Division, Translational Genomics Research Institute, Phoenix, AZ 85004, USA. [3] Department of Electrical and Computer Engineering, The Ohio State University, Columbus, OH 43210, USA.

References

1. ER Dougherty, U Braga-Neto, Epistemology of computational biology: mathematical models and experimental prediction as the basis of their validity. J. Biol. Syst. **14**, 65–90 (2006)
2. H Reichenbach, *The Rise of Scientific Philosophy* (University of California Press, Berkeley, 1971)
3. ER Dougherty, ML Bittner, *Epistemology of the Cell: A Systems Perspective on Biological Knowledge*. IEEE Press Series on Biomedical Engineering (John Wiley, New York, 2011)
4. R Feynman, *QED: The Strange Theory of Light and Matter* (Princeton University Press, Princeton, 1985)
5. P Frank, *Modern Science and Its Philosophy* (Collier Books, New York, 1961)
6. ER Dougherty, On the epistemological crisis in genomics. Curr. Genomics **9**(2), 69–79 (2008)
7. M Brun, C Sima, J Hua, J Lowey, B Carroll, E Suh, ER Dougherty, Model-based evaluation of clustering validation measures. Pattern Recognit. **40**(3), 807–824 (2007)
8. L Devroye, L Györfi, G Lugosi, *A Probabilistic Theory of Pattern Recognition*. Stochastic Modelling and Applied Probability (Springer, New York, 1996)
9. ER Dougherty, Biomarker development: prudence, risk, and reproducibility. BioEssays **34**(4), 277–279 (2012)
10. B Hanczar, J Hua, ER Dougherty, Decorrelation of the true and estimated classifier errors in high-dimensional settings. EURASIP J. Bioinformatics Syst. Biol. **2007**, 12 (2007). Article ID 38473
11. U Braga-Neto, ER Dougherty, Exact performance of error estimators for discrete classifiers. Pattern Recognit. **38**(11), 1799–1814 (2005)
12. M Hills, Allocation rules and their error rates. J. R. Stat. Soc. Ser. B (Stat. Methodology) **28**, 1–31 (1966)
13. D Foley, Considerations of sample and feature size. IEEE Trans. Inf. Theory **18**(5), 618–626 (1972)
14. MJ Sorum, Estimating the conditional probability of misclassification. Technometrics **13**, 333–343 (1971)
15. GJ McLachlan, An asymptotic expansion of the expectation of the estimated error rate in discriminant analysis. Aust. J. Stat. **15**(3), 210–214 (1973)
16. M Moran, On the expectation of errors of allocation associated with a linear discriminant function. Biometrika **62**, 141–148 (1975)
17. M Goldstein, E Wolf, On the problem of bias in multinomial classification. Biometrics 1977, **33**, 325–331 (1975)
18. A Davison, P Hall, On the bias and variability of bootstrap and cross-validation estimates of error rates in discrimination problems. Biometrica **79**, 274–284 (1992)
19. Q Xu, J Hua, UM Braga-Neto, Z Xiong, E Suh, ER Dougherty, Confidence intervals for the true classification error conditioned on the estimated error. Technol. Cancer Res. Treat. **5**, 579–590 (2006)
20. A Zollanvari, UM Braga-Neto, ER Dougherty, On the sampling distribution of resubstitution and leave-one-out error estimators for linear classifiers. Pattern Recognit. **42**(11), 2705–2723 (2009)
21. A Zollanvari, UM Braga-Neto, ER Dougherty, On the joint sampling distribution between the actual classification error and the resubstitution and leave-one-out error estimators for linear classifiers. IEEE Trans Inf. Theory **56**(2), 784–804 (2010)
22. A Zollanvari, UM Braga-Neto, ER Dougherty, Exact representation of the second-order moments for resubstitution and leave-one-out error estimation for linear discriminant analysis in the univariate Heteroskedastic Gaussian Model. Pattern Recognit. **45**(2), 908–917 (2012)
23. A Zollanvari, UM Braga-Neto, ER Dougherty, Analytic study of performance of error estimators for linear discriminant analysis. IEEE Trans. Signal Process. **59**(9), 4238–4255 (2011)
24. F Wyman, D Young, D Turner, A comparison of asymptotic error rate expansions for the sample linear discriminant function. Pattern Recognit. **23**, 775–783 (1990)
25. V Pikelis, Comparison of methods of computing the expected classification errors. Automatic Remote Control **5**, 59–63 (1976)
26. ER Dougherty, A Zollanvari, UM Braga-Neto, The illusion of distribution-free small-sample classification in genomics. Curr. Genomics **12**(5), 333–341 (2011)
27. LA Dalton, ER Dougherty, Bayesian minimum mean-square error estimation for classification error–part I: definition and the Bayesian MMSE error estimator for discrete classification. IEEE Trans. Signal Process. **59**, 115–129 (2011)
28. LA Dalton, ER Dougherty, Exact sample conditioned MSE performance of the Bayesian MMSE estimator for classification error–part I: representation. IEEE Trans. Signal Process. **60**(5), 2575–2587 (2012)
29. LA Dalton, ER Dougherty, Optimal classifiers with minimum expected error within a, Bayesian framework–part I: discrete and Gaussian models. Pattern Recognit. **46**(5), 1301–1314 (2013)
30. LA Dalton, ER Dougherty, Application of the Bayesian MMSE estimator for classification error to gene expression microarray data. Bioinformatics **27**(13), 1822–1831 (2011)
31. LA Dalton, ER Dougherty, Exact sample conditioned MSE performance of the Bayesian MMSE estimator for classification error–part II: consistency and performance analysis. IEEE Trans. Signal Process. **60**(5), 2588–2603 (2012)
32. LA Dalton, ER Dougherty, Optimal classifiers with minimum expected error within a Bayesian framework–part II: properties and performance analysis. Pattern Recognit. **46**(5), 1288–1300 (2013)
33. LA Dalton, ER Dougherty, Bayesian minimum mean-square error estimation for classification error–part II: the Bayesian MMSE error estimator for linear classification of Gaussian distributions. IEEE Trans. Signal Process. **59**, 130–144 (2011)
34. ER Dougherty, J Hua, Z Xiong, Y Chen, Optimal robust classifiers. Pattern Recognit. **38**(10), 1520–1532 (2005)
35. T Kailath, A view of three decades of linear filtering theory. IEEE Transact. Inf. Theory **20**(2), 146–181 (1974)

Relationships between kinetic constants and the amino acid composition of enzymes from the yeast *Saccharomyces cerevisiae* glycolysis pathway

Peteris Zikmanis[*] and Inara Kampenusa

Abstract

The kinetic models of metabolic pathways represent a system of biochemical reactions in terms of metabolic fluxes and enzyme kinetics. Therefore, the apparent differences of metabolic fluxes might reflect distinctive kinetic characteristics, as well as sequence-dependent properties of the employed enzymes. This study aims to examine possible linkages between kinetic constants and the amino acid (AA) composition (AAC) for enzymes from the yeast *Saccharomyces cerevisiae* glycolytic pathway. The values of Michaelis-Menten constant (K_M), turnover number (k_{cat}), and specificity constant ($k_{sp} = k_{cat}/K_M$) were taken from BRENDA (15, 17, and 16 values, respectively) and protein sequences of nine enzymes (HXK, GADH, PGK, PGM, ENO, PK, PDC, TIM, and PYC) from UniProtKB. The AAC and sequence properties were computed by ExPASy/ProtParam tool and data processed by conventional methods of multivariate statistics. Multiple linear regressions were found between the log-values of k_{cat} (3 models, $85.74\% < R_{adj}^2 < 94.11\%$, $p < 0.00001$), K_M (1 model, $R_{adj}^2 = 96.70\%$, $p < 0.00001$), k_{sp} (3 models, $96.15\% < R_{adj}^2 < 96.50\%$, $p < 0.00001$), and the sets of AA frequencies (four to six for each model) selected from enzyme sequences while assessing the potential multicollinearity between variables. It was also found that the selection of independent variables in multiple regression models may reflect certain advantages for definite AA physicochemical and structural propensities, which could affect the properties of sequences. The results support the view on the actual interdependence of catalytic, binding, and structural residues to ensure the efficiency of biocatalysts, since the kinetic constants of the yeast enzymes appear as closely related to the overall AAC of sequences.

Keywords: Michaelis-Menten constant, Turnover number, Specificity constant, Glycolytic enzymes, Sequence-dependent properties, Multivariate relationships

Introduction

According to the concepts of systems biology, metabolic fluxes are net sums of underlying enzymatic reaction rates represented by integral outputs of three biological quantities which interact at the level of enzyme kinetics: kinetic parameters, enzyme and reactant concentrations [1]. Integrated view of enzymes suggests to consider them as dynamic assemblies whose variable structures are closely related to catalytic functions [2,3]. It is therefore an important task to extend the knowledge of the enzyme sequence, structure and function relationships which allow to specify a chemical mechanism of catalytic

reaction and to be predictive for targeted modification of enzymes [4]. Site-directed mutagenesis has proved to be a powerful tool to probe certain amino acids (AA) within an enzyme, yet still somewhat less focusing on other residues and, therefore, tempted to ignore the actual interdependence of catalytic, binding, and structural residues being considered as a key feature of such complex cooperative systems [2,3,5]. Moreover, statistical evaluation of the relation between functionally and structurally important AA of the enzyme sequences reveals contribution of the catalytic residues to the structural stabilization of the respective proteins, which indicates both residue sets as rather overlapping than segregated [6]. In addition, the modest success of creating artificial enzymes also points to currently unknown,

* Correspondence: zikmanis@lanet.lv
Institute of Microbiology and Biotechnology, University of Latvia, Kronvalda Boulevard 4, Riga LV-1010, Latvia

probably crucial, parameters that could significantly affect enzyme catalysis [7]. AA composition (AAC) is a simplest attribute of proteins among the so-called global sequence descriptors [8] which represents the frequencies of occurrence of the natural AA thereby creating a 20-dimensional feature for a given protein sequence [8,9]. AAC appears as a simple, yet powerful feature for a successful prediction of several protein properties, including protein folding and mutual interactions [10-12].

On the other hand, these complex events can be measured in many respects, including protein conformational heterogeneity and structural dynamics [7,13,14]. For these reasons, there could be certain links between the enzyme kinetic constants and AAC of the sequences. The goal of this study was to check this assumption.

Methods

The dataset consisted of the enzyme characteristics, representing the yeast *Saccharomyces cerevisiae* glycolysis pathway, together with the reaction directly branching (pyruvate carboxylase) from it. It includes the data for the following enzymes: Hexokinase (HXK, EC 2.7.1.1), Glyceraldehyde-3-phosphate dehydrogenase (GADH, EC 1.2.1.12), 3-phosphoglycerate kinase (PKG, EC 2.7.2.3), Phosphoglycerate mutase (PGM, EC 5.4.2.1), Enolase (ENO, EC 4.2.1.11), Pyruvate kinase (PK, EC 2.7.1.40), Pyruvate decarboxyase (PDC, EC 4.1.1.1), Triose-phosphate isomerase (TIM, EC 5.3.1.1),

and Pyruvate carboxylase (PYC, EC 6.4.1.1). The kinetic constants and the enzyme AA sequences were taken from the BRENDA [15] and UniProtKB [16] databases, respectively. The numerical values of kinetic constants retrieved from BRENDA and the UniProtKB accession numbers of enzyme sequences are summarized in Additional file 1: Table S1. The relatively limited volume of this dataset is due to the fact that only these glycolytic enzymes from *S. cerevisiae* are currently represented in BRENDA database [15] by both fundamental constants [17]: the turnover number ($k$cat), the Michaelis-Menten constant (K_M) and, consequently, the derived specificity constant ($k$sp = $k$cat/K_M) [17,18]. The values of $k$cat and K_M obtained from the same literature source were used for the direct calculation of $k$sp. If the several kinetic constants with the different numerical values come from various literature sources (m*n) values for $k$sp were calculated, where m and n represent the numbers of $k$cat and K_M, respectively (Additional file 1: Table S1). In this way, the calculated smallest and largest $k$sp values were excluded from subsequent use to form a more even balance for the number of sequences under study. Consequently, 16 $k$sp values were included in the data set (Additional file 1: Table S1).

The AAC (frequencies of AA occurrence) of sequences was computed using ExPASy/ProtParam tool [19]. The average AA property, Pave(i), for each sequence (or an extracted group of AA) was computed using the standard formula [20], where $P(j)$ is the property value for jth

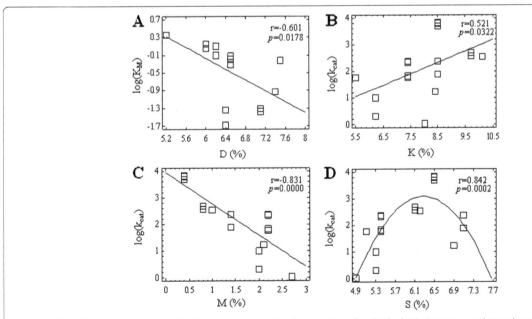

Figure 1 The relationships between kinetic constants and the frequencies of individual AA. Bivariate correlations between the log-values of kinetic constants and frequencies of occurrence for individual AA in the yeast *S. cerevisiae* enzyme sequences, where K_M is the Michaelis-Menten constant **(A)** and $k$cat is the catalytic constant **(B–D)**. All the linear correlations are significant at the non-parametric assessment (Kendall's τ, Spearman's ρ correlation coefficients).

residue and the summation over N, the total number of residues in a protein.

The data were processed by correlation analysis (parametric and non-parametric) using the Statgraphics®Plus (Manugistics Inc., Maryland, USA) and SPSS 11.0 for Windows (SPSS Inc., Illinois, USA) and subjected to the multiple linear regression analysis using the same software. Explanatory variables in the models were selected by stepwise forward selection procedures by finding the significant one-variable models (20 AA × 3 kinetic constants) as well as significant two-variable models (190 possible ways/$C(20,2)$/to arrange 20 AA in groups of 2 at a time for each kinetic constant). The best three-variable models were formed by adding another variable one-by-one from the remaining ones and the variables that yield the greatest increase in the adjusted $R2$ value

were included. And so forth to obtain the four-variable and larger models until no variables could increase the criterion. The logarithmic transformation of the kinetic constant values was used to increase the normality of the dependent variables. The Fisher's F-test for analysis of variance (ANOVA) was performed to evaluate the statistical significance of regression models and the Student's t-test was employed to check the significance of regression coefficients. The leave-one-out cross-validation (LOOCV) procedure was employed to validate developed regression models [21]. The linear plots of the actual kinetic constants against those predicted by the multiple regression models were used throughout the study to assess the goodness-of-fit for observed multivariate relationships according to adjusted $R2$ values. Conventional non-parametric tests, including the Friedman

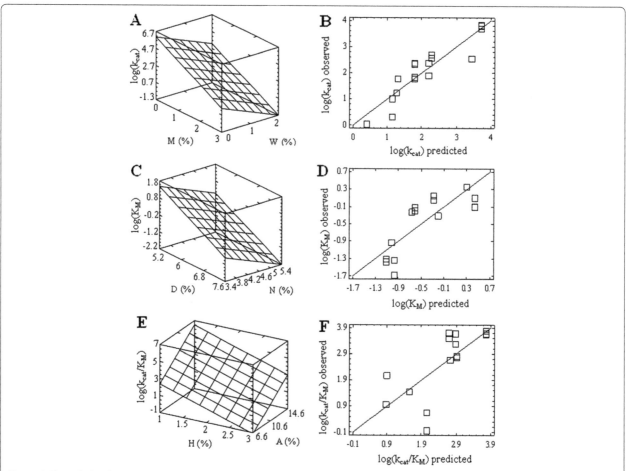

Figure 2 The relationships between kinetic constants and frequencies of two AA. The multiple linear regressions showing changes of the log-values of kinetic constants as dependent variables upon the frequencies of occurrence for two AA in the yeast *S. cerevisiae* sequences, where *k*cat is the catalytic constant (**A**), *K*M is the Michaelis-Menten constant (**C**), and *k*sp = *k*cat/*K*M is the specificity constant (**E**). The observed versus predicted plots (**B,D,F**) for the values of dependent variables (*k*cat, *K*M, and *k*sp, respectively). The predicted values were calculated from the regression equations: log(*k*cat) = 5.556 −1.620*M −0.984*W (*R*adj.2 = 82.88%, *p* = 0.0000); log(*K*M) = 8.593 −0.596*N −0.998*D (*R*adj.2 = 53.72%, *p* = 0.0039); log(*k*cat/*K*M) = 0.818 +0.501*A −1.736*H (*R*adj.2 = 46.50%, *p* = 0.0068). All the multiple and pair correlations (A–F) are significant at the non-parametric assessment (Kendall's τ, Spearman's ρ correlation coefficients).

ANOVA for ranks and the Wilcoxon signed rank test, were used to evaluate the $Pave(i)$ for each protein in respect of the AA groups selected/non-selected as the predictor variables.

The p values < 0.05 were considered to be statistically significant for both parametric and non-parametric tests.

A conventional single letter code was used throughout to denote AA representing their frequencies of occurrence as the independent variables.

Results

Already a bivariate correlation analysis of 60 possible relationships (3 kinetic constants × 20 AA) revealed 12 significant parametric and/or rank correlations, confirming that the enzyme constants can be linked up even with the individual AA frequencies. Furthermore, the observed relationships (Figure 1) for different AA can be as direct (B) as well the reverse (A, C) or even a nonlinear (D).

Subsequent analysis of the data by means of the forward selection procedures showed that the stepwise inclusion of additional variables leads to a statistically significant multiple regression, where the kinetic constants appear to depend on two or more AA frequencies, thus substantially increasing the proportion of the "explained" variance (Figures 2 and 3). Furthermore, the increasing adjusted $R2$ values indicate that the "explained" variance substantially rises with the growing number of variables in the regression model, although in a nonlinear proportion, due to a more pronounced contribution of the few "strongest" AA frequencies (Figure 3). Therefore, four to six variables turned out to be enough to form statistically robust multiple linear regression models linking the enzyme kinetic constants with the AAC of corresponding sequences (Table 1). The matching quality of the data obtained by the proposed models was evaluated by the linear plots (Figure 4A,C,E,) of the actual kinetic constants against those predicted by proposed regression models (Table 1). The highly significant adjusted $R2$ values also point out that the models (Table 1) adequately represent the actual relationships between the AAC and kinetic constants of the enzymes, since only a relatively small proportion (3.30–14.26%) of the total variance remains unexplained. In addition, the validation of models using the LOOCV procedure although resulted in the certain reduction of the $R2$ values (Table 1, Figure 4B,D,F), but still remained within the limits of high ($p < 0.00001$) statistical significance.

It is noted that rather small or moderate values of the variance inflation factor (VIF) [22] (Table 1) also indicate that the observed multivariate relationships are not significantly affected by the multicollinearity of independent variables.

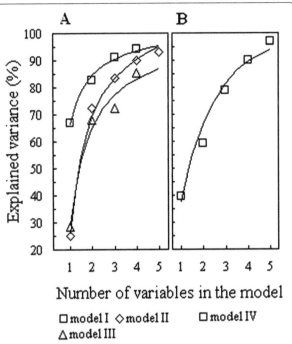

Figure 3 The changes of explained variance upon the growing number of variables in the models. Relationships between an increase in the percentage of explained variance and the number of independent variables (AA frequencies of occurrence) included in multiple regressions, where **A** and **B** represent the variety of cases for log($kcat$) and log(KM), respectively. Variables in the models: model I: 1 – M, 2 – M, W, 3 – M, W, R, and 4 – M, W, R, L; model II: 1 – T, 2 – T, V, 3 – T, V, H, 4 – T, V, H, A, and 5 – T, V, H, A, K; model III: 1 – H, 2 – H, A, 3 – H, A, E, and, 4 – H, A, E, V; model IV: 1 – D, 2 – D, N, 3 – D, N, W, 4 – D, N, W, L, and 5 – D, N, W, L, A.

The ANOVA for the regression models are summarized in Additional file 2: Table S2.

Comparison of multiple regression models (Table 1) showed that they include a broad, although uneven, representation of AA where some of them occur more frequently, while others rarely or not, thus creating ranked series (A > N > Q, H, L, T, W > R, V > D, C, E, G, K, M, F > I, P, S, Y) under the downward distribution of AA occurrences. Moreover, it was found that ranked differences of AAC are reflected in their rankings for physicochemical and structural propensities as confirmed by significant multiple rank as well as by parametric correlations: Kendall's $\tau1.23 = 0.372$ ($p < 0.05$), Spearman's $\rho1.23 = 0.609$ ($p < 0.01$), Pearson's $r1.23 = 0.623$ ($p < 0.01$), where 1 is the AA occurrence, 2 is the average flexibility index [23], and 3 is the propensity for AA hydrophobicity (OMH) [24]. These correlations indicate that the selection of independent variables in multiple regression models may reflect certain advantages for definite AA properties, which, in turn, could affect the overall properties of sequences. This possibility was also confirmed by assessing the enzyme sequences as well as the groups

Table 1 The characteristics of the obtained models

Regression model	Dependent variable	Parameters [a]	Regression coefficient	S.E.	t value	P value	R^2%	$R^2_{adjusted}$%	VIF [b]	R^2% [c]	$R^2_{adjusted}$% [c]
I	log(k$_{cat}$)	constant	5.2073	0.5003	10.408	0.0000	95.58	94.11		90.72	90.10
		M	−1.6219	0.1169	−13.879	0.0000			1.853		
		W	−0.5258	0.2147	−2.449	0.0307			3.329		
		R	0.3558	0.07329	4.855	0.0004			1.103		
		L	−0.1697	0.06309	−2.691	0.0196			2.180		
II	log(k$_{cat}$)	constant	3.9385	1.3200	2.984	0.0124	95.22	93.05		80.32	79.01
		T	−0.4482	0.07274	−6.161	0.0001			2.851		
		V	0.2756	0.05350	5.151	0.0003			1.530		
		H	−1.3861	0.2088	−6.639	0.0000			2.003		
		A	0.2840	0.06859	4.141	0.0016			1.868		
		K	−0.2333	0.09633	−2.422	0.0339			2.857		
III	log(k$_{cat}$)	constant	−6.3103	1.7275	−3.653	0.0033	89.30	85.74		71.62	69.73
		A	0.4367	0.07955	5.489	0.0001			1.224		
		H	−0.9759	0.3015	−3.237	0.0071			2.034		
		V	0.2728	0.07752	3.519	0.0042			1.564		
		E	0.5900	0.1564	3.773	0.0027			1.498		
IV	log(K$_M$)	constant	13.2588	0.8236	16.098	0.0000	97.88	96.70		93.18	92.66
		D	−1.1379	0.06612	−17.209	0.0000			1.365		
		N	−0.9961	0.07256	−13.729	0.0000			1.932		
		W	1.0535	0.08387	12.561	0.0000			1.948		
		L	−0.2347	0.03077	−7.628	0.0002			2.140		
		A	−0.09888	0.02288	−4.321	0.0019			1.093		
V	log(k$_{cat}$/K$_M$)	constant	−11.0119	1.5657	−7.052	0.0001	97.77	96.29		88.86	88.06
		A	−0.5525	0.05736	9.632	0.0000			1.705		
		H	−1.2042	0.1817	−6.626	0.0001			2.082		
		R	1.1894	0.1006	11.829	0.0000			2.373		
		G	0.6911	0.09445	7.317	0.0000			2.520		
		Q	−0.5142	0.1009	−5.098	0.0006			1.672		
		N	0.4252	0.1246	3.412	0.0077			2.176		
VI	log(k$_{cat}$/K$_M$)	constant	9.4887	0.8188	11.589	0.0000	97.69	96.15		88.86	88.07
		L	−0.4399	0.05548	−7.929	0.0000			1.902		
		T	−0.9367	0.07023	−13.338	0.0000			3.267		
		N	1.1552	0.1032	11.194	0.0000			1.437		
		W	−1.0394	0.2182	−5.012	0.0007			3.420		
		Q	−0.3207	0.1191	−2.692	0.0247			2.244		
		F	−0.2690	0.09349	−2.877	0.0183			1.349		
VII	log(k$_{cat}$/K$_M$)	constant	2.5597	0.8288	3.088	0.0115	97.00	96.50		90.44	89.77
		T	−0.8156	0.06297	−12.953	0.0000			2.249		
		Q	−0.7700	0.1050	−7.331	0.0000			1.495		
		C	2.4452	0.2845	8.593	0.0000			3.581		
		N	0.5745	0.1162	4.943	0.0006			1.561		
		A	0.2605	0.06600	3.946	0.0027			2.027		

Elements and the statistical indices for multiple linear regression models which link the log-values of kinetic constants and the AAC of the yeast S. cerevisiae enzyme sequences.

a Elements of multiple linear regression which represent the frequencies of AA (a single letter code) occurrence in the yeast S. cerevisiae enzyme sequences and the constant (intercept) of equation.

b The variance inflation factor which indicates the impact of multicollinearity between the independent variables [22].

c Obtained by the LOOCV [21] of models.

Relationships between kinetic constants and the amino acid composition of enzymes from the yeast...

129

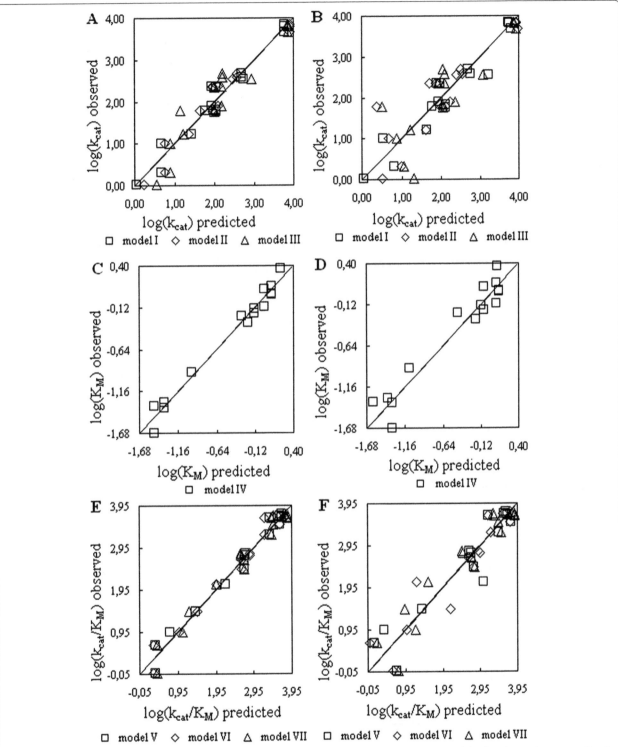

Figure 4 Linear plots of the actual kinetic constants against those predicted by linear regression models. The observed versus predicted plots (**A,C,E**) for the values of dependent variables log(*k*cat), log(*K*M), and log(*k*cat/*K*M), respectively. The predicted values were calculated from the statistically robust model equations as specified in Table 1, including those obtained by the LOOCV of models (**B,D,F**).

of the selected and non-selected (rest) variables in terms of "the average AA property for each protein" [20] in respect of given regression models (Table 1). Such an evaluation revealed that the groups of selected and non-selected AA frequencies can make substantially different contributions to the combined set of average physico-chemical [25] and structural [26] properties for the enzyme sequences (Figure 5).

Compiling the data [16] on the enzyme active sites, 63 residues representing 11 AA (E, H, K, D, R, N, T, G, S, C, Y) were found to be responsible for the activity of the nine studied enzymes. These almost exclusively charged (E, H, K, D, R) or polar (N,T,S,C,Y) residues represent only a small portion (up to 1.5%) of the total amount (4,406 residues) in the sequences. Even those active site residues also involved as variables (K, D, H, R, N) in the regression models (Table 1) constitute rather low proportion (2.74–3.14%) of their total number in sequences, as well as both sets of frequencies are not correlated. These considerations suggest that the AA represented in the regression models (Table 1) are mainly eligible for the so-called structural residues [3] in enzymes, since the contribution of active center AA frequencies might not be great. This was supported by further control applications of the regression models when the active center AA were "excluded" from the dataset, overall AA frequencies recalculated and the same variables (Table 1) employed. As a result, $R2$ values of the regression models were affected (Figure 6), to a limited extent and close to the proportion of active site residues in sequences whereas all the multiple regressions remained at a high level of statistical significance. Nevertheless, it was observed that the small and unevenly distributed active center frequencies, independently of the overall AAC of the enzyme sequences, can also form multiple linear regressions with the kinetic

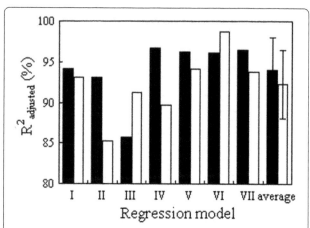

Figure 6 Adjusted coefficients of determination for the multiple regression models which represent the full AA sequences (filled bars) and those which do not take into account the quantities of catalytic and binding residues in the active sites of enzymes and formed by the recalculated AA frequencies (open bars). Both model types contain the same independent variables.

constants. Thus, the selected sets of relevant variables (E, H, K, S), (N, D, S, T, Y), and (R, H, K, T) form highly significant ($p < 0.00001$) multiple linear regressions with the values of $k$cat, KM, and $k$cat/KM, respectively, as well as reach the high values of determination coefficients (Radj.2: 89.14, 97.63, and 98.84%, respectively). The full set of the respective results is summarized in Additional file 3: Table S3.

It is noted that statistically robust multivariate relationships could also occur in cases where the values of kinetic constants have come from different sources. Thus, the KM values which are represented for only seven enzymes of *S. cerevisiae* TCA cycle in the BRENDA database [15] were found to be closely related (Radj.2 = 91.81%; $p = 0.0006$) to the selected frequencies

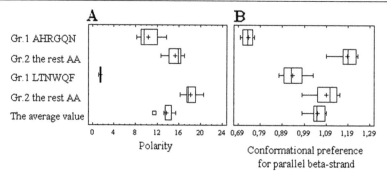

Figure 5 Different contributions of the selected and non-selected AA into the properties of enzyme sequences. The Box-and-Whisker plot of the average AA property estimates for the selected/non-selected groups of independent variables in respect of the $k$cat/KM regression models (models V and VI, Table 1). The upper and lower bounds of the bars represent maximum and minimum values of estimates, the upper and lower bounds of each box represent the upper and lower quartiles of estimations and the lines in the middle of each box represent the median values. The effects of group selection and all pair differences between the groups are significant (Friedman ANOVA and Wilcoxon signed rank tests, respectively).

of AA (A, R, L, M, P). Besides, the KM values included in the Teusink's model for yeast glycolysis [27] also were closely linked to the frequencies of selected AA (K, Y, C, M, I) in sequences of 10 corresponding enzymes (Radj.^{2} = 98.87%; p = 0.0001). Extended sets of these results are summarized in Additional file 4: Figure S1 and Additional file 5: Figure S2, respectively. In this case, the essential differences between the sets of variables for regression models (Table 1) are due to the fact that the KM values included in BRENDA have been obtained in "optimized" *in vitro* conditions, while the model uses the estimates (experimental and computational) which are more in line to the environment of living cell [27,28].

Discussion

The obtained results indicate that the basic kinetic constants [17,18] of yeast glycolytic enzymes appear as closely related to the AAC of the sequences and, therefore, support the view on the actual interdependence of catalytic, binding, and structural residues to ensure the full-scale efficiency of biocatalysts [3] as well as suggest that a certain functional overlap may occur between these sets of AA [6]. Furthermore, the observed relationships fit well with the up-to-date concepts on the structural and functional properties of proteins, including structural, energy and conformational networks [28], conformational dynamics, heterogeneity and selection [7], AA networks [12,29]. A broad representation of AA frequencies as the strong predictor variables for the developed regression models (Table 1) as well as findings about the different impact of the selected AA groups on predicted features of enzyme sequences (Figure 5) most likely reflect the potential of protein adjustments to keep the kinetic parameters of enzymes within a definite range and, consequently, their efficient operation under varied external conditions.

In general, such relationships between the kinetic constants and AAC of the enzymes might include the quadratic effects and interactions between the variables actually making them more complex. Nevertheless, it should be noted that a multiple linear regression still offers a best linear approximation to the unknown regression function even if it is nonlinear [30]. Really, the refinement of the observed multiple linear regressions (Figure 2) by means of the second-order polynomial equations resulted in a marked reduction of unexplained variance which characterize substantially stronger relationships between the variables (Additional file 6: Figure S3). However, it should be taken into account that the practical use of second-order equations are strongly restricted due to a sharp increase of required regression coefficients and degrees of freedom to obtain statistically robust regression models.

It should be noted that this study well corresponds to a certain line of research in recent years where the set of primary structure-derived features [31,32] or integral physicochemical indices of proteins [33] have been used to predict the values of kinetic constants for particular enzymes.

Conclusions

The multivariate linear relationships broadly confirm the actual link between the kinetic constants of yeast enzymes and the AAC of the respective sequences. The results of this study suggest to some possible outputs. Regression models of such kind could be used, at least in principle, to specify and co-ordinate the appropriate values of kinetic constants especially if there is a need to include any additional enzyme currently not represented in a given metabolic pathway (e.g., metabolic engineering, dynamic modeling). There is a possibility that the metabolic fluxes could be directly linked to the enzyme sequence-dependent properties including AAC, in particular because they are largely determined by enzyme kinetic parameters [1].

Although, prospects of such an approach apparently now are rather limited due to lack of necessary kinetic parameters and, therefore, are dependent on further data accumulation and specification in the enzyme databases.

Additional files

Additional file 1: Table S1. Kinetic constants and enzyme AA sequences of the yeast S. cerevisiae.

Additional file 2: Table S2. The variance analysis of the regression models.

Additional file 3: Table S3. The characteristics of the models obtained by using the set of AA from enzyme active sites.

Additional file 4: Figure S1. The linkage of kinetic constants and AAC for enzymes of the TCA pathway.

Additional file 5: Figure S2. The linkage of kinetic constants and AAC for glycolytic enzymes employed in the Teusink's model.

Additional file 6: Figure S3. The second-order multiple relationships of kinetic constants and AAC.

Abbreviations
AA: Amino acid; AAC: Amino acid composition; *k*cat: Turnover number; *K*M: Michaelis-Menten constant; *k*sp: Specificity constant; LOOCV: Leave-one-out cross-validation; VIF: Variance inflation factor.

Competing interests
The authors declare that they have no competing interests.

Acknowledgment
This study was funded by the European Structural Fund Nr. 2009/0207/1DP/1.1.1.2.0/09/APIA/VIAA/128 "Latvian Interdisciplinary Interuniversity Scientific group of Systems Biology".

References
1.   L Gerosa, U Sauer, Regulation and control of metabolic fluxes in microbes. Curr. Opin. Biotechnol. **22**, 1–10 (2011). doi:10.1016/j.copbio.2011.04.016

2. PK Agarwal, Enzymes: an integrated view of structure, dynamics and function. Microbial Cell. Fact **5**, 2 (2006). doi:10.1186/1475-2859-5-2

3. DA Kraut, KS Carroll, D Herschlag, Challenges in enzyme mechanism and energetics. Annu. Rev. Biochem. **72**, 517–571 (2003). doi:10.1146/annurev.biochem.72.121801.161617

4. SC Pegg, SD Brown, S Ojha, J Seffernick, EC Meng, JH Morris, PJ Chang, CC Huang, TE Ferrin, PC Babbitt, Leveraging enzyme structure-function relationships for functional inference and experimental design: the structure-function linkage database. Biochemistry **45**, 2545–2555 (2006). doi:10.1021/bi0521011

5. E Nevoigt, Progress in metabolic engineering of *Saccharomyces cerevisiae*. Microbiol. Mol. Biol. Rev **72**, 379–412 (2008). doi:10.1128/MMBR.00025-07

6. C Magyar, E Tudos, I Simon, Functionally and structurally relevant residues of enzymes: are they segregated or overlapping? FEBS Lett **567**, 239–242 (2004)

7. DD Boehr, R Nussinov, PE Wright, The role of dynamic conformational ensembles in biomolecular recognition. Nat. Chem. Biol **5**, 789–796 (2009). doi:10.1038/nchembio.232

8. Z Zhang, S Kochhar, MG Grigorov, Descriptor-based protein remote homology identification. Protein Sci **14**, 431–444 (2005). doi:10.1110/ps.041035505

9. S Rackovsky, Sequenced physical properties encode the global organization of protein structure space. Proc. Natl Acad. Sci. USA **106**, 14345–14348 (2009). doi:10.1073/pnas.0903433106

10. A Deiana, A Giansanti, Predictors of natively unfolded proteins: unanimous consensus score to detect a twilight zone between order and disorder in generic datasets. BMC Bioinforma **11**, 198 (2010). doi:10.1186/1471-2105-11-198

11. MM Gromiha, Intrinsic relationship of amino acid composition/occurrence with topological parameters and protein folding rate. Open Struct. Biol. J **3**, 126 (2009)

12. S Roy, D Martinez, H Platero, T Lane, M Werner-Washburne, Exploiting amino acid composition for predicting protein-protein interactions. PLoS One **4**(11), e7813 (2009)

13. MA Antal, C Böde, P Csermely, Perturbation waves in proteins and protein networks: Applications of percolation and game theories in signaling and drug design. Curr. Protein Peptide Sci **10**, 161 (2009)

14. KA Johnson, Role of induced fit in enzyme specificity: a molecular forward/reverse switch. J Biol. Chem **283**, 26297–26301 (2008). doi:10.1074/jbc.R800034200

15. BRENDA (D Schomburg, Braunschweig, 2002). http://www.brenda-enzymes.org/. Accessed 27 December 2011

16. UniProtKB (The UniProt Consortium, 2008). http://www.uniprot.org. Accessed 27 December 2011

17. C Bauer, G Cercignani, GM Mura, M Paolini, A unified theory of enzyme kinetics based upon the systematic analysis of the variations of k_{cat}, K_M, and k_{cat}/K_M and the relevant $\Delta G0{\neq}$ values—possible implications in chemotherapy and biotechnology. Biochem. Pharmacol **61**, 1049–1055 (2001). doi:10.1016/S0006-2952(01)00579-2

18. SA Benner, Enzyme kinetics and molecular evolution. Chem. Rev **89**, 789–806 (1989). doi:10.1021/cr00094a004

19. E Gasteiger, A Gattiker, C Hoogland, I Ivanyi, RD Appel, A Bairoch, ExPASy: the proteomics server for in-depth protein knowledge and analysis. Nucleic Acids Res **31**, 3784–3788 (2003). doi:10.1093/nar/gkg563

20. MM Gromiha, AM Thangakani, S Selvaraj, Fold-rate: prediction of protein folding rates from amino acid sequence. Nucleic Acids Res **34**, W70–W74 (2006)

21. S Arlot, A Cellise, A survey of cross-validation procedures for model selection. Stat. Surv **4**, 40–79 (2010). doi:10.1214/09-SS054

22. RM O'Brien, A caution regarding rules of thumb for variance inflation factors. Qual. Quant **41**, 673–690 (2007). doi:10.1007/s11135-006-9018-6

23. R Bhaskaran, PK Ponnuswamy, Positional flexibilities of amino acid residues in globular proteins. Int. J Pept. Protein Res **32**, 242–255 (1988). doi:10.1111/j.1399-3011.1988.tb01258.x

24. G Deleage, B Roux, Algorithm for protein secondary structure prediction based on class prediction. Protein Eng **1**, 289–294 (1987). doi:10.1093/protein/1.4.289

25. JM Zimmerman, N Eliezer, R Simha, The characterization of amino acid sequences in proteins by statistical methods. J Theor. Biol **21**, 170–201 (1968)

26. S Lifson, C Sander, Nature **282**, 109 (1979)

27. B Teusink, J Passage, CA Reijenga, E Esgalhado, CC van der Wejden, M Schepper, MC Walsh, BM Bakker, HV Westerhoff, JL Snoep, Can yeast glycolysis be understood in terms of in vitro kinetics of the constituent enzymes? Testing Biochemistry. Eur. J. Biochem **267**, 1 (2000). doi:10.1046/j.1432-1327.2000.01527.x

28. K van Eunen, J Bouwman, P Daran-Lapujade, J Postmus, AB Canelas, FIC Mensonides, R Orij, I Tuzun, J van den Brink, GJ Smits, WM van Gulik, S Brul, JJ Heijnen, JH de Winde, MJT de Mattos, C Kettner, J Nielsen, HV Westerhoff, BM Bakker, Measuring enzyme activities under standardized *in vivo*-like conditions for systems biology. FEBS J **277**, 749 (2010). doi:10.1111/j.1742-4658.2009.07524.x

29. C Böde, IA Kovács, MS Szalay, R Palotai, T Korcsmáros, P Csermely, Network analysis of protein dynamics. FEBS Lett **281**, 2776–2782 (2007)

30. K.C. Li, Nonlinear confounding in high dimensional regression. Ann. Stat **25**, 577–612 (1997). doi:10.1214/aos/1031833665

31. SM Yan, DQ Shi, H Nong, G Wu, Predicting K_M values of beta-glucosidases using cellobiose as substrate. Interdiscip. Sci. Comput. Life Sci **4**, 1–8 (2012)

32. SM Yan, G Wu, Prediction of Michaelis-Menten constant of beta-glucosidases using nitrophenyl-beta-D-glucopyranoside as substrate. Protein Peptide Lett **18**, 1053 (2011)

33. RR Gabdoulline, M Stein, RC Wade, qPIPSA: relating enzymatic kinetic parameters and interaction fields. BMC Bioinforma **8**, 373 (2007). doi:10.1186/1471-2105-8-373

Analysis of gene network robustness based on saturated fixed point attractors

Genyuan Li and Herschel Rabitz[*]

Abstract

The analysis of gene network robustness to noise and mutation is important for fundamental and practical reasons. Robustness refers to the stability of the equilibrium expression state of a gene network to variations of the initial expression state and network topology. Numerical simulation of these variations is commonly used for the assessment of robustness. Since there exists a great number of possible gene network topologies and initial states, even millions of simulations may be still too small to give reliable results. When the initial and equilibrium expression states are restricted to being saturated (i.e., their elements can only take values 1 or −1 corresponding to maximum activation and maximum repression of genes), an analytical gene network robustness assessment is possible. We present this analytical treatment based on determination of the saturated fixed point attractors for sigmoidal function models. The analysis can determine (a) for a given network, which and how many saturated equilibrium states exist and which and how many saturated initial states converge to each of these saturated equilibrium states and (b) for a given saturated equilibrium state or a given pair of saturated equilibrium and initial states, which and how many gene networks, referred to as viable, share this saturated equilibrium state or the pair of saturated equilibrium and initial states. We also show that the viable networks sharing a given saturated equilibrium state must follow certain patterns. These capabilities of the analytical treatment make it possible to properly define and accurately determine robustness to noise and mutation for gene networks. Previous network research conclusions drawn from performing millions of simulations follow directly from the results of our analytical treatment. Furthermore, the analytical results provide criteria for the identification of model validity and suggest modified models of gene network dynamics. The yeast cell-cycle network is used as an illustration of the practical application of this analytical treatment.

Keywords: Robustness of gene networks; Fixed point attractor; Sigmoidal function; Yeast cell-cycle network

1 Introduction

A subset of genes in a cell whose protein products mutually regulate one another's expression at the transcriptional level will be referred to as a 'gene network' in this paper. The concentration of proteins encoded by the genes changes in time due to auto- and cross-regulation by the gene products. Each of such network is considered as a dynamical system. Gene networks must be robust with respect to ever-changing environments. Robustness here refers to the ability of a gene network to respond to short-term changes in the environment and quickly return to its functional steady state. Moreover, a gene network itself may endure small structural changes and mutations, while still retaining its desired steady state. The robustness of

gene networks depends on their topology with some networks being more stable than others. The analysis of the relationship between the topology of a gene network and its robustness to environmental and structural perturbations is important both theoretically and practically [1-10].

Recently, Wagner and coworkers considered the robustness of gene networks [11-14], and a similar assessment was given by Cho et al. [15] In these works, a simplified model proposed by Wagner was used to describe the dynamics of the gene expression states [11,12]. Let $\mathbf{G} = (G_1, \ldots, G_n)$ represent the n genes in a network. The concentration of proteins encoded by the genes $(G_1, \ldots, G_n)$ is denoted by $\mathbf{P} = (P_1, \ldots, P_n)$. For computational convenience, the admissible concentration range for each P_i is normalized and restricted to the interval $[0, 1]$, where

*Correspondence: hrabitz@princeton.edu
Department of Chemistry, Princeton University, Princeton, NJ 08544, USA

$P_i = 1$ corresponds to the maximum possible concentration, i.e., the corresponding gene G_i is in a state of maximum transcriptional activation. It is also assumed that $P_i = 0.5$ means that gene i is 50% 'on'. The dynamics of the expression states of the genes in a network is often described by some sigmoidal function $g_c(x)$

$$P_i(t + \tau) = g_c \left(\sum_{j=1}^{n} w_{ij} P_j(t) \right), \quad (i = 1, 2, \ldots, n) \quad (1)$$

where τ is a time constant characteristic of the process under consideration. In some work, τ was set to be 1. The constant $w_{ij} \in \Re$ describes the strength of interaction (i.e., transcriptional regulation) of the product of gene j with gene i, i.e., the degree of transcriptional activation ($w_{ij} > 0$), repression ($w_{ij} < 0$), or absence ($w_{ij} = 0$). These constants define a matrix of connectivities $W = (w_{ij})$ within the network. To facilitate the analytical treatment, the variable transformation

$$\mathbf{S} = 2\mathbf{P} - (1 \ldots 1)^T \quad (2)$$

is employed. Using the sigmoidal function σ proposed by Siegal [16] and Cho [15] for g_c, (1) becomes

$$S_i(t + \tau) = \sigma \left(\sum_{j=1}^{n} w_{ij} S_j(t) \right)$$

$$= \frac{2}{1 + \exp\left[-\sum_{j=1}^{n} w_{ij} S_j(t) \right]} - 1, \quad (i = 1, 2, \ldots, n)$$

$$(3)$$

with $S_i \in [-1, 1]$, and $S_i = 0$ corresponding to 50% of gene i being 'on'. Notwithstanding the simplicity of (3), variants of this model have been successfully used to study (a) the robustness of gene regulatory networks [12,16,17], (b) the role of robustness in evolutionary innovation [18,19], and (c) how recombination can produce negative epistasis [20].

Mjolsness at al. [21] proposed a model

$$\tau_a \frac{dv_i^a}{dt} = g_a \left(\sum_{b=1}^{n} T^{ab} v_i^b + h^a \right) - \lambda_a v_i^a, \quad (a = 1, 2, \ldots, n)$$

$$(4)$$

to describe the dynamics for each element of primitive objects $\mathbf{v}_i$ (cells, nuclei, fibers, and synapses), where g_a is a sigmoidal threshold function, T^{ab} is similar to w_{ij} in (3); v_i^a, v_i^b denote the elements of vector $\mathbf{v}_i$; h^a determines the threshold of g_a. The long-time behavior of this system has been studied, and, in some cases, is controlled by a simple limit set

$$v_i^a = \frac{1}{\lambda_a} g_a \left(\sum_{b=1}^{n} T^{ab} v_i^b + h^a \right), \quad (5)$$

which is similar to (3) with the additional parameters λ_a and h^a. This model has been successfully applied to treat the blastoderm of *Drosophila melanogaster* [21].

Similarly, Mendoza and Alvarez-Buylla [22] used a model

$$x_i(t + 1) = H \left(\sum_{j=1}^{n} w_{ij} x_j(t) - \theta_i \right), \quad (6)$$

where H is the Heaviside step function

$$H(x) = \begin{cases} 1, & \text{if } x > 0, \\ 0, & \text{if } x \leq 0 \end{cases} \quad (7)$$

to describe the dynamics of a genetic regulatory network for *Arabidopsis thaliana* flower morphogenesis. This model is also similar to (3) except that the sigmoidal function σ is replaced by the Heaviside step function and a threshold parameter θ_i is included.

All these models present simplified descriptions of gene network dynamics. Nevertheless, the models are still useful for obtaining insights into the dynamics of gene networks. In the following analysis for gene network robustness, we will employ the sigmoidal function model in (3), and its modification with threshold parameters.

The robustness of a gene network specified by W to noise (environmental) and mutation (structural) perturbations may be expressed as the stability of the final equilibrium (or steady) expression state $\mathbf{S}(\infty)$ obtained from the solution of (3), respectively, to changes of initial expression state $\mathbf{S}(0)$ and to changes of W. A complete and reliable robustness analysis would seem to call for an exhaustive sampling over the space of possible initial states for a given network and then repeating the same simulations for all possible networks. This task is infeasible as there are many possible networks W, and each W may have many initial/final equilibrium expression states. Consider a simple case where $S_i(0)$ and $S_i(\infty)$ ($i = 1, 2, \ldots, n$) can only take values $-1, 1$ and w_{ij} can only take values $-1, 0, 1$. In this case, there are 2^n possible initial/final states and 3^{n^2} possible gene networks. For a modest network of size $n = 20$, there are $2^{20} = 1,048,576$ initial/final expression states and $3^{400} \approx 7 \times 10^{190}$ gene networks. Even if one arbitrarily makes the restriction that 75% of the w_{ij} interactions are zero, and that the remaining 25% of the w_{ij} interactions can only take nonzero values $-1, 1$ to reduce the possible number of networks [13], for $n = 20$ there are still $C_{400}^{100} \times 2^{100}$ possible gene networks. Further restriction may also be applied to reduce the possible number of initial expression states [13]. Even under these restrictions, solving (3) for all possible initial expression states and gene networks is still infeasible, and only a small fraction of them can be randomly sampled and simulated. Such limitations leave open the reliability of the conclusions obtained from the simulations.

Previous work [13] concerned networks with connectivity W whose expression dynamics start from a pre-specified initial state $\mathbf{S}(0)$ at some time $t = 0$ and arrive at a prespecified stable equilibrium or 'target' expression state $\mathbf{S}(\infty)$; these networks are referred to as 'viable'. Then, the values of some elements of $\mathbf{S}(0)$ or W were changed for each viable network to check whether $\mathbf{S}(\infty)$ is reached. These studies entailed performing millions of simulations with different network topologies and initial expression states. Although the number of simulations is much smaller than 2^n and 3^{n^2} for $n = 20$, some specific conclusions were obtained. First, the fraction of viable networks, that is, networks that arrive at a prespecified target expression state $\mathbf{S}(\infty)$ given an initial gene expression state $\mathbf{S}(0)$ to the total number of possible networks, is generally very small. For moderately sized networks of $n = 20$ genes (with the number M of nonzero w_{ij} set to be 200, and the fraction d of elements different between $\mathbf{S}(0)$ and $\mathbf{S}(\infty)$ set to 0.5), the fraction of viable networks was found to be $v_f = 5.1 \times 10^{-9} \pm 1.7 \times 10^{-10}$. Due to the large numbers 2^n and 3^{n^2}, the qualitative correctness of this conclusion is clear. Since there are 2^n possible equilibrium states, even if we only consider the factor of expression states, the probability that a network W arrives at a prespecified $\mathbf{S}(\infty)$ is expected on the order of $1/2^n$. The viable networks in this prior work could be organized as a graph with each node corresponding to a network of a given topology, and two nodes are connected by an edge if they differ by a single regulatory interaction (i.e., they differ in one element w_{ij}). Remarkably, this graph is connected and can be easily traversed by gradual changes of the network topology. Thus, highly robust topologies can evolve from topologies with low robustness through gradual Darwinian topological changes. These results are claimed to be valid for discrete and continuous w_{ij} taking values $[-1, 0, 1]$ and over the interval $[-a, a]$, respectively. While simulations are valuable, they do not provide a complete picture.

Ciliberti et al. [13] considered the case where each element of the initial and equilibrium expression states, $\mathbf{S}(0)$ and $\mathbf{S}(\infty)$, can only take the values 1 or -1 corresponding to maximum and minimum possible protein concentrations. We call them *saturated* expression states. Under this condition, the present paper provides an analytical robustness assessment of gene networks whose dynamics can be described by (3) and its modification with threshold parameters. This analysis can determine (a) for a given network, which and how many saturated equilibrium states exist, and which and how many saturated initial states converge to each of these saturated equilibrium states; (b) for a given saturated equilibrium state, or a given pair of saturated equilibrium and initial states, which and how many gene networks, referred to as viable, share this saturated equilibrium state or the pair

of saturated equilibrium and initial states. We also show that the viable networks sharing a given saturated equilibrium state must follow certain patterns. These capabilities of the analytical treatment make it possible to properly define and accurately determine robustness to noise and mutation for gene networks. Previous network research conclusions drawn from performing millions of simulations follow directly from the results of our analytical treatment. Furthermore, the analytical results provide criteria for identification of model validity and suggest modified models of gene network dynamics.

The paper is organized as follows: Section 2 first defines the saturated state and saturated fixed point attractor for dynamics (3), and then gives the necessary and sufficient condition for a gene network to have a given saturated equilibrium state. Sections 3 and 4 analyze the robustness to noise and mutation, respectively. Section 5 proposes a modification of dynamics (3) with threshold parameters. Section 6 gives an illustration of the practical application of this analytical treatment: the model construction of the yeast cell-cycle network and its robustness assessment. The details of the treatment of the yeast cell-cycle network are given in an Additional file 1: Supplementary information. Finally, Section 7 presents conclusions. Mathematical proofs of the theorems in the main text are given in the Appendix.

2 Saturated states and fixed point attractors

In this work, the initial and equilibrium expression states $S_i(0)$ and $S_i(\infty)$ for gene i can only be either active ($S_i(0)$ and $S_i(\infty) = 1$) or inactive ($S_i(0)$ and $S_i(\infty) = -1$) [11,12,14]. The initial and equilibrium expression states with $S_i(0)$ and $S_i(\infty) = \pm 1$ are referred to as *saturated* initial and equilibrium expression states. *Under the condition that the initial and equilibrium expression states $\mathbf{S}(0)$ and $\mathbf{S}(\infty)$ are saturated, we may analyze the robustness and evolvability of gene networks analytically*, as explained below.

2.1 Saturated sigmoidal function

A continuous function $f(x)$ defined on $\Re$ satisfying

(f1) $f(x) = 1$ if $x \geq 1, f(x) = -1$ if $x \leq -1$,
(f2) $f(x)$ is a strictly increasing and continuous function for $x \in [-1, 1]$ and $f(0) = 0$,

is called a saturated sigmoidal function. Furthermore, if

(f3) $f(x) \geq x$ for $x \in (0, 1]$ and $f(x) \leq x$ for $x \in [-1, 0)$,

we call $f(x)$] a dissipative saturated sigmoidal function.

Note that for the particular sigmoidal function $\sigma_\beta(x)$ in domain [-1, 1]

$$x(t + \tau) = \sigma_\beta(x(t)) = \frac{2}{1 + e^{-\beta x(t)}} - 1, \tag{8}$$

the conditions (**f1**) to (**f3**) are approximately satisfied when β is sufficiently large. For example, when $\beta = 5$ and 10, we have $\sigma_\beta(1) = 0.9866$ and 0.9999 (approximately 1); and $\sigma_\beta(-1) = -0.9866$ and -0.9999 (approximately -1), respectively. Therefore, in numerical simulation, $\sigma_\beta(x)$ can be considered as a dissipative saturated sigmoidal function for a sufficiently large β. We refer to $\beta = 5$ and 10 as having 0.99 and 0.9999 confidence levels for the dissipative saturated sigmoidal function (8), because $|\sigma_\beta(\pm 1)|$ is equal to 0.99 and 0.9999, respectively (see Figure 1). In the sequel, we set $\beta \geq 5$.

2.2 Necessary and sufficient condition for a saturated state S to be an equilibrium state or a fixed point attractor of dynamics (3) with a given W

When the equilibrium states $\mathbf{S}(\infty)$ are saturated, the analysis of robustness and evolvability for gene networks can be readily performed by utilizing Feng and Tirozzi's treatment for neural networks [23].

Definition 1. A saturated state $\mathbf{S}$ in $[-1, 1]^n$ is called a saturated fixed point attractor (or saturated equilibrium state) of dynamics (3), if there exists a nonempty neighborhood $B(\mathbf{S})$ of $\mathbf{S}$ such that

$$\lim_{t \to \infty} \mathbf{S}(t) = \mathbf{S}$$

for $\mathbf{S}(0) \in B(\mathbf{S})$ and $\sum_{j=1}^{n} w_{ij} S_j \neq 0$, for all i.

It is easy to see that a saturated state $\mathbf{S}$ is a saturated fixed point of dynamics (3) with 0.99 ($\beta = 5$) or 0.9999 ($\beta = 10$) confidence level when

$$\sum_{j=1}^{n} w_{ij} \operatorname{sign}(S_j) \geq \beta, \qquad \text{if } S_i = 1, \tag{9}$$

$$\sum_{j=1}^{n} w_{ij} \operatorname{sign}(S_j) \leq -\beta, \qquad \text{if } S_i = -1, \tag{10}$$

and

$$\lim_{t \to \infty} S_i(t) \approx \begin{cases} 1, & \text{if } S_i = 1 \\ -1, & \text{if } S_i = -1 \end{cases} \qquad (i = 1, 2, \ldots, n), \tag{11}$$

i.e., $\mathbf{S}$ is a saturated fixed point with 0.99 ($\beta = 5$) or 0.9999 ($\beta = 10$) confidence level. When

$$\left| \sum_{j=1}^{n} w_{ij} \operatorname{sign}(S_j) \right| < 5,$$

for any i, then $-0.99 < S_i(t + \tau) < 0.99$ for any t, and the gene network cannot have a saturated fixed point.

Let $\mathbf{S}$ be a saturated state. We define

$$J^+(\mathbf{S}) = \{i, S_i = 1\}, \qquad J^-(\mathbf{S}) = \{i, S_i = -1\} \tag{12}$$

which denote, respectively, the two sets of all integers in $\{1, 2, \ldots, n\}$ with $S_i = 1$ and $S_i = -1$.

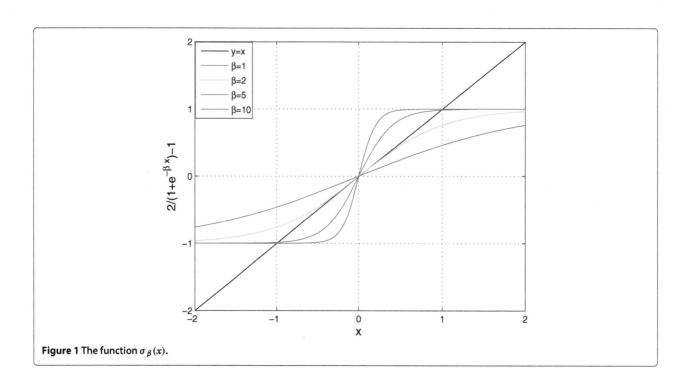

Figure 1 The function $\sigma_\beta(x)$.

Theorem 1. The necessary and sufficient condition for a saturated state $\mathbf{S}$ to be an equilibrium expression state or a fixed point attractor of dynamics (3) with a given matrix W is

$$\sum_{j \in J^+(\mathbf{S})} w_{ij} - \sum_{j \in J^-(\mathbf{S})} w_{ij} \geq \beta, \quad \text{if } i \in J^+(\mathbf{S}), \tag{13}$$

$$\sum_{j \in J^+(\mathbf{S})} w_{ij} - \sum_{j \in J^-(\mathbf{S})} w_{ij} \leq -\beta, \quad \text{if } i \in J^-(\mathbf{S}), \tag{14}$$

or equivalently

$$S_i \left(\sum_{j=1}^{n} w_{ij} S_j \right) \geq \beta, \quad (i = 1, 2, \ldots, n). \tag{15}$$

Proof. If a saturated state $\mathbf{S}$ is a fixed point of (3), it must satisfy (9,10), i.e., (13,14). If (13,14) are satisfied, so are (9,10), then (11) is satisfied and $\mathbf{S}$ is a fixed point. A saturated state $\mathbf{S}$ satisfying (13,14) (or equivalently (15)) is a fixed point attractor. The proof is given in Theorem A2 in the Appendix. $\qquad\square$

There are a total 2^n saturated states $\mathbf{S}$. Since (15) only involves simple multiplication and summation, for a modest n one can test all 2^n saturated vectors $\mathbf{S}$ for a given W and find all of its saturated fixed point attractors without iteratively solving the sigmoidal function (3). For $n = 11$ and $2^{11} = 2,048$, the test takes 0.01 s by Matlab on a Dell Precision Workstation T3400.

Example 1. Consider the network model proposed by Azevedo et al. [20] for the gap gene system of *Drosophila melanogaster* shown in Figure 2.

The authors obtained the equilibrium state $\mathbf{S}_1 = (-11 -11)$ by iteratively solving a sigmoidal function similar to (3). Using (9,10), we can determine this solution by noting

$$W \cdot \mathbf{S}_1 = \begin{bmatrix} 2 & -1 & -1 & -5 \\ -8 & 1 & 0 & 1 \\ -1 & -1 & 1 & -4 \\ 0 & -1 & -6 & 1 \end{bmatrix} \begin{bmatrix} -1 \\ 1 \\ -1 \\ 1 \end{bmatrix} = \begin{bmatrix} -7 \\ 10 \\ -5 \\ 6 \end{bmatrix}$$

which shows that the necessary and sufficient condition is satisfied with 0.99 confidence level

$$\sum_{j=1}^{4} w_{ij} S_j \geq 5, \quad i = 2, 4 \in J^+(\mathbf{S}_1),$$

$$\sum_{j=1}^{4} w_{ij} S_j \leq -5, \quad i = 1, 3 \in J^-(\mathbf{S}_1).$$

There are $2^4 = 16$ saturated states. Similar tests for the other 15 saturated states were performed. The case $\mathbf{S}_2 = -\mathbf{S}_1 = (1 - 11 - 1)$ is the only other saturated equilibrium state for the network.

3 Robustness to noise

Robustness to noise may be assessed for (a) each saturated equilibrium expression state or (b) a specified pair of saturated equilibrium and initial expression states. In case 1, we need to *compare* how many of 2^n possible saturated initial expression states converge to each saturated equilibrium expression state; in case 2, we need to determine how many *neighbours* (differing only in one element) of the $\mathbf{S}(0)$ converge to the same saturated equilibrium expression state for a given W [13]. In either case, we need to establish the condition under which a saturated initial expression state converges to a given saturated equilibrium expression state of W.

3.1 Relationship between saturated initial expression states and saturated equilibrium expression states

Theorem 2. If $\mathbf{S}$ is a saturated equilibrium expression state (or a fixed point attractor) of dynamics (3) with a given W, so is $-\mathbf{S}$.

Proof. Since $\mathbf{S}$ is a saturated fixed point attractor of (3) with a given W, then (15) is satisfied. Multiplying by -1 within and outside the parentheses in (15) will not change its right-hand side:

$$(-1)S_i \left((-1) \sum_{j=1}^{n} w_{ij} S_j \right) \geq \beta, \quad (i = 1, 2, \ldots, n),$$

$$(-S_i) \left(\sum_{j=1}^{n} w_{ij}(-S_j) \right) \geq \beta, \quad (i = 1, 2, \ldots, n) \tag{16}$$

which proves that $-\mathbf{S}$ is also a saturated fixed point attractor, i.e., a saturated equilibrium expression state for W. Example 1 demonstrates its validity. $\qquad\square$

Corollary 1. Dynamics (3) either does not have a saturated equilibrium expression state, or has an even number of saturated equilibrium expression states.

This result can be obtained immediately from Theorem 2.

Example 2. Consider a gene network given by

$$W = \begin{bmatrix} 0 & 1 & 1 & -1 & -1 & -1 \\ 1 & 0 & 1 & -1 & -1 & -1 \\ 1 & 1 & 0 & -1 & -1 & -1 \\ -1 & -1 & -1 & 0 & 1 & 1 \\ -1 & -1 & -1 & 1 & 0 & 1 \\ -1 & -1 & -1 & 1 & 1 & 0 \end{bmatrix} \tag{17}$$

with the discrete values [-1, 0, 1] for w_{ij}, and there is no auto-regulation ($w_{ii} = 0$). The six genes are separated into two groups {1, 2, 3} and {4, 5, 6}. The regulations are

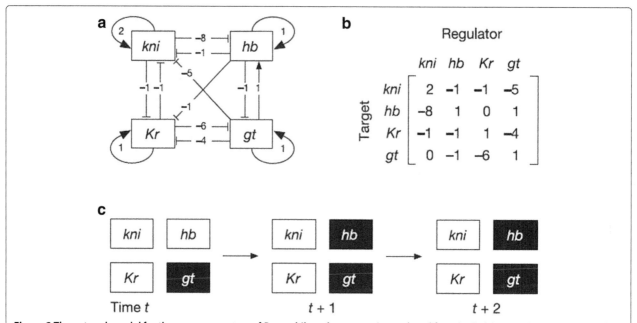

Figure 2 The network model for the gap gene system of *Drosophila melanogaster* (reproduced from [20]). (a) Network representation of the regulatory interactions between four gap genes (*gt*, giant; *hb*, hunchback; *kni*, knirps; *Kr*, Krüppel). **(b)** Corresponding matrix *W*. **(c)** graphic representation of the gene expression states of each gap gene over three successive time steps of a sigmoidal function similar to (3) where a filled box denotes 'on' (1), and an open box denotes 'off' (−1).

activating within each group, but repressing between the two groups. For such a simple system, it is easy to find by observation that amongst the $2^6 = 64$ saturated states only two states

$$S_1 = (1\ 1\ 1\ -1\ -1\ -1\ ),$$
$$S_2 = (-1\ -1\ -1\ 1\ 1\ 1\ )$$

satisfy the necessary and sufficient condition (15) to be saturated equilibrium expression states with 0.99 confidence level. An examination of (15) for all 64 saturated states proved this to be the case. Moreover,

$$S_2 = -S_1$$

satisfies Theorem 2 and Corollary 1.

Theorem 3. If $S(t)$ converges to a saturated equilibrium expression state S, then $-S(t)$ converges to $-S$.

Proof. See Theorem A3 in the Appendix. □

Example 3. The gene network given in (17) is used to show the validity of Theorem 3. The following two initial saturated states

$$S_1(0) = (1\ 1\ -1\ 1\ 1\ 1\ ),$$
$$S_2(0) = (-1\ -1\ 1\ -1\ -1\ -1\ ),$$

with $S_2(0) = -S_1(0)$, were used for dynamics (3). The two solution trajectories are found to satisfy Theorem 3.

Figure 3 gives the projections of the two trajectories onto the two-dimensional (S_1, S_5)-subspace.

Corollary 2. In the hypercube $[-1, 1]^n$, the volume of the region where points converge to a saturated equilibrium state S is equal to the volume of the region where points converge to $-S$.

Proof. Considering that $S(t)$ and $-S(t)$ are symmetric and have the same distance to the origin (see Figure 3), then in $[-1, 1]^n$ (which is symmetric to the origin) the volume of the region where points converge to S is equal to the volume of the region where points converge to $-S$. However, if S_1 and S_2 are two saturated fixed point attractors, but $S_2 \neq -S_1$, for a given W, generally in $[-1, 1]^n$ the volume of the region where points converge to S_1 may not be equal to the volume of the region where points converge to S_2. □

Theorem 4. $S = 0$ is a fixed point, but may not be a fixed point attractor for a W having a saturated fixed point attractor S.

Proof. $S = 0$ is a fixed point because

$$S_i(t + \tau) = \frac{2}{1 + \exp\left[-\sum_{j=1}^{n} w_{ij}0\right]} - 1 = \frac{2}{1 + 1} - 1 = 0, \quad \forall i.$$

(18)

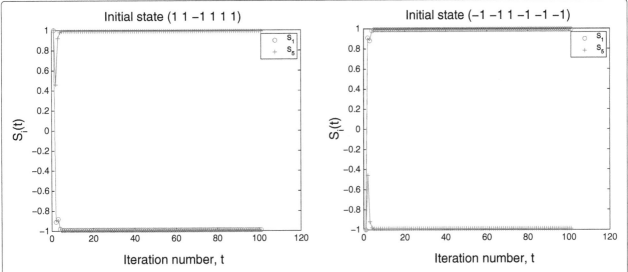

Figure 3 Projections of two trajectories with initial states $S_1(0)$ and $S_2(0)(= -S_1(0))$, respectively, in Example 3 onto two-dimensional (S_1, S_5)-subspace.

Let $B_\epsilon = \{\hat{S} \in \Re^n \mid \|\hat{S}\| < \epsilon\}$ be an open ball of radius ϵ centered at the origin in $\Re^n$ where ϵ is chosen sufficiently small such that there is only a single fixed point $\mathbf{0}$ within B_ϵ. The *sufficient* condition for $\mathbf{0}$ to be a unique fixed point attractor is (see (110) of Theorem A1 in the Appendix)

$$\sum_{j=1}^{n} |w_{ij}| \leq 2, \qquad (i = 1, 2, \ldots, n). \tag{19}$$

A saturated fixed point attractor $\mathbf{S}$ of W must satisfy (15). Then, we have

$$\sum_{j=1}^{n} |w_{ij}| \geq \sum_{j=1}^{n} w_{ij} S_i S_j$$

$$= S_i \left(\sum_{j=1}^{n} w_{ij} S_j \right) \geq \beta > 2, \quad (i = 1, 2, \ldots, n). \tag{20}$$

Therefore, $\mathbf{0}$ may not be a fixed point attractor, but an unstable fixed point. For an unstable fixed point, there exist *divergent* or both *convergent and divergent* neighborhoods of $\mathbf{0}$. In the convergent region, trajectories will be attracted to $\mathbf{0}$; In the divergent region, trajectories will leave from the neighbourhood of $\mathbf{0}$. Therefore, it is possible upon starting from a saturated initial expression state $\mathbf{S}(0)$ that the solution trajectory arising from the sigmoidal function (3) may converge to $\mathbf{0}$, or first approach $\mathbf{0}$, but then enter the divergent region, and move away from that neighborhood. □

Theorem 5. A saturated initial expression state $\mathbf{S}(0)$ converges to a saturated equilibrium expression state $\mathbf{S}$ if

the following condition is satisfied after a finite number k of iteration steps of (3) starting from $\mathbf{S}(0)$

$$\sum_{j=1}^{n} w_{ij} S_j(t \geq k) > -\ln\left[(\alpha_i - 1) - \sqrt{(\alpha_i - 1)^2 - 1}\right], \quad i \in J^+(\mathbf{S}),$$
$$\tag{21}$$

$$\sum_{j=1}^{n} w_{ij} S_j(t \geq k) < \ln\left[(\alpha_i - 1) - \sqrt{(\alpha_i - 1)^2 - 1}\right], \quad i \in J^-(\mathbf{S}),$$
$$\tag{22}$$

where

$$\alpha_i = \sum_{j=1}^{n} |w_{ij}| \tag{23}$$

under the constraint that $\alpha_i \geq 2$.

Proof. See Theorem A4 in the Appendix. □

Theorem 5 provides a way to determine all possible saturated initial expression states converging to a saturated equilibrium expression state of a W. The constraint $\alpha_i \geq 2$ implies that the gene network must contain more than one gene if w_{ij} only takes values in $[-1, 0, 1]$. This is always true.

Example 4. For the gene network given in (17) all $\alpha_i = 5$, and the sufficient condition for a saturated initial expression state converging to a given saturated equilibrium expression state $\mathbf{S}$ is then

$$\sum_{j=1}^{n} w_{ij} S_j(t \geq k) > \quad 2.0634, \quad i \in J^+(\mathbf{S}), \tag{24}$$

$$\sum_{j=1}^{n} w_{ij} S_j(t \geq k) < \quad -2.0634, \quad i \in J^-(\mathbf{S}), \tag{25}$$

where $\mathbf{S}(t \geq k)$ is the solution of (3) after k iterations starting from a saturated state $\mathbf{S}(0)$. All $2^6 = 64$ saturated states are used as initial expression states for dynamics (3). The results are given in Table 1.

Using the condition in (24,25), we found that each saturated equilibrium expression state for the gene network given in (17) has 22 saturated initial expression states (including the saturated equilibrium expression state itself). The remaining 20 saturated initial states, which do not satisfy (24,25), converge to $\mathbf{0}$.

For saturated initial expression states converging to one of the two saturated equilibrium expression states, the condition in (24,25) is satisfied starting from the iteration number k as either 0 or 1. For saturated initial expression states converging to $\mathbf{0}$, the condition given in (24,25) is never satisfied. Therefore, in this gene network, the sigmoidal function (3) either does not need to be solved, or only needs to be solved just once, to determine which and how many saturated initial expression states converge to a particular saturated equilibrium expression state. The computational effort will be reduced. For a network with 11 genes, using Theorem 5 has approximately 60% CPU time saving compared to completely solving (3).

Figure 4 gives the projection of a trajectory converging to the final state $\mathbf{0}$ onto the two-dimensional (S_1, S_5)-subspace. Since $\mathbf{0}$ may be an unstable fixed point, and the values of the elements of $\mathbf{S}(t)$ are not exactly zero, but are within a small region around $\mathbf{0}$. Therefore, the trajectory is sensitive to computational precision, that determines which region the trajectory enters. Continued iteration may lead to the trajectory entering the diverging region of $\mathbf{0}$ and leaving away from $\mathbf{0}$. When there are no limit cycles for the W, the trajectory must converge to one of the two saturated equilibrium expression states. The outcome depends on the precision used in the computation.

Table 1 Number of saturated initial states converging to different final states for the gene network given in (17)

Final state	Number of saturated initial states
$(1\ 1\ 1\ -1\ -1\ -1)$	22
$(-1\ -1\ -1\ 1\ 1\ 1)$	22
$(0\ 0\ 0\ 0\ 0\ 0)$	20

Figure 5 shows two trajectories that first approach to $\mathbf{0}$ and then leave the neighborhood of $\mathbf{0}$ and converge to one of the two saturated equilibrium expression states $(1\ 1\ 1\ -1\ -1\ -1)$ and $(-1\ -1\ -1\ 1\ 1\ 1)$, respectively. Such a property of $\mathbf{0}$ for dynamics (3) may not be meaningful biologically and causes confusion. This problem will be discussed in Section 5.

3.2 Definition for robustness to noise

Robustness to noise may be defined as follows for a network W, for each of its saturated equilibrium expression states, and for a specified pair of saturated equilibrium and initial expression states, respectively.

Definition 2. The robustness to noise R_{n_t} of a given gene network W is specified as inversely proportional to the total number m of fixed points.

$$R_{n_t} = \begin{cases} 0, & \text{if } m = 0, \\ 1/m, & \text{otherwise.} \end{cases} \tag{26}$$

The subscript n_t denotes 'noise' and 'total'.

According to the definition, larger values of m correspond to worse robustness to noise. This definition is reasonable because more fixed points a W has, then less saturated initial states converging to each of its equilibrium states. Changing an initial state has more chances to cause change of the equilibrium state.

In this definition, m should also include limit cycles. Since there is no simple way (like the Banach fixed point theorem for the existence of fixed point attractor) to determine the existence of limit cycle for sigmoidal functions, in the current work, we are unable to include it. The robustness R_{n_t} takes on values in $[0, 1]$. For W given in Example 2, there are three fixed points: $\mathbf{0}$, $(1\ 1\ 1\ -1\ -1\ -1)$ and $(-1\ -1\ -1\ 1\ 1\ 1)$. Therefore, $R_{n_t} = 1/3$, which implies that there is a 2/3 probability for having a saturated equilibrium expression state change caused by a saturated initial expression state change.

Definition 3. The robustness to noise R_{n_i} of a given saturated equilibrium expression state $\mathbf{S}_i$ for a gene network W is specified by the ratio of the number N_i of saturated initial expression states converging to $\mathbf{S}_i$, to the total number 2^n of possible saturated initial states

$$R_{n_i} = N_i/2^n. \tag{27}$$

The subscripts n and i denote 'noise' and the ith saturated equilibrium expression state. For saturated equilibrium expression states $(1\ 1\ 1\ -1\ -1\ -1)$ and $(-1\ -1\ -1\ 1\ 1\ 1)$ in Example 2, $R_{n_i} = 22/64 \approx 1/3\ (i = 1, 2)$.

Ciliberti et al. [13] argued that the pair of saturated equilibrium and initial expression states, $\mathbf{S}(\infty)$ and $\mathbf{S}(0)$, play

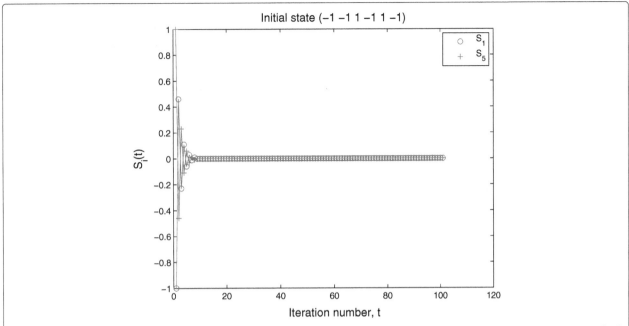

Figure 4 Projection of trajectory onto two-dimensional (S_1, S_5)-subspace starting from initial state $(-1 -1 1 -1 1 -1)$ converging to final state **0** (Example 4).

a central role for a viable network, but the variation of initial expression state in realistic cases is often mild. They define one measure of robustness to noise as the probability $R_{v,I}$ that a change in *one* gene's expression state in the saturated initial expression state $\mathbf{S}(0)$ leaves the unchanged network's saturated equilibrium state $\mathbf{S}(\infty)$. Following this pattern, we also define the measure of robustness to noise for a given pair of saturated equilibrium and initial expression states with a viable network as follows.

Definition 4. The robustness to noise $R_{n_{ij}}$ of a given pair of saturated equilibrium and initial expression states $\mathbf{S}_i$ and $\mathbf{S}_j(0)$ for a viable gene network W is specified by the ratio of the number N_{ij} of neighboring saturated initial expression states differing from $\mathbf{S}_j(0)$ by only one element and still converging to $\mathbf{S}_i$, with respect to the total number n of possible one element differing saturated initial states

$$R_{n_{ij}} = N_{ij}/n. \tag{28}$$

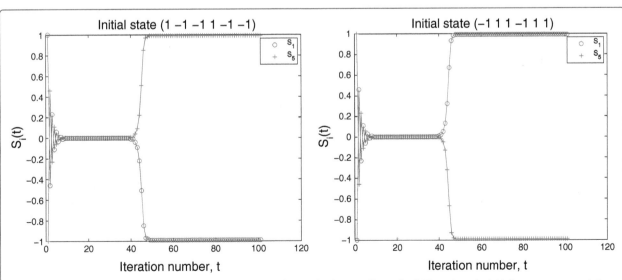

Figure 5 Projections of two trajectories onto two-dimensional (S_1, S_5)-subspace (Example 4). The trajectories initially converge towards **0** and then leave the divergent neighborhood of **0** and converge to one of the two saturated equilibrium expression states.

Example 5. Determination of $R_{n_{ij}}$ for the network in Example 2.

The network (17) has two equilibrium states S_1, S_2 with 22 saturated initial states $S_j(0)$ converging to each. The $R_{n_{ij}}$ for each pair of S_i and $S_j(0)$ was determined from solving dynamics (3) for all n one-element differing saturated initial states. The measure $R_{n_{ij}}$s for all possible pairs take only two values 1, 1/3 (i.e., N_{ij} only takes value 6 or 2). The distribution of $R_{n_{ij}}$ (i.e., how may pairs have the same $R_{n_{ij}}$) is given in Table 2.

For S_i, the seven $S_j(0)$s in the 22 saturated initial states with $R_{n_{ij}} = 1$ are S_i itself and those differing from S_i by only one element; the other fifteen $S_j(0)$s in the 22 saturated initial states with $R_{n_{ij}} = 1/3$ are those differing from S_i by two elements. The $S_j(0)$ differing from S_i by more than two elements does not converge to the S_i.

4   Robustness to mutations

For robustness to noise, we need to find all possible saturated equilibrium expression states for a given gene network W. In contrast, for robustness to mutations, we have the opposite task: for a given saturated equilibrium expression state we need to determine which and how many Ws share this saturated equilibrium expression state.

4.1   Conditions under which gene networks share the same saturated equilibrium expression state

Theorem 6. For a given saturated expression state S, all possible networks specified by particular Ws having it as a saturated equilibrium expression state can be completely constructed by solving the following inequalities:

$$\sum_{j\in J^+(S)} w_{ij} - \sum_{j\in J^-(S)} w_{ij} \geq \quad \beta, \text{ if } i \in J^+(S), \quad (29)$$

$$\sum_{j\in J^+(S)} w_{ij} - \sum_{j\in J^-(S)} w_{ij} \leq -\beta, \text{ if } i \in J^-(S), \quad (30)$$

under the condition $w_{ij} \in [-a, a]$.

Proof. Note that the rows of W are independent. When S is the saturated equilibrium expression state of W, the elements of each row (for example, the ith row $w_{ij}(j = 1, 2, \ldots, n)$) of W must satisfy either (13) or (14), i.e., (29) or (30) which is an inequality with n variables. The

Table 2 Distribution of $R_{n_{ij}}$ for the network W in Example 2

Final state	$R_{n_{ij}}$	
	1	1/3
(1 1 1 -1 -1 -1)	7	15
(-1 -1 -1 1 1 1)	7	15

inequality is solvable and has an infinite number of solutions. Those are the desired solutions with each w_{ij} located within the required range $[-a, a]$. For discrete w_{ij} (only taking values $[-1, 0, 1]$), the number of solutions is finite. All the solutions can be completely counted and determined by solving (29) or (30).   □

From (29) or (30), we may draw the following conclusions:

1. For $i \in J^+(S)$, increasing the value of the first term of (29) (if the increase does not make the value of w_{ij} larger than the upper bound a) will not violate the inequality, i.e., increasing the value of $w_{ij}(j \in J^+(S))$ will keep the same saturated equilibrium state S. This behavior implies that either increasing the activation or decreasing the repression influence of active gene j on active gene i at equilibrium state S will not change the saturated equilibrium state.

2. For $i \in J^+(S)$, decreasing the value of the second term of (29) (if the decrease does not make the value of w_{ij} smaller than the lower bound $-a$) will not violate the inequality, i.e., decreasing the value of $w_{ij}(j \in J^-(S))$ will keep the same saturated equilibrium state S. This behavior implies that either decreasing the activation or increasing the repression influence of inactive gene j on active gene i at equilibrium state S will not change the saturated equilibrium state.

3. Similarly, for $i \in J^-(S)$, either increasing the activation or decreasing the repression influence of inactive gene j on inactive gene i at equilibrium state S will not change the saturated equilibrium state.

4. For $i \in J^-(S)$, either decreasing the activation or increasing the repression influence of active gene j on inactive gene i at equilibrium state S will not change the saturated equilibrium state.

Example 6. Consider the determination of all possible gene networks W with the given saturated equilibrium expression state

$$S = (1\ 1\ 1\ -1\ -1\ -1).$$

Here, the discrete values $[-1, 0, 1]$ are required for the elements w_{ij}. Thus, we seek to determine all gene networks W sharing the same *two* saturated equilibrium expression states given in Example 2 (due to Theorem 2, $-S$ is also a saturated equilibrium expression state).

First, consider $i \in J^+(S)$. Set $\beta = 5$ for the 0.99 confidence level. In this case, (29) becomes

$$\sum_{j=1}^{3} w_{ij} - \sum_{j=4}^{6} w_{ij} \geq 5, \quad (i = 1, 2, 3). \quad (31)$$

Rearrange (31) as

$$\sum_{j=1}^{3} w_{ij} \geq 5 + \sum_{j=4}^{6} w_{ij}. \tag{32}$$

Note that the second term on the right-hand side of (32) takes on integer values from -3 to 3 corresponding to all three w_{ij} having the value either -1 or 1, respectively. We treat each circumstance separately:

1. $\sum_{j=4}^{6} w_{ij} = -3$

In this case, (32) is

$$\sum_{j=1}^{3} w_{ij} \geq 2. \tag{33}$$

It is easy to see that there is only one choice for

$$(w_{i4}\ w_{i5}\ w_{i6}) = (-1\ -1\ -1)$$

and four choices for

$$(w_{i1}\ w_{i2}\ w_{i3}) = (1\ 1\ 1),\ (0\ 1\ 1),\ (1\ 0\ 1),\ (1\ 1\ 0).$$

Thus, we have four choices for $w_{ij}(j = 1, 2, \ldots, 6)$

$$w_1^+ = (1\ 1\ 1\ -1\ -1\ -1),$$
$$w_2^+ = (0\ 1\ 1\ -1\ -1\ -1),$$
$$w_3^+ = (1\ 0\ 1\ -1\ -1\ -1),$$
$$w_4^+ = (1\ 1\ 0\ -1\ -1\ -1).$$

Here, w_k^+ denotes the kth permitted pattern for the ith row of W with $i \in J^+(\mathbf{S})$.

2. $\sum_{j=4}^{6} w_{ij} = -2$

In this case, (32) is

$$\sum_{j=1}^{3} w_{ij} \geq 3. \tag{34}$$

It is easy to see that there is only one choice for

$$(w_{i1}\ w_{i2}\ w_{i3}) = (1\ 1\ 1)$$

and three choices for

$$(w_{i4}\ w_{i5}\ w_{i6}) = (0\ -1\ -1),\ (-1\ 0\ -1),\ (-1\ -1\ 0).$$

Thus, we have another three choices for $w_{ij}(j = 1, 2, \ldots, 6)$

$$w_5^+ = (1\ 1\ 1\ \ 0\ -1\ -1),$$
$$w_6^+ = (1\ 1\ 1\ -1\ \ 0\ -1),$$
$$w_7^+ = (1\ 1\ 1\ -1\ -1\ \ 0).$$

3. $\sum_{j=4}^{6} w_{ij} \geq -1$

In this case, (32) is

$$\sum_{j=1}^{3} w_{ij} \geq 4. \tag{35}$$

This criterion is impossible because $\sum_{j=1}^{3} w_{ij}$ cannot be larger than 3. Therefore, altogether, there are only seven choices or permitted rows for w_{ij} when $i \in J^+(\mathbf{S})$.

$$W^+ = \begin{bmatrix} w_1^+ \\ w_2^+ \\ w_3^+ \\ w_4^+ \\ w_5^+ \\ w_6^+ \\ w_7^+ \end{bmatrix} = \begin{bmatrix} 1 & 1 & 1 & -1 & -1 & -1 \\ 0 & 1 & 1 & -1 & -1 & -1 \\ 1 & 0 & 1 & -1 & -1 & -1 \\ 1 & 1 & 0 & -1 & -1 & -1 \\ 1 & 1 & 1 & 0 & -1 & -1 \\ 1 & 1 & 1 & -1 & 0 & -1 \\ 1 & 1 & 1 & -1 & -1 & 0 \end{bmatrix}. \tag{36}$$

Now consider $i \in J^-(\mathbf{S})$. In this case, (30) becomes

$$\sum_{j=1}^{3} w_{ij} - \sum_{j=4}^{6} w_{ij} \leq -5, \qquad (i = 4, 5, 6). \tag{37}$$

Rearrange (37) as

$$\sum_{j=4}^{6} w_{ij} \geq 5 + \sum_{j=1}^{3} w_{ij}. \tag{38}$$

Note that (38) is the same as (32) except that $(w_{i1}w_{i2}w_{i3})$ and $(w_{i4}w_{i5}w_{i6})$ interchange their positions. Therefore, there are seven choices or permitted rows for w_{ij} when $i \in J^-(\mathbf{S})$:

$$W^- = \begin{bmatrix} w_1^- \\ w_2^- \\ w_3^- \\ w_4^- \\ w_5^- \\ w_6^- \\ w_7^- \end{bmatrix} = \begin{bmatrix} -1 & -1 & -1 & 1 & 1 & 1 \\ -1 & -1 & -1 & 0 & 1 & 1 \\ -1 & -1 & -1 & 1 & 0 & 1 \\ -1 & -1 & -1 & 1 & 1 & 0 \\ 0 & -1 & -1 & 1 & 1 & 1 \\ -1 & 0 & -1 & 1 & 1 & 1 \\ -1 & -1 & 0 & 1 & 1 & 1 \end{bmatrix}. \tag{39}$$

In the construction of w_k^+, for a given (w_{i4}, w_{i5}, w_{i6}), all possible patterns of (w_{i1}, w_{i2}, w_{i3}) are considered. For a given (w_{i1}, w_{i2}, w_{i3}), a similar treatment for (w_{i4}, w_{i5}, w_{i6}) was performed. Thus, for any w_k^+, we can always find a w_l^+ differing from it only by a single w_{ij}. This is also true for w_k^-. In this example, w_k^+ and $w_k^-(k = 2, 3, \ldots, 7)$ differ from w_1^+ and w_1^- only by a single w_{ij}, respectively.

Since each row of W has seven choices, altogether, there are $7^6 = 117,649$ gene networks, each specified by a particular W, sharing the same saturated equilibrium expression states

$$\mathbf{S} = (1\ \ 1\ \ 1\ -1\ -1\ -1),$$
$$-\mathbf{S} = (-1\ -1\ -1\ \ 1\ \ 1\ \ 1).$$

These gene networks sharing the same saturated equilibrium expression states are referred to as 'viable' networks (see [20]). This definition is different from that given by Ciliberti et al. [13], where viable networks were those sharing a prespecified pair of saturated initial and equilibrium expression states. The viable networks defined by sharing a pair of saturated initial and equilibrium expression states are a subset of the viable networks defined by sharing a saturated equilibrium expression state only.

The analysis here about viable networks implies that for a given saturated state, all viable networks having it as an equilibrium state must follow certain patterns, i.e., its rows must be chosen from finite permitted rows. The permitted rows for a given saturated equilibrium state have specific biological meaning and reflect the required connectivity patterns of each gene to other genes. This restriction distinguishes viable networks for a given equilibrium state from other viable networks with distinct equilibrium states as well as inviable networks.

4.2 Definitions of robustness to mutation

The number of viable networks in the example above $7^6 = 117,649$ itself is large, but the total number of possible gene networks with $n = 6$ is $3^{6^2} \approx 1.5 \times 10^{17}$. The fraction of viable gene networks in the total number of possible gene networks is $7^6/3^{36} \approx 7.8383 \times 10^{-13}$, even smaller than that obtained previously in numerical simulations [13] for $n = 20$. Based on the above analysis for viable gene networks, it seems plausible to define robustness to mutation for a given saturated equilibrium state as the ratio of the number of viable networks to the total number of possible networks for a given n. If so, it would appear that none of the viable gene networks is robust to mutation because the ratio is very small.

The latter inference is misleading because most of the possible gene networks have no similarity in topology with the viable gene networks having a specific saturated equilibrium state, and there is rarely a chance that a viable gene network will suddenly change to one of them. In normal circumstances, the structure perturbations due to mutation are small and the topology can only change gradually. A viable network may experience topology changes step-by-step, and in each step, only one w_{ij} changes. Ciliberti et al. [13] defined mutational robustness for a viable gene network as the fraction of its one-mutant neighbors that are also viable, and we follow the same criterion. In the following discussion, w_{ij} is restricted only to take the discrete values $[-1, 0, 1]$.

We will use Example 5 as an illustration. A gene network W is viable if and only if its ith row belongs to one of the seven rows in W^+ (if $i \in J^+(S)$) or W^- (if $i \in J^-(S)$), respectively. Since w_{ij} only takes on three values $[-1, 0, 1]$, each w_{ij} may have two possible changes from its original value, and there is a total $2n^2 = 2 \times 6^2 = 72$ single w_{ij} changes (i.e., $2n^2 = 72$ one-mutant neighbors) for any W.

Suppose that only one w_{ij} can change. From W^+, we see that each element w_{1j}^+ in w_1^+ changing to 0 yields one of $w_k^+(k = 2, ..., 7)$, which is still viable. Other changes are not viable. Therefore, the total number of viable single w_{1j}^+ changes in w_1^+ is

$$N_{w_1^+}^v = 6. \tag{40}$$

However, for each w_{kj}^+ in $w_k^+(k = 2, \ldots, 7)$ only 0 changing to 1 (if $j \in J^+(S)$) or -1 (if $j \in J^-(S)$) gives w_1^+ which is still viable, and other changes are not viable. Thus, the total number of viable single w_{kj}^+ changes in $w_k^+(k = 2, \ldots, 7)$ is

$$N_{w_k^+}^v = 1, \qquad (k = 2, \ldots, 7). \tag{41}$$

It can be proved that this is also true for w_1^- and $w_k^-(k = 2, \ldots, 7)$, i.e.,

$$N_{w_1^-}^v = 6, \qquad N_{w_k^-}^v = 1, \qquad (k = 2, \ldots, 7). \tag{42}$$

We then define robustness to mutation as follows:

Definition 5. Robustness to mutation for a viable gene network W with a specified saturated equilibrium state S_i is

$$R_{m_i} = \begin{cases} 0, & \text{if } W \text{ is inviable}, \\ \dfrac{N_W^v}{N_W} = \sum_{i=1}^{n} \dfrac{N_{w_i}^v}{2n^2}, & \text{if } W \text{ is viable}. \end{cases} \tag{43}$$

Here the subscripts m and i in R_{m_i} denote 'mutation' and the ith saturated equilibrium expression state; N_W^v and $N_{w_i}^v$ respectively are the total numbers of viable single w_{ij} changes (which is also the number of one-mutant viable neighbors) of W and its ith row; N_W is the total number of possible single w_{ij} changes of W. For a given W with a specified saturated equilibrium state, its robustness to mutation can be readily calculated from $N_{w_i}^v$ of each row. In Example 5, since each row of a viable network must be one of the seven rows in W^+ or W^-, and $N_{w_1^+}^v = N_{w_1^-}^v = 6$, $N_{w_k^+}^v = N_{w_k^-}^v = 1(k = 2, \ldots, 7)$, the value of R_{m_i} depends on how many w_1^+ and w_1^- are contained in W.

Example 7. Some inviable and viable networks $W_k(k = 1, \ldots, 8)$ with respect to the saturated equilibrium expression state $(1\ 1\ 1\ -1\ -1\ -1)$ (and $(-1\ -1\ -1\ 1\ 1\ 1)$ by

Theorem 2) are given below and their N_W^v and R_{m_i} are given in Table 3.

$$W_1 = \begin{bmatrix} 0 & 0 & 1 & -1 & -1 & -1 \\ 1 & 0 & 1 & -1 & -1 & -1 \\ 1 & 1 & 0 & -1 & -1 & -1 \\ -1 & -1 & -1 & 1 & 0 & 1 \\ -1 & -1 & -1 & 1 & 0 & 1 \\ -1 & -1 & -1 & 1 & 1 & 0 \end{bmatrix} \quad W_2 = \begin{bmatrix} 0 & 1 & 1 & -1 & -1 & -1 \\ 1 & 0 & 1 & -1 & -1 & -1 \\ 1 & 1 & 0 & -1 & -1 & -1 \\ -1 & -1 & -1 & 0 & 1 & 1 \\ -1 & -1 & -1 & 1 & 0 & 1 \\ -1 & -1 & -1 & 1 & 1 & 0 \end{bmatrix}$$

$$W_3 = \begin{bmatrix} 1 & 1 & 1 & -1 & -1 & -1 \\ 1 & 0 & 1 & -1 & -1 & -1 \\ 1 & 1 & 0 & -1 & -1 & -1 \\ -1 & -1 & -1 & 0 & 1 & 1 \\ -1 & -1 & -1 & 1 & 0 & 1 \\ -1 & -1 & -1 & 1 & 1 & 0 \end{bmatrix} \quad W_4 = \begin{bmatrix} 1 & 1 & 1 & -1 & -1 & -1 \\ 1 & 0 & 1 & -1 & -1 & -1 \\ 1 & 1 & 0 & -1 & -1 & -1 \\ -1 & -1 & -1 & 0 & 1 & 1 \\ -1 & -1 & -1 & 1 & 0 & 1 \\ -1 & -1 & -1 & 1 & 1 & 1 \end{bmatrix}$$

$$W_5 = \begin{bmatrix} 1 & 1 & 1 & -1 & -1 & -1 \\ 1 & 1 & 1 & -1 & -1 & -1 \\ 1 & 1 & 0 & -1 & -1 & -1 \\ -1 & -1 & -1 & 0 & 1 & 1 \\ -1 & -1 & -1 & 1 & 0 & 1 \\ -1 & -1 & -1 & 1 & 1 & 1 \end{bmatrix} \quad W_6 = \begin{bmatrix} 1 & 1 & 1 & -1 & -1 & -1 \\ 1 & 1 & 1 & -1 & -1 & -1 \\ 1 & 1 & 0 & -1 & -1 & -1 \\ -1 & -1 & -1 & 0 & 1 & 1 \\ -1 & -1 & -1 & 1 & 1 & 1 \\ -1 & -1 & -1 & 1 & 1 & 1 \end{bmatrix}$$

$$W_7 = \begin{bmatrix} 1 & 1 & 1 & -1 & -1 & -1 \\ 1 & 1 & 1 & -1 & -1 & -1 \\ 1 & 1 & 1 & -1 & -1 & -1 \\ -1 & -1 & -1 & 0 & 1 & 1 \\ -1 & -1 & -1 & 1 & 1 & 1 \\ -1 & -1 & -1 & 1 & 1 & 1 \end{bmatrix} \quad W_8 = \begin{bmatrix} 1 & 1 & 1 & -1 & -1 & -1 \\ 1 & 1 & 1 & -1 & -1 & -1 \\ 1 & 1 & 1 & -1 & -1 & -1 \\ -1 & -1 & -1 & 1 & 1 & 1 \\ -1 & -1 & -1 & 1 & 1 & 1 \\ -1 & -1 & -1 & 1 & 1 & 1 \end{bmatrix}$$

W_1 is inviable because its first row does not belong to any row of W^+ or W^-. The other W_k s are viable. As mentioned above, the value of R_{m_i} of a viable W depends on how many w_1^+ and w_1^- are contained in the network. From W_2 to W_8, more and more w_1^+ and w_1^- are included. Thus, the corresponding N_W^v and R_{m_i} become larger and larger, and W_8 is the most stable one with $N_W^v = 36$ (i.e., having 36 one-mutant viable neighbors) and $R_{m_i} = 1/2$.

For $n = 6$ and the saturated equilibrium expression states $(1\ 1\ 1\ -1\ -1\ -1)$ and $(-1\ -1\ -1\ 1\ 1\ 1)$, the viable gene networks can only take seven distinct values of R_{m_i} given in Table 3 corresponding to W containing $0,1,\ldots,6$ of w_1^+ and w_1^-. Suppose k rows of a viable network are w_1^+ and w_1^-, then the value of its mutational robustness $R_{m_i}(k)$ is given by

$$R_{m_i}(k) = \sum_{i=1}^{6} V_{w_i}^v / (2 \times 6^2) = [6k + 1(6-k)]/72$$

$$= (5k+6)/72, \quad (k = 0,1,\ldots,6). \tag{44}$$

It can be readily proved that the number $N(k)$ of all possible viable networks with robustness to mutation equal to $R_{m_i}(k)$ is

$$N(k) = C_6^k \times 6^{6-k}, \quad (k = 0,1,\ldots,6), \tag{45}$$

Table 3 The robustness to mutation R_{m_i} of W_k

W_k	N_W^v	R_{m_i}	W_k	N_W^v	R_{m_i}
W_1	0	0	W_5	21	21/72
W_2	6	6/72	W_6	26	26/72
W_3	11	11/72	W_7	31	31/72
W_4	16	16/72	W_8	36	36/72

where the first term C_6^k denotes the number of combinations of k elements taken from six elements, representing how many possible positions that k rows of w_1^+ or w_1^- can take in six rows of W. Each of the remaining $6 - k$ rows of W has six choices from w_k^+ and w_k^- ($k = 2,\ldots,7$), and the second term 6^{6-k} gives the total possible number of combinations for the $6-k$ rows. Figure 6 gives the distribution of R_{m_i}.

Following [13], we also define robustness to mutation, $R_{m_{ij}}$, as follows:

Definition 6. Robustness to mutation for a viable gene network W with specified saturated equilibrium and initial states $\mathbf{S}_i$ and $\mathbf{S}_j(0)$ is

$$R_{m_{ij}} = \frac{N_{m_{ij}}^v}{N_W} = \frac{N_{m_{ij}}^v}{2n^2}. \tag{46}$$

Here, the subscript m and i,j in $R_{m_{ij}}$ respectively denote 'mutation' and the ith saturated equilibrium expression state $\mathbf{S}_i$ and jth saturated initial expression state $\mathbf{S}_j(0)$; $N_{m_{ij}}^v$ is the total numbers of viable single w_{ij} changes of W with respect to $\mathbf{S}_i$ and $\mathbf{S}_j(0)$, which can be obtained by testing how many viable networks in N_W^v share $\mathbf{S}_j(0)$.

Example 8. Determination of $R_{m_{ij}}$ for W_2 and W_3 in Example 7.

$R_{m_{ij}}$ values were determined for the networks W_2 and W_3 given in Example 7. Both W_2 and W_3 have the same saturated equilibrium states $\mathbf{S}_1$, $\mathbf{S}_2$. For W_2 each $\mathbf{S}_i$ has 22 saturated initial states converging to it. For W_3 each $\mathbf{S}_i$ has 32 saturated initial states converging to it. The numbers N_W^v of one-mutant viable networks sharing the same saturated equilibrium state $\mathbf{S}_i(i = 1,2)$ for W_2 and W_3 are 6 and 11, respectively (see Table 3). For W_2, all 6 one-mutant neighbours sharing $\mathbf{S}_i$ also share all 22 $\mathbf{S}_j(0)(j = 1 - 22)$, i.e., $N_{m_{ij}}^v = N_W^v = 6$, $R_{m_{ij}} = 6/72$ for all 22 pairs. For W_3, $N_{m_{ij}}^v$ is different not only for distinct $\mathbf{S}_i$ but also for distinct initial states. For $\mathbf{S}_1$, $N_{m_{ij}}^v(\leq N_W^v)$ takes values: 5,7,11; for $\mathbf{S}_2$, $N_{m_{ij}}^v(\leq N_W^v)$ takes values: 5,6,9,11, respectively. Table 4 gives the distribution of $R_{m_{ij}}$ values for W_3, i.e., how many pairs of $\mathbf{S}_i$ and $\mathbf{S}_j(0)$ take these values.

4.3 Topology evolution of gene networks

From the procedure to construct viable networks given in Example 6, we know that for each permitted row there always exists another permitted row differing by only a single w_{ij} from it. Therefore, for a viable network W_i, we can always find one or more viable networks, W_j's, differing by only one w_{ij} from it. The above eight networks $W_k(k = 1, 2,\ldots, 8)$ are an example. They only differ from one another as adjacent neighbors with a single changed w_{ij}. These changes in topology correspond to the loss of a

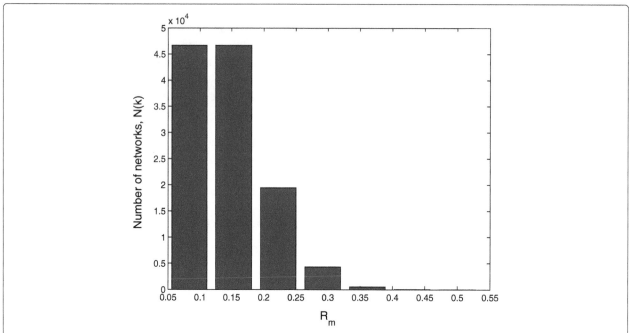

Figure 6 Distribution of mutational robustness for viable gene networks. *n* = 6; saturated equilibrium expression states (1 1 1 −1 −1 −1) and (−1 −1 −1 1 1 1).

regulatory interaction ($w_{ij} \rightarrow 0$), or to the appearance of a new regulatory interaction that was previously absent. The changes can be represented as a reversible path

$$
\begin{array}{c}
W_1 \Leftrightarrow W_2 \Leftrightarrow W_3 \Leftrightarrow W_4 \\
\Updownarrow \\
W_8 \Leftrightarrow W_7 \Leftrightarrow W_6 \Leftrightarrow W_5
\end{array}
\tag{47}
$$

In going from W_2 to W_1, the gene network no longer attains the saturated equilibrium expression state. Thus, we may consider W_1 as 'dead'. In going from W_2 to W_3, however, not only is the saturated equilibrium expression state retained, but also the robustness to mutation becomes higher. Suppose that all possible single w_{ij} changes have the same probability, then the gene network with higher R_{m_i} has a greater chance to 'survive'. This implies that highly robust topologies can evolve from topologies with low robustness through gradual Darwinian topological changes or 'natural selection'.

Ciliberti et al. [13] suggested that all viable networks attaining a given gene expression state can be organized into a graph whose nodes are networks that differ in their topology. Two networks (nodes) in the graph are connected by an edge if they differ in the value of only one regulatory interaction (w_{ij}). As proved above, for a viable network W_i, we can always find one or more viable networks, W_js differing by only one w_{ij} from it. The number of viable neighbors differing by a single w_{ij} for a viable network W is simply the value of its N_W^v (see Table 2). Therefore, any two viable networks W_i and W_j with k different elements w_{ij} can be connected by a path with k edges and $k - 1$ viable networks between them. For example, W_2 and W_8 have six different diagonal w_{ij}s, and they are connected by a path with six edges and five viable networks between them. This circumstance implies that all viable networks can be organized to comprise a large graph which can be easily traversed by a sequence of single w_{ij} changes of network topology. Thus, robustness is an evolvable property. To draw this conclusion, a previous study performed millions of simulations [13], but the analytical treatment here directly leads to this result.

5   Modified sigmoidal function with threshold parameters

All the results obtained here are based on the sigmoidal function model (3) for gene networks. This model is a simplified picture, and caution is called for so as to not over-interpret the conclusions obtained from our analytical treatment. For example, we proved that $-\mathbf{S}$ is also a saturated equilibrium expression state if $\mathbf{S}$ is one; this conclusion may not be biologically meaningful. Another

Table 4 The distribution of $R_{m_{ij}}$ for the network W_3

Final state	$R_{m_{ij}}$				
	5/72	6/72	7/72	9/72	11/72
S_1	7	0	3	0	22
S_2	1	6	0	3	22

conclusion from our analysis is that $\mathbf{0}$ may be an unstable fixed point. Following a previous definition, $\mathbf{0}$ corresponds to all genes being 'half-on'. This definition may not be appropriate under some circumstances, and instability of $\mathbf{0}$ introduces difficulty for biological interpretation. However, these considerations provide criteria to modify the mathematical model, for example, by using the more general sigmoidal function proposed in [23] to describe network dynamics. To remove $-\mathbf{S}$ and $\mathbf{0}$ from being an equilibrium state or a fixed point, the complex sigmoidal function given in [23] is unnecessary, we only need to slightly modify the sigmoidal model (3) by introducing a threshold parameter θ_i [21,22]:

$$S_i(t+\tau) = \frac{2}{1 + \exp\left[-\left(\sum_{j=1}^{n} w_{ij}S_j(t) - \theta_i\right)\right]} - 1,$$
$$(i = 1, 2, \ldots, n). \tag{48}$$

Using (48), $\mathbf{0}$ is no longer a fixed point because

$$S_i(t+\tau) = \frac{2}{1 + \exp\left[-\left(\sum_{j=1}^{n} w_{ij}0 - \theta_i\right)\right]} - 1 \tag{49}$$

$$= \frac{2}{1 + e^{\theta_i}} - 1 \neq 0, \qquad \theta_i \neq 0.$$

The necessary and sufficient condition for $\mathbf{S}$ to be an equilibrium state for (48) becomes

$$\sum_{j=1}^{n} w_{ij}S_j \geq \beta + \theta_i, \qquad \text{if } i \in J^+(\mathbf{S}), \tag{50}$$

$$\sum_{j=1}^{n} w_{ij}S_j \leq -\beta + \theta_i, \qquad \text{if } i \in J^-(\mathbf{S}). \tag{51}$$

Multiplying both sides by -1 and interchanging $\geq$ and $\leq$ and changing $J^+(\mathbf{S})$ to $J^-(-\mathbf{S})$ and $J^-(\mathbf{S})$ to $J^+(-\mathbf{S})$ yield

$$\sum_{j=1}^{n} w_{ij}(-S_j) \leq -\beta - \theta_i, \qquad \text{if } i \in J^-(-\mathbf{S}), \tag{52}$$

$$\sum_{j=1}^{n} w_{ij}(-S_j) \geq \beta - \theta_i, \qquad \text{if } i \in J^+(-\mathbf{S}). \tag{53}$$

If $\theta_i > 0$ for all i,

$$\beta - \theta_i < \beta + \theta_i, \tag{54}$$

and it is possible that

$$\sum_{j=1}^{n} w_{ij}(-S_j) \ngeq \beta + \theta_i, \qquad \text{if } i \in J^+(-\mathbf{S}), \tag{55}$$

i.e., (50) may not be satisfied, and $-\mathbf{S}$ may not be a saturated equilibrium state. If $\theta_i < 0$ for all i, then

$$-\beta - \theta_i > -\beta + \theta_i, \tag{56}$$

and it is possible that

$$\sum_{j=1}^{n} w_{ij}(-S_j) \nleq -\beta + \theta_i, \qquad \text{if } i \in J^-(-\mathbf{S}). \tag{57}$$

In this case, (51) may not be satisfied, and $-\mathbf{S}$ may not be a saturated equilibrium state.

If $\theta_i < 0$ for all $i \in J^+(\mathbf{S})$ and $\theta_i > 0$ for all $i \in J^-(\mathbf{S})$, then both (50) and (51) may not be satisfied for $-\mathbf{S}$, and $-\mathbf{S}$ may not be a saturated equilibrium state for W. In Example 2, when the model (48) is used with $\theta_i = -2$ ($i = 1, 2, 3$) and $\theta_i = 2(i = 4, 5, 6)$, then the network given in (17) only has a single saturated equilibrium state $(1\ 1\ 1\ -1\ -1\ -1)$, and all saturated initial states converge to it. Thus, the problem reduces to choosing the parameter θ_i and giving it biological interpretation. Then, we have

Theorem 7. The necessary and sufficient condition for a saturated state $\mathbf{S}$ to be an equilibrium expression state or a fixed point attractor of the dynamics (48) with a given matrix W is

$$\sum_{j\in J^+(\mathbf{S})} w_{ij} - \sum_{j\in J^-(\mathbf{S})} w_{ij} - \theta_i \geq \beta, \text{ if } i \in J^+(\mathbf{S}), \tag{58}$$

$$\sum_{j\in J^+(\mathbf{S})} w_{ij} - \sum_{j\in J^-(\mathbf{S})} w_{ij} - \theta_i \leq -\beta, \text{ if } i \in J^-(\mathbf{S}), \tag{59}$$

or equivalently

$$S_i\left(\sum_{j=1}^{n} w_{ij}S_j - \theta_i\right) \geq \beta, \quad (i = 1, 2, \ldots, n). \tag{60}$$

Proof. If a saturated state $\mathbf{S}$ is a fixed point of (48), it must satisfy (58,59), which implies that

$$\lim_{t\to\infty} S_i(t) \approx \begin{cases} 1, & \text{if } S_i = 1 \\ -1, & \text{if } S_i = -1 \end{cases} \quad (i = 1, 2, \ldots, n), \tag{61}$$

i.e., $\mathbf{S}$ is a saturated fixed point with 0.99 ($\beta = 5$) or 0.9999 ($\beta = 10$) confidence level. A saturated state $\mathbf{S}$ satisfying (58,59, or 60) is a fixed point attractor. The proof is given in Theorem A5 in the Appendix. $\square$

Similarly, we can have

Theorem 8. For a given saturated expression state $\mathbf{S}$, all possible networks specified by particular Ws having it as a saturated equilibrium expression state for dynamics (48) can be completely constructed by solving the following system of inequalities

$$\sum_{j\in J^+(\mathbf{S})} w_{ij} - \sum_{j\in J^-(\mathbf{S})} w_{ij} - \theta_i \geq \beta, \text{ if } i \in J^+(\mathbf{S}), \quad (62)$$

$$\sum_{j\in J^+(\mathbf{S})} w_{ij} - \sum_{j\in J^-(\mathbf{S})} w_{ij} - \theta_i \leq -\beta, \text{ if } i \in J^-(\mathbf{S}), \quad (63)$$

under the condition $w_{ij} \in [-a, a]$, and $\theta_i \in [-b, b]$.

Proof. The proof is the same as that for Theorem 6. □

6 Application to a yeast cell-cycle network

A simple yeast cell-cycle network shown in Figure 7b with 11 nodes was proposed by Li et al. [24].

The dynamics of the network was defined by Li et al. as

$$S_i(t+1) = \begin{cases} 1, & \sum_j a_{ij}S_j(t) > 0, \\ 0, & \sum_j a_{ij}S_j(t) < 0, \\ S_i(t), & \sum_j a_{ij}S_j(t) = 0, \end{cases} \quad (64)$$

where 1 and 0 correspond to active and inactive states of the gene, i.e., 0 instead of -1 is used to represent the inactive state, and a_{ij} is w_{ij} in (3). Using model (64), Li et al. found that there exist 7 saturated fixed point attractors (considering 0 as -1) and all of the $2^{11} = 2,048$ possible saturated initial expression states converge to one of the seven fixed point attractors (see Table 5).

Note that dynamics (64) is different from dynamics (3). For $\sum_j a_{ij}S_j(t) = 0$, dynamics (3) gives $S_i(t+1) = 0$, not $S_i(t)$. Dynamics (3) with the W constructed directly from the connectivities in Figure 7b will not give the same result as that given by dynamics (64). All the information given by the simplified model for yeast cell-cycle network (Figure 7b) will be considered as 'available experimental information' for budding yeast, and used as an example to

illustrate our analytical treatment for network construction and its robustness analysis. Hereafter, 0 representing the inactive state by Li et al. will be replaced by -1. Only the main results are presented here; see the online Supplementary information (Additional file 1) for more details.

6.1 Construction of viable networks

Define the node order from 1 to 11 as specified in Table 5, i.e., Cln3 is node 1, MBF is node 2, etc. We first construct all viable networks sharing the most stable saturated equilibrium expression state, the first fixed point attractor in Table 5

$$\mathbf{S}_1 = (-1 \ -1 \ -1 \ -1 \ 1 \ -1 \ -1 \ -1 \ 1 \ -1 \ -1) \quad (65)$$

for dynamics (3). According to Theorem 2, these viable networks will also share the other saturated equilibrium expression state

$$\mathbf{S}_2 = -\mathbf{S}_1. \quad (66)$$

As mentioned by Li et al. [24], 'the overall dynamic properties of the network are not very sensitive to the choice of these parameters' (w_{ij}), but the connectivity patterns of the network, i.e., the regulatory influence between genes (activation, repression, and absence) is important for determining gene network robustness. Therefore, we restrict w_{ij} to only take the discrete values 1 (activation), -1 (repression), and 0 (absence).

Theorem 6 gives the criterion to construct all of such networks W. When w_{ij} only takes values $[-1, 0, 1]$, to satisfy (29,30) each row of W must have five or more nonzero elements due to $\beta \geq 5$. Otherwise, the network would not have any saturated equilibrium states. This problem occurs not only for networks with less than five genes, but also for larger networks with sparse connectivities

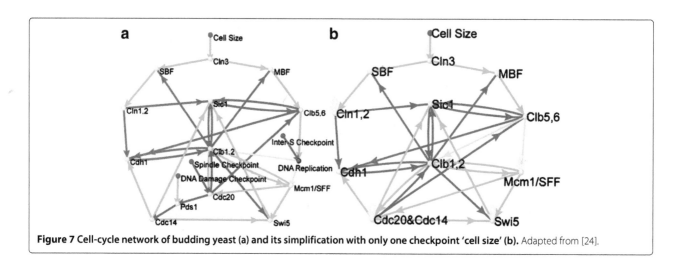

Figure 7 Cell-cycle network of budding yeast (a) and its simplification with only one checkpoint 'cell size' (b). Adapted from [24].

Table 5 Fixed point attractors of the cell-cycle network and the number of saturated states (basin size) converging to them

Basin size	Cln3	MBF	SBF	Cln1,2	Cdh1	Swi5	Cdc20	Clb5,6	Sic1	Clb1,2	Mcm1
1,764	0	0	0	0	1	0	0	0	1	0	0
151	0	0	1	1	0	0	0	0	0	0	0
109	0	1	0	0	1	0	0	0	1	0	0
9	0	0	0	0	0	0	0	0	1	0	0
7	0	1	0	0	0	0	0	0	1	0	0
7	0	0	0	0	0	0	0	0	0	0	0
1	0	0	0	0	1	0	0	0	0	0	0

between genes. For example, Node 1 (Cln3) in Figure 7b is a pure 'parent' node, which does not have any regulation coming from all other 'children' nodes, i.e., all $w_{1j} = 0$ for $j \neq 1$, and for $\mathbf{S}_1$ the condition (30) does not hold:

$$\sum_{j \in J^+(\mathbf{S}_1)} w_{1j} - \sum_{j \in J^-(\mathbf{S}_1)} w_{1j} = -w_{11} \not\leq -\beta. \quad (67)$$

To avoid this problem, the factor β may be introduced such that

$$W = \beta \hat{W}, \quad (68)$$

so to satisfy condition (29,30), $\hat{w}_{ij}$ can only take values $[-1, 0, 1]$ without any restriction on the number of nonzero elements in each row of $\hat{W}$. For the sake of notational simplicity, in the sequel, we still use W instead of $\hat{W}$, but write dynamics (3) as

$$S_i(t + \tau) = \sigma \left(\sum_{j=1}^{n} w_{ij} S_j(t) \right)$$
$$= \frac{2}{1 + \exp \left[-\beta \sum_{j=1}^{n} w_{ij} S_j(t) \right]} - 1. \quad (69)$$

Conditions (29,30) then become

$$\sum_{j \in J^+(\mathbf{S})} w_{ij} - \sum_{j \in J^-(\mathbf{S})} w_{ij} \geq 1, \text{ if } i \in J^+(\mathbf{S}), \quad (70)$$

$$\sum_{j \in J^+(\mathbf{S})} w_{ij} - \sum_{j \in J^-(\mathbf{S})} w_{ij} \leq -1, \text{ if } i \in J^-(\mathbf{S}). \quad (71)$$

For saturated equilibrium state $\mathbf{S}_1$, (70,71) may be rewritten as

$$-\sum_{j=1, j \neq 5,9}^{11} w_{ij} \geq 1 - w_{i5} - w_{i9}, \text{ if } i = 5,9, \quad (72)$$

$$-\sum_{j=1, j \neq 5,9}^{11} w_{ij} \leq -1 - w_{i5} - w_{i9}, \text{ if } i \neq 5,9, \quad (73)$$

or

$$\sum_{j=1, j \neq 5,9}^{11} w_{ij} \leq -1 + w_{i5} + w_{i9}, \text{ if } i = 5,9, \quad (74)$$

$$\sum_{j=1, j \neq 5,9}^{11} w_{ij} \geq 1 + w_{i5} + w_{i9}, \text{ if } i \neq 5,9. \quad (75)$$

Using the condition (74,75), all permitted row patterns sharing saturated equilibrium state $\mathbf{S}_1$ for dynamics (69) have been completely counted and determined (see Additional file 1: Supplementary information). Each row has **72,219** permitted patterns. Thus, the total number of viable networks sharing saturated equilibrium state $\mathbf{S}_1$ is

$$72,219^{11} \approx 2.7872 \times 10^{53}.$$

As shown below, for the yeast cell-cycle network, the first row of W is restricted to be

$$(1\ 0\ 0\ 0\ 0\ 0\ 0\ 0\ 0\ 0\ 0),$$

then the total number of viable networks for dynamics (69) is

$$72,219^{10} \approx 3.8594 \times 10^{48}.$$

There are many choices of practically relevant networks.

Similarly, the dynamics with threshold parameters (48) is also modified as

$$S_i(t + \tau) = \sigma \left(\sum_{j=1}^{n} w_{ij} S_j(t) \right)$$
$$= \frac{2}{1 + \exp \left[-\beta (\sum_{j=1}^{n} w_{ij} S_j(t) - \theta_i) \right]} - 1. \quad (76)$$

The necessary and sufficient condition to have $\mathbf{S}$ as a saturated equilibrium state for dynamics (76) becomes

$$\sum_{j \in J^+(\mathbf{S})} w_{ij} - \sum_{j \in J^-(\mathbf{S})} w_{ij} - \theta_i \geq 1, \text{ if } i \in J^+(\mathbf{S}), \quad (77)$$

$$\sum_{j \in J^+(\mathbf{S})} w_{ij} - \sum_{j \in J^-(\mathbf{S})} w_{ij} - \theta_i \leq -1, \text{ if } i \in J^-(\mathbf{S}). \quad (78)$$

and for $\mathbf{S}_1$ (77,78) become

$$\sum_{j=1,j\neq 5,9}^{11} w_{ij} + \theta_i \leq -1 + w_{i5} + w_{i9}, \quad \text{if } i = 5,9, \quad (79)$$

$$\sum_{j=1,j\neq 5,9}^{11} w_{ij} + \theta_i \geq \quad 1 + w_{i5} + w_{i9}, \quad \text{if } i \neq 5,9. \quad (80)$$

Condition (79,80) can be used to construct all viable networks W for dynamics (76) with a given set of θ_is sharing the saturated equilibrium state $\mathbf{S}_1$. Since there is no unambiguous biological interpretation for the values of θ_i, as $[-1, 0, 1]$, to represent activation, repression, absence for w_{ij}, we will not construct all such viable networks here.

6.2   Construction of yeast cell-cycle networks
According to the definition for the green and red arrows along with the yellow loop in [24], the network directly constructed from the connectivities of Figure 7b is

$$W_0 = \begin{bmatrix} -1 & 0 & 0 & 0 & 0 & 0 & 0 & 0 & 0 & 0 & 0 \\ 1 & 0 & 0 & 0 & 0 & 0 & 0 & 0 & 0 & -1 & 0 \\ 1 & 0 & 0 & 0 & 0 & 0 & 0 & 0 & 0 & -1 & 0 \\ 0 & 0 & 1 & -1 & 0 & 0 & 0 & 0 & 0 & 0 & 0 \\ 0 & 0 & 0 & -1 & 0 & 0 & 1 & -1 & 0 & -1 & 0 \\ 0 & 0 & 0 & 0 & 0 & -1 & 1 & 0 & 0 & -1 & 1 \\ 0 & 0 & 0 & 0 & 0 & 0 & -1 & 0 & 0 & 1 & 1 \\ 0 & 1 & 0 & 0 & 0 & 0 & -1 & 0 & -1 & 0 & 0 \\ 0 & 0 & 0 & -1 & 0 & 1 & 1 & -1 & 0 & -1 & 0 \\ 0 & 0 & 0 & 0 & -1 & 0 & -1 & 1 & -1 & 0 & 1 \\ 0 & 0 & 0 & 0 & 0 & 0 & 0 & 1 & 0 & 1 & -1 \end{bmatrix}.$$
$$(81)$$

W_0 does not satisfy condition (70,71) for any saturated state and does not have a saturated equilibrium state for dynamics (69). However, W_0 will be used as the basis for the connectivities of the network to construct networks for dynamics (69) with the saturated equilibrium expression state $\mathbf{S}_1$. *The construction of networks reduces to satisfying condition (74, 75) or (79, 80) as much as possible consistent with experimental observation.*
Two yeast cell-cycle networks for dynamics (69)

$$W_1 = \begin{bmatrix} 1 & 0 & 0 & 0 & 0 & 0 & 0 & 0 & 0 & 0 & 0 \\ 1 & 1 & 0 & 0 & 0 & 0 & 0 & 0 & 0 & -1 & 0 \\ 1 & 0 & 1 & 0 & 0 & 0 & 0 & 0 & 0 & -1 & 0 \\ 0 & 0 & 1 & 0 & 0 & 0 & 0 & 0 & 0 & 0 & 0 \\ 0 & 0 & 0 & -1 & 0 & 0 & 1 & -1 & 0 & -1 & 0 \\ 0 & 0 & 0 & 0 & 0 & 0 & 1 & 0 & 0 & -1 & 1 \\ 0 & 0 & 0 & 0 & 0 & -1 & 0 & 0 & 1 & 1 & \\ 0 & 1 & 0 & 0 & 0 & 0 & -1 & 1 & -1 & 0 & 0 \\ 0 & 0 & 0 & -1 & 0 & 1 & 1 & -1 & 0 & -1 & 0 \\ 0 & 0 & 0 & 0 & -1 & 0 & -1 & 1 & -1 & 0 & 1 \\ 0 & 0 & 0 & 0 & 0 & 0 & 0 & 1 & 0 & 1 & -1 \end{bmatrix}, \quad (82)$$

and

$$W_2 = \begin{bmatrix} 1 & 0 & 0 & 0 & 0 & 0 & 0 & 0 & 0 & 0 & 0 \\ 1 & 1 & 0 & 0 & 0 & 0 & 0 & 0 & 0 & -1 & 0 \\ 1 & 0 & 1 & 0 & 0 & 0 & 0 & 0 & 0 & -1 & 0 \\ 0 & 0 & 1 & 0 & 0 & 0 & 0 & 0 & 0 & 0 & 0 \\ 0 & 0 & 0 & -1 & 0 & 0 & 1 & -1 & 0 & -1 & 0 \\ 0 & 0 & 0 & 0 & 0 & 0 & 1 & 0 & 0 & -1 & 1 \\ 0 & 0 & 0 & 0 & 0 & 0 & -1 & 0 & 0 & 1 & 1 \\ 0 & 1 & 0 & 0 & 0 & 0 & -1 & 1 & -1 & 1 & 0 \\ 0 & 0 & 0 & -1 & 0 & 1 & 1 & -1 & 0 & -1 & 0 \\ 0 & 0 & 0 & 0 & -1 & 0 & -1 & 1 & -1 & 0 & 1 \\ 0 & 0 & 0 & 0 & 0 & 0 & 0 & 1 & 0 & 1 & -1 \end{bmatrix} \quad (83)$$

have been obtained (the detailed procedure for their construction can be found in the Additional file 1: Supplementary information). W_1 and W_2 differ only for $w_{8,10}$.
We can also use W_0 without any change, but introduce the threshold parameters

$$\Theta^T = (\,\theta_1\ \theta_2\ \theta_3\ \theta_4\ \theta_5\ \theta_6\ \theta_7\ \theta_8\ \theta_9\ \theta_{10}\ \theta_{11}\,) \quad (84)$$

for dynamics (76) satisfying condition (79, 80). One choice with the smallest magnitudes of θ_is

$$\Theta^T = (\,2\ 1\ 1\ 1\ 0\ 1\ 0\ 0\ 0\ 0\ 0\,) \quad (85)$$

is obtained by using

$$\sum_{j=1,j\neq 5,9}^{11} w_{ij} + \theta_i = -1 + w_{i5} + w_{i9}, \quad \text{if } i = 5,9, \quad (86)$$

$$\sum_{j=1,j\neq 5,9}^{11} w_{ij} + \theta_i = \quad 1 + w_{i5} + w_{i9}, \quad \text{if } i \neq 5,9. \quad (87)$$

6.3   Saturated equilibrium expression states for constructed networks
The saturated equilibrium expression states for a given network W in dynamics (69) can be determined by using the modified condition of (15) in Theorem 1

$$S_i \left(\sum_{j=1}^{n} w_{ij}S_j \right) \geq 1, \qquad (i = 1,2,\ldots,11). \quad (88)$$

For $n = 11$, there are $2^{11} = 2,048$ saturated states. All of the 2,048 states were tested by condition (88) for W_1 and W_2, respectively, to determine which of them are saturated equilibrium states for W_1 and W_2. The test for 2,048 states took only **0.01** s by Matlab on a Dell Precision Workstation T3400. The saturated equilibrium expression states for a given network W with threshold vector Θ in dynamics (76) can be determined by using the condition

$$S_i \left(\sum_{j=1}^{n} w_{ij}S_j - \theta_i \right) \geq 1, \qquad (i = 1,2,\ldots,11). \quad (89)$$

The saturated equilibrium expression states for W_1, W_2, and W_0 with Θ are shown below.

1. W_1
   W_1 has two saturated equilibrium expression states for dynamics (69)

   $$S_1 = (-1 \ -1 \ -1 \ -1 \ \ 1 \ -1 \ -1 \ -1 \ \ 1 \ -1 \ -1),$$
   $$S_2 = (1 \ \ \ 1 \ \ \ 1 \ \ \ 1 \ -1 \ \ \ 1 \ \ \ 1 \ \ \ 1 \ -1 \ \ \ 1 \ \ \ 1)$$

   with

   $$S_2 = -S_1.$$

2. W_2
   W_2 has four saturated equilibrium expression states for dynamics (69)

   $$S_1 = (-1 \ -1 \ -1 \ -1 \ \ 1 \ -1 \ -1 \ -1 \ \ 1 \ -1 \ -1),$$
   $$S_2 = (1 \ \ \ 1 \ \ \ 1 \ \ \ 1 \ -1 \ \ \ 1 \ \ \ 1 \ \ \ 1 \ -1 \ \ \ 1 \ \ \ 1),$$
   $$S_3 = (-1 \ \ \ 1 \ -1 \ -1 \ \ \ 1 \ -1 \ -1 \ -1 \ \ \ 1 \ -1 \ -1),$$
   $$S_4 = (1 \ -1 \ \ \ 1 \ \ \ 1 \ -1 \ \ \ 1 \ \ \ 1 \ \ \ 1 \ -1 \ \ \ 1 \ \ \ 1).$$

   with

   $$S_2 = -S_1, \qquad S_4 = -S_3.$$

   The S_1 and S_3 are just the 1st and 3rd fixed point attractors in Table 5.

3. W_0 with Θ given in (85)
   There is only a single saturated equilibrium state for dynamics (76)

   $$S_1 = (-1 \ -1 \ -1 \ -1 \ \ 1 \ -1 \ -1 \ -1 \ \ 1 \ -1 \ -1).$$

6.4 Robustness to noise

First, the number of saturated initial expression states converging to each equilibrium expression state for W_1, W_2 is determined by either directly solving the dynamics (69) or using modified condition of Theorem 5

$$\beta \left(\sum_{j=1}^{n} w_{ij}S_j(t \geq k) \right) > -\ln\left[(\alpha_i - 1) - \sqrt{(\alpha_i - 1)^2 - 1} \right],$$

$$i \in J^+(\mathbf{S}), \qquad (90)$$

$$\beta \left(\sum_{j=1}^{n} w_{ij}S_j(t \geq k) \right) < \ln\left[(\alpha_i - 1) - \sqrt{(\alpha_i - 1)^2 - 1} \right],$$

$$i \in J^-(\mathbf{S}). \qquad (91)$$

For W_1, the CPU times are **0.8** and **0.3** s, respectively to check all 2,048 saturated states, i.e., using Theorem 5 the CPU time is approximately 41% of that for the direct solving of the sigmoidal function. The results are given in Table 6. Note that for W_1, W_2, no saturated initial state converges to the unstable fixed point **0**. Therefore, in the calculation of R_{n_t}, we ignore **0** and only consider

Table 6 The number of saturated initial states converging to different equilibrium states for different gene networks

Final state	Number of saturated initial states		
	W_0 with Θ	W_1	W_2
S_1	2,048	1,024	979
S_2		1,024	979
S_3			45
S_4			45

the saturated equilibrium states. The resultant robustness to noise measures R_{n_t} and R_{n_i} are given in Table 7. There are significant differences between $R_{n_i}(i = 1, 2, 3, 4)$ for W_2. Obviously, the saturated equilibrium states S_1, S_2 are much more stable than S_3, S_4.

The robustness to noise $R_{n_{ij}}$ for each pair of saturated equilibrium and initial expression states was calculated. The distribution of $R_{n_{ij}}$, i.e., how many pairs with the same value of $R_{n_{ij}}$, is given in Tables 8 and 9.

The results show that W_0 with Θ is completely stable for any viable pair; for W_1, there is one neighbour of $S_j(0)$ differing at the first element, which causes changes in the saturated equilibrium state S_i; for W_2, the distribution of $R_{n_{ij}}$ is divergent, and S_1 and S_2 are much more stable than S_3 and S_4.

6.5 Robustness to mutation

The R_{m_i} values have been calculated for W_1, W_2, and W_0 with the Θ given in (85) as shown in Table 10. Note that for S_1, R_{m_i} is almost the same for W_1, W_2, and W_0 with Θ.

Robustness to mutation $R_{m_{ij}}$ for a viable pair of specified saturated equilibrium and initial states S_i and $S_j(0)$ has also been calculated for W_1, W_2, and W_0 with Θ. The resultant distribution, i.e., how many pairs having the same $R_{m_{ij}}$ for W_1, W_2, and W_0 with the Θ given above is shown in Figure 8 and Table S12 in Additional file 1: Supplementary information.

7 Conclusion

Based on the determination of saturated fixed point attractors for the sigmoidal function model in (3) with a given gene network, W, one can analytically determine

Table 7 The Robustness to noise R_{n_t} and R_{n_i} for different gene networks

Network	R_{n_t}	R_{n_i}			
		S_1	S_2	S_3	S_4
W_0 with Θ	1	1			
W_1	1/2	1/2	1/2		
W_2	1/4	0.478	0.478	0.022	0.022

Table 8 The distribution of $R_{n_{ij}}$ for the networks W_0 with Θ and W_1

Final state	$R_{n_{ij}}$ (for W_0 with Θ)	$R_{n_{ij}}$ (for W_1)
	11/11	10/11
S_1	2,048	1,024
S_2		1,024

Table 10 The robustness to mutation R_{m_i} of W_0 with Θ, W_1, and W_2

Final state	W_0 with Θ		W_1		W_2	
	N_W^v	R_{m_i}	N_W^v	R_{m_i}	N_W^v	$R_{m_{si}}$
S_1	137	0.57	140	0.58	143	0.59
S_2			140	0.58	143	0.59
S_3					131	0.54
S_4					131	0.54

which and how many saturated equilibrium expression states exist. Furthermore, for each saturated equilibrium expression state of a W, which and how many saturated initial expression states converging to it can also be determined. These results make it possible to establish the robustness of a given gene network to noise without performing a large number of simulations. Based on the necessary and sufficient condition for gene networks to share the same saturated equilibrium expression state, one can determine all the viable gene networks for a specified saturated equilibrium state. This result also makes it possible to establish the robustness to mutation for a network with a specified saturated equilibrium expression state or a specified pair of saturated equilibrium and initial expression states.

The analytical treatment presented here proved that for a given saturated state, all viable gene networks having it as an equilibrium state must follow certain patterns, i.e., the rows of the corresponding W must be chosen from a finite number of permitted rows. The permitted rows for a given saturated equilibrium state have specific biological meaning and reflect the required connectivity patterns of each gene to other genes. This restriction distinguishes the viable networks for a given saturated equilibrium state from other viable networks with distinct saturated equilibrium states as well as inviable networks. The analysis also proved, without performing a very large numbers of simulations, that all viable networks can be organized as a large graph which can be easily traversed by a sequence of single w_{ij} changes of network topology. Thus, robustness is an evolvable property. Highly robust topologies can evolve from topologies with low robustness through gradual Darwinian topological changes or natural selection. The analytical treatment presented in this paper may be employed not only for robustness analysis but also for the

model construction and analysis of other properties for gene networks.

Appendix

The appendix proves several theorems in the main text.

Lemma 1 (Banach Fixed Point Theorem [25]). Let (X, d) be a non-empty complete metric space with a contraction mapping $\mathbf{g} : X \rightarrow X$. Then $\mathbf{g}$ admits a unique fixed point $\mathbf{x}^*$ in X (i.e. $\mathbf{g}(\mathbf{x}^*) = \mathbf{x}^*$). Furthermore, $\mathbf{x}^*$ can be found as follows: start with an arbitrary element $\mathbf{x}_0 \in X$ and define a sequence $\{\mathbf{x}_n\}$ by $\mathbf{x}_n = \mathbf{g}(\mathbf{x}_{n-1})$, then $\mathbf{x}_n \rightarrow \mathbf{x}^*$.

A map $\mathbf{g} : X \rightarrow X$ is called a contraction mapping on X if there exists $q \in [0, 1)$ such that

$$d(\mathbf{g}(\mathbf{x}), \mathbf{g}(\mathbf{y})) \le q\, d(\mathbf{x}, \mathbf{y}) \tag{92}$$

where d denotes the distance, for all $\mathbf{x}, \mathbf{y} \in X$.

A continuous function $\mathbf{g}$ satisfies the Lipschitz condition

$$\|\mathbf{g}(\mathbf{x}) - \mathbf{g}(\mathbf{y})\|_p \le \sup_{\mathbf{t} \in X} \|J(\mathbf{t})\|_p \|\mathbf{x} - \mathbf{y}\|_p \tag{93}$$

where $J(\mathbf{x})$ is the Jacobian of $\mathbf{g}(\mathbf{x})$. Its (i, j)th entry is

$$J_{ij}(\mathbf{x}) = \left[\frac{\partial g_i(\mathbf{x})}{\partial x_j} \right] \tag{94}$$

and $\|J(\mathbf{t})\|_p$ is the L_p-norm:

$$\|J\|_1 = \max_{\substack{j \\ \mathbf{t} \in X}} \left(\sum_{i=1}^n |J_{ij}(\mathbf{t})| \right), \qquad (j = 1, 2, \cdots, n), \tag{95}$$

$$\|J\|_\infty = \max_{\substack{i \\ \mathbf{t} \in X}} \left(\sum_{j=1}^n |J_{ij}(\mathbf{t})| \right), \qquad (i = 1, 2, \cdots, n), \tag{96}$$

$$\|J\|_2 = \max_{\mathbf{t} \in X} \sqrt{\max \lambda_{J^T(\mathbf{t})J(\mathbf{t})}}. \tag{97}$$

From (95 to 97) we see that $\|J\|_1$ is the largest sum of the absolute values of the elements in each column; $\|J\|_\infty$ is the largest sum of the absolute values of elements in each row; and $\|J\|_2$ is the square root of the largest eigenvalue for matrix $J^T(\mathbf{t})J(\mathbf{t})$. Now define d of $\mathbf{g}(\mathbf{x})$ and $\mathbf{g}(\mathbf{y})$ as the L_p-norm of their difference. If $\mathbf{g}$ is a contraction

Table 9 The distribution of $R_{n_{ij}}$ for the network W_2

Final state	$R_{n_{ij}}$							
	2/11	3/11	4/11	5/11	6/11	7/11	8/11	9/11	10/11
S_1					1	12	29	146	791
S_2					1	12	29	146	791
S_3	1	6	21	7	3	7			
S_4	1	6	21	7	3	7			

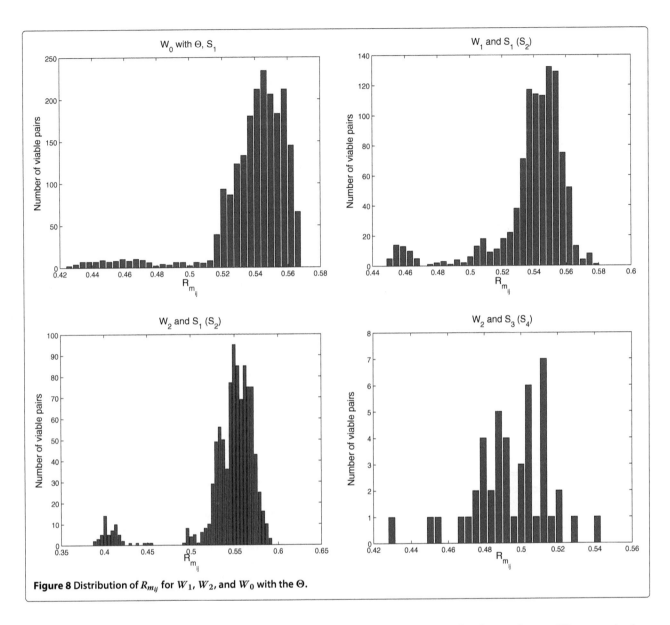

Figure 8 Distribution of $R_{m_{ij}}$ for W_1, W_2, and W_0 with the Θ.

mapping, (92) requires that at least one of the L_p-norms of its Jacobian satisfies

$$\|J\|_p \leq q < 1. \tag{98}$$

This condition is sufficient, but not necessary. It is possible that one of (95 to 97) is satisfied, but the other two may not. Such examples can be constructed.

Theorem A1. The sufficient condition for the sigmoidal function in (3) to have a unique fixed point attractor $\mathbf{0}$ is

$$\sum_{j=1}^{n} |w_{ij}| \leq 2, \quad (i = 1, 2, \ldots, n). \tag{99}$$

Proof. Since $\mathbf{0}$ is a fixed point for any W, to see whether it is a unique fixed point attractor, we need to determine under what condition (3) is a contraction mapping.

The (i, j)th entry of the Jacobian $J^{(k+\tau)}(\mathbf{S}(k))$ for (3) with $\tau = 1$ is

$$J_{ij}^{(k+1)}(\mathbf{S}(k)) = \frac{\partial S_i(k+1)}{\partial S_j(k)} = \frac{2e^{-u_i(k)}}{\left(1 + e^{-u_i(k)}\right)^2} w_{ij}$$

$$= \frac{2e^{-u_i(k)}}{1 + 2e^{-u_i(k)} + e^{-2u_i(k)}} w_{ij} \tag{100}$$

$$= \frac{2}{e^{u_i(k)} + 2 + e^{-u_i(k)}} w_{ij}$$

where

$$u_i(k) = \sum_{j=1}^{n} w_{ij} S_j(k). \tag{101}$$

The matrix form of the Jacobian $J^{(k+1)}(\mathbf{S}(k))$ is

$$J^{(k+1)}(\mathbf{S}(k)) = V(k)W \tag{102}$$

where $V(k)$ is a diagonal matrix with

$$V_{ii}(k) = \frac{2}{e^{u_i(k)} + 2 + e^{-u_i(k)}}. \tag{103}$$

The ∞-norm is

$$\|J^{(k+1)}(\mathbf{S}(k))\|_\infty = \max_{\substack{i \\ \mathbf{s}\in[-1,1]^n}} \frac{2}{e^{u_i(k)} + 2 + e^{-u_i(k)}} \sum_{j=1}^n | w_{ij} |,$$
$$(i = 1, 2, \cdots, n). \tag{104}$$

Because $e^{u_i(k)}, e^{-u_i(k)} > 0$, the maximum of $2/(e^{u_i(k)} + 2 + e^{-u_i(k)})$ is given by the minimum of $e^{u_i(k)} + e^{-u_i(k)}$ which can be obtained from

$$\frac{d\left(e^{u_i(k)} + e^{-u_i(k)}\right)}{du_i(k)} = e^{u_i(k)} - e^{-u_i(k)} = 0. \tag{105}$$

This is true if and only if

$$e^{u_i(k)} = e^{-u_i(k)} \tag{106}$$

which yields $u_i(k) = 0$, $e^{u_i(k)} = e^{-u_i(k)} = 1$. The minimum for $e^{u_i(k)} + e^{-u_i(k)}$ is 2, and then

$$\max_{\substack{i \\ \mathbf{s}\in[-1,1]^n}} \frac{2}{e^{u_i(k)} + 2 + e^{-u_i(k)}} = \frac{1}{2}. \tag{107}$$

Figure 9 gives the comparison of $e^x + e^{-x}$ and $2/(e^x + 2 + e^{-x})$.

Therefore, we have

$$\|J^{(k+1)}(\mathbf{S}(k))\|_\infty = \max_i \frac{1}{2} \sum_{j=1}^n | w_{ij} |, \qquad (i = 1, 2, \cdots, n). \tag{108}$$

To be a contraction mapping requires

$$\|J^{(k+1)}(\mathbf{S}(k))\|_\infty < 1 \tag{109}$$

i.e.,

$$\sum_{j=1}^n | w_{ij} | < 2, \qquad (i = 1, 2, \cdots, n). \tag{110}$$

Notice that $1/2$ is the superior value in (107). In many cases, not all $S_i = 0$ (i.e., $u_i(k)$'s are not zero), then the factor in (107) has values smaller than $1/2$, which implies that the condition for a contraction mapping given in (110) may be softened as

$$\sum_{j=1}^n | w_{ij} | \le 2, \qquad (i = 1, 2, \cdots, n). \tag{111}$$

The condition in (111) is sufficient, but not necessary. $\square$

Theorem A2. A saturated state $\mathbf{S}$ satisfying (13) and (14) is a fixed point attractor.

Proof. Suppose $\mathbf{S}$ is a fixed point of (3). Let $B_\epsilon = \{\hat{\mathbf{S}} \in \Re^n \mid \|\mathbf{X} = \hat{\mathbf{S}} - \mathbf{S}\| < \epsilon\}$, where ϵ is chosen sufficiently small such that there is only a single fixed point $\mathbf{S}$ within B_ϵ. $\mathbf{X} = \mathbf{0}$ is a fixed point in B_ϵ with representation $\mathbf{X}$ because $\mathbf{S}$ is a fixed point for $\hat{\mathbf{S}}$ in B_ϵ. If we can prove that $\mathbf{X} = \mathbf{0}$ is a fixed point attractor in B_ϵ, then so is $\mathbf{S}$.

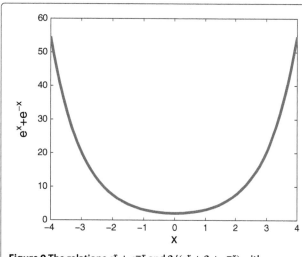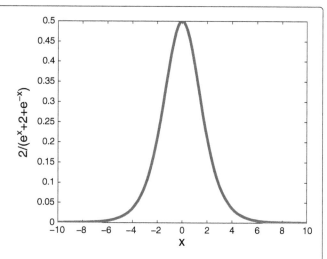

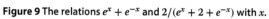
Figure 9 The relations $e^x + e^{-x}$ and $2/(e^x + 2 + e^{-x})$ with x.

Subtracting S_i on the both sides of (3) yields

$$
\begin{aligned}
X_i(t+\tau) = S_i(t+\tau) - 1 &= \frac{2}{1 + \exp\left[-\sum\limits_{j=1}^{n} w_{ij} S_j(t)\right]} - 1 - 1 \\
&= \frac{2}{1 + \exp\left[-\sum\limits_{j=1}^{n} w_{ij}\left(S_j(t) - 1 + 1\right)\right]} - 2 \\
&= \frac{2}{1 + \exp\left[-\sum\limits_{j=1}^{n}\left(w_{ij} X_j(t) + w_{ij} S_j\right)\right]} - 2 \\
&= \frac{2}{1 + e^{-\beta'} \exp\left[-\sum\limits_{j=1}^{n} w_{ij} X_j(t)\right]} - 2, \quad i \in J^+(\mathbf{S})
\end{aligned}
\tag{112}
$$

where $\beta' \geq \beta$.

The (i,j)th entry of the Jacobian is

$$
\begin{aligned}
J_{ij}^{(t+\tau)}(\mathbf{X}(t)) &= \frac{2e^{-\beta'} \exp\left[-\sum\limits_{j=1}^{n} w_{ij} X_j(t)\right]}{\left(1 + e^{-\beta'} \exp\left[-\sum\limits_{j=1}^{n} w_{ij} X_j(t)\right]\right)^2} w_{ij} \\
&= \frac{2e^{-\beta'} \exp\left[-\sum\limits_{j=1}^{n} w_{ij} X_j(t)\right]}{1 + 2e^{-\beta'} \exp\left[-\sum\limits_{j=1}^{n} w_{ij} X_j(t)\right] + e^{-2\beta'} \exp\left[-2\sum\limits_{j=1}^{n} w_{ij} X_j(t)\right]} w_{ij} \\
&= \frac{2}{e^{\beta'} \exp\left[\sum\limits_{j=1}^{n} w_{ij} X_j(t)\right] + 2 + e^{-\beta'} \exp\left[-\sum\limits_{j=1}^{n} w_{ij} X_j(t)\right]} w_{ij} \\
&\approx \frac{2}{e^{\beta'} + 2 + e^{-\beta'}} w_{ij}, \quad i \in J^+(\mathbf{S}).
\end{aligned}
\tag{113}
$$

Here, the condition $\mathbf{X}(t) < \epsilon \approx 0$ and $\exp\left[\sum_{j=1}^{n} w_{ij} X_j(t)\right] \approx \exp\left[-\sum_{j=1}^{n} w_{ij} X_j(t)\right] \approx 1$ were used. The L_1-norm of row vector $J_i^{(t+\tau)}$ is

$$
\|J_i^{(t+\tau)}(\mathbf{X}(t))\|_1 \approx \frac{2}{e^{\beta'} + 2 + e^{-\beta'}} \sum_{j=1}^{n} |w_{ij}|.
\tag{114}
$$

When

$$
\begin{aligned}
\sum_{j=1}^{n} |w_{ij}| &< \frac{e^{\beta'} + 2 + e^{-\beta'}}{2} \\
&\geq \frac{e^{\beta} + 2 + e^{-\beta}}{2} > \begin{cases} 75, & \text{if } \beta = 5, \\ 11{,}014, & \text{if } \beta = 10, \end{cases}
\end{aligned}
\tag{115}
$$

which is often the case in practice for W satisfying (13) and (14), we have

$$
\|J_i^{(t+\tau)}(\mathbf{X}(t))\|_1 < 1, \quad i \in J^+(\mathbf{S}).
\tag{116}
$$

The same result can be obtained for $i \in J^-(\mathbf{S})$. Therefore, we have

$$\|J^{(t+\tau)}(\mathbf{X}(t))\|_\infty = \max_i \|J_i^{(t+\tau)}(\mathbf{X}(t))\|_1 < 1, \tag{117}$$

i.e., $\mathbf{X} = \mathbf{0}$ is a fixed point attractor, and thus so is $\mathbf{S}$. $\square$

Theorem A3. If an $\mathbf{S}(t)$ converges to a saturated equilibrium expression state $\mathbf{S}$, then $-\mathbf{S}(t)$ converges to the saturated equilibrium expression state $-\mathbf{S}$.

Proof. For $\mathbf{S}(t)$ and $-\mathbf{S}(t)$, the corresponding equations are

$$S_i(t+\tau) = \frac{2}{1 + \exp\left[-\sum_{j=1}^n w_{ij} S_j(t)\right]} - 1, \quad (i = 1, 2, \ldots, n), \tag{118}$$

and

$$\tilde{S}_i(t+\tau) = \frac{2}{1 + \exp\left[-\sum_{j=1}^n w_{ij}(-S_j(t))\right]} - 1, \quad (i = 1, 2, \ldots, n), \tag{119}$$

respectively. It can be proved that

$$\tilde{S}_i(t+\tau) = -S_i(t+\tau). \tag{120}$$

The proof is given below.

$$
\begin{aligned}
\tilde{S}_i(t+\tau) &= \frac{2}{1 + \exp\left[-\sum_{j=1}^n w_{ij}(-S_j(t))\right]} - 1 = \frac{2}{1 + \exp\left[\sum_{j=1}^n w_{ij} S_j(t)\right]} - 1 \\[2ex]
&= \frac{1 - \exp\left[\sum_{j=1}^n w_{ij} S_j(t)\right]}{1 + \exp\left[\sum_{j=1}^n w_{ij} S_j(t)\right]} = \frac{1 + \exp\left[\sum_{j=1}^n w_{ij} S_j(t)\right] - 2\exp\left[\sum_{j=1}^n w_{ij} S_j(t)\right]}{1 + \exp\left[\sum_{j=1}^n w_{ij} S_j(t)\right]} \\[2ex]
&= \frac{\left(1 + \exp\left[\sum_{j=1}^n w_{ij} S_j(t)\right] - 2\exp\left[\sum_{j=1}^n w_{ij} S_j(t)\right]\right)\left(1 + \exp\left[-\sum_{j=1}^n w_{ij} S_j(t)\right]\right)}{\left(1 + \exp\left[\sum_{j=1}^n w_{ij} S_j(t)\right]\right)\left(1 + \exp\left[-\sum_{j=1}^n w_{ij} S_j(t)\right]\right)} \\[2ex]
&= 1 - \frac{2\left(\exp\left[\sum_{j=1}^n w_{ij} S_j(t)\right] + 1\right)}{\left(1 + \exp\left[\sum_{j=1}^n w_{ij} S_j(t)\right]\right)\left(1 + \exp\left[-\sum_{j=1}^n w_{ij} S_j(t)\right]\right)} \\[2ex]
&= 1 - \frac{2}{1 + \exp\left[-\sum_{j=1}^n w_{ij} S_j(t)\right]} = -S_i(t+\tau).
\end{aligned}
\tag{121}
$$

Equation (121) implies that there is an one-to-one relation between $\tilde{S}_i(t)$ and $-S_i(t)$. Since $\mathbf{S}(\infty) = \mathbf{S}$, we have

$$\tilde{\mathbf{S}}(\infty) = -\mathbf{S}. \tag{122}$$

Therefore, starting from $-\mathbf{S}(t)$ will converge to $-\mathbf{S}$. $\quad\square$

Theorem A4. A saturated initial expression state $\mathbf{S}(0)$ converges to a saturated equilibrium expression state $\mathbf{S}$ if the following condition is satisfied after a finite number k of iteration steps of (3) starting from $\mathbf{S}(0)$

$$\sum_{j=1}^{n} w_{ij}S_j(t \geq k) > -\ln[(\alpha_i - 1) - \sqrt{(\alpha_i - 1)^2 - 1}],$$

$$i \in J^+(\mathbf{S}), \tag{123}$$

$$\sum_{j=1}^{n} w_{ij}S_j(t \geq k) < \ln[(\alpha_i - 1) - \sqrt{(\alpha_i - 1)^2 - 1}],$$

$$i \in J^-(\mathbf{S}), \tag{124}$$

where

$$\alpha_i = \sum_{j=1}^{n} |w_{ij}| \tag{125}$$

under the constraint that $\alpha_i \geq 2$.

Proof. First, consider $i \in J^+(\mathbf{S})$. If $\mathbf{S}$ is the fixed point attractor for the initial state $\mathbf{S}(0)$, then $\mathbf{X} = \mathbf{0}$ is the fixed point attractor for the initial expression state $\mathbf{X}(0) = \mathbf{S}(0) - \mathbf{S}$ of (112). This is equivalent to finding the condition under which (112) is a contraction mapping. According to the Banach fixed point theorem, the sufficient condition is that the norm of the Jacobian matrix satisfies $\|J\|_\infty < 1$. To prove Theorem A4, we try to seek the largest $B_a = \{\mathbf{X} \in \Re^n \mid \|\mathbf{X}\| < a\}$ where a is the upper bound to have $\|J\|_\infty < 1$, i.e., $\|J_i^{(t+\tau)}(\mathbf{X}(t))\|_1 < 1$, for all $i \in J^+(\mathbf{S})$.

Set

$$y = e^{-\beta'} \exp\left[-\sum_{j=1}^{n} w_{ij}X_j(t)\right]. \tag{126}$$

From (113) the L_1-norm of row vector $J_i^{(t+\tau)}$ can be represented as

$$\|J_i^{(t+\tau)}(\mathbf{X}(t))\|_1 = \frac{2y}{(1+y)^2} \sum_{j=1}^{n} |w_{ij}|$$

$$= \frac{2\alpha_i y}{(1+y)^2} < 1, \quad i \in J^+(\mathbf{S}), \tag{127}$$

which gives the quadratic equation

$$y^2 + 2(1 - \alpha_i)y + 1 = (y - y_1)(y - y_2) > 0, \tag{128}$$

where

$$y_1 = (\alpha_i - 1) + \sqrt{(\alpha_i - 1)^2 - 1}, \tag{129}$$

$$y_2 = (\alpha_i - 1) - \sqrt{(\alpha_i - 1)^2 - 1}. \tag{130}$$

It is easy to check that y_1, y_2 are all nonnegative when $\alpha_i \geq 2$, and $y_2 < 1$.

Equation (128) is valid if and only if y is chosen within the two disjoint ranges

$$(-\infty, y_2) \ (y_1, \infty) \ \text{if } \alpha_i > 2,$$
$$(-\infty, \ 1) \ (1, \ \infty) \ \text{if } \alpha_i = 2,$$

i.e., either smaller than y_2 or larger than y_1. This implies that

$$e^{-\beta'} \exp\left[-\sum_{j=1}^{n} w_{ij}X_j(t)\right] = \exp\left[-\sum_{j=1}^{n} w_{ij}S_j(t)\right] \begin{cases} > y_1 \\ < y_2 \end{cases}$$
$$\tag{131}$$

or

$$\sum_{j=1}^{n} w_{ij}S_j(t) \begin{cases} < -\ln[(\alpha_i - 1) + \sqrt{(\alpha_i - 1)^2 - 1}] < 0, \\ > -\ln[(\alpha_i - 1) - \sqrt{(\alpha_i - 1)^2 - 1}] > 0. \end{cases}$$
$$\tag{132}$$

Using (15), we know that when $\mathbf{S}(t)$ is close to the fixed point attractor $\mathbf{S}$,

$$\sum_{j=1}^{n} w_{ij}S_j > 0, \quad i \in J^+(\mathbf{S}). \tag{133}$$

Therefore, we obtain

$$\sum_{j=1}^{n} w_{ij}S_j(t) > -\ln[(\alpha_i - 1) - \sqrt{(\alpha_i - 1)^2 - 1}]. \tag{134}$$

If $\mathbf{S}(t = k)$ satisfies (134), then the trajectory starting from $\mathbf{S}(t = k)$ will converge to $\mathbf{S}$. Therefore, $\mathbf{S}(t \geq k)$ will also satisfy (134). Thus,

$$\sum_{j=1}^{n} w_{ij}S_j(t \geq k) > -\ln[(\alpha_i - 1) - \sqrt{(\alpha_i - 1)^2 - 1}]. \tag{135}$$

Equation (135) proves the condition for $i \in J^+(\mathbf{S})$ given in Theorem A4.

For $i \in J^-(\mathbf{S})$, (112) becomes

$$X_i(t + \tau) = S_i(t + \tau) - (-1)$$

$$= \frac{2}{1 + e^{\beta'} \exp\left[-\sum_{j=1}^{n} w_{ij}X_j(t)\right]}, \quad i \in J^-(\mathbf{S}).$$
$$\tag{136}$$

Set

$$y = e^{\beta'} \exp\left[-\sum_{j=1}^{n} w_{ij} X_j(t)\right]. \tag{137}$$

Then the proof procedure is the same as above except that for $i \in J^-(S)$

$$\sum_{j=1}^{n} w_{ij} S_j < 0, \qquad i \in J^-(S) \tag{138}$$

when $S(t)$ is close to the fixed point attractor S. Thus, we obtain

$$\sum_{j=1}^{n} w_{ij} S_j(t) < -\ln[(\alpha_i - 1) + \sqrt{(\alpha_i - 1)^2 - 1}]. \tag{139}$$

Note that

$$-\ln[(\alpha_i - 1) + \sqrt{(\alpha_i - 1)^2 - 1}]$$
$$= \ln \frac{1}{(\alpha_i - 1) + \sqrt{(\alpha_i - 1)^2 - 1}}$$
$$= \ln \frac{(\alpha_i - 1) - \sqrt{(\alpha_i - 1)^2 - 1}}{[(\alpha_i - 1) + \sqrt{(\alpha_i - 1)^2 - 1}][(\alpha_i - 1) - \sqrt{(\alpha_i - 1)^2 - 1}]}$$
$$= \ln \frac{(\alpha_i - 1) - \sqrt{(\alpha_i - 1)^2 - 1}}{(\alpha_i - 1)^2 - (\alpha_i - 1)^2 + 1}$$
$$= \ln[(\alpha_i - 1) - \sqrt{(\alpha_i - 1)^2 - 1}]. \tag{140}$$

Then we have

$$\sum_{j=1}^{n} w_{ij} S_j(t) < \ln[(\alpha_i - 1) - \sqrt{(\alpha_i - 1)^2 - 1}], \tag{141}$$

and similarly we obtain

$$\sum_{j=1}^{n} w_{ij} S_j(t \geq k) < \ln[(\alpha_i - 1) - \sqrt{(\alpha_i - 1)^2 - 1}], \tag{142}$$

i.e., the condition for $i \in J^-(S)$ given in Theorem A4. $\square$

Theorem A5. A saturated state S satisfying (58) and (59) is a fixed point attractor.

Proof. Suppose S is a fixed point of (48). Let $B_\epsilon = \{\hat{S} \in \Re^n \mid \|X = \hat{S} - S\| < \epsilon\}$ where ϵ is chosen sufficiently small such that there is only a single fixed point S within B_ϵ. $X = 0$ is a fixed point in B_ϵ with representation X because S is a fixed point for $\hat{S}$ in B_ϵ. If we can prove that $X = 0$ is a fixed point attractor in B_ϵ, then so is S.

Subtracting S_i on the both sides of (48) yields

$$X_i(t + \tau) = S_i(t + \tau) - 1$$
$$= \frac{2}{1 + \exp\left[-\left(\sum_{j=1}^{n} w_{ij} S_j(t) - \theta_i\right)\right]} - 1 - 1$$
$$= \frac{2}{1 + \exp\left[-\left(\sum_{j=1}^{n} w_{ij}(S_j(t) - 1 + 1) - \theta_i\right)\right]} - 2$$
$$= \frac{2}{1 + \exp\left[-\left(\sum_{j=1}^{n} (w_{ij} X_j(t) + w_{ij} S_j) - \theta_i\right)\right]} - 2$$
$$= \frac{2}{1 + e^{-\beta'} \exp\left[-\sum_{j=1}^{n} w_{ij} X_j(t)\right]} - 2, \quad i \in J^+(S) \tag{143}$$

where

$$\beta' = \sum_{j=1}^{n} w_{ij} S_j - \theta_i \geq \beta. \tag{144}$$

The following step of proof is exactly the same as that in Theorem A2, and will not repeat here. $\square$

Additional file

Additional file 1: **Supplementary information.** Application to the yeast cell-cycle network.

Competing interests
The authors declare that they have no competing interests.

Acknowledgements
Support for this work was provided by DOE of USA.

References
1. R Thornhill, A Moller, Developmental stability, disease and medicine. Biol. Rev. Camb. Philos. Soc. **72**, 497–548 (1997)
2. H McAdams, A Arkin, It's a noisy business! Genetic regulation at the nanomolar scale. Trends. Genetics. **15**, 65–69 (1999)
3. G von Dassow, E Meir, E Munro, G Odell, The segment polarity network is a robust development module. Nature. **406**, 188–192 (2000)
4. M Morohashi, A Winn, M Borisuk, H Bolouri, J Doyle, H Kitano, Robustness as a measure of plausibility in models of biochemical networks. J. Theor. Biol. **216**, 19–30 (2002)
5. A Eldar, R Dorfman, D Weiss, H Ashe, B Shilo, N Barkai, Robustness sof the BMP morphogen gradient in Drosophila embryonic patterning. Nature. **419**, 304–308 (2002)
6. E Ozbudak, M Thattai, I Kurtser, A Grossman, A van Oudenaarden, Regulation of noise in the expression of a single gene. Nat. Genet. **31**, 69–73 (2002)
7. M Elowitz, A Levine, E Siggia, P Swain P, Stochastic gene expression in a single cell. Science. **297**, 1183–1186 (2002)
8. F Isaacs, J Hasty, C Cantor, J Collins, Prediction of measurement of an autoregulatory genetic module. Proc. Natl. Acad. Sci. USA. **100**, 7714–7719 (2003)

9. W Blake, M Kaern, C Cantor, J Collins, Noise in eukaryotic gene expression. Nature. **422**, 633–637 (2003)
10. N Ingolia, Topology and robustness in the Drosophila segment polarity network. PLoS Biol. **2**(6), 805–815 (2004)
11. A Wagner, Evolution of gene networks by gene duplications: a mathematical model and its implications on genome organization. Proc Nati. Acad. Sci. USA. **91**, 4387–4391 (1994)
12. A Wagner, Dose evolutionary plastcity evolve? Evolution. **50**(3), 1008–1023 (1996)
13. S Ciliberti, O Martin, A Wagner, Robustness can evolve gradually in complex regulatory gene networks with varying topology. PLoS Comput. Biol. **3**(2), 0164–0173 (2007)
14. C Espinosa-Soto, A Wagner, Specialization can drive the evolution of modularity. PLoS Comput. Biol. **6**(3), 1–10 (2010)
15. Y Kwon, K Cho, Quantitative analysis of robustness and fragility in biological networks based on feedback dynamics. Bioinformatics. **24**(7), 987–994 (2008)
16. M Siegal, A Bergman, Waddington's canalization revisited: developmental stability and evolution. Proc. Nati. Acad. Sci. USA. **99**, 8–10532 (2002)
17. O Matin, A Wagner, Multifunctionality and robustness trade-offs in model genetic circuits. Biophys. J. **94**, 2927–2937 (2008)
18. S Ciliberti, O Martin, A Wagner, Innovation and robustness in complex regulatory networks. Proc. Nati. Acad. Sci. USA. **104**, 13591–13596 (2007)
19. J Draghi, O Matin, A Wagner, The evolutionary dynamics of evolvability in a gene network model. J. Evov. Biol. **22**, 599–611 (2009)
20. R Azevedo, R Lohaus, S Srinivasan, K Dang, C Burch, Sexual reproduction selects for robustness and negative epistasis in artificial gene networks. Nature. **440**, 87–90 (2006)
21. E Mjoisness, D Sharp, J Reinitz, A connectionist model of development. J. Theor. Biol. **152**, 429–453 (1991)
22. I Mendoza, E Alvarez-Buylla, Dynamics of the genetic regulatory network of Arabidopsis thaliana flower morphogenesis. J. Theor. Biol. **193**, 307–319 (1998)
23. T Feng, B Tirozzi, An analysis on neural dynamics with saturated sigmoidal functions. Comput. Math. Appl. **34**, 71–99 (1997)
24. F Li, T Long, Y Lu, Q Quyang, C Tang, The yeast cell-cycle network is robustly designed. PNAS. **101**(14), 4781–4786 (2004). Copyright 2004 National Academy of Sciences, USA
25. A Granas, J Dugundji, *Fixed Point Theory*. (Springer-Verlag, New York, 2003)

Effective gene prediction by high resolution frequency estimator based on least-norm solution technique

Manidipa Roy[1] and Soma Barman[2*]

Abstract

Linear algebraic concept of subspace plays a significant role in the recent techniques of spectrum estimation. In this article, the authors have utilized the noise subspace concept for finding hidden periodicities in DNA sequence. With the vast growth of genomic sequences, the demand to identify accurately the protein-coding regions in DNA is increasingly rising. Several techniques of DNA feature extraction which involves various cross fields have come up in the recent past, among which application of digital signal processing tools is of prime importance. It is known that coding segments have a 3-base periodicity, while non-coding regions do not have this unique feature. One of the most important spectrum analysis techniques based on the concept of subspace is the least-norm method. The least-norm estimator developed in this paper shows sharp period-3 peaks in coding regions completely eliminating background noise. Comparison of proposed method with existing sliding discrete Fourier transform (SDFT) method popularly known as modified periodogram method has been drawn on several genes from various organisms and the results show that the proposed method has better as well as an effective approach towards gene prediction. Resolution, quality factor, sensitivity, specificity, miss rate, and wrong rate are used to establish superiority of least-norm gene prediction method over existing method.

Keywords: Periodogram; Deoxyribonucleic acid; Least-norm solution; Eigenvector; Eigenvalue

1 Introduction

It has been observed that the most significant scientific and technological endeavour of the 21st century is mostly related to genomics. Therefore, researchers from various cross fields have concentrated in the field of genomic analysis in order to extract the vast information content hidden in it. Deoxyribonucleic acid (DNA) is the hereditary material present in all living organisms. In eukaryotic organisms, genes (sequences of DNA) consist of exons (coding segments) and introns (non-coding segments). It has been established that genetic information is stored in the particular order of four kinds of nucleotide bases, Adenine (a), Thymine (t), Cytosine (c) and Guanine (g) which comprise the DNA biomolecule along with sugar-phosphate backbone. Exons of a DNA sequence are specified as the most information-bearing part because only the exons take part in protein coding while the

introns are spliced off during protein synthesis process. Gene prediction means detecting locations of the protein-coding regions of genes in a long DNA chain. Since DNA encodes information of proteins, various statistical and computational techniques have been studied and explored to extract the information content carried by DNA and distinguish exons from introns.

Genomic information is made up of a finite number of nucleotides in the form of alphabetical characters; hence, it is discrete in nature. As a result, digital signal processing (DSP) techniques can be used as effective tools to analyze DNA in order to capture its periodic characteristics. The main objective of spectrum estimation is determination of power spectrum density of a random process. Power spectral density (PSD) describes how the average power of a signal $x[n]$ is distributed with frequency, where $x[n]$ is a sequence of random variables defined for every integer n. The estimated PSD provides information about the structure of a random process which can be used for refined modeling, prediction, or filtering. Estimation of power spectrum of discretely sampled processes is generally

* Correspondence: barmanmandal@gmail.com
[2]Institute of Radio Physics & Electronics, University of Calcutta, 92, A.P.C. Road, Kolkata 700 009, India
Full list of author information is available at the end of the article

based on procedures employing the fast Fourier transform (FFT). This approach is computationally efficient and produces reasonable results, but in spite of the advantages, it has certain performance limitations. The most important limitation lies in its frequency resolution. Moreover, spectral estimation by the Fourier method generates various harmonics which often lead to false prediction of coding regions. Among the recently introduced techniques, the eigendecomposition-based noise subspace method, known as the least-norm solution is found to be of great interest. In the present paper the authors addressed the problems posed by standard FFT method and proposed a least-norm algorithm based on the concept of subspace frequency estimation for effective and accurate prediction of coding regions in DNA sequence.

Application of DSP methods to find periodicities in DNA sequences has been studied by various researchers [1-4]. It is established that exon regions of DNA molecules exhibit a period-3 property because of the codon structure involved in the translation of nucleotide bases into amino acids [5-7]. Yin and Yau explained the phenomenon of three-base periodicity in the Fourier power spectrum of protein-coding regions resulting from nonuniform distribution of nucleotides in the three codon positions [8]. An improved algorithm for gene finding by period-3 periodicity using the nonlinear tracking differentiator is presented by Yin et al. [9]. Peng et al. discussed about statistical properties of genes in their article [10]. A universal graphical representation method based on S.S.-T. Yau's technique employing trigonometric functions which denotes the four nucleotide bases to predict coding regions is presented by Jiang et al. [11]. Application of digital filters to extract period-3 components and effectively eliminate background noise present in DNA sequence has given good results [12-14]. Yu et al. have used in their paper probability distributions to study similarity in DNA sequences employing symmetrized Kullback–Leibler convergence [15]. Kwan et al. introduced novel codes for one-sequence numerical representation for spectral analysis and compared them with existing mapping techniques [16]. Roy et al. introduced positional frequency distribution of nucleotides (PFDN), an algorithm for prediction of coding regions [17]. Parametric techniques of gene prediction where autoregressive all-pole models were used for identifying coding and non-coding regions provided better results [18,19]. Yu et al. proposed a novel method to construct moment vectors for DNA sequences using a two-dimensional graphical representation and proved that the two had one-to-one correspondence [20]. In another work, Deng et al. introduced a novel method of characterizing genetic sequence defining genome space with biological distance for subsequent applications in analyzing and annotating genomes [21]. An exclusive survey of various gene prediction techniques is presented by Pradhan

et al. [22]. The fundamental theory of principal component analysis is explained by Shlens and its application is discussed by Ubeyli et al. [23,24].

In this article, authors have compared and analyzed power spectral peaks obtained by modified periodogram method with pseudo-spectrum obtained by least-norm solution method for detecting the presence of coding regions in DNA sequence and established superiority of the later technique [25-28]. The algorithm has been successfully tested on several sample databases downloaded from NCBI GenBank [29].

2 Materials and methods

PSD estimation of DNA sequence requires conversion of DNA character string into numerical form. Different researchers have adopted different mapping methods to achieve this objective. The Voss representation is a very popular technique giving four binary indicator sequences $x_a[n]$, $x_t[n]$, $x_c[n]$ and $x_g[n]$ which takes a value of either 1 or 0 at location n depending on whether the corresponding character exists at that location or not [7,13,14]. These indicator sequences show redundancy because

$$x_a[n] + x_t[n] + x_c[n] + x_g[n] = 1 \text{ for all n} \qquad (1)$$

Therefore, three out of these four binary sequences would be enough to uniquely determine the DNA character string. There are several other techniques such as complex numbers [2], paired numeric [6], universal graphical representation [11], weak-strong hydrogen bonding [18], EIIP [30], quaternion [31] etc. each having a certain special feature of its kind. Rao and Shepherd [19] in their study found that complex mapping was one of the most effective and compact mapping rules. In a recent work, Kwan et al. [16] introduced several novel codes for single-sequence numerical representations for spectral analysis and studied their relative performances. They focused on direct and simple numerical representations which satisfied the following requirements:

(a). Single-sequence mapping for a nucleotide sequence
(b). Fixed value mapping for each nucleotide
(c). Accessible to digital signal processing analysis

Seven single-sequence complex-value numerical representations were derived by them in which each nucleotide of sequence was mapped to a single real value element (+1 or −1) and a single imaginary value element (+j or −j). According to the main findings of their study, the K-Quaternary Code-I was most attractive whereas Rao and Shepherd found K-Quaternary Code-III to be more suitable. Details of these codes are furnished in Table 1. In this article, the authors have adopted a novel mapping rule in which K-Quaternary Code-III has been flipped about

Table 1 Numerical representations

Name	c	g	a	t	Remarks
K-Quaternary Code-III	−j	−1	+1	+j	Rao and Shepherd
K-Quaternary Code-I	−1	−j	+1	+j	Kwan et al.
Quaternary Code proposed	−j	+1	−1	+j	Proposed mapping

Y-axis assigning numerical values, a = −1, c = −j, g = 1 and t = j to nucleotide sequence x[n] as shown in the following example in order to provide location accuracy to predicted exons.

$$x[n] = [a\,t\,g\,c\,c\,t\,t\,a\,g\,g\,a\,t] \tag{2}$$

After mapping,

$$x_m[n] = [\text{-1 j 1-j-j j j-1 1 1-1 j}] \tag{3}$$

Once numerical conversion of DNA sequence is obtained, DSP technique can easily be applied to estimate its power spectrum. Spectral estimation by non-parametric method can be broadly classified as direct and indirect. These two methods are equivalent and are popularly known as the periodogram method. The direct method takes discrete Fourier transform (DFT) of the signal and then averages the square of its magnitude. The indirect method is based on the concept of first estimating the autocorrelation of data sequence and then taking its Fourier transform (FT).

In the first part of this section, spectral analysis of DNA by periodogram method is discussed in brief. The basic of eigendecomposition is given in the second subsection. Mathematical background of the least-norm solution is explained in the third subsection followed by algorithm of the least-norm solution technique. In the next section of this article, results and discussion have been presented. In the first subsection of this section, performance of proposed method has been compared with the modified periodogram method. Model order selection by eigenvalue ratio technique has been elaborated in the next subsection. In the final and last section of the article, conclusion has been drawn. MATLAB 7.1 software has been used to show performance of the estimators.

2.1 Spectral analysis by modified periodogram method

In the direct method mentioned above, periodogram $P_{per}(f_k)$ for signal $x(n)$ can be computed by DFT or more efficiently by fast Fourier transform (FFT) for N data points as shown in Equation 4:

$$P_{per}(k/N) = 1/N |\sum_{n=0}^{N-1} x(n) e^{-j2\Pi nk/N}|^2 \tag{4}$$

where $f_k = k/N$, for $k = 0, 1, 2, ..., N-1$

To enhance performance of the periodogram method, at first, the N-point data sequence is divided into K overlapping segments of length M each, then the periodogram is computed applying the Bartlett window; finally, the average is computed from the result.

2.2 Spectral analysis by eigendecomposition

In this article, eigendecomposition of the autocorrelation matrix has been motivated as an approach for frequency estimation of DNA sequence. Here, the signal $x(n)$ is modeled as a sum of p complex exponentials in white noise $w(n)$ as shown in the following equation:

$$x(n) = \sum_{i=1}^{p} A_i e^{jnw_i} + w(n), \tag{5}$$

where amplitude A_i are complex values given by $A_i = |A_i|\, e_i^{j\phi}$ with ϕ_i being uncorrelated random variables that are uniformly distributed over the interval $[\pi, -\pi]$. The power spectrum of $x(n)$ consists of a set of p impulses of amplitude $|A_i|$ at frequencies w_i for $i = 1,2,3,...,p$ plus power spectrum of white noise $w(n)$ having variance σ_n^2.

The $M \times M$ autocorrelation sequence of the process with lag size M is given by

$$R_{xx}(k) = \sum_{i=1}^{p} P_i e^{jkw_i} + \sigma_n^2 \delta(k), \tag{6}$$

where $P_i = |A_i|^2$ is the power in the ith component. Therefore, the autocorrelation matrix R_{xx} is the sum of autocorrelation matrix due to signal R_s and autocorrelation matrix due to noise R_n which may be written concisely as

$$R_{xx} = R_s + R_n = EPE^H + \sigma_n^2 I, \tag{7}$$

where $E = [e_1, e_2,..., e_p]$ is an $M \times p$ matrix containing p signal vectors e_i and E^H signifies its Hermitian transpose. $P = \{P_1, P_2,..., P_p\}$ is a diagonal matrix of signal powers. The eigenvalues of R_{xx} is $\lambda_i = \lambda_i^s + \sigma_n^2$ where λ_i^s are eigenvalues of R_s having rank p corresponding to signal subspace and the last (M-p) eigenvalues approximately equal to σ_n^2 are noise eigenvalues. Hence, the eigenvalues and eigenvectors of R_{xx} may be divided into two groups as shown below. Assuming that the eigenvectors have been normalized to have unit norm, we may use spectral theorem to denote R_{xx} as

$$R_{xx} = \sum_{i=1}^{p} \lambda_i v_i v_i^H + \sum_{i=p+1}^{M} \lambda_i v_i v_i^H \tag{8}$$

The set of eigenvectors $\{v_1, v_2,..., v_p\}$, associated with largest eigenvalues span the signal subspace and are called principal eigenvectors. The second subset of eigenvectors $\{v_{p+1}, v_{p+2},..., v_M\}$ span the noise subspace and have σ_n^2 as their eigenvalue. Since the signal and noise eigenvectors are orthogonal, it follows that the signal subspace and the noise subspace are also orthogonal.

After eigendecomposition of the autocorrelation matrix, the eigenvalues are arranged in decreasing order $\lambda_1 \geq \lambda_2 \geq \lambda_3,..., \geq \lambda_M$ as depicted in Figure 1. From this plot of eigenvalues, one can distinguish initial steep slope representing signal and a more or less flat floor representing noise level.

An issue that is of central importance to successful implementation of principal-component analysis (PCA) is the selection of appropriate model order p since the accuracy of estimated spectrum is critically dependent on this choice. In this article, the eigenvalue-ratio technique has been adopted for optimum model order selection. A plot of λ_p/λ_{p+1} vs integer values p indicates a large eigenvalue gap at the threshold of signal subspace and noise subspace. This p value is chosen as the required model order and eigenvalues λ_{p+1} to λ_M are assumed to be the noise eigenvalues corresponding to the noise subspace.

The pseudo-spectrum estimation by noise subspace method involves three generic steps:

1. Formation of autocorrelation matrix from data vector.
2. Derivation of noise subspace with the help of eigendecomposition.
3. Identification of signal components from noise subspace by frequency estimation function.

2.3 Frequency estimation by least-norm solution

Frequency estimation is the process in which complex frequency components of a signal are estimated in the existence of noise [32]. The least-norm algorithm developed in this paper uses a single vector $\vec{a}$ that is constrained to lie on the noise subspace and the complex exponential

frequencies are estimated from the peaks of the frequency estimation function:

$$\hat{P}_{LN}(e^{jw}) = 1/\left| \vec{e}^H \vec{a} \right|^2, \tag{9}$$

where $\{\vec{e}\}$ is an auxiliary vector given by

$$\vec{e} = \left[1 \; e^{jw} \; e^{j2w} \; e^{j3w} ....e^{j(N-1)w} \right] \tag{10}$$

with $\vec{a}$ constrained to lie in the noise subspace, if the autocorrelation function is known exactly, then $\left| \vec{e}^H \vec{a} \right|^2$ will have nulls at the frequencies of each complex exponentials. Therefore, Z-transform of coefficients of $\vec{a}$ may be factored as

$$A(z) = \sum_{k=0}^{M-1} a(k)z^{-k} = \prod_{k=1}^{p} \left(1 - e^{jwk}z^{-1}\right) \prod_{k=p+1}^{M-1} \left(1 - z_k z^{-1}\right) \tag{11}$$

where Z_k for $k = (p + 1),...,(M - 1)$ are the spurious roots that in general do not lie on the unit circle. The least-norm method attempts to eliminate the effects of spurious zeros by pushing them inside the unit circle leaving the desired zeros on the unit circle. The problem then is to determine which vector in the noise subspace minimizes the effects of spurious zeros on the peaks of $\hat{P}_{LN}(e^{jw})$.

The approach used in the least-norm algorithm is to find a vector $\vec{a}$ that satisfies the three following constraints:

1. The vector $\vec{a}$ lies on the noise subspace ensuring that p roots of $A(z)$ are on the unit circle.
2. The vector $\vec{a}$ has least Euclidean norm ensuring that spurious roots of $A(z)$ lie inside unit circle.
3. The first element of $\vec{a}$ is unity, i.e. least-norm solution is not the zero vector.

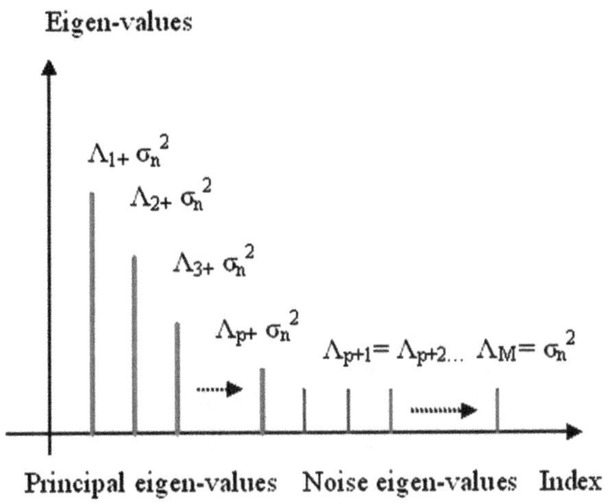

Figure 1 Decomposition of the eigenvalues of noisy signal into the principal and noise eigenvalues.

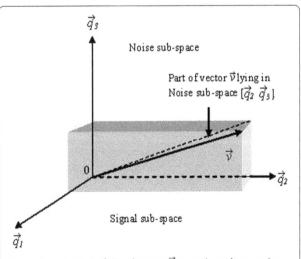

Figure 2 Projection of signal vector $\vec{v}$ on noise sub-space in a three-dimensional vector space.

Table 2 Summary of statistical parameters and computation time of modified periodogram and least-norm methods for various genes

Gene	Sliding DFT method				Least-norm method			
	Q.F. (mean)^2/var	CPU Time (s)	Window Length M	K No. of segments	Q.F. (mean)^2/var	CPU Time (s)	Model Order p	Percent Rise in Q.F.
F56F11.4a	4.83	0.24	351	23	121.89	104.86	20	2.42e + 003
T12B5.1G-1	6.32	0.14	252	07	347.96	48.72	08	5.41e + 003
T12B5.1G-2	5.58	0.14	252	08	305.51	50.37	16	5.37e + 003
T12B5.1G-3	3.54	0.09	252	04	742.96	06.68	02	2.09e + 004
T12B5.1G-4	8.38	0.15	252	09	221.09	54.15	17	2.54e + 003
T12B5.1G-5	5.88	0.13	252	06	227.29	07.76	17	3.76e + 003
C30C11-1	10.43	0.18	252	12	498.41	11.37	07	4.68e + 003
C30C11-2	3.92	0.10	210	04	107.79	06.21	17	2.65e + 003
D13156	4.84	0.15	351	05	246.08	37.38	17	4.98e + 003

To solve this constrained minimization problem, we begin by noting the constraint that $\vec{a}$ lies on the noise subspace which is given by the following equation:

$$\vec{a} = P_n \vec{v}, \tag{12}$$

where $P_n = V_n V_n^H$ is the projection matrix projecting an arbitrary vector $\vec{v}$ on the noise subspace as shown in Figure 2 [25].

The least-norm method involves projection of signal vector $\vec{v}$ on to the entire noise space.

The third constraint is expressed as

$$\vec{a}^H \vec{u}_1 = 1, \tag{13}$$

where $\vec{u}_1 = [1, 0, 0, ..., 0]^T$

This may be combined with the constraint in Equation 12 giving

$$\vec{v}^H \left(P_n^H \vec{u}_1 \right) = 1 \tag{14}$$

The norm of $\vec{a}$ may be written as

$$\| \vec{a} \|^2 = \| P_n \vec{v} \|^2 = \vec{v}^H \left(P_n^H P_n \right) \vec{v} \tag{15}$$

Since projection matrix P_n is Hermitian, therefore $P_n = P_n^H$ and also idempotent, hence $P_n^2 = P_n$, we get

$$\| \vec{a} \|^2 = \| P_n \vec{v} \|^2 = \vec{v}^H \left(P_n^H P_n \right) \vec{v} \tag{16}$$

Minimizing $\vec{a}$ is equivalent to finding vector $\vec{v}$ that minimizes the quadratic form of $\vec{v}^H P_n \vec{v}$

After reformulating the constrained minimization problem,

i.e., $\quad \min \vec{v}^H P_n \vec{v} \quad$ subject to $\vec{v}^H \left(P_n^H \vec{u}_1 \right) = 1$

$$\tag{17}$$

Once the solution of Equation 14 is found, the least-norm solution is formed by projecting $\vec{v}$ onto noise subspace using Equation 12 and using Optimization Theory, the least-norm solution is found to be

$$\vec{a} = P_n \vec{v} = \lambda P_n \vec{u}_1 = \left(P_n \vec{u}_1 \right) / \vec{u}_1^H P_n \vec{u}_1 \tag{18}$$

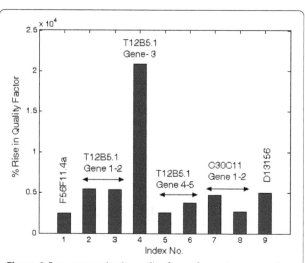

Figure 3 Percentage rise in quality factor for various genes by least-norm and periodogram methods.

which is the projection of the unit vector onto normalized noise subspace such that the first coefficient is unity, and the Lagrange multiplier λ is given by

$$\lambda = 1/ \left(\vec{u}_1^{\,H} P_n \vec{u}_1 \right) \tag{19}$$

In terms of eigenvectors of the autocorrelation matrix, the least-norm solution is given using quadratic factorization (QR) by the following equation:

$$\vec{a} = \left((V_n V_n^H) \vec{u}_1 \right) / \left(\vec{u}_1^{\,H} (V_n V_n^H) \vec{u}_1 \right) \tag{20}$$

2.4 Algorithm of proposed least-norm solution technique for estimating period-3 peaks

Step 1 Convert the samples of data vectors to column vector.

Step 2 Compute autocorrelation matrix of data with pre-determined lag size (M).

Step 3 Diagonalize the autocorrelation matrix. Produce diagonal matrix D of eigenvalues and a full matrix V whose columns are the corresponding eigenvectors so that X*V = V*D, where X is the signal matrix.

Step 4 Sort diagonal matrix D in ascending order for eigendecomposition. Take into account noise subspace spanned by the eigenvectors corresponding to nonsignificant eigenvalues.

Table 3 Summary of performance analysis of data for least-norm and modified periodogram methods

Gene	DSP methods	Threshold value	Prediction measures				
			S_n	S_p	$(S_n + S_p)/2$	M_r	W_r
F56F11.4a	Periodogram	1.75	0.4	1.0	0.70	0.6	0.0
	Periodogram	1.50	0.8	0.66	0.73	0.2	0.4
	Least-norm	*	1.0	1.00	1.00	0.0	0.00
T12B5 Gene-1	Periodogram	1.75	1.0	0.43	0.71	0.0	0.55
	Periodogram	1.50	1.0	0.33	0.66	0.0	0.66
	Least-norm	*	1.0	1.0	1.0	0.0	0.0
T12B5 Gene-2	Periodogram	1.75	1.0	0.6	0.8	0.0	0.4
	Periodogram	1.50	1.0	0.5	0.75	0.0	0.5
	Least-norm	*	1.0	1.0	1.0	0.0	0.0
T12B5 Gene-3	Periodogram	1.75	1.0	0.15	0.57	0.0	0.84
	Periodogram	1.50	1.0	0.12	0.56	0.0	0.87
	Least-norm	*	1.0	1.0	1.0	0.0	0.0
T12B5 Gene-4	Periodogram	1.75	0.5	0.4	0.45	0.5	0.6
	Periodogram	1.50	0.75	0.33	0.54	0.25	0.66
	Least-norm	*	1.0	1.0	1.0	0.0	0.0
T12B5 Gene-5	Periodogram	1.75	0.66	0.22	0.44	0.33	0.77
	Periodogram	1.50	1.0	0.25	0.62	0.0	0.75
	Least-norm	*	1.0	1.00	1.00	0.0	0.0
C30C11 Gene-1	Periodogram	1.75	0.5	0.4	0.45	0.5	0.6
	Periodogram	1.50	1.0	0.4	0.7	0.0	0.6
	Least-norm	*	1.0	1.0	1.0	0.0	0.0
C30C11 Gene-2	Periodogram	1.75	1.0	0.33	0.66	0.0	0.66
	Periodogram	1.50	1.0	0.21	0.60	0.0	0.78
	Least-norm	*	1.0	1.0	1.0	0.0	0.0
D13156	Periodogram	1.75	1.0	0.22	0.61	0.0	0.77
	Periodogram	1.50	1.0	0.15	0.57	0.0	0.86
	Least-norm	*	1.0	0.5	0.75	0.0	0.5

*Threshold value not required.

Step 5 Project signal vector $\vec{v}$ onto the noise space using projection matrix.

Step 6 Find Least Norm vector $\vec{a}$ on noise subspace with first element equal to unity using QR factorization and applying the Optimization Theory.

Step 7 Estimate pseudo-spectrum (in dB) by computing absolute FFT of vector $\vec{a}$

Step 8 Plot the result (in dB) to observe period-3 spectral peaks.

3 Results and discussion

The proposed algorithm has been tested on several eukaryotic genes to predict location of coding regions of varying lengths of a few base-pairs to thousand base-pairs and simulation results are compared with that of modified periodogram on the same DNA data. The segments of test data used for analysis contain both exons and introns of fully constructed genes. According to period-3 property of DNA, a prominent peak should be observed in the PSD plot of each exon segment. It is observed that the proposed method produces very sharp and well-defined period-3 peaks indicating existence and numbers of protein-coding regions of very short to long coding segments present in the test data. Once the existence and locations of exons in the enormous length of DNA are confirmed, further statistical or computational methods may be applied on the DNA sequence to find the boundaries of protein-coding regions. The statistical parameters and computation times for modified periodogram and least-norm methods for genes F56F11.4a, T12B5.1, C30C11 and D13156 are indicated in Table 2.

It is observed that the proposed approach removes the entire noise and reveals the hidden periodicities prominently. A comparison has been drawn with periodogram method applying Bartlett (triangular) sliding window with 50% overlap and suitable segment lengths M and number of segments K. Window length M should be chosen subjectively based on a trade-off between spectral resolution and statistical variance. If M is very small, important features may be smoothed out, while if M is very large, the behavior becomes more like unmodified periodogram with erratic variation. Hence, a compromise value is selected between range $1/25 < M/N < 1/3$ where N is nucleotide sequence length. Quality factor (Q.F.) which measures the ratio of variance to square of mean of PSD has been used as comparison metric between the two methods which are shown in Table 2. It is observed that quality factor of spectrum by the least-norm method is much higher than modified periodogram method. Figure 3 shows bar plot of percentage rise in quality factor for various genes. Table 2 also indicates that computation time required in the least-norm method is more than modified periodogram method.

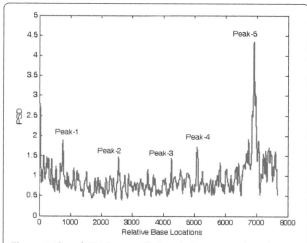

Figure 4 Plot of PSD by modified periodogram method for F56F11.4a gene.

3.1 Performance comparison of proposed method with existing method

The analysis of performance of both the methods can be made by prediction measures such as sensitivity (S_n), specificity (S_p), miss rate (M_r) and wrong rate (W_r). Their definitions are stated below:

$$S_n = T_p/(T_p + F_n) \tag{21}$$

$$S_p = T_p/(T_p + F_p) \tag{22}$$

$$M_r = M_e/A_e \tag{23}$$

$$W_r = W_e/P_e \tag{24}$$

where M_e = missing exons, A_e = actual exons, W_e = wrong exons, P_e = predicted exons, T_p = true positive, F_p = false positive, and F_n = false negative. T_p corresponds to those genes that are accurately predicted by the algorithm and

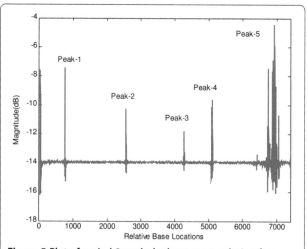

Figure 5 Plot of period-3 peaks by least-norm solution for F56F11.4a gene.

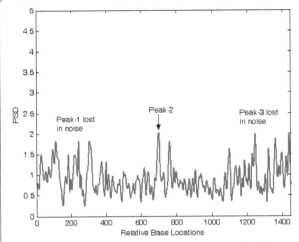

Figure 6 Plot of PSD by modified periodogram method for T12B5.1 gene-1.

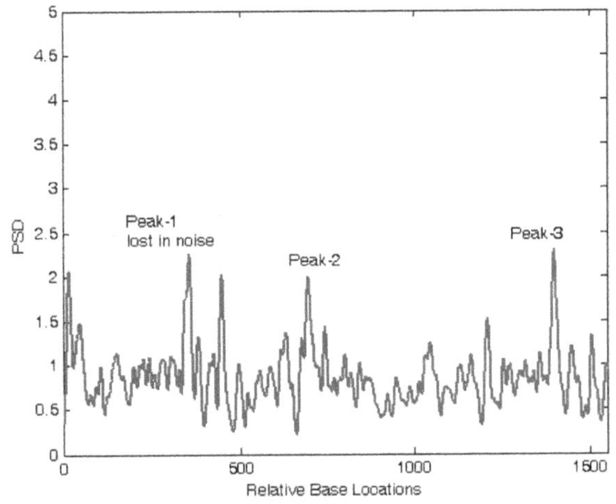

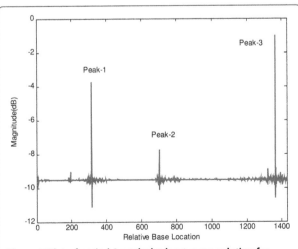

Figure 7 Plot of period-3 peaks by least-norm solution for T12B5.1 gene-1.

Figure 8 Plot of PSD by modified periodogram method for T125B.1 gene-2.

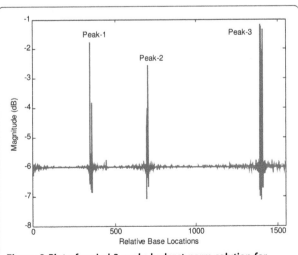

Figure 9 Plot of period-3 peaks by least-norm solution for T12B5.1 gene-2.

also exist in the GenBank annotation. F_p corresponds to the exon regions which are identified by the given algorithm but are not specified in the standard annotation. F_n is coding region that is present in the GenBank annotation but is not predicted as a coding segment by the algorithm. The average value of S_n and S_p gives the overall exon sensitivity and specificity. Table 3 summarizes the simulation results of the eight genes used as test data. It is evident from tabulated data that S_n, S_p and the average of S_n and S_p of the proposed method are significantly higher than existing method in all the cases whereas the miss rate and wrong rate are much lower indicating superior performance of the proposed algorithm over the existing technique [33].

At first, both modified periodogram technique and proposed least-norm algorithm are applied to *C. elegans*

cosmid F56F11.4a gene having 8060-base pair (bp) length test data starting from 7021-bp location. It has five known exons between locations 7948 to 8059, 9548 to 9877, 11,134 to 11397, 12485 to 12664 and 14275 to 14625 bp. The modified periodogram result is shown in Figure 4 and the proposed algorithm result is plotted in Figure 5. In the PSD plot shown in Figure 4, there are five visible exon peaks in the presence of background noise. But it is evident from Figure 5 by the proposed method that the five sharp period-3 spectral peaks visible in the specific coding regions are well defined, accurately positioned and without any noise component.

Figures 6 and 7 show the results of application of conventional modified periodogram method and proposed least-norm solution method to 32488-bp length *C. elegans* cosmid T12B5.1 DNA (Accession no. FO081674.1

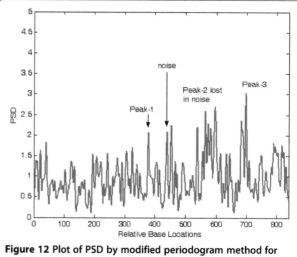

Figure 10 Plot of PSD by modified periodogram method for *C. elegans* C30C11 gene-1.

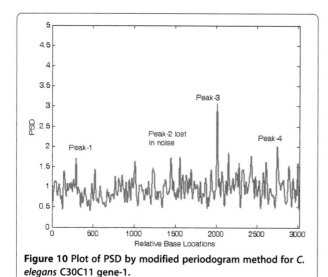

Figure 12 Plot of PSD by modified periodogram method for C30C11 gene-2.

AF100307). The plots indicate three exons in gene-1 between locations 17332 to 17402, 17645 to 18266, and 18311 to 18505 bp. In Figure 6, the exon peaks are present along with other peaks; therefore, prediction becomes ambiguous. In Figure 7, obtained by the proposed algorithm, there are only three sharp period-3 peaks corresponding to the exons present in the gene. They are in proper location and are absolutely devoid of noise. Hence, there is no scope of any ambiguity. Similar results are seen in Figures 8 and 9 for gene-2 with three exons between locations 18994 to 19064, 19349 to 19997 and 20059 to 20253 bp. The technique was applied to the remaining three genes of this DNA and was verified successfully.

Next, both the methods were applied to DNA C30C11 (Accession no. FO080722.7 L09634) from *C. elegans*chromosome-III having length 30866 bp. Figures 10 and 11

mention spectral peaks by modified periodogram and least-norm solution method respectively for gene-1 with exons between locations 4874 to 4985, 5034 to 5408, 5452 to 6179 and 6227 to 6526 bp. In Figure 11 it is observed that peak-2 is shifted to right from actual position. Figures 12 and 13 indicate accurate results for gene-2 with exon segments between locations 7320 to7503, 7555 to 7757 and 7804 to 7923 bp. All these plots showing results of both the existing and proposed methods reflect the superiority of proposed technique over the conventional method because the peaks obtained with proposed algorithm are sharp, well defined, unambiguous, and noise-free. The threshold values for performance analysis of modified periodogram method have been chosen judiciously as 1.75 and 1.5, respectively. Table 3 indicates a list of genes studied and analysis summary of modified periodogram

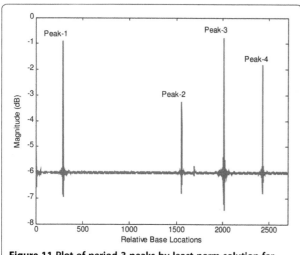

Figure 11 Plot of period-3 peaks by least-norm solution for C30C11 gene-1.

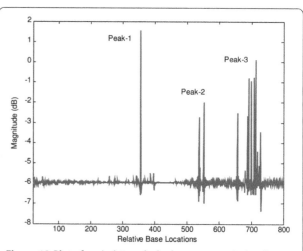

Figure 13 Plot of period-3 peaks by least-norm solution for C30C11 gene-2.

Table 4 Details of organisms with short exons

Gene ID	GenBank accession no.	DNA length in bp	Length of exons in bp	Source
DMPROTP1	L17007.1	624	177 (122 to 248, 376 to 425)	*Didelphis marsupialis* (Southern opossum)
			Exon1-127 and Exon2-50	
OAMTTI	X07975.1	2055	186 (995 to 1022, 1312 to 1377, 1697 to 1,788) Exon1-28, Exon2-66, Exon3-92	*Ovis aries* (sheep)
CALEGLOBIM	L25363.1	1698	444 (144 to 235, 364 to 586, 1399 to 1527)	*Callithrix jacchus* (white tufted ear marmoset)
PIGAPAI	L00626.1	3333	Exon1-92, Exon2-223, Exon3-129	*Sus scorfa* (pig)
			798 (751 to 793, 975 to 1128, 1770 to 2,370)	
			Exon1-43, Exon2-154,	
			Exon3-601	

and least-norm solution approaches. In all the above examples cited, the proposed method shows better result than the existing method giving a higher value of sensitivity, specificity and their average as well as lower value of miss rate and wrong rate.

Next, least-norm algorithm has been applied to organisms with very short exon segments. It is known that prediction of exons with less than 100-bp length is difficult but the proposed least-norm method is found to be very suitable for detecting presence of exons as small as 28 bp length. Table 4 shows details of the organisms with short exons used as test data. Spectral plots for DMPROTP1 and CALEGLOBIM have been shown in Figures 14 and 15 respectively. The figures show very sharp, well defined and noise-free peaks in exon regions even for very small exon segments. Similar tests were performed on other organisms too giving satisfactory results. Hence, it is established that our method is robust and equally suitable for short as well as long exons.

The proposed least-norm algorithm though offers high predictive accuracy compared to existing SDFT method, it has certain limitations on its part. It is a key issue to select model order judiciously for accurate exon detection. In the least-norm method, the time of execution is more compared to the other existing methods since computation time depends on the autocorrelation lag size which is determined depending on the length of nucleotide sequence being tested. The computation of many lags is required in estimation of periodicity which requires great deal of arithmetic, increasing the execution time of the proposed technique. It is desirable to exploit certain properties of autocorrelation function that are known to reduce the computational load. This can be done by taking advantage of the special technique based on reduction in number of multiplications given by Kendall [34]. Another method for speeding up the autocorrelation computation is by the well-known FFT method, which can also help in reducing computation time of proposed least-norm technique [35].

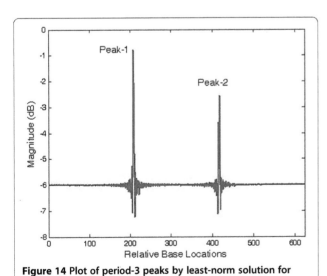

Figure 14 Plot of period-3 peaks by least-norm solution for DMPROTP1 gene.

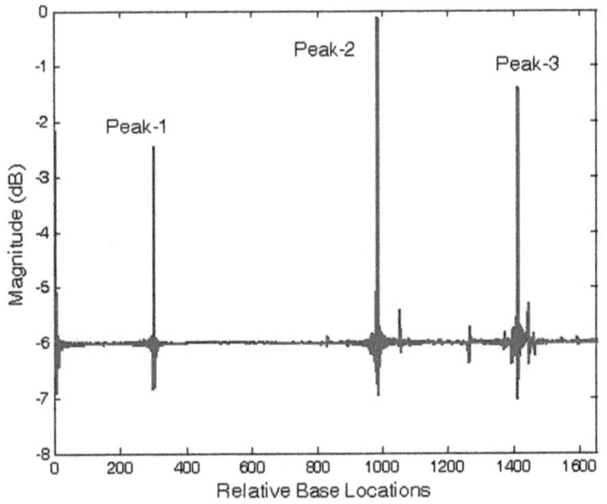

Figure 15 Plot of period-3 peaks by least-norm solution for CALEGLOBIM gene.

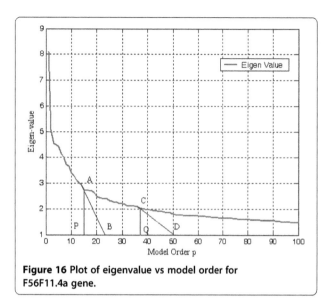

Figure 16 Plot of eigenvalue vs model order for F56F11.4a gene.

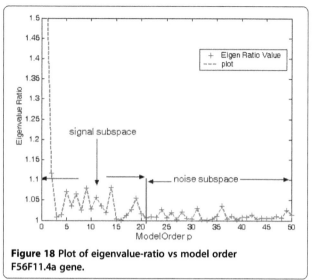

Figure 18 Plot of eigenvalue-ratio vs model order F56F11.4a gene.

3.2 Eigenvalue-ratio based model order selection approach

A key issue in developing the eigendecomposition-based model is proper selection of model order p. In order to estimate least-norm solution-based pseudo-spectrum, the dimension M-p of the noise subspace must be determined accurately. If value of p taken is less than required, then few prominent peaks may go unnoticed. On the other hand, if selected model order is more than the required value, undesired peaks are introduced in the plot leading to false prediction. The most common approach is to calculate and sort the eigenvalues of the correlation matrix R_{xx} of the noisy signal. The plot of eigenvalues sorted in decreasing order is termed as Scree-plot. The prime eigenvalues of dimension p having steep slope correspond to the signal subspace. The set of smallest eigenvalues having

dimension M-p with values equal to noise variance σ_n^2 is more or less flat in nature (Figure 1). Decrease in negativity of the derivative from higher value to lower value is determined by the slope of tangents drawn from the Scree-plot to the X-axis. At first, two points are chosen carefully on the Scree-plot such that the first is on steep slope and second is on less steep portion of the eigen-curve. The values of model order p intercepted by the two projections drawn vertically downward from the point of the tangent touching the eigen-curve (Scree plot) to the X-axis are identified. A 'large gap' or 'elbow' is looked for within this segment by eigenvalue-ratio technique to be treated as the threshold value between signal and noise subspaces (Figures 16 and 17).

A very simple method based on eigenvalue ratio has been adopted by the authors to find model order p is discussed

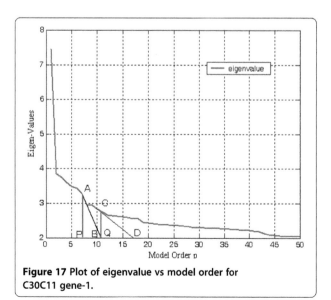

Figure 17 Plot of eigenvalue vs model order for C30C11 gene-1.

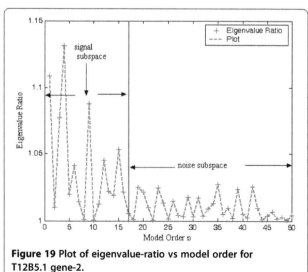

Figure 19 Plot of eigenvalue-ratio vs model order for T12B5.1 gene-2.

in this subsection [32,36]. As shown in Figures 18 and 19 the authors have plotted eigenvalue ratio λ_p/λ_{p+1} vs model order p. It is noted that there exists an eigenvalue gap of high magnitude between orders $p = 20$ and 21 and $p = 16$ and 17, in the figures, respectively. Satisfactory estimates of rank of R_{xx} by suggested method was found to be 20 for F56F11.4a gene, 16 for T12B5.1 gene-2, and 7 for C30C11 gene-1 Thus, it may be considered that eigenvalues λ_{21}, λ_{17} and λ_8 onwards can be treated as noise eigenvalues in the three successive cases.

In this article, spectral content measure techniques based on sliding DFT was compared with proposed least-norm technique. In an early work, Tiwari et al. (1997) employed Fourier technique to analyze the three-base periodicity in order to recognize coding regions in genomic DNA. They observed that a few genes in *Saccharomyces cerevisiae* do not exhibit period-3 property at all. Anastassiou (2000, 2001) was inspired by the work of Tiwari et al. and introduced computational and visual tools for analysis of biomolecular sequences. He developed optimization procedure for improving performance of traditional Fourier technique. Later, Vaidyanathan and Yoon (2004) designed multistage narrowband band-pass filter for reducing background 1/f noise. Recently, Sahu and Panda (2011) in their work improved computational efficiency by employing SDFT with the help of the Goertzel algorithm, but the method is constrained by frequency resolution and spectral leakage effects.

The least-norm algorithm presented in this paper provides an absolutely novel approach. The first important feature of the proposed algorithm is that it produces very sharp and well-defined period-3 peaks in the protein-coding regions. The second significant feature is that it eliminates noise completely; hence, there is no requirement of setting threshold value. The third significant feature of this algorithm is that it is able to effectively detect very short exons as well. Moreover, this method offers very high sensitivity and specificity and very low miss rate and wrong rate compared to other available techniques.

4 Conclusion

DNA sequence analysis through power spectrum estimation by traditional non-parametric methods is in use since long. These are methodologically straightforward, computationally simple, and easy to understand, but due to low SNR, spectral features are difficult to distinguish as noise artifacts appear in spectral estimates. Therefore, effective identification of protein-coding region becomes difficult. The application of least-norm frequency estimator to capture period-3 peaks in coding regions has been introduced here. We used a constrained vector that lies on the noise subspace and the algorithm completely filters out the spurious peaks. Selection of proper model order is a fundamental issue in application of the eigendecomposition

approach. The eigenvalue-ratio 'gap' or 'elbow' located on the Scree plot is treated as threshold between signal and noise spaces. Application of eigendecomposition-based methods to various DNA sequences has given amazing results as compared to standard classical methods in terms of resolution, quality factor, sensitivity, specificity, miss rate, and wrong rate. It was observed that high-resolution pseudo-spectrum estimator based on least-norm solution could identify protein-coding regions in DNA accurately. Another important feature of the proposed technique is that it can detect the presence of extremely short exon segments which is difficult for other existing methods. Unfortunately the computational effort for this high-resolution method is significantly higher than FFT processing. This limitation may be tackled by applying Kendall's algorithm or incorporating the well-known FFT method to speed up the autocorrelation computation. Hence, it can be concluded that identification of protein-coding regions in DNA can be done effectively in a much superior way by applying the least-norm solution technique.

Competing interests
The authors declare that they have no competing interests.

Author details
[1]The Calcutta Technical School, Govt. of West Bengal, 110,S.N.Banerjee Road, Kolkata 700013, India. [2]Institute of Radio Physics & Electronics, University of Calcutta, 92, A.P.C. Road, Kolkata 700 009, India.

References
1. L Zhao, *Application of spectral analysis to DNA sequences* (CSD, Purdue University, TR #06-003, 2006)
2. D Anastassiou, Frequency-domain analysis of biomolecular sequences. Bioinformatics **16**(12), 1073–1081 (2000)
3. D Anastassiou, DSP in genomics: processing and frequency-domain analysis of character strings, in *Proceedings of the IEEE International Conference on Acoustics, Speech, and Signal Processing, 2001. (ICASSP '01), Salt Lake City, 7–11 May, vol. 2* (IEEE, Piscataway, 2001). pp 1053–1056, 0-7803-7041-2001
4. PP Vaidyanathan, BJ Yoon, The role of signal-processing concepts in genomics and proteomics. J. Franklin Inst. **351**, 111–135 (2004)
5. JW Ficket, CS Tung, Recognition of protein coding regions in DNA sequences. Nucleic Acids Res. **10**(17), 5303–5318 (1982)
6. S Tiwari, S Ramachandran, A Bhattacharya, S Bhattacharya, R Ramaswamy, Prediction of probable genes by Fourier analysis of genomic sequences. CABIOS **3**(3), 263–270 (1997)
7. C Yin, SS-T Yau, Prediction of protein coding regions by the 3-base periodicity analysis of a DNA sequence. J. Theor. Biol. **247**, 687–694 (2007)
8. C Yin, SS-T Yau, A Fourier characteristic of coding sequences: origins and a non-Fourier approximation. J. Comput. Biol. **12**(9), 1153–1165 (2005)
9. C Yin, D Yoo, SS-T Yau, Denoising the 3-base periodicity walk of DNA sequences in gene finding. J. Med. Bio-Eng **2**(2), 80–83 (2013)
10. CK Peng, SV Buldyrev, AL Goldberger, S Havlin, RN Mantegna, M Simons, HE Stanley, Statistical properties of DNA sequences. J. Physica. **A-221**, 180–192 (1995)
11. X Jiang, D Lavenier, SS-T Yau, Coding region prediction based on a universal DNA sequence representative method. J. Comput. Biol. **15**(10), 1237–1256 (2008)
12. AS Nair, S Sreenadhan, An improved digital filtering technique using nucleotide frequency indicators for locating exons. J. CSI **36**(1), 54–60 (2006)
13. J Tuqan, A Rushdi, A DSP approach for finding the codon bias in DNA sequences. IEEE J. Signal Process. **2**(3), 345–355 (2008)

14. SS Sahu, G Panda, Identification of protein coding regions in DNA sequences using a time frequency filtering approach. Genomics Proteomics Bioinformatics **9**(1–2), 45–55 (2011)

15. C Yu, M Deng, SS–T Yau, DNA sequence comparison by a novel probabilistic method. Information Sci. **181**, 1484–1492 (2011)

16. HK Kwan, K Benjamin YM, K Jennifer YY, Novel methodologies for spectral classification of exon and intron sequences. EURASIP J. Adv. Signal Process. **2012**, 50 (2012). doi: 10.1186/1687-6180-2012-50

17. M Roy, S Biswas, S Barman (Mandal), *Identification and analysis of coding and non-coding regions of a DNA sequence by positional frequency distribution of nucleotides (PFDN) algorithm* (Paper presented at the international conference on computers and devices for communication CODEC-09, Kolkata, India, 2009)

18. M Roy, S Barman (Mandal), Spectral analysis of coding and non-coding regions of a DNA sequence by parametric and non-parametric methods: a comparative approach. Annals of Faculty Engineering Hunedoara. Int. J. Eng. Romania **3**, 57–62 (2011)

19. N Rao, SJ Shepherd, Detection of 3-periodicity for small genomic sequences based on AR technique, International Conference on Communications. IAC and Systems **2**, 1032–1036 (2004). 27–29 June

20. C Yu, Q Liang, C Yin, RL He, SS–T Yau, A novel construction of genome space with biological geometry. DNA Res **18**(6), 435–449 (2010)

21. M Deng, C Yu, Q Liang, RL He, SS–T Yau, A novel method of characterizing genetic sequences: genome space with biological distance and applications. PLOS ONE **6**(3), e17293 (2011)

22. M Pradhan, RK Sahu, An exclusive survey on gene prediction methodologies. Int. J. Comp. Sci. Info. Sec **8**(7), 88–103 (2010)

23. J Shlens, A Tutorial on principal component analysis, derivation, discussion and singular value decomposition. Version-I, pp.1-16 25 March (2003), http://www.cs.princeton.edu/picasso/mats/PCA-Tutorial-Intuition_jp.pdf

24. ED Ubeyli, I Guler, Comparison of eigenvector methods with classical and model-based methods in analysis of internal carotid arterial doppler signals. Comput. Biol. Med. **33**, 473–493 (2003)

25. MH Hayes, *Statistical Digital Signal Processing and Modeling* (Wiley, New York, 1996), pp. 393–474

26. S Haykin, *Adaptive Filter Theory*, 4th edn. (Upper Saddle River, Prentice Hall, 2002). pp. 809–822. ISBN 978-81-317-0869-9

27. P Stoica, R Moses, *Spectral Analysis of Signals* (PHI Pvt. Learning Ltd, New Dehli, 2011), pp. 23–67. ISBN 978-81-203-4359-7

28. JG Praokis, DG Manolakis, *Digital Signal Processing: Principles, Algorithms and Applications*, 4th edn. (PHI Learning Pvt. Ltd, New Dehli, 2008), pp. 960–985

29. NCBI Database http://www.ncbi.nlm.nih.gov. Accessed 20 July 2012

30. AS Nair, SP Sreenadhan, A coding measure scheme employing electron-ion interaction pseudopotential (EIIP). Bioinformation **1**(6), 197–202 (2006)

31. AK Brodzik, O Peters, Symbol-balanced quaternionic periodicity transform for latent pattern detection in DNA sequences. ICASSP **5**, 373–376 (2005)

32. T Lobos, Z Leonowicz, J Rezmer, H-J Koglin, Harmonics and interharmonics estimation using advanced signal processing methods, in *Proceedings of the 9th International Conference on Harmonics and Quality Power* (Orlando). 1–4 October 2000, Vol-I, pp. 335–340

33. J Meher, PK Meher, G Dash, Improved comb filter based approach for effective prediction of protein coding regions in DNA sequences. J. Sig. Info. Proc **2**, 88–99 (2011)

34. WB Kendall, A New algorithm for computing autocorrelations. IEEE Trans. Computers **C-23**(1), 90–93 (1974)

35. LR Rabiner, RW Schafer, *Digital Processing of Speech Signals* (Pvt. Ltd., Noida, Dorling Kindersley (India, 2013), pp. 178–180. ISBN 978-81-317-0513-1

36. AP Liavas, PA Regalia, On the behavior of information theoretic criteria for model order selection. IEEE Trans. Signal. Process. **49**(8), 1689–1695 (2001)

On the impoverishment of scientific education

Edward R Dougherty

Abstract

Hannah Arendt, one of the foremost political philosophers of the twentieth century, has argued that it is the responsibility of educators not to leave children in their own world but instead to bring them into the adult world so that, as adults, they can carry civilization forward to whatever challenges it will face by bringing to bear the learning of the past. In the same collection of essays, she discusses the recognition by modern science that Nature is inconceivable in terms of ordinary human conceptual categories - as she writes, 'unthinkable in terms of pure reason'. Together, these views on scientific education lead to an educational process that transforms children into adults, with a scientific adult being one who has the ability to conceptualize scientific systems independent of ordinary physical intuition. This article begins with Arendt's basic educational and scientific points and develops from them a critique of current scientific education in conjunction with an appeal to educate young scientists in a manner that allows them to fulfill their potential 'on the shoulders of giants'. While the article takes a general philosophical perspective, its specifics tend to be directed at biomedical education, in particular, how such education pertains to translational science.

Review

Introduction

Between Past and Future is a collection of essays written by Hannah Arendt between 1954 and 1968 in which, among many other issues, she makes basic points regarding education and science that when taken together entail a certain kind of scientific education [1]. From a general perspective, education should provide students with the knowledge to renew the world, that is, to refresh and keep vibrant a civilization that, except for the ability to take on new and unforeseen crises, would succumb to the vicissitudes of Nature and the human condition.

In *The Crisis in Education*, Arendt writes,

Education is the point at which we decide whether we love the world enough to assume responsibility for it and by the same token save it from that ruin which, except for renewal, except for the coming of the new and young, would be inevitable. And education, too, is where we decide whether we love our children enough not to expel them from our world and leave them to their own devices, nor to strike from their

hands their chance of undertaking something new, something unforeseen by us, but to prepare them in advance for the task of renewing a common world [2].

Sound education is not an option; society depends upon it, for otherwise humans would lack the capacity to renew their world since, in an endless cycle, the old must pass on and leave it to the young to carry on. This places a heavy responsibility upon educators. They must not leave the young to fend for themselves; rather, they must provide them with the fundamentals required to maintain and extend human knowledge. These fundamentals apply not only to a specialized field of research; they encompass a wide range of learning across many fields, including science, mathematics, philosophy, and history. Significant scientific knowledge does not rest on particular technical relationships alone but rather on the integration of myriad philosophical-scientific sources that facilitate deep conceptualizations. Absent the ability to conceptualize, one cannot engage in the creative thought needed to discover new knowledge and address the crises lurking in the future. To provide the young with the fundamentals necessary for renewal, the educator must transform children into adults.

Correspondence: edward@ece.tamu.edu
Center for Bioinformatics and Genomic Systems Engineering, Department of Electrical and Computer Engineering, Texas A&M University, 3128 TAMU, College Station, TX 77843-3128, USA

Nature is unthinkable

For aspiring young scientists, this transformation is governed by the nature of scientific knowledge. This leads us to Arendt's basic point regarding scientific knowledge. In *The Conquest of Space and the Stature of Man*, she writes,

> To understand physical reality seems to demand not only the renunciation of an anthropocentric or geocentric world view, but also a radical elimination of all anthropomorphic elements and principles, as they arise either from the world given to the five senses or from the categories inherent in the human mind [3].

In a similar vein, in *The Concept of History: Ancient and Modern*, she writes,

> The trouble, in other words, is not that the modern physical universe cannot be visualized, for this is a matter of course under the assumption that Nature does not reveal itself to the human senses; the uneasiness begins when Nature turns out to be inconceivable, that is, unthinkable in terms of pure reasoning as well [4].

Not only need we reject an anthropocentric world view, as one might do when accepting the Copernican hypothesis, and not only need we accept the inability of our senses to reveal Nature in her true form, but much more than either of these limitations, we must accept that Nature is so strange to us that it is not even thinkable in terms of the human categories of understanding.

It became quite clear in the first half of the twentieth century, with the advent of the quantum theory and general relativity, that ideas such as particle, wave, and force, whose origins lay in pre-scientific perceptual experience, and frames of reference, such as Euclidean three-dimensional space and linear time, and underlying hypotheses concerning regularity, such as causality and continuity, were inadequate, or even detrimental, to scientific conceptualization. Erwin Schrodinger puts the matter this way:

> As our mental eye penetrates into smaller and smaller distances and shorter and shorter times, we find nature behaving so entirely differently from what we observe in visible and palpable bodies of our surrounding that no model shaped after our large-scale experiences can ever be 'true'. A completely satisfactory model of this type is not only practically inaccessible, but not even thinkable. Or, to be precise, we can, of course, think it, but however we think it, it is wrong; not perhaps quite as meaningless as a 'triangular circle', but much more so than a 'winged lion' [5].

Because science concerns relations between measurable variables and it is these relations that constitute the subject matter of science, scientific knowledge *ipso facto* is mathematically constituted. Nonetheless, scientists had historically attached physical descriptions in the sense of our ordinary categories of understanding to their mathematical systems; however, once it is recognized that the behavior of the phenomena is unthinkable in terms of our ordinary pre-scientific categories, such descriptions are no longer satisfactory. While they might be useful in organizing one's thinking, they are superfluous; indeed, they can be misleading. In the words of James Jeans, 'The final truth about phenomena resides in the mathematical description of it; so long as there is no imperfection in this, our knowledge is complete. We go beyond the mathematical formula at our own risk' [6]. Scientific knowledge is not constrained by the limitations of human physical understanding developed in our everyday world of experience; indeed, everyday physical thinking can be an impediment to scientific knowledge. Lack of sensible experience applies not only to the quantum world; it also applies to complexity. Humans have no perceptual experience with systems, such as cells, involving hundreds of thousands of interacting components. The mind boggles and intuition crashes when confronted with such immense complexity.

Whatever the reason might be for our inability to think about Nature *qua* Nature, human knowledge of Nature is not limited by our understanding of Nature. Arendt writes, 'What defies description in terms of the "prejudices" of the human mind defies description in every conceivable way of human language; it can no longer be described at all, and it is being expressed, but not described, in mathematical processes' [3]. The prejudices to which she refers are, in the words of Niels Bohr, the categories of 'our necessarily prejudiced conceptual frame', [7] and include categories such as causality and determinism. In sum, our scientific knowledge of Nature is not given by description of the phenomena; rather, it is constituted by mathematical processes.

As for the validity (or 'truth') of such processes, the sole criterion is their functionality as predictors of future behavior. This means that a scientific theory consists of two parts: (1) the mathematical theory itself and (2) a set of relations, called *operational definitions*, that connects the theory to the phenomena so that the predictive capacity of the theory can be tested. The operational definitions themselves are mathematical in form since the accuracy of prediction must be understood within the framework of statistics. Without going into detail on the statistical issues involved, the key point in the present exposition is that the mathematical theory must be formally connected to future observations and the firmness of this connection determines the truth of the theory.

One's personal predilections, such as a metaphysical belief in causality, play no role in the acceptance or rejection of a theory. Richard Feynman writes, 'It is whether or not the theory gives predictions that agree with experiment. It is not a question of whether a theory is philosophically delightful, or easy to understand, or perfectly reasonable from the point of view of common sense' [8]. The latter point is crucial. As stated by Arendt, Nature is 'unthinkable in terms of pure reasoning', so reasoned arguments can play no role in validating a scientific theory.

The most remarkable aspect of modern science is that when confronted with the inability to understand Nature, human beings do not stand helpless before Nature. Modern science has turned away from the ancient and medieval attempts to describe Nature to building mathematical systems that can predict phenomena. Arendt writes, 'Man can *do*, and successfully do, what he cannot comprehend and cannot express in everyday human language' [3]. That is, although the theory cannot be put into words, given the operational definitions, it can be tested. Mathematical reasoning allows us to go beyond our physical reasoning in characterizing phenomenal relations. Historian Morris Kline writes, 'What science has done, then, is to sacrifice physical intelligibility for the sake of mathematical description and mathematical prediction' [9]. Notice that Kline refers to 'mathematical description', not description in terms of the 'prejudices' of the human mind. Intelligibility resides in these 'prejudices', and therefore, we should not expect scientific theories to be intelligible. This is why Feynman says, 'I hope you can accept Nature as she is — absurd' [8]. Indeed, Nature is *ipso facto* absurd because it is unintelligible.

While it may be true that our inability to think about Nature in terms of our ordinary categories of physical understanding has been brought into clear focus on account of general relativity and the quantum theory, as Arendt points out, the issue has been with us since the dawn of modern science in the seventeenth century. In *Dialogues Concerning Two New Sciences*, Galileo puts these words into the mouth of Salviati:

> The present does not seem to me to be an opportune time to enter into the investigation of the cause of the acceleration of natural motion... For the present, it suffices our Author that we understand him to want us to investigate and demonstrate some attributes of a motion so accelerated (whatever be the cause of its acceleration) that the momenta of its speed go increasing, after its departure from rest, in that simple ratio with which the continuation of time increases, which is the same as to say that in equal times, equal additions of speed are made [10].

Galileo does not deny causality; he simply *brackets* it (puts it aside), ignores it, and gets on with the business of obtaining mathematical relations between phenomena. He writes that there would be 'little gain' in examining the kind of 'fantasies' put forth by philosophers to explain acceleration in terms of causality. It is more beneficial to 'investigate and demonstrate some attributes of motion'. Although Galileo does not deny causality, as opposed to Aristotle, he rejects it as a requirement for knowledge.

Like Galileo, Newton believes in causality but brackets it outside of science. Near the beginning of *The Principia: Mathematical Principles of Natural Philosophy*, he writes, 'For I here design only to give a mathematical notion of these forces, without considering their physical causes and seats' [11]. Near the end of *The Principia*, he states, 'Hitherto I have not been able to discover the cause of those properties of gravity from the phenomena, and I frame no hypothesis; for whatever is not deduced from the phenomena is to be called an hypothesis; and hypotheses, whether metaphysical or physical, whether of occult qualities or mechanical, have no place in experimental philosophy' [11].

Ancient and medieval science comes to an end with Galileo and Newton, who are thoroughly modern in recognizing that human language and the concepts constructed within that language are not sufficient for science. Kline writes, 'The insurgent seventeenth century found a qualitative world whose study was aided by mathematical abstractions. It bequeathed a mathematical, quantitative world that subsumed under its mathematical laws the concreteness of the physical world' [9].

It would be David Hume who would fully comprehend that causality cannot be logically or empirically deduced from natural phenomena and therefore is not a scientific category. He notes that a cause and its effect are contiguous and related via temporal priority, with the cause prior to the effect. But causality corresponds to more than contiguity and temporal priority; it relates to a 'necessary connection' between the cause and the effect. However, the principle of causality is neither intuitively certain nor provable by logical means, and according to Hume, our belief in the principle rests not on reason, but on habit and custom.

Immanuel Kant agrees with Hume that the principle of causality is not a scientific principle; however, whereas for Hume, habit underlies belief in causality, for Kant, causality is a category of understanding that imposes forms on the data of sensation, and scientific knowledge is limited by these forms. The way things appear, such as being spatially coordinated and connected by causality, is due to subjective *a priori* conditions for human knowledge. One cannot know things apart from the manner in which they conform to these *a priori* mental forms.

While Kant differs from Hume on the ground of causality, regarding Nature, the basic point remains. Kant writes, '[Hume] justly maintains that we cannot comprehend by reason the possibility of causality, that is, of the reference of the existence of one thing to the existence of another, which is necessitated by the former' [12]. Rather, causality is automatically imposed upon the phenomena to make them thinkable.

Even if this is so, why should they be thinkable? Jeans states the matter concisely: 'We need no longer discuss whether light consists of particles or waves; we know all there is to be known about it if we have found a mathematical formula which accurately describes its behavior, and we can think of it as either particles or waves according to our mood and the convenience of the moment' [6]. One can think about the phenomena in terms of ordinary physical categories of understanding, but the choice of how one chooses to think about them depends on one's predilections of the moment. The danger is that the intuitions associated with the phenomena might have nothing to do with them - or worse, be completely misleading.

Educational implications

Two major educational implications arise from the inconceivability of Nature. One is technical and relates to the ability to conceptualize and hence form scientific theories. The other is more general and has to do with appreciating and working within an epistemology that presupposes conceptualizations outside those of the ordinary understanding and outside of ordinary language.

Technical implications

Broad mathematical knowledge gives a scientist greater capability for conceptualization. Thus, it is obvious that budding scientists should be armed with a large mathematical tool box rich in the mathematics appropriate to one's field - the deeper the mathematical knowledge, the more suitable for framing fundamental scientific knowledge. For instance, since the characterization of cellular behavior involves massive stochastic systems of interacting genes and proteins, to constitute biological knowledge at more than a superficial level, a biologist must be armed with a working knowledge of stochastic processes. How else would it be possible to conceptualize the processes that will inevitably constitute the theory characterizing signaling pathways within the cell? This does not simply mean that a biologist needs to possess a mathematical understanding of existing stochastic models for cellular behavior; more to the point, being a biologist means to formulate scientific theories, not simply to read about the theories of others. The biologist must also formulate experiments that elicit relevant behavior of cellular pathways and use the resulting

observations to formulate network models. The need for a rich tool box is not an esoteric requirement for a small group of theoretical academicians; it applies directly to those studying regulatory diseases such as cancer.

None of this is new. In 1948, Norbert Wiener wrote, 'The group of scientists about Dr. Rosenblueth and myself had already become aware of the essential unity of the set of problems centering about communication, control, and statistical mechanics, whether in the machine or in living tissue' [13]. By 1948, Wiener had recognized the epistemological unity of systems-based sciences, be they electrical, economic, or biological systems. The fact that biology concerns systems was noted in 1935 by Conrad Waddington, who wrote, 'To say that an animal is an organism means in fact two things: firstly, that it is a system made up of separate parts, and secondly, that in order to describe fully how any one part works one has to refer either to the whole system or to the other parts' [14].

Today, given the vast body of relevant knowledge accumulated since the 1930s, would it not behoove our educational system to educate biologists so that they possess a working knowledge of stochastic systems? What could possibly be the point of not educating biologists so that they have the knowledge to address biological problems at a deep level? Why send out young researchers to try to engineer solutions to cancer without first educating them in the well-established theory of stochastic control? As M. L. Bittner and I have written elsewhere, 'Isaac Newton published his *Principia* in 1646; Pierre-Simon Laplace published the first volume of his *Celestial Mechanics* 150 years later in 1796. Laplace's system depends on the calculus of Newton and its subsequent developments over a century and a half. Laplace did not ignore the well-developed mathematics of his day and try to develop his mechanics without it; rather, he used the relevant available tools' [15]. Is there any rationale for sending young scientists out into the research world with the vain hope that elementary mathematics will suffice for the investigation of complex regulatory networks? We return to Arendt's first point: Do 'we love our children enough not to…leave them to their own devices?'

This is not to argue that biologists or physicists need to be mathematicians. Albert Einstein was not a mathematician and had the assistance of a number of outstanding and great mathematicians, including David Hilbert. What Einstein had, however, was sufficient mathematical knowledge to give him the power of conceptualization. He writes, 'Experience, of course, remains the sole criterion for the serviceability of mathematical constructions for physics, but the truly creative principle resides in mathematics' [16]. The creative principle must lie in mathematics because scientific theory is conceived in mathematics. While a scientist need not be a mathematician, there is a threshold that must be crossed. Wiener clarifies the issue very well: 'The mathematician need not have the skill to conduct a physiological experiment, but he must have the skill to understand one, to criticize one, and to suggest one. The physiologist need not be able to prove a certain mathematical theorem, but he must be able to grasp its physiological significance and tell the mathematician for what he should look for' [13].

Referring to my 2012 book with M. L. Bittner, *Epistemology of the Cell* [17], Terrence McGarty writes, 'The authors place a stake in the ground to say what would be expected for those to work in the field, that the books by Loeve and Cramer be used as standard bearers!... Thus they set a high hurdle, but a necessary one for those to work in the field' [18]. Two points can be made regarding McGarty's comment. First, Michel Loeve published his *Probability Theory* in 1955 and Harald Cramer published his *Mathematical Methods in Statistics* in 1946. Surely more than half a century later, statisticians involved in scientific research should at least be at the level of these seminal books; however, perusal of the bioinformatics literature provides convincing evidence that a large number of recent Ph.D.s lack proficiency in the basics of their subject. The second point regarding McGarty's comment is that these books set a 'necessary' standard for medical research based on cell dynamics. Given that this standard is not being met, can we expect any more from the billions of dollars poured into biomedical research than the meager, and often meaningless or even erroneous, results now being published [19-24]?

The situation is far worse than statisticians not knowing fundamental theory. There is growing evidence that statisticians in major research groups apparently cannot even properly utilize rudimentary statistics. John Ioannidis writes, 'There is increasing concern that in modern research, false findings may be the majority or even the vast majority of published research claims.... Simulations show that for most study designs and settings, it is more likely for a research claim to be false than true' [19]. Mehta et al. write, 'Many papers aimed at the high dimensional biology community describe the development or application of statistical techniques. The validity of many of these is questionable, and a shared understanding about the epistemological foundations of the statistical methods themselves seems to be lacking' [22]. Alain Dupuy and Richard Simon, Chief of the Biometric Research Branch, Division of Cancer Treatment and Diagnosis, of the National Cancer Institute, state, 'Both the validity and the reproducibility of microarray-based clinical research have been challenged' [23]. Based on a detailed analysis of 42 studies published in 2004, Dupuy and Simon report that 21 (50%) of them contain at least

one of three basic flaws. The situation is actually much worse because, as will shortly be discussed, many use error estimation methods, that while properly computed, are not applicable under the experimental conditions in which they are being employed (Dupuy and Simon only consider an error estimate to be flawed if it is calculated incorrectly). Needless to say, the vast majority of erroneous research findings are favorable to the authors' claims. This phenomenon has been politely termed 'over-optimism' [24]. Anne-Laure Boulesteix writes, 'The difficulty to publish negative results obviously encourages authors to find something positive in their study by performing numerous analyses until one of them yields positive results by chance, i.e. to fish for significance' [24].

Lest one think that Ioannidis and Boulesteix, and others, are being overly pessimistic, according to a recent report regarding comments by Janet Woodcock, Director of the Center for Drug Evaluation and Research at the FDA, she has estimated that as much as 75% of published biomarker associations are not replicable. She states, 'This poses a huge challenge for industry in biomarker identification and diagnostics development' [25]. Much of the blame for these non-reproducible findings rests with a cavalier attitude towards the application of statistical methods [26].

There are various ways to fish for significance, but the sport often revolves around bogus error estimation: use an error estimation procedure with large variance so that when the analysis is repeated with different data analysis methods, it is highly probable that a good-looking (but phony) result will occur and then report that result. When trying to find sets of genes to classify a disease, two popular fishing methods are to try a number of different data sets [27] or try numerous methods to design the classifier [28]. In the first case, an error estimate is computed for each data set, and in the second, an error estimate is computed for each attempted classifier. Such fishing can be hard to detect unless the authors' reveal how many data sets and classification schemes they have tried.

One should not jump to the conclusion that fishing represents a deliberate attempt to publish fraudulent research; rather, the widespread use of error estimation techniques such as cross-validation makes it much more likely that it is simply a matter of inadequate education. Given that these estimates can be used by a sixth grader and appear in text books absent any proof that they should provide accurate results, and given ample evidence going back to 1978 showing that they should not be expected to produce accurate results when samples are small [29-34] as is very often the case in real-world situations, one can reasonably conclude that society is reaping the rewards of educational impoverishment. One can hardly imagine a statistician brought up on Cramer being so cavalier with statistical methods.

Epistemological implications

Science has a rich and varied history. Its epistemological ground has shifted from its totally empirical Egyptian-Mesopotamian beginnings through its integration with metaphysics with Aristotle to the beginnings of the experimental-mathematical duality with Francis Bacon and Galileo and onto complete freedom from conception within the ordinary categories of understanding in the twentieth century. A deep appreciation of this history allows a scientist to see his work in the stream of civilization and to avoid falling into the myriad of fruitless paths that have beguiled our predecessors.

For those who truly wish to be scientists, Einstein's following words penned in a letter should be taken to heart:

> I fully agree with you about the significance and educational value of methodology as well as history and philosophy of science. So many people today – and even professional scientists – seem to me like somebody who has seen thousands of trees but has never seen a forest. A knowledge of the historic and philosophical background gives that kind of independence from prejudices of his generation from which most scientists are suffering. This independence created by philosophical insight is – in my opinion – the mark of distinction between a mere artisan or specialist and a real seeker after truth [35].

It is natural for Einstein to refer to the 'prejudices of his generation'. As a young man he had broken free from the Newtonian world that had been regnant since Newton's *Principia*.

Three centuries before Einstein, Francis Bacon urged mankind to break free from prejudices of two millennia when in his *Novum Organum*, he called upon natural philosophers to go beyond haphazard observation of Nature to directed and purposeful observation:

> There remains simple experience which, if taken as it comes, is called accident; if sought for, experiment. But this kind of experience is no better than a broom without its band, as the saying is — a mere groping, as of men in the dark, that feel all round them for the chance of finding their way, when they had much better wait for daylight, or light a candle, and then go. But the true method of experience, on the contrary, first lights the candle, and then by means of the candle shows the way; commencing as it does with experience duly ordered and digested, not bungling or erratic, and from it educing axioms, and from established axioms again new experiments [36].

Reflecting on the rapid advance of post-Galilean science in comparison to the scanty achievements of the preceding 2,000 years, in the preface of the second edition of the *Critique of Pure Reason*, Kant writes,

> Reason must approach nature with the view, indeed, of receiving information from it, not, however, in the character of a pupil, who listens to all that his master chooses to tell him, but in that of a judge, who compels the witnesses to reply to those questions which he himself thinks fit to propose. To this single idea must the revolution be ascribed, by which, after groping in the dark for so many centuries, natural science was at length conducted into the path of certain progress [37].

As opposed to groping about amid unstructured observations, in accordance with his own mental constructs, the scientist imposes himself upon Nature by setting up conditions that constrain Nature to behave in ways that provide answers to targeted questions.

We hear the reverberation of Bacon and Kant in the words of statistician Douglas Montgomery: 'By the statistical design of experiments we refer to the process of planning the experiment so that appropriate data will be collected, which may be analyzed by statistical methods resulting in valid and objective conclusions. The statistical approach to experimental design is necessary if we wish to draw meaningful conclusions from the data' [38]. Statistical experimental design is a key part of the evolution of scientific thinking over the last four centuries. Moreover, the validity of scientific knowledge is characterized by the predictive capacity of a theory, and the predictive capacity must be evaluated using proper statistical theory. Groping and fishing are out of place here.

Contemporary efforts at groping and fishing go under the name of 'data mining'. Massive amounts of unstructured data are being collected via all sorts of expensive technology without any experimental design. The data set is said to be 'big' when it contains an enormous number of measurements. A so-called big data set often arises from measuring tens of thousands of variables with only a small number of replicates. Hence, from a statistical perspective, the data set is extremely small, because the number of replicates required to assure good inference typically grows faster than the number of variables being measured. Therefore, 100 replicates for 10,000 variables is a scanty data set. Once this supposedly big data set is obtained, it is 'mined' by various groping algorithms, usually going under the name of 'machine learning' and generally trying to discover patterns in the data. Clustering algorithms cluster data to group together data points that are similar relative to some criterion. Classification algorithms generate classifiers that will then be used to classify future observations. Of course, clustering algorithms form clusters and classification algorithms form classifiers. Whether these clusters and classifiers possess any scientific content is generally not seriously addressed. Some so-called 'validation index' may be computed for the clusters and some error estimate might be computed for the classifier, but these are rarely probabilistically justified. Clustering validation indices generally lack any substantiating theory and have been shown to often possess very little correlation with clustering error [39]. Simulation studies have shown small-sample error estimators to typically be inaccurate [29-33]. Moreover, only recently has there been any theoretical analysis of their accuracy [40-43], and this has only scratched the surface. Hence, the scientific literature is littered with thousands of null or erroneous papers referring back and forth to each other in some sort of nihilistic waltz.

This is not to say that data collected without experimental design cannot lead to major discoveries. Perhaps the most salient illustration in this regard is the heliocentric theory. Nicolaus Copernicus used data collected by Claudius Ptolemy about 1,400 years earlier to develop his heliocentric theory, and Johannes Kepler used data collected by Tycho Brahe, who by the way rejected the heliocentric theory, to develop his laws of planetary motion.

It is not that thinking about unplanned data cannot bear fruit; rather, greater progress can typically be achieved by having an idea and then obtaining data directly in response to questions emanating from that idea. Hans Reichenbach states the matter in terms relating to complexity when he writes, 'An experiment is a question addressed to Nature.... As long as we depend on the observation of occurrences not involving our assistance, the observable happenings are usually the product of so many factors that we cannot determine the contribution of each individual factor to the total result' [44]. What is the question? This is the question that a scientist must address in his role as a scientist. The more precise the question, the more likely he is to draw from Nature the desired knowledge. According to Arturo Rosenblueth and Norbert Wiener, 'An experiment is a question. A precise answer is seldom obtained if the question is not precise; indeed, foolish answers – i.e., inconsistent, discrepant or irrelevant experimental results – are usually indicative of a foolish question' [45]. Finally, let it be noted that Arendt is in full agreement with these assessments. In *The Concept of History: Ancient and Modern*, she states, 'The natural sciences turned toward the experiment, which, by directly interfering with nature, assured the development whose progress has ever since appeared to be limitless' [4].

Data mining and Copernicus share a lack of experimental design; however, in contradistinction to data mining, Copernicus thought about unplanned data and

changed the world, the key word being 'thought.' Copernicus was not an algorithm numerically crunching data until some stopping point, very often with no adequate theory of convergence or accuracy. Copernicus had a mind and ideas. William Barrett writes, 'The absence of an intelligent idea in the grasp of a problem cannot be redeemed by the elaborateness of the machinery one subsequently employs' [46]. Or as M. L. Bittner and I have asked, 'Does anyone really believe that data mining could produce the general theory of relativity' [17]?

Data mining represents a regression from the achievements of three and a half centuries of epistemological progress to a radical empiricism, in regard to which Reichenbach writes, 'A mere report of relations observed in the past cannot be called knowledge. If knowledge is to reveal objective relations of physical objects, it must include reliable predictions. A radical empiricism, therefore, denies the possibility of knowledge' [44]. A collection of measurements together with statements about the measurements is not scientific knowledge, unless those statements are tied to verifiable predictions concerning the phenomena to which the measurements pertain.

One only need read Siddhartha Mukherjee's *The Emperor of All Maladies: A Biography of Cancer* to be shocked by the suffering inflicted on patients by a radical empiricism. Concerning chemotherapy in the 1970s, he writes,

> The NCI meanwhile was turning into a factory of toxins. The influx of money from the National Cancer Act had potently stimulated the institute's drug-discovery program, which had grown into an even more gargantuan effort and was testing hundreds of thousands of chemicals each year to discover new cytotoxic drugs. The strategy of discovery was empirical – throwing chemicals at cancer cells in test tubes to identify cancer killers – but, by now, unabashedly and defiantly so...

> Chemicals thus came pouring out of the NCI's cauldrons, each one with a unique personality. There was Taxol, one gram purified from the bark of a hundred Pacific yew trees.... Adriamycin,...even at therapeutic doses, it could irreversibly damage the heart. Etoposide came from the fruit of the poisonous mayapple. Bleonmycin, which could scare lungs without warning, was an antibiotic derived from mold.

> The greatly expanded coffers of the NCI also stimulated enormous, expensive, multi-institutional trials, allowing academic centers to trot out ever more powerful permutations of cytotoxic drugs. Cancer hospitals, also

boosted by the NCI's grants, organized themselves into efficient and thrumming trial-running machines....

It was trial and error on a giant human scale.... In another particularly tenacious trial, known as the eight-in-one study, children with brain tumors were given eight drugs in a single day. Predictably, horrific complications ensued. Fifteen percent of the patients needed blood transfusions. Six percent were hospitalized with life-threatening infections. Fourteen percent of the children suffered kidney damage; three lost their hearing. One patient died of septic shock.... Most of the children in the eight-in-one trial died soon afterward, having only marginally responded to chemotherapy.

This pattern was repeated with tiresome regularity for many forms of cancer.... Like lunatic cartographers, chemotherapists frantically drew and redrew their strategies to annihilate cancer [47].

This, in the 1970s, after engineers had put men on the moon! What profound ideas lay behind 'throwing chemicals at cancer cells in test tubes?'

While ignorance of basic scientific method is a serious problem, it is necessary to probe further than simply methodological ignorance to get at the full depth of the educational problem. Science does not stand alone, disjoint from the rest of culture. Science takes place within the general human intellectual condition. Biology cannot be divorced from physics, nor can either be divorced from mathematics and philosophy. One's total intellectual repertoire affects the direction of inquiry: the richer one's knowledge, the more questions that can be asked. Schrodinger comments, 'A selection has been made on which the present structure of science is built. That selection must have been influenced by circumstances that are other than purely scientific' [48]. If one is intellectually and culturally impoverished, then one's set of possible selections will be small. Fundamental issues arise in the presence of deep conflicts or inadequacies within scientific theory. Serious study of historical antinomies and their resolutions enriches the mind, provides it with the perspective to see new fundamental issues, and trains it with the ability to think orthogonally to the attacks that have heretofore been thrown against the problem without success.

Can one truly appreciate the present without knowledge of the great past ruptures in human thinking? The Ptolemaic system assured man's position at the center of the universe until Copernicus put humans on a planet revolving around the sun. From Euclid through Kant, Euclidean geometry provided the framework for human sensibility before this worldview was shattered by the non-Euclidean geometry of Janos Bolyai and Nikolai Lobachevsky. From Aristotle into the eighteenth century,

philosophers and scientists accepted a causal world view, even with its bracketing by Galileo and Newton, until David Hume showed with relative ease that there was no logical or empirical support for cause in Nature and mankind was shaken from a comfortable causal, deterministic outlook and tossed into probabilistic insecurity. The Newtonian world of absolute space seemed all too obvious until Einstein shattered the obvious. And from Euclid into the twentieth century, man's hope for some safe harbor of consistency in his thinking was believed to lie in mathematics until in 1931 Kurt Godel proved that the consistency of any mathematical system rich enough to include whole number arithmetic (which is not much) cannot be proven by the ordinary basic principles of logic. Each of these ruptures was a shock to human understanding and the human position in the universe. All that came before was overturned, and a new human condition came into being. Study of these events, along with the historical and other scientific events surrounding them, forms the intellect. There have been many more disruptive events, perhaps of lesser cosmic import. Some of these pertain to one's individual scientific pursuits. These, too, need to be placed into historical context so that a student understands what has come before, what the situation is today, and the possibilities of where it will go tomorrow.

Arendt emphasizes that the proper role of education is to raise the child out of the world of children into the adult world. Admittedly, this is a painful process. Nonetheless, it is necessary if the child is to take his place in the adult world and contribute to the maintenance and furtherance of that world. Nothing is more disheartening than to discuss causality and be forced to listen to sophomoric arguments insisting on a causal science. You ask the bright young scientist if he has read Hume's *An Enquiry Concerning Human Understanding* or Kant's *Prolegomena to Any Future Metaphysics*, and there is a blank look. Something terribly important for a scientist (or, for that matter, any supposedly educated person) is missing. You are confronting an educational impoverishment that precludes the possibility of a serious discussion and has resulted in the person's thinking processes being centuries out of date.

Hume and Kant have transformed human reason, and a student must drink that transformation to the dregs or remain intellectually stunted. All that comes after, including twentieth century science, statistics, and engineering, would not be what it is without this transformation. In a few short pages, Hume rocks the scientific and philosophic worlds. Einstein comments, 'If one reads Hume's books, one is amazed that many and sometimes even highly esteemed philosophers after him have been able to write so much obscure stuff and even find grateful readers for it. Hume has permanently influenced the development of the best philosophers who came after him' [49]. William Barrett calls Kant the 'pivot' [50]. Barrett provides a diagram in which pre-Kantian rationalism and empiricism enter into Kant and outcome idealism, positivism, pragmatism, and existentialism into the post-Kantian world. There is much here to chew on for the scientist, who is often torn between rationalism and empiricism. After Kant, the phenomena, which are somehow constructed in the mind from sense data, are ever separated from the noumena, which are the things-in-themselves (actual Nature). How one perceives this separation tells much about one's scientific perspective. As Jose Ortega y Gasset says, 'Einstein needed to saturate himself with Kant and Mach before he could reach his own keen synthesis. Kant and Mach – the names are mere symbols of the enormous mass of philosophic and psychological thought which has influenced Einstein – have served to liberate the mind of the latter and leave the way open for his innovation' [51]. Building on the century and a half of philosophic and scientific development beginning with Bacon, Hume and Kant redefine adulthood. To intellectually become an adult, one must walk the path they trod.

When one ponders the massively complex regulatory machinery of the cell, its parallelism, non-linearity, feedback, redundancy, multiple time scales, and stochasticity, it helps immensely to have struggled through Hume's dismantling of causality and Kant's analysis of the categories of understanding. A scientific adult views this complex regulatory network in the light of stochastic systems theory, not through the eyes of a child who thinks it possible to gain knowledge of system dynamics by looking at some computer-generated visualization, as if scientific knowledge were somehow akin to gazing at colorful pictures. It is immensely beneficial to have suffered the anguish of maturation in undergraduate school and thereby freed the mind for the non-intuitive peculiarities of a stochastic world, a place in which one's intuition is constantly shocked. More than that, having broken free of the 'prejudices' of the mind and having recognized the mind's inability to describe Nature in terms of its ordinary physical categories, one learns that story telling has no place in science and that one must stick closely to rigorous mathematical and statistical analysis.

Playing children's games

Scientific epistemology has developed so as to formalize quantitative predictive relations between phenomena and to characterize the truth of those relations based upon the efficacy of predictions regarding those phenomena. Not only has this epistemology led to a grounding of scientific knowledge that overcomes the skepticism of Hume, it has also resulted in mankind's

ability to alter the course of Nature in ways beneficial to human existence.

Peering into a future ubiquitous with data mining and the oxymoronic data science, troubling questions arise. How many patients will be improperly treated based on gene- or protein-based diagnostic tests developed using statistically meaningless performance estimates? How many billions of dollars will be wasted on studies so poorly designed that they cannot possibly produce useful results? How many petabytes of unstructured data will be generated by academic centers to be groped through in mindless darkness? It all sounds utterly childish to those who have walked the epistemological path from Aristotle to Galileo to Newton to Hume to Kant to Einstein to Schrodinger. Oblivious to the demands of science, the educationally impoverished proponents of this latest incarnation of radical empiricism are playing children's games, except that these games will not pay off in candy, but in human suffering on a grand scale - even if it is only the result of the billions of wasted dollars that could have been spent on serious research.

What has brought our civilization to this point? Again we turn to Arendt: 'In education this responsibility for the world takes the form of authority.... Authority has been discarded by the adults, and this can mean only one thing: that the adults refuse to assume responsibility for the world into which they have brought the children' [2]. Irresponsibility has led to the impoverishment of education and a consequent loss of scientific capability. One might laugh at the ignorance that Mukherjee repeatedly highlights, but the suffering of innocent patients at the hands of those whose reasoning lies somewhere in the fifteenth century is not a laughing matter. More recently, the world witnessed a bizarre fiasco in the Gulf of Mexico, where we were assured that the 'best' engineers were on hand to stop an oil spill. These 'best' engineers demonstrated their fifteenth century capability by pouring rocks into a hole and surrounding floating oil with poles dragged by ships, something that Odysseus might have done. The ludicrousness of the whole operation can easily be seen by comparing this woeful episode with the engineering operations run by Robert Oppenheimer and Werner von Braun.

The plight of science is not a scientific problem. It lies outside of science, in a general collapse of authority. Ortega y Gasset places the matter in the wider context:

> Whoever wishes to have ideas must first prepare himself to desire truth and to accept the rules of the game imposed by it. It is no use speaking of ideas when there is no acceptance of a higher authority to regulate them, a series of standards to which it is possible to appeal in a discussion. These standards are the principles on which culture rests. I am not

concerned with the form they take. What I affirm is that there is no culture where there are no standards to which our fellow-men can have recourse.... Barbarism is the absence of standards to which appeal can be made [51].

The scientific epistemology posits standards developed over centuries to ground knowledge with a functional, phenomenal, and inter-subjective concept of truth. The theory can be understood by anyone possessing the requisite mathematical knowledge. The experimental protocols can be understood by anyone possessing knowledge of the experimental apparatus. The operational definitions, corresponding statistics, and validation criteria take logical or mathematical form and again can be understood by anyone possessing the requisite knowledge. The overall theory, mathematical and experimental, is therefore inter-subjective. This is not to say that two people cannot disagree on whether to accept a theory. That will depend on their validation criteria. One may impose stronger, or different, validation criteria than the other. There is inter-subjectivity because each understands the other's criteria. This is not to say that the truth of the theory is universally applicable. On the contrary, it is constrained by the context in which the relations (equations) of the theory are purported to hold. Outside that context, the relations might fail, so that the context in which the operational definitions can be applied must be specified. All of this provides the standards by which the higher authority is constituted. But that authority must be manifested by human beings, and these must be sufficiently educated so that they can make judgments in accordance with that authority. If educators fail in their responsibility to educate, then the higher authority becomes vacuous because in practice there will be no one, or an insufficient number, to exercise it.

If educators fail to educate, then civilization, not just science, is at grave risk. Will Durant, who spent his life studying the rise and fall of civilizations, puts the matter starkly: 'For civilization is not something inborn or imperishable; it must be acquired anew by every generation, and any serious interruption in its financing or its transmission may bring it to an end. Man differs from the beast only by education, which may be defined as the technique of transmitting civilization' [52]. And what is the relationship of science to civilization? Perhaps this question can best be answered by noting that Will and Ariel Durant list three books as 'the basic events in the history of modern Europe': *Philosophiae Naturalis Principia Mathematica* (Isaac Newton), *De Revolutionibus Orbium Coelestium* (Nicolaus Copernicus), and *The Origin of the Species* (Charles Darwin) [53]. For Will and Ariel Durant, these books are not simply the basic events of science; they are the fundamental events that have driven the overall philosophic, religious, and political evolution of Western Civilization - more profound than Martin Luther nailing his 95 theses to the door of the Castle Church in Wittenberg, than Renes Descartes' systematic doubt, than Jean-Jacques Rousseau and the French Revolution. To appreciate the monumental roles of Copernicus, Newton, and Darwin, one must be able to place and understand them in the historic stream of philosophic thought. To bring students into the university and leave them ignorant of Plato, Aristotle, Bacon, Hume, Kant, et al. is to deny them a meaningful education. It is to leave them outside the course of civilization and to stunt their growth into intellectual adulthood. In Arendt's words, it is to 'strike from their hands their chance of undertaking something new, something unforeseen by us'. And the horrific cost will be borne by future generations.

Once lost or seriously diminished, modern science will not be easily resuscitated. It is a unique and precious gift to our civilization, one whose continuance is not guaranteed: Ortega y Gasset recognizes its tenuous character when he writes,

> Has any thought been given to the number of things that must remain active in men's souls in order that there may still continue to be 'men of science' in real truth?... Experimental science is one of the most unlikely products of history. Seers, priests, warriors and shepherds have abounded in all times and places. But this fauna of experimental man apparently requires for its production a combination of circumstances more exceptional than those that engender the unicorn. Such a bare, sober fact should make us reflect on the supervolatile, evaporative character of scientific inspiration [51].

Whatever 'must remain active in men's souls', to a great extent it must come from educators who recognize that it is not their duty to make children happy; rather, it is their duty to transform children into adults.

Conclusions

Transforming children into adults - this has been the theme of this essay and it is also the theme of Arendt's *The Crisis in Education*, in which she notes, 'Childhood is a temporary stage, a preparation for adulthood'. This essay is not about lack of innate intelligence or a lack of desire to accomplish great things. A student may enter the academy with both a brilliant mind and a longing to join the community that has driven the great scientific enterprise, but if the academy shirks its responsibility and impoverishes that student, then that brilliant and ambitious mind will not come close to achieving its true potential. The manner in which human beings scientifically perceive the world has gone through at least four radically transforming periods that can be marked by certain names: (1) Plato and Aristotle, (2) Galileo and Newton, (3) Hume and Kant, and (4) Einstein and Heisenberg. Here we are not talking about radical theories, but rather radical transformations of mind. In that sense, these are maturing transformations, in each case the notion of intellectual adulthood being redefined. The young student enters the academy as a wet-behind-the-ears babe and must be transformed through these stages, perhaps kicking and screaming, into an adult who appreciates the road humans have traveled in two and half millennia to achieve the current state of maturity. Only then does the aspiring scientist appreciate the limitations of science and the mathematical, logical, and experimental rigor necessary to achieve scientific truth.

Competing interests

The author declares that he has no competing interests.

References

1. H Arendt, *Between Future and Past* (Penguin, New York, 1977)
2. H Arendt, *The crisis in education, in Between Future and Past* (Penguin, New York, 1977)
3. H Arendt, *The conquest of space and the stature of man, in Between Future and Past* (Penguin, New York, 1977)
4. H Arendt, *The concept of history: ancient and modern, in Between Future and Past* (Penguin, New York, 1977)
5. E Schrodinger, *Between Future and Past* (Penguin, New York, 1977)
6. JH Jeans, *The Mysterious Universe* (Cambridge University Press, Cambridge, 1930)
7. N Bohr, *Between Future and Past* (Penguin, New York, 1977)
8. R Feynman, *QED: The Strange Theory of Light and Matter* (Princeton University Press, Princeton, 1985)
9. M Kline, *Mathematics and the Search for Knowledge* (Oxford University Press, Oxford, 1985)
10. G Galilei, *Dialogues Concerning Two New Sciences* (Dover, New York, 1954). originally published 1638
11. I Newton, Mathematical principles of natural philosophy, in *in Great Books of the Western World*, ed. by RM Hutchins, MJ Adler. vol. 34 (Encyclopedia Britannica, Chicago, 1952). originally published 1687
12. I Kant, *Prolegomena to Any Future Metaphysics* (Hackett Publishing Company, Indianapolis, 1977). Originally published 1783
13. N Wiener, *Cybernetics or Control and Communication in the Animal and Machine* (MIT Press, Cambridge, 1948)
14. CH Waddington, *How Animals Develop* (Allen & Unwin, London, 1935)
15. ML Bittner, ER Dougherty, Newton, Laplace, and the epistemology of systems biology. Cancer. Informat. **5**, 185–190 (2012). doi:10.4137/CIN.S10630, 2012
16. A Einstein, *Herbert Spencer Lecture* (Oxford University Press, New York, 1933)
17. ER Dougherty, ML Bittner, *Epistemology of the Cell: A Systems Perspective on Biological Knowledge (IEEE Press Series on Biomedical Engineering* (John Wiley, New York, 2011)
18. TP McGarty, *Epistemology of Cancer Genomic Systems* (White Paper No. 84, The Telmarc Group, 2012)
19. JPA Ioannidis, Why most published research findings are false. PLoS. Med. **2**(8), e124 (2005). doi:10.1371/journal.pmed.0020124
20. HM Colhoun, PM McKeigue, G Smith Davey, Problems of reporting genetic associations with complex outcomes. Lancet. **361**, 865–872 (2003)
21. ER Dougherty, On the epistemological crisis in genomics. Curr. Genomics. **9**(2), 69–79 (2008)
22. T Mehta, T Murat, DB Allison, Towards sound epistemological foundations of statistical methods for high-dimensional biology. Nat. Genet. **36**, 943–947 (2004)
23. A Dupuy, RM Simon, Critical review of published microarray studies for cancer outcome and guidelines on statistical analysis and reporting. J. Natl. Canc. Inst. **99**, 147–157 (2007)
24. AL Boulesteix, Over-optimism in bioinformatics research. Bioinformatics. **26**(3), 437–439 (2010)
25. T Ray, FDA's Woodcock says personalized drug development entering 'long Slog' phase. Pharmacogenomics. Rep. (2011)
26. ER Dougherty, Prudence, risk, and reproducibility in biomarker discovery. Bioessays. **34**(4), 277–279 (2012)
27. MR Yousefi, J Hua, C Sima, ER Dougherty, Reporting bias when using real data sets to analyze classification performance. Bioinformatics. **26**(1), 68–76 (2010)
28. MR Yousefi, J Hua, ER Dougherty, Multiple-rule bias in the comparison of classification rules. Bioinformatics. **27**((1), 2), 1675–1683 (2011)
29. N Glick, Additive estimators for probabilities of correct classification. Pattern. Recogn. **10**, 211–222 (1978)
30. UM Braga-Neto, ER Dougherty, Is cross-validation valid for small-sample microarray classification. Bioinformatics. **20**(3), 374–380 (2004)
31. B Hanczar, J Hua, ER Dougherty, Decorrelation of the true and estimated classifier errors in high-dimensional settings. EURASIP. J. Bioinforma. Syst. Biol. **38473**(12), 2007 (2007)
32. B Hanczar, J Hua, C Sima, J Weinstein, ML Bittner, ER Dougherty, Small-sample precision of ROC-related estimates. Bioinformatics. **26**(6), 822–830 (2010)
33. ER Dougherty, C Sima, J Hua, B Hanczar, UM Braga-Neto, Performance of error estimators for classification. Curr. Bioinforma. **5**(1), 53–67 (2010)
34. UM Braga-Neto, ER Dougherty, Exact correlation between actual and estimated errors in discrete classification. Pattern. Recogn. Lett. **31**, 407–413 (2010)
35. A Einstein, *In a letter to Robert A* (Thornton, December, 1944)
36. F Bacon, Novum organum, in *Great Books of the Western World, 35*, ed. by RM Hutchins, MJ Adler (Encyclopedia Britannica, Chicago, 1952). originally published 1620
37. I Kant, Critique of pure reason, in *Great Books of the Western World, 42*, ed. by RM Hutchins, MJ Adler, 2nd edn. (Encyclopedia Britannica, Chicago, 1952). originally published 1787
38. DC Montgomery, *Design and Analysis of Experiments* (John Wiley, New York, 1976)
39. M Brun, C Sima, J Hua, J Lowey, B Carroll, E Suh, ER Dougherty, Model-based evaluation of clustering validation measures. Pattern. Recogn. **40**(3), 807–824 (2007)
40. U Braga-Neto, ER Dougherty, Exact performance of error estimators for discrete classifiers. Pattern. Recogn. **38**(11), 1799–1814 (2005)
41. A Zollanvari, UM Braga-Neto, ER Dougherty, On the joint sampling distribution between the actual classification error and the resubstitution and leave-one-out error estimators for linear classifiers. IEEE. Trans. Inf. Theory **56**(2), 784–804 (2010)
42. A Zollanvari, UM Braga-Neto, ER Dougherty, Analytic study of performance of error estimators for linear discriminant analysis. IEEE. Trans. Signal Process. **59**(9), 4238–4255 (2011)
43. LA Dalton, ER Dougherty, Exact MSE performance of the Bayesian MMSE estimator for classification error – part I: representation. IEEE. Trans. Signal Process. **60**(5), 2575–2587 (2012)
44. H Reichenbach, *The Rise of Scientific Philosophy* (University of California Press, Berkeley, 1971)
45. A Rosenblueth, N Wiener, The role of models in science. Philos. Sci. **12**, 316–321 (1945)
46. W Barrett, *The Illusion of Technique* (Anchor Books, New York, 1979)
47. S Mukherjee, *The Emperor of All Maladies: A Biography of Cancer* (Scribner, New York, 2010)
48. E Schrodinger, *Science Theory and Man* (Dover, New York, 1957)
49. A Einstein, *Einstein's Reply to criticisms, in Albert Einstein: Philosopher-Scientist.* Library of Living Philosophers Series (Cambridge University Press, Cambridge, 1949)
50. W Barrett, *Death of the Soul: From Descartes to the Computer* (Doubleday, New York, 1986)
51. Y Ortega, J Gasset, *The Revolt of the Masses* (W. W. Norton and Company, New York, 1932)
52. W Durant, *The Story of Civilization: Part I, Our Oriental Heritage* (Simon and Schuster, New York, 1954)
53. W Durant, A Durant, *The Story of Civilization: Part VIII: The Age of Louis XI* (Simon and Schuster, New York, 1963)

15

Tracking of time-varying genomic regulatory networks with a LASSO-Kalman smoother

Jehandad Khan[1], Nidhal Bouaynaya[1*] and Hassan M Fathallah-Shaykh[2,3,4,5,6]

Abstract

It is widely accepted that cellular requirements and environmental conditions dictate the architecture of genetic regulatory networks. Nonetheless, the status quo in regulatory network modeling and analysis assumes an invariant network topology over time. In this paper, we refocus on a dynamic perspective of genetic networks, one that can uncover substantial topological changes in network structure during biological processes such as developmental growth. We propose a novel outlook on the inference of time-varying genetic networks, from a limited number of noisy observations, by formulating the network estimation as a target tracking problem. We overcome the limited number of observations (small n large p problem) by performing tracking in a compressed domain. Assuming linear dynamics, we derive the LASSO-Kalman smoother, which recursively computes the minimum mean-square sparse estimate of the network connectivity at each time point. The LASSO operator, motivated by the sparsity of the genetic regulatory networks, allows simultaneous signal recovery and compression, thereby reducing the amount of required observations. The smoothing improves the estimation by incorporating all observations. We track the time-varying networks during the life cycle of the *Drosophila melanogaster*. The recovered networks show that few genes are permanent, whereas most are transient, acting only during specific developmental phases of the organism.

1 Introduction

1.1 Motivation

A major challenge in systems biology today is to understand the behaviors of living cells from the dynamics of complex genomic regulatory networks. It is no more possible to understand the cellular function from an informational point of view without unraveling the underlying regulatory networks than to understand protein binding without knowing the protein synthesis process. The advances in experimental technology have sparked the development of genomic network inference methods, also called *reverse engineering* of genomic networks. Most popular methods include (probabilistic) Boolean networks [1,2], (dynamic) Bayesian networks [3-5], information theoretic approaches [6-9], and differential equation models [10-12]. A comparative study is compiled in [13]. The Dialogue on Reverse Engineering Assessment and Methods (DREAM) project, which built a blind framework for performance assessment of methods for gene network inference, showed that there is no single inference method that performs optimally across all data sets. In contrast, integration of predictions from multiple inference methods shows robust and high performance across diverse data sets [14].

These methods, however, estimate one single network from the available data, independently of the cellular 'themes' or environmental conditions under which the measurements were collected. In signal processing, it is senseless to find the Fourier spectrum of a non-stationary time series [15]. Similarly, time-dependent genetic data from dynamic biological processes such as cancer progression, therapeutic responses, and developmental processes cannot be used to describe a unique time-invariant or static network [16,17]. Inter- and intracellular spatial cues affect the course of events in these processes by rewiring the connectivity between the molecules to respond to specific cellular requirements, e.g., going through the successive morphological stages during development. Inferring a unique static network from a time-dependent dynamic biological process results in an 'average' network that cannot reveal the regime-specific and key transient interactions that cause cell biological changes to occur. For a long time, it has been clear that

*Correspondence: bouaynaya@rowan.edu
[1]Department of Electrical and Computer Engineering, Rowan University, 201 Mullica Hill Rd, Glassboro, NJ 08028, USA
Full list of author information is available at the end of the article

the evolution of the cell function occurs by change in the genomic program of the cell, and it is now clear that we need to consider this in terms of change in regulatory networks [16,17].

1.2 Related work

While there is a rich literature on modeling static or time-invariant networks, much less has been done towards inference and learning techniques for recovering topologically rewiring networks. In 2004, Luscombe et al. made the earliest attempt to unravel topological changes in genetic networks during a temporal cellular process or in response to diverse stimuli [17]. They showed that under different cellular conditions, transcription factors, in a genomic regulatory network of *Saccharomyces cerevisiae*, alter their interactions to varying degrees, thereby rewiring the network. Their method, however, is still based on a static representation of known regulatory interactions. To get a dynamic perspective, they integrated gene expression data for five conditions: cell cycle, sporulation, diauxic shift, DAN damage, and stress response. From these data, they traced paths in the regulatory network that are active in each condition using a trace-back algorithm [17].

The main challenge facing the community in the inference of time-varying genomic networks is the unavailability of multiple measurements of the networks or multiple observations at every instant t. Usually, one or at most a few observations are available at each instant. This leads to the 'large p small n' problem, where the number of unknowns is smaller than the number of available observations. The problem may seem ill defined because no unique solution exists. However, we will show that this hurdle can be circumvented by using prior information.

One way to ameliorate this data scarcity problem is to presegment the time series into stationary epochs and infer a static network for each epoch separately [18,18-23]. The segmentation of the time series into stationary pieces can be achieved using several methods including estimation of the posterior distribution of the change points [19], HMMs [20], clustering [18], detecting geometric structures transformed from time series [21], and MCMC sampling algorithm to learn the times of non-stationarities (transition times) [22,23]. The main problem with the segmentation approach for estimating time-varying gene networks is the limited number of time points available in each stationary segment, which is a subset of the already limited data. Since the time-invariant networks are inferred in each segment using only the data points within that segment and disregarding the rest of the data, the resulting networks are limited in terms of their temporal resolution and statistical power.

A semi-flexible model based on a piecewise homogeneous dynamic Bayesian network, where the network structure in each segment shares information with adjacent segments, was proposed in [24]. This setting allows the network to vary gradually through segments. However, some information is lost by not considering the entire data samples for the piecewise inference. A more flexible model of time-varying Bayesian networks based on a non-parametric Bayesian method for regression was recently proposed in [25]. The non-parametric regression is expected to enable capturing of non-linear dynamics among genes [24]. However, a full-scale study of a time-varying system was lacking; the approach was only tested on an 11-gene *Drosophila melanogaster* network.

Full resolution techniques, which allow a time-specific network topology to be inferred from samples measured over the entire time series, rely on model-based approaches [26,27]. However, these methods learn the structure (or skeleton) of the network, but not the detailed strength of the interactions between the nodes. Dynamic Bayesian networks (DBNs) have been extended to the time-varying case [28-31]. Among the earliest models is the time-varying autoregressive (TVAR) model [29], which describes nonstationary linear dynamic systems with continuously changing linear coefficients. The regression parameters are estimated recursively using a normalized least-squares algorithm. In time-varying DBNs (TVDBN), the time-varying structure and parameters of the networks are treated as additional hidden nodes in the graph model [28].

In summary, the current state-of-the-art in time-varying network inference relies on either chopping the time-series sequence into homogeneous subsequences [18-23,32-35] (concatenation of static networks) or extending graphical models to the time-varying case [28-31] (time modulation of static networks).

1.3 Proposed work and contributions

In this paper, we propose a novel formulation of the inference of time-varying genomic regulatory networks as a tracking problem, where the target is a set of incoming edges for a given gene. We show that the tracking can be performed in parallel: there are p independent trackers, one for each gene in the network, thus avoiding the curse of dimensionality problem and reducing the computation time. Assuming linear dynamics, we use a constrained and smoothed Kalman filter to track the network connections over time. At each time instant, the connections are characterized by their strength and sign, i.e., stimulative or inhibitive. The sparsity constraint allows simultaneous signal recovery and compression, thereby reducing the amount of required observations. The smoothing improves the estimation by incorporating all observations for each smoothed estimate. The paper is organized as follows: In Section 2, we formulate the network inference problem in a state-space framework, where the target state, at each time point, is the network connectivity vector. Assuming linear dynamics of gene expressions, we further show that the model can be decomposed into p independent linear models, p being the number of genes. Section 3 derives the LASSO-Kalman smoother, which renders the optimal network connectivity at each time point. The performance of the algorithm is assessed using synthetic data in Section 4. The LASSO-Kalman smoother is subsequently used to recover the time-varying networks of the *D. melanogaster* during the time course of its development spanning the embryonic, larval, pupal, and adulthood periods.

2   The state-space model

Static gene networks have been modeled using a standard state-space representation, where the state x_k represents the gene expression values at a particular time k, and the microarray data y_k constitutes the set of noisy observations [36,37]. A naive approach to tackle the time-varying inference problem is to generalize this representation of time-invariant networks and augment the gene profile state vector by the network parameters at all time instants. This approach, however, will result in a very poor estimate due to the large number of unknown parameters. Instead, we propose to re-formulate the state-space model as a function of the time-varying connections or parameters rather than the gene expression values. In order to do so, we need to model the time evolution of the parameters using, for instance, prior knowledge about the biological process. Denoting by a_k the network parameters to be estimated, the state-space model of the time-varying network parameters can be written as

$$a(k + 1) = f_k(a(k)) + w(k), \quad (1)$$

$$y(k) = g_k(a(k)) + v(k). \quad (2)$$

The function f_k models the dynamical evolution of the network parameters, e.g., smooth evolution or abrupt changes across time. The observation function g_k characterizes the regulatory relationships among the genes and can be, for instance, derived from a differential equation model of gene expression (see Equation 8). In particular, observe that the state-space model in (1) to (2) does not incorporate the 'true' gene expression values, which have to be estimated and subsequently discarded. It only includes the measured gene expression values with an appropriate measurement noise term.

2.1   The observation model

We model the concentrations of mRNAs, proteins, and other molecules using a time-varying ordinary differential equation (ODE). More specifically, the concentration of each molecule is modeled as a linear function of the concentrations of the other components in the system. The

time-dependent coefficients of the linear ODE capture the rewiring structure of the network. We have

$$\dot{x}_i(t) = -\lambda_i(t)x_i(t) + \sum_{j=1}^{p} w_{ij}(t)x_j(t) + b_i u(t) + v_i(t), \quad (3)$$

where $i = 1, \cdots, p$, p being the number of genes, $x_i(t)$ is the expression level of gene i at time t, $\dot{x}_i(t)$ is the rate of change of expression of gene i at time t, λ_i is the self degradation rate, $w_{ij}(t)$ represents the time-varying influence of gene j on gene i, b_i is the effect of the external perturbation $u(t)$ on gene i, and $v_i(t)$ models the measurement and biological noise. The goal is to infer the time-varying gene interactions $\lambda_i(t), \{w_{ij}(t)\}_{i,j=1}^{p}$, given a limited number of measurements $n < p$.

To simplify the notation, we absorb the self-degradation rate $\lambda_i(t)$ into the interaction parameters by letting $a_{ij}(t) = w_{ij}(t) - \lambda_i(t)\delta_{ij}$, where δ_{ij} is the Kronecker delta function. The external perturbation is assumed to be known. The model in (3) can be simplified by introducing a new variable

$$y_i(t) = \dot{x}_i(t) - b_i u(t). \quad (4)$$

The discrete-time equivalent of (3) can, therefore, be expressed as

$$y_i(k) = \sum_{j=1}^{p} a_{ij}(k)x_j(k) + v_i(k), \ i = 1, \cdots, p, \ k = 1, \ldots, n. \quad (5)$$

Writing (5) in matrix form, we obtain

$$\mathbf{y}(k) = A(k)\,\mathbf{x}(k) + \mathbf{v}(k), \quad (6)$$

where $\mathbf{y}(k) = [y_1(k), \ldots, y_p(k)]^T$, $A(k) = \{a_{ij}(k)\}$ is the matrix of time-dependent interactions, $\mathbf{x}(k) = [x_1(k), \ldots x_p(k)]^T$, and $\mathbf{v}(k) = [v_1(k), \ldots, v_p(k)]^T$.

Let $1 \leq m_k < p$ be the number of available observations at time k. Taking into account all m_k observations, Equation 6 becomes

$$\mathbf{Y}(k) = A(k)\,\mathbf{X}(k) + \mathbf{V}(k), \quad (7)$$

where $Y(k), X(k)$, and $V(k) \in \mathbb{R}^{p \times m_k}$ with the m_k observations ordered in the columns of the corresponding matrices.

The linear model in Equation 7 can be decomposed into p independent linear models as follows:

$$\mathbf{y}_i^t(k) = \mathbf{a}_i^t(k)\mathbf{X}(k) + \mathbf{v}_i^t(k), \quad (8)$$

where $\mathbf{y}_i^t(k), \mathbf{a}_i^t(k)$, and $\mathbf{v}_i^t(k)$ are the ith rows of $\mathbf{Y}(k), A(k)$, and $V(k)$, respectively. In particular, the vector $\mathbf{a}_i(k)$ represents the set of incoming edges to gene i at time k. Equation 8 represents the observation equation for gene i.

2.2 The linear state-space model

The state equation models the dynamics of the state vector $a_i(k)$ given a priori knowledge of the system. In this work, we assume a random walk model of the network parameters. The random walk model is chosen for two reasons. First, it reflects a flat prior or a lack of a priori knowledge. Second, it leads to a smooth evolution of the state vector over time (if the variance of the random walk is not very high). The state space model of the incoming edges for gene i is, therefore, given by

$$\begin{cases} a_i(k+1) = a_i(k) + w_i(k) \\ y_i(k) = X^t(k)a_i(k) + v_i(k), \end{cases} \quad (9)$$

where $i = 1, \cdots, p$, and $w_i(k)$ and $v_i(k)$ are, respectively, the process noise and the observation noise, assumed to be zero mean Gaussian noise processes with known covariance matrices, $Q(k)$ and $R(k)$, respectively. In addition, the process and observation noises are assumed to be uncorrelated with each other and with the state vector $a_i(k)$. In particular, we have p independent state-space models of the form (9) for $i = 1, \cdots, p$. Thus, the connectivity matrix A can be recovered by simultaneous recovery of its rows. Another important advantage of the representation in (9) is that the state vector $a_i(k)$ has dimension p (the number of genes in the network) rather than p^2 (the number of possible connections in the network), thus avoiding the curse of dimensionality problem. For instance, in a network of 100 genes, the state vector will have dimension 100 instead of 10,000!. Though the number of genes p can be large, we show in simulations that the performance of the Kalman tracker is unchanged for p as large as 5,000 genes by using efficient matrix decompositions to find the numerical inverse of matrices of size p. A graphical representation of the parallel architecture of the tracker is shown in Figure 1.

It is well known that the minimum mean square estimator, which minimizes $E[\|a(k) - \hat{a}(k)\|_2^2]$, can be obtained using the Kalman filter if the system is observable. If the system is unobservable, then the classical Kalman filter cannot recover the optimal estimate. In particular, it seems hopeless to recover $a_i(k) \in \mathbb{R}^p$ in (9) from an under-determined system where $m_k < p$. Fortunately, this problem can be circumvented by taking into account the fact that $a_i(k)$ is sparse. Genomic regulatory networks are known to be sparse: each gene is governed by only a small number of the genes in the network [11].

3 The LASSO-Kalman smoother

3.1 Sparse signal recovery

Recent studies [38,39] have shown that sparse signals can be exactly recovered from an under-determined system of linear equations by solving the optimization problem

$$\min \|\hat{z}\|_0 \text{ s.t. } \|y - H\hat{z}\|_2^2 \le \epsilon, \quad (10)$$

for a sufficiently small ϵ and where the l_0-norm, $\|z\|_0$, denotes the support of z or the number of non-zero elements in z. The optimization problem in (10) can be extended to the stochastic case as follows:

$$\min \|\hat{z}\|_0 \text{ s.t. } E_{z|y}[\|z - \hat{z}\|_2^2] \le \epsilon. \quad (11)$$

Unfortunately, the above optimization problem is, in general, NP-hard. However, it has been shown that if the observation matrix H obeys the restricted isometry property (RIP), then the solution of the combinatorial problem (10) can be recovered by solving instead the convex optimization problem

$$\min \|\hat{z}\|_1 \text{ s.t. } \|y - H\hat{z}\|_2^2 \le \epsilon. \quad (12)$$

This is a fundamental result in the emerging theory of *compressed sensing*(CS) [38,39]. CS reconstructs large dimensional signals from a small number of measurements, as long as the original signal is sparse or admits a sparse representation in a certain basis. Compressed sensing has been implemented in many applications including digital tomography [38], wireless communication [40], image processing [41], and camera design [42]. For a further review of CS, the reader can refer to [38,39].

Inspired by the compressed sensing approach given that genomic regulatory networks are sparse, we formulate a constrained Kalman objective

$$\min_{\hat{z}} E_{z|y}\left[\|z - \hat{z}\|_2^2\right] \text{ s.t. } \|\hat{z}\|_1 \le \epsilon. \quad (13)$$

The constrained Kalman objective in (13) can be seen as the regularized version of least squares known as least absolute shrinkage and selection operator (LASSO) [43], which uses the l_1 constraint to prefer solutions with fewer non-zero parameter values, effectively reducing the number of variables upon which the given solution is dependent. For this reason, the LASSO and its variants are fundamental to the theory of compressed sensing.

3.2 Constrained Kalman filtering

Constrained Kalman filtering has been mainly investigated in the case of linear equality constraints of the form $Dx = d$, where D is a known matrix and d is a known vector [44]. The most straightforward method to handle linear equality constraints is to reduce the system model parametrization [45]. This approach, however, can only be used for linear equality constraints and cannot be used for inequality constraints (i.e., constraints of the form $Dx \le d$). Another approach is to treat the state constraints as perfect measurements or pseudo-observations (i.e., no measurement noise) [46]. The perfect measurement technique applies only to equality constraints as it augments the measurement equation with the constraints. The third approach is to project the standard

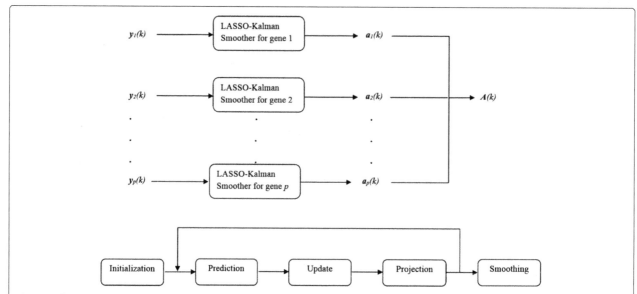

Figure 1 The LASSO-Kalman smoother tracker. Top row: parallel architecture of the tracker. The tracking is performed for each gene separately to find its incoming edges. The connectivity matrix $\mathbf{A}(k) = [\mathbf{a}_1^t; \cdots ; \mathbf{a}_p^t]$. Bottom row: the LASSO-Kalman smoother: the prior estimate is predicted to give $\mathbf{a}_{k|k-1}$. The filter is updated with the observations to give the unconstrained estimate $\mathbf{a}_{k|k}$. The projection operator projects this estimate to enforce the constraint. This procedure is repeated for all time steps $k = 1, \cdots , n$. Then, a forward-backward smoother is applied to reduce the covariance of the estimate and lead to the final constrained and smoothed estimate.

(unconstrained) Kalman filter estimate onto the constraint surface [44]. Though non-linear constraints can be linearized and then treated as perfect observations, linearization errors can prevent the estimate from converging to the true value. Non-linear constraints are, thus, much harder to handle than linear constraints because they embody two sources of errors: truncation errors and base point errors [47,48]. Truncation errors arise from the lower order Taylor series approximation of the constraint, whereas base point errors are due to the fact that the filter linearizes around the estimated value of the state rather than the true value. In order to deal with these errors, iterative steps were deemed necessary to improve the convergence towards the true state and better enforce the constraint [47-49]. The number of necessary iterations is a tradeoff between estimation accuracy and computational complexity.

In this work, the non-linear constraint is the l_1-norm of the state vector. We adopt the projection approach, which projects the unconstrained Kalman estimate at each step onto the set of sparse vectors, as defined by the constraint in (13). Denoting by $\tilde{a}$ the unconstrained Kalman estimate, the constrained estimated, $\hat{a}$, is then obtained by solving the following (convex) LASSO optimization:

$$\hat{a} = \underset{a}{\arg\min} \|\tilde{a} - a\|_2^2 + \lambda\|a\|_1, \qquad (14)$$

where λ is a parameter controlling the tradeoff between the residual error and the sparsity. This approach is

motivated by two reasons: First, we found through extensive simulations that the projection approach leads to more accurate estimates than the iterative pseudo-measurement techniques (PM) in [47-49]. Additionally, the sparsity constraint is controlled by only one parameter, namely λ, whereas in PM, the number of iterations is a second parameter that needs to be properly tuned and presents a tradeoff between accuracy and computational time. Second, for large-scale genomic regulatory networks (few thousands of genes), the iterative PM approaches render the constrained Kalman tracking problem computationally prohibitive.

3.3   The LASSO-Kalman smoother
The Kalman filter is causal, i.e., the optimal estimate at time k depends only on past observations $\{y(i), i \leq k$. In the case of genomic measurements, all observations are recorded and available for post-processing. By using all available measurements, the covariance of the optimal estimate can be reduced, thus improving the accuracy. This is achieved by smoothing the Kalman filter using a forward-backward approach [44]. The forward-backward approach obtains two estimates of $a(j)$. The first estimate, $\hat{a}_f$, is based on the standard Kalman filter that operates from $k = 1$ to $k = j$. The second estimate, $\hat{a}_b$, is based on a Kalman filter that runs backward in time from $k = n$ back to $k = j$. The forward-backward approach combines the two estimates to form an optimal smoothed estimate. The LASSO-Kalman smoother algorithm is summarized below (see also Figure 1).

Algorithm 1 The LASSO-Kalman smoother algorithm

1. *Initialization*: Initialize the state vector $a_{0|0} = \hat{a}$ and state estimation error covariance $V_{0|0} = 0$.

2. *Constrained Kalman Filtering*: For $k = 1, \cdots, n$, do

   - *Prediction*:

   $$a_{k|k-1} = a_{k-1|k-1} \qquad (15)$$

   $$V_{k|k-1} = V_{k-1|k-1} + Q_k \qquad (16)$$

   - *Filtering*:

   $$K_k = V_{k|k-1} X_k (X_k^t V_{k|k-1} H_k^t + R_k)^{-1}, \ (17)$$

   $$a_{k|k} = a_{k|k-1} + K_k(y_k - X_k^t a_{k|k-1}), \qquad (18)$$

   $$V_{k|k} = (I - K_k X_k^t) V_{k|k-1}. \qquad (19)$$

   - *Projection*: Project the estimated state onto a sparse space by solving the LASSO problem in (14).

3. *Smoothing*: Smooth the estimate $a_{k|n}$ as follows

   $$\Phi_k = V_{k|k} V_{k+1|k}^{-1}, \qquad (20)$$

   $$a_{k|n} = a_{k|k} + \Phi_k(a_{k+1|n} - a_{k+1|k}), \qquad (21)$$

   $$V_{k|n} = V_{k|k} + \Phi_k(V_{k+1|n} - V_{k+1|k})\Phi_k^t. \qquad (22)$$

---

4 Results and discussion

4.1 Synthetic data

In order to assess the efficacy of the proposed LASSO-Kalman smoother in estimating the connectivity of time-varying networks, we first perform Monte Carlo simulations on the generated data to assess the prediction error using the following criterion:

$$\|a_{ij} - \hat{a}_{ij}\| \leq \alpha |a_{ij}| \qquad (23)$$

where a_{ij} is the (i,j)th true edge value and $\hat{a}_{ij}$ is the corresponding predicted edge value. The criterion in (23) counts an error if the estimated edge value is outside an α-vicinity of the true edge value. In our simulations, we adopted a value of α equal to 0.2. That is, the error tolerance interval is $\pm 20\%$ of the true value. The percentage of total correct or incorrect edges in a connectivity matrix is used to determine the accuracy of the algorithm.

We first investigate the effect of the network size on the estimation error. We generate networks of different sizes according to the model in (7) and calculate the prediction error. Figure 2a shows the prediction error as a function of the network size with a number of measurements equal to 70% of the network size p. We observe that the network estimation error is about constant between $p = 100$ to $p = 1,000$ and is thus unaffected by how large the network is, at least for networks of size few thousand genes. The reason for this outcome may be the linear increase of

the size vector with the number of genes, which is due to the splitting of the original connectivity estimation problem (p^2 parameters) into p smaller problems, that can be solved simultaneously.

We subsequently investigated the effect of the number of measurements m on the prediction accuracy. Figure 2b shows the prediction error as a function of the number of observations for a network of size $p = 100$. The estimation error seems to be constant up to 50 measurements then decreases rapidly as the number of observations increase to 100. But even for a small number of observations (10% of the network size), the estimation error is fairly small (less than 18%). This is an important result because in real-world applications, the number of available observations is very limited. We believe that the reason the error stays about constant for a small number of measurements (up to 50) is due to the good initial condition that is adopted in these simulations (see below for details on the estimation of the initial condition). For randomly chosen initial conditions, the LASSO-Kalman smoother takes a longer time, and thus requires more observations, to converge.

Figure 3 shows a ten-gene directed time-varying network over five time points Figure 3a. For each time point, we assume that seven observations are available. The thickness of the edge indicates the strength of the interaction. Blue edges indicate stimulative interactions, whereas red edges indicate repressive or inhibitive interactions. In order to show the importance of the LASSO formulation and the smoothing, we track the network using the classical Kalman filter Figure 3d, the LASSO online Kalman filter Figure 3c, and the LASSO Kalman smoother Figure 3b. It can be seen that the LASSO constraint is essential in imposing the sparsity of the network, hence significantly reducing the false positive rate. The smoothing improves the estimation accuracy by reducing variance of the estimate.

In order to obtain a more meaningful statistical evaluation of the proposed LASSO-Kalman, we randomly generated 10,000 sparse ten-gene networks evolving over five time points. The true-positive (TP), true-negative (TN), false-positive (FP), and false-negative (FN) rates, and the sensitivity, specificity, accuracy, and precision are shown in Table 1. The results reported in Table 1 do not take into account the sign or strength of the interactions, but consider only the presence or absence of an interaction between two genes. Observe that the TP rate of the classical Kalman filter is high because the Kalman filter is very dense and contains many spurious connections. This leads to an 'artificially' high sensitivity (97% ability to detect edges) but a very low specificity (50% ability to detect the absence of an interaction or sparsity) for the Kalman filter. The smoothed LASSO-Kalman results in a sparser network, missing more edges

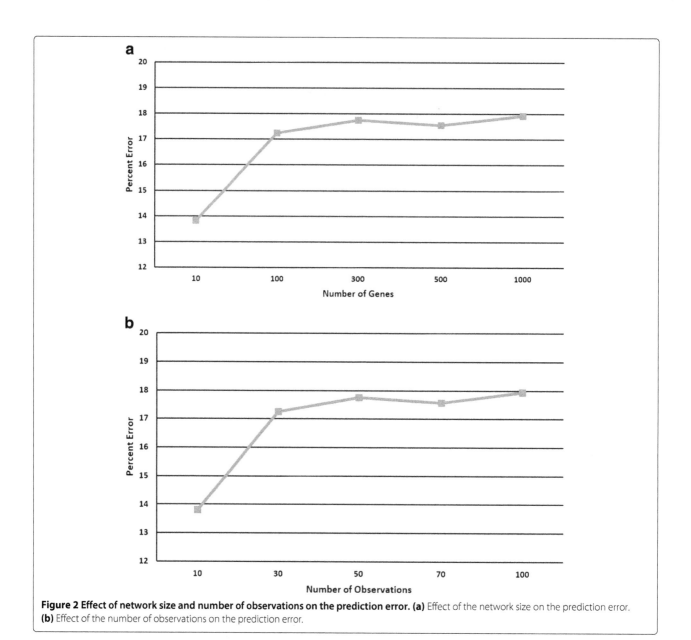

Figure 2 Effect of network size and number of observations on the prediction error. (a) Effect of the network size on the prediction error. **(b)** Effect of the number of observations on the prediction error.

than the unsmoothed LASSO-Kalman. In particular, the FP rate of the smoothed LASSO-Kalman is higher than its unsmoothed counterpart, but the FN rate of the smoothed LASSO-Kalman is lower, resulting in less spurious connections.

4.1.1 Estimation of λ

Equation 14 introduces the penalty parameter λ. This parameter controls the sparsity of the resulting estimate, and hence, a correct estimate of λ is of paramount importance. Tibshirani [43] enumerates three methods for the estimation of the sparsity parameter: cross-validation, generalized cross-validation, and an analytical unbiased estimate of risk. The first two methods assume that

the observations (X, Y) are drawn from some unknown distribution, and the third method applies to the X-fixed case. We adopt the second approach with a slight variation to improve the estimation accuracy. As proposed in [43], this method is based on a linear approximation of the LASSO estimate by the ridge regression estimator. In this paper, instead of calculating the ridge regression estimate as an approximation to the LASSO, we calculate the actual LASSO and determine the number of its effective parameters in order to construct the generalized cross-validation style statistic. The sparsity of the constrained solution is directly proportional to the value of λ. If λ is small, the solution will be less sparse and if it is large, the solution will be very sparse. At the limit, when $\lambda \longrightarrow \infty$,

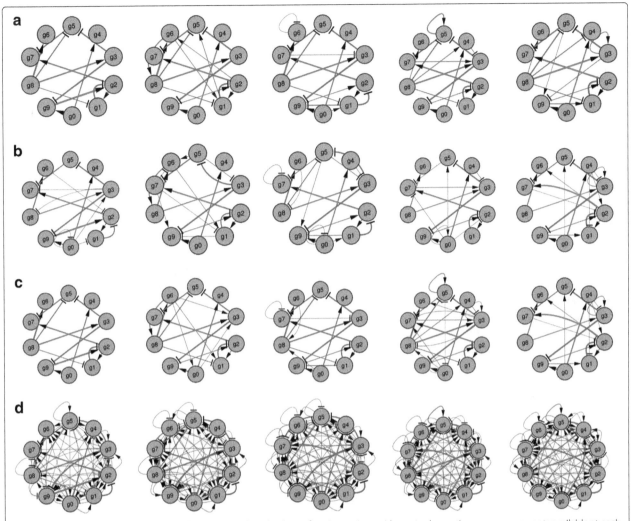

Figure 3 Tracking of a ten-gene network. The network evolved over five time points, with seven observations or measurements available at each time point. **(a)** Time-varying true network evolving over five time points, with seven observations available per time point. **(b)** Estimated time-varying network using the LASSO-Kalman smoother. **(c)** Estimated time-varying network using the LASSO-Kalman filter (no smoothing). **(d)** Estimated time-varying network using the classical Kalman filter.

the solution to (14) is the zero vector. To find the optimum value for λ for the specific data at hand, we compute the generalized cross-validation statistic for different values of λ with a coarse step size to determine the neighborhood of the optimum value of λ. Then, we perform a finer search in this neighborhood to find the optimal λ for the data. This two-step procedure finds an accurate estimate of λ while keeping the computational cost low.

4.1.2 Estimation of the initial condition
The fact that very few observations are available (at each time point) implies that the Kalman filter may take considerable time to converge to the true solution. To make the tracker converge faster, we generate an initial condition based on the maximum likelihood estimate of the static network, as proposed in [11]. This gives the Kalman filter the ability to start from an educated guess of the initial

Table 1 Performance analysis of the smoothed LASSO-Kalman, unsmoothed LASSO-Kalman, and the classical Kalman filter

	TP (%)	TN (%)	FP (%)	FN (%)	Sensitivity	Specificity	Accuracy	Precision
Classical Kalman	71.06	13.60	13.11	2.22	0.97	0.50	0.85	0.84
Unsmoothed LASSO-Kalman	80.21	11.52	4.32	3.93	0.95	0.72	0.91	0.94
Smoothed LASSO-Kalman	81.11	10.21	5.63	3.02	0.96	0.64	0.91	0.93

state estimate, which will increase the convergence time of the filter and hence its estimation accuracy over time.

4.2 Time-varying gene networks in *Drosophila melanogaster*

A genome-wide microarray profiling of the life cycle of the *D. melanogaster* revealed the evolving nature of the gene expression patterns during the time course of its development [50]. In this study, cDNA microarrays were used to analyze the RNA expression levels of 4,028 genes in wild-type flies examined during 66 sequential time periods beginning at fertilization and spanning embryonic, larval, pupal, and the first 30 days of adulthood. Since early embryos change rapidly, overlapping 1-h periods were sampled; the adults were sampled at multiday intervals [50]. The time points span the embryonic (samples 1 to 30; time E01h until E2324h), larval (samples 31 to 40; time L24h until L105h), pupal (samples 41 to 58; M0h until M96h), and adulthood (samples 59 to 66; A024h until A30d) periods of the organism.

Costello et al. [51] normalized the Arbeitman et al. raw data [50] using the optimized local intensity-dependent normalization (OLIN) algorithm [52]. Details of the normalization protocol can be found at http://www.sciencemag.org/content/suppl/2002/09/26/297.5590.2270.DC1/ArbeitmanSOM.pdf. In their procedure, a gene may be flagged for several reasons: the corresponding transcript not being expressed under the considered condition, the amplification of the printed cDNA was reported as 'failed' in the original data, or the data is missing for technical reasons. A statistical test was also conducted to determine if the expression of a labeled sample is significantly above the distribution of background values. Spots with a corrected p value greater than 0.01 were considered absent (or within the distribution of background noise). In this study, we downloaded the Costello et al. dataset [51] and considered the unflagged genes only, which amount to a total of 1,863 genes.

The LASSO-Kalman smoother was used to estimate 21 dynamic gene networks, one per three time points, during the life cycle of *D. melanogaster*. Figure 4 shows the estimated networks, where edges with absolute strength less than 10^{-3} were set to zero. The networks were visualized in Cytoscape using a force-directed layout [53]. Markov clustering [54] was used to identify clusters within each network. Clusters containing more than 30 genes were tested for functional enrichment using the BiNGO plugin for Cytoscape [55]. The Gene Ontology term with the highest enrichment in a particular cluster was used to label the cluster on the network. The changing connectivity patterns are an evident indication of the evolution of gene connectivity over time.

Figure 5 shows the evolution of the degree connectivity of each gene as a function of time. This plot helps visualize the hubs (high degree nodes) at each time point and shows which genes are active during the phases of the organism's development. It is clear that certain genes are mainly active during specific developmental phases (transient genes), whereas others seem to play a role during the entire developmental process (permanent genes).

We quantified the structural properties of the temporal network by its degree distribution and clustering coefficient. We found that the degree distribution of each snapshot network follows a power law distribution, which indicates that the networks self-organize into a scale-free state (a global property). The power law exponents of the snapshot networks are plotted in Figure 6a. The clustering coefficient, shown in Figure 6b, measures the cliquishness of a typical neighborhood (a local property) or the degree of coherence inside potential functional modules. Interestingly, the trends (maximums and minimums) of the degree distribution and the clustering coefficients over time corroborate the results in [56], except for the clustering coefficient during early embryonic period. The LASSO-Kalman found a small clustering coefficient in early embryonic, whereas the model-based Tesla algorithm in [56] reported a high clustering coefficient for that phase.

To show the advantages of dynamic networks over a static network, we compared the recovered interactions against a list of known undirected gene interactions hosted in FlyBase (http://flybase.org/). The LASSO-Kalman algorithm was able to recover 1,065 gene interactions (ignoring all interactions smaller or equal than 10^{-3}). The static network, computed as one network across all time periods using the algorithm in [11], recovers 248 interactions. Using the segmentation approach, we also computed four networks, where each network uses the number of samples in each developmental phase of the organism (embryonic, larval, pupal, and adulthood). The embryonic-stage network uses the 30 time points sampled during the embryonic phase and recovers 121 interactions. The larval-stage network uses nine time points available for the larval phase and recovers 28 known interactions. The pupal-stage network uses 18 time points collected during the pupal period and recovers 125 interactions. The adult-stage network utilizes eight time points sampled during adulthood and recovers 41 interactions. Hence, in total, the segmentation approach recovers 315 interactions. The dynamic networks of Tesla [56] were able to recover 96 known interactions. We mention that, in [56], the network size was 4,028 genes, whereas we considered a subset of 1,863 unflagged genes. Thus, Tesla's recovery rate is 2.4%, whereas the LASSO-Kalman recovery rate is 57.2%. The low recovery rate of Tesla in [56] may be due to the presence of spurious samples since the flagged genes were included in the networks.

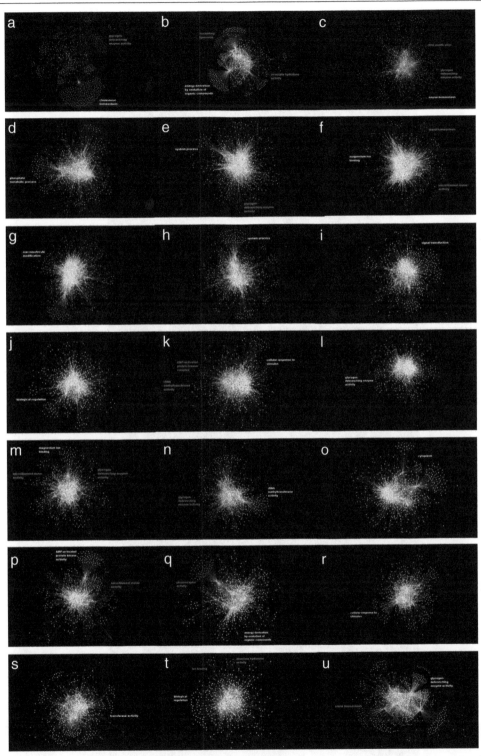

Figure 4 Snapshots of the time-varying networks at 21 time epochs during the *Drosophila melanogaster* development cycle. The genes are represented as nodes and interactions as edges. Colored nodes are sets of genes enriched for Gene Ontology summarized by the indicated terms. The nodes were distributed using a force-directed layout in Cytoscape. **(a)** t_1 to t_3 (embryonic), **(b)** t_4 to t_6 (embryonic), **(c)** t_7 to t_9 (embryonic), **(d)** t_{10} to t_{12} (embryonic), **(e)** t_{13} to t_{15} (embryonic), **(f)** t_{16} to t_{18} (embryonic), **(g)** t_{19} to t_{21} (embryonic), **(h)** t_{22} to t_{24} (embryonic), **(i)** t_{25} to t_{27} (embryonic), **(j)** t_{28} to t_{30} (embryonic), **(k)** t_{31} to t_{33} (larval), **(l)** t_{34} to t_{36} (larval), **(m)** t_{37} to t_{39} (larval), **(n)** t_{40} to t_{42} (pupal), **(o)** t_{43} to t_{45} (pupal), **(p)** t_{46} to t_{48} (pupal), **(q)** t_{49} to t_{51} (pupal), **(r)** t_{52} to t_{54} (pupal), **(s)** t_{55} to t_{57} (pupal), **(t)** t_{58} to t_{60} (adult), **(u)** t_{61} to t_{63} (adult).

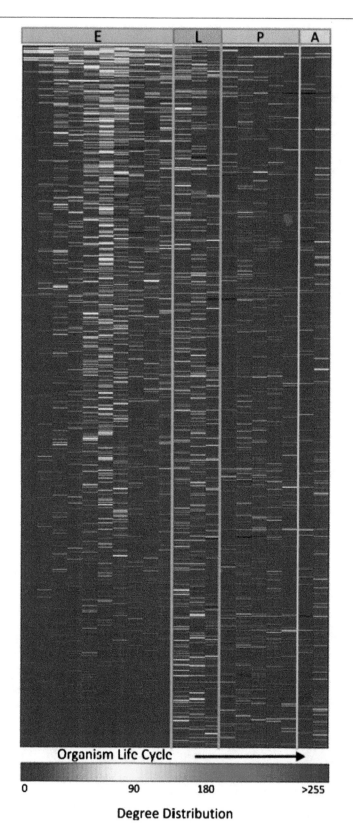

Figure 5 Gene degree connectivity ordered by the onset of their first increase. Each row represents data for one gene, and each column is a developmental time point. Blue indicates low degrees, and red indicates high degrees.

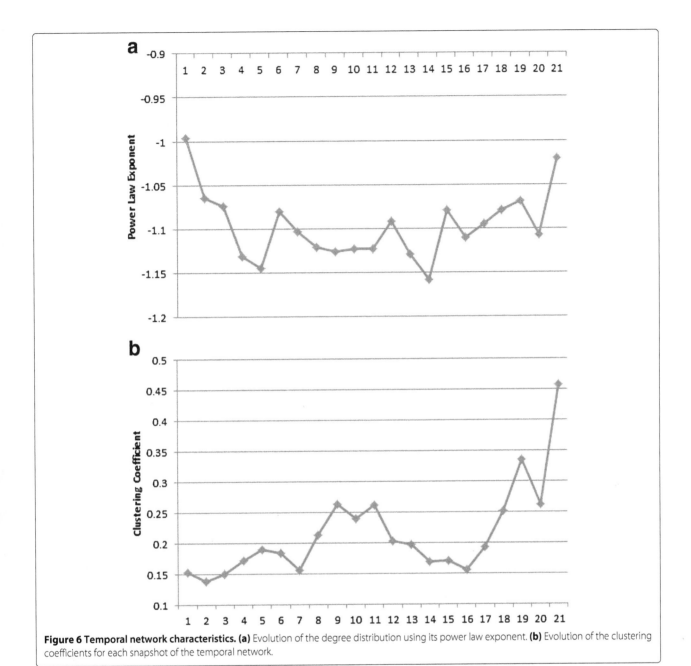

Figure 6 Temporal network characteristics. (a) Evolution of the degree distribution using its power law exponent. **(b)** Evolution of the clustering coefficients for each snapshot of the temporal network.

4.3 High-performance computing implementation

The proposed LASSO-Kalman smoother algorithm was first tested and validated in MATLAB. Subsequently, a high-performance computing (HPC)-based implementation of the algorithm was developed to allow a large number of genes. Each HPC core computes the interactions of one gene at a time. The communication between the individual processes is coordinated by the open message passing interface (open MPI). Due to the large scale of the problem, both the Intel® C++ Compiler and the Intel® Math Kernel Library (Intel® MKL) (Intel Corporation, Santa Clara, CA, USA) were used on a Linux-based platform for maximum performance. This approach enabled an implementation that is highly efficient, inherently parallel, and has built-in support for the HPC architecture. The implementation starts by the main MPI process spawning the child processes: each child process is assigned an individual gene to compute, based on the gene expression data that is made available to it using the file system. The child process returns the computed result to the main process, which then assigns the next gene until all genes are processed. Finally, the master process compiles the computed results in a contagious matrix. Figure 7 summarizes the HPC implementation

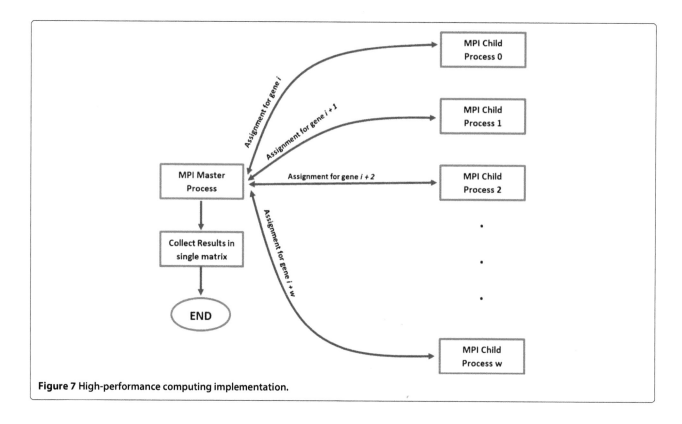

Figure 7 High-performance computing implementation.

process. The memory requirement of the algorithm, however, is still high. At each time point, two $p \times p$ covariance matrices must be stored and computed (the *a priori* and *a posteriori* error covariance matrices), where p is the number of genes. In order to alleviate the memory requirement, we used a memory mapped file, which swaps the data between the local disk and the memory. We used the Razor II HPC system at the Arkansas High Performance Computing Center (AHPCC) at the University of Arkansas at Fayetteville. The AHPCC has 16 cores per node, with 32 GB of memory; each node is interconnected using a 40-Gbps QLogic quad-data rate QDR InfiniBand (Aliso Viejo, CA, USA). In our implementation, we were allowed to use 40 such nodes at a given time. This implementation is scalable and supports a larger number of genes for future investigations. Further details of the implementation are available at http://users.rowan.edu/~bouaynaya/EURASIP2014.

5   Conclusions

Due to the dynamic nature of biological processes, biological networks undergo systematic rewiring in response to cellular requirements and environmental changes. These changes in network topology are imperceptible when estimating a static 'average' network for all time points. The dynamic view of genetic regulatory networks reveals the temporal information about the onset and duration of genetic interactions, in particular showing that few genes are permanent players in the cellular function while others act transiently during certain phases or 'regimes' of the biological process. It is, therefore, essential to develop methods that capture the temporal evolution of genetic networks and allow the study of phase-specific genetic regulation and the prediction of network structures under given cellular and environmental conditions.

In this paper, we formulated the reverse-engineering of time-varying networks, from a limited number of observations, as a tracking problem in a compressed domain. Under the assumption of linear dynamics, we derived the LASSO-Kalman smoother, which provides the optimal minimum mean-square sparse estimate of the connectivity structure. The estimated networks reveal that genetic interactions undergo significant rewiring during the developmental process of an organism such as the *D. melanogaster*. We anticipate that these topological changes and phase-specific interactions apply to other genetic networks underlying dynamic biological processes, such as cancer progression and therapeutic treatment and development.

Finally, we anticipate that the rapid breakthroughs in genomic technologies for measurement and data collection will make the static representation of biological networks obsolete and establish instead the dynamic perspective of biological interactions.

Competing interests

The authors declare that they have no competing interests.

Acknowledgements

The authors would like to thank Mr. Lee Henshaw and Adam Haskell, undergraduate students with the Department of Electrical and Computer Engineering at Rowan University, for their contribution to the network visualization. This project is supported by the Award Number R01GM096191 from the National Institute of General Medical Sciences (NIH/NIGMS). The content is solely the responsibility of the authors and does not necessarily represent the official views of the National Institute Of General Medical Sciences or the National Institutes of Health. This project is also supported in part by the National Science Foundation through grants MRI-R2 #0959124 (Razor), ARI #0963249, #0918970 (CI-TRAIN), and a grant from the Arkansas Science and Technology Authority, with resources managed by the Arkansas High Performance Computing Center. Partial support has also been provided by the National Science Foundation through grants CRI CNS-0855248, EPS-0701890, EPS-0918970, MRI CNS-0619069, and OISE-0729792.

Author details

[1]Department of Electrical and Computer Engineering, Rowan University, 201 Mullica Hill Rd, Glassboro, NJ 08028, USA. [2]Department of Neurology, University of Alabama at Birmingham, 1720 2nd Ave S, Birmingham, AL 35233, USA. [3]Department of Mathematics, University of Alabama at Birmingham, 1720 2nd Ave S, Birmingham, AL 35233, USA. [4]Department of Electrical and Computer Engineering, University of Alabama at Birmingham, 1720 2nd Ave S, Birmingham, AL 35233, USA. [5]Department of Biomedical Engineering, University of Alabama at Birmingham, 1720 2nd Ave S, Birmingham, AL 35233, USA. [6]Department of Cell, Developmental and Integrative Biology, University of Alabama at Birmingham, 1720 2nd Ave S, Birmingham, AL 35233, USA.

References

1. SA Kauffman, Metabolic stability and epigenesis in randomly constructed genetic nets. J Theor. Biol. **22**, 437–467 (1969)
2. I Shmulevich, ER Dougherty, S Kim, W Zhang, Probabilistic Boolean networks: a rule-based uncertainty model for gene regulatory networks. Bioinformatics. **18**(2), 261–274 (2002)
3. N Friedman, M Linial, I Nachman, D Peter, Using Bayesian networks to analyze expression data. J. Comput. Biol. **7**(3-4), 601–620 (2000)
4. K Murphy, S Mian, Modeling gene expression data using dynamic Bayesian networks. Technical report, Computer Science Division, University of California, Berkeley, 1999
5. N Friedman, Inferring cellular networks using probabilistic graphical models. Science. **303**(5659), 799–805 (2004)
6. PE Meyer, K Kontos, F Lafitte, G Bontempi, Information-theoretic inference of large transcriptional regulatory networks. EURASIP J. Bioinformat. Syst. Biol. **2007**, 79879 (2007). doi:10.1155/2007/79879
7. W Zhao, E Serpedin, ER Dougherty, Inferring connectivity of genetic regulatory networks using information-theoretic criteria. IEEE/ACM Trans. Comput. Biol. Bioinf. **5**(2), 262–274 (2008)
8. V Chaitankar, P Ghosh, EJ Perkins, P Gong, Y Deng, C Zhang, A novel gene network inference algorithm using predictive minimum description length approach. BMC Syst. Biol. **4**(Suppl 1), S7 (2010)
9. P Zoppoli, S Morganella, M Ceccarelli, TimeDelay-ARACNE: reverse engineering of gene networks from time-course data by an information theoretic approach. BMC Bioinformatics. **11**(154) (2010). doi: 10.1186/1471-2105-11-154
10. HM Fathallah-Shaykh, JL Bona, S Kadener, Mathematical model of the *drosophila* circadian clock: loop regulation and transcriptional integration. Biophys. J. **97**(9), 2399–2408 (2009)
11. G Rasool, N Bouaynaya, HM Fathallah-Shaykh, D Schonfeld, Inference of genetic regulatory networks using regularized likelihood with covariance estimation. Paper presented at the IEEE statistical signal processing workshop, Aug. 2012, pp. 560–563
12. J Cao, X Qi, H Zhao, Modeling gene regulation networks using ordinary differential equations. Methods Mol. Biol. **802**, 185–197 (2012)
13. H Hache, H Lehrach, R Herwig, Reverse engineering of gene regulatory networks: a comparative study. EURASIP J. Bioinform. Syst. Biol. **2009**, 617281 (2009). doi:10.1155/2009/617281

14. D Marbach, JC Costello, R Küffner, NM Vega, RJ Prill, DM Camacho, KR Allison, Wisdom of crowds for robust gene network inference. Nature Methods. **9**(8), 796–804 (2012)
15. NE Huang, Z Shen, SR Long, MC Wu, HH Shih, Q Zheng, NC Yen, CC Tung, HH Liu, The empirical mode decomposition and the Hilbert spectrum for nonlinear and non-stationary time series analysis. Proc. R. Soc. A. **454**(1971), 903–995 (1998)
16. EH Davidson, JP Rast, P Oliveri, A Ransick, C Calestani, CH Yuh, T Minokawa, G Amore, V Hinman, C Arenas-Mena, O Otim, CT Brown, CB Livi, PY Lee, R Revilla, AG Rust, ZJ Pan, MJ Schilstra, PJC Clarke, MI Arnone, L Rowen, RA Cameron, DR McClay, L Hood, H Bolouri, A genomic regulatory network for development. Science. **295**(5560), 1669–1678 (2002)
17. NM Luscombe, MM Babu, H Yu, M Snyder, SA Teichmann, M Gerstei, Genomic analysis of regulatory network dynamics reveals large topological changes. Lett. Nature. **431**, 308–312 (2004)
18. A Rao, AO Hero, DJ States, JD Engel, Inferring time-varying network topologies from gene expression data. EURASIP J. Bioinform. Syst. Biol. **2007**, 51947 (2007). doi:10.1155/2007/51947
19. P Fearnhead, Exact and efficient Bayesian inference for multiple change point problems. Stat. Comput. **16**(2), 203–213 (2006)
20. J Ernst, O Vainas, CT Harbison, I Simon, Z Bar-Joseph, Reconstructing dynamic regulatory maps. Mol. Syst. Biol. **3**(3), 74 (2007)
21. KW Xidian, J Zhang, F Shen, L Shi, Adaptive learning of dynamic Bayesian networks with changing structures by detecting geometric structures of time series. Knowl. Inf. Syst. **17**, 121–133 (2008)
22. JW Robinson, EJ Hartemink, Non-stationary dynamic Bayesian networks, Paper presented at the twenty-first annual conference on neural information processing systems, (Vancouver, Canada, 11–13 Dec 2008), pp. 1369–1376
23. M Grzegorczyk, D Husmeier, Non-stationary continuous dynamic Bayesian networks, Paper presented at the twenty-second annual conference on neural information processing systems, (Vancouver, Canada, 6–11 Dec. 2009), pp. 682–690
24. F Dondelinger, S Lébre, D Husmeier, Non-homogeneous dynamic Bayesian networks with Bayesian regularization for inferring gene regulatory networks with gradually time-varying structure. Mach. Learn. **90**(2), 191–230 (2013)
25. H Miyashita, T Nakamura, Y Ida, T Matsumoto, T Kaburagi, Nonparametric Bayes-based heterogeneous Drosophila melanogaster gene regulatory network inference: T-process regression. Paper presented at the international conference on artificial intelligence and applications, (Innsbruck, Austria, 11–13 Feb. 2013), pp. 51–58
26. A Ahmed, EP Xing, Recovering time-varying networks of dependencies in social and biological studies. Proc. Nat. Acad. Sci. **106**(29), 11878–11883 (2009)
27. F Guo, S Hanneke, W Fu, EP Xing, Recovering temporally rewiring networks: a model-based approach. Paper presented at the twenty-fourth international conference on machine learning, (Corvalis, OR, USA, 20–24 June 2007), pp. 321–328
28. Z Wang, EE Kuruoğlu, X Yang, Y Xu, TS Huang, Time varying dynamic Bayesian network for nonstationary events modeling and online inference. IEEE Trans. Signal Process. **59**(4), 1553–1568 (2011)
29. R Prado, G Huerta, M West, Bayesian time-varying autoregressions: theory, methods and applications. Resenhas. **4**, 405–422 (2000)
30. JW Robinson, AJ Hartemink, Learning non-stationary dynamic Bayesian networks. J. Mach. Learn. Res. **11**, 3647–3680 (2010)
31. L Song, M Kolar, E Xing, Time-varying dynamic Bayesian networks. Paper presented at the twenty-second annual conference on neural information processing systems, (Vancouver, Canada, 6–11 Dec. 2009)
32. A Tucker, X Liu, A Bayesian network approach to explaining time series with changing structure. Intell. Data Anal. **8**(8), 469–480 (2004)
33. SH Nielsen, TD Nielsen, Adapting Bayes network structures to non-stationary domains. Int. J. Approx. Reason. **49**(2), 379–397 (2008)
34. SM Oh, JM Rehg, T Balch, F Dellaert, Learning and inferring motion patterns using parametric segmental switching linear dynamic systems. Int. J. Comput. Vis. **77**, 103–124 (2008)
35. E Fox, EB Sudderth, MI Jordan, AS Willsky, Bayesian nonparametric inference of switching dynamic linear models. IEEE Trans. Signal Process. **59**(4), 1569–1585 (2011)
36. Z Wang, X Liu, Y Liu, J Liang, V Vinciotti, An extended Kalman filtering approach to modeling nonlinear dynamic gene regulatory networks via

short gene expression time series. IEEE/ACM Trans. Comput. Biol. Bioinform. **6**(3), 410–419 (2009)

37. A Noor, E Serpedin, M Nounou, HN Nounou, Inferring gene regulatory networks via nonlinear state-space models and exploiting sparsity. IEEE Trans. Comput. Biol. Bioinform. **9**(4), 1203–1211 (2012)

38. EJ Candes, J Romberg, T Tao, Robust uncertainty principles: exact signal reconstruction from highly incomplete frequency information. IEEE Trans. Inf. Theory. **52**(2), 489–509 (2006)

39. M Fornasier, H Rauhut, Compressive sensing, in *Handbook of Mathematical Methods in Imaging*, ed. by O Scherzer (Springer, New York, 2011), pp. 187–228

40. G Tauböck, F Hlawatsch, D Eiwen, H Rauhut, Compressive estimation of doubly selective channels in multicarrier systems: leakage effects and sparsity-enhancing processing. IEEE J. Sel. Top. Sign. Proces. **4**(2), 255–271 (2010)

41. J Bobin, JL Starck, R Ottensamer, Compressed sensing in astronomy. IEEE J. Sel. Top. Sign. Proces. **2**(5), 718–726 (2008)

42. M Duarte, M Davenport, D Takhar, J Laska, T Sun, K Kelly, R Baraniuk, Single-pixel imaging via compressive sampling. IEEE Signal Process. Mag. **25**(2), 83–91 (2008)

43. R Tibshirani, Regression shrinkage and selection via the lasso. J. R. Stat. Soc. Series B. **58**, 267–288 (1996)

44. D Simon, *Optimal State Estimation*. (Wiley, New York, 2006)

45. W Wen, HF Durrant-Whyte, Model-based multi-sensor data fusion, in *proceedings of the IEEE international conference on robotics and automation*, vol. 2, pp 1720–1726, May 1992

46. S Hayward, Constrained Kalman filter for least-squares estimation of time-varying beamforming weights, in *Mathematics in, Signal Processing IV*, ed. by J Mc Whirter, I Proudler (Oxford University Press, Oxford, 1999), pp. 113–125

47. JD Geeter, HV Brussel, JD Schutter, M Decreton, A smoothly constrained Kalman filter. IEEE Trans. Pattern Anal. Mach. Intell. **19**(10), 1171–1177 (1997)

48. SJ Julier, JJ LaViola, On Kalman filtering with nonlinear equality constraints. IEEE Trans. Signal Process. **55**(6), 2774–2784 (2007)

49. A Carmi, P Gurfil, D Kanevsky, Methods for sparse signal recovery using Kalman filtering with embedded pseudo-measurement norms and quasi-norms. IEEE Trans. Signal Process. **58**(4), 2405–2409 (2010)

50. M Arbeitman, E Furlong, F Imam, E Johnson, B Null, B Baker, M Krasnow, M Scott, R Davis, K White, Gene expression during the life cycle of Drosophila melanogaster. Science. **297**, 2270–2275 (2002)

51. JC Costello, MM Dalkilic, JR Andrews, *Microarray normalization protocols*. (FlyBase Consortium, FlyBase, 2008)

52. ME Futschik, T Crompton, OLIN: optimized normalization, visualization and quality testing of two-channel microarray data. Bioinformatics. **21**(8), 1724–1726 (2005)

53. P Shannon, A Markiel, O Ozier, NS Baliga, JT Wang, D Ramage, N Amin, B Schwikowski, T Ideker, Cytoscape: a software environment for integrated models of biomolecular interaction networks. Genome Res. **13**(11), 2498–2504 (2003)

54. SV Dongen, Performance criteria for graph clustering and Markov cluster experiments. Technical report, National Research Institute for Mathematics and Computer Science, 2000

55. S Maere, K Heymans, M Kuiper, BiNGO: a Cytoscape plugin to assess overrepresentation of gene ontology categories in biological networks. Bioinformatics. **21**, 3448–3449 (2005)

56. A Ahmed, L Song, EP Xing, Time-varying networks: recovering temporally rewiring genetic networks during the life cycle of *Drosophila melanogaster*. Technical report, Carnegie Mellon University, 2009

16

From microscopy data to *in silico* environments for *in vivo*-oriented simulations

Noriko Hiroi[1,*,†], Michael Klann[2†], Keisuke Iba[1], Pablo de Heras Ciechomski[3], Shuji Yamashita[4], Akito Tabira[1], Takahiro Okuhara[1], Takeshi Kubojima[1], Yasunori Okada[4], Kotaro Oka[1], Robin Mange[2], Michael Unger[2], Akira Funahashi[1] and Heinz Koeppl[2*]

Abstract

In our previous study, we introduced a combination methodology of Fluorescence Correlation Spectroscopy (FCS) and Transmission Electron Microscopy (TEM), which is powerful to investigate the effect of intracellular environment to biochemical reaction processes. Now, we developed a reconstruction method of realistic simulation spaces based on our TEM images. Interactive raytracing visualization of this space allows the perception of the overall 3D structure, which is not directly accessible from 2D TEM images. Simulation results show that the diffusion in such generated structures strongly depends on image post-processing. Frayed structures corresponding to noisy images hinder the diffusion much stronger than smooth surfaces from denoised images. This means that the correct identification of noise or structure is significant to reconstruct appropriate reaction environment *in silico* in order to estimate realistic behaviors of reactants *in vivo*. Static structures lead to anomalous diffusion due to the partial confinement. In contrast, mobile crowding agents do not lead to anomalous diffusion at moderate crowding levels. By varying the mobility of these non-reactive obstacles (NRO), we estimated the relationship between NRO diffusion coefficient (D_{nro}) and the anomaly in the tracer diffusion (α). For $D_{nro} = 21.96$ to $44.49\ \mu m^2/s$, the simulation results match the anomaly obtained from FCS measurements. This range of the diffusion coefficient from simulations is compatible with the range of the diffusion coefficient of structural proteins in the cytoplasm. In addition, we investigated the relationship between the radius of NRO and anomalous diffusion coefficient of tracers by the comparison between different simulations. The radius of NRO has to be 58 nm when the polymer moves with the same diffusion speed as a reactant, which is close to the radius of functional protein complexes in a cell.

Introduction

The complex physical structure of the cytoplasm has been a long-standing topic of interest [1,2]. The physiological environment of intracellular biochemical reactants is not one of well diluted, homogeneous space. This fact is in contradiction with the basic assumption underlying the standard theories for reaction kinetics [3]. The difference may render actual *in vivo* reaction processes deviate from those *in vitro* or *in silico*. Lately, we showed the results of a combined investigation of Fluorescence Correlation Spectroscopy (FCS) and Transmission Electron Microscopy (TEM) [4,5]. We examined the effects of intracellular crowding and inhomogeneity on the mode of reactions *in vivo* by calculating the spectral dimension (d_s) which can be translated into the reaction rate function. We compared estimates of the anomaly parameter, obtained from FCS data, with the fractal dimension from an analysis with transmission electron microscopy images. Therefrom we estimated a value of $d_s = 1.34 \pm 0.27$. This result suggests that the *in vivo* reactions run faster at initial times when compared to the reactions in a homogeneous space. The result is compatible with the result of our Monte Carlo simulation. Also, in our further investigation, we confirmed by the simulation that the above-mentioned *in vivo* like properties are different from those of homogeneously concentrated environments. Also other simulation results indicated that the crowding level

*Correspondence: hiroi@bio.keio.ac.jp; koepplh@ethz.ch
†Equal contributors
[1] Department of BioSciences and Informatics, Keio University, Yokohama, Kanagawa, Japan
[2] Automatic Control Laboratory, Swiss Federal Institute of Technology, Zurich, Switzerland
Full list of author information is available at the end of the article

of an environment affects the diffusion and reaction rate of reactants [6-9]. Such knowledge of the spatial condition enables us to construct realistic models for *in vivo* diffusion and reaction systems.

The novel points of this study are the following three:

(i) we investigated the influence of the mobility of non-reactive obstacles (NRO) on the anomaly coefficient,

(ii) we investigated the influence of the size of the NROs, and

(iii) we reconstructed the static simulation space based on TEM images and run diffusion tests in these virtual volumes as well

in order to make the *in silico* simulation environment more realistic. The *in vivo* NROs have a wide size distribution and complex shapes. Based on our simulations we can suggest simpler systems with just one class of NROs which result in the same properties in the observed effective diffusion of the tracer molecules in the complex environment and experimental results.

While several projects investigated diffusion and reaction within compartments like the ER [10,11], this study aims at resolving the diffusion and reaction of cytosolic proteins outside of these structures, for instance signaling molecules that have to travel from the plasma membrane to the nucleus [12,13]. Cryoelectron tomography can be used to obtain a 3D reconstruction of only the scanned cell section [14,15]. Statistical methods, in contrast, can be used to learn the properties of the 3D space and to generate many samples from it [16,17]. In order to generate reaction volumes with the same properties like the TEM images, we therefore learned the image statistics. This enables us to test the influence of the structures such as mitochondria and membrane enclosed compartments on the diffusion and reaction of molecules in the cytosol. By using state-of-the-art volume visualization techniques we can also show the shape of the generated volumes.

The generated structures are used for a volumetric 3D pixel (voxel)-driven graphical representation, which was further filtered into a smooth analytic surface using the software package BioInspire [18,19]. This analytic conversion for the visualization was done to better understand the properties of the 3D structure, which is not obvious from single 2D slices. The analytic surface is also the natural description of large intracellular objects like membrane enclosed compartments or mitochondria [11,16] and avoids the discreteness of pixel/voxel-based approaches [20]. The 3D ray tracing visualization package BioInspire is used to interactively sample the analytical surface to create the final image; therefore, never losing any details by going over some intermediate representation such as a triangle mesh as is common in literature [21,22].

Generally, TEM images visualize the information of scattering/absorption or permeation of electron rays through a sample slice of the cell. The electron rays are detected by charge-coupled devices and converted to grey scale images. The part in a sample section where electrons have been scattered or absorbed appear darker on the image, while the parts permeating electron rays appear white. There exist many imaging studies which investigated intracellular structures by electron microscopy. In those images, organelle, such as nucleus, mitochondria, rough endoplasmic reticulum, zymogen granules, Golgi complex, etc., appear as clear shadows, resulting from scattered or absorbed electron rays.

Based on the above reasons, we assumed that the black segment in the TEM images consisted of solid structures comprising the non-reactive obstacle. Simultaneously, the non-reactive surface can provide anchorage for small mobile molecules. The faint segment areas in TEM images presumed to be made up of sol proteins, which formed the main reaction chamber for the intracellular reactants.

Besides the (at least temporarily) static structures the cytoplasm is known to be filled with all kinds of mobile-crowding molecules [2]. Therefore, we added the mobility of the NRO and their size to the parameters that are investigated in this study.

In our former simulation, we used just one size of NRO, which could, e.g., represent single molecular obstacles [4,5]. But in a cell, many of those molecules representing the NRO exist as complexes or polymers, for instance cytoskeletal proteins. In order to include this information, we analyzed if the overall radius of the obstacles would affect the diffusion and reaction processes. Especially, we checked the results obtained in such simulations for anomalous diffusion, which is a sensitive probe for crowding conditions [9].

Anomalous diffusion is a common phenomenon in cell biology [23] but was previously defined by using a random walker on percolation clusters [24]. Percolation theory deals with the number and properties of clusters which are formed as follows [25]; each site of a very large lattice is occupied randomly with probability p, independent of its neighbors. The resulting network structure is the target of percolation theory [26]. When the probability p is over the critical value (p_c), the cluster reaches from one side to the opposite side of the lattice. This p_c is the threshold to undergo phase transition like the gelation of polymer sol. Anomalous diffusion is observed when the reaction space is occupied inhomogeneously with obstacles until the relative volume of obstacles reaches close to the threshold. The value of p_c for the 3D cube is 0.312 [27].

In several numerical simulations including our model, a percolation lattice is used as a simple example of the disordered medium [7,28,29] and we found that it is similar to the *in vivo* reaction space. Likewise the structured *in vivo* reaction space is similar to porous media [6,30]. Such structures, which are often self-similar, can readily be seen under the TEM and are easily generated for instance by self-organizing molecules such as titanium dioxide and sol–gel powders.

When $p = 1$, the cluster becomes a regular lattice without disorder. If the non-obstructed space in the cell forms such a regular lattice, the time dependency of the mean squared displacement (MSD) of a random walker on the lattice grows linear with time. On the other hand, if the random walker is confined at a specific volume, the MSD converges to a constant [31]. The case between these two extreme cases was named anomalous diffusion by Gefen et al. [24]. The exponent α represents the anomaly of the MSD [23]:

$$\langle(\vec{x}(t) - \vec{x}(0))^2\rangle = \Gamma t^\alpha \qquad (1)$$

We estimated diffusion constants of NRO based on simulation results in different environments. Our *in silico* models enables us to verify the consistency of the hypothesis that the intracellular component is built using a self-organization and that the structure provides a percolation cluster-like environment for soluble molecules. We computed α from the Monte Carlo simulations in these virtual environments, as well as $D(t)$, and compared it with the experimental results from FCS measurements to find the

parameters of the *in silico* models which match the *in vivo* results.

Main text

Reconstruction of reaction space based on TEM image data

Based on TEM images (Figure 1) the intracellular environment was reconstructed (Figures 2 and 3) as described in Methods,"Generation of virtual cellular structures". The 3D visualization of the static NRO structure helps to grasp the properties of the volume, which cannot be seen from single 2D images. A video showing the complete volume and sweeping through it is available as Supporting material (see Additional file 1).

The 1D statistics about neighboring pixels/voxels is sufficient to generate similar structures in two and three dimension applying an isotropy assumption. The structures show a wide size distribution in 2D images and a tubular network in the 3D volume. Only completely spherical structures are not generated in the present approach. The applied filters in the volume generation process have a tendency to increase the size of structures (eroding) or to reduce it (dilation). By controlling the NRO volume fraction in the process we could create volumes which have the same NRO volume fraction like the TEM images. Note that the smoothing of the surface for visualization likewise can increase the volume occupied by NROs (cf. Figure 3).

With respect to the diffusion of molecules through such structures the identification of the true fine-grained structure becomes very important. The diffusion test simulations in these 3D structures were performed with the

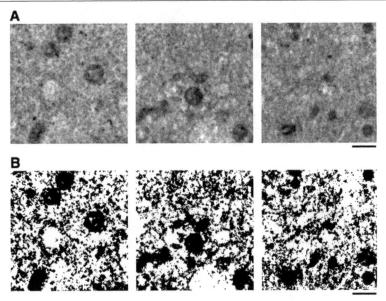

Figure 1 Material TEM images.(A) Original TEM images of the cytoplasmic region of 3Y1 cell for reaction space reconstruction.These images were captured by 1,000 magnifications. bar $= 1.0\,\mu$m $= 56.8$ pixels. **(B)** The binarized images of the photos **(A)**. The binarizing algorithm is described in "Methods".

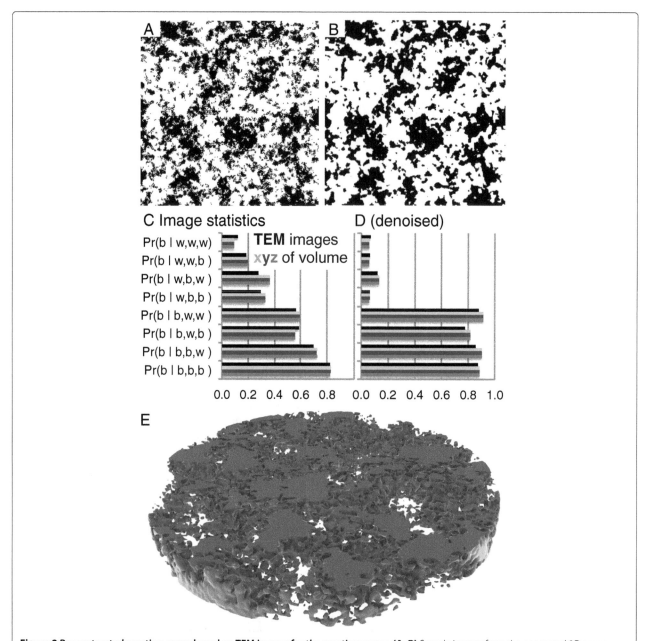

Figure 2 Reconstructed reaction space based on TEM images for the reaction space. (A, B) Sample images from the generated 3D space. **(C, D)** Comparison of original TEM image statistics and generated volume statistics. The reconstructed space has 17.6 × 17.6 × 17.6 nm resolution. **(B, D)** Low pass filtered by a median filter in order to reduce noise. **(E)** Visualization of the 3D structure by raytracing. See SI movie for a complete overview of the 3D reaction space.

continuous space discrete time Brownian dynamics simulation [6,32,33] (see Methods "Diffusion simulations in the virtual environment"). In the rather noisy structure corresponding to the thresholded TEM images, the diffusion is hindered much stronger than in a smoothed structure. We fitted the observed MSD to Equation (1) yielding $\Gamma = 3.37 \pm 0.14$ in the noisy volume and $\Gamma = 3.79 \pm 0.15$ in the smooth volume, i.e., the MSD grows faster in the smooth volume. The anomaly is $\alpha = 0.940 \pm 0.004$ and

$\alpha = 0.948 \pm 0.005$, respectively. All simulations stopped, when the first of the 10,000 molecules starting from the center had reached the surface of our test volume—which restricts a further increase of the MSD. This time span/distance is not sufficient to leave the anomalous regime. The effective diffusion coefficient is on average reduced to 63% of the input value in the noisy volume and to 70% in the smooth volume at this point in time. Especially, the larger surface of the noisy volume leads to an

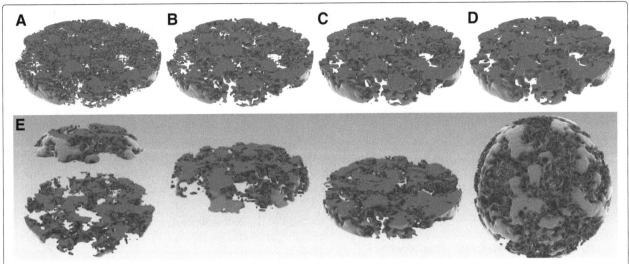

Figure 3 Surface generation of the NRO structure. Filtered versions of the above images going from left to right (**A**: 0%, **B**: 15%, **C**: 25%, and **D** 50% of the original voxel resolution) require (1.26, 1.21, 1.07, and 0.89 GB) of memory with an initial memory footprint of 0.49 GB, which amounts to around 50 MB per 1 million voxels. This reflects a linear memory usage with predictable performance requirements as the number of input voxels grow. Depending on the number of control points and coarse graining of the data points the surface becomes smoother, thus improving the perception of the overall 3D structure. The excluded volume grows slightly with the coarse graining and at the high value of D too many details of the structure are lost. **(E)** different slices of the reaction volume. The complete volume is also shown in the SI video (Additional file 1) .

increase in the excluded volume for finite particle radii, which is consistent with an increased reduction of the diffusion. Therefore, the more fragmented space leads to a stronger reduction in the diffusion [6].

Also depending on the local structure the effective diffusion varies. As indicated in Figure 4, the structures can (locally) vary in their isotropy, leading to an anisotropic diffusion. It is especially important that the reaction space reconstruction process leads to isotropic structures because even slight deviations are sensitively recognized by the diffusion process. Likewise the original microscope data where each voxel is $17.6 \times 17.6 \times 60$ nm are non-isotropic.

The comparison of the diffusion properties in the reconstructed reaction space and FCS measurements shows that the static (or at least temporarily static) structures are not sufficient to explain *in vivo* diffusion. The anomaly coefficient $\alpha = 0.94$ does not match the values observed in *in vivo* FCS measurements ($\alpha = 0.768 \pm 0.14$) [4,5]. Especially, the molecular crowding by mobile NROs seems to have an important effect [9,34]. The computational complexity of the multitude of interactions between all particles and the dimension of the simulation-parameter space however renders the analysis within such a detailed 3D volume structure impossible. Therefore, we investigated the influence of mobile NROs within a scalable discrete lattice-based simulation framework.

Dynamics of NRO change the diffusion and reaction speed
We performed Monte Carlo simulation with mobile NRO in our lattice-based simulation space described in Methods "Lattice-based Monte Carlo simulation" (the lattice-based simulator is also included as Additional file 2 and available from [35]). The motivation to move the NRO despite the increased computational complexity is to make the simulation environment compatible with realistic intracellular conditions, and to investigate if we can find a simulation-parameter regime matching our former FCS results [4,5].

First, if the jump probability describing the mobility of the particles (P_f) of the reactants equals the jump probability of the NROs (i.e., $P_f = 1$), the diffusion of reactants was independent from the crowding level of their

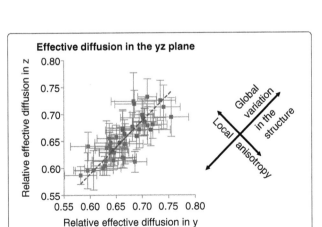

Figure 4 Isotropy of the effective diffusion in the virtual cytoplasm. Local anisotropy and global variation in the observed diffusion in different structures .

environment. They show normal diffusion instead of anomalous diffusion (Figure 5A). By FCS analyses, we observed anomalous diffusion of green fluorescent protein (GFP) in cytoplasm. The simulation results with the NRO jump probability $P_f = 1$ thus was not compatible with experimental results. Especially, when the relative volume of NROs is lower than 50%, the diffusion of the reactants shows no anomalous subdiffusive behavior.

Starting from this incompatibility with the experimental results, we varied the following two parameters: (i) the probability which determines the mobility of NRO in the simulation space and (ii) the radius of NROs to analyze the effect of the size of NROs on the diffusion of the reactants.

NRO mobility which leads to matching diffusion with experimental results

We varied the jump probability P_f, which determines the mobility of NRO in the simulation space (Figure 5B). In

this analysis, we fixed the size of NRO to occupy only one lattice site (i.e., single or small crowding molecules). The frequency of NRO movement was given in the range from 1/40 to 1/10 of the frequency of reactant moves, which move in every simulation step. This means that the NRO move once per 10 steps ($P_f = 1/10$), once per 20 steps ($P_f = 1/20$), once per 30 steps ($P_f = 1/30$), once per 40 steps ($P_f = 1/40$), or never ($P_f = 0$), respectively.

The results in Figure 5A show that if P_f is less than 1/10, diffusing reactants show the anomalous subdiffusive behavior for all tested NRO levels from 10 to 70%. This result is in agreement with previous works which indicated that the more static NROs result in a stronger confinement of the reactants [6,31], hence a more anomalous behavior (smaller α).

For all $P_f < 1$, we can obtain an anomalous parameter compatible with our experimental results ($\alpha = 0.768 \pm 0.14$) with about 20% relative volume of NRO in the reaction space. The estimated P_f value to reproduce the compatible α is 0.2383 to 0.3689. This means that the reactants move 2 to 5 times faster than the NROs in the reaction volume. However, the estimated relative volume amount is less than the occupied volume in the TEM images of 37%. Previous studies showed that the NRO-effect on the diffusion strongly depends on the size of the NROs [6,36]. Therefore, also the size has to be taken into account.

NRO size which leads to matching diffusion with experimental results

We also varied the aggregation level of NRO in the simulation space (Figure 5B). In this analysis, we fixed the mobility of the NROs to the same rate like the mobility of the reactants ($P_f = 1$).

The radius of the NRO was varied from 1 to 5 pixels. The original size ($r_{nro} = 1$) means that the object occupies 8 pixels. We assumed the reactants diffuse in cytoplasm. Because the reactants affect the moves of the NROs in the same way like the NROs block the way of the reactants, the concentrations of both NROs and reactants have to set in the right proportion. In order to adopt our simulation environment to the case of cytoplasmic enzyme, we chose 1.0 μM as the approximate concentration of the reactant. Our simulation environment for varying NRO radius is 1000 reactants in the lattice with $50 \times 50 \times 50$ total sites. To reconstruct the realistic intracellular environment by our simulation space, we assume the size of 1 pixel equals to 77.8 nm. This is about 15 times larger than the diameter of GFP, which is the molecule for which we analyzed the diffusion in a cytoplasmic region. Also, the approximate compartment size is $64\,\mu m^3 = 64\,fl$. This volume is acceptable as a part of cytoplasm; the expected whole volume of cytoplasm of a cell is 2.8 pl [37]. Now the radius of NRO varied from 1 to 5 pixels means the diameter of NRO is 155.6 to 778 nm.

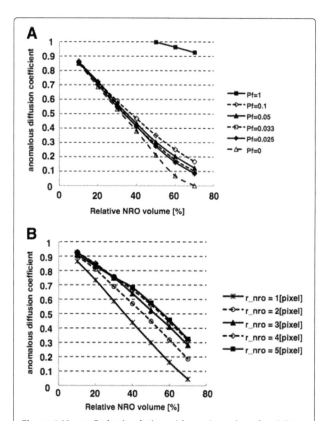

Figure 5 Monte Carlo simulation with varying value of mobility and aggregation level of NRO. (A) If all NRO are mobile with the same speed as the reactant and have the same size like it, the reactants in a cell show nearly a normal diffusion independent from the level of crowdedness. If the mobility of NRO is lower than the reactant diffusion in the reaction space, the reactants show anomalous diffusion as observed by FCS experiments. The different lines show the results produced by the different levels of crowding (0–70% of the volume is occupied by NRO). **(B)** Mobility of NRO is the same as the mobility of the reactant while the size is varied.

By changing the size of NRO, we find that the relative NRO volume is different for each different NRO size to produce compatible anomalous diffusion coefficient with experimental results. When the NRO size is small (155.6 nm, i.e., 30 times larger than a reactant), a cell can involve only 15 to less than 20% relative volume of NRO to produce a compatible anomalous diffusion coefficient with experimental results. If the NRO size is large (778 nm, i.e., 150 times larger than a reactant), a cell can involve over 30% relative volume of NRO to produce a compatible anomalous diffusion coefficient. This result is also consistent with a previous studies which showed that smaller objects have a much bigger influence on the diffusion of test molecules [6,36].

Empiric relationship between α, D_{nro}, and r_{nro}

We fitted the empiric functions given in Table 1 to the results of our Monte Carlo simulation with various conditions in order to find parameter ranges which are consistent with the results from FCS measurements. Note that these empiric functions do not need to have a physical meaning, but for instance show that the Stokes–Einstein relation $D \propto 1/r$ is not valid in the cytoplasm, because due to the microscopic structure different radii exhibit different viscosity. For instance large molecules sense a bigger hindrance in their mobility and can even be trapped by the meshes of the cytoskeleton [2,6].

The relation between D_{nro} and r_{nro} (Table 1, third equation) is calculated from the first two equations in Table 1 for the condition $P_f = 1$. Based on the appropriate size of the NRO from the previous section and the relationship with r_{nro} we conclude that $D_{nro} = 21.96$ to $44.49\,\mu m^2/s$ in order to obtain the desired α in the simulation at the target NRO fraction of 37%.

This diffusion coefficient is still in the same range like the diffusion coefficient of GFP in cytoplasm. On the one hand it is rather fast for large molecules but on the other hand our model in silico cytoplasm is just constructed out of one class of NROs compared to the complex size distribution in vivo [9,34]. The diffusion coefficient is not more than 10 times faster than the diffusion coefficient of large macromolecules (e.g., microtubule) in cytoplasm, thus supporting that our results are in a realistic physiological regime.

On the other hand, if the diffusion of NRO occurs at the physiological macromolecule level (ex. tubulin in cytoplasm is measured as 4–$10\,\mu m^2/s$ [39]), the diameter of NRO must be about 33–43 nm. This is smaller than the single NRO in our simulation. That means if the reaction space is crowded only with this size of obstacles, the anomalous diffusion constant will be smaller than the physiological value at the relative NRO volume fraction of 37%, which we found in our TEM image data. This value of relative NRO volume should be independent from the mobility state of the NROs.

Conclusions

We can conclude from simulation results in the reconstructed reaction space that the correct identification of noise or concrete structures in TEM images is very important because the diffusion strongly depends on it. The reconstructed tubular structures are consistent with, e.g., ER structures [11]. The structures are static in simulations of that reconstructed space (at least on the short timescales of the simulation), but future work aims at modeling the spatial dynamics of such membrane enclosed compartments [40]. The present generated structures could serve as a starting point for the size distribution of the compartments. Finally, a detailed and multi-scale simulation should include both the quasi-static cellular structures and the mobile NROs responsible for the majority of the molecular crowding effects. At the same time, investigation of the mixing ratio of differently sized NROs is also necessary in order to find a functional size distribution.

As the microscope data are discretizing the cell internal structures one could argue that the simulation should also use the 3D analytical surface representation, reconstructed inside the BioInspire visualization software. At the moment the simulation is not using this surface as the interfaces between the simulation and visualization are currently being defined. For an investigation of transient anomalous diffusion in such structures [23], much longer time spans need to be covered, which means that particles will diffuse much further away. Therefore, periodic boundary conditions for the volume are necessary. The reaction space might also be reconstructed based on the Fourier transform of the TEM images, which would lead to smooth boundaries under periodic boundary conditions.

The TEM image-reconstruction for a realistic simulation space gave us (i) an impression how the microscopic intracellular environment is structured in 3D and (ii) lets us further compare the results with that of lattice based and more scalable simulations, which also includes mobile NROs. By searching a compatible condition between the results of TEM-reconstructed space and artificial space, we could estimate the parameters for in silico simulation

Table 1 Empiric relations between α, D_{nro}, and r_{nro}

Relationship between α and D_{nro}	$\alpha = 0.0093 D_{nro} + 0.4606$
Relationship between α and r_{nro}	$\alpha = 0.1302 \times \ln r_{nro} + 0.0976$
Relationship between D_{nro} and r_{nro}	$D_{nro} = 14.0 \ln r_{nro} - 39.0$

The empiric relations are fitted to the simulation results. We used the value $D_{GFP} = 82 \pm 2\,\mu m^2/s$ for GFP and its mutant protein in solution [38]. The last relation is then deduced from the first two for $P_f = 1.0$ and a NRO volume fraction of 37%.

environments with realistic intracellular structures and dynamics.

Due to computational limitations these environments have to be tremendously simplified compared to the complexity of the *in vivo* system. Thus, our efforts match for instance the approach of Hou et al. [41] trying to create a simplified yet realistic *in vitro* model of the cytoplasm.

We confirmed that the diffusion characteristics of inert test molecules in a crowded space are preserved in the characteristics of molecules which take part in a Michaelis-Menten reaction by using discrete reaction space [42]. The reaction proceeds quickly at the beginning, but later on the reactants are exhausted slowly in our simulations. This result may mean that the intracellular environment transforms reaction processes in a cell from the *in vitro* reaction in a fractal manner [8]. It is comparable to the classic mass action system with a time-dependent rate constant. Also the observable effective reaction rate constant depends on the level of crowding and the effective diffusion, and might sensitively react in the case of anomalous diffusion [32]. These results support the importance to confirm detailed structures of the reaction space because the reaction environment affects the reaction process.

Therefore, the next challenge for *in vivo* oriented simulations will be performing simulations of bimolecular enzymatic reaction processes in the reconstructed reaction volume based on true cell environment, also by estimating the concrete value of environmental dynamics, and possibly by mixing static structures and mobile NROs.

Methods
Cell culture
Cell culture reagents for 3Y1 cells were obtained from Wako Pure Chemical Industries, Ltd. (Japan). The cell lines were routinely cultured in Dulbecco's Minimal Essential Medium supplemented with 10% fetal bovine serum in a 5% CO_2 incubator. We obtained 3Y1 cell line from Japanese Collection of Research Bioresources (JCRB) Cell Bank for use at Keio University.

Transmission electron microscopy
We obtained 101 images of rat fibroblast 3Y1 cells. We selected those images from the cytoplasmic regions, mainly at a magnification 1000.

The cells were collected on the day when the cells reached at the confluent condition in order to obtain a homogeneous population in their cell cycle (G1 to G0 cells).

In preparation for TEM, the cells were fixed with 4% formaldehyde and 2% glutaraldehyde in 0.1-M phosphate buffer (pH 7.4) for 16 h at 4°C, and successively with 1% osmium tetraoxide in 0.1-M phosphate buffer (pH 7.4).

The cells were dehydrated in graded ethanol and embedded in epoxy resin. Ultrathin sections (approximately 60-nm thick) were prepared with a diamond knife and were electron-stained with uranyl acetate and lead citrate, and were examined using an electron microscope (H-7650; Hitachi Ltd.).

First, the TEM images were binarized into objects and background using the auto-thresholding function of ImageJ (http://rsbweb.nih.gov/ij/; see Figure 1). Briefly, this algorithm computes the average intensity of the pixels at below or above, a particular threshold. It then computes the average of these two values, increments the threshold, and iterates the process until the threshold is larger than the composite average. That is,

$$\text{threshold} = \frac{(\text{average background} + \text{average objects})}{2}.$$

Subsequently, the binary images were translated into a 1-0 matrix in Matlab to reconstruct the simulation space. The simulation space for Figures 2, 3, and 4 was reconstructed based on TEM images as indicated below.

Generation of virtual cellular structures
In order to reconstruct the intracellular environment we learned the following statistics from the thresholded binary TEM images (cf. Figure 1B): $P_b(I(px_i) = 1|I(px_{i-1}), I(px_{i-2}), I(px_{i-3}))$, the probability that this pixel px_i is black ($I(px_i) = 1$), given the sequence of the neighboring three pixels, averaged over all directions (cf. Figure 2C). Likewise, we learned the probability of a pixel being black which is between two other pixels (separated by a distance j), and the average blackness (0.3755).

The $300 \times 300 \times 300\,\text{px}$ *in silico* volume is generated by drawing lines from P_b, each separated by 16 px in all directions. Next, we interpolated the pixels in between the lines (distance 8, 4, 2, and 1 px) to generate the complete volume. The generated volume is then iteratively processed by filtering it (erosion and dilation) until its $\hat{P}_b$ in all directions equals the empirical P_b of the images (cf. Figure 2A,C). In order to preserve not only big structures but also finer objects in the processed volume, the raw volume was fed back into the processed volume repeatedly by averaging over both images, while the weight of the raw image was reduced in each iteration. In order to produce a smoother surface, the volume was also low pass filtered (cf. Figure 2A–D). The necessary 3D filters were created based on ordfilt3 by Olivier Salvado from the Matlab central File Exchange (File ID: #5722). The present Matlab code to generate the volumes is available as Additional file 3.

In order to avoid boundary effects only the pixels 10-290 are used subsequently in the simulations, and accordingly a sphere with a diameter of $4.928\,\mu\text{m}$ is created at the scale of 1 px = 17.6 nm.

Visualization

The 3D NRO structure described in the previous section—even if filtered twice, once in 2D with ImageJ (section "Transmission electron microscopy") and once in 3D in Matlab (cf. Figure 2A,B)—still contains high-frequency components from image noise and the discretization of data into voxels. Image stacks acquired from TEM are discretizations of the actual natural analytic (or at least very highly detailed) environment of the cell's internal structures, which is why the direct visualization of the voxel space itself only reveals the coarse grained, cubic 3D environment. As input to the BioInspire raytracing engine, a total of 12.5 million voxels (4.5 million of which are occupied by NROs) were given, corresponding to the spherical subvolume of the simulation space. As touched upon in the introduction a 3D filter of the software package BioInspire was used to create a smooth surface by averaging over the 3D structure. The difference in non-processed data and filtered data can be seen in Figure 3 where the number of control points and parameters is adjusted. Clearly, the filtered version with a smoother surface is preferable for a clear visualization of the 3D structure. A section of the volume is shown in Figure 2 for comparison with the 2D 300×300 pixel image of single slices.

Diffusion simulations in the virtual environment

The continuous space discrete time diffusion simulator as described in [32] is used to simulate the diffusion of inert tracer molecules through a cell which contains the generated structures. The structures are represented by a binary 3D grid of spheres at the positions of black voxels of the generated volume. The static spheres had a radius of $r_s = 10.92$ nm, such that their volume matches the volume of each pixel of $(17.6 \text{ nm})^3$. We performed the simulations in 20 different structures to average over the different realizations. The diffusion of tracer molecules with molecular radii of $r_i = 2.6$ nm was simulated with 10 sets of 1000 molecules each. All original diffusion coefficients are arbitrarily set to $D_0 = 1 \mu m^2/s$, and Δt is chosen such that $\max \Delta x/(r_i + r_s) = 0.08$, i.e. $\Delta t = 1.27 \times 10^{-7} s$. The effective diffusion $D_{eff} = \langle (x(t) - x(t_0))^2 \rangle / (2d(t - t_0))$ was obtained in 3 dimensions ($d = 3$) as well as in each dimension separately ($d = 1$). The test volume was a cell with a diameter of $4.928 \mu m$ and was accordingly filled with approximately 4.5 million obstacles. The simulations were performed on the Brutus computing cluster at ETH Zurich, needed 10 h for 0.15 s of physical time and 400 MB memory at max (non-parallelized, but the different sets were running in parallel). With a Intel Core i7 2600K at 3.5 GHz and 8 GB RAM 1×10^6 steps, (i.e., 0.127s) of all 10000 particles of one set needed 3 h. The simulation is available from [33]. We used this virtual environment for the calculation of effective diffusion constant and for the investigation of the local anisotropy of the volume.

Lattice-based Monte Carlo simulation

We also performed a scalable lattice-based Monte Carlo simulation and compared it with the results from the simulations in our virtual environment as well as experimental results from [4,5] by changing the size and mobility of NRO, in order to clarify the characteristics of such a crowded environment. This simulation is available from [35] or Additional file 2.

Diffusion simulation with immobile NRO

The simulation space is a $50 \times 50 \times 50$ cubic lattice with periodic boundary conditions. The reaction space is randomly interspersed with NRO. The random walkers representing the diffusing reactants can jump to a neighboring lattice site in each iteration, which is selected randomly. If the chosen lattice site was previously empty, the reactant fills the site; if the site was occupied by an NRO, a new position is randomly allocated for the reactant. The simulator is implemented in the C++ programming language.

Reaction simulation with immobile NRO

The reaction simulated in our model is $A + A \rightarrow A$. If the chosen lattice site of reactant $A1$ in a diffusion step is occupied by another reactant $A2$, $A2$ is obliterated and only $A1$ remains at the new lattice site.

Pseudo-mono reaction process simulation with mobile NRO

We changed the characteristics of NRO such that they can move randomly as well. Their probability to move P_f was varied from the same as reactants ($P_f = 1$) to 40 times smaller ($P_f = 1/40$), i.e., slower, to investigate the effect of NRO mobility to the reactants behaviors.

All NRO move as single independent molecules. The other conditions for this simulation remain unchanged.

Pseudo-mono reaction process simulation with aggregated NRO

We also varied the diameter of NRO to test the effect of NRO size to the reactant behaviors. By this analysis, we investigated the condition relating with NRO aggregation level, which move with $P_f = 1$, i.e., with the same probability as the reactants. The other conditions for this simulation remain the unchanged.

Additional files

Additional file 1: Video of the 3D volume. Dynamic exploration of the generated 3D virtual cytoplasm.

> **Additional file 2:** Lattice-based simulator. Zip folder contains reaction–diffusion simulator with mobile and fixed lattice-based NROs of variable size. Code is written in C++ and requires the respective compilers.
>
> **Additional file 3:** MATLAB code for volume generation. Zip folder contains original images to learn statistics from and MATLAB code to generate the 3D volumes. Requires MATLAB.

Competing interests
Dr.Pablo de Heras Ciechomski is the founder of ScienceVisuals, Sarl, which is developing products related to the research described in this article and developed through the Swiss Agency KTI for promotion of medical technologies. The terms of this arrangement have been reviewed and approved by the swiss Federal Institute of Technology, Zurich, Switzerland, in accordance with their respective conflict of interest policies.

Authordetails
[1]Department of BioSciences and Informatics, Keio University, Yokohama, Kanagawa, Japan. [2]Automatic Control Laboratory, Swiss Federal Institute of Technology, Zurich, Switzerland. [3]ScienceVisuals Sarl, Lausanne, Switzerland. [4]Department of Pathology,School of Medicine, Keio University, Shinjuku-ku, Tokyo, Japan.

Acknowledgements
MK and RM acknowledge the funding through the Swiss Confederation's Commission for Technology and Innovation (CTI) project 12532.1 PFLS-LS. HK acknowledges the support from the Swiss National Science Foundation, grant no. PP00P2_128503. TEM microscope imaging and the culturing the material cells by NH have been supported by SUNBOR grant (provided by SUNTORY Institute for Bioorganic Research, Japan) and Keio University (Japan).

References
1. A Fulton, How crowded is the cytoplasm? Cell. **30**, 345–347 (1982)
2. K Luby-Phelps, Cytoarchitecture and physical properties of cytoplasm: volume, viscosity, diffusion, intracellular surface area. Int. Rev. Cytol. **192**, 189–221 (2000)
3. AP Minton, The influence of macromolecular crowding and macromolecular confinement on biochemical reactions in physiological media. J. Bio. Chem. **276**(14), 10577–10580 (2001)
4. N Hiroi, J Lu, K Iba, S Tabira, A Yamashita, Y Okada, G Köhler, A Funahashi, A study into the crowdedness of intracellular environment: estimation of fractal dimensionality and anomalous diffusion. in *The 8th Workshop in Computational Systems Biology.* (Tampere, Finland, 77–80, 2011)
5. N Hiroi, J Lu, K Iba, S Tabira, A Yamashita, Y Okada, K Oka, G Köhler, A Funahashi, Physiological environment induces quick response-slow exhaustion reactions. Front. Syst. Physiol. **2**(50), 1–16 (2011)
6. M Klann, A Lapin, M Reuss, Stochastic simulation of signal transduction: impact of the cellular architecture on diffusion. Biophys. J. **96**(12), 5122–5129 (2009)
7. I Novak, P Kraikivski, Slepchenko B, Diffusion in cytoplasm: effects of excluded volume due to internal membranes and cytoskeletal structures. Biophys. J. **97**(3), 758–767 (2009)
8. S Schnell, Turner T, Reaction kinetics in intracellular environments with macromolecular crowding: simulations and rate laws. Prog. Biophys. Mol. Biol. **85**(2–3), 235–260 (2004)
9. M Weiss, M Elsner, F Kartberg, T Nilsson, Anomalous subdiffusion is a measure for cytoplasmic crowding in living cells. Biophys. J. **87**, 3518–3524 (2004)
10. A Verkman, et al., Monte carlo analysis of obstructed diffusion in three dimensions: application to molecular diffusion in organelles. Biophys. J. **74**(5), 2722–2730 (1998)
11. I Sbalzarini, A Mezzacasa, A Helenius, P Koumoutsakos, Effects of organelle shape on fluorescence recovery after photobleaching. Biophys. J. **89**(3), 1482–1492 (2005)
12. B Kholodenko, Cell-signalling dynamics in time and space. Nat. Rev. Mol. Cell Biol. **7**(3), 165–176 (2006)
13. A Lapin, M Klann, M Reuss, Multi-scale spatio-temporal modeling: lifelines of microorganisms in bioreactors and tracking molecules in cells. Biosystems Eng. II, Adv. Biochem. Eng./Biotechnol. **121**, 23–43 (2010)
14. O Medalia, I Weber, AS Frangakis, D Nicastro, Gerisch G, W Baumeister, Macromolecular architecture in eukaryotic cells visualized by cryoelectron tomography. Science. **298**, 1209–1213 (2002)
15. A Nans, N Mohandas, D Stokes, Native ultrastructure of the red cell cytoskeleton by cryo-electron tomography. Biophys. J. **101**(10), 2341–2350 (2011)
16. T Peng, R Murphy, Image-derived, three-dimensional generative models of cellular organization. Cytometry Part A. (2011)
17. C Rose, C Taylor, A statistical model of texture for medical image synthesis and analysis. Med. Image Understand Anal., 1–4 (2003)
18. P De Heras Ciechomski, R Mange, A Peternier, Two-phased real-time rendering of large neuron databases. *2008 Int. Conference Innovations Inf. Technol.*, 712–716, (2008). http://ieeexplore.ieee.org/lpdocs/epic03/wrapper.htm?arnumber=4781778
19. P de Heras Ciechomski, R Mange. in *Proceedings of the First International Conference on Biomedical Electronics and Devices, BIOSIGNALS 2008, Funchal, Madeira, Portugal, January 28-31, 2008, Vol 2,* ed. by Encarnacao P, Veloso A, and Realtime neocortical column visualization: INSTICC - Institute for Systems and Technologies of Information, Control and Communication, 283–288, 2008)
20. C Crassin, F Neyret, S Lefebvre, E Eisemann, GigaVoxels : ray-guided streaming for efficient and detailed voxel rendering. in *ACM SIGGRAPH Symposium on Interactive 3D Graphics and Games (I3D).* (ACM, Boston, MA, Etats-Unis: ACM Press, 2009. http://maverick.inria.fr/Publications/2009/CNLE09
21. R Concheiro, M Amor, M Boo, M Doggett, Dynamic and adaptive tessellation of Bezier surfaces. in *VISIGRAPP 2011, International Joint Conference on Computer Vision, Imaging and Computer Graphics Theory and Applications,* (2011)
22. WJ Schroeder, LS Avila, W Hoffman, Visualizing with VTK: a tutorial. IEEE Comput. Graph. Appl. **20**, 20–27 (2000). http://dx.doi.org/10.1109/38.865875
23. M Saxton, A biological interpretation of transient anomalous subdiffusion. I. Qualitative model. Biophys. J. **92**(4), 1178–1191 (2007)
24. Y Gefen, A Aharony, S Alexander, Anomalous diffusion percolating clusters. Phys. Rev. Lett. **50**, 77–80 (1983)
25. SR Broadbent, JMT Hammersley, T Taittaja, GG Guru, SR Broadbent, JM Hammersley, Percolation processes. in *Mathematical Proceedings of the Cambridge Philosophical Society 53,* 629–541, (1957)
26. D Stauffer, A Aharony, Percolation processes. Phys. Rev. Lett. **50**, 77–80 (1983)
27. S Kirkpatrick, Percolation and conduction. Rev. Modern Phys. **45**(4), 574 (1973)
28. M Saxton, Two-Dimensional continuum percolation threshold for diffusing particles of nonzero radius. Biophys. J. **99**(5), 1490–1499 (2010)
29. O Seksek, J Biwersi, A Verkman, Translational diffusion of macromolecule-sized solutes in cytoplasm and nucleus. J. Cell Biol. **138**, 131–142 (1997)
30. S Trinh, P Arce, Effective diffusivities of point-like molecules in isotropic porous media by Monte Carlo Simulation. Transport Porous Media. **38**, 241–259 (2000)
31. D Hall, M Hoshino, Effects of macromolecular crowding on intracellular diffusion from a single particle perspective. Biophys. Rev. **2**, 39–53 (2010)
32. M Klann, A Lapin, M Reuss, Agent-based simulation of reactions in the crowded and structured intracellular environment: Influence of mobility and location of the reactants. BMC Syst. Biol. **71**(5) (2011)
33. BISON Group spatial simulation package. http://www.bison.ethz.ch/research/spatial_simulations
34. D Ridgway, G Broderick, A Lopez-Campistrous, M Ru'aini, P Winter, M Hamilton, P Boulanger, A Kovalenko, M Ellison, Coarse-grained molecular simulation of diffusion and reaction kinetics in a crowded virtual cytoplasm. Biophys. J. **94**(10), 3748–3759 (2008)
35. InVivoCrowdingSimulator: A 3D lattice-based simulator for studying the dynamics of particles in the crowded environment. http://fun.bio.keio.ac.jp/software/invivosim/
36. J Sun, H Weinstein, Toward realistic modeling of dynamic processes in cell signaling: Quantification of macromolecular crowding effects. J. Chem. Phys. **127**, 155105 (2007)

37. K Aoki, M Yamada, K Kunida, S Yasuda, M Matsuda, Processive phosphorylation of ERK MAP kinase in mammalian cells. Proc. Natl. Acad. Sci, 1–6 (2011). [Pnas.1104030108. MEK 1.2 μM, ERK 0.74 μM].

38. Z Wang, J Shah, Z Chen, C Sun, M Berns, Fluorescence orrelation spectroscopy investigation of a GFP mutant-enhanced cyan fluorescent protein and its tubulin fusion in living cells with two-photon excitation. J. Biomed. Opt. **9**(2), 395–403 (2004). [The diffusion constants of ECFP were determined to be 20+/-7 microm(2)/s in the nucleus and 21+/-8 microm(2)/s in the cytoplasm. The diffusion constant of ECFP in solution 82+/-2microm(2)/s].

39. ED Salmon, WM Saxton, RJ Leslie, ML Karow, JR Mcintosh, Diffusion coefficient od fluorescein-labeled tubulin in the cytoplasm of embryonic cells of a sea urchin: video image analysis of fluorescence redistribution after photobleaching. J. Cell. Biol. **99**, 2157–2164 (1984). [The viscosity of the cytoplasm which slows down tubulin diffusion (about 5.101 x 2 m^2/s as measured in sea urchin extracts].

40. M Klann, H Koeppl, M Reuss, Spatial modeling of vesicle transport and the cytoskeleton: the challenge of hitting the right road. PLoS ONE. **7**, e29645 (2012). http://dx.plos.org/10.1371/journal.pone.0029645.

41. L Hou, F Lanni, K Luby-Phelps, Tracer diffusion in F-actin and Ficoll mixtures. Toward a model for cytoplasm. Biophys. J. **58**, 31–43 (1990)

42. K Iba, A Tabira, T Okuhara, T Kubojima, N Hiroi, A Funahashi, Intracellular environment affects the properties of molecular behaviors and the reaction properties. in *2011 Winter Simulation Conference Simulation For A Sustainable World*: Omnipress, 75, 2011)

17

Simultaneous identification of robust synergistic subnetwork markers for effective cancer prognosis

Navadon Khunlertgit[1] and Byung-Jun Yoon[1,2]*

Abstract

Background: Accurate prediction of cancer prognosis based on gene expression data is generally difficult, and identifying robust prognostic markers for cancer remains a challenging problem. Recent studies have shown that modular markers, such as pathway markers and subnetwork markers, can provide better snapshots of the underlying biological mechanisms by incorporating additional biological information, thereby leading to more accurate cancer classification.

Results: In this paper, we propose a novel method for simultaneously identifying robust synergistic subnetwork markers that can accurately predict cancer prognosis. The proposed method utilizes an efficient message-passing algorithm called affinity propagation, based on which we identify groups – or subnetworks – of discriminative and synergistic genes, whose protein products are closely located in the protein-protein interaction (PPI) network. Unlike other existing subnetwork marker identification methods, our proposed method can simultaneously identify multiple nonoverlapping subnetwork markers that can synergistically predict cancer prognosis.

Conclusions: Evaluation results based on multiple breast cancer datasets demonstrate that the proposed message-passing approach can identify robust subnetwork markers in the human PPI network, which have higher discriminative power and better reproducibility compared to those identified by previous methods. The identified subnetwork makers can lead to better cancer classifiers with improved overall performance and consistency across independent cancer datasets.

Keywords: Cancer classification; Subnetwork marker identification; Protein-protein interaction network; Message-passing algorithm

Introduction

Identifying disease-related biological markers is an important problem in translational genomics, and there have been significant research efforts to find robust markers for disease diagnosis and prognosis from gene expression data obtained from microarrays or next-generation sequencing (NGS). However, the small sample size and the high dimensionality of the typical genomic data makes the prediction of such biomarkers very challenging. A large number of approaches have been proposed so far to

deal with these issues, where it has been recently shown that the concept of 'modular markers' have potentials for detecting better disease markers that are more robust and reproducible across independent datasets. In the past, it has been a common practice to look for the so-called 'key genes' that show significant differential expression under different conditions or between distinct phenotypes to discover gene markers that may be used for discriminating between different classes of biological/clinical samples. Unlike these traditional gene markers, where each gene is viewed as a potential biomarker, a *modular marker* consists of multiple genes that belong to the same functional module and show coordinated behaviors to fulfill a common biological function. The utilization of modular markers allows us to interpret and analyze the gene

*Correspondence: byoon@qf.org.qa
[1] Department of Electrical and Computer Engineering, Texas A&M University, 77843-3128 College Station, TX, USA
[2] College of Science, Engineering, and Technology, Hamad Bin Khalifa University (HBKU), P.O. Box 5825 Doha, Qatar

expression data in a more system-oriented way, which may facilitate the prediction of system-level properties based on the markers.

Examples of such modular markers include the pathway markers [1-5] and the subnetwork markers [6,7]. A pathway marker consists of multiple genes that belong to the same functional pathway. In order to use a pathway marker in a classification task, we first need to infer the activity level of the pathway based on the expression levels of its member genes, after which the inferred pathway activity can be used as a feature in a classifier. So far, several different methods have been proposed for pathway activity inference [1-5], and it has been shown that pathway markers tend to be more effective and robust compared to traditional gene markers. Unfortunately, the usefulness of pathway markers is practically limited by our incomplete pathway knowledge. In fact, currently known pathways cover only a relatively small number of genes; hence, the reliance on pathway markers may result in excluding crucial genes that may play important roles in determining the phenotypes of interest.

The concept of subnetwork markers has been originally proposed to address the weakness of pathway markers [6,8]. The main idea is to overlay the protein-protein interaction (PPI) network with the gene expression data to identify potential 'subnetwork markers,' which consist of discriminative genes whose protein products interact with each other, hence, connected in the PPI network. Conceptually, we can find such subnetwork markers by identifying subnetwork regions that undergo significant differential expression across different phenotypes, and the detected subnetwork markers may potentially correspond to functional modules – such as signaling pathways or protein complexes – in the underlying biological network. PPI networks provide a much better gene coverage compared to the set of currently known pathways; hence, this network-based approach can essentially overcome the major shortcoming of the pathway-based approach.

Until now, several different strategies have been proposed for identifying subnetwork markers. For example, Chuang et al. [6] proposed an efficient algorithm for finding subnetwork markers, where they first identify highly discriminative seed genes and then greedily grow the subnetworks around the seed genes to maximize the mutual information between the average z-score of the member genes and the class label. More recently, Su et al. [7] proposed a different strategy, where differentially expressed linear paths are found by dynamic programming and overlapping paths are combined to obtain discriminative subnetwork markers. Both studies [6,7] have shown that subnetwork markers can lead to more accurate and robust classifiers, compared to pathway markers.

In this paper, we propose a novel method for identifying effective subnetwork markers for predicting cancer prognosis. The proposed method is based on an efficient message-passing algorithm, called affinity propagation, which can be used to efficiently identify clusters of discriminative and synergistic genes whose protein products are either connected or closely located in the PPI network. Unlike previous subnetwork marker identification methods, the proposed method can simultaneously predict multiple subnetwork markers, which are mutually exclusive and have the potential to accurately predict cancer prognosis in a synergistic manner. Based on several independent breast cancer datasets, we demonstrate that the proposed method can identify better prognostic markers that have improved reproducibility and higher discriminative power compared to the markers identified by previous methods.

Materials and methods
Datasets
We obtained four independent breast cancer microarray gene expression datasets from previous studies, which we refer to as the USA dataset (GEO:GSE2034) [9], Netherlands dataset (NKI-295) [10], Belgium dataset (GEO:GSE7390) [11], and Sweden dataset (GEO:GSE1456) [12], respectively. The USA, Belgium, Sweden datasets were profiled on the Affymetrix U133a platform and downloaded from the Gene Expression Omnibus (GEO) website [13]. The Netherlands dataset was profiled on a custom Agilent microarray platform, and it was downloaded from the Stanford website [14]. The USA dataset contains the gene expression profiles of 286 breast cancer patients, the Netherlands dataset contains the profiles of 295 patients, the Belgium dataset contains the profiles of 198 patients, and the Sweden dataset contains the profiles obtained from 159 patients. In this study, gene expression profiles of the patients for whom metastasis had been detected within 5 years of surgery were labeled as 'metastatic', while the remaining profiles were labeled as 'non-metastatic'. The USA, Netherlands, Belgium, and Sweden datasets respectively contain 106, 78, 35, and 35 metastatic profiles. The human protein-protein interaction network used in this paper was obtained from a previous study on subnetwork marker identification by Chuang et al. [6], which consists of 11,203 proteins and 57,235 interactions. We overlaid the gene expression data in the four breast cancer datasets with this PPI network, by mapping each gene to the corresponding protein in the network. After removing the proteins that do not have corresponding genes in all four datasets, we obtained an induced network with 26,150 interactions among 4,936 proteins.

The affinity propagation algorithm: a brief overview
In order to identify discriminative subnetwork markers, we apply *affinity propagation* [15], an efficient clustering

algorithm based on a message-passing approach. In affinity propagation, real-valued messages are iteratively exchanged between data points until a good set of exemplars (i.e., representative data points) are identified. The data points are clustered around the exemplars that best represent them, which gives rise to clusters that consist of similar data points. During the message-passing process, two different types of messages are exchanged between data points: *responsibility* and *availability*. The responsibility $r(i,k)$ measures the suitability of the data point k to be an exemplar of the data point i, considering other potential exemplars. The availability $a(i,k)$ measures the appropriateness of choosing the data point k as the exemplar for the data point i, based on the choice of other data points. At each iteration, these messages are updated as follows:

$$r(i,k) \leftarrow s(i,k) - \max_{k' \text{ s.t. } k' \neq k} \left\{ a(i,k') + s(i,k') \right\} \qquad (1)$$

$$a(i,k) \leftarrow \min \left\{ 0, r(k,k) + \sum_{i' \text{ s.t. } i' \notin \{i,k\}} \max \left\{ 0, r(i',k) \right\} \right\}, \qquad (2)$$

where $s(i,k)$ is the similarity between the data points i and k, used as the input of the clustering algorithm. This similarity $s(i,k)$ can be asymmetric. The self-availability is updated in a slightly different way, as shown below:

$$a(k,k) \leftarrow \sum_{i' \text{ s.t. } i' \neq k} \max \left\{ 0, r(i',k) \right\}. \qquad (3)$$

The data point k that maximizes the sum $a(i,k) + r(i,k)$ is chosen as the exemplar for the data point i, and the algorithm converges if the set of exemplars does not change further.

So far, affinity propagation has been applied to various applications – such as predicting genes from microarray data and clustering facial images – and it has been shown to effectively identify meaningful clusters of data points at a much lower computational cost than traditional clustering methods [15]. One important advantage of affinity propagation is that the number of clusters need not be specified in advance. This is especially useful in our current application, since we neither know how many functional modules are embedded in the biological network at hand nor how many of them are relevant to cancer prognosis, which makes it practically difficult to determine how many subnetwork markers we should look for.

Computing the similarity between genes

In our proposed method, we use affinity propagation to identify clusters – or subnetworks – of discriminative and synergistic genes, whose protein products either interact with each other or are closely located in the PPI network. In order to use affinity propagation to identify the gene clusters, we first have to define the similarity $s(i,k)$ between genes g_i and g_k for all gene pairs. The characteristics of the final clusters – especially, their usefulness as potential subnetwork markers – will critically depend on how we define this similarity. For this reason, we take the following points into consideration when defining $s(i,k)$:

1. The proteins corresponding to the genes in the same cluster should have direct interaction or should be closely located in the PPI network.
2. Every gene in a potential subnetwork marker should have sufficient discriminative power to distinguish between the two class labels (metastatic vs. non-metastatic).
3. The discriminative power to distinguish between the two class labels should be increased by combining genes within the same cluster.

Based on these considerations, we define the similarity $s(i,k)$ as follows:

$$s(i,k) = t_k + \min \{t_{ik} - t_i, t_{ik} - t_k\} - \alpha \, |t_i - t_k| \qquad (4)$$

if the shortest distance $d(i,k)$ between the protein products of the genes g_i and g_k in the PPI network satisfies $d(i,k) \leq 2$. Otherwise, we set the similarity to $s(i,k) = -\infty$. The discriminative power of a given gene is measured in terms of the t-test statistics score of the log-likelihood ratio (LLR) between the two class labels, and t_i and t_k are the t-test scores of g_i and g_k, respectively. Similarly, t_{ik} is the t-test score of the combined LLRs of g_i and g_k which is computed by summing up the LLRs of the two genes. This term, t_{ik}, reflects the discriminative power of the gene pair (g_i, g_k) after combining them. The self-similarity was set to $s(k,k) = c$ for all k, where the constant c was chosen such that $s(i,k) \geq c$ for only 1% of all gene pairs (g_i, g_k). Uniform initialization of the self-similarity $s(k,k) = c$ guarantees that every gene in the dataset gets equal chance to be an exemplar at the beginning of the message-passing process.

As shown in (4), the similarity $s(i,k)$ between g_i and g_k is defined in an asymmetric way, where the first term corresponds to the discriminative power of the gene g_k, the second term measures the improvement in discriminative power after combining the two genes g_i and g_k, and the last term corresponds to a penalty term for the difference between t_k and t_i. The parameter $\alpha \in [0,1]$ is used to control the penalty term. According to the above definition, gene g_i regards gene g_k as being 'similar' to itself:

1. if g_k has high discriminative power (first term);
2. if combining the two genes increases the overall discriminative power;
3. if both genes have similar discriminative power.

The main reason underlying the asymmetric definition of the similarity $s(i, k)$ is to indicate the direction of similarity. Based on our asymmetric definition, the exemplars of the identified clusters tend to have higher discriminative power compared to other non-exemplars. Intuitively, the gene similarity defined in (4) will make the affinity propagation algorithm identify gene clusters that consist of highly discriminative genes that are synergistic to each other and whose protein products are closely located in the PPI network.

Post-processing the identified gene subnetworks

Although the affinity propagation algorithm can effectively identify subnetworks that consist of discriminative and synergistic genes, the clustering process does not completely rule genes with relatively lower discriminative power out of those subnetworks. As a result, the initial subnetworks that are predicted by affinity propagation may still contain genes with relatively lower discriminative power compared to other genes in the same subnetwork. In order to improve the overall discriminative power of the potential subnetwork markers, we post-processed the initial subnetworks as follows. First, we clustered the genes in a given subnetwork into k groups based on their t-test statistics scores using the k-means clustering algorithm, where k was chosen to be $k = \lfloor \log(\# \text{ of gene in considered subnetwork}) + 1 \rfloor$. After clustering, the genes in the group with the lowest average t-test score were removed from the subnetwork.

Probabilistic inference of subnetwork activity

For estimating the activity level of a subnetwork based on the gene expression profile of a patient, we adopted the probabilistic pathway activity inference method introduced in [4]. Given a subnetwork (or a pathway) with n member genes $\mathcal{G} = \{g_1, g_2, \ldots, g_n\}$ and the gene expression profile $\boldsymbol{x} = \{x^1, x^2, \ldots, x^n\}$ of a patient, where x^i is the expression level of the gene g_i, the activity level of the subnetwork is computed by:

$$A(\boldsymbol{x}) = \sum_{i=1}^{n} \lambda_i \left(x^i \right), \tag{5}$$

where $\lambda_i(x^i)$ is the log-likelihood ratio between the two class labels (in this work, metastatic vs. non-metastatic). This is given by

$$\lambda_i(x^i) = \log \left[f_i^1(x^i) / f_i^2(x^i) \right], \tag{6}$$

where $f_i^j(x^i)$ is the conditional probability density function (PDF) of x^i under phenotype j. We assume that the gene expression level of g_i under phenotype j follows a Gaussian distribution.

Results

Statistics of the identified subnetwork markers

For each of the four datasets, we identified potential subnetwork markers using the proposed method and selected the top 50 markers based on their discriminative power, measured in terms of the t-test statistics score of the subnetwork activity. Three different values of $\alpha (= 0.2, 0.5, 0.8)$ were used in our experiments to investigate the effect of the penalty term in (4) on the subnetwork marker identification result. Table 1 shows the average size of the top 50 subnetwork markers for each dataset and α. The last two columns in the table show the average size of the subnetwork markers identified using the method proposed by Chuang et al. [6], which we refer to as the 'greedy' method, for simplicity. Two different values of r were used for this greedy method. This parameter r specifies the minimum improvement rate of the discriminative power of a subnetwork marker. The greedy method stops when extending the subnetwork marker by adding a neighboring gene that does not improve the marker's discriminative power by at least the specified rate r. We tested the greedy method with $r = 0.05$ (or 5% minimum required improvement) which is the same as in [6]. We also tested the method with a lower rate $r = 0.001$ (or 0.1% minimum required improvement) in order to allow the greedy search to continue even if the improvement is not very significant and find out how a lower rate affects the subnetwork size and its discriminative power. As we can see from Table 1, the size of the network decreases as α gets larger. In fact, a large α tends to cluster only genes with similar discriminative power (i.e., genes with similar t-test scores), thereby yielding smaller subnetworks with fewer genes. Similar trends can be also observed in Table 2, which shows the total number of unique genes in the top 50 subnetwork markers. As see can see in this table, a larger α results in a smaller number of unique genes in the top subnetwork markers, as each marker tends to get smaller.

Table 3 shows the total number of the common genes between the identified subnetworks using different α. We can see that around 77% of genes included in the identified subnetworks using smaller α are also found in the subnetworks identified with larger α. We examined the overlap between the subnetworks identified on different datasets,

Table 1 Average size of the identified subnetwork markers

Dataset	Proposed method			Greedy	
	$\alpha = 0.2$	$\alpha = 0.5$	$\alpha = 0.8$	$r = 0.05$	$r = 0.001$
USA	52.58	35.58	16.96	3.94	5.22
Netherlands	52.62	31.2	15.9	5.18	7.20
Belgium	37.64	20.2	12.3	4.12	5.48
Sweden	33.18	21.38	14.16	3.66	4.82

Table 2 Total number of unique genes in the identified subnetwork markers

Dataset	Proposed method			Greedy	
	$\alpha = 0.2$	$\alpha = 0.5$	$\alpha = 0.8$	$r = 0.05$	$r = 0.001$
USA	2,629	1,779	848	169	217
Netherlands	2,631	1,560	795	158	222
Belgium	1,916	1,010	615	113	149
Sweden	1,695	1,069	708	123	166

which is defined as the number of genes in the intersection divided by the number of genes in the union. As shown in Table 4, we can see that the average overlap is typically close to (or above) 20%, which is larger than the greedy method as well as the overlap reported in [6] (12.7%).

Computational cost for subnetwork marker identification
In order to evaluate the computational complexity of the proposed method, we computed the total CPU time that is needed for identifying the top 50 subnetwork markers on each dataset. We considered three different values of α (= 0.2, 0.5, 0.8) that were used in our simulations. For comparison, we also estimated the total CPU time for the greedy method that was previously proposed. It should be noted that the two methods take completely different approaches for identifying multiple markers. In our proposed method, all potential subnetwork markers (whose total number exceeds 50) are *simultaneously* identified; hence, we need to rank the potential markers to select the top 50 markers with the highest discriminative power. As a result, for our proposed method, the total CPU time includes the time for calculating the similarity between genes, potential subnetwork marker identification through affinity propagation, and post-processing and ranking the subnetwork markers. On the other hand, for the greedy method, we measured the CPU time for calculating the discriminative power of the genes and iteratively searching for the top 50 markers. Since the greedy method finds one marker at a time, the search process needs to be repeated to find multiple markers. Figure 1 shows the total CPU time of the two methods for different parameters. All experiments were performed on a

Table 3 Total number of common genes between the top subnetwork markers identified using different α

Dataset	$\alpha = 0.2 \cap$ $\alpha = 0.5$	$\alpha = 0.2 \cap$ $\alpha = 0.8$	$\alpha = 0.5 \cap$ $\alpha = 0.8$
USA	1,612	660	561
Netherlands	1,382	646	488
Belgium	767	454	372
Sweden	802	466	387

Table 4 Overlap between the top subnetwork markers identified on different datasets

Dataset	Proposed method	Greedy	
	($\alpha = 0.5$)	$r = 0.05$	$r = 0.001$
USA - Netherlands	25.10%	8.28%	7.60%
USA - Belgium	19.04%	5.22%	6.09%
USA - Sweden	19.71%	5.32%	5.51%
Netherlands - Belgium	18.11%	8.84%	10.09%
Netherlands - Sweden	18.85%	7.92%	7.78%
Belgium - Sweden	17.13%	11.57%	11.31%

desktop computer with a 3.06 GHz Intel Core i3 CPU and 4GB 1333 MHz DDR3 memory. The results show that the proposed method is computationally more efficient for the given task as it can simultaneously identify all potential markers without repeating the search process multiple times. Unless one is interested in predicting only a few top markers, the proposed method provides a clear advantage over the previous greedy method. Figure 1 also shows that using different parameters does not affect the overall CPU time significantly.

Discriminative power of the subnetwork markers
We evaluated the discriminative power of the predicted subnetwork markers by following a similar procedure as in previous studies [3,4]. For each subnetwork marker identified using the proposed method, we first inferred its activity level for the gene expression profile of each patient and then computed the t-test score of the the inferred subnetwork activity level. Next, we sorted the subnetwork markers according to their absolute t-test score in a descending order. We then computed the average absolute t-test score of the top $K = 10, 20, 30, 40, 50$ subnetwork markers, as shown in Figure 2.

The horizontal axis in Figure 2 corresponds to K, and the vertical axis corresponds to the mean absolute t-test score of the top K subnetwork markers. We compared the discriminative power of the subnetwork markers predicted by the proposed method with the discriminative power of the subnetworks predicted by the greedy method proposed in [6]. The activity level of these subnetworks (identified by the greedy method) was inferred based on the same scheme that was originally used in [6]. As we can see from Figure 2, the proposed method typically finds subnetwork markers with comparable or slightly higher discriminative power compared to the previous greedy method, although both methods work very well. In this experiment, the parameter α did not significantly affect the average discriminative power of the subnetwork markers identified by the proposed method.

We also investigated the impact of the post-processing step by comparing the discriminative power of the

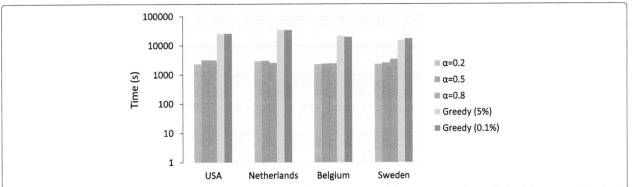

Figure 1 Total CPU Time for identifying the top 50 subnetwork markers. We evaluated the computational complexity of the proposed method by estimating the total CPU time needed for identifying the top 50 subnetwork markers in a given dataset. We compared our method with the previously proposed greedy method for a number of different parameters.

subnetwork markers before and after post-processing. Additional file 1: Figure S1 shows the results obtained using $\alpha = 0.5$. We can see that the discriminative power of the top 50 subnetwork markers improves as a result of the post-processing step, during which we remove the genes that have relatively lower discriminative power.

Next, to test the reproducibility of the subnetwork markers identified by the proposed method, we performed cross-dataset experiments as follows. First, we identified subnetwork markers using the proposed method on one of the datasets and ranked the markers based on their absolute t-test statistics score. After ranking the subnetwork markers, we re-evaluated the discriminative power of the top 50 markers on a different dataset.

This experiment allows us to find out how much discriminative power is retained by the top predicted markers in a different, and independent, dataset. The cross-dataset experiments are shown in Figure 3 and Additional file 1: Figure S2, where we can see that the markers identified by the proposed method remain highly discriminative across datasets. This is in clear contrast to the subnetwork markers identified by the greedy method [6], for which we can typically observe a sharp decrease in discriminative power when applied to an independent dataset that was not used for predicting the markers. Interestingly, we can also see that the proposed method finds effective markers that retain high discriminative power even on an independent gene expression dataset profiled on a different microarray

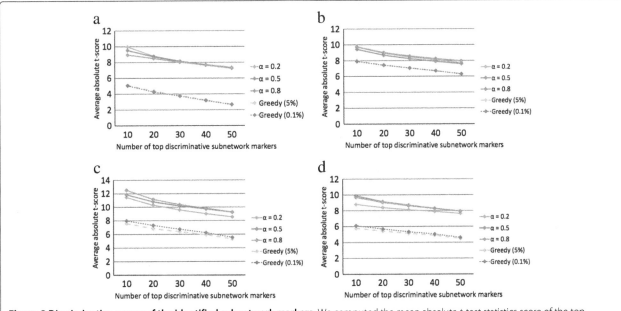

Figure 2 Discriminative power of the identified subnetwork markers. We computed the mean absolute t-test statistics score of the top $K = 10, 20, 30, 40$, and 50 subnetwork markers identified by different methods for the following datasets: **(a)** USA, **(b)** Netherlands, **(c)** Belgium, and **(d)** Sweden.

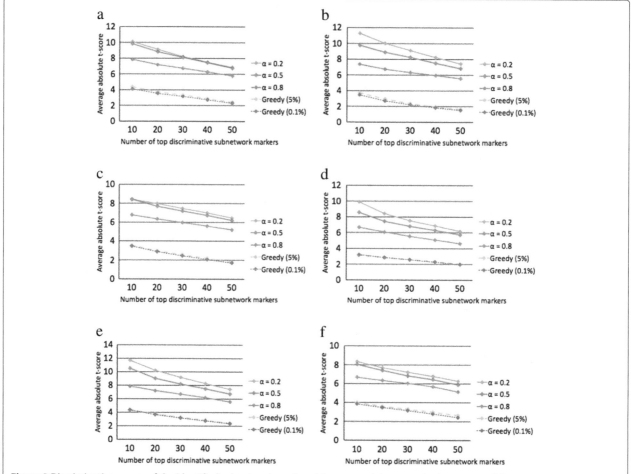

Figure 3 Discriminative power of the identified subnetwork markers. We computed the mean absolute *t*-score of the top *K* = 10, 20, 30, 40, and 50 markers for all datasets. The markers were identified using the first dataset and their discriminative power was evaluated on the second dataset. The experiments were performed for the following dataset pairs: **(a)** USA-Netherlands, **(b)** USA-Belgium, **(c)** USA-Sweden, **(d)** Netherlands-USA, **(e)** Netherlands-Belgium, and **(f)** Netherlands-Sweden.

platform. For example, in Figure 3a, the subnetwork markers were first identified using the USA dataset profiled on an Affymetrix chip and then evaluated on the Netherlands dataset profiled on a custom Agilent chip. Figure 3a shows that the markers predicted by the proposed method using the first dataset can also effectively discriminate between the two class labels based on the gene expression profiles in the second dataset. Similar trends can also be observed in Figure 3d,e,f and Additional file 1: Figures S2b,e.

One interesting observation we can make from these figures is that a smaller α tends to yield subnetwork markers that retain their discriminative power relatively better across independent datasets. This observation makes an intuitive sense, since a larger α tends to penalize genes with different discriminative power thereby giving rise to relatively smaller subnetwork markers that mostly consist of a few highly discriminative genes that may not be necessarily synergistic. This increases the risk of overfitting the

data, thereby degrading the effectiveness of the predicted markers on other independent datasets.

Evaluating the reproducibility of the predicted subnetwork markers

In order to evaluate the efficacy of the predicted subnetwork markers in cancer prognosis, we performed five-fold cross-validation experiments based on a similar set-up that has been commonly used in previous studies [3-7].

Considering that our ultimate goal is to identify effective subnetwork markers that can be used for building robust classifiers that can accurately predict breast cancer prognosis, it is important to verify whether the predicted markers can actually lead to better classifiers whose performance can be reproduced on independent datasets. For this purpose, we performed the following cross-dataset experiments.

First of all, we selected one of the four breast cancer datasets just for identifying the potential subnetwork markers and selecting the optimal feature set (i.e., the set of markers to be used for building the classifier). To select the optimal set of features, we randomly divided the chosen dataset into three folds, where two folds (marker-evaluation set) were used for evaluating the discriminative power of the subnetwork markers and the remaining one fold (feature-selection set) was used for selecting the features to be used in the classifier. We used the entire set for estimating the class conditional probability density functions that are needed for the pathway activity inference [4].

We evaluated the discriminative power of all potential subnetwork markers based on the marker-evaluation set, selected the top 50 markers, and sorted them according to their absolute t-test score in a descending order. Initially, we built a classifier based on linear discriminant analysis (LDA), where only the top subnetwork marker was included in the feature set. The classifier was trained on the marker-evaluation set, and its classification performance was assessed by measuring the area under ROC curve (AUC) on the feature-selection set. Subsequently, we added the next best subnetwork marker to the feature set, re-trained and re-evaluated the classifier, and kept the subnetwork marker only if the AUC increased. We repeated this process for the top 50 subnetwork markers.

Next, we chose a different dataset to train an LDA classifier (using the markers selected from the first dataset) and evaluate its performance. For this, the second dataset was randomly divided into five folds, where four folds were used for training (without reselecting the features) and the rest was used for computing the AUC. The entire process was repeated for 100 random partitions, and we report the average AUC as the performance measure. Similar experiments have been performed to evaluate the classification performance of previous methods, including the greedy subnetwork marker identification method [6] as well as a number of pathway-based classification methods: Rank-LLR [5], LLR [4], Mean, and Median [2]. Each method uses a different way to infer the pathway activity level based on the expression levels of its gene members. For example, Mean (or Median) method uses the mean (or median) expression value of the member genes that belong to the same pathway. LLR and Rank-LLR both utilize the log-likelihood ratio between different phenotypes based on the expression level of each member gene. For pathway markers, we selected the top 50 pathways among the 880 pathways in the C2 curated gene sets in Molecular Signatures Database (MsigDB) [16]. Figure 4 summarizes the classification performance of different methods, where we can clearly see that the proposed method leads to more

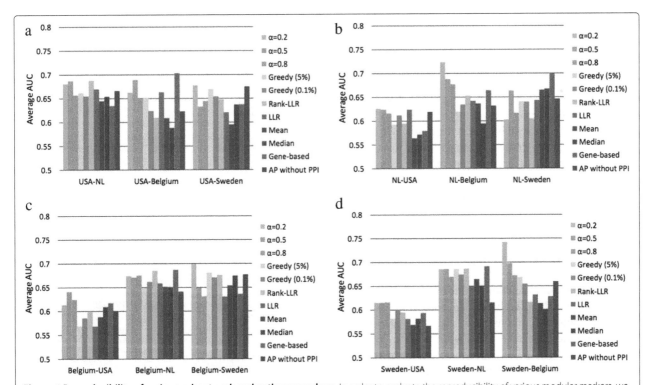

Figure 4 Reproducibility of various subnetwork and pathway markers. In order to evaluate the reproducibility of various modular markers, we used the first dataset to identify potential markers and select the optimal set of features and the second dataset to train the classifier (using the selected features) and evaluate its performance. Average classification performance is shown when the markers were selected based on **(a)** the USA dataset, **(b)** the Netherlands dataset, **(c)** the Belgium dataset, and **(d)** the Sweden dataset.

reliable classifiers with a much more consistent performance across different breast cancer datasets.

Finally, we also performed within-dataset experiments to investigate the performance of the proposed method and compare it with previous subnetwork and pathway-based methods. In these experiments, the classifiers were trained and evaluated on different folds of the same dataset, where a similar five-fold cross-validation set-up was used as before. We first selected a dataset and then randomly divided it into five folds. Four out of the five folds were used as a training set for building the classifier. The remaining one fold was used as a test set for evaluating the classification performance. The subnetwork markers were identified using the entire dataset, and not just the four fold training set, due to the high computational burden for re-identifying the subnetwork markers every time for a large number of random partitions. The results are depicted in Additional file 1: Figure S3. We can see that classifiers based on subnetwork markers performed significantly better compared to those based on pathway markers. The main reason for this significant performance improvement is the substantially increased coverage of genes, which was the main motivation for identifying subnetwork markers and using them for cancer classification. The proposed subnetwork marker identification method and the greedy method performed both well in the within-dataset experiments, although our proposed method outperformed the greedy method in terms of robustness and reproducibility across different datasets as we have shown before.

Conclusions

In this paper, we proposed a novel method for identifying robust and synergistic subnetwork markers that can be used to accurately predict breast cancer prognosis. Our proposed method utilizes an efficient message-passing algorithm called affinity propagation [15] to identify gene subnetworks that consist of discriminative and synergistic genes whose protein products are known to interact with each other or to be closely located in the protein-protein interaction network. The proposed method allows us to simultaneously identify multiple mutually exclusive subnetwork markers that have the potential to synergistically improve the prediction of breast cancer prognosis. Extensive evaluation based on four large-scale breast cancer datasets demonstrates that the proposed method can predict effective subnetwork markers with high discriminative power and reproducible performance across independent datasets. Furthermore, the predicted markers can be used to construct robust cancer classifiers that can yield more consistent classification performance across datasets compared to other existing methods.

Additional file

Additional file 1: **Supplementary material.** This supplement contains figures for additional experimental results. **Figure S1.** shows the discriminative power of the subnetwork markers identified by the proposed method with and without the post-processing step. **Figure S2.** contains charts showing the discriminative power of the subnetwork and pathway markers across different datasets. **Figure S3.** shows the classification results of the within-dataset experiments.

Competing interests
The authors declare that they have no competing interests.

Authors' contributions
NK and BJY conceived and designed the experiments, analyzed the data, and wrote the paper. NK performed the experiments. Both authors read and approved the final manuscript.

Acknowledgements
NK was supported by a scholarship from the Royal Thai Government. BJY was supported in part by the National Science Foundation, through NSF Award CCF-1149544.

References
1. L Tian, SA Greenberg, SW Kong, J Altschuler, IS Kohane, PJ Park, Discovering statistically significant pathways in expression profiling studies. Proc. Natl. Acad. Sci. U S A. **102**, 13544–13549 (2005)
2. Z Guo, T Zhang, X Li, Q Wang, J Xu, H Yu, J Zhu, H Wang, C Wang, EJ Topol, Q Wang, S Rao, Towards precise classification of cancers based on robust gene functional expression profiles. BMC Bioinformatics. **6**, 58 (2005)
3. E Lee, HY Chuang, JW Kim, T Ideker, D Lee, Inferring pathway activity toward precise disease classification. PLoS Comput. Biol. **4**(1000217) (2008)
4. J Su, B-J Yoon, ER Dougherty, Accurate and reliable cancer classification based on probabilistic inference of pathway activity. PLoS ONE **4**(12), 8161 (2009)
5. N Khunlertgit, B-J Yoon, Identification of robust pathway markers for cancer through rank-based pathway activity inference. Adv. Bioinformatics. **2013**(618461) (2013). doi:10.1155/2013/618461
6. HY Chuang, E Lee, YT Liu, D Lee, T Ideker, Network-based classification of breast cancer metastasis. Mol. Syst. Biol. **3**, 140 (2007)
7. J Su, B-J Yoon, ER Dougherty, Identification of diagnostic subnetwork markers for cancer in human protein-protein interaction network. BMC Bioinformatics **11**, 8 (2010)
8. C Auffray, Protein subnetwork markers improve prediction of cancer outcome. Mol. Syst. Biol. **3**, 141 (2007)
9. Y Wang, JG Klijn, Y Zhang, AM Sieuwerts, MP Look, F Yang, D Talantov, M Timmermans, MM-v Gelder, J Yu, T Jatkoe, EM Berns, D Atkins, JA Foekens, Gene-expression profiles to predict distant metastasis of lymph-node-negative primary breast cancer. Lancet. **365**, 671–679 (2005)
10. MJ van de Vijver, YD He, LJ van't Veer, H Dai, AA Hart, DW Voskuil, GJ Schreiber, JL Peterse, C Roberts, MJ Marton, M Parrish, D Atsma, A Witteveen, A Glas, L Delahaye, T van der Velde, H Bartelink, S Rodenhuis, ET Rutgers, SH Friend, R Bernards, A gene-expression signature as a predictor of survival in breast cancer. N Engl J Med. **347**(25), 1999–2009 (2002)
11. C Desmedt, F Piette, S Loi, Y Wang, F Lallemand, B Haibe-Kains, G Viale, M Delorenzi, Y Zhang, MS d'Assignies, J Bergh, R Lidereau, P Ellis, AL Harris, JGM Klijn, JA Foekens, F Cardoso, MJ Piccart, M Buyse, C Sotiriou, Strong time dependence of the 76-gene prognostic signature for node-negative breast cancer patients in the transbig multicenter independent validation series. Clin. Cancer Res. **13**(11), 3207–3214 (2007)
12. Y Pawitan, J Bjohle, L Amler, A-L Borg, S Egyhazi, P Hall, X Han, L Holmberg, F Huang, S Klaar, E Liu, L Miller, H Nordgren, A Ploner, K Sandelin, P Shaw, J Smeds, L Skoog, S Wedren, J Bergh, Gene expression profiling spares early breast cancer patients from adjuvant therapy: derived and validated in two population-based cohorts. Breast Cancer Res. **7**(6), 953–964 (2005)

13. R Edgar, M Domrachev, AE Lash, Gene expression omnibus: NCBI gene expression and hybridization array data repository. Nucleic Acids Res. **30**(1), 207–210 (2002)

14. HY Chang, DSA Nuyten, JB Sneddon, T Hastie, R Tibshirani, T Sørlie, H Dai, YD He, LJ van't Veer, H Bartelink, M van de Rijn, PO Brown, MJ van de Vijver, Robustness, scalability, and integration of a wound-response gene expression signature in predicting breast cancer survival.Proc. Natl. Acad. Sci. U S A. **102**(10), 3738–3743 (2005)

15. BJ Frey, D Dueck, Clustering by passing messages between data points. Science. **315**(5814), 972–976 (2007)

16. A Liberzon, A Subramanian, R Pinchback, H Thorvaldsdóttir, P Tamayo, JP Mesirov, Molecular signatures database (msigdb) 3.0. Bioinformatics. **27**(12), 1739–1740 (2011)

Application of discrete Fourier inter-coefficient difference for assessing genetic sequence similarity

Brian R King[1*], Maurice Aburdene[2], Alex Thompson[2] and Zach Warres[2]

Abstract

Digital signal processing (DSP) techniques for biological sequence analysis continue to grow in popularity due to the inherent digital nature of these sequences. DSP methods have demonstrated early success for detection of coding regions in a gene. Recently, these methods are being used to establish DNA gene similarity. We present the inter-coefficient difference (ICD) transformation, a novel extension of the discrete Fourier transformation, which can be applied to any DNA sequence. The ICD method is a mathematical, alignment-free DNA comparison method that generates a genetic signature for any DNA sequence that is used to generate relative measures of similarity among DNA sequences. We demonstrate our method on a set of insulin genes obtained from an evolutionarily wide range of species, and on a set of avian influenza viral sequences, which represents a set of highly similar sequences. We compare phylogenetic trees generated using our technique against trees generated using traditional alignment techniques for similarity and demonstrate that the ICD method produces a highly accurate tree without requiring an alignment prior to establishing sequence similarity.

Keywords: Discrete Fourier transform; Sequence analysis; Sequence similarity

Introduction

Substantial technological advances continue to be made in modern DNA sequencing instrumentation. Next-generation sequencing (NGS) systems generate genetic and genomic data at unprecedented rates. Methods that can be used to help us understand these data are being researched in earnest. In general, the most common, biologically meaningful approach to understand new sequence data are based on methods that can compare new data against a large set of data that is well understood.

When a new biological sequence with unknown function has been identified, researchers search for the most 'similar' sequence in a database of annotated sequence data, under the premise that similar sequences imply similar biological functionality, and in the case of proteins, similar structural characteristics. Similarity between two biological sequences forms the basis for determining whether the sequences are homologous, i.e., there is shared ancestry between them [1]. Phylogenetics, the study of evolutionary relationships between organisms, relies on methods that can quantitatively measure differences between these organisms, with the premise that larger differences between organisms imply a larger span of time before the organisms split from a common ancestor. Phylogenies are most commonly inferred from pairwise comparisons performed on the underlying genetic sequence data obtained from the organisms being analyzed [2,3]. For these and many other reasons, sequence analysis methods are among the most researched and sought after methods in bioinformatics. We encourage the reader to consult a text on biological sequence analysis to learn about existing methods [1,4].

Generally speaking, the predominant methods for biological sequence comparison are based on sequence alignments, such as the popular BLAST and the ClustalW series of methods [5,6]. Alignment methods have represented the *de facto* standard for sequence analysis, comparison, and retrieval. However, the advent of NGS sequencing has pushed traditional alignment methods to their limits. There are numerous user-defined parameters

* Correspondence: brk009@bucknell.edu
[1]Department of Computer Science, Bucknell University, Lewisburg, PA 17837, USA
Full list of author information is available at the end of the article

for dealing with gaps and mismatches between sequences, and it is difficult to determine the ideal parameters to achieve an optimal alignment. The computational resources required for these methods can increase quadratically or more with respect to the length of the sequences and the number of sequences being aligned [1]. Moreover, there is an increased risk of errors being introduced with multiple sequence alignments as the average pairwise sequence identity of the data being aligned decreases. Another source of alignment error arises if the order of significant regions in sequences is not conserved [7]. If an optimal alignment has been found, it is difficult to determine an accurate metric of distance between sequences [8]. Despite these challenges, alignment methods continue to be used. With appropriate parameter selection, they excel at visually indicating regions that are highly conserved among many sequences.

To overcome these challenges, there has been increased interest in techniques that can compare sequences without an alignment, referred to as alignment-free methods [7-9]. The most popular alignment-free methods are based on computing various transformations of fixed-length words of length n (or n-mers, n-grams), with common approaches involving computing a frequency vector over all possible n-mers for each sequence [2]. Other methods search for a shared set of the longest common subsequences [10]. These methods tend to be among the most efficient, as their computational complexity is linear [9]. However, they may lose valuable information with respect to positioning of important subsequences within the whole sequence. Moreover, like alignment-based methods, they often require multiple runs to select the most ideal parameters.

Digital signal processing (DSP) techniques have been used effectively for efficient searching and comparison of sequential data [11,12]. They are emerging as another alternative alignment-free approach used to analyze both genomic and proteomic data. In order for these data to be processed using DSP techniques, they must be converted to a numeric sequence. There are several numeric representations available, each with their own strengths and weaknesses [13-15]. In the case of DNA, there are a limited number of numeric transformations available. DNA encodes the genetic blueprint of every organism as a sequence over four possible nucleotides, represented as A, C, G, or T. Encoded in DNA are genes, which contain the instructions to make proteins, and intergenic regions, which fill in the large gaps between genes. Within each gene are coding regions (exons) and noncoding regions (introns). The information content, which is critical to understanding the biological function of the gene, is hidden in the coding regions in the gene. Coding regions are comprised of codons, nucleotide triplets that code for individual amino acids, and represent a very

small portion of the entire genome. In the human genome, only about 5% of it contains coding instructions. These complexities make the process of identifying genes and coding regions within these genes a daunting task.

Proteins have more choices of possible numeric transformations available, owed in part to the physicochemical properties of amino acids. Proteins themselves are long polypeptide chains of amino acids. There are 20 possible amino acids that exist in proteins, each having many physicochemical properties, such as hydropathy, charge, and solubility. These properties provide useful numeric representations for protein sequences, making a translation to a numeric sequence a relatively easy process. For example, the MAFFT method is a protein sequence alignment method that converts converted proteins into numeric sequences that represent the polarity and volume values of each amino acid residue in the proteins being aligned [16].

Regardless of the numeric transformation chosen, preservation of information content in the sequence is critical. This is perhaps one reason for the most common representation of a DNA, the binary indicator sequence, also commonly known as the Voss representation [17]. In this representation, each DNA sequence is transformed into a sequence of binary occurrence vectors. (This is the transformation used in our research, and is described in detail in the Methods and materials section). Some methods use variations of the binary indicator sequence. For example, Afrexio et al. introduced a variant of the Voss representation that converts the occurrence vector into a vector of inter-nucleotide distances [18]. There is a wide range of transformations available [13]. Hota et al. analyzed the performance of several common DNA to numerical mapping techniques. They provide a good description of each transformation method used in practice [19].

DSP based methods have continued to emerge in recent years for the purpose of genomic analysis. The most prevalent use has been to locate reading frames in DNA, as well as different regions in the genome, including genes and coding (or exon) regions within these genes [14,20,21]. Sharma et al. analyzed the performance of several DNA mapping schemes for detecting the coding region of genes [15]. DSP techniques have been used to address other problems in genomics and proteomics. For example, methods have been developed for splice site detection within the gene [20], the identification of active sites in a protein using Morlet wavelets [22] and identification of acceptor splicing sites and the visual identification of patterns and motifs in DNA through spectral analysis [14,23].

Regardless of the domain, the field of digital signal processing has provided a plethora of methods for analyzing sequential data. Most methods use variations of the Fourier transform [24], with the discrete Fourier transform (DFT) being among the most popular signal processing technique [25,26]. Typically, the fast Fourier transform (FFT) is used to compute the DFT, as it is among the most computationally efficient algorithms for this purpose [24]. These transforms have been successfully used for general sequential data comparison and retrieval [11,12], and are readily suitable for biological sequence comparison, owed to the inherent discrete, symbolic nature of biological sequences [14,27,28]. In fact, FFTs have been used to analyze DNA data before [20,29,30]. In addition to some of the methods listed previously, Cheever et al. measured the cross correlation of two DNA sequences to explore significant regions of similarity between the DNA, where the cross correlation was computed using a FFT [31]. The FFT has also been used for protein sequence alignments in the MAFFT method [16].

There have been many DSP-based methods introduced in recent years for biological data analysis; however, very few were designed to report a biologically relevant measure of evolutionary distance between sequences being analyzed, particularly when a large number of sequences are being analyzed. Multiple sequence alignments have been used successfully for this purpose, but these methods can be computationally expensive and are prone to errors, particularly as the set of sequences being analyzed increase in size and diversity. We developed a novel signal processing technique that characterizes genetic sequence data through a simple transformation of the coefficients generated by the DFT of a specific numeric representation of the original DNA sequence. In our work, we compute a transformation on the set of coefficients generated that we call the *inter-coefficient difference* or ICD. We show that this characterization effectively produces a signature for a given sequence and can be used to compare genetic sequences among different species. The ICD method provides comparisons between genes from evolutionarily distant species, as well as subtle variants from identical genes from the same species. We demonstrate its effectiveness through analysis of datasets that have different levels of pairwise similarity. The method effectively generates a pairwise distance matrix representing the level of similarity between each genetic sequence with remarkable running times. The resulting matrix can be used to induce a dendrogram representing phylogenetic relationships between species from which the sequences were obtained. Our results show that we produce alignment-free dendrograms that are highly similar to those trees produced using alignment-based techniques and other alignment-free methods.

Methods and materials

Our method is based on the application of the DFT to four numeric sequences that are derived from the original DNA sequence. We use a binary indicator sequence representation of a DNA sequence, which is among the most popular numeric representation used in this area in literature [17,20]; it allows for an easy transformation from the original sequence on which many DSP and other numeric transformations can be computed [18,20,27].

The inter-coefficient difference

Let S represent a set of DNA sequences, where s_i represents an arbitrary sequence in S. Each DNA sequence s_i is defined over the alphabet. Let N be the length of the longest sequence in S. Each sequence s_i in S goes through a series of transformations to produce the corresponding ICD vector. The first transformation computes a unique binary indicator sequence from s_i. Next, we apply the DFT on the indicator sequence, yielding a vector of coefficients. Basic mathematical transformations are applied to the coefficient vector, resulting in the ICD vector. The details of this algorithm are given below.

For a given sequence s_i, we define four binary indicator sequences $x_A[n]$, $x_C[n]$, $x_G[n]$, and $x_T[n]$, which indicate the presence (i.e., a 1) or absence (i.e., a 0) of a symbol in s_i at position n. Each indicator sequence is padded with zeros to ensure that every indicator sequence in S has an identical length of N. Zero padding is a common technique with FFT computations that can increase the spectral resolution and can increase the efficiency of the computation when the length of the original sequence is padded to a power of 2 [26]. For example, let $s_i = GAC GACTCAT$, which has a length of 10. However, suppose that N, which is the length of the longest sequence in S, is 12. Then:

$$s_i = GACGACTCAT$$

$$x_A = 010010001000$$

$$x_C = 001001010000$$

$$x_G = 100100000000$$

$$x_T = 000000100100$$

For each indicator sequence, we compute the DFT, which converts the finite-length sequence $x_A[n]$ into a series of coefficients $X_A[k]$ resulting from the DFT computation, defined in Equation 1:

$$X_A[k] = \sum_{n=0}^{N-1} x_A[n]e^{-j\left(\frac{2\pi n k}{N}\right)} \quad k = 0, 1, ..., N-1 \quad (1)$$

The coefficients produced are complex, and thus the absolute value of each coefficient is computed, yielding a series of real valued numbers. $X_A[0]$ represents the number of 1 s in the indicator sequence x_A. It is discarded because it is substantially larger than all other coefficients and is highly dependent on the length of the original unpadded sequence. We retain coefficients $X_A[1], X_A[2], ..., X_A[^N/_2]$, eliminating half of the coefficients because of the symmetric nature of the coefficients produced by the DFT [26]. The remaining coefficients are denoted as vector $\mathbf{X}_A^*$. We normalize $\mathbf{X}_A^*$ by dividing by its Euclidean norm, $\|\mathbf{X}_A^*\|$, resulting in $\mathbf{X}_A$. Equation 2 illustrates this transformation, introducing variable η for simplicity:

$$\eta = \left[{N}/{2} \right] \tag{2}$$

$$\mathbf{X}_A^* = [|X_A[1]|, |X_A[2]|, ..., |X_A[\eta]|]$$

$$\mathbf{X}_A = \frac{\mathbf{X}_A^*}{\|\mathbf{X}_A^*\|}$$

For each vector $\mathbf{X}_A$, we compute the inter-coefficient difference of $\mathbf{X}_A$, denoted ICD($\mathbf{X}_A$), by computing the difference between each adjacent number in the sequence as shown in Equation 3:

$$\text{ICD}(\mathbf{X}_A) = [\mathbf{X}_A[2] - \mathbf{X}_A[1], \mathbf{X}_A[3] - \mathbf{X}_A[2], ..., \mathbf{X}_A[\eta] - \mathbf{X}_A[\eta - 1]] \tag{3}$$

The same computations are repeated for indicator sequences x_C, x_G, and x_T, yielding vectors $\mathbf{X}_C$, $\mathbf{X}_G$, and $\mathbf{X}_T$ separately.

For example, continuing from our previous example indicator sequence, $x_A = 010010001000$, and $N = 12$. We apply Equations 1 and 2 above on x_A, which computes the DFT on x_A and normalizes it, resulting in the vector of coefficients $\mathbf{X}_A$:

$$\mathbf{X}_A^* = [0.5176, 1.0000, 2.2361, 1.7321, 1.9319, 1.0000]$$

$$\|\mathbf{X}_A^*\| = 3.7417$$

$$\mathbf{X}_A = [0.1383, 0.2673, 0.5976, 0.4629, 0.5163, 0.2673]$$

Then, the inter-coefficient difference of $\mathbf{X}_A$ is computed, resulting in:

$$\text{ICD}(\mathbf{X}_A) = [0.1289, 0.3304, -0.1347, 0.0534, -0.2490]$$

The ICD of each coefficient vector resulting from vectors $\mathbf{X}_C$, $\mathbf{X}_G$, and $\mathbf{X}_T$ is concatenated to produce a single numeric vector, denoted $\mathbf{X}$.

$$\mathbf{X} = [\text{ICD}(\mathbf{X}_A)\text{ICD}(\mathbf{X}_C)\text{ICD}(\mathbf{X}_G)\text{ICD}(\mathbf{X}_T)]$$

It is important to mention that all ICD vectors will have an equal length for every sequence in S, regardless of the length of the original sequence. Each indicator sequence transformation is padded to have a length of N, which is the length of the longest sequence in S. The final concatenated vector $\mathbf{X}$ will have a length of $4\lfloor N/2 \rfloor = 4\eta$.

Establishing distance between DNA sequences

Given two arbitrary DNA sequences, s_1 and s_2 in set S, we can compute the ICD transformation yielding numeric vectors $\mathbf{X}_1$ and $\mathbf{X}_2$, respectively. A single numeric value that represents a measure of biological distance is computed from these vectors by computing the correlation between the two vectors. We compute Dist ($\mathbf{X}_1$, $\mathbf{X}_2$), a single measure of distance between the ICD vectors, as follows:

$$\text{Dist}(\mathbf{X}_1, \mathbf{X}_2) = 1.0 - \frac{\sum_{i=1}^{4\eta} (X_1[i] - \bar{X}_1)(X_2[i] - \bar{X}_2)}{\sqrt{\sum_{i=1}^{4\eta} (X_1[i] - \bar{X}_1)^2 \sum_{i=1}^{4\eta} (X_2[i] - \bar{X}_2)^2}} \tag{4}$$

Equation 4 is 1.0 minus a standard correlation calculation between two sets of data. We know that a standard correlation falls in the range [–1.0, 1.0], where –1.0 is a perfect negative correlation and 1.0 is a positive correlation. Two vectors of identical values would have perfect positive correlation, and thus their Dist calculation would be 0.0, implying that there is no distance between them. A value of 2.0 is perfect negative correlation, implying opposing numerical trends around the means.

Data

To test the efficacy of this method, we assembled two sets of DNA data. Our first set consisted of mRNA insulin sequences from 19 different animals, called *INS19* (Table 1). Insulin is an important hormone found throughout the animal kingdom for regulating carbohydrate and fat metabolism and for managing glucose levels in the blood. All sequences were downloaded from NCBI's RefSeq database (http://www.ncbi.nlm.nih.gov/refseq/). This dataset was chosen to measure the ability of the method to assess pairwise similarity over a set of sequences that have highly conserved regions in its genetic sequence owed to its similar function among all species while exhibiting substantial regions of low conservation in proportion to the evolutionary distance between species. The length of the sequences in the data ranged between 291 and 774 nucleotides in length.

Our second set of data was chosen to test the ability of the method to accurately distinguish subtle differences among a large set of sequences from the same gene obtained from the same viral species. To this end, we selected 60 influenza type A sequences collected from the NCBI Influenza Virus Sequence Database (http://www.ncbi.nlm.nih.gov/genomes/FLU/). Influenza is an RNA virus that affects a wide range of mammals and birds; in extreme cases, it can lead to death. Influenza A viruses are broken down into different subtypes that are

Table 1 mRNA insulin sequences from 19 animal species in the INS19 dataset

Species	Common name	Accession	Length
H. sapiens	Human	NM_000207	469
P. troglodytes	Chimp	NM_001008996	416
O. baboon	Olive baboon	XM_003909376	505
M. fascicularis	Monkey	J00336	392
B. taurus	Cow	NM_173926	434
S. scrofa	Pig	NM_001109772	435
G. gallus	Chicken	NM_205222	453
C. familiaris	Dog	NM_001130093	463
F. catus	Cat	AB043535	420
C. procellus	Guinea pig	NM_001172891	442
C. cristata	Star-nosed mole	XM_004695041	291
E. telfairi	Hedgehog	XM_004717178	327
M. auratus	Hamster	XM_005064148	450
O. cuniculus	Rabbit	NM_001082335	433
D. rerio	Zebrafish	AF036326	468
P. buchholzi	Butterfly fish	AF199588	459
C. chitala	Clown knifefish	AF199586	375
F. albicollis	Flycatcher	XM_005046804	324
X. laevis	Clawed frog	NM_001085882	774

Table 2 Avian influenza A subtype frequency in FLU60

Influenza A subtype	Frequency
H1N1	3
H1N3	1
H3N1	1
H3N6	1
H3N8	13
H4N6	25
H6N1	2
H7N3	6
H9N2	1
H10N7	4
H11N9	2
H12N5	1

named based on two specific proteins that are on the surface of the virus: hemagglutinin (HA) and neuraminidase (NA). There are 17 types of the HA protein and 10 types of neuraminidase NA protein. Each virus receives a designation labeled HxNy, where x represents a specific subtype of the HA gene and y represents a subtype of the NA gene in the virus. Our dataset, denoted FLU60, contains 60 examples of avian influenza sequences (influenza sequences known to affect birds) for the HA gene only, collected from various locations in the United States between January and July of 2010. Avian flu strands were selected because all known subtypes of influenza A can affect birds. The length of all sequences in FLU60 ranged between 1,683 and 1,746 nucleotides in length. The frequency of influenza A subtypes in the dataset are detailed in Table 2. The most dominant variant in the data is H4N6 at 25 examples, with H3Nx variants coming in second. Because we collected only examples of the HA gene, only the Hx part of the subtype name should play a role in determining similarity. Additional file 1: Table S1 has detailed information about the dataset, including the accession number, subtype, date and place that specimen was acquired, and the length of each sequence [see Additional file 1].

Results

To assess the capability of the ICD method to measure sequence similarity, we generated a dendrogram based on a hierarchical clustering using the unweighted pair group method average (UPGMA) method for constructing the tree. This was performed for both *INS19* and FLU60 datasets. For comparative purposes, we computed an all-against-all pairwise global alignment using the standard Needleman-Wunsch algorithm for each set of sequences being tested [32], utilizing a uniform nucleotide substitution matrix (as defined by the nuc44 function in the Matlab® Bioinformatics Toolbox) for the purpose of finding the best alignment. Though computing a pairwise alignment for all possible pairs of sequences is computationally expensive, this will yield a superior alignment than any single multiple sequence alignment (MSA), as it significantly reduces the likelihood of introducing alignment errors that result from an MSA. The distance between each pair of aligned sequences was computed by measuring the proportion of sites in the alignment at which the two sequences are different, yielding a score of 1 for entirely dissimilar sequences and 0 if they were identical. This distance measure yields identical groupings to those that are generated directly from the alignment score itself but has a comparative advantage of producing numbers that are in an identical range to the distance values that are produced with the ICD method. ICD uses a correlation coefficient between coefficient differences and likewise always produces a distance value between 0 and 1. We also compared our results to an alignment-free sequence comparison method called feature frequency profile (FFP), which is a popular tool for phylogenetic analysis [2]. We used default parameters on all FFP tools to generate a tree, with the exception of word size; we evaluated word sizes between 6 and 20 and determined that a word size of 16 achieved results that produced the most biologically correct phylogenetic groupings. Finally, the Robinson-Foulds (RFdist) tree distance metric is computed on the INS19 test using the treedist function in the phangorn package in R [33,34].

RFdist is computed between all combinations of pairs of trees to assist in measuring tree similarity.

ICD method on INS19 dataset

Our first test was conducted to measure the ability for the ICD method to accurately assess similarity between sequences that are relatively divergent, where the data was collected from a wide range of eukaryotic species. The INS19 dataset contains data from the insulin gene, taken from 19 species in the eukaryotic kingdom. The range of pairwise sequence identity after alignment ranged between 32% and 89% identity, with an average observed percent identity at 60% (see Figure 1). A dendrogram was built based on the pairwise similarity computed from the ICD method and is shown in Figure 2. For comparison purposes, an all-against-all pairwise global alignment (denoted AAP) was performed on all sequences, and a dendrogram was built revealing the relationships between the sequences based on the alignment. A dendrogram was also computed based on the alignment-free FFP method [2]. The resulting dendrograms from each of these comparative methods are shown in Figures 3 and 4, respectively.

All trees exhibit strong similarities within major groupings, closely resembling phylogenetic relationships observed in nature, with some subtle, yet biologically significant differences between each method. In particular, both ICD and AAP methods place monkey and chimp as the most similar among all species, whereas FFP places human and chimp as most similar. All methods suggest the African clawed frog as most distant from others species used in this study. The FFP method grouped the zebrafish with the clawed frog, whereas the ICD and AAP methods correctly cluster all three fish species. The AAP method grouped a

hedgehog, a type of rodent, with a flycatcher, a type of bird. In contrast, the ICD and FFP methods correctly grouped the flycatcher with a chicken, which are both types of birds, and the hedgehog with other similar mammals. The AAP method grouped the hamster, a rodent, with the cow and pig, which are both even-toed ungulates; the FFP method fared a bit better, placing a hamster between a rabbit and hedgehog. In contrast, the ICD method correctly grouped the hamster with the guinea pig, which are both rodents.

The RFdist distance metric was computed between all pairs of trees. The RFdist between the ICD and FFP phylogenetic trees is 26, between ICD and AAP is 24, and between FFP and AAP is 22. These values suggest that, though the trees have similar groups, they have a relatively equal number of different partitions of data that are implied by each tree, with the final tree produced by the ICD method being only slightly more similar to the tree produced by the all-against-all pairwise alignment than the FFP method.

ICD method on FLU60 dataset

Our next test was conducted on the FLU60 dataset, which contains 60 DNA sequences of the HA gene from avian influenza A virus. Conducting an all-against-all pairwise alignment revealed a pairwise sequence identity range of 57% to 99.9%, with an average identity of 70.5%. Additional file 1: Figure S1 shows a histogram revealing the sequence identity over all pairs of sequences (see Additional file 1). We performed identical analyses on these data to the analyses performed with the INS19 data, resulting in dendrograms from each method. The dendrogram for the ICD method is shown in Figure 5. The dendrograms for the AAP and FFP methods are shown in Additional file 1: Figures S2 and S3 (see Additional file 1). The RFdist metric was not measured for this test.

Close evaluation of these dendrograms will reveal remarkably similar groupings among each individual subtype of influenza A. We were pleased to see that all influenza HA subtypes were grouped together correctly by all methods. In particular, in the case of H3 and H4 subtypes, all three methods indicated two very distinct strains. H3 is divided into a strain that hit Mississippi and one that hit Alaska. H4 was divided into three distinct strains, with all methods agreeing on the divisions. When looking at similarity between subtypes, all methods group together influenza A subtype H7 with H10, suggesting that each of these groups share a common ancestor. However, they differ slightly on the ancestry relationships between H9, H11, and H12. These findings, as well as most of the other relationships observed in this study, are confirmed by Air's work on sequence relationships in the hemagluttinin genes of 12 different variants of influenza A

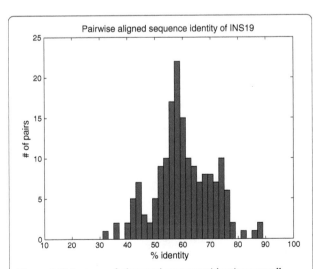

Figure 1 Histogram of observed sequence identity over all pairs of aligned sequences in INS19 dataset. The percent identity is computed for all possible pairs of sequences in the INS19 dataset. Most data averaged between 55% and 75% sequence identity.

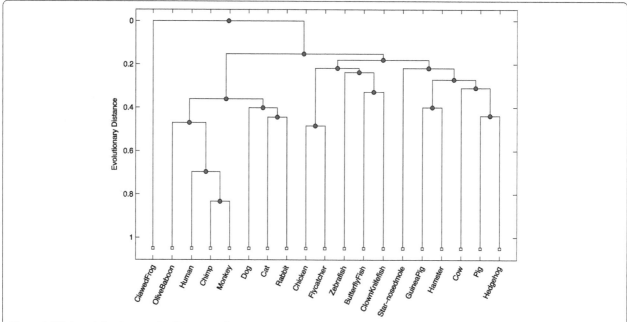

Figure 2 ICD-based dendrogram for INS19. This figure shows the resulting dendrogram generated based on the ICD method applied on the ICD19 dataset, which contains mRNA sequences taken from 19 different eukaryotic species for the insulin (INS) gene.

[35]. The methods differ on the divergence point of subtype H6; the AAP and FFP methods suggest that H6 and H1 have a common ancestor, whereas the ICD method suggests that H6 diverged much earlier from a subgroup consisting of H4, H9, and H12. The AAP and FFP method are closer to the similarity observed in Air's work. However, the level of similarity computed by the ICD method

between H6 and subgroup H4, H9, and H12 is remarkably similar to the alternative group H1, H11, and H3, suggesting that the common ancestor could have been from either group.

The execution times were recorded for each of the methods we investigated. In addition, we included the timing results of ClustalW2 [36] and Clustal Omega

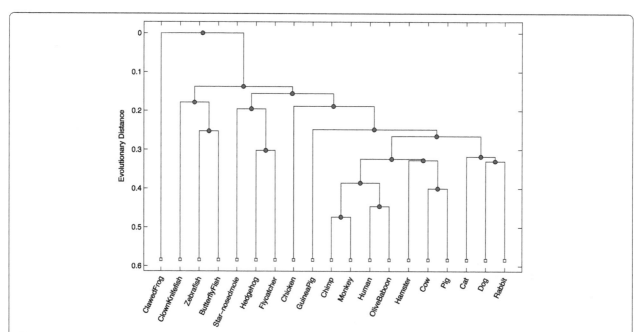

Figure 3 Alignment-based dendrogram for INS19. This figure shows the resulting dendrogram generated from phylogenetic relationships inferred from pairwise alignments computed over all pairs from the INS19 dataset, which contains mRNA sequences taken from 19 different eukaryotic species for the insulin (INS) gene.

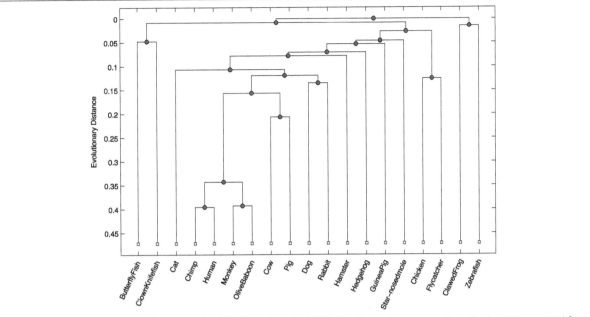

Figure 4 Alignment-free-based dendrogram using FFP [2] method for INS19. This figure shows the resulting dendrogram generated from phylogenetic relationships inferred using the FFP method on the INS19 dataset, which contains mRNA sequences taken from 19 different eukaryotic species for the insulin (INS) gene.

[37], which are two other popular multiple sequence alignment methods widely used today. All methods were run on a laptop computer running Mac OS X 10.9 with a 2.2 GHz Intel Core i7 processor equipped with 16 GB of memory. The ICD and AAP methods were run as Matlab® applications, while FFP, ClustalW2, and Clustal Omega were compiled and installed as native applications. All methods were executed multiple times with similar loads. The first time was discarded to eliminate bias resulting from file system latency. All methods ran under one second of execution time on the INS19 dataset. This is not surprising given the small size of the dataset and the short length of each sequence. The FLU60 dataset provided a much more informative comparison. Table 3 shows the results for all five methods tested. The results clearly indicate the strength of alignment-free methods with respect to running times. Among the alignment-free methods, the ICD method outperformed FFP, despite the fact that it is running within the Matlab® framework. This suggests that even better execution times may be observed with the ICD method if it was redesigned as a native application.

Discussion

The binary indicator representation of DNA is a common representation to use on methods that treat DNA as a digital signal [19]. Some suggest that this representation is common because it inherently retains the important three-base periodicity which is important for detecting coding regions in DNA [15]. Some methods make interesting transformations to the original indicator sequence, such as the inter-nucleotide distance utilized by Afreixo et al. [18], with the goal of strengthening signals in the original digital signal that are discriminatory between different sequences. We applied the DFT on the indicator sequence. The DFT is a common DSP technique on digital signals and has been used in other methods for DNA sequence analysis. Each coefficient of the DFT represents a cross correlation of the entire input sequence and a complex sinusoid at a specific frequency, notably k/N [25]. As noted, DFTs have been successfully used in detecting coding regions of genes, where a strong peak is observed at frequency $N/3$. Our work was largely motivated by an interest in investigating how the differences of the magnitudes of the sinusoids between adjacent frequencies might improve sequence characterization in DNA. The ICD method presents a novel use of the DFT by computing the inter-coefficient difference from the resulting set of coefficients computed by the DFT transformation. The analysis presented here demonstrates its potential as a viable alternative approach toward DNA sequence analysis. In particular, the ability to distinguish differences between sequences having both low and high measures of homology, without computing an alignment, is particularly useful, compared to the challenges from computing multiple sequence alignments over large amounts of biological sequence data.

One may wonder about the likelihood of two different sequences producing an identical ICD vector. The critical part of the ICD method is the DFT. Two different DNA sequences will produce a unique set of coefficients,

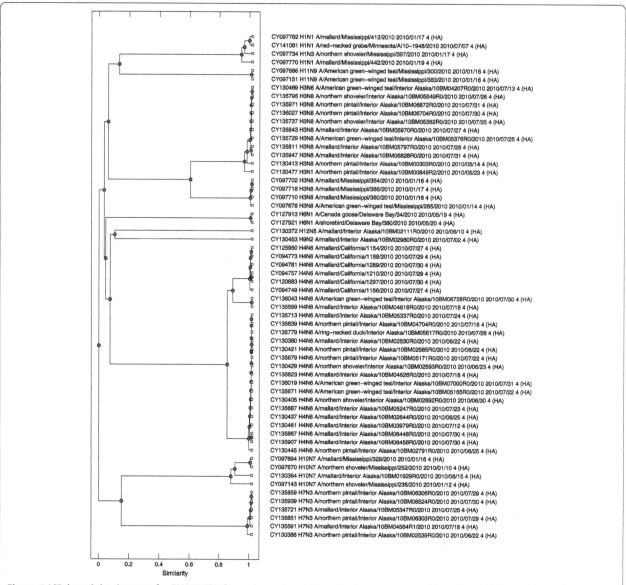

Figure 5 ICD-based dendrogram for FLU60. This figure shows the resulting dendrogram generated based on the ICD method applied on the FLU60 dataset, which contains 60 sequences of the HA gene of different subtypes of avian influenza type A.

and likewise, our ICD transformation applied to these coefficients is thus also unique, except under one condition: when one sequence is a rotational shift of the other, and both of these sequences represent the longest sequences in the set of DNA being analyzed, meaning, there will be

Table 3 Observed execution time for FLU60

Method	Exec time (sec)
Clustal W	157.0
Clustal Omega	27.0
Pairwise alignment	53.8
FFP	7.1
ICD	0.2

no zeros appended to either sequence. For example, if the sequences GACGACTCAT and TGACGACTCA (the second sequence is equivalent to the first sequence right-shifted by 1 with rotation) were both in the set of DNA being analyzed and were the longest sequences in the data, they will both yield the same X_A^*, X_C^*, X_G^*, and X_T^* vectors. However, the likelihood of two biologically meaningful DNA sequences being an entire rotational shift of the other is highly unlikely, particularly when analyzing entire genes. If this event were to actually occur in nature, then our method will yield these sequences as being identical, rightfully drawing the attention of the researcher.

Though we tested several datasets to determine the efficacy of the method, it does have a limitation worth noting.

The ICD method works well when assessing similarity of identical genes over many different species, such as the INS19 dataset. It also works well when assessing similarity over many variants of the same gene from the same species, such as the FLU60 dataset. However, for evaluating the similarity over large, genomic regions or entire genomes from different species, the ICD method is limited. The reason for this is due to the requirement of padding zeros to the indicator sequences to ensure all sequences have equal length. Sequences that are significantly shorter than the longest sequence will likewise have a substantial vector of zeros padded and thus will yield comparatively poor ICD vectors.

The results of the ICD method compared favorably to other methods tested. In fact, we observed examples in the INS19 test where the ICD analysis yielded a more phylogenetically correct tree than those produced from other methods tests, backed up by simple phylogenetic relationships observed in any biological text. We opted to perform an all-against-all pairwise alignment over a multiple sequence alignment to ensure the highest degree of accuracy of the measure of similarity of alignments. In the FLU60 data, the ICD methods ability to detect the correct measure of similarity among even those sequences that had a high measure of pairwise sequence identity was remarkable.

A significant disadvantage of alignment-based sequence comparison methods is that they assume that important regions in the genetic sequence will follow the same order between similar species. However, as noted by Pinello et al., this is not always the case [7]. As a method based on the DFT, the ICD method capitalizes on recurrent patterns, regardless of the position of those patterns in the whole sequence. It is robust to possible reordering of conserved regions between genetic sequences.

The ICD method offers a significant advantage over alignment and alignment-free methods by eliminating the need for parameters. Other methods often require multiple runs to determine the best parameter set. In comparison, our ICD method is a pure mathematical, alignment-free transformation that requires no user-defined parameters prior to the analysis.

Depending on the alignment algorithm chosen, the running time to compare m sequences of length n and produce a tree based on alignment methods can vary between $O(m^2n^2)$ for ClustalW [6] to as high as $O(n^m)$ for dynamic programming approaches. More recently, Clustal Omega implemented substantial improvements over its predecessors in the Clustal family, improving the running time to $O(nm \log m)$, making it suitable for large-scale multiple sequence alignments. Alignment-free methods often have a performance advantage, particularly those that are based on k-mer frequencies. These methods can be run in $O(knm)$ time, noting that selection of word size will have an

effect on the final performance. This is particularly important for DNA, which requires longer word lengths for meaningful results. In contrast, the FFT runs in $O(mn \log n)$, suggesting that it is an efficient technique, comparable with other alignment-free methods. Our results in Table 3 confirm the theoretical running times, with the alignment-free methods having a superior advantage over the alignment methods.

Alignment-based methods have their advantages. In particular, an alignment will often produce a better *absolute* value of evolutionary distance between sequences by incorporating a substitution matrix such as BLOSUM62. In contrast, it is relatively difficult to infer a precise measure of evolutionary distance from alignment-free methods, and this is particularly true of the correlation computed from the ICD vector. This is not uncommon, as this is a limitation with any phylogenetic approach that involves computing a distance matrix based on sequence homology. Despite this limitation, most of the relative distances observed between species in the INS19 dataset and between different variants of avian flu in the FLU60 dataset were consistent with the alignments produced. More interestingly, we demonstrated a few differences between the results from the methods applied to the INS19 data, where the ICD approach produced evolutionary relationships that were more consistent with our biological understanding of evolution among species that the other approaches we evaluated failed to capture.

The use of a correlation coefficient for distance is part of the novel approach in this work. Even though the theoretical value of the Dist computation is [0.0, 2.0], all pairs of sequences analyzed had values between 0.0 and 1.0. In other words, sequences were either found to have a strong positive correlation, which is implied for Dist values near 0, or no correlation, for Dist values near 1.0. Our observations on all tests never observed Dist computations of more than 1.0. If this had happened, it would have implied that the two biological sequences being tested had a negative correlation with respect to their ICD vector. From a biological viewpoint, different species, genes, or even different variants within the same genes arise due to evolution; more specifically, due to selective pressures placed on the genome to become more 'fit' than its ancestors. The processes behind natural selection that are so important for breeding new species and genetic functions are not random. However, the underlying genetic mutations that occur over eons are generally considered to be random events [38]. The fact that we never observed a negative correlation might offer a metric to numerically confirm the random nature of evolution. This needs further investigation over a much larger set of genetic data to draw any conclusions.

Conclusions

In this paper, we present a novel use of the discrete Fourier transform to establish sequence similarity through incorporating a simple transform of the coefficient vector. We demonstrated its efficacy on two datasets designed to measure the method's capability on establishing similarity among datasets with different levels of sequence identity. The ICD approach produced a high quality dendrogram representing phylogenetic relationships of sequences with different levels of sequence identity. Our results were nearly identical with those obtained using traditional alignment-based approaches.

Additional file

> **Additional file 1: Application of the discrete Fourier transform on DNA for sequence similarity. Table S1.** Avian Flu Sequences (FLU60). **Figure S1.** Histogram of % identity in FLU60. **Figure S2.** Alignment based dendogram for *FLU60*. **Figure S3.** FFP based dendogram for *FLU60*.

Abbreviations

AAP: all-against-all pairwise global alignment; DFT: discrete Fourier transform; DNA: deoxyribonucleic acid; DSP: digital signal processing; FFP: feature frequency profile method; FFT: fast Fourier transform; FLU60: dataset of 60 variants of avian influenza; HA: hemagglutinin (an influenza gene); ICD: inter-coefficient difference; INS19: dataset of the insulin gene from 19 species; MSA: multiple sequence alignment; NA: neuraminidase (an influenza gene); RFdist: Robinson-Foulds tree distance metric; UPGMA: unweighted pair group method average; $\lfloor x \rfloor$: the floor of x; $\|X\|$: the euclidean norm of vector X.

Competing interests

The authors declare that they have no competing interests.

Acknowledgements

Part of this work was funded through a grant awarded to Brian King from the Bucknell Geisinger Research Initiative. Additional funding was provided through the Bucknell Presidential Fellowship program. We wish to thank the reviewers for insightful comments that helped strengthen our work.

Author details

[1]Department of Computer Science, Bucknell University, Lewisburg, PA 17837, USA. [2]Department of Electrical and Computer Engineering, Bucknell University, Lewisburg, PA 17837, USA.

References

1. R Durbin, SR Eddy, A Krogh, G Mitchison, *Biological Sequence Analysis: Probabilistic Models of Proteins and Nucleic Acids* (Cambridge University Press, Cambridge, UK, 1998), p. 356
2. GE Sims, S-R Jun, GA Wu, S-H Kim, Whole-genome phylogeny of mammals: evolutionary information in genic and nongenic regions. Proc Natl Acad Sci U S A. **106**, 17077–82 (2009)
3. A Phillips, D Janies, W Wheeler, Multiple sequence alignment in phylogenetic analysis. Mol Phylogenet Evol. **16**, 317–30 (2000)
4. T Samuelsson, *Genomics and bioinformatics: an introduction to programming tools for life scientists*, 1st edn. (Cambridge University Press, Cambridge, UK, 2012), p. 356
5. S Altschul, W Gish, W Miller, E Myers, D Lipman, Basic local alignment search tool. J Mol Biol. **215**, 403–410 (1990)
6. JD Thompson, DG Higgins, TJ Gibson, CLUSTAL W: improving the sensitivity of progressive multiple sequence alignment through sequence weighting, position-specific gap penalties and weight matrix choice. Nucleic Acids Res. **22**, 4673–4680 (1994)
7. L Pinello, G Lo Bosco, G-C Yuan, Applications of alignment-free methods in epigenomics. Brief Bioinform. **15**, 419–430 (2013)
8. S Vinga, J Almeida, Alignment-free sequence comparison–a review. Bioinformatics. **19**, 513–523 (2003)
9. O Bonham-Carter, J Steele, D Bastola, Alignment-free genetic sequence comparisons: a review of recent approaches by word analysis. Brief Bioinform. online only, published July 31, 2013
10. M Domazet-Lošo, B Haubold, Alignment-free detection of local similarity among viral and bacterial genomes. Bioinformatics. **27**, 1466–72 (2011)
11. D Rafiei, A Mendelzon, Efficient Retrieval of Similar Time Sequences Using DFT, in *Proceedings of 5th International Conference of Foundations of Data Organization – FODO '98* (Kobe, Japan, 1998), pp. 249–257
12. Y-L Wu, D Agrawal, A El Abbadi, A comparison of DFT and DWT based similarity search in time-series databases, in *Proc. ninth Int. Conf. Inf. Knowl. Manag. - CIKM '00* (ACM Press, New York, USA, 2000), pp. 488–495
13. PD Cristea, Conversion of nucleotides sequences into genomic signals. J Cell Mol Med. **6**, 279–303 (2002)
14. D Anastassiou, Genomic signal processing. IEEE Signal Process Mag. **18**, 8–20 (2001)
15. SD Sharma, K Shakya, SN Sharma, Evaluation of DNA mapping schemes for exon detection. Int Conf Comput Commun Electr Technol. **2011**, 71–74 (2011)
16. K Katoh, K Misawa, K Kuma, T Miyata, MAFFT: a novel method for rapid multiple sequence alignment based on fast Fourier transform. Nucleic Acids Res. **30**, 3059–3066 (2002)
17. RF Voss, Evolution of long-range fractal correlations and 1/f noise in DNA base sequences. Phys Rev Lett. **68**, 3805–3808 (1992)
18. V Afreixo, CAC Bastos, AJ Pinho, SP Garcia, PJSG Ferreira, Genome analysis with inter-nucleotide distances. Bioinformatics. **25**, 3064–70 (2009)
19. MK Hota, VK Srivastava, Performance analysis of different DNA to numerical mapping techniques for identification of protein coding regions using tapered window based short-time discrete Fourier transform. Int Conf Power, Control Embed Syst. **3**, 1–4 (2010)
20. M Akhtar, J Epps, E Ambikairajah, Signal processing in sequence analysis: advances in eukaryotic gene prediction. IEEE J Sel Top Signal Process. **2**, 310–321 (2008)
21. H Saberkari, M Shamsi, M Sedaaghi, F Golabi, Prediction of protein coding regions in DNA sequences using signal processing methods, in *Proc. 2012 IEEE Symp. Ind. Electron. Appl. (ISIEA2012)* (Bandung, Indonesia, 2012), pp. 355–360
22. KD Rao, S Member, MNS Swamy, L Fellow, Analysis of genomics and proteomics using DSP techniques. IEEE Trans Circuits Syst I Regul Pap. **55**, 370–378 (2008)
23. SA Marhon, SC Kremer, Gene prediction based on DNA spectral analysis: a literature review. J Comput Biol. **18**, 639–76 (2011)
24. EO Brigham, RE Morrow, The fast Fourier transform. IEEE Spectr. **4**, 63–70 (1967)
25. RG Lyons, *Understanding Digital Signal Processing* (Pearson Education, Upper Saddle River, NJ, 2004)
26. AV Oppenheim, RW Schafer, *Discrete-Time Signal Processing*, 3rd edn. (Prentice Hall, Upper Saddle River, NJ, USA, 2010)
27. P Vaidyanathan, The role of signal-processing concepts in genomics and proteomics. J Franklin Inst. **341**, 111–135 (2004)
28. JA Berger, SK Mitra, M Carli, A Neri, New approaches to genome sequence analysis based on digital signal processing, in *IEEE Work. Genomic Signal Process. Stat. (GENSIPS)* (IEEE Press, Raleigh, North Carolina, USA, 2002)
29. J Tuqan, A Rushdi, S Member, A DSP approach for finding the codon bias in DNA sequences. IEEE J Sel Top Signal Process. **2**, 343–356 (2008)
30. D Anastassiou, Frequency-domain analysis of biomolecular sequences. Bioinformatics. **16**, 1073–1081 (2000)
31. EA Cheever, DB Searls, W Karunaratne, GC Overton, Using Signal Processing Techniques for DNA Sequence Comparison, in *Proc. Fifteenth Annu. Northeast Bioeng. Conf* (IEEE Press, Boston, MA, 1989), pp. 173–174
32. SB Needleman, CD Wunsch, A general method applicable to the search for similarities in the amino acid sequence of two proteins. J Mol Biol. **48**, 443–453 (1970)
33. DF Robinson, LR Foulds, Comparison of phylogenetic trees. Math Biosci. **53**, 131–147 (1981)
34. KP Schliep, phangorn: phylogenetic analysis in R. Bioinformatics. **27**, 592–3 (2011)
35. GM Air, Sequence relationships among the hemagglutinin genes of 12 subtypes of influenza A virus. Proc Natl Acad Sci U S A. **78**, 7639–43 (1981)
36. MA Larkin, G Blackshields, NP Brown, R Chenna, PA McGettigan, H McWilliam, F Valentin, IM Wallace, A Wilm, R Lopez, JD Thompson, TJ

Gibson, DG Higgins, Clustal W and Clustal X version 2.0. Bioinformatics. **23**, 2947–8 (2007)

37. F Sievers, A Wilm, D Dineen, TJ Gibson, K Karplus, W Li, R Lopez, H McWilliam, M Remmert, J Söding, JD Thompson, DG Higgins, Fast, scalable generation of high-quality protein multiple sequence alignments using Clustal Omega. Mol Syst Biol. **7**, 539 (2011)

38. S Kaufmann, *The origins of order, vol. 209* (Oxford University Press, Oxford, UK, 1993), p. 709

Discovering irregular pupil light responses to chromatic stimuli using waveform shapes of pupillograms

Minoru Nakayama[1*], Wioletta Nowak[2], Hitoshi Ishikawa[3], Ken Asakawa[3] and Yoshiaki Ichibe[4]

Abstract

Background: The waveforms of the pupillary light reflex (PLR) can be analyzed in a diagnostic test that allows for differentiation between disorders affecting photoreceptors and disorders affecting retinal ganglion cells, using various signal processing techniques. This procedure has been used on both healthy subjects and patients with age-related macular degeneration (AMD), as a simple diagnostic procedure is required for diagnosis.

Results: The Fourier descriptor technique is used to extract the features of PLR waveform shapes of pupillograms and their amplitudes. To detect those patients affected by AMD using the extracted features, multidimensional scaling (MDS) and clustering techniques were used to emphasize stimuli and subject differences. The detection performance of AMD using the features and the MDS technique shows only a qualitative tendency, however. To evaluate the detection performance quantitatively, a set of combined features was created to evaluate characteristics of the PLR waveform shapes in detail. Classification performance was compared across three categories (AMD patients, aged, and healthy subjects) using the Random Forest method, and weighted values were optimized using variations of the classification error rates. The results show that the error rates for healthy pupils and AMD-affected pupils were low when the value of the coefficient for a combination of PLR amplitudes and features of waveforms was optimized as 1.5. However, the error rates for patients with age-affected eyes was not low.

Conclusions: A classification procedure for AMD patients has been developed using the features of PLR waveform shapes and their amplitudes. The results show that the error rates for healthy PLRs and AMD PLRs were low when the Random Forest method was used to produce the classification. The classification of pupils of patients with age-affected eyes should be carefully considered in order to produce optimum results.

Introduction

The pupillary response has long been used for diagnostic procedures [1] and psycho-physiological studies [2-4]. The pupillary response, a reaction to light intensity, is well-known, and the pupillary light response controls the dilation and constriction of the pupil in response to changes in light intensity. The response is usually observed and recorded using pupillograms which consist of pupil diameter and time diagrams [5].

This response is often called the pupillary light reflex (PLR). It has also been used as an objective measure of

retinal and optic nerve functions. In recent years, a growth in interest in the examination of PLR has been observed. It is the result of the discovery of a new type of retinal ganglion cells [6,7]. Since the melanopsin-associated photoreceptive system (ipRGCs, intrinsically photosensitive retinal ganglion cells) in the human retina was discovered [8], various diagnostic procedures have been proposed and introduced.

In particular, the difference between the response behavior of this photoreceptive system to some types of chromatic stimuli and the behavior of the conventional rod-cone system has been compared [8] to determine the possibility of detecting the condition of the retina. In addition to receiving rod and cone inputs, the responses based on the newly discovered system have been studied

*Correspondence: nakayama@cradle.titech.ac.jp
[1] Department of Human System Science, Tokyo Institute of Technology, Ookayama, Meguro, Tokyo 152-8552, Japan
Full list of author information is available at the end of the article

as intrinsically photosensitive [9,10]. Those cells are interchangeably referred to as ipRGC or melanopsin-mediated retinal ganglion cells (mRGC), and according to recent studies, they drive pupillary responses and circadian rhythms [6-8]. Also, this phenomenon has been applied to diagnostic procedures for patients with glaucoma [11] or retinas pigmentosa [12,13]. Feature extraction and analysis of PLRs has made a significant contribution to the development of diagnostic procedures for these patients, as opthalmologically scientific evidence was discovered. Another well-known disease which is observed in aging patients is age-related macular degeneration (AMD) [14]. This disease is related to the condition of the retina, and thus, PLRs are affected by the progress of the disease. Unfortunately, this disease spreads gradually. Therefore, detection and prediction procedures are required. A simple procedure which detects prominent symptoms, such as an easy at home test, is necessary.

In addition to some types of portable pupillometers currently available, a PC web camera and a smart phone with an additional lens can be used to observe pupillography. Some types of clinical consultations can be conducted anywhere using either of these pieces of equipment.

As mentioned above, PLRs can be applied to extract features and to detect irregular responses. This means that a record of temporal pupillary changes as pupillograms is a time series signal, requiring various types of signal processing techniques. This suggests that a simple signal processing technique may be used to extract some symptoms of the disease. For example, the Fourier descriptor technique is often used to indicate the shapes of waveforms [15-17], and the possibility of using this method should be examined.

In this paper, feature expressions of PLR waveform shapes of pupillograms are introduced to identify pupil characteristics. Also, the possibility of detecting eyes which are affected by AMD and other factors is examined. Therefore, the following topics are addressed:

1. A procedure for extracting features of PLR waveforms of pupillograms is created, and the features used to compare these waveforms are analyzed to detect irregular responses.
2. To determine the possibility of detection in diseased eyes, several classifying techniques were applied to features of PLRs, and the performance of the techniques is discussed.

Related works

The study of ipRGC mentioned in related research work currently being conducted is concerned mainly with, on the one hand, the study of the ipRGC structure and functions and on the other hand, with the diagnostic use of their specific activity. A brief review of literature regarding this research is presented below.

The ipRGCs are atypical retinal photoreceptors distinct from classical rod and cone photoreceptors [18]. They express the photopigment melanopsin and are intrinsically photosensitive, since they showed sluggish melanopsin-mediated responses. They can also act as conventional RGCs by receiving synaptic rod/cone input via bipolar cells. This integrated information is then transmitted to numerous discrete brain regions involved in both non-image and image-forming vision [19]. The ipRGCs ultimately modulate a multiplicity of behaviors including circadian photoentrainment, PLR, activity masking, sleep/arousal, anxiety, light aversion, and even make a significant contribution to visual functions. Recently, it has been discovered that ipRGCs consist of several subtypes that are morphologically and physiologically distinct, which contribute differentially to the abovementioned non-image and image-forming functions [19,20]. Detailed study of the ipRGC's different types and their behaviour with varying attributes of light are being still analyzed. In particular, intensive research involving the relationship between melanopsin activity and PLR reflex is now being conducted [21,22]. These studies have direct applications in clinical conditions for the diagnosis of retinal degeneration and sleep disturbances under clinical conditions [22,23].

The application of ipRGCs to the study of retinal degeneration is focused mainly on the use of pupil responses to chromatic light as a clinical marker, to allow differentiation between disorders affecting rod/cone photoreceptors (the outer retina) and those affecting retinal ganglion cells (the inner retina). As used above, the terms 'inner retina' and 'outer retina' are the consequence of the anatomical distribution of ipRGC photoreceptors (the inner nuclear layer) and rod/cone photoreceptors (the outer retinal layer) in the retina [24]. Where a disease affects multiple retinal layers, the pupillary light reflex could be a useful tool in determining the contributions of the inner and outer retina to the disease process.

Kankipati et al. focused on the post illumination pupil response (PIPR) analysis of glaucoma patients, and compared them with normal subjects [25,26]. They used a 10-s light stimulus (retinal irradiance, 13 log quanta/cm^2/s; light wavelengths, 470 nm (blue), and 623 nm (red)) and recorded pupillary response for 50 s after light cessation. They found that normal subjects displayed a significant PIPR for blue light (but not for red light), which is consistent with the proposed melanopsin-mediated response. When glaucoma patients are compared to patients using age-matching controls, there was a significant decrease in melanopsin-mediated PIPR. They concluded that PIPR has the potential for use as a clinical tool for evaluating patients with glaucoma. Feigl et al. [11] also tested PIPR to analyze whether glaucoma alters the function of ipRGC. They use a 10-s light stimuli with 488 nm and 610 nm light wavelengths and retinal irradiance of 14.2 log photons cm^2/s. They have found that patients with advanced glaucoma have a dysfunctional ipRGC-mediated PIPR. It has been confirmed that PIPR may be a clinical indicator of progressive changes in glaucoma.

Kardon et al. focused on the percentage of pupil contraction in transient and sustained pupil responses in patients with retinas pigmentosa [12,13]. They used a stimulus paradigm using red and blue light as a continuous Ganzfeld stimulus which produced a 13-s stepwise increase in intensity over a 2 log-unit range (low ($1\ cd/m^2$), medium ($10\ cd/m^2$), and high ($100\ cd/m^2$)). They have found that pupil responses to red and blue light stimuli which are weighed to favor cone or rod input are significantly reduced in patients with retinas pigmentosa. Their preliminary results suggest that pupil response to a low-intensity blue light, to a high-intensity red light, and to a high-intensity blue light may be reasonable markers of rod activity, cone-driven responses, and direct, intrinsic activation of mRGC, respectively.

AMD is another concern regarding retinal disease. This disease causes impairment of both the inner and outer retinal layers, depending on the stage of the disease, and pupil chromatic response measurements may allow the monitoring of the progression of the disease or facilitate the determination of different stages of the disease [27]. In particular, the function of ipRGC concerns the PLR while AMD influences the waveforms of PLR [22].

Brozou et al. tested outer retinal contributions to pupil responses in patients with AMD [28]. The study showed that AMD significantly affects the pupil's response to light stimulus (20 msec duration and $24.6\ cd/m^2$ intensity), when compared to normal subjects. Feigl and Zele present a new experimental paradigm for the first time that allows the differentiation of inner and outer retinal contributions to the pupil response in AMD [22]. They used a 11.9-s duration 0.5 Hz sine wave stimulus with 464 and 635 nm light wavelengths and retinal irradiance of 15.1 log photon $cm^{-2}s^{-1}$. Additionally, they introduced a new metric called 'a phase amplitude percentage' (PAP) that reflects inner and outer interactions. PAP is determined from the average long-wavelength and short-wavelength peak-to-through phase amplitudes. PAP approaches zero for retinal irradiances below a certain melanopsin threshold, as PLR is driven by rods and cones. PAP is non-zero for retinal irradiances above a certain melanopsin threshold, as PLR is predominantly driven by cones with ipRGC contributions. They also showed that application of this paradigm to AMD patients can provide information that ipRGCs are altered. This result can be a very important step toward using PLR to determine the inner and outer retinal dysfunction of AMD patients. Future work will be focused on quantifying retinal inputs to the pupil response in order to determine the different stages of AMD or to monitor the disease's progression.

Our work presents an attempt to use the pupil response to chromatic rectangular light pulses, which are routinely measured in clinical studies, as a simple and fast tool (indicator) for early detection of AMD. AMD (both the dry and wet forms) is the one of the most common irreversible causes of severe loss of vision. It usually affects older adults and results in a loss of vision because of damage to the central part of the retina, known as the macula. The gradual disappearance of the retina pigment epithelium (RPE) in the dry form results in patches of chorioretinal atrophy lacking any visual function. In the wet form, the damage is due to the escape of subretinal fluid/intraretinal fluid, blood, or destruction of photoreceptors and RPE by fibrous or fibrovascular tissue. Since AMD destroys photoreceptors which are initial receptors for PLR, it may reduce the PLR. The type or localization of the damaged photoreceptors may then be indicated using a pupil response to chromatic light. AMD is painless and, consequently, the lack of early warning signals in existing retinal pathology necessitates an indicator which will allow for earlier and easier detection (prediction) of this type of disorder. It is believed that the pupil reaction to chromatic light could be such an indicator.

Methods
Subjects
Six healthy young subjects (20 to 21 years old) and six elderly AMD-affected patients (59 to 86 years old) participated. Each elderly patient had a diseased eye and a normal eye, according to a medical doctor.

Diseased eyes with choroidal neovascularization (CNV) in the macular region are often affected by new blood vessels, which bleed and form dense macular scars [14]. Also, CNV is a major cause of visual loss due to AMD [14].

Patient details are summarized in Table 1. Regarding fluorescein angiographic assessment as a medical diagnostic [14], the diseased eyes are classified into *predominantly classic CNV lesion* (the area of classic CNV occupies 50% or more of the entire lesion) and *occult lesion* (either fibrovascular pigment epithelial detachments or late leakage from an undetermined source [29]). As regards to the clinical consultation, there is no significant difference in the seriousness of disease between the two types. Table 1 shows patients with normal eyes that have sufficient visual acuity.

This study followed the tenets of the Declaration of Helsinki regarding research involving human subjects; informed consent was obtained from all subjects. The study protocol was approved at the Kitasato University School of Medicine Institutional Ethics Committee. This test does not determine the risk, however.

Table 1 Patient information

	Age	Sex	Type of disease	Visual acuity D	N
Patient 1	82	Male	Predominantly	0.2	1.0
Patient 2	66	Male	Predominantly	0.04	1.0
Patient 3	74	Male	Predominantly	0.4	0.9
Patient 4	86	Male	Occult	0.6	1.0
Patient 5	59	Male	Occult	0.5	1.2
Patient 6	63	Male	Occult	0.2	1.0

Predominantly, predominantly classic CNV; Occult, occult without classic CNV; D, disease eye; N, normal eye.

Experimental procedure

Pupil responses were measured using a PLR observation procedure and without any procedures to stimulate mydriasis, to determine the level of functionality of the melanopsin-associated photoreceptors [9,10].

Pupil responses were recorded using Iriscorder Dual equipment (Hamamatsu Photonics, Hamamatsu, Japan) at a sampling rate of 30 Hz. This equipment is designed for observing PLRs with ipRGCs activation in accordance with the measurements taken in previous studies [10,12] and consists of a measurement controller and a pair of goggles which have an infrared camera and a LED light source for each eye of the goggles. Therefore, the stimulus light presentation was binocular, and the recordings were also binocular. In the experiment, a long wavelength (635 ± 5 nm) red light and a short wavelength (470 ± 7 nm) blue light were used at two different light intensities (10 and 100 cd/m^2). The light stimulation conditions were adjusted in accordance with the method of Kawasaki and Kardon [10,12] while the measurement validity was also confirmed [30,31]. PLRs for light stimuli were simply recorded as single trial measure. The light pulses were projected within the housing of a pair of goggles. Subjects were asked to not blink for 20 s while their pupil diameter was recorded. The observation period consisted of a 10-s light pulse which caused a restriction of the pupil size, followed by 10 s without a light pulse during which restoration of the pupil size was allowed to occur. These measurements were taken in a dark room with constant lighting conditions. A dark adaptation period of 5 min was allowed prior to the taking of measurements.

Responses for both left and right pupils were recorded as pupillograms for each subject. In this paper, the four conditions for the left (L) and right (R) eyes are defined as follows: 'r10' (long wavelength and low light intensity), 'r100' (long and high intensity), 'b10' (short wavelength and low intensity), and 'b100' (short wavelength and high intensity). The pupil responses of a healthy subject are illustrated in Figure 1, and the pupil responses of a patient diseased eye with AMD are illustrated in Figure 2. In both

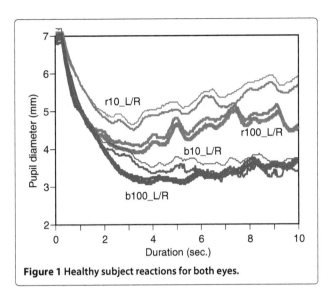

Figure 1 Healthy subject reactions for both eyes.

figures, the red line indicates pupil responses for red light, and the blue line indicates responses for blue light. In Figure 1, the very fine line shows the pupil response of the left eye for 10 cd/m^2, the less fine line shows the pupil response of the right eye for 10 cd/m^2, while the bold line shows pupil response of left eye for 100 cd/m^2 and the bolder line shows pupil response for the right eye for 100 cd/m^2.

In Figure 1, there is little difference in PLR waveform shapes between the left and right eyes. Pupil sizes are sustained during both blue light pulses, and restoration of pupil sizes can be observed after both red light pulses. These phenomena confirm pupil behavior using blue and red light pulses observed in previous studies. However, these phenomena influenced diseased eyes, as shown in Figure 2.

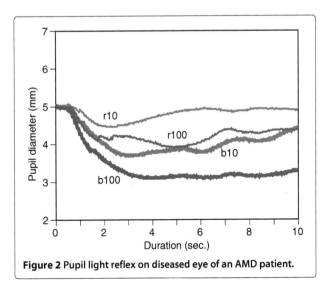

Figure 2 Pupil light reflex on diseased eye of an AMD patient.

To emphasize the difference in PLR waveforms between patient's diseased eye and healthy eyes, averaged PLRs are illustrated for all healthy eyes in Figure 3 and for all diseased eyes in Figure 4. Regarding Figure 3, the order of mean pupil diameters clearly shows the degree of pupil restrictions for stimuli. The order for patient with diseased eyes may be influenced by the disease. Table 2 shows mean pupil diameters and STDs for four stimuli across healthy subjects, patients with normal eyes, and patients with diseased eyes. The order of means is maintained across three types of eyes, and it does not seem easy to classify eye conditions using these statistics.

During all observations for pupil reactions, repeated measures were not taken and so the test-retest reliability of the paradigm has not been evaluated.

Fourier descriptors

The feature vectors for PLR waveforms were extracted using the discrete Fourier transform (DFT) procedure [16,17]. As mentioned above, PLRs were sampled as discrete signals. Here, the length N of a discrete signal is defined as $x(n)$, which is sampled at time t with spacing Δ. The signal $x(n)$ can be noted as an Equation 1 using DFT [32].

$$x(n) = a_0 + \sum_{k=1}^{N/2} \left(a(k)\cos\left(2\pi k \frac{t(n)}{N\Delta} \right) \right.$$
$$\left. + b(k)\sin\left(2\pi k \frac{t(n)}{N\Delta} \right) \right) \tag{1}$$

$$a_0 = X(1)/N$$
$$a(k) = 2\,\mathrm{real}(X(k+1))/N$$
$$b(k) = 2\,\mathrm{imag}(X(k+1))/N$$

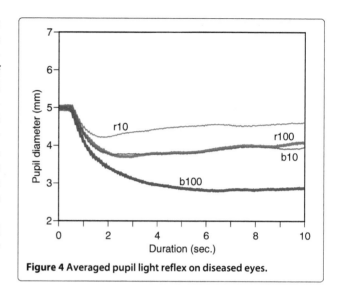

Figure 4 Averaged pupil light reflex on diseased eyes.

This suggests that PLR waveforms can be represented using coefficients a_0, $a(k)$, and $b(k)$ with periodical sine and cosine functions. To present the features of the waveforms of pupillograms, the magnitudes of the coefficients are preferred because coefficient $b(k)$ is the imaginary part of a value. The magnitudes of coefficients, including a_0, $\mathrm{FD}_i (i = 0, \ldots, N/2-1)$ are used as Fourier descriptors (FD) in vector (2) as follows:

$$f = [\mathrm{FD}_0, \mathrm{FD}_1, \ldots, \mathrm{FD}_{N/2-1}] \tag{2}$$

In general, the components FD_0 and a_0 in the Equation 1 show the DC components of the signal. These DC components represent the amplitude; however, the waveform shape consists of frequency components. Also, the features are affected by individual factors, so that a standardized feature using a component, such as FD_1 for example, is preferred in vector (3), which is converted from the above vector (2), as follows [17]:

$$f = \left[\frac{\mathrm{FD}_2}{\mathrm{FD}_1}, \frac{\mathrm{FD}_3}{\mathrm{FD}_1}, \ldots, \frac{\mathrm{FD}_{N/2-1}}{\mathrm{FD}_1} \right] \tag{3}$$

Prediction procedure for AMD disease

This paper proposes a procedure for detecting AMD patients and diseased eyes. The procedure is summarized

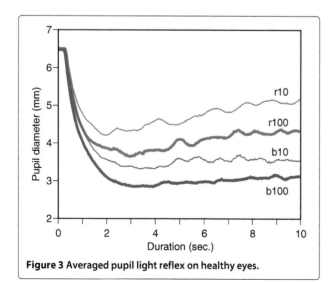

Figure 3 Averaged pupil light reflex on healthy eyes.

Table 2 Mean pupil diameters for the stimuli

	Healthy subject		Patient normal		Patient diseased	
	Mean	STD	Mean	STD	Mean	STD
r10	4.82	0.86	3.98	0.68	4.50	0.74
r100	4.30	0.90	3.41	0.73	3.99	0.74
b10	3.74	0.85	3.23	0.61	3.96	0.78
b100	3.16	0.85	2.65	0.69	3.18	0.74

in a flowchart in Figure 5. The first step is the definition of feature vectors of PLR waveforms for four stimuli using the FD technique mentioned above. Both eyes should be observed. The second step is to measure the (dis)similarity as distances between feature vectors of PLR waveforms for individuals for each eye. Finally, prediction in this paper is conducted using multidimensional scaling (MDS) and Random Forest techniques. The process of analysis is represented as follows.

Processing and prediction can be conducted for a few subjects without repeated measurements. Of course, the validity may not be sufficient, but it can be improved step by step when data from additional subjects is gathered. In this way, all of the techniques employed in this procedure are simple.

Feature descriptions

Feature definition

The features of observed PLRs are presented using the procedure specified in the 'Experimental procedure' section. The actual calculations were conducted using MATLAB (Mathworks, Inc., Natick, MA, USA). To extract features of pupil constriction in transient and sustained pupil reactions, pupil responses mainly during the first 10 s are analyzed because they are melanopsin-based reactions. Every individual observation of the pupillogram for a stimulus was set to a signal $x(n)$ in Equation 1, then FD vectors were extracted such as in Equation 2.

First, FD_0 were extracted in order to compare waveform amplitudes which were extracted from the transform. The amplitudes for PLR waveforms of all responses were calculated. Here, the amplitudes were standardized using the maximum peaks of the waveforms, such as b100, which suppresses individual differences for example [12]. The means were summarized into three categories: patients

with diseased eyes, patients with normal eyes and healthy eyes. The results are shown in Figure 6. The error bars indicate standard errors. According to previous studies and Figure 1, the amplitude increases from the r10 condition to the b100 condition. The mean amplitude of healthy eyes responds to the order. However, these orders are influenced in patients with one normal and one diseased eye. Regarding Figures 1 and 2, pupil diameters at stimulus onset as baselines are different. The mean diameter for patients is 4.87 mm, and the mean for healthy subjects is 6.46 mm while there is a significant difference between them ($t(10) = 4.88, p < 0.05$). The factor of this difference is not determined, however. There is no significant difference in mean pupil diameters between patients with diseased and normal eyes ($t(10) = 0.60, p = 0.56$). The above result shows that the amplitudes present differences which are independent of baseline pupil diameters, since the differences change with the stimulus conditions in Figure 6.

The waveform shape can be noted as a vector in the Fourier descriptors section. A number of components of the feature vector represent the characteristics of most signals at only the low-order values of four or five FDs [16]. Therefore, four dimensions have been employed as feature vectors (f) in this paper. Also, FD_0 was too large in this observation, so FD_1 was used for the standardization. As an example, Fourier descriptors of r10 for the left eye of the healthy subject in Figure 1 are given as Equation 2:

$$f_{r10\_L} = [501.0, 83.6, 50.6, 28.2, 23.3, 30.0, \ldots] \quad (4)$$

This vector is converted using Equation 3:

$$f_{r10\_L} = \left[\frac{50.6}{83.6}, \frac{28.2}{83.6}, \frac{23.3}{83.6}, \frac{30.0}{83.6} \right] \quad (5)$$

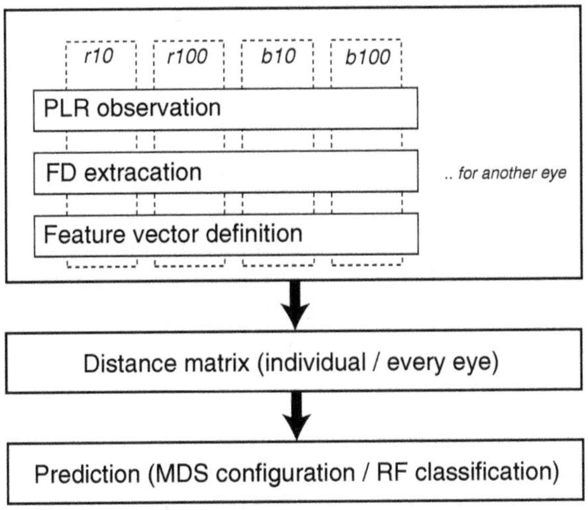

Figure 5 Flowchart of signal processing and prediction.

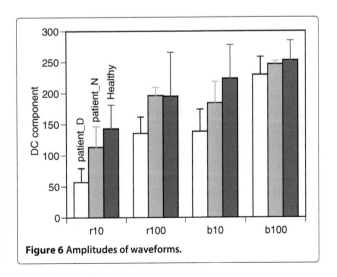

Figure 6 Amplitudes of waveforms.

Therefore, the feature vectors are noted as follows:

$$f_{r10\_L} = [0.61, 0.34, 0.28, 0.36] \tag{6}$$
$$f_{r100\_L} = [0.68, 0.52, 0.40, 0.36]$$
$$f_{b10\_L} = [0.68, 0.47, 0.48, 0.33]$$
$$f_{b100\_L} = [0.64, 0.43, 0.33, 0.30]$$

Similarity/dissimilarity

As both Figures 1 and 2 show, the waveforms of PLRs in response to stimuli are different between subjects. To compare the shapes of waveforms quantitatively, the metrics of similarity and dissimilarity should be defined using waveform feature vectors which are noted above. This is a very popular approach for pattern recognition, such as categorization and discrimination of waveforms [33]. Here, the Euclidean distance (or Minkowski's power metric) can be defined as the Euclidean norm between two feature vectors. This is the dissimilarity metric. The distances between stimuli conditions mentioned above for a set of PLRs of an eye (left eye) are summarized in the following matrix (Ed_L) as a triangular matrix.

$$\text{Ed\_L} = \begin{pmatrix} & r10 & r100 & b10 & b100 \\ r10 & 0 & 0.23 & 0.25 & 0.12 \\ r100 & 0.23 & 0 & 0.10 & 0.13 \\ b10 & 0.25 & 0.10 & 0 & 0.16 \\ b100 & 0.12 & 0.13 & 0.16 & 0 \end{pmatrix} \tag{7}$$

These components indicate dissimilarity between the two waveform shapes when their amplitude factors are excluded.

Comparing PLRs between eyes

Features of two eyes

There are many cases where one of the eyes is diseased and the other is not. As Table 1 shows visual acuities of both diseased (D) and normal (N) eyes, where all patients have a level of visual acuity in one eye that is comparable to healthy people and a diseased eye with poor acuity. Regarding the progress of AMD, the disease seldom progresses simultaneously in both eyes. This means that there is a difference in retinal condition between the left and right eyes of most patients with AMD. Since the retinal condition is different, the PLR waveforms are also different, as shown in Figures 1 and 2 while both healthy eyes respond similarly in Figure 1. This phenomenon suggests that quantitative differences in PLRs between two eyes may provide some information regarding symptoms of AMD. Therefore, a procedure of feature extraction from PLRs and the creation of a distance matrix in the above section can be applied to other cases with two eyes.

Here is a set of feature vectors of PLR waveform shapes of a patient:

$$f_{r10\_D} = [10.54, 0.22, 0.21, 0.17] \tag{8}$$
$$f_{r100\_D} = [0.62, 0.38, 0.30, 0.24]$$
$$f_{b10\_D} = [0.59, 0.37, 0.25, 0.20]$$
$$f_{b100\_D} = [0.69, 0.49, 0.37, 0.30]$$
$$f_{r10\_N} = [0.65, 0.23, 0.23, 0.14]$$
$$f_{r100\_N} = [0.55, 0.42, 0.19, 0.08]$$
$$f_{b10\_N} = [0.23, 0.56, 0.29, 0.26]$$
$$f_{b100\_N} = [0.72, 0.48, 0.36, 0.28]$$

In this notation, D means diseased eye and N means normal eye for each experimental stimulus condition, such as r10.

Regarding the procedure and feature vectors, a distance matrix across two eyes for one subject can be created as follows:

$$\text{Ed\_D/N} = \begin{pmatrix} & r10\_D & r100\_D & b10\_D & b100\_D & r10\_N & r100\_N & b10\_N & b100\_N \\ r10\_D & 0 \\ r100\_D & 0.23 & 0 \\ b10\_D & 0.55 & 0.40 & 0 \\ b100\_D & 0.32 & 0.32 & 0.50 & 0 \\ r10\_N & 0.11 & 0.22 & 0.47 & 0.36 & 0 \\ r100\_N & 0.19 & 0.21 & 0.43 & 0.16 & 0.21 & 0 \\ b10\_N & 0.17 & 0.15 & 0.41 & 0.22 & 0.17 & 0.07 & 0 \\ b100\_N & 0.34 & 0.32 & 0.47 & 0.04 & 0.36 & 0.16 & 0.22 & 0 \end{pmatrix}$$
$$\tag{9}$$

To maintain the presentation of distance matrix for two eyes, both the left and right eyes (L/R) are allotted instead of diseased and normal eyes (D/N) for healthy subjects since they have two healthy eyes.

The distances between PLR waveforms for subjects with normal eyes are relatively shorter than the distances between diseased eyes and distances between one normal and one diseased eye. A matrix can be created for every subject based on this procedure.

According to the matrix of one patient, the distances representing the dissimilarity between the conditions for diseased eyes are longer than the distances for one normal eye and one diseased eye and the distances for two normal eyes. The distances for subjects with two healthy normal eyes are the shortest. Distance matrices were created for all subjects.

Configurations using MDS

To create an overall structure of the relationship between PLR waveforms, the MDS method [34] was applied to the distance matrix [35].

The basic approach of MDS is as follows:

There are n samples which have feature vectors of waveforms, the distance can be defined using Euclidean distance such as o_{ij} between samples i and j. The diagonal distance components are 0. Here, a n by A matrix X of the waveform coordinates is introduced, another distance d_{ij} can be defined as the following equation:

$$d_{ij} = \left\{ \sum_{a=1}^{A} (x_{ia} - x_{ja})^2 \right\}^{1/2} \quad (10)$$

Additionally, the monotonic transformation of the data g is introduced, and the following equation is minimized:

$$\phi(g, \mathbf{X}) = \sum_{j<i} (g(o_{ij}) - d_{ij})^2 \quad (11)$$

As a result, MDS produces a low-dimensional projection of the data which can present the paired distances between data points. As the low-dimensional projection provides a way to configure the data, the illustration can be used to visually understand the relationship between the data.

The individual difference MDS procedure has been introduced to extend conventional MDS analysis to multiple distance matrices using the features of every subject [36,37]. The actual calculation was conducted using R. During MDS analysis, the number of dimensions was set to three. Again, the dimensions are defined in order to present a low-dimensional projection regarding MDS calculations. Therefore, the dimension may present the features of the spatial layout of the data. The dimensional values are summarized in Table 3. The contributions of both dimension 1 and dimension 2 to the classification have the same tendency as in the case of a two-dimensional analysis. Following this, dimensions 1 and 3 were then compared. The stimulus is configured in a two-dimensional space which was created using MDS analysis, as shown in Figure 7. The horizontal axis shows dimension 1, and the vertical axis shows dimension 3. According to the distance matrix, one of the waveforms of a stimulus includes a diseased and a normal eye (D/N), the other

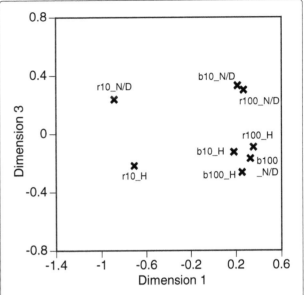

Figure 7 Light pulse condition configurations using three-dimensional scales.

includes eyes which are both healthy (H). The conditions are indicated in Figure 7 as 'D/N' for the former and 'H' for the latter. All normal conditions are gathered in one cluster except 'r10H', and only 'b100-D/N' belongs to a cluster which consists of normal responses. This suggests that for normal responses, stimuli conditions are configured outside of the cluster when the conditions include abnormal responses. This means that the possibility of detecting abnormal responses exists. According to the configuration, it is interesting that the r10 condition always shows a different tendency. This stimuli condition may provide significant information about the abnormal responses of diseased eyes.

All results for the eight conditions of the six healthy subjects and six patients are mapped in Figure 8. The stimuli conditions produce clusters in response to the configurations of stimuli, as shown in Figure 8 where all subjects' data is mapped in a similar style. However, the plots for the patient subjects are positioned in a different area. In particular, the values for patient subjects deviate from the norm in dimension 3. Even the plots of normal eyes of patient subjects are more widely distributed. The features of most patients show a different tendency. All subjects can be configured using their own individual two-dimensional information, as shown in Figure 9. In this figure, the value of dimension 3 clearly indicates the differences between healthy subjects and patient subjects. The healthy subjects produce a cluster in the lower area, and the patient subjects' plots are distributed around the cluster. If the borders between the classes could be defined mathematically, classification according to health

Table 3 Three-dimensional information of MDS for stimuli

	D/N			H		
	dim1	dim2	dim3	dim1	dim2	dim3
r10	-.89	0.16	0.24	-.71	0.17	-.22
r100	0.27	0.26	0.30	0.35	0.37	-.09
b10	0.21	-.38	0.33	0.18	-.44	-.13
b100	0.33	-.05	-.17	0.25	-.08	-.26

D/N, diseased and normal eyes of AMD patients; H, healthy eyes.

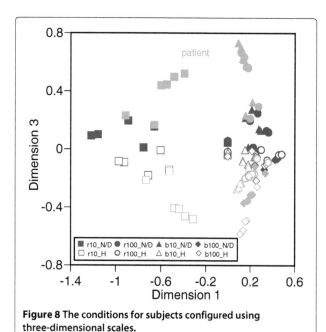

Figure 8 The conditions for subjects configured using three-dimensional scales.

condition may also be possible. The meaning of dimension 3 cannot be defined mathematically in response to the nature of MDS analysis, however. The dimension is created as a deviation of distances each of the targeted data. A detailed analysis of this will be a subject of our further study.

Since MDS analysis also provides a three-dimensional feature for every subject and patient, grouping of participants is possible using cluster analysis and data of the

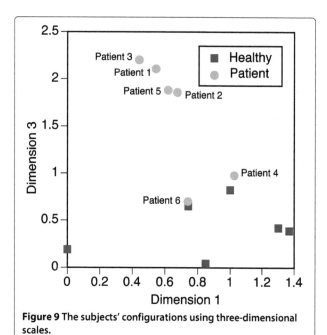

Figure 9 The subjects' configurations using three-dimensional scales.

feature set. The dendrogram as a result of cluster analysis is summarized in Figure 10. The horizontal axis shows averaged distance between subjects. The clustering process responds to the distribution of subjects in Figure 7. Most patients (the predominant type) are classified apart from other subjects.

This procedure can illustrate some of the differences between healthy subjects and patient subjects, and the clustering results show the tendency toward deviations. Therefore, the subject categories (healthy or patient) are ambiguous. Regarding the specific purpose of this work, more quantitative classification may be required as a result.

In the next section, a possible procedure for this will be introduced and discussed.

Classification using a combination of amplitudes and features of waveform shapes of pupillograms
Feature combinations

In the previous section, the features of waveform shapes were extracted as amplitudes and Fourier descriptors. There were significant differences in the mean amplitudes between the eye conditions when the features of waveform shapes were used to separate the subjects. Though they can indicate some of the conditions affecting the eyes, they are not used collaboratively. Since they are recognized as different scales of features, some consideration is required in order to combine them. Also, a more robust classification technique should be considered.

To include FD_0 components with features, the FD_0 values were standardized using the means for each eye. In the case of the left eye of the healthy subject in Figure 1, the FD_0' of the standardized FD_0 uses a mean of components. Both are noted as follows:

$$FD_{0:L}' = [FD_{0:r10\_L}', FD_{0:r100\_L}', FD_{0:b10\_L}', FD_{0:b100\_L}']$$
$$[FD_{0:r10\_L}', FD_{0:r100\_L}', FD_{0:b10\_L}', FD_{0:b100\_L}',]$$
$$= [0.65, 0.95, 1.16, 1.25]$$

$$(12)$$

$$FD_{0:L}' = \frac{FD_{0:L}}{\frac{1}{n}|FD_{0:L}|} \tag{13}$$

$$FD_{0:L}' = [0.65, 0.95, 1.16, 1.25]$$

Combined vector f' can be noted as a modified feature vector using weight coefficient w.

$$f' = \left[\frac{FD_2}{FD_1}, \frac{FD_3}{FD_1}, \ldots, \frac{FD_5}{FD_1}, wFD_0' \right] \tag{14}$$

Here, w is a coefficient used as a weighted value to create a balance between the features of waveform shapes and standardized FD_0 (FD_0'). To optimize the coefficient

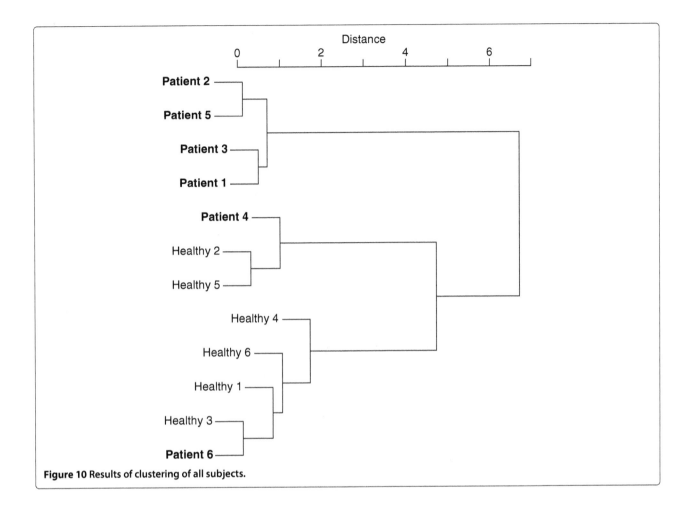

Figure 10 Results of clustering of all subjects.

w, the performance of this classification is evaluated in response to variations of w in the section which follows.

Classification procedure

In this paper, the number of subjects is small, and the number of trials for taking measurements is limited because the experimental stimuli influences the response. The Random Forest method [38], which uses an ensemble learning procedure to analyze the classification of a small sample, is used frequently. Also, the Random Forest method can show contributions of features and can be used to conduct cross validation calculations. Since the structure of the feature data set is not clear, the results of the Random Forest method may provide useful information to improve the detection procedure. The statistical package R and the 'RandomForest' package [39,40] were used for this analysis.

The number of decision trees was set at 500 as a default value, and the sample size was set at 6. The total number of samples was 24 (2 × (6 + 6 subjects)). One third of the samples were assigned as test data, and the rest of

data was assigned as OOB (Out of Bag) training data. The selection of the data set was initially random. This selection was performed 10 times, in order to calculate the generalized performance of the data throughout all conditions. To optimize the coefficient w, performance was evaluated according to the value of w, as follows:

$$w = [0, 0.3, 0.5, 1.0, 1.5, 2.0, 3.0, \infty] \tag{15}$$

Here, ∞ means a case using only FD_0'.

Classification of the modified set of features into two classes: healthy and normal (HN) and AMD (D), or into three classes: fealthy (H), AMD patient (D), and patient normal age-affected eyes (N) was conducted using the RF technique.

According to the preliminary analysis, the performance was low when the feature set of Equation 1 was used. Next, Euclidean distances between the four conditions were analyzed in the same way as in the previous assessment [41].

Here, a Euclidean distance matrix is shown as $Ed_{Healthy\ L}$ for the example of the healthy subject's left eye, and the distance feature is noted as FE. The FE vector consists of distance components without zero distance such as diagonal components in Ed matrix.

$$\text{Ed}_{\text{Healthy } L} = \begin{pmatrix} & r10 & r100 & b10 & b100 \\ \hline r10 & 0 & 0.37 & 0.57 & 0.62 \\ r100 & 0.37 & 0 & 0.24 & 0.33 \\ b10 & 0.57 & 0.24 & 0 & 0.18 \\ b100 & 0.62 & 0.33 & 0.18 & 0 \end{pmatrix} \quad (16)$$

$$\text{FE} = [r10 - r100, r10 - b10, r10 - b100, r100 \quad (17)$$
$$- b10, r100 - b100, b10 - b100]$$
$$\text{FE}_{\text{Healthy } L} = [0.37, 0.57, 0.62, 0.24, 0.33, 0.18]$$

Two-class performance

For two-class classification of PLRs of healthy and normal (HN) and AMD-affected diseased (D) eyes, 10 times calculations were conducted using w values. Mean error rates of classifications are summarized in Figure 11. The horizontal axis shows weight w, and the vertical axis shows the error rate. The error bar in the figure shows the standard deviation (STD). The minimum error rate appears at $w = 1.5$. In the case of $w = 0.5$ or only FD_0', the error rates are high.

The estimation performance for $w = 1.5$ is summarized as a contingency table in Table 4. The table shows that healthy and normal eyes (HN) can almost always be correctly classified, but the error rate of classification for AMD-affected diseased eyes (D) is low, at 17%.

Table 4 Contingency table for two classes

	D	HN	Err.
AMD (D, $n = 6$)	5	1	0.17
Healthy and normal (HN, $n = 18$)	0	18	0.00

w for $FD_0' = 1.5$.

Three-class performance

For three-class classification of PLRs of healthy (H), AMD-affected disease (D), and age-affected normal (N) eyes, 10 times calculations were conducted using w values. Mean error rates across w values are summarized in Figure 12 using the same format as in Figure 11. Error bars in the figure show the STDs of all 10 results. The minimum error rate also appears when $w = 1.5$, while the rate changes with the w values.

The results for three classifications are summarized as a contingency table in Table 5, as mean rates for all 10 results. According to the results, healthy eyes are almost always correctly classified, while the error rate for AMD-affected diseased eyes is once again 17%. The performance for age-affected normal eyes is not good, as the error rate is over 50%. The age-affected normal eyes class may include eyes which respond in the same manner as healthy eyes or eyes which affected by AMD. Therefore, further observation of the condition of the subject's eyes may be required.

The error rates for the three-class classifications are summarized in Figure 13. The rates of both healthy and AMD-affected eyes are almost always small, and the minimum rate appears at $w = 1.5$. The rates for age-affected

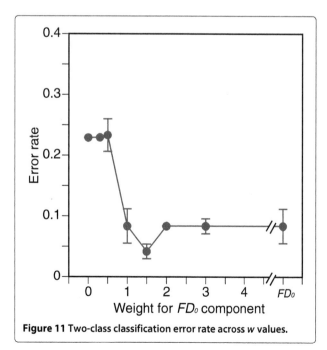

Figure 11 Two-class classification error rate across w values.

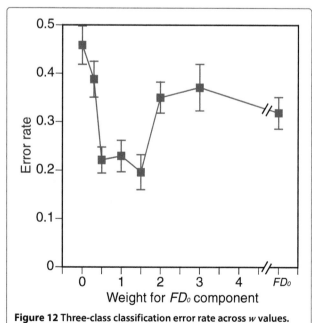

Figure 12 Three-class classification error rate across w values.

Table 5 Contingency table for three classes

	D	N	H	Err.
AMD (D, $n = 6$)	5	0	1	0.17
Normal (N, $n = 6$)	1	3	2	0.50
Healthy (H, $n = 12$)	0	0.7	11.3	0.06

w for $FD_0' = 1.5$.

eyes are relatively higher than the ones for the other two classes.

Features contributing to estimations

According to the classification results in the previous section, pupils can be classified accurately using features of PLR waveforms, except for the performance of age-affected normal eyes.

The next question was which components of features make it possible to classify PLRs. After that, the contributions of features were evaluated using the Random Forest tool. The degrees of contribution of each feature are summarized in Figure 14. The figure suggests that Euclidean distances are dissimilar between PLRs for blue light and PLRs for red light at low intensities such as $r10$ to $b100$ or $r10$ to $b10$ and denote the level of performance. Also, color differences at high intensities in PLRs such as $r100$ to $b100$ or $b10$ to $b100$ present the ability to distinguish the condition of the pupil.

These results coincide with the visual differences in PLRs between healthy and AMD-affected patients.

Clustered PLRs

The similarities of the features of waveform shapes in PLRs were also identified using the Random Forest

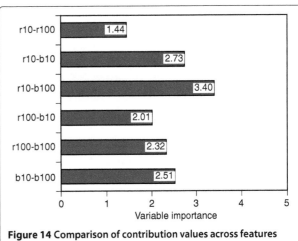

Figure 14 Comparison of contribution values across features ($w = 1.5$).

procedure, and cluster analysis of these distances was then conducted using the Ward method. Figure 15 shows the resulting dendrogram of the clusters of PLR features with $w = 1.5$ as the optimized value. In this figure, all subjects and eyes are indicated as healthy/patient and left/right or normal/diseased.

As the figure shows, the upper cluster displays a group of healthy subjects except for one patient with age-affected eyes. A sub-cluster consists of both eyes of most

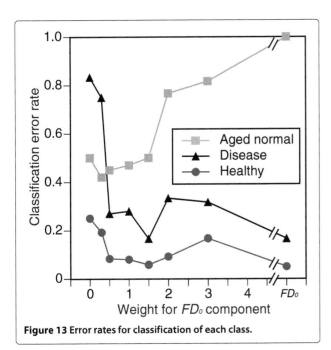

Figure 13 Error rates for classification of each class.

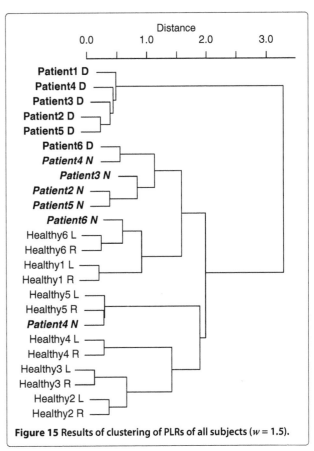

Figure 15 Results of clustering of PLRs of all subjects ($w = 1.5$).

subjects. The lower clusters consist of patients with age-affected eyes in the upper part and patients with AMD-affected eyes in the lower part. Some healthy subjects and some patients with AMD-affected eyes have been incorrectly classified into these groups. These occurrences have been explained in the above section where performance was classified and evaluated.

To improve the performance of the test, responses should be ophthalmologically diagnosed. For the classification procedure, many different data mining tools have been developed, so a more effective procedure should be devised. The characteristics of features of pupillary response waveform shapes of pupillograms which result from using the Random Forest method will be a subject of our further study.

Conclusions

This paper proposes a possible procedure for detecting AMD-affected eyes and age-affected eyes using features of PLR waveforms. The Fourier descriptor technique was applied to extract the features of PLR waveform shapes of pupillograms and their amplitudes.

To detect affected patients using the extracted features, MDS and clustering techniques were applied to emphasize certain stimuli and subject differences, since there were restrictions on gathering patient data. The performance is shown as a qualitative tendency.

To quantitatively evaluate detection performance, an appropriate classifier such as the Random Forest method was introduced. For this classification, a combination of features was used in order to obtain detailed features of waveform shapes of pupillograms. This was a balanced combination of the two features, and was controlled using weighted values. As a result of classification analysis using the Random Forest method, the performance of the three categories (patients, aged, and healthy subjects) was compared after the weighted values were optimized using variations of the classification error rate.

The results show that the error rates for healthy pupils and AMD-affected pupils were low when the value of the coefficient for a combination of PLR amplitudes and feature of waveforms was optimized as 1.5. However, the error rates for patients with age-affected eyes was not low.

The pupils of patients with age-affected eyes were influenced by various factors, so it may not be easy to classify healthy and AMD-affected patients in some cases. Additional feature processing, such as processing of the pupil diameter [42,43] and having a sufficient number of patients for statistical analysis [11] may be required.

Also, the evaluation of additional diagnostic procedures will be a subject of our further study in the future.

Competing interests
The authors declare that they have no competing interests.

Author details
[1]Department of Human System Science, Tokyo Institute of Technology, Ookayama, Meguro, Tokyo 152-8552, Japan. [2]Institute of Biomedical Engineering and Instrumentation, Wroclaw University of Technology, Wroclaw 50-370, Poland. [3]School of Allied Health Sciences, Kitasato University, Kitasato, Minami, Sagamihara 252-0373, Japan. [4]School of Medicine, Kitasato University, Kitasato, Minami, Sagamihara 252-0373, Japan.

References
1. S Ishikawa, K Ukai, Pupillary escape and visual fatigue phenomena in optic nerve disease. Adv. Diagn. Vis. Opt. **41**, 187–195 (1983)
2. EH Hess, JM Polt, Pupil size in relation to mental activity during simple problem solving. Science. **143**(3611), 1190–1192 (1964)
3. J Beatty, Task-evoked pupillary response, processing load, and the structure of processing resources. Psychol. Bull. **91**(2), 276–292 (1982)
4. H Lüdtke, B Wilhelm, M Adler, F Schaeffel, H Wilhelm, Mathematical procedures in data recording and processing of pupillary fatigue waves. Vis. Res. **38**, 2889–2896 (1998)
5. H Wilhelm, B Wilhelm, H Lüdtke, Pupillography - priciples and applications in basic and clinical research, in *Pupillography: Principles, Methods and Applications, Volume 18 of Clinical Pharmacology, ed by J Kuhlmann, M Böttcher* (W. Zuckschwerdt Verlag Munchen Germany, 1999), pp. 1–12
6. S Hattar, HW Liao, M Takao, Melanopsin-containing retinal ganglion cells: architecture, projections, and intrinsic photosensitivity. Science. **295**, 1065–1070 (2002)
7. DM Dacey, HW Liao, BB Peterson, FR Robinson, VC Smith, J Pokorny, KW Yau, PD Gamlin, Melanopsin-expressing ganglion cells in primate retina signal color and irradiance and project to the LGN. Nature. **433**, 749–754 (2005)
8. PD Gamlin, DH McDougal, J Pokorny, Human and macaque pupil responses driven by melanopisn-containing retinal ganglion cells. Vis. Res. **47**, 946–954 (2007)
9. R Young, E Kimura, Pupillary correlates of light-evoked melanopsin activity in humans. Vis. Res. **48**, 862–871 (2008)
10. A Kawasaki, RH Kardon, Intrinsically photosensitive retinal ganglion cells. J. Neuroophthalmol. **27**, 195–204 (2007)
11. B Feigl, D Mattes, R Thomas, AJ Zele, Intrinsically photosensitive (Melanopsin) retinal ganglion cell function in glaucoma. Invest. Opthalmol. Vis. Sci. **52**(7), 4362–4367 (2011)
12. RH Kardon, SC Anderson, TG Damarjian, EM Grace, E Stone, A Kawasaki, Chromatic pupil responses -preferential activation of the melanopsin-mediated versus outer photoreceptor-mediated pupil light reflex. Ophthalmology. **116**(8), 1564–1573 (2009)
13. RH Kardon, SC Anderson, TG Damarjian, EM Grace, E Stone, A Kawasaki, Chromatic pupillometry in patients with retinitis pigmentosa. Ophthalmology. **118**(2), 376–381 (2011)
14. TAP Study Group, Photodynamic therapy of subfoval choroidal neovascularization in age-related macular degeneration with verteprofin. Arch. Ophthalmol. **117**, 1329–1346 (1999)
15. CT Zahn, RZ Roskies, Fourier descriptors for plane closed curves. IEEE Trans. Comput. **C-21**(3), 269–281 (1971)
16. B Pinkowski, Robust Fourier descriptions for characterizing amplitude-modulated waveform shapes. J. Acoust. Soc. Am. **95**(6), 3419–3423 (1994)
17. D Zhang, G Lu, A comparative study on shape retrieval using Fourier Descriptors with different shape signatures, in *Proceedings of the 5th Asian Conference on Computer Vision* (Springer-Verlag Berlin, Germany, 2002), pp. 646–651
18. TM Schimidt, Do M T H, D Dacey, R Lucas, S Hatter, A Matynia, Melanopsin-positive intrisically photosensitive retinal ganglion cells: from form to function. J. Neurosci. **31**(45), 4–16101 (2011)
19. Schimidt T M, SK Chen, S Hatter, Intrinsically photosensitive retinal ganglion cells: many subtypes, diverse functions. Trends Neurosci. **34**(11), 572–580 (2011)
20. M Hatori, S Panda, The emerging roles of melanopsin in behavioral adaptation to light. Trends Mol. Med. **16**(10), 435–446 (2010)
21. JC Park, AL Moura, Raza A S, DW Rhee, RH Kardon, DC Hood, Toward a clinical protocol for assessing rod, cone, and melanopsin contributions to

the human pupil response. Invest. Ophthalmol. Vis. Sci. **52**(9), 6624–6635 (2011)

22. B Feigl, AJ Zele, Melanopsin-expressing intrinsically photosensitive retinal ganglion cells in retinal disease. Ophthalmol. Vis. Sci. **91**(8), 894–903 (2014)

23. CL Morgia, FN Ross-Cisneros, J Hannibal, P Montagna, AA Sadun, Melanopsin-expressing retinal ganglion cells: implications for human diseases. Vis. Res. **51**, 296–302 (2011)

24. EL Markwell, B Feigl, AJ Zele, Intrinsically photosensitive melanopsin retinal ganglion cell contributions to the pupillary light reflex and circadian rhythm. Clin. Exp. Optom. **93**(3), 137–149 (2010)

25. L Kankipati, CA Girkin, PD Gamlin, Post-illumination pupil response in subjects without ocular disease. Vis. Neurophysiol. **51**(5), 2764–2769 (2010)

26. L Kankipati, CA Girkin, PD Gamlin, The post-illumination pupil response is reduced in Glaucoma patients. Vis. Neurophysiol. **52**(5), 2287–2292 (2011)

27. B Feigl, Age-related maculopathy - Linking aetiology and pathophysiological changes to the ischaemia hypothesis. Prog. Retin. Eye. Res. **28**, 63–86 (2009)

28. CG Brozou, D Fotiou, S Androudi, E Theodoridou, C Giantselidis, A Alexandridis, P Brazitikos, Pupillometric characteristics in patients with choroidal neovascularisation due to age-related macular degeneration. Eur. J. Ophthalmol. **19**(2), 254–262 (2009)

29. TW Olsen, X Feng, Kasper T J, PP Rath, ER Steuer, Fluorescein angiographic lesion type frequency in neovascular age-related macular degeneration. Ophthalmology. **111**(2), 250–255 (2004)

30. H Ishikawa, A Onodera, K Asakawa, S Nakadomari, K Shimizu, Effects of selective-wavelength block filters on pupillary light reflex under red and blue light stimuli. Jpn. J. Ophthalmol. **56**, 181–186 (2012)

31. A Narita, K Shrai, N Kubota, R Tkayama, Y Tkahashi, T Onuki, C Numakura, M Kato, Y Hamada, N Sakai, A Ohno, Asami M S Matsushita, A Hayashi, T Kumada, T Fujii, A Horino, T Inoue, I Kuki, K Asakawa, H Ishikawa, K Ohno, Y Nishimura, A Tamasaki, Y Maegaki, Abnormal pupillary light reflex with chromatic pupillometry in Gacher disease. Ann. Clin. Transl. Neurol. **1**(2), 135–140 (2014)

32. I Morishita, H Kobatake, *Signal Processing (In Japanese)*. (The Society of Instrument and Control Engineers, Tokyo, Japan, 1982)

33. DGR Stork, O Duda, Hart P E, *Pattern Classification*, 2nd edn. (John Wiley & Sons Inc.,2001). [Japanese translation by M. Onoue, New Technology Communications Co., Ltd., Tokyo, Japan]

34. Y Takane, Applications of Multidimensional Scaling in Psychometrics, in *handbook of statistics 26 – Psychometrics. ed by C Rao, S Sinharay* (North-Holland, Amsterdam, Netherlands, 2007), pp. 359–400

35. M Nakayama, W Nowak, H Ishikawa, K Asakawa, An assessment procedure involving waveform shapes for pupil light Reflex, in *Proceedings of BIOSIGNALS2010* (INSTICC Portugal, 2010), pp. 322–326

36. J Leeuw, P Mair, Multidimensional scaling using majorization: SMACOF in R. J. Stat. Softw. **31**(3), 1–30 (2009)

37. Package smacof. http://cran.r-project.org/web/packages/smacof/smacof.pdf. Accessed date (07/03/2011)

38. J Mingzhe, M Murakami, Authorship identification using random forests, in *Proceedings of the Institute of Statistical Mathematics, Volume 55* (ISM Tokyo, Japan, 2007), pp. 255–268

39. J Mingzhe, Toukeiteki Tekisuto Kaiseki 15. ESTRELA1 (No. 182), 44–49 (2009)

40. Package randomForest. http://www.stat.berkeley.edu/~breiman/RandomForests/. accessed date (14/03/2012)

41. M Nakayama, W Nowak, H Ishikawa, K Asakawa, Y Ichibe, Waveform Shapes for Pupil Light Responses and Their Analyzing Procedure, in *IEICE Technical Report* (IEICE Tokyo, Japan, 2011), pp. 1–6

42. P Ren, A Barreto, Y Gao, M Adjouadi, Affective assessment by digital processing of the pupil diameter. IEEE Trans. Affect Comput. **4**, 2–14 (2013)

43. P Ren, A Barreto, J Huang, Gao Y, FR Ortega, M Adjoudadi, Off-line and on-line stress detection through processing of the pupil diameter signal. Ann. Biomed. Eng. **42**, 162–176 (2014)

A comparison study of optimal and suboptimal intervention policies for gene regulatory networks in the presence of uncertainty

Mohammadmahdi R Yousefi[1]* and Edward R Dougherty[2]

Abstract

Perfect knowledge of the underlying state transition probabilities is necessary for designing an optimal intervention strategy for a given Markovian genetic regulatory network. However, in many practical situations, the complex nature of the network and/or identification costs limit the availability of such perfect knowledge. To address this difficulty, we propose to take a Bayesian approach and represent the system of interest as an uncertainty class of several models, each assigned some probability, which reflects our prior knowledge about the system. We define the objective function to be the expected cost relative to the probability distribution over the uncertainty class and formulate an optimal Bayesian robust intervention policy minimizing this cost function. The resulting policy may not be optimal for a fixed element within the uncertainty class, but it is optimal when averaged across the uncertainly class. Furthermore, starting from a prior probability distribution over the uncertainty class and collecting samples from the process over time, one can update the prior distribution to a posterior and find the corresponding optimal Bayesian robust policy relative to the posterior distribution. Therefore, the optimal intervention policy is essentially nonstationary and adaptive.

Keywords: Optimal intervention; Markovian gene regulatory networks; Probabilistic Boolean networks; Uncertainty; Prior knowledge; Bayesian control

Introduction

A fundamental problem of translational genomics is to develop optimal therapeutic methods in the context of genetic regulatory networks (GRNs) [1]. Most previous studies rely on perfect knowledge regarding the state transition rules of the network; however, when dealing with biological systems such as cancer cells, owing to their intrinsic complexity, little is known about how they respond to various stimuli or how they function under certain conditions. Moreover, if there exists any knowledge regarding their functioning, it is usually marginal and insufficient to provide a perfect understanding of the full system. To address uncertainty, one can construct an uncertainty class of models, each representing the system of interest to some extent, and optimize an objective function across the entire uncertainty class. In this way, success in therapeutic applications is fundamentally bound to the degree of *robustness* of the designed intervention method.

Markovian dynamical networks, especially probabilistic Boolean networks (PBNs) [2], have been the main framework in which to study intervention methods due to their ability to model randomness that is intrinsic to the interactions among genes or gene products. The stochastic state transition rules of any PBN can be characterized by a corresponding Markov chain with known transition probability matrix (TPM) [3]. Markov decision processes (MDPs), on the other hand, are a standard framework for characterizing optimal intervention strategies. Many GRN optimization problems have been formulated in the context of MDPs - for instance - infinite-horizon control [4], constrained intervention [5], optimal intervention in asynchronous GRNs [6], optimal intervention when there are random-length responses to drug intervention [7], and optimal intervention to achieve the maximal beneficial

*Correspondence: yousefi@ece.osu.edu
[1] Department of Electrical and Computer Engineering, The Ohio State University, Columbus, OH 43210, USA
Full list of author information is available at the end of the article

shift in the steady-state distribution [8]. Herein, PBNs will be our choice of reference model for GRNs.

The first efforts to address robustness in the design of intervention policies for PBNs assumed that the errors made during data extraction, discretization, gene selection and network generation introduce a mismatch between the PBN model and the actual GRN [9,10]. Therefore, uncertainties manifest themselves in the entries of the TPM. A *minimax* approach was taken in which robust intervention policies were formulated by minimizing the worst-case performance across the uncertainty class [9]. Thus, the resulting policies were typically conservative. To avoid the detrimental effects of extreme, but rare, states on minimax design and motivated by the results of Bayesian robust filter design [11], the authors in [10] adopted a Bayesian approach whereby the optimal intervention policy depends on the prior probability distribution over the uncertainty class of networks. Constructing a collection of optimal policies, each being optimal for a member of the uncertainty class, the goal was to pick a single policy from this collection that minimizes the average performance relative to the prior distribution. The corresponding policy provides a *model-constrained robust* (MCR) policy. It was noted that this model-constrained policy may not yield the best average performance among all possible policies (we will later define the set of all possible policies for this problem). The authors also considered a class of *globally robust* (GR) policies, which are designed optimally only for a centrality parameter, such as the mean or median, to represent the mass of the uncertainty distribution.

Since [10] was concerned only with stationary policies, it did not consider the possibility of finding nonstationary policies under a Bayesian updating framework, where state transitions observed from the system are used directly to enrich the prior knowledge regarding the uncertainty class. The resulting nonstationary intervention policy, which we refer to it as the *optimal Bayesian robust* (OBR) policy, is our main interest in the present paper. As our main optimization criterion, we use the expected total discounted cost in the long run. This choice is motivated by the practical implications of discounted cost in the context of medical treatment, where the discounting factor emphasizes that obtaining good treatment outcomes at an earlier stage is favored over later stages.

Since the early development of MDPs, it was recognized that when dealing with a real-world problem it seldom happens that the decision maker is provided with the full knowledge of the TPM, but rather some prior information often expressed in a probabilistic manner. Taking a Bayesian approach, an optimal control policy may exist in the expected value sense specifying the best choice of control action in each state. Since the decision maker's state of knowledge about the underlying true process evolves in time as the process continues, the best choice of control action at each state might also evolve. Because the observations are acquired through a controlled process (a control action is taken at every stage of the process), the optimal policy derived through the Bayesian framework may not necessarily ever coincide with a policy that is optimal for the true state of nature. In fact, frequently, the optimal policy is not *self-optimizing* [12]; rather, optimal control will provide the best trade-off between exploration rewards and immediate costs.

Bellman [13] considered a special case of this problem - the two-armed bandit problem with discounted cost - and later used the term *adaptive control* for control processes with incompletely known transition probabilities. He suggested transforming the problem into an equivalent dynamic program with completely known transition laws for which the state now constitutes both the physical state of the process and an *information* state summarizing the past history of the observed state transitions from the process [14]. This new state is referred to as the *hyperstate*. Along this line of research, authors in [15-17] developed the theory of the OBR policy for Markov chains with uncertainty in their transition probabilities, where there is a clear notion of optimality defined with respect to all possible scenarios within the uncertainty class. This approach is in contrast with the MCR methodology because the resulting policy may not be optimal for any member of the uncertainty class but it yields the best performance when averaged over the entire uncertainty class.

Following the methodology proposed in [17] and assuming that the prior probability distribution of a random TPM belongs to a conjugate family of distributions which are closed under consecutive observations, one can formulate a set of functional equations, similar to those of fully known controlled Markov chains, and use a method of successive approximation to find the unique set of solutions to these equations. In this paper, we adopt this approach for the robust intervention of Markovian GRNs and provide a simulation study demonstrating the performance of OBR policies compared with several suboptimal methods, such as MCR and two variations of GR policies, when applied to synthetic PBNs with various structural properties and parameters, as well as to a mutated mammalian cell cycle network.

The paper is organized as follows. First, we give an overview of controlled PBNs and review the nominal MDP problem where the TPMs of the underlying Markov chain are completely known. We then formulate the OBR policy for PBNs with uncertainty in their TPMs and provide the dynamic programming solution to this optimization problem. We demonstrate a conjugate family of probability distributions over the uncertainty class where each row of the random TPM follows a Dirichlet distribution with certain parameters. Assuming that the rows are independent, the posterior probability distribution will again be a Dirichlet distribution with updated parameters. This provides a compact representation of the dynamic programming equation and facilitates the computations involved in the optimization problem. Several related suboptimal policies are also discussed in detail. Finally, we provide simulation results over both synthetic and real networks, comparing the performance of different design strategies discussed in this paper.

Methods
Controlled PBNs
PBNs constitute a broad class of stochastic models for transcriptional regulatory networks. Their construction takes into account several random factors, including effects of latent variables, involved in the dynamical genetic regulation [3]. The backbone of every PBN is laid upon a collection of Boolean networks (BNs) [18]. A BN is composed of a set of n nodes, $V = \{v^1, v^2, \ldots, v^n\}$ (representing expression level of genes $g^1, g^2, \ldots, g^n$ or their products) and a list of Boolean functions $F = \{f^1, f^2, \ldots, f^n\}$ describing the functional relationships between the nodes. We restrict ourselves to binary BNs, where we assume that each node takes on value of 0, corresponding to an unexpressed (OFF) gene and 1, corresponding to an expressed (ON) gene. This definition extends directly to any finitely discrete-valued nodes. The Boolean function $f^i : \{0,1\}^{j_i} \to \{0,1\}$ determines the value of node i at time $k+1$ given the value of its predictor nodes at time k by $v^i_{k+1} = f^i(v^{i1}_k, v^{i2}_k, \ldots, v^{ij_i}_k)$, where $\{v^{i1}, v^{i2}, \ldots, v^{ij_i}\}$ is the *predictor set* of node v^i. In a BN, all nodes are assumed to update their values synchronously according to F. The dynamics of a BN are completely determined by its state transition diagram composed of 2^n states. Each state corresponds to a vector $\mathbf{v}_k = (v^1_k, v^2_k, \ldots, v^n_k)$ known as the *gene activity profile* (GAP) of the BN at time k. To make our analysis more straightforward, we will replace each GAP, $\mathbf{v}_k$, with its decimal equivalent denoted by $x_k = 1 + \sum_{i=1}^n 2^{n-i} v^i_k$, where $x_k \in \mathcal{S} = \{1, \ldots, 2^n\}$ for all k.

A PBN is fully characterized by the same set of n nodes, V, and a set of m constituent BNs, $\mathbf{F} = \{F^1, F^2, \ldots, F^m\}$, called *contexts*, a selection probability vector $R = \{r^1, r^2, \ldots, r^m\}$ over $\mathbf{F}$ ($r^i \geq 0$ for $i = 1, \ldots, m$ and $\sum_{i=1}^m r^i = 1$), a network switching probability $q > 0$, and a random gene perturbation probability $p \geq 0$. At any updating epoch, depending on the value of a random variable $\xi \in \{0,1\}$, with $P(\xi = 1) = q$, one of two mutually exclusive events will occur. If $\xi = 0$ then the values of all nodes are updated synchronously according to an operative constituent BN; if $\xi = 1$ then another operative BN, $F^l \in \mathbf{F}$, is randomly selected with probability r^l, and the values of the nodes are updated accordingly. The

current BN may be selected consecutively when a switch is called for [1]. PBNs also admit random gene perturbations where the current state of each node in the network can be randomly flipped with probability p.

A PBN is said to be *context-sensitive* if $q < 1$; otherwise, a PBN is called *instantaneously random*. The number of states in a context-sensitive PBN is $m2^n$, whereas the state transition diagram of an instantaneously random PBN is composed of the same 2^n states in $\mathcal{S}$. It is shown in [19] that averaging over the various contexts, relative to R, reduces the transition probabilities of a context-sensitive PBN to an instantaneously random PBN with identical parameters. PBNs with only one constituent BN, i.e., $m = 1$, are called BNs with perturbation and are of particular interest in some applications [8,20]. For the sake of simplicity and reducing the computational time, we will focus only on instantaneously random PBNs.

Since the nature of transitions from one state to another in a PBN is stochastic and has the Markov property, we can model any PBN by an equivalent homogeneous Markov chain, whose states are members of $\mathcal{S}$ and the TPM of this Markov chain can be calculated as described in [19]. We denote the TPM of an instantaneously random PBN by $\mathcal{P}$ and let $\{Z_k \in \mathcal{S}, k = 0, 1, \ldots\}$ be the stochastic process of the state transitions for this PBN. Originating from state $i \in \mathcal{S}$, the successor state $j \in \mathcal{S}$ is selected randomly according to the transition probability $\mathcal{P}_{ij} = P(Z_{k+1} = j \mid Z_k = i)$, the (i,j) element of the TPM. For every $i \in \mathcal{S}$, the transition probability vector $(\mathcal{P}_{i1}, \mathcal{P}_{i2}, \ldots, \mathcal{P}_{i|\mathcal{S}|})$ is a stochastic vector such that $\mathcal{P}_{ij} \geq 0$ and $\sum_{j \in \mathcal{S}} \mathcal{P}_{ij} = 1$ for every $i \in \mathcal{S}$. Random gene perturbation guarantees the ergodicity of the equivalent Markov chain, resulting in a unique invariant measure equal to its limiting distribution.

To model the effect of interventions, we assume that PBNs admit an external control input, A, from a set of possible inputs signals, $\mathcal{A}$, that determines a specific type of intervention on a set of *control genes*. It is common to assume that the control input is binary, i.e., $\mathcal{A} = \{0, 1\}$, where $A = 0$ indicates no-intervention and $A = 1$ indicates that the expression level of a single control gene, g^c (or equivalently v^c), for a given $c \in \{1, 2, \ldots, n\}$, should be flipped. For this control scheme, $A = 0$ does not alter the TPM of the original uncontrolled PBN. However, assuming that the network is in state i, the action $A = 1$ replaces the row corresponding to this state by the row that corresponds to the state $\tilde{i}$, where the binary representation of $\tilde{i}$ is the same as i except v^c being flipped. The effect of this binary control scheme on any PBN can be easily generalized to more than one control gene with more than two control actions; in this paper, we only consider the binary control scheme.

Let $\{(Z_k, A_k), Z_k \in \mathcal{S}, A_k \in \mathcal{A}, k = 0, 1, \ldots\}$ denote the stochastic process of a state-action pair. The law of motion for the controlled network, with binary external control, is represented by a matrix $\mathcal{P}(a)$ with its (i, j) element defined as

$$
\begin{aligned}
\mathcal{P}_{ij}(a) &= P(Z_{k+1} = j \mid Z_k = i, A_k = a) \\
&= \begin{cases} \mathcal{P}_{ij}, & \text{if } a = 0, \\ \mathcal{P}_{\tilde{i}j}, & \text{if } a = 1. \end{cases}
\end{aligned} \tag{1}
$$

$\mathcal{P}_{ij}(a)$ is the probability of going to state $j \in \mathcal{S}$ at time $k+1$ from state $i \in \mathcal{S}$, while taking action $a \in \mathcal{A}$, at time k. By this construction, it is clear that the controlled TPM, $\mathcal{P}(a)$, can be calculated directly from $\mathcal{P}$.

The nominal problem

External intervention in the context of Markovian networks refers to a class of sequential decision making problems in which actions are taken at discrete time units to alter the dynamics of the underlying GRN. It is usually assumed that the decision maker can observe the state evolution of the network at consecutive time epochs $k = 0, 1, \ldots, N$, where the *horizon* N may be finite or infinite. At each k, upon observing the state, the decision maker chooses an action from $\mathcal{A}$ that will subsequently alter the dynamics of the network. Hence, the stochastic movement of the GRN from one state to another is completely characterized based on the current state and action taken at this state by (1).

Associated with each state and action, there is an immediate cost function $g : \mathcal{S} \times \mathcal{A} \times \mathcal{S} \to \mathbb{R}$ to be accrued until the next decision epoch, which we assume is nonnegative and bounded. This cost may reflect the degree of desirability of different states and/or the cost of intervention that is applied. Whenever the process moves from state i to j under action a, a known cost $g_{ij}(a)$ is incurred. We also assume that $\lambda \in (0, 1)$ is the discount factor reflecting the present value of the future cost. An *intervention policy*, denoted by μ, is a prescription for taking actions from the set $\mathcal{A}$ at each point k in time. In general, one can allow a policy for taking an action at time k to be a mapping from the entire history of the process up to time k to the action space. This mapping need not be deterministic; on the contrary, it might involve a random mechanism that is a function of the history. However, for the problem we consider, there exists a deterministic policy that is optimal. We denote the set of all admissible policies by $\mathcal{M}$. The TPM $\mathcal{P}$, initial state $Z_0 = i$, and any given policy $\mu = \{\mu_0, \mu_1, \ldots\}$ in $\mathcal{M}$ determine a unique probability measure, P_i^{μ}, over the space of all trajectories of states and actions, which correspondingly defines the stochastic processes Z_k and A_k of the states and actions

for the controlled network [12]. In the nominal optimization problem, we desire an intervention policy $\mu \in \mathcal{M}$ such that the objective function

$$
J_{\mathcal{P}}^{\mu}(i) = \lim_{N \to \infty} E_i^{\mu} \left\{ \sum_{k=0}^{N-1} \lambda^k g_{Z_k Z_{k+1}}(A_k) \right\}, \tag{2}
$$

is minimized, i.e., $J_{\mathcal{P}}^*(i) = \min_{\mu \in \mathcal{M}} J_{\mathcal{P}}^{\mu}(i)$ for all $i \in \mathcal{S}$. In the above equation, E_i^{μ} denotes expectation relative to the probability measure P_i^{μ}.

This optimization problem is usually solved by formulating a set of simultaneous functional equations and a mapping $TJ : \mathcal{S} \to \mathbb{R}$, obtained by applying the dynamic programming mapping to any function $J : \mathcal{S} \to \mathbb{R}$, for all $i \in \mathcal{S}$ defined by

$$
(TJ)(i) = \min_{a \in \mathcal{A}} \left\{ \sum_{j \in \mathcal{S}} \mathcal{P}_{ij}(a) g_{ij}(a) + \lambda \sum_{j \in \mathcal{S}} \mathcal{P}_{ij}(a) J(j) \right\}. \tag{3}
$$

The optimal cost function J^* uniquely satisfies the above functional equation, i.e., it is the fixed point of the mapping T. One can determine the optimal policy with the help of convergence, optimality, and uniqueness theorems for the solution, proven in [21]. These results furnish an iterative method for successive approximation of the optimal cost function, which in turn gives the optimal intervention policy. It can be further shown that the optimal intervention policy belongs to the class of *stationary deterministic* policies, meaning that $\mu_k = \mu$ for all k and $\mu : \mathcal{S} \to \mathcal{A}$ is a single-valued mapping from states to actions.

OBR intervention policy

In many real-world intervention scenarios, perfect knowledge regarding $\mathcal{P}$ may be unavailable or very expensive to acquire. Therefore, we resort to a probabilistic characterization of the elements of $\mathcal{P}$ and optimize relative to this uncertainty. Our results in this section are mainly derived from the Bayesian treatment of MDPs by [17]. Let

$$
\Omega = \Big\{ \mathcal{P} : \mathcal{P} \text{ is } |\mathcal{S}| \times |\mathcal{S}|, \mathcal{P}_{ij} \geq 0, \\ \sum_{j \in \mathcal{S}} \mathcal{P}_{ij} = 1 \text{ for all } i, j \in \mathcal{S} \Big\}, \tag{4}
$$

denote the set of all valid uncontrolled TPMs. The uncertainty about the random matrix $\mathcal{P}$ is characterized by the prior probability density $\pi(\mathcal{P})$ over the set Ω. Given $\pi(\mathcal{P})$ and some initial state i, we define

$$
J^{\mu}(i, \pi) = \lim_{N \to \infty} E_{i, \pi}^{\mu} \left\{ \sum_{k=0}^{N-1} \lambda^k g_{Z_k Z_{k+1}}(A_k) \right\}, \tag{5}
$$

where the expectation is taken not only with respect to the random behavior of the state-action stochastic process but also with respect to the random choice of $\mathcal{P}$ according to its prior distribution, $\pi(\mathcal{P})$. The goal is to find an optimal policy μ^* such that (5) is minimized for any $i \in \mathcal{S}$ and any prior distribution π, i.e., $\mu^* = \operatorname{argmin}_{\mu \in \mathcal{M}} J^\mu(i, \pi)$. We denote the optimal cost by $J^*(i, \pi)$.

Suppose that we could find optimal intervention policies for every element of Ω. Letting $J^*_{\mathcal{P}}(i)$ denote the optimal cost for any $\mathcal{P} \in \Omega$ and $i \in \mathcal{S}$ and assuming that the optimal cost $J^*(i, \pi)$ exists, we have $E_\pi[J^*_{\mathcal{P}}(i)] \leq J^*(i, \pi)$ for all $i \in \mathcal{S}$ and any π. In other words, $E_\pi[J^*_{\mathcal{P}}(i)]$ is the best that could be achieved if we were to optimize for every element of the uncertainty class for fixed i and π.

Since at every stage of the problem an observation is made immediately after taking an action, we can utilize this additional information and update the prior distribution to a posterior distribution as the process proceeds in time. Therefore, we can treat $\pi(\mathcal{P})$ as an additional state and call (i, π) the hyperstate of the process. From this point of view, we seek an intervention policy that minimizes the total expected discounted cost when the process starts from a hyperstate (i, π). Suppose the true, but unknown, TPM is $\hat{\mathcal{P}}$. At time 0, the initial state z_0 is known and $\mathcal{P}$ is distributed according to π. Based on z_0 and π, the controller chooses an action a_0 according to some intervention policy. Based on $(z_0, a_0, \hat{\mathcal{P}})$ the new state z_1 is realized according to the probability transition rule $\hat{\mathcal{P}}_{z_0 z_1}(a_0)$ and a cost $g_{z_0 z_1}(a_0)$ is incurred. Based on (z_0, π, a_0, z_1), the controller chooses an action a_1 according to some (possibly another) intervention policy and so on [12]. Although the number of states in $\mathcal{S}$ and actions in $\mathcal{A}$ are finite, the space of all possible hyperstates is essentially uncountable. Therefore, finding an optimal intervention policy which provides a mapping from the space of hyperstates to the space of actions in a sense similar to the nominal case is rather difficult. However, as we will see, it is possible to find an optimal action for a fixed initial hyperstate using an equivalent dynamic program.

Dynamic programming solution

We assume that the rows of $\mathcal{P}$ are mutually independent. Note that this assumption might not hold true for a large class of problems; however, the analysis becomes overwhelmingly complicated if one is willing to relax this assumption. The posterior probability density of $\mathcal{P}$, when the process moves from state i to state j under control a, is found via Bayes' rule:

$$\pi'(\mathcal{P}; i, a, j) = \begin{cases} c\mathcal{P}_{ij}\pi(\mathcal{P}), & \text{if } a = 0, \\ c'\mathcal{P}_{ij}\pi(\mathcal{P}), & \text{if } a = 1, \end{cases} \quad (6)$$

where c and c' are normalizing constants depending on i, a, and j. Under the sequence of events described above,

Martin [17] showed that the minimum expected discounted cost over an infinite period, $N = \infty$, exists and formulated an equivalent dynamic program with a set of simultaneous functional equations. The dynamic programming operator T, similar to (3) but now with the hyperstate (i, π), takes the following form:

$$(TJ)(i, \pi(\mathcal{P})) = \min_{a \in \mathcal{A}} \left\{ \sum_{j \in \mathcal{S}} \bar{\mathcal{P}}_{ij}(a) g_{ij}(a) + \lambda \sum_{j \in \mathcal{S}} \bar{\mathcal{P}}_{ij}(a) J(j, \pi'(\mathcal{P}; i, a, j)) \right\}, \quad (7)$$

for all $i \in \mathcal{S}$, where $\bar{\mathcal{P}}_{ij}(a) = E[\mathcal{P}_{ij}(a)]$ with respect to the prior probability density function π. It is shown in [17] that there exists a unique bounded set of optimal costs J^* satisfying

$$J^*(i, \pi(\mathcal{P})) = \min_{a \in \mathcal{A}} \left\{ \sum_{j \in \mathcal{S}} \bar{\mathcal{P}}_{ij}(a) g_{ij}(a) + \lambda \sum_{j \in \mathcal{S}} \bar{\mathcal{P}}_{ij}(a) J^*(j, \pi'(\mathcal{P}; i, a, j)) \right\},$$

which is the fixed point of the operator T. Since the space of all possible hyperstates (i, π) is uncountable, construction of an optimal intervention policy for all (i, π), except for some special cases, may not be feasible. However, given that the process starts at (i, π), the minimization argument in the above equation yields an optimal action to take only for the current hyperstate.

The difficulty in solving (7), which makes it more complicated than (3), is that the total expected discounted cost when different actions are taken now involves the difference in expected immediate costs and the expected difference in future costs due to being in different states at the next period as well as the effect of different information states resulting from these actions [22]. It should be noted that since the decision maker's knowledge regarding the uncertainty about $\mathcal{P}$ evolves with each transition, the intervention policy will also evolve over time. In a sense, the optimal policy will adapt, implying that stationary optimal policies as defined for the nominal problem do not exist. The optimal nonstationary intervention policy derived through the process discussed above is referred to as the OBR policy.

Special case: independent Dirichlet priors

Suppose that both prior and posterior distributions belong to the same family of distributions, i.e., they are conjugate distributions. Then, instead of dealing with prior and posterior at every stage of the problem, we will only need to keep track of the *hyperparameters* of the prior/posterior distributions. A special case of the families of distributions closed under consecutive observations is the Dirichlet distribution, which is the conjugate prior of the multinomial distribution.

Let the initial state z_0 be known and $\mathbf{z}_n = (z_0, z_1, z_2, \ldots, z_n)$ represent a sample path of n independent transitions recorded from the network under the influence of an intervention policy. Then the posterior probability density of $\mathcal{P}$, $\pi'(\mathcal{P})$, can be found using Bayes' rule:

$$\pi'(\mathcal{P}) \propto \pi(\mathcal{P}) \prod_{i \in S} \prod_{j \in S} (\mathcal{P}_{ij})^{\beta_{ij}}, \tag{8}$$

where β_{ij} denotes the number of transitions in $\mathbf{z}_n$ from state i to state j. The right product in (8) is called the *likelihood function* and the constant of proportionality can be found by normalizing the integral of $\pi'(\mathcal{P})$ over Ω to 1. Note that although the transitions made in $\mathbf{z}_n$ result from an intervention policy, we have formulated the likelihood function only in terms of the elements of $\mathcal{P}$ (and not $\mathcal{P}(a)$). This is a consequence of our particular intervention model, where we can substitute for $\mathcal{P}_{ij}(a)$ with $\mathcal{P}_{ij}$ whenever $a = 1$ as shown in (1). To be more precise, we have $\beta_{ij} = \beta_{ij}(0) + \beta_{\bar{i}j}(1)$, where $\beta_{ij}(a)$ is the number of transitions in $\mathbf{z}_n$ from state i to state j under control a.

For a fixed state i, a transition to state j is an outcome of a multinomial sampling distribution with parameters $\{\mathcal{P}_{i1}, \mathcal{P}_{i2}, \ldots, \mathcal{P}_{i|S|}\}$ constituting the standard $(|S| - 1)$-simplex. As stated in the beginning of this section, the conjugate prior for the multinomial distribution is given by the Dirichlet distribution. By the independence assumption imposed on the rows of $\mathcal{P}$, one can write the prior for $\mathcal{P}$ as

$$\pi(\mathcal{P}) = c(\alpha) \prod_{i \in S} \prod_{\in S} (\mathcal{P}_{ij})^{\alpha_{ij} - 1}, \tag{9}$$

where $\alpha_{ij} > 0$ and $\alpha = [\alpha_{ij}]$ is the hyperparameter matrix with the rows arranged in the same manner as $\mathcal{P}$. The constant of proportionality is given by

$$c(\alpha) = \prod_{i \in S} \frac{\Gamma\left(\sum_{j \in S} \alpha_{ij}\right)}{\prod_{j \in S} \Gamma(\alpha_{ij})}, \tag{10}$$

where Γ is the gamma function. The uniform prior distribution is obtained if $\alpha_{ij} = 1$ for all $i, j \in S$. As we increase a specific α_{ij}, it is as if we bias the posterior distribution on the corresponding element of $\mathcal{P}$ with some transition samples before ever observing any samples. It can be verified that

$$E[\mathcal{P}_{ij}] = \frac{\alpha_{ij}}{\sum_{l \in S} \alpha_{il}} = \bar{\mathcal{P}}_{ij}, \tag{11}$$

and

$$\text{var}[\mathcal{P}_{ij}] = \frac{\bar{\mathcal{P}}_{ij}(1 - \bar{\mathcal{P}}_{ij})}{\sum_{l \in S} \alpha_{il} + 1}.$$

We also have the following theorem, which is due to Martin [17].

Theorem 1. *Let $\mathcal{P}$ have a probability density function given in (9) and (10) with the hyperparameter matrix α and suppose that a sample with a transition count matrix $\beta = [\beta_{ij}]$ is observed. Then the posterior probability density function of $\mathcal{P}$ will have the same form as in (9) and (10), but with the hyperparameter matrix $\alpha + \beta$.*

Assuming α as the hyperparameter representing $\pi(\mathcal{P})$ and using Theorem 1, one can rewrite Equation 7 as

$$(TJ)(i, \alpha) = \min_{a \in \mathcal{A}} \left\{ \sum_{j \in S} \bar{\mathcal{P}}_{ij}(a) g_{ij}(a) + \lambda \sum_{j \in S} \bar{\mathcal{P}}_{ij}(a) J(j, \alpha + \gamma) \right\},$$

where γ is a matrix of all zeros except $\gamma_{ij} = 1$ if $a = 0$ or $\gamma_{\bar{i}j} = 1$ if $a = 1$, and

$$\bar{\mathcal{P}}_{ij}(a) = \begin{cases} \bar{\mathcal{P}}_{ij}, & \text{if } a = 0, \\ \bar{\mathcal{P}}_{\bar{i}j}, & \text{if } a = 1. \end{cases}$$

The optimal cost $J^*(i, \alpha)$ is defined by

$$J^*(i, \alpha) = \min_{\mu \in \mathcal{M}} J^\mu(i, \alpha),$$

for a given $i \in S$ and prior hyperparameter α. Taking an approach based on the method of successive approximation, let $J_k(i, \alpha)$ for $k = 0, 1, \ldots$ be defined recursively for all $i \in S$ and any valid hyperparameter matrix α by

$$J_{k+1}(i, \alpha) = \min_{a \in \mathcal{A}} \left\{ \sum_{j \in S} \bar{\mathcal{P}}_{ij}(a) g_{ij}(a) + \lambda \sum_{j \in S} \bar{\mathcal{P}}_{ij}(a) J_k(j, \alpha + \gamma) \right\}, \tag{12}$$

with $\{J_0(i, \alpha)\}$ as a set of bounded initial functions. Under some mild conditions, the sequence of functions $\{J_k(i, \alpha)\}$ converges monotonically to the optimal solution $J^*(i, \alpha)$ for any $i \in S$ and uniformly for all valid α [17]. Faster rates of convergence can be achieved for smaller values of λ. Assuming that the method of successive approximation converges in K steps, then for a specific value of (i, α), one needs to evaluate $(|\mathcal{A}| \times |S|)^K$ terminal values necessary for the computation of $J^*(i, \alpha)$. Therefore, to minimize computational time, we restrict ourselves to small values for λ and K. Once the successive approximation converges, an action a^* that minimizes the RHS of (12) is optimal.

The intervention policy optimally adapts to the consecutive observations as follows: we start with an initial hyperstate (z_0, α_0), with α_0 reflecting our prior knowledge regarding the unknown network (or equivalently $\mathcal{P}$). We can calculate $\bar{\mathcal{P}}$ using (11) with respect to α_0 and utilize the successive approximation method in (12) for a fixed K to find an optimal action a^*. We then apply the action a^* to the network and let it transition from state z_0, or $\tilde{z}_0$ depending on the optimal action, to a new random state z_1 according to $\hat{\mathcal{P}}$. We incorporate the new observation into our prior knowledge and update the hyperparameter matrix to α_1 by incrementing the entry at (z_0, z_1) or $(\tilde{z}_0, z_1)$ of the hyperparameter matrix α_0 by 1. We repeat the entire optimization procedure, but now with the new hyperstate (z_1, α_1), etc. A schematic diagram of this procedure is demonstrated in Figure 1.

The extreme computational complexity of finding the OBR intervention policy for MDPs with large state-space poses a major obstacle when dealing with real-world problems. It is relatively straightforward to implement the procedure described above for networks with three or four genes. However, for larger networks, one should resort either to clever ways of indexing all possible transitions, such as hash tables or a branch-and-bound algorithm, or to approximation methods, such as reinforcement learning. See [12,22,23] for more details. An alternative approach, as we will demonstrate, is to implement suboptimal methods that, in general, have acceptable performance. Yet another potential approach to circumvent the explosion of the space of all hyperstates is to reduce the size of the uncertainty class. For example, we can assume that some rows of the underlying TPM are perfectly known and uncertainty is only on some other rows, with the implication that the regulatory network is partially known. We will leave the analysis of such approaches to future research.

Suboptimal intervention policies

Besides the OBR policy, three suboptimal policies are of particular interest: *MCR*, *GR*, and *adaptive GR* (AGR). Similar to the previous section, let $\mathcal{P}$ be random, having a probability density $\pi(\mathcal{P})$ over the set of valid TPMs, Ω, defined in (4).

Let $\mathcal{M}_{MCR}$ denote the set of all policies that are optimal for some element $\mathcal{P} \in \Omega$. Each policy in $\mathcal{M}_{MCR}$ is stationary and deterministic (each corresponds to a problem with known TPM). Because Ω is uncountable and there exits a finite number of stationary deterministic policies, one might find policies that are optimal for many elements of Ω. Assuming that the initial state Z_0 is randomly distributed according to some probability

distribution η, the policy μ_{MCR} yields the minimum cost, which is defined by

$$J_{MCR}(i) = \min_{\mu \in \mathcal{M}_{MCR}} E_\pi \left[E_\eta \left[J_\mathcal{P}^\mu(Z_0) \right] \right], \qquad (13)$$

where $J_\mathcal{P}^\mu(Z_0)$ is defined in (2) for any fixed Z_0 and $\mathcal{P}$. Since we are limiting ourselves to policies in $\mathcal{M}_{MCR}$, it is seldom the case that a single policy minimizes $E_\pi [J_\mathcal{P}^\mu(Z_0)]$ for all $Z_0 \in \mathcal{S}$. Hence, we take the expected value of $J_\mathcal{P}^\mu(Z_0)$ with respect to η in (13) as a single value representing the expected cost. The resulting MCR intervention policy is therefore fixed for a given prior distribution in the sense that it will not adapt to the observed transitions.

We define the GR policy as the minimizing argument for the optimization problem given by $J_{GR}(i) = \min_{\mu \in \mathcal{M}} J_{\bar{\mathcal{P}}}^\mu(i)$, for all $i \in \mathcal{S}$, where $\bar{\mathcal{P}} \in \Omega$ is the mean of the uncertainty class Ω with respect to the prior distribution π. The optimization method presented for the nominal problem can be readily applied. Hence, the resulting policy, μ_{GR}, is stationary and deterministic. In the case of independent Dirichlet priors, $\bar{\mathcal{P}}$ is given by Equation 11. Here we are considering the mean as an estimate for unknown $\mathcal{P}$. However, one can use any other estimate of $\mathcal{P}$ and find the optimal policy in a similar fashion. Similar to the MCR policy, this intervention method is also fixed for a given prior distribution and it will not adapt to the observed transitions.

The AGR policy is similar to the GR policy in the sense that it is optimal for the mean of the uncertainty class Ω. However, instead of taking the mean with respect to the prior distribution π and using the same policy for the entire process, we update π to a posterior π', defined in (6), whenever a transition is made and calculate the mean of Ω with respect to π'. Since the posterior evolves as we observe more and more transitions, the AGR policy also evolves - therefore, the name adaptive. We denote the cost and the corresponding policy resulting from this procedure, for any initial hyperstate (i, π), by $J_{AGR}(i, \pi)$ and μ_{AGR}, respectively. In the case of independent Dirichlet priors, we can simply replace π with α.

Results

In this section, we provide a comparison study on the performance of optimal and suboptimal policies based on simulations on synthetically generated PBNs and a real network. Since we implement the method of successive approximation to calculate μ_{OBR}, we restrict ourselves to synthetic networks with $n = 3$ genes. Given that, as we will show, μ_{AGR} yields very similar performance compared to the optimal policy, we can implement μ_{AGR} for networks of larger size and use it as the baseline for comparison with other suboptimal policies, keeping in mind that the optimal policy should and will outperform any suboptimal method.

Synthetic networks

We first consider randomly generated PBNs with $n = 3$ genes and $m = 3$ equally likely constituent BNs (total number of states being 8) with the maximum number of predictors for each node set to 2 ($j_i \leq 2$ for all $i \in \{1, 2, \ldots, n\}$). The *bias* of a randomly generated PBN is the probability that each of its Boolean regulatory functions takes on the value 1 in its truth table. We assume that the bias is taken randomly from a beta distribution with mean 0.5 and standard deviation 0.01. The gene perturbation probability is assumed to be $p = 0.001$. In the context of gene regulation, there are some genes associated with phenotypes (typically undesirable ones). We refer to these genes as *target genes* and our goal in controlling the network is to push the dynamics of these genes away from undesirable states towards desirable ones. Once the set of target genes is identified, one can partition the state space $\mathcal{S}$ into subsets of desirable and undesirable states, denoted by $\mathcal{D}$ and $\mathcal{U}$, respectively. In our synthetic network simulations, we choose the control and target genes to be the least and most significant bits in the binary representation of states, respectively, and assume that downregulation of the target gene is undesirable. As for the discount factor and the immediate cost function $g_{ij}(a)$, we set $\lambda = 0.2$ and

$$
g_{ij}(a) = \begin{cases} 2.1, & \text{if } j \in \mathcal{U} \text{ and } a = 1, \\ 2.0, & \text{if } j \in \mathcal{U} \text{ and } a = 0, \\ 0.1, & \text{if } j \in \mathcal{D} \text{ and } a = 1, \\ 0, & \text{otherwise,} \end{cases} \tag{14}
$$

the interpretation being that a cost will be incurred if the future state in undesirable or there is an intervention in the network.

To design an OBR policy for a given network, we need to assign the prior probability distribution to the set Ω. As discussed earlier, independent Dirichlet priors parameterized by α constitute a natural choice for this application. Therefore, we only need to assign values to α. The choice of prior hyperparameters plays a crucial role in the design of an optimal policy: the tighter the prior around the true, but unknown, TPM $\hat{\mathcal{P}}$, the closer the OBR cost is to that

of $\hat{\mathcal{P}}$. Since our synthetic networks are generated randomly and not according to some biologically motivated GRN, it would be difficult to assign prior probabilities for individual networks. Therefore, we use the randomly generated PBNs themselves for this purpose and perturb and scale the elements of the TPMs via the ε-contamination method.

A random PBN, $\hat{\mathcal{P}}$, is first generated. This network will serve as the true, but unknown, PBN. Then a contamination matrix $\mathcal{Q}$ of the same size ($|\mathcal{S}| \times |\mathcal{S}|$) is generated, where each row is sampled uniformly from the $|\mathcal{S} - 1|$-simplex. Note that $\mathcal{Q}$ is a valid TPM. We now define the hyperparameter matrix α by

$$
\alpha = \kappa \left((1 - \varepsilon)\hat{\mathcal{P}} + \varepsilon\mathcal{Q} \right), \tag{15}
$$

where $\kappa > 0$ controls the tightness of the prior around the true PBN and $\varepsilon \in [0, 1]$ controls the level of contamination. For networks with three genes, we assume that $\varepsilon = 0.1$ and demonstrate the effect of κ on the performance of intervention policies.

We generate 500 random PBNs, denoted by $\{\mathcal{N}^l\}$ for $l = 1$ to 500, for each set of parameters and calculate their TPMs, denoted by $\{\hat{\mathcal{P}}^l\}$. These networks will serve as the ground-truth for our simulation study. For a given pair of κ and ε, we then construct hyperparameter matrices, denoted by $\{\alpha^l\}$, using (15), each corresponding to a random network. To compare the performance of different intervention policies, for each randomly generated network $\mathcal{N}^l$, we take a Monte Carlo approach and generate 500 random TPMs, denoted by $\{\hat{\mathcal{P}}^{l,l'}\}$ for $l' = 1$ to 500, from the α^l-parameterized independent Dirichlet priors. The set $\{\hat{\mathcal{P}}^{l,l'}\}$ will essentially represent Ω and the prior distribution.

To design and evaluate the performance of μ_{MCR} for each random PBN $\mathcal{N}^l$, we proceed as follows: We find the optimal intervention policy for each $\hat{\mathcal{P}}^{l,l'}$, apply this policy to every element in the set $\{\hat{\mathcal{P}}^{l,l'}\}$, and calculate the average over all equally likely initial states, $Z_0 \in \mathcal{S}$, of the infinite-horizon expected discounted cost using (2) for that element. The expected performance of the each

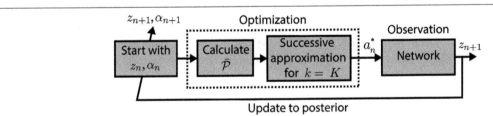

Figure 1 Optimization procedure for an OBR policy. We start with a hyperstate (z_n, α_n). We calculate $\bar{\mathcal{P}}$ using α_n and utilize the successive approximation method for a fixed K to find an optimal action a_n^*. We then apply the action a_n^* to the network and let it transition from state z_n, or $\tilde{z}_n$, depending on the optimal action, to a new random state z_{n+1} according to $\hat{\mathcal{P}}$. We incorporate the new observation into our prior knowledge and update the hyperparameter matrix to α_{n+1} by incrementing the entry at (z_n, z_{n+1}) or $(\tilde{z}_n, z_{n+1})$ of the hyperparameter matrix α_n by 1. We repeat the entire optimization procedure, but now with the new hyperstate (z_{n+1}, α_{n+1}).

policy optimal for $\hat{\mathcal{P}}^{l,l'}$, relative to the prior distribution, can be computed by taking the average of the resulting costs over all $\hat{\mathcal{P}}^{l,l'}$. We repeat this procedure for every element of $\{\hat{\mathcal{P}}^{l,l'}\}$ and declare a policy MCR if it yields the minimum expected performance. We denote the expected cost function for a random PBN $\mathcal{N}^l$ obtained via an MCR policy by J^l_{MCR}.

Finding μ_{GR} for each PBN $\mathcal{N}^l$, on the other hand, is easier and it requires only the value of the hyperparameter α^l. Once found, the performance of this policy is evaluated by applying it to all elements of $\{\hat{\mathcal{P}}^{l,l'}\}$ and taking the average of the resulting costs. Similar to the MCR policy, we assume that the initial states are equally likely and calculate the average over all possible initial states. We denote the expected cost function corresponding to the GR policy derived for $\mathcal{N}^l$ by J^l_{GR}.

To quantify the performance of the OBR policy for each random PBN $\mathcal{N}^l$, we directly evaluate the cost function defined in (5) relative to the independent Dirichlet prior distribution, π^l, parameterized by α^l. This is accomplished using the sample set of 500 random TPMs, $\{\hat{\mathcal{P}}^{l,l'}\}$. Starting from a hyperstate and a TPM $\hat{\mathcal{P}}^{l,l'}$, we derive an optimal action from (12) using the method of successive approximations with $K = 5$ and some initial cost function. We then observe a transition according to $\hat{\mathcal{P}}^{l,l'}$ and find the incurred discounted immediate cost according to (14), depending on the new observed state and the optimal action just taken. We update our prior hyperparameter and carry out the optimization problem again, but now with the updated hyperparameter and the recently observed state, and accumulate the newly incurred discounted immediate cost. We iterate this for seven epochs, thus observing seven different hyperstates for a sampling path, and record the total accumulated discounted cost over this period. We then repeat this entire process, for the same $\hat{\mathcal{P}}^{l,l'}$ for 100 iterations (although the same TPM is used, different sampling paths will result due to random transitions), and take the average of all 100 total accumulated discounted cost values. This will represent the cost associated with $\hat{\mathcal{P}}^{l,l'}$ and the initial state. We implement a similar procedure for all initial states (assuming all equally likely) and all elements of $\{\hat{\mathcal{P}}^{l,l'}\}$ and take the average of the resulting costs, yielding the expected optimal cost, $E_\eta[J^*(Z_0, \pi^l)]$, with respect to the uniform probability distribution η over the initial states in $\mathcal{S}$. Since we use the

same hyperparameter α^l in our Monte Carlo simulation for a given random PBN $\mathcal{N}^l$, we denote the expected optimal cost obtained from a OBR policy by J^l_{OBR}.

We take a similar approach for evaluating the performance of μ_{AGR}. Instead of using the method of successive approximations at every epoch, we use the current value of the hyperparameter to calculate the mean of Ω and use this to find the optimal action to take at that hyperstate. Every other step of the process is essentially the same to those of the OBR policy. We denote the expected optimal cost obtained from this policy by J^l_{AGR}.

We also evaluate three other cost functions for each PBN $\mathcal{N}^l$: $J^l_{\text{LB}} := E_\pi\left[E_\eta[J^*_{\mathcal{P}}(Z_0)]\right]$, $J^l_{\text{T}} := E_\eta[J^*_{\hat{\mathcal{P}}^l}(Z_0)]$, and $J^l_{\text{ET}} := E_\pi\left[E_\eta[J^l_{\mathcal{P}}(Z_0)]\right]$, where $J^l_{\mathcal{P}}$ is the cost of applying an optimal intervention policy corresponding to $\hat{\mathcal{P}}^l$ to an element $\mathcal{P}$ of Ω. The first cost function, J^l_{LB}, is a lower bound on the performance of the OBR policy, J^l_{BA}. The second cost function, J^l_{T}, corresponds to the cost of applying an optimal intervention policy as if we knew the true network, $\hat{\mathcal{P}}^l$, to the true network itself. The third cost function, J^l_{ET}, is the expected cost, relative to the prior, of applying an intervention policy that is optimal for the true network. We can calculate these cost functions assuming that Ω and the prior distribution π^l are represented by the set $\{\hat{\mathcal{P}}^{l,l'}\}$ corresponding to each PBN $\mathcal{N}^l$.

All cost functions discussed above are defined relative to a given random PBN $\mathcal{N}^l$. Since we have 500 such networks, for each parameter value, we report the average performance across all random networks and provide a statistical comparison on the performance of different intervention policies. The results are presented in Table 1. As seen in the table, the optimal policy performance, in the average sense, is consistently better than all suboptimal policies. The closest performance to the optimal method is achieved by the AGR policy, which is not surprising, since this policy adapts to the process over time by updating the prior distribution to a posterior distribution and optimizes with respect to the mean of the posterior.

As it has been reported in the previous studies [7,8,24], the performance of an optimal policy might not significantly exceed those of suboptimal policies when averaged across random PBNs; nonetheless, there are networks for which the optimal policy notably outperforms the suboptimal ones. To demonstrate this, we use the difference

Table 1 Average costs across all 500 randomly generated PBNs with $n = 3$ genes and $\varepsilon = 0.1$

	$E[J^l_{\text{LB}}]$	$E[J^l_{\text{T}}]$	$E[J^l_{\text{ET}}]$	$E[J^l_{\text{MCR}}]$	$E[J^l_{\text{GR}}]$	$E[J^l_{\text{AGR}}]$	$E[J^l_{\text{OBR}}]$
$\kappa = 0.1$	0.7626	1.0803	1.0998	1.0948	1.0991	1.0816	1.0812
$\kappa = 1.0$	0.8078	1.0296	1.0531	1.0520	1.0526	1.0458	1.0457
$\kappa = 5.0$	0.9417	1.0209	1.0525	1.0518	1.0513	1.0502	1.0501

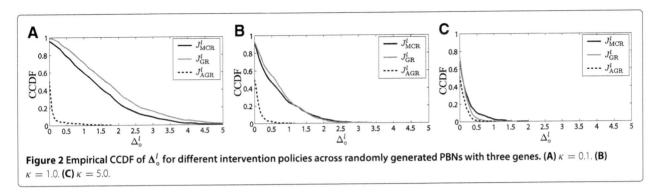

Figure 2 Empirical CCDF of Δ_o^l for different intervention policies across randomly generated PBNs with three genes. **(A)** $\kappa = 0.1$. **(B)** $\kappa = 1.0$. **(C)** $\kappa = 5.0$.

between the optimal and suboptimal costs to quantify the gain made by implementing an optimal policy. We define *percent decrease* by

$$\Delta_o^l = 100 \times \frac{J_o^l - J_\bullet^l}{J_o^l},$$

where J_o^l and $J_\bullet^l$ denote two different intervention policies. Since PBNs are randomly generated, Δ_o^l will also be a random variable with a probability distribution. We estimate the complementary cumulative distribution function (CCDF) of this distribution for different values of Δ_o^l using its empirical distribution function.

For networks with three genes, we assume that $J_\bullet^l = J_{OBR}^l$ and J_o^l is any suboptimal policy. Figure 2 shows the empirical CCDF of Δ_o^l for 500 random PBNs for different values of κ and different intervention policies. The graphs illustrate that as the prior distribution gets tighter around the true TPM by increasing κ, the difference between the optimal and suboptimal policies vanishes. Again, the best performance among the suboptimal policies is achieved by J_{AGR}^l.

As suggested by these results, we may use the suboptimal AGR policy instead of an optimal method for larger networks without a significant lose of optimality. For this

purpose, we carry out a similar set of simulations with 500 randomly generated PBNs of size $n = 4$ genes. We assume that each PBN consists of $m = 3$ equally likely constituent BNs with the maximum number of predictors for each node set to 2, the total number of states being 16. The network bias is drawn randomly from a beta distribution with mean 0.5 and standard deviation 0.01. The gene perturbation probability is $p = 0.001$. We generate prior distributions using (15) for each network and different parameter values for κ and ε. To model Ω, we draw 5,000 random TPMs from each prior distribution. We assume that each random sampling path has length 10 and set the discounting factor λ to 0.2. We emulate different sampling paths during the calculation of J_{AGR}^l by repeating the entire process for each randomly generated TPM for 1,000 iterations and take the average. The results averaged over 500 random PBNs are presented in Table 2. The AGR policy yields the best performance relative to other suboptimal policies.

We graph the empirical CCDF of Δ_o^l for these networks in Figure 3 for different values of the pair (κ, ε) and different suboptimal policies. Here, we have that $J_\bullet^l = J_{AGR}^l$ and J_o^l is any other suboptimal policy. Similar to networks with three genes, as the prior distributions get more concentrated around the true parameters, the

Table 2 Average costs across all 500 randomly generated PBNs with $n = 4$ genes

	$E[J_{LB}^l]$	$E[J_T^l]$	$E[J_{ET}^l]$	$E[J_{MCR}^l]$	$E[J_{GR}^l]$	$E[J_{AGR}^l]$
$(\kappa, \varepsilon) = (0.1, 0.0)$	0.7559	1.0878	1.0869	1.0856	1.0869	1.0773
$(\kappa, \varepsilon) = (1.0, 0.0)$	0.8702	1.0888	1.0888	1.0918	1.0888	1.0854
$(\kappa, \varepsilon) = (5.0, 0.0)$	0.9510	1.0579	1.0578	1.0612	1.0578	1.0572
$(\kappa, \varepsilon) = (0.1, 0.1)$	0.7711	1.1099	1.1260	1.1248	1.1258	1.1156
$(\kappa, \varepsilon) = (1.0, 0.1)$	0.8722	1.1106	1.1278	1.1314	1.1276	1.1236
$(\kappa, \varepsilon) = (5.0, 0.1)$	0.9714	1.0826	1.1011	1.1049	1.1009	1.1002
$(\kappa, \varepsilon) = (0.1, 0.25)$	0.7177	1.0796	1.1289	1.1234	1.1248	1.1133
$(\kappa, \varepsilon) = (1.0, 0.25)$	0.8307	1.0853	1.1348	1.1325	1.1305	1.1257
$(\kappa, \varepsilon) = (5.0, 0.25)$	0.9729	1.0629	1.1178	1.1157	1.1137	1.1130

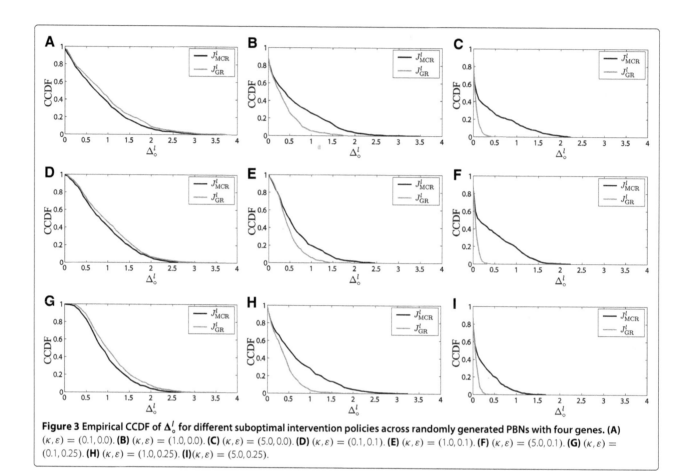

Figure 3 Empirical CCDF of Δ_o^l for different suboptimal intervention policies across randomly generated PBNs with four genes. **(A)** $(\kappa, \varepsilon) = (0.1, 0.0)$. **(B)** $(\kappa, \varepsilon) = (1.0, 0.0)$. **(C)** $(\kappa, \varepsilon) = (5.0, 0.0)$. **(D)** $(\kappa, \varepsilon) = (0.1, 0.1)$. **(E)** $(\kappa, \varepsilon) = (1.0, 0.1)$. **(F)** $(\kappa, \varepsilon) = (5.0, 0.1)$. **(G)** $(\kappa, \varepsilon) = (0.1, 0.25)$. **(H)** $(\kappa, \varepsilon) = (1.0, 0.25)$. **(I)** $(\kappa, \varepsilon) = (5.0, 0.25)$.

difference between these suboptimal policies gets smaller and smaller. However, it can be seen that the GR policy outperforms MCR for larger κ, which could be due to the fact that GR and AGR policies differ very little when the effect of observations on the posterior distribution is dominated by the prior hyperparameters.

Real network

We construct a PBN corresponding to a reduced network from a mutated mammalian cell cycle network proposed

in [25]. The original GRN is a BN with ten genes. Three key genes in the model are Cyclin D (CycD), retinoblastoma (Rb), and p27, where cell division is coordinated with the overall growth of the organism through extracellular signals controlling the activation of CycD in the cell. A proposed mutation for this network is that p27 can never be activated (always OFF), creating a situation where both CycD and Rb might be inactive [25]. Under these conditions, the cell can cycle in the absence of any growth factor, thereby causing undesirable proliferation. Table 3 lists the Boolean functions for this real network.

Since the size of the network is too large for the Bayesian treatment, we need to first reduce the number of genes to a more manageable size while preserving important

Table 3 Boolean regulatory functions of a mutated mammalian cell cycle

Gene	Node	Predictor functions
CycD	v_1	Extracellular signal
Rb	v_2	$(\overline{v_1} \wedge \overline{v_4} \wedge \overline{v_5} \wedge \overline{v_9})$
E2F	v_3	$(\overline{v_2} \wedge \overline{v_5} \wedge \overline{v_9})$
CycE	v_4	$(v_3 \wedge \overline{v_2})$
CycA	v_5	$(v_3 \wedge \overline{v_2} \wedge \overline{v_6} \wedge (\overline{v_7 \wedge v_8})) \vee (v_5 \wedge \overline{v_2} \wedge \overline{v_6} \wedge (\overline{v_7 \wedge v_8}))$
Cdc20	v_6	v_9
Cdh1	v_7	$(\overline{v_5} \wedge \overline{v_9}) \vee v_6$
UbcH10	v_8	$\overline{v_7} \vee (v_7 \wedge v_8 \wedge (v_6 \vee v_5 \vee v_9))$
CycB	v_9	$(\overline{v_6} \wedge \overline{v_7})$

Table 4 Boolean regulatory functions of a reduced mutated mammalian cell cycle

Gene	Node	Predictor functions
CycD	v_1	Extracellular signal
Rb	v_2	$(\overline{v_1} \wedge v_2 \wedge \overline{v_3} \wedge \overline{v_5})$
CycA	v_3	$(\overline{v_2} \wedge v_3 \wedge \overline{v_5}) \vee (\overline{v_2} \wedge \overline{v_4} \vee \overline{v_5})$
UbcH10	v_4	$(v_4 \wedge v_5) \vee (v_3 \wedge \overline{v_5})$
CycB	v_5	$v_3 \wedge \overline{v_5}$

Table 5 Total discounted cost of different suboptimal policies for the reduced cell cycle network

	J_{LB}	J_T	J_{ET}	J_{MCR}	J_{GR}	J_{AGR}
$(\kappa, \varepsilon) = (0.1, 0.0)$	0.7507	0.9685	0.9326	0.9465	0.9326	0.9316
$(\kappa, \varepsilon) = (1.0, 0.0)$	0.4990	0.9685	0.9675	0.9614	0.9675	0.9571
$(\kappa, \varepsilon) = (5.0, 0.0)$	0.6136	0.9685	0.9658	0.9774	0.9658	0.9605
$(\kappa, \varepsilon) = (0.1, 0.1)$	0.4501	0.9685	0.9239	0.9268	0.9239	0.9144
$(\kappa, \varepsilon) = (1.0, 0.1)$	0.5752	0.9685	0.9340	0.9526	0.9340	0.9294
$(\kappa, \varepsilon) = (5.0, 0.1)$	0.7507	0.9685	0.9326	0.9465	0.9326	0.9316
$(\kappa, \varepsilon) = (0.1, 0.25)$	0.3885	0.9685	0.8643	0.8674	0.8623	0.8550
$(\kappa, \varepsilon) = (1.0, 0.25)$	0.5140	0.9685	0.8728	0.8860	0.8730	0.8694
$(\kappa, \varepsilon) = (5.0, 0.25)$	0.7014	0.9685	0.8864	0.9002	0.8864	0.8861

dynamical properties of the network. We have implemented the methodology proposed in [26] and reduced the size of the network to the five genes shown in Table 4. Even for a network of this size, finding the OBR policy is computationally too expensive. Therefore, we only report results for suboptimal policies.

We first construct an instantaneously random PBN for the reduced network. The PBN consists of five genes, CycD, Rb, CycA, UbcH10 and CycB, ordered from the most significant bit to the least significant bit in the binary representation. In the mutated network, depending on the state of the extracellular signal determining the state of CycD as being ON or OFF, we obtain two BNs. These two will serve as two equally likely constituent BNs. It is also assumed that the gene perturbation probability is 0.01. Since cell growth in the absence of growth factors is undesirable, we define undesirable states of the state space to be those for which CycD and Rb are both downregulated. We also choose CycA as the control gene. The immediate cost function is defined similarly to that of the synthetic network simulations (Equation 14). The discounting factor is $\lambda = 0.2$. We calculate the TPM of this network and construct prior hyperparameter matrices α using (15) for various pairs of κ and ε. We generate $10,000$ random TPMs from the prior distribution to represent the uncertainty class Ω. We also generate $10,000$ different sampling paths of length 10 for each random TPM. The total costs are reported in Table 5, where we can see that the results are consistent with those obtained from synthetic networks.

Conclusions

Due to the complex nature of Markovian genetic regulatory networks, it is commonplace not to possess accurate knowledge of their parameters. Under the latter assumption, we have treated the system of interest as an uncertainty class of TPMs governed by a prior distribution. The goal is to find a robust intervention policy minimizing the expected infinite-horizon discounted cost relative to the prior distribution. We have taken a Bayesian approach and formulated the intervention policy optimizing this cost, thereby resulting in an intrinsically robust policy. Owing to extreme computational complexity, the resulting OBR policy is, from a practical sense, infeasible. Using only a few genes, we have compared it to several suboptimal polices on synthetically generated PBNs. In this case, although there are PBNs where the OBR policy significantly outperforms the suboptimal AGR policy, on average there is very little difference. Hence, one can feel somewhat comfortable using the AGR policy while losing only negligible performance. Unfortunately, even the AGR policy is computationally burdensome. Hence, when applying it to the mammalian cell cycle network, we are restricted to five genes.

The twin issues of uncertainty and computational complexity are inherent to translational genomics. Here we have examined the problem in the context of therapy, where the uncertainty is relative to network structure. It occurs to also in the other major area of translational genomics, gene-based classification. Whereas here the prior distribution is over an uncertainty class of networks, in classification it is over an uncertainty class of feature-label distributions and one looks for a classifier that is optimal, on average, across that prior distribution [27,28]. There is no doubt, however, that the complexity issue is much graver in the case of dynamical intervention. Hence, much greater effort should be placed on gaining knowledge regarding biochemical pathways and thereby reducing the uncertainty when designing intervention strategies [29]. This means more attention should be paid to classical biological regulatory experiments and less reliance on blind data mining [30].

Competing interests
The authors declare that they have no competing interests.

Authors' contributions
MRY contributed to the main idea, designed and implemented the algorithms, designed and carried out the simulation, analyzed the results, and drafted the manuscript. ERD conceived the study, contributed in the design of the simulation, and revised the manuscript. Both authors read and approved the final manuscript.

Acknowledgements
The authors thank the High-Performance Biocomputing Center of TGen for providing the clustered computing resources used in this study; this includes the Saguaro-2 cluster supercomputer, partially funded by NIH grant 1S10RR025056-01.

Author details
[1]Department of Electrical and Computer Engineering, The Ohio State University, Columbus, OH 43210, USA. [2]Center for Bioinformatics and Genomic Systems Engineering, Department of Electrical and Computer Engineering, Texas A & M University, College Station, TX 77843, USA.

References
1. ER Dougherty, R Pal, X Qian, ML Bittner, A Datta, Stationary and structural control in gene regulatory networks: basic concepts. Int. J. Syst. Sci. **41**(1), 5–16 (2010)
2. I Shmulevich, ER Dougherty, *Genomic Signal Processing* (Princeton University, Princeton, 2007)
3. I Shmulevich, ER Dougherty, S Kim, W Zhang, Probabilistic, Boolean networks: a rule-based uncertainty model for gene regulatory networks. Bioinformatics. **18**(2), 261–274 (2002)
4. R Pal, A Datta, ER Dougherty, Optimal infinite-horizon control for probabilistic Boolean networks. IEEE Trans. Signal Process. **54**(6), 2375–2387 (2006)
5. B Faryabi, G Vahedi, J-F Chamberland, A Datta, ER Dougherty, Optimal constrained stationary intervention in gene regulatory networks. EURASIP J. Bioinform. Syst. Biol. **2008**, 620767 (2008)
6. B Faryabi, J-F Chamberland, G Vahedi, A Datta, ER Dougherty, Optimal intervention in asynchronous genetic regulatory networks. IEEE J. Sel. Top. Signal. Process. **2**(3), 412–423 (2008)
7. MR Yousefi, A Datta, ER Dougherty, Optimal intervention in Markovian gene regulatory networks with random-length therapeutic response to antitumor drug. IEEE Trans. Biomed. Eng. **60**(12), 3542–3552 (2013)
8. MR Yousefi, ER Dougherty, Intervention in gene regulatory networks with maximal phenotype alteration. Bioinformatics. **29**(14), 1758–1767 (2013)
9. R Pal, A Datta, ER Dougherty, Robust intervention in probabilistic Boolean networks. IEEE Trans. Signal Process. **56**(3), 1280–1294 (2008)
10. R Pal, A Datta, ER Dougherty, Bayesian robustness in the control of gene regulatory networks. IEEE Trans. Signal Process. **57**(9), 3667–3678 (2009)
11. AM Grigoryan, ER Dougherty, Bayesian robust optimal linear filters. Signal Process. **81**(12), 2503–2521 (2001)
12. PR Kumar, A survey of some results in stochastic adaptive control. SIAM J. Contr. Optim. **23**(3), 329–380 (1985)
13. R Bellman, A problem in the sequential design of experiments. Sankhya: Indian J. Stat. **16**(3/4), 221–229 (1956)
14. R Bellman, R Kalaba, Dynamic programming and adaptive processes: mathematical foundation. IRE Trans. Automatic Control. **AC-5**(1), 5–10 (1960)
15. EA Silver, Markovian decision processes with uncertain transition probabilities or rewards. Technical report, DTIC document, (1963)
16. JM Gozzolino, R Gonzalez-Zubieta, RL Miller, Markovian decision processes with uncertain transition probabilities. Technical report, DTIC document (1965)
17. JJ Martin, *Bayesian Decision Problems and Markov Chains* (Wiley, New York, 1967)
18. SA SA Kauffman, Metabolic stability and epigenesis in randomly constructed genetic nets. J. Theor. Biol. **22**(3), 437–467 (1969)
19. B Faryabi, G Vahedi, J-F Chamberland, A Datta, ER Dougherty, Intervention in context-sensitive probabilistic Boolean networks revisited. EURASIP J. Bioinform. Syst. Biol. **2009**(5) (2009)
20. X Qian, ER Dougherty, Effect of function perturbation on the steady-state distribution of genetic regulatory networks: optimal structural intervention. IEEE Trans. Signal Process. **56**(10), 4966–4976 (2008)
21. C Derman, *Finite State Markovian Decision Processes* (Academic, Orlando, 1970)
22. JK Satia, RE Lave, Markovian decision processes with uncertain transition probabilities. Oper. Res. **21**(3), 728–740 (1973)
23. MO Duff, Optimal learning: computational procedures for Bayes-adaptive Markov decision processes. PhD thesis, University of Massachusetts, Amherst (2002)
24. MR Yousefi, A Datta, ER Dougherty, Optimal intervention strategies for therapeutic methods with fixed-length duration of drug effectiveness. IEEE Trans. Signal Process. **60**(9), 4930–4944 (2012)
25. A Faure, A Naldi, C Chaouiya, D Thieffry, Dynamical analysis of a generic Boolean model for the control of the mammalian cell cycle. Bioinformatics. **22**(14), 124–131 (2006)
26. A Veliz-Cuba, Reduction of Boolean network models. J. Theor. Biol. **289**, 167–172 (2011)
27. LA Dalton, ER Dougherty, Optimal classifiers with minimum expected error within a Bayesian framework - Part I: discrete and gaussian models. Pattern Recogn. **46**(5), 1301–1314 (2013)
28. LA Dalton, ER Dougherty, Optimal classifiers with minimum expected error within a Bayesian framework - Part II: properties and performance analysis. Pattern Recogn. **46**(5), 1288–1300 (2013)
29. B-J Yoon, X Qian, ER Dougherty, Quantifying the objective cost of uncertainty in complex dynamical systems. IEEE Trans. Signal Process. **61**(9), 2256–2266 (2013)
30. ER Dougherty, ML Bittner, *Epistemology of the Cell: A Systems Perspective on Biological Knowledge* (Wiley, Hoboken, 2011)

Permissions

List of Contributors

Florian Nigsch
Developmental and Molecular Pathways, Novartis Institutes for BioMedical Research, Forum 1, Novartis Campus Basel, CH-4056, Basel, Switzerland

Janna Hutz, Ben Cornett, Douglas W Selinger, Gregory McAllister, Joseph Loureiro and Jeremy L Jenkins
Developmental and Molecular Pathways, Novartis Institutes for BioMedical Research, 220 Massachusetts Avenue, 02139 Cambridge, MA, USA

Somnath Bandyopadhyay
Immunology Clinical Biomarkers, Bristol Myers Squibb, Princeton, New Jersey

Daniela Besozzi
Universitàdegli Studi di Milano, Dipartimento di Informatica, Via Comelico 39, 20135 Milano, Italy

Paolo Cazzaniga
Università degli Studi di Bergamo, Dipartimento di Scienze della Persona, Piazzale S. Agostino 2, 24129 Bergamo, Italy

Dario Pescini
Universit`a degli Studi di Milano-Bicocca, Dipartimento di Statistica, Via Bicocca degli Arcimboldi 8, 20126 Milano, Italy

Giancarlo Mauri
Università degli Studi di Milano-Bicocca, Dipartimento di Informatica, Sistemistica e Comunicazione,Viale Sarca 336, 20126 Milano, Italy

Sonia Colombo and Enzo Martegani
Università degli Studi di Milano-Bicocca, Dipartimento di Biotecnologie e Bioscienze, Piazza della Scienza 2, 20126 Milano, Italy

Tomasz M Ignac and David J Galas
Institute for Systems Biology, 401 N. Terry Avenue, Seattle, WA 98109, USA
Luxembourg Centre for Systems Biomedicine, University of Luxembourg, Campus Belval, 7, Avenue des Hauts-Fourneaux, L-4362 Esch-sur-Alzette, Luxembourg

Nikita A Sakhanenko
Institute for Systems Biology, 401 N. Terry Avenue, Seattle, WA 98109, USA

Aleksandr Andreychenko, Linar Mikeev, David Spieler and Verena Wolf
Computer Science Department, Saarland University, 66123 Saarbrücken, Germany

Amin Ahmadi Adl
Department of Computer Science and Engineering, University of South Florida, Tampa, FL, 33620, USA

Xiaoning Qian
Department of Computer Science and Engineering, University of South Florida, Tampa, FL, 33620, USA
Department of Electrical & Computer Engineering, Texas A&M University, College Station, TX, 77843, USA

Ping Xu, Kendra Vehik and Jeffrey P Krischer
Department of Pediatrics, College of Medicine, University of South Florida, Tampa, FL, 33613, USA

Wenlong Tang and Junbo Duan
Department of Biomedical Engineering, Tulane University, New Orleans, LA, USA

Ji-Gang Zhang
Department of Biostatistics and Bioinformatics, Tulane University, New Orleans, LA, USA

Yu-Ping Wang
Department of Biomedical Engineering, Tulane University, New Orleans, LA, USA
Department of Biostatistics and Bioinformatics, Tulane University, New Orleans, LA, USA
Center for Systems Biomedicine, Shanghai University for Science and Technology, Shanghai, China

Bilal Wajid
Department of Electrical and Computer Engineering, Texas A&M University, College Station,TX 77843-3128, USA Department of Electrical Engineering, University of Engineering & Technology, Lahore, Punjab 54890, Pakistan

Erchin Serpedin
Department of Electrical and Computer Engineering, Texas A&M University, College Station,TX 77843-3128, USA

Mohamed Nounou
Department of Chemical Engineering, Texas A&M University, Doha, Qatar

Hazem Nounou
Department of Electrical and Computer Engineering, Texas A&M University, Doha, Qatar

Ahmad Rushdi
Department of Electrical and Computer Engineering at the University of California, Davis, CA 95616, USA, and is now with Cisco Systems, Inc., San Jose CA 95134, USA

Jamal Tuqan
Department of Electrical and Computer Engineering at the University of California, Davis, CA 95616, USA

Thomas Strohmer
Department of Mathematics, University of California, Davis, CA 95616, USA

Tzu-Hung Hsiao and Hung-I Harry Chen
Greehey Children's Cancer Research Institute, University of Texas Health Science Center at San Antonio, San Antonio, TX 78229, USA

Stephanie Roessler
Institute of Pathology, University Hospital, Im Neuenheimer Feld 224, Room 2.034, Heidelberg 69120, Germany

Xin Wei Wang
Laboratory of Human Carcinogenesis, National Cancer Institute, NIH, Bethesda, MD 20892, USA

Yidong Chen
Greehey Children's Cancer Research Institute, University of Texas Health Science Center at San Antonio, San Antonio, TX 78229, USA
Department of Epidemiology and Biostatistics, University of Texas Health Science Center at San Antonio, San Antonio, TX 78229, USA

Edward R Dougherty
Department of Electrical and Computer Engineering, Texas A&M University, College Station, TX 77843, USA
Computational Biology Division, Translational Genomics Research Institute, Phoenix, AZ 85004, USA

Lori A Dalton
Department of Electrical and Computer Engineering, The Ohio State University, Columbus, OH 43210, USA

Peteris Zikmanis and Inara Kampenusa
Institute of Microbiology and Biotechnology, University of Latvia, Kronvalda Boulevard 4, Riga LV-1010, Latvia

Genyuan Li and Herschel Rabitz
Department of Chemistry, Princeton University, Princeton, NJ 08544, USA

Manidipa Roy
The Calcutta Technical School, Govt. of West Bengal, 110,S.N.Banerjee Road, Kolkata 700013, India

Soma Barman
Institute of Radio Physics & Electronics, University of Calcutta, 92, A.P.C. Road, Kolkata 700 009, India

Edward R Dougherty
Center for Bioinformatics and Genomic Systems Engineering, Department of Electrical and Computer Engineering, Texas A&M University, 3128 TAMU, College Station, TX 77843-3128, USA

Jehandad Khan and Nidhal Bouaynaya
Department of Electrical and Computer Engineering, Rowan University, 201 Mullica Hill Rd, Glassboro, NJ 08028, USA

Hassan M Fathallah-Shaykh
Department of Neurology, University of Alabama at Birmingham, 1720 2nd Ave S, Birmingham, AL 35233, USA
Department of Mathematics, University of Alabama at Birmingham, 1720 2nd Ave S, Birmingham, AL 35233, USA
Department of Electrical and Computer Engineering, University of Alabama at Birmingham, 1720 2nd Ave S, Birmingham, AL 35233, USA
Department of Biomedical Engineering, University of Alabama at Birmingham, 1720 2nd Ave S, Birmingham, AL 35233, USA
Department of Cell, Developmental and Integrative Biology, University of Alabama at Birmingham, 1720 2nd Ave S, Birmingham, AL 35233, USA

Noriko Hiroi, Akito Tabira, Takahiro Okuhara, Takeshi Kubojima, Keisuke Iba, Kotaro Oka and Akira Funahashi
Department of BioSciences and Informatics, Keio University, Yokohama, Kanagawa, Japan

Michael Klann, Robin Mange, Michael Unger and Heinz Koeppl
Automatic Control Laboratory, Swiss Federal Institute of Technology, Zurich, Switzerland

Pablo de Heras Ciechomski
ScienceVisuals Sarl, Lausanne, Switzerland

Shuji Yamashita and Yasunori Okada
Department of Pathology, School of Medicine, Keio University, Shinjuku-ku, Tokyo, Japan

Navadon Khunlertgit
Department of Electrical and Computer Engineering, Texas A&M University, 77843-3128 College Station, TX, USA

Byung-Jun Yoon
Department of Electrical and Computer Engineering, Texas A&M University, 77843-3128 College Station, TX, USA
College of Science, Engineering, and Technology, Hamad Bin Khalifa University (HBKU), P.O. Box 5825 Doha, Qatar

Brian R King
Department of Computer Science, Bucknell University, Lewisburg, PA 17837, USA

Maurice Aburdene, Alex Thompson and Zach Warres
Department of Electrical and Computer Engineering, Bucknell University, Lewisburg, PA 17837, USA

Minoru Nakayama
Department of Human System Science, Tokyo Institute of Technology, Ookayama, Meguro, Tokyo 152-8552, Japan

Wioletta Nowak
Institute of Biomedical Engineering and Instrumentation, Wroclaw University of Technology, Wroclaw 50-370, Poland

Hitoshi Ishikawa and Ken Asakawa
School of Allied Health Sciences, Kitasato University, Kitasato, Minami, Sagamihara 252-0373, Japan

Yoshiaki Ichibe
School of Medicine, Kitasato University, Kitasato, Minami, Sagamihara 252-0373, Japan

Mohammadmahdi R Yousefi
Department of Electrical and Computer Engineering, The Ohio State University, Columbus, OH 43210, USA

Edward R Dougherty
Center for Bioinformatics and Genomic Systems Engineering, Department of Electrical and Computer Engineering, Texas A & M University, College Station, TX 77843, USA